Aristophanes'
Old-and-New
Comedy

Aristophanes' Old-and-New Comedy

VOLUME 1

SIX ESSAYS IN PERSPECTIVE

BY KENNETH J. RECKFORD

THE UNIVERSITY OF

NORTH CAROLINA PRESS

CHAPEL HILL & LONDON

I am grateful for permission from the following publishers to quote from copyright materials. To Harcourt Brace Jovanovich, New York, and Harold Ober Associates, for excerpts from "Full Moon" in P. L. Travers's *Mary Poppins and Mary Poppins Comes Back*, © 1962, 1963. To Grove Press, New York, and Fraser and Dunlop Scripts, London, for lines from Tom Stoppard's *Travesties*, © 1975. To Grove Press, New York, and Faber & Faber, London, for lines from Trevor Griffiths's *Comedians*, © 1976. To Dodd, Mead, New York, and A. P. Watt, London, for a passage from G. K. Chesterton's *Orthodoxy*, © 1908, 1936. And to Holt, Rinehart & Winston, New York, for a passage from G. B. Trudeau's *The Doonesbury Chronicles*, © 1975.

© 1987 The University of North Carolina Press

Manufactured in the United States of America

Library of Congress Cataloging-in-Publication Data

Reckford, Kenneth J., 1933–
   Aristophanes' old-and-new comedy.

   Bibliography: p.
   Includes index.
   Contents: v. 1. Six essays in perspective
   1. Aristophanes—Criticism and
      interpretation.
2. Comedy. I. Title.
PA3879.R4   1987   882'.01   86-16188
ISBN 0-8078-1720-1 (v. 1)

The publication of this work was made possible in part through a grant from the National Endowment for the Humanities, a federal agency whose mission is to award grants to support education, scholarship, media programming, libraries, and museums, in order to bring the results of cultural activities to a broad, general public.

FRONTISPIECE

Dionysus on shipboard, with magical transformations, by the Exekias painter, ca. 535 B.C., black-figure Attic cup with red glaze from Vulci. Courtesy Museum Antiker Kleinkunst, Munich (no. 2044).

Contents

Illustrations

Preface

THIS book emerged from what seemed a simple wish back in 1967, to vindicate Aristophanes' *Clouds* against detractors. I had come to love the play as an undergraduate and later had directed the 1959 Harvard production, in Greek, in the courtyard of the Fogg Museum; and so, when my teacher Cedric Whitman gave it less praise in his book than I thought right, I began to argue its merits, first in letters, then in essays meant for publication. All I wanted was to convince Whitman, and a somewhat incredulous world along with him, that the *Clouds* is— and was—a wise, beautiful, and very funny play.

Over the years, however, as I reread and taught Aristophanes and went on arguing, it became clear that the *Clouds* could not be vindicated by analysis of that play in isolation. Something more was needed; I wanted to fight for a comic perspective within which Aristophanes' comedies generally and the *Clouds* in particular could be enjoyed, understood, and rightly appreciated. So I planned a tripartite book, in dialectic form. The thesis (part 1) would be the power and fun of Old Comedy, as I saw it; the antithesis (part 2), the threat posed by cultural change in the later fifth century B.C.; the synthesis (part 3), the *Clouds* itself, or Old Comedy Meets Cultural Change. But although I was right in thinking that the long way around would be the shortest way home, the book grew unwieldy. It came to resemble Saint-Exupery's boa constrictor that had eaten an elephant. (The result, to grown-ups, looked like a hat.) So, after working extensively on parts 2 and 3, I decided in 1980 to pull part 1 out of the hat and rewrite it to stand independently, as "Six Essays in Perspective." The rest will appear in the sequel, "Clouds of Glory."

The order of these six essays matters. I have tried to put first things first: not from the viewpoint of most readers or scholars, but from that of the comic poet, to which reading and scholarship alike need to become adjusted. The book therefore proceeds through a descending series of defining essays, each with its own dominant concern and method of approach:

1. Religious: deriving the force and meaning of Old Comedy from festive play and celebration, now become artistically self-conscious (as, for example, Shakespeare's *Midsummer Night's Dream* is).
2. Psychological: going beyond the usual Freudian approaches, which stress pent-up impulses of hostility and obscenity and their discharge in laughter, to a new theory, that Aristophanes builds to

larger "clarifications of wishing and hoping" in his plays, to which fairy tales offer the best analogy today.

3. Theatrical: exploring the development of Aristophanes' plays from comic idea to comic performance, in ways suggested by what we may observe of Tom Stoppard's procedure today.

4. Poetic and fantastic: comparing the symbolic transformations and comic recognitions in one play, the *Wasps*, with dream experience and dream interpretation (an analogy toward which Aristophanes himself directs our attention).

5. (And only at this stage in the argument) political: arguing inductively for certain basic loyalties, comic, human, and democratic, to which Aristophanes holds throughout his artistic career, and which underlie his complex and dizzying insights about man and society; and

6. Literary-historical: redefining the achievement of Aristophanes and the place of his Old-and-New Comedy within the larger story.

The Appendix, on comedy's emergence from ritual and play, would logically have followed (or still more logically, have preceded) chapter 1; but its speculative argument and complicated subject matter would have impeded the easy, natural movement into Aristophanes' comedy, based on the extant plays, that I wanted to provide. (My *daimonion* made me take out a second Appendix, on catharsis. The main ideas are indicated in the text and notes; I promise a more detailed treatment of Aristotle's concept, or what might have been Aristotle's concept, at a later time.)

To analyze all eleven plays at length would have distracted me, and distracted the reader, from the balanced perspective that I was struggling to establish, and to maintain; and detailed considerations of image and metaphor, diction and word arrangement, meter and rhythm, scene-building, comic business, and the structuring of Aristophanes' plays would obviously have swollen the book to many times its present (and, to my mind, necessary) length. I am grateful to be able to refer to many outstanding books and articles on these subjects. The reader should be warned, however, that I have treated some plays more fully than others, have discussed different aspects of different plays, and have not presented the plays in the usual chronological order. This would be:

Period 1: *Acharnians* (425), *Knights* (424), *Clouds* (423), *Wasps* (422), *Peace* (421).
Period 2: *Birds* (414), *Lysistrata* and *Thesmophoriazusae* (411).
Period 3: *Frogs* (405).
Period 4: *Ecclesiazusae* (392 or 391), *Plutus* (388).

(These plays represent slightly more than one-quarter of Aristophanes' total production. A fuller account of his literary and dramatic career appears in sections 13 and 33.) I have dealt most extensively with the *Wasps*, in chapter 4; also at some length with the *Peace* in chapter 1, the *Acharnians* in chapter 3, the *Birds* in chapter 5, and the *Frogs* in chapter 6. Other plays come in more briefly, though not for lack of affection. In order to avoid tendentiousness and circular argument, I have postponed treatment of my beloved *Clouds* until volume 2, merely commenting on its reception, and Aristophanes' reaction to this, in chapter 6.

Aristophanes wrote for performance. For him, the play came alive in the theater of Dionysus for perhaps ninety minutes, after many long months of writing and rehearsal. He was not concerned to provide posterity with an abiding text; and the "Aristophanes" that we are so very grateful to possess today is derived ultimately from the playwright's working (and much changed) script, which, even before performance, was supplemented by the poet-director's oral instructions to experienced comic actors. It is hardly surprising that modern scholars prefer to ask questions about structural organization and technique that can be answered from the text. It will be clear that I have profited from their studies. But because I care passionately about living theater, I have tried to keep alive, for myself and for the reader, the vast distance between "the event and the text" (the phrase is Tom Stoppard's); and I have asked questions about the playwright's creative experience, and about the emotional impact of comedy on an Athenian audience, that are not susceptible of precise answers such as scholars like to produce, and yet that *need* to be asked, and tentatively answered, if we are to revive that sense of living comedy by which all our interpretations of specific plays must be affected. Otherwise, we too much resemble the wife who tried to shame her husband by imitating his foul cursing: "You have the words, dear," he retorted, "but you don't catch the tone."

The overall approach here used is eclectic, in keeping with its peculiar and playful subject. It might perhaps be called *arrière-garde* criticism. I have written, first, for nonspecialists who care about comedy and who wish to become more familiar with Aristophanes; and second, for students and teachers of the classics who may welcome this new perspective. Because I have wanted to provide an introduction of feeling as well as thought (an *Einfühlung* as well as an *Einführung*) into Aristophanes' plays for both groups of readers, and because this book is written *sub specie ludi*, I have given more than usual attention to qualities of comic feeling and tone in the passages and scenes that I have treated. The translations, which are my own, are playful; they are about eighty percent literal: all puns and anachronisms are intentional. I must apologize, not for the sexual and scatological obscenities, but for the loss of the Aristophanic elegance and grace, or *charis*, with which these once were joined. To regain the sense of Old Comedy as something still vital and funny, and very moving, I have added a few personal excursuses, much as I do in class, and I have leaned heavily on analogies: with Shakespeare (for great writers are best compared with great); with Tom Stoppard, who brilliantly combines farce today with the comedy of ideas; and with fairy tale, which I have always loved, and to which, I am convinced, Aristophanic comedy comes close in its essential spirit.

Acknowledgments

ONE of the joys of scholarship is the sense of companionship with others who have cared. And anyone who writes about Aristophanes knows how much he or she owes to the long tradition of textual criticism and commentary, as well as to twentieth-century interpretations of poetry and drama. I have tried in the notes to indicate how much I have learned, and continue to learn, from so many scholars both living and dead, at home and abroad. Although my bibliography ends with what was available to me before December 1984, good books and articles on Aristophanes continue almost relentlessly to emerge. Some of these will be acknowledged in my second volume.

I want next to thank so many people who have, over the years, given me help, advice, and encouragement toward this book. These include: Edwin Brown, Peter Burian, John Davies, Mark Davies, Nan Dunbar, Alfred Engstrom, Joseph Ewbank, Marie-Henriette Gates, Leon Golden, Henry and Sara Immerwahr, George Kennedy, Kimball King, Bernard Knox, David Konstan, Mallory Masters, Anna Morpurgo-Davies, Gregory Nagy, Alison Parker, James Peacock, Michael Putnam, Nicholas Richardson, Amy Richlin, Kenneth Sams, Charles Segal, Erich Segal, Beatrix and Peter Smith, Friedrich Solmsen, Philip Stadter, Hans-Peter Stahl, Max Steele, Douglas Stewart, Laura Stone, Dana Sutton, Oliver Taplin, Theodore Tarkow, Nancy Vickers, William West, Garry Wills, and Terry Zug. And many, many others.

In shape and spirit the book owes most to a teacher, a colleague, and two students. John H. Finley, Jr., Eliot Professor of Greek at Harvard and Master of Eliot House, made me free of Greek scholarship through his teaching and his example, as he proclaimed the "god-given radiance" that, amid struggle and defeat, still lights up human life. Douglass Parker, in our one glorious year at the Center for Hellenic Studies, first showed me how to read Aristophanes as *poetry*, and how to avoid calling Aristophanes serious about less than everything. Fontaine Belford, in her brilliant 1974 dissertation "Comedy's Play," put play, ritual, myth, and game into exemplary perspective for me. And Lois-Jenny Hinckley has believed in the book since its inception and has reminded me often (in the words of her song) of its premise that "joy is the basic, and not routine."

The daily support and encouragement that I have received from colleagues and students at Chapel Hill over twenty-five years have been incalculable. In a colder atmosphere I could not have written this book.

Three successive chairmen, the late Albert Suskin, George Kennedy, and Philip Stadter, have protected me somewhat from those unreasonable pressures and demands ("What have you done for us lately?") that are so common nowadays, and that make it impossible for teachers and scholars to do their best work. I owe much to the generations of graduate students who have read Aristophanes with me, and to the brave undergraduates who took my honors seminar in fairy tale and comedy in the spring of 1982. I am grateful to the University of North Carolina for an assignment to research duties in 1978–79 and for a Kenan leave in the fall of 1984, as well as a grant from the University Research Council that aided in the publication of this work; to Lynda (Johnson) Myers and George Garrett, who helped me with bibliography; to Maura Lafferty, who saw the footnotes and bibliography through the computer; to Nancy Honeycutt, Juanita Mason, Mark Masterson, and especially Erline Nipper, for all their patient typing and retyping, and word processing; and to John Kirby, who ventured into my sibyl's cave and put my papers into remarkable order, leading me to imagine that the book could actually be finished. From here, my thanks pass to two generous, unnamed readers for The University of North Carolina Press, and to the editors, notably Laura Oaks, who have guided the book toward its safe delivery. And to Susan Foutz, who has energetically read proof and compiled the index.

In the end it is perhaps family life that has most challenged and shaped my own comic perspective. Mary, my wife, has guided me through Dante in so many companionable evenings. She has also played Martha, answering literally thousands of telephone calls over the years so that I could continue working in my attic study. Our children, Rachel, Joe, Sam, Jon, and Sarah, have treated the whole project as a teasing chorus might have done: "But you *said*, you'd be finished in 1978!" I owe so much to their companionship, and to their laughter. A still older debt is to my late mother, Janet R. Limburg, née Sidenberg (1910–77). Born of a sports- and laughter-loving family, she matched my father's self-ironic intellectualism and work ethic with her own overriding sense of disciplined play. Her sense of humor was remarkable, and what Samuel Johnson would have called her ability to be pleased. Her stories of Maisie the Magic Motor-Bus first nurtured my child's imagination, which has remained incorrigible. This book is dedicated to her memory.

Chapel Hill
Thanksgiving 1985

Chapter One

Aristophanes' Festive

Comedy

The return of Hephaistus to Olympus (with Dionysus as escort), by the Kleophon Painter, ca. 435–430 B.C., red-figure Attic pelike from Gela. Courtesy Museum Antiker Kleinkunst, Munich (no. 2361).

I   *Relaxation, Recovery, and Recognition:* Peace

I *don't want to do these dance-steps,*
really I don't—but out of joy
my legs, even if I don't move them,
will *go dancing on their own,*
dancing, dancing, dancing, dancing. . . .

S o the farmer-chorus sings at a crucial moment in Aristophanes' *Peace.* Trygaeus, the peasant-hero, has "flown to Olympus" on his dung beetle to confront Zeus with the question, "Why does the war drag on?" But the gods have moved to regions more remote. Only Hermes, the folksy, lower-class god, remains to watch over the Olympian pots and pans. Zeus and the rest, he explains, became fed up with the Greeks after they rejected so many godsent opportunities for making peace; so now, the Greeks have been handed over to the untender mercies of War—a great hulking giant out of folktale. War has cast the lady Peace into a deep pit, and when Trygaeus arrives, he is on the verge of pounding all Greece into a salad in his huge mortar. By punning associations, all the Greek cities become salad ingredients. Not even the "dear" Attic honey will be spared. But War can't find a pestle: the notorious Athenian and Spartan ones (Cleon and Brasidas, those hawkish generals) have just recently become unavailable; and War's withdrawal to fashion a new pestle gives Trygaeus his chance to summon the chorus to pull out Peace. Hence their joyful entrance, singing and dancing.

What is immediately funny is the way the exuberant chorus rebel against any constraint.[1] Trygaeus is forced into a spoilsport role when he insists, sensibly enough, that they pull out Peace first and celebrate afterwards. But the chorus of Greek farmers won't stop dancing. They claim that they are stopping, but they don't stop. The right leg has to have its fling, then the left leg. It seems that joy will not be postponed—which is, in a curious way, the recognition on which this play turns and from which it draws its resiliency, its almost manic vitality, and its hope.

Now critics whose attention is focused on what I might call "the real Athens" of March, 421 B.C., will be tempted to interpret this scene, and indeed the entire play, in one of two ways. First, they may treat it as reflecting actual hopes for peace. For almost a year, Athens and Sparta had been negotiating peace; now a settlement drew near—and a peace treaty was actually signed only a short while after the performance of *Peace*.[2] Even if, as seems likely, Aristophanes wrote his play in the summer or early fall of 422, it seems reasonable to think that he wrote it in a spirit of hope and confidence, which would account for the unusual lightness, cheerfulness, and ease of movement that still strikes its readers today.

The other historically based interpretation of *Peace* would be less optimistic. In this view, Aristophanes raises strong doubts whether the peace that everyone anticipates so hopefully can be real or lasting. His exaggeration of the ease with which Peace is recovered *on the stage* should remind us by contrast of all those difficulties in real life that call for skepticism. In the theater, there is virtually no conflict. Everything comes easily, naturally, and spontaneously; it only takes a little communal effort to "pull out" Peace—and the rest is celebration. By contrast, an enormous amount of political effort seems required in real life, in history, to take advantage of the opportunity or *kairos* when it offers itself, and not to let it slip, as had happened many times before. In short: the Athenians in the audience are being told *not* to take peace for granted as the silly, dancing chorus do, but rather to work, and to continue to work, toward its achievement and preservation.

There is much truth in both these views. Aristophanes *was* heartened by the real, historical prospect of a peace treaty; Aristophanes *was* sensible enough not to take a lasting peace for granted. Yet both views are misleading insofar as they treat comedy as a pale reflection of historical hopes or fears. In ordinary life, celebration and joy may depend, or seem to depend, on right-thinking politics. In Aristophanic comedy, the reverse is true. Celebration and joy are an end in themselves. The first thing to do is to sing and dance with abandon; everything else will follow, in good time. Right action depends on right intention, which springs in turn from the recovery of good feeling and good will. And it is just this recovery that must not be postponed, for the Athenians, and presumably the other Greeks, have become prisoners of a vicious cycle of distrust, bad temper, and unimaginative politics. How can you break out of this cycle? Only by *preempting* the better temper and outlook of peacetime—which is exactly what Aristophanes' play manages to accomplish.

Recovery is a great and central gift of comedy, but it is not easy to describe. Even as I write these words, my tense posture and anxious mind distance me, a sedentary scholar, from precisely the experience of good humor and fun which Aristophanes' dancers celebrate and with which I am centrally concerned. It helps to relax first, to look up from my typewriter, perhaps to contemplate the five-colored jester's cap (green, yellow, red, purple, and blue) that I wear on Mardi Gras; or perhaps, to think back to the remarkably funny farce by Tom Stoppard, *On the Razzle*, that I saw in Washington last week. Already it would be hard to explain why I laughed so hard, why the production (which was superb) gave such delight. The gorgeous sets and costumes, the slapstick and running about and music and wild punning and sexual innuendo and general confusion—all this was wonderful fun, and most of this would be lost in the telling. How then can I as critic recapture the gift of recovery that Aristophanes' comedy provided if I have no living performance before me, not even before my mind's eye, but only a Greek text—only printed words that come to us at several removes from the living play with its singing and dancing, its music and color and clowning and make-believe and interplay with the audience? How, except by analogy with my experience and yours, can the gift of recovery be explained?

Trygaeus himself is at a loss for words when Peace reappears, together with her handmaids, Opora and Theoria. The latter are personifications—Autumn Harvest and Festive Sightseeing—played by mute actors; for the emotional flavor, I translate them as Thanksgiving and Holiday.[3] Here is Trygaeus' greeting:

> *Tryg.* Lady goddess! How can I greet you properly?
> Where could I find a million-gallon word
> to address you by? I've had none at home.
> Greetings to you, Thanksgiving, and you too,
> Holiday. What splendid—features you have,
> dear goddess. And what a scent. Its sweetness
> goes right to the heart, like a breath of
> freedom-from-army-service mixed with myrrh.
> *Hermes* Not like a military knapsack, then?
> *Tryg.* I reject a hated man's most hated—bag.
> Your knapsack smells, you know, of onion-belching,
> but she—
> she brings a scent
> of autumn-time, entertaining
> guests, Dionysia, flutes,
> tragic players, Sophoclean
> lyrics, thrushes, clever little
> sayings of Euripides—
> *Herm.* You'll be sorry, casting aspersions

> on the lady. She doesn't like
> a man who puts
> court-arguments in plays.

Tryg.   —ivy, new-wine strainers, bleating
> sheep, bosomy women jogging
> into the fields, drunken slavegirls,
> jugs of wine tilted skyward,
> lots and lots of other blessings. . . .   (520–38)

Aristophanes' list of sensual delights of peacetime is twice difficult to translate here: first, because the imaginative sensual appeal of "Sophoclean lyrics" and "thrushes" loses much of its immediacy and (so to speak) mouth-watering appeal in English translation, and over time and space; and second, because Aristophanes takes poetic delight in juxtaposing pleasurable images of sight and sound, taste and touch and smell, partly for their comic incongruity, but still more for the sake of their combined associations and their power to evoke happy occasions.[4] If "thrushes" came individually and exemplified only something delicious to eat, I might translate them as "squabs," which my mother used to serve on special occasions—just as, elsewhere, I would translate Aristophanes' often-mentioned *enkelys* and *lagōa* and *plakountes* not literally as "eel" and "hare's-meat stew" and "layered cheesecakes," but rather more freely as filet of sole Walewska (to be eaten with a *very* dry Riesling), or roast beef (rare, but not too rare), or strawberry shortcake (just the way Annie used to make it when I was a boy). Please make your own nostalgic substitutions at this point. Even so, something is lost if we turn thrushes into squabs. They may belong next to Sophoclean lyrics, and not just for fun: for these good thrushes may have sung very brightly indeed before they came to provide the even greater delight of roast fowls with a good rich gravy poured over them. The accumulation of images, their sensual profusion and confusion, evokes the overwhelming beauty and richness of peace, which made Trygaeus feel the need of that "million-gallon word." This also reflects a basic comic axiom of Aristophanes', that all good things are related to all other good things. Food and drink, sex and rejuvenation, peace, holiday, sport, leisure, country doings, and unrestrained laughter—all rush in together like a troupe of comic revelers, once they are given the chance. Asked to help, a recent class of students suggested the smell of Thanksgiving turkey being cooked; Christmas trees; barbecued hamburgers and fireworks on the Fourth of July; and maybe a mixture of guitars, new-mown hay, Shakespeare, and honeysuckle. That is something like what Trygaeus (and Aristophanes) has in mind.

Furthermore, these accumulated pleasures are enhanced against their dark wartime background. Pleasure is always intensified by contrast: children laugh when they get out of school, and grown-ups when they leave their offices; and there is nothing like army life to make one appreciate the sheer luxuriousness of ordinary existence. That stinking knapsack is more than an uncalled-for interruption of Trygaeus' list: it is necessary as a reminder of contrast and of the feeling of liberation. Had anyone realized how special things can be that are taken for granted normally, like those "bosomy women jogging / into the fields"? We read *astrateias kai myrou* as a comic zeugma, "freedom-from-army-service mixed with myrrh"; but by poetic suggestion, that release has a delightful odor. We forget it at our peril.

We do forget, and often; hence the particular quality of nostalgia with which Aristophanes invests the imagined recovery of Peace. In ordinary life nostalgia is released very powerfully by an old song heard once more, or by a remembered taste (as of Proust's madeleine dipped in tea), or most of all, by familiar smells. I myself am strongly affected by the scent of lilacs, and of some old books (and conversely, when I visited my old school, the stench of the locker room brought back many miserable hours spent in athletics). Just so, it is the lovely scent of the goddess that brings back so much remembered happiness in a flood of sensual and mixed images. Later, too, the chorus are urged to join Trygaeus in that same strong nostalgia, that *newly remembered* enjoyment of things past:

> Come now, people, and recall
>   your older way of life
> that *she* used to provide for us:
>
>   the dried fruit and the cakes,
>   the figs and myrtles burgeoning,
>   the taste of sweet new wine,
>   violets growing near the well,
>   olive trees,
>   all the things we long for:
>   in the name of all good things,
>   welcome the goddess now!
>
> *Chorus* Hail to you, all hail,
>   most gracious lady!
> We welcome you,
> we longed for you
>   overwhelmingly, and waited
> back into the countryside
>   at long last to return.
>
> You were our greatest good:
>   we know that now,
>   honored, most longed-for lady—
> all of us who led the farmer's life.

> Earlier, when you were with us,
>   we could enjoy
>   many ordinary things,
>   nice and cheap and comfortable things,
> back in the good old days
>   when you were there.
>
> You were groats and salvation
>   for the farmers:
> so all the little baby vines
> and all the little fig trees
> and all the other little
>   things that grow
> will laugh, they'll be so happy then
>   to get you back!   (571–600)

It is obvious that, beyond the chorus of farmers, the Athenian audience in the theater of Dionysus is meant to feel that same remembered stab of yearning (*pothos*), to desire the recovery of peace with the same erotic fervor that some people idiotically save for war and empire. And here a paradox suggests itself. Peace cannot be regained until it is strongly enough desired; cannot be desired until it is remembered; cannot be remembered until it is rightly imagined—under the guidance of the comic poet employing the magic of poetry and stage. Aristophanes pre-celebrates with and for us a future that can only be built on good, hopeful feelings, and on such memories as inspire longing with hope. This is the central recovery. All other right decisions and actions must follow after it, not come before.

That is why Hermes "explains" what has been happening in wartime Greece only after Peace has been recovered and reimagined.[5] The god is evidently a persona for the comic poet here. With full Olympian authority he makes the usual Aristophanic points: that the flame of war was fanned by Pericles, and later by others, out of private political and economic interests; that war escalated of its own momentum, tending increasingly to grow harsher and more violent, and to perpetuate itself through suspiciousness and hostility; and that the country folk, normally sensible but now hungry, impoverished, and confused, were cheated by the politicians, losing their chance of peace:

> Then, when the working folk arrived,
>   packed together, from the country,
> they didn't realize how they
>   were bought and sold for someone's profit,
> but wanting grapes, and wanting figs,
>   they kept their eyes on the politicians:
> and they, the speakers, well aware

that the poor were weak, and sick, and breadless,
threw out this goddess (like manure)
   with two-pronged—screams, though she came back
many times over, out of fondness
   for her dear Athens. Then they'd squeeze
some rich and fruitful allies, claiming,
   "This man collaborates with Sparta!"
Then you'd worry the man to pieces
   like a pack of starving puppies:
pale and sick and scared, our city
   snapped up any slanders going.
Foreigners saw men take a beating;
   they stopped the speakers' mouths with money,
so *they* got rich; but all of Hellas
   could go to waste, for all you noticed.
And all these things were organized
   by just one man. A LEATHER-SALESMAN.   (634–48)

Aristophanes never tired of displaying the gullibility of the Athenian people, their subservience to tricky orators and politicians—most notably, the late unlamented Cleon. What is more striking here is his awareness, which he means the audience to share, of the dynamics by which war worsens and perpetuates itself, and especially of the role played in this process by war neurosis, or bad public temper.[6] In similar ways, Thucydides and Euripides demonstrate how war is "a harsh teacher," how it produces public and private demoralization. Aristophanes makes the point in terms of diet. It was a commonplace of modern Athenian medicine that good health depended largely on diet, on a sensible and balanced regimen of life. In wartime, however, the Athenian farmers were crowded into the cities and deprived of their ordinary good food, their healthy diet; being weak and discouraged, physically and (still more) spiritually, they allowed the politicians to feed them on a diet of slanders, which only heightened their distemper. There is a further, grotesque suggestion that the Athenians were kept on a diet of shit, like scavenging dogs, like the great dung beetle, and, by a curious inversion, like the monstrous "shit-eater" Cleon himself. But only after Peace is recovered, and the joyful perspective of peace and the countryside is regained, can the Athenians realize to what foul smells and tastes they had become habituated as the war crept on. Part of Aristophanes' intent in writing the play is therefore to act as a "good humor man," to bring his audience to the point where they could say about Peace something very like what Shakespeare has Demetrius say about Helena in *A Midsummer Night's Dream*:

> To her, my lord,
> was I betrothed ere I saw Hermia,
> but, like a sickness, did I loathe this food;
> but, as in health, come to my natural state,
> now do I wish it, love it, long for it,
> and will for evermore be true to it.   (4.1)

To "remember" the older love of peace, and the older life of the country-side, is not just nostalgic: it is the best way, by Aristophanes' comic strategy, to begin to get it back.

I would like now to describe this strategy as consisting of three basic steps: relaxation, recovery, and recognition. And I want to illustrate these in a manner appropriate to Aristophanes' comic muse, by lingering on the uses of dung in the *Peace*.

As the play opens, two slaves are kneading great shitcakes and conveying them to what turns out to be a monstrous dung beetle, not yet visible to us. The creature is curiously fastidious. ("Another one, quick! A young male whore's, this time: he says he wants it *mashed*.") The dirty jokes build. They are, to some extent, an end in themselves. At the same time, Aristophanes teases his audience: what is the point of these messy go-ings-on? Eventually, we learn that Trygaeus will ride the dung beetle to Olympus (for the queer creature has evidently been bred from Euripidean tragedy out of Aesopic fable:[7] it is a cross between the winged horse ridden by Bellerophon and the dung beetle that flew to Olympus, to the very lap of Zeus, to get revenge on his enemy, the eagle); but earlier, one of the slaves expresses the curiosity that we must feel about what the dung beetle stands for, and where the jokes are leading:

> So then, one of the spectators might say,
> a young man who thinks he's clever: "What's
> going on here? What's the point of the dung beetle?"
> And a man sitting next to him—a man from Ionia—
> says, "In my opinion, the riddle points to
> Cleon—seeing that *he* is eating shit in Hades!"
> Oh well. I'm going in, to give the beetle a drink.   (43–49)

The joke, like so many in Aristophanes, scores extra points. It is a won-derfully roundabout attack on Cleon, who is dead but not forgotten: Aristophanes' old enemy, the monstrous muckraker of earlier comedies, is here imagined as receiving his offal but just desserts down in Hell. But the joke is also on the literary critic, then or now. What a hurry we are always in to get the point, to interpret the "symbolic relevance" of jokes, whether as political satire or as comedy of ideas. It would be better to relax first, to enjoy what should be obvious even to a critic. The dirty jokes are comedy's lowest common denominator.[8] They bring us back a little to the bathroom humor of five-year-olds, back even to the feces-

and mud-pie pleasures of earlier childhood. They draw us together in loud, coarse, fundamental laughter. And they produce the preliminary relaxation required by the comic catharsis: for even as Trygaeus, mounted paratragically on his flying steed, calls out urgently to the commoners below to keep a tight asshole, lest the beetle swoop after its proper nourishment and throw its rider, the actual audience in the theater of Dionysus, tense and anxious from wartime griefs and pressures and anxieties, are given (for this moment at least) the gift of relaxation, which is the necessary catalyst for their larger recovery of good temper.

This recovery has already been described, and the poetry in which it is conveyed: not least, through images of good taste and good smell. We are now, with Aristophanes' audience, able to make the full contrast: between the pleasures of peace and the pains of war; between the lovely sights, sounds, tastes, and smells of peacetime and the countryside, and the foul experiences of war and the wartime temper, which the prologue helps us to imagine now with a proper revulsion. It is all a matter of taste—or of smell. One problem of sick people is that they lose their taste for normal, healthy food. One problem of people at war is that they lose their peacetime perspective of things, that they become reduced to a thoroughly foul temper and to feeding on—shitty slanders. Conversely, the recovery of good temper, which the comic poet provides—by professional habit of funmaking, and almost by a kind of prevenient grace inherent in comedy—in turn supplies the good will, the good hope, and the good perspective on which any specific right decisions in day-to-day politics must finally depend.

With recovery, then, comes recognition. Aristophanes' business is to make people laugh; it also aims, by means of good humor, to bring them (together with himself) to see the world through a clearer lens. Interpreters of Aristophanes' plays have usually pointed to certain limited attitudes, and limited purposes: that he wants to end the war; that he disapproves of demagogues like Cleon; that he wants the Athenians to be less gullible, and less suspicious, and quicker to cooperate with the rest of Greece, and especially with Sparta. Now all this may be true, but like the man from Ionia's comment, it may not do full justice to the nature or the effect of Aristophanes' comedy. Rather, all those separate political, social, psychological, or aesthetic recognitions embodied in the plays and conveyed to the audience should be seen as subordinate to the larger recognition that goes closely with the recovery of feeling and of perspective. The flight of the dung beetle, the "Olympian" view gained by Trygaeus, are partly metaphors for the renewal of perspective enjoyed by the comic poet and communicated to his audience. Within this clearer view of things, it becomes possible fully to "recognize" Peace: not only in the dictionary definition of "identifying" her "from knowledge of appearance or character," but in the equally important sense of "taking notice of her, treating her as valid, acknowledging her worth." Since the sense of gratitude is still prominent among the connotations of the French verb *reconnaître*, we might best describe Trygaeus' comic flight in the *Peace* as a *vol de reconnaissance*.

Aristotle used the term "recognition" (*anagnōrismos*), together with "reversal" (*peripeteia*), to describe a key moment in tragedy on which its meaning pivots, like Oedipus' recognition of who his parents are, or Iphigenia's recognition that the Greek stranger whom she is ready to sacrifice is her brother Orestes. It is not clear how Aristotle might have applied the term to comedy, if indeed he did. But if we can speak of a more general tragic recognition, involving pity and fear, of what it is to be a human being subject to suffering, pain, loss, disease, and death, could we not equally speak of a general and opposite recognition mediated by comedy, and especially by Old Comedy: a recognition of the comic helplessness shared by human beings, but also of the possibilities of happiness that they are invited to share? The business of a tragic hero like Bellerophon is to attempt to override human limitations, to fly up toward an Olympian power denied to men. Inevitably, he falls to earth, a miserable cripple. The business of a comic hero like Trygaeus is to find a low-down steed that will serve our common human purpose: to find the ordinary but very real and very great happiness that is ours by right. The two visions are competitive but also complementary, as Trygaeus succeeds where Bellerophon failed; and the two recognitions enhance one another by contrast within the total theatrical experience presided over by Dionysus.

Using a medical metaphor that has provoked endless controversy, Aristotle described the function of tragedy in part as effecting a catharsis of pity and fear through (the artistic expression of) the corresponding emotional experiences in the theater. Although he clearly intended to give a similar account of the comic catharsis, this is lost to us, and we can say little with certainty except that tears were replaced with laughter.[9] Still, the concept of catharsis seems a rich and fruitful way of approaching comedy as well as tragedy. It had (what Aristotle largely ignored) a religious dimension, of "purification"; it had a psychological dimension of "purgation"; it had further possibilities of an aesthetic and intellectual dimension, which Aristotle seems to have become increasingly interested in as he contemplated the relation of tragedy's effect to its artistic structure. To my mind, the concept of catharsis is richer, and more largely applicable to tragedy, than Aristotle realized or (as he used it) intended. I want, in the present book, to apply it to the full experience of Aristophanic comedy. I shall take my time, constructing a cumulative account of comic catharsis in my first four chapters, which approach the problem from different angles (festive, psychological, theatrical, and playful); but I shall return again and again to the same basic sequence, of relaxation, recovery, and recognition, that I have sketched out for the *Peace*.

Very provisionally, I shall translate catharsis as "clarification through release," a phrase used by C. L. Barber in his splendid book *Shakespeare's Festive Comedy*.[10] It suggests nicely both the emotional experience of comedy and the lucidity of mind that this can bring. It also returns us to the atmosphere of Athenian festival, and to Dionysus.

2   Theōria *as Festive Release*

PEACE'S first attendant, Opora, whom Trygaeus will marry, personifies the bounty of the Athenian countryside. Her companion Theoria, who is presented to the Council, is harder to define. The name suggests "gazing" or "sight-seeing"; and indeed, Trygaeus includes among the recovered joys of peace the possibility that now you can "go where you like," freed from military call-up; that you can "sail or stay, screw or sleep, / or see the sights and fairs" (*eis panēgyreis theōrein*, 342). Sight-seeing is therefore one of many embodiments of the holiday spirit indicated by *theōria*. Usually it suggests a journey to participate in some religious celebration like the great Games at Olympia.[11] Later in the play, Theoria as a "naked woman" lends herself to a series of jokes about sex and sports taken from such occasions: people will find places to put up their tentpoles; they will wrestle, dig in, ride bareback or astride, and so forth. The sports all turn sexual, in a marvelous series of double entendres. But the sex is also sportive. Everything reflects the exuberance of holiday leisure and entertainment, in town delights as well as country matters.

One special manifestation of *theōria* is the enjoyment of the theater (*theatron*) by the spectators (*theatai*). Trygaeus lists "Dionysia, flutes, tragic players, Sophoclean lyrics" among the pleasures sponsored by peace (Euripides is rejected by Hermes as being too controversial). Although comedy is not mentioned here, the Dionysian festivals alluded to included tragic and comic plays, and there is surely a hint of the Great Dionysia of 421 B.C., in which the spectators of the *Peace* are presently engaged. Briefly, Aristophanes pauses to enjoy and celebrate his comedy's festive context. The parodos of the *Clouds* shows a comparable moment of self-regard. There the mist maidens exhort themselves, in lovely lyric verses, to rise (as natural clouds might) from Ocean's waters to the mountain heights, whence they can behold the entire earth with far-seeing eye: mountain peaks, watered farmlands, the sounding rivers and deep-roaring sea. But then, like a camera's eye, their sight-seeing focuses in on Athens as the home of religious celebrations, of temples and dedications and processions, "well garlanded sacrifices to the gods, and festivities in all seasons,"

> and as the spring enters in,
> the grace of the Roaring One,
> excitement of sounding choruses
> and deep-roaring
> music of the shawms.

The ode is very joyful. It celebrates the liturgical calendar of Athens, the continuous flow of feasts and holidays that brighten the year and give it meaning and excitement. The chorus move imaginatively from a far-off perspective of the whole earth to a close-up view of the occasion in which the singers and dancers who play clouds are actually participating. They tell us that the year is for making holiday, and holidays are for plays, and the best sort of play is a new comedy by Aristophanes! It all seems encouraging—even in a play about intellectual and cultural changes that might, in the end, banish the Olympian gods and quite take away the point of holidays and feasts.

How can we understand Aristophanes' plays adequately when we ourselves disregard holidays? When we appreciate conflict but not celebration? It seems that, so long as the comic hero is struggling against odds to carry his point or win his victory, we are with him; but afterwards, when he settles down to enjoy the fruits of victory, we tend to lose interest, to feel that the play is falling apart. Too many literary critics end up resembling the spoilsport and imposter types who regularly turn up during these later scenes to interrupt a sacrifice, to claim a share in a feast—and to be beaten and kicked and whipped ignominiously offstage. We talk about conventions, but we miss their meaning. We speak as though Aristophanes threw in a *kōmos* and *gamos* (revel and marriage) at a play's end because he had to, because he didn't have anything else to do. We lick our lips over obscene jokes; we pride ourselves on having outgrown Victorian inhibitions—but we divorce these jokes from the living holiday context from which they derive their vitality, their fun, and, in the end, their meaning. If the sex jokes cited earlier are so very funny, and even rejuvenating, it is because they remain playful at heart—because they have not yet become detached from cakes and wine and games and worship of the gods. Holiday is not a pretext for obscenity. Rather, obscenity is one way of expressing and celebrating the richness of life—which is what religious festivals are mainly about. Hence the sacrifices and prayers onstage (especially in the later part of comedies) and the thanksgiving rituals in which the *theatai* imaginatively or actually participate are a way of recalling and focusing the holiday meanings on which the spirit of Old Comedy depends.

In a central ode in the *Peace*, the chorus invoke the Muse, asking her to "dance with me, your friend, making tell of marriages of gods, banquets of men, and celebrations: for these are, from the beginning, your concern." And after much funmaking, the ode ends, "Goddess Muse, play out the holiday with us" (*sympaisde tēn heortēn*). It is hard to join in "sympaisthetically" if we cannot reconstruct that intimate connection between play and holiday from our own experience; but art and archaeology can help greatly, and comparative anthropology, if we bring receptive minds and hearts to what they offer. The *choes*, those little squat pitchers depicting scenes of Athenian children playing with new toys during the Anthesteria, may (if we look closely) help us remember our own childhood presents under the Christmas tree.[12] The pictures of tops, of hobbyhorses, of little wagons, recall the richness of such times. Again (to return to sex and jokes among older people, which may yet keep a childlike aspect in areas innocent of Freud): a student tells me how living on Amorgos helped him understand Aristophanes. For the Greeks today, and especially the islanders, the high point of the year is still Easter, its week-long liturgies culminating first in the tragic ritual, the age-old lamentation, of Good Friday, and then, beyond that, in the glorious and joyful celebration of Easter Sunday, of the Resurrection. But after that? It seems that on the afternoon of Easter—often an anticlimactic time—the people of Amorgos sit around in a great circle and make jokes, old familiar jokes with double entendres about cucumbers and bananas and other fruits and vegetables.[13] It is very good fun, and it has, on Easter Sunday afternoon, its place.[14]

The Parthenon frieze conveys the deep seriousness and excitement of an Athenian holiday. It shows one of those rare moments when liberty and order march (or ride) together, when different ages, sexes, and classes are reconciled in communal celebration. For a blessed moment of time, or almost out of time, they all cooperate in the great procession and offering to Athena, and they all have their place: the maidens carrying chairs, the aristocratic young riders, the middle-aged marshals, the older priests and priestesses, and beyond them, quietly receiving their homage, the seated Olympian gods and goddesses who are the true center of life's order and meaning for families and for the polis. Pericles speaks in the Funeral Oration of the psychological benefit of such holidays:

> Not only this: but we provided many respites from toil for the mind, through traditional games and sacrifices throughout the year, and also through excellent private furnishings from which we derive a pleasure that, day by day, casts out pain. (Thuc. 2.38)

Here, as elsewhere, Pericles is justifying the importance given to leisure and culture in Athenian life. On the one hand he defends Athens against the charge made by quieter, more conservative states that the Athenians "take no rest themselves, and allow none to other people";[15] on the other, he justifies the abundance of holidays (which some critics of the democracy thought excessive, and extremely expensive);[16] and he argues that leisure and enjoyment promote, even as they are balanced by, self-discipline and the constant capacity to act. "We are lovers of beauty, but with economy," he will say later. "We are lovers of wisdom, but without becoming soft." The ideal was, and is, impressive. Notice, however, that Pericles (here as elsewhere) largely ignores the gods in his panegyric of Athens. His emphasis is psychological. He stresses what holidays *do* for people, along with those handsome tables and couches and red-figured drinking cups that rest the mind. In short, the aesthetic pleasure and psychological relief afforded by periodic holidays make up one part of a complex formula, a Periclean balancing act that marshals the diverse forces and tensions and aspirations of Athenian life. But are the gods behind those holidays quite real? The man of reason, nourished on the new sciences of music, physics, and psychology, does not say.

I do not mean, in noting the gods' absence from Pericles' idealizing picture of Athens, either to belittle his humanism or (returning to my subject, the theater) to play down the contributions of the polis, and especially the Periclean polis, to the dramatic festivals of Athens. To do so would be ungrateful. Tragedy and comedy grew out of the worship of Dionysus, the fertility rituals of late winter and early spring, and the play forms, of singing and dancing, masking and acting, that became attached to these rituals.[17] For the gift, and the inner meaning, of the play forms that became tragedy and comedy, we should thank Dionysus. For the theater in which dramatic art reached mature excellence, we must thank the polis, and especially those leaders who, from Peisistratus to Pericles, and from whatever personal or political motives, believed in strengthening Athenian culture, and greatly succeeded.

Athenian comedy, like Athenian tragedy, exists in time and depends on many historical conditions for its beauty, its richness, and its freedom of spirit. Aristophanes' artistic maturity, his brilliant and sure control of poetic and theatrical conventions, depends on a long process of artistic maturation from comedy's rustic and spontaneous beginnings (to which Aristotle rightly but somewhat vaguely points), on the cumulative skill of generations of comic playwrights, on the stimulus and example of the earlier development of Greek tragedy. The unusual freedom of Old Comedy, in word and gesture and act, rests also on the unusual freedom of Athenian, and Periclean, democracy (not least when it makes fun of Pericles); the unusual energy of Old Comedy reflects the riches, power, and assertive self-confidence of later fifth-century Athens, which was imperialistic as well as democratic. Plays were produced at the Great Dionysia after the year's tribute money was publicly displayed. The comic poets could, and often did, criticize Athens' exploitation of her subject "allies," but they enjoyed state payment for themselves and for their actors, and, still more, enjoyed the costuming and costly training of their choruses by rich sponsors, aristocrats and businessmen and politicians, who sometimes accepted these and other "liturgies" less from public spirit and love of the arts than for other, less pure motives. Perhaps gratitude takes hindsight. The decline in drama after the Peloponnesian War shows how much the spirit of tragedy and comedy depended on Athens' power and prosperity. The stimulus of competition counted for much also. And finally, however much I want to praise the holiday spirit as being central to comedy (as it is to tragedy), we need to remember that, practically speaking, festive release was always supported and shaped by public discipline and order.[18] After all, you can't enjoy Aristophanes' *Peace* if your drunken neighbor is hitting you with a whip or pouring wine down your back. Many carnivals today, whether in Munich or Rio or New Orleans, can teach us much about festive release and social solidarity: they are vital institutions for recovering good civic feeling and for reenergizing the human spirit; but although their band music and jazz and popular singing are splendid, they have not, as a rule, produced very great comedy. Without great order and great discipline (and the training of a Greek chorus was sometimes compared to military training), Aristophanes' comedies would never have existed.

How far did the Great Dionysia retain the force of religious holiday in the later fifth century, and how far had it become secularized, as just one more excuse for a good time? The question is relative, of course, since *all* Greek holidays were times off from ordinary work or routine: times to eat roast meat, to drink more wine than usual, to dress up, to make noise, and to watch processions or games (*agōnes*) or other forms of entertainment.[19] Plato's account of a festival of Bendis, the Thracian Artemis, in *Republic* 1 gives a point of comparison. Socrates is tempted to dine with friends in the Piraeus in order to enjoy an unusual spectacle: a relay race with torches on horseback, which will be part of the all-night celebration (*pannychis*) of the goddess. For the sophisticated young Athenians whom Socrates meets, a little bored with ordinary religious occasions, the festival of Bendis provides new excitement, something new to "look at" (*theōrein*). Indeed, their interest exemplifies that "fondness for sight-seeing" (*philotheōria*) that Socrates later decries as a rival, or deterrent, to the serious study of philosophy.

It may be that interest in exotic gods and goddesses like the Thracian Sabazios or Bendis reflects a falling-off from the Olympians. Yet I would argue that this did not yet hold true of Dionysus. In his festivals, the old seasonal revelry and fertility magic took on heightened power, and new meaning, as part of the worship of a god whose gifts of ecstasy and release were very beautiful but also very dangerous—who was not yet a tame god to be taken for granted by his festivalgoers.[20]

In Greek myth and art Dionysus is special, different, the giver of release (Lyaios, Lysios). He is typically shown as escaping from bondage or helping others to escape. Thus, in the Homeric Hymn to Dionysus, he is kidnapped by pirates, but his hands and feet cannot stay bound: suddenly wine streams through the ship, swelling grapevines enwrap the sails, ivy grows around the mast; the god, now a lion, devours the captain, but the other sailors leap overboard and are changed to dolphins. (The Exekias Cup makes us feel that, leaping and sporting, they are now better off.) "The god himself will release me, at my desire," says the disguised god in Euripides' *Bacchae*. For his followers, as for him, fetters are loosed, prison doors swing open wide. Everyday labor too can be a prison: so the loom on which Minyas' daughters weave is suddenly overgrown with ivy and grapevines, while milk and wine trickle down from the ceiling. In the lost myth of the Return of Hephaestus, Hera is released from a magic golden chair contrived by her son. Ares tried and failed: Hephaestus could not be appeased; but finally Dionysus made him drunk and conveyed him back to Olympus in great revelry and joy. (The procession back is splendidly represented on vases.)[21] Why was this myth so appealing? It almost seems a parable of the psyche's return, through wine and revelry, to its natural wholeness and freedom. We are rescued ourselves from bonds, and from stubborn isolation, by the god's gift. We laugh to see the all-too-relaxed Hephaestus borne helplessly along on the donkey's back, but this laughter is sign and token of our own release.

Dionysus was long known in Greece as the giver of joy, through his sacrament of wine. His coming as liberator from cares and troubles and ordinary labors could be felt in the leisure of a dinner party or in the unusual exaltation of religious revelry and celebration. That full range of joy is conveyed in two great odes of the *Bacchae*; but we can hear it throughout Greek drama if we listen receptively to the language and feeling of choral songs: for example, to Sophocles' breathtaking

> *iō pyr pneiontōn chorag' astrōn, nychiōn*
> *phthegmatōn episkope*

> (O chorus-leader of the fire-breathing stars,
> who watch over
>   voices in the night)

from the *Antigone*. Let me turn again to the strong emotional witness of vase painting. A magnificent red-figured vase by the Berlin Painter, formerly at Castle Ashby, shows a maenad of exceptional beauty, humanized yet wild.[22] She holds a thyrsus in her right hand; the left is outflung in a gesture of adoration; her feet are turned to the right, but the rest of her body turns effortlessly to the left, toward the dignified, commanding presence of the god. With others—a piping satyr, another maenad—she is caught up in the dance; yet she shows the tranquility and gracefulness of an utterly relaxed personality at harmony with itself. She is ecstatic with joy, yet beautifully human—an Athenian worshiper.

I have dwelt on these representations of Dionysus partly out of love, for they are beautiful and moving, but partly too because they remind us of the force *behind* the holiday. For it was the god's advent in early spring, celebrated in festive procession, in hymn and prayer and sacrifice by day, in torch-lit revelry by night, *and* in dithyramb, tragedy, comedy, and satyr play, that gave release and rejoicing. You cannot have a holiday just because (as Pericles says) the mind needs frequent resting places from toil. A holiday is sacred time. The theater was, or once again became, sacred space. Both were Dionysus' gift. The state could organize the holiday magnificently, could shape the occasion by public and private generosity and by the provision of good order; but in the end, it was the god's felt presence that gave the holiday games their liberating force and made it possible to play.

A few known details from the ceremonies of the Great Dionysia may be suggestive.[23] It came, first of all, around the beginning of March. A dithyramb of Pindar written for the Athenians celebrates Dionysus' coming in spring, inviting him to take his share of "violet-wreathed garlands and songs culled in springtime."[24] Here he is associated with the earth's gentle and gracious awakening in spring; elsewhere, with the violent equinoctial storms that accompany it. In any event the connection between Dionysus and spring must have been a potent, joyous one. The Great Dionysia came after the opening of the sailing season, for allied cities sent their representatives to Athens, bearing tribute to be displayed at the festival. Aristophanes makes us aware of the presence of foreigners at his comedies, which Cleon seized upon as a pretext for trying to censor them. Something of the feeling of Dionysian release may be reflected in legal provisions for the holiday. A scholiast tells us that prisoners were let out on bail to attend the festival; sometimes they took the chance of escaping. There was also a law forbidding legal proceedings or seizure or the taking of security for debt during this festival. Not that these provisions are uniquely attested for the Dionysia: but they do suggest the force of holidays, much as, today, the customary force of religious holidays in Italy or Spain may be measured by the degree to which everything closes down (banks, shops, restaurants), to the dismay of American tourists.

Pickard-Cambridge describes how, perhaps before the festival proper began, the Athenians reenacted the original coming of Dionysus from Eleutherai, on the Boeotian border:

> The statue of Dionysus Eleuthereus was taken to a temple in the neighborhood of the Academy, on the road to Eleutherai, and placed by the *eschara* there. There sacrifice was offered, and hymns

were sung, and the statue was escorted back to the theatre in a torchlight procession in which the leading part was taken by the *ephēboi*, the young men of military age.[25]

This ceremony must have helped the Athenians to feel the force of the god's coming, much as, at the Anthesteria, he arrived in his magical ship-car, as from overseas, and was drawn through the streets, surrounded by a crowd of revelers. The Great Dionysia did not have the special carnival flavor of the Anthesteria, that late winter festival when the new wine was opened and dangerous spirits walked abroad—a time for widespread drunkenness and carousing, for dressing up, for daemon masquerading, and for hurling indecent remarks and insults at bystanders from the Dionysian floats. The Anthesteria had something of the special danger-ousness and excitement that we associate with such remaining carnival times as Halloween and New Year's Eve. The Lenaea, an earlier winter festival of Dionysus, was derived from his ecstatic worship by companies of "madwomen" (*lēnai*) and so may have shared in this carnival atmo-sphere. The Great Dionysia, by contrast, had departed from its rustic origins and had become more a national patriotic celebration. Tribute was displayed in the theater; the grown children of dead Athenian sol-diers were paraded in new armor, and blessed; honors were proclaimed; ambassadors came from other states. Yet the god's presence, as a bringer of release and freedom, must have remained central. His epithet, Eleu-thereus, indicates this too: for besides meaning "from Eleutherai," it must also have suggested Eleutherios, the god "of freedom," a special patron of the Athenian democracy.

Tragedy and comedy are set off from the ordinary Athenian world; they belong to sacred space, and to sacred time. This must have been felt by the Athenian theatergoer as few tourists feel it today, except for the occasional very imaginative archaeologist: for the theater of Dionysus on the south slope of the Acropolis was closed off by a precinct wall, or *peribolos*, that also included the temple of Dionysus in which the ancient cult image was housed.[26] It seems likely that sacrifices and prayers were offered to Dionysus daily during the festival; likely, too, that the statue was escorted each day into the theater, with some ceremony. There it stood, recalling the sacred origin and meaning of the plays. So, too, did the priest of Dionysus, enthroned in the center of the first row of specta-tors, as though presiding over the games. Still more, the enclosing *peri-bolos* must have conveyed a sense of protection, of sacred space. For a time the theatergoers left their ordinary world, entered into a world belonging to Dionysus. The religious sanctions of tragedy, and still more (for our purposes) of comedy, could still be felt.

The Great Dionysia had grown out of the much simpler Country Di-onysia of early winter, which was marked by a phallic procession and song, the sacrifice of a goat, and a *kōmos*, or night-revel, in the god's honor. It seems likely that, from early times, groups of worshipers formed choruses to sing, dance, and play, perhaps in animal masquerade, and later to compete with other such choruses. These may have been the original "goat-singers" (*tragōidoi*) and "revel-singers" (*kōmōidoi*) from whom the later, specialized dramatic forms take their name. Similarly, at the Great Dionysia, sacred time was marked out by the ceremonies of the opening day. It began with a great procession escorting the god's image into the theater, where a sacrifice and prayers were held; it closed with a torchlit *kōmos*. The most striking feature of the day must have been the carrying of great wooden phalluses in procession, sent by all the tribute-paying cities of the empire. Evidently this had its political side, like so much else at the Dionysia. It was a clear demonstration of Athenian potency—of the allies' surrender, so to speak, of their masculine force to Athens. But also, it kept a continuity with the old fertility rites by which blessings were invoked upon the crops, animals, and people, and blighting influences were expelled or warded off. Phales became, in Aristophanes' words, the "fellow reveler of Dionysus." Differently, we could say that the old forms of festive play from which tragedy and comedy sprang were taken up into Dionysian worship, from which they received continuing protection, and heightened meaning. This is the more specially true for Old Comedy, as it retains, or integrates into a sophisticated art form, such old festive elements as the singing and dancing in animal or daemon disguise, the ritual combats (*agōnes*), the various uses of obscenity and invective (*aischrologia*), or teasing, in combination with hymns and prayers for blessings, and the representation, though in burlesque form, of a sacrifice and feast.

All this is sacred play. It also gives healing. If you could ask an Athenian why the phallic procession was included in the festival, you would be given not an anthropological answer but an explanation traditionally couched in the shape of a myth.[27] It seems that in Athens, as elsewhere, people resisted the coming of the god, and the men of Athens were afflicted with a disease (presumably a sexual one); on consulting an oracle, they were told to manufacture phalluses in the god's honor. They did so, and were cured. The story is typical in the way it provides an ex post facto explanation for a cult practice. Obscenity is right, in this sacred time and place, because the god requires it. But we could put it differently: that the occasional expression of pent-up libidinal and aggressive feelings has its own strong healing force in any civilized society. And being cathartic, it is especially appropriate to the festive worship of Dionysus, the giver of release. Yet this brings us to his other, his dangerous side, as the god who destroys self-possession, who can bring on madness.

For Dionysus (to return to my earlier point) cannot be taken for granted. He does not exist just to provide wine, fun, and relaxation for people. He is not like Santa Claus. Myth and cult, art and drama, constantly remind us that he and his gifts are ambivalent, that they can be intensely dangerous. Release is joyful, but utter release is into madness. The daughters of Minyas were not just rescued from working at the loom: they were driven mad. The landscape of myth is full of the god's victims, and of *their* victims. Euripides' *Bacchae*, for all its hymns to joy, tells the most frightful of stories: how the rationalist Pentheus resists the god; how little by little, he succumbs to the god's seductive power, and to his own repressed instincts; how he dons women's clothing, goes to spy on the Bacchantes, and is torn to pieces by them (and especially by his own delirious mother). We ourselves may choose to rationalize, to draw a psychological moral, to say that people who "let go" a little are saved from the greater madness. That is sometimes true. But it is not what Euripides saw. It does not make his tragedy any the less frightful.

I think, then, that behind Greek tragedy and comedy we must see a god who has a double nature. On the one hand, Dionysus is a naturalized Olympian god, a friend and equal of Apollo (with whom he is so often represented in vase paintings, Apollo with his lyre, Dionysus in a trailing robe, his head graciously bent, holding a vine branch in one hand and a wine cup in the other). This is the god of Athenian state worship, including the dramatic festivals. Indeed it is helpful to see tragedy and comedy as ventures co-sponsored by Dionysus and Apollo, passion and the ordering intelligence working together to achieve highest art. And yet Dionysus is never fully assimilated into the Olympian pantheon, the rational order of things. He always remains a little the Stranger God. The parallel with Aphrodite is striking. On the East Pediment of the Parthenon both Dionysus and Aphrodite turn away from the other Olympians. Both are tigers, not kittens to sport with. The Greeks knew the overpowering force of *erōs*, of sexual passion, and so prayed to Aphrodite for gentle loves, for happy marriage. Likewise, even as they gratefully celebrated Dionysus' gift of joyful release from care, they cried to the same god to protect them from the strong insanity for which he also stood, and stands. Like Aphrodite, Dionysus was a god to be loved, but also a god strongly to be feared.

It remains true that human life is enriched, indeed made most fully human by the inclusion and integration of strong, potentially destructive emotions. Even Plato, who usually saw emotion as the great enemy of reason, has Socrates speak in the *Phaedrus* of four beneficial, creative, and god-fostered types of "madness" (*mania*): (1) prophetic madness, inspired by Apollo; (2) "cathartic" madness (such as that of the Corybantes, a religious form of psychotherapy characterized by loud music and violent dancing); (3) poetic madness, under the patronage of the Muses; and (4) Socrates' special subject here, the madness of love. In the end we are not surprised when the Platonic *erōs* is sublimated, made philosophical in its striving, a powerful instrument of the soul's return to the divine realm of Forms where it rightly belongs. Yet Plato's myth of the soul's chariot and the wingedness of love gives strong testimony to the value of the irrational—to how much creativity, inspiration, and friendship with the gods would be lost if we ignored our irrational, even daemonic powers. The life commonly praised as "sensible" and "rational" is a poor, dry, unwinged life by comparison.

And so, to return to Aristophanes' *Peace*: there is a link between the "madness" of the comic hero and the Dionysian catharsis of which comedy and its audience partake. From any normal standpoint a comic hero like Trygaeus is evidently mad. He makes little ladders to climb to Heaven. He attempts (despite Bellerophon's failure on Pegasus) transportation by dung beetle. And yet: it takes some *mania* to break through the limits of what is usually called feasibility in the affairs of nations. If everyone knows (to paraphrase the imposter and oracle-monger Hierocles) that peace cannot be made until the moon turns blue, then it is up to the comic hero to go after peace, which we all want and need, and to obtain it somehow in that queer blue light. Trygaeus is mad, but there is comic method in his madness. The chorus, as said before, are also maniacal in their singing and dancing and celebrating; and we too are called to a healing touch of madness, to leave behind our usual cares and strategies, to join in the comic revel. The ultimate question asked by comedy is, "Will you, won't you, will you, won't you, won't you join the dance?" Comedy invites us all to the wedding feast and revel, though a few spoilsports—munitions makers, oracle-mongers, literary critics—will have to be kicked out of the party in the old ritual way. "If you follow me," say the departing chorus of the *Peace*, "you will eat cheesecakes." We are being invited one last time to enjoy (after securing them) the blessings of peace. But before that, we are invited to join in the comic revel. Only by joining in will we experience the full recovery; only by letting go a little, in Dionysian release, will we receive the god's gift of catharsis that wards off larger insanity. For what we gain is not just a better intellectual or ethical understanding of life. It is more a "clarification through release," akin to the lucidity born of relaxation that (sometimes) comes from drinking wine. It is, if I may pun, a comic revel-ation.

3   Theōria *as Playful Awareness*

UP to now, I have been arguing for the importance of holiday participation to our appreciation of Aristophanic comedy. Even before the spectators enter the theater, even before the comedy begins, Dionysus' holiday provides escape from the ordinary cares and constraints of life. The holiday sanctions and protects comedy's jokes, its strategies of relaxation and recovery; and comedy in its turn mirrors holiday values and meanings and reminds us feelingly of what they mean. There is a similar relation between the comic gift of recovery and the good political life. Theoria is an attendant of Peace, on whom holiday leisure and merrymaking depend; yet we must preempt *theōria* imaginatively, must accept the comic perspective in advance, in our hearts and minds, if we are even going to desire Peace sufficiently to make a sustained effort to get her back.

Not surprisingly, then, there is a great deal of audience participation in the *Peace*. As they sit, row on row, beyond and above the chorus, they may be imagined as pulling with them, joining in the common effort of drawing Peace out of the deep cave where she has been hidden.[28] (I think of the Beatles' song "All together now!" at the end of their comic fantasy *The Yellow Submarine*.) They may also be imagined to share in the dedication of Peace and the concomitant festivities and rewards. Theoria herself is "handed over" into the keeping of the Council, who (in the theater) welcome her lustfully. The front rows are sprinkled, and possibly drenched, with lustral water for the ritual sacrifice onstage; barley grains (from the same ritual) are hurled into the audience; later on, they are invited to join in tasting the *splanchna* or viscera of the sacrificial victim. In this way, the old trick of throwing candy to the audience takes on new meaning, of communion in the blessings of peace that they have helped to secure.

But Theoria has another side. The very act of "looking attentively" at something suggests detachment as well as participation; and the audience of the *Peace* are constantly reminded that they are watching a play, are *theatai* in a *theatron*. The play is rich in what are called "violations of the dramatic illusion." There are all the jokes about the flight of the dung beetle to Olympus: actually, a large wooden "flying machine" is hoisted up by a crane (the famous *mēchanē*) from behind the facade representing Trygaeus' house; it carries him over the stage in a series of jerky motions, and finally it deposits him at "Olympus," which is either the other side of the stage or else midstage again, just where he started.[29] All this illustrates on a large scale the fun of *mimēsis*, of "pretend" or "make-believe": something that gives great pleasure in comedy, as in tragedy, but that calls attention to itself in comedy in wonderfully funny ways that were not (then) possible in tragedy: as when the actor playing Trygaeus bellows from aloft,

> Boy, am I scared! It's not a joke any longer!
> Hey there, stage manager, pay attention, will you?
> I've already got butterflies in my tummy,
> and if you don't watch out, I really mean it,
>   I'll—*I'll feed the beetle!*

And so it goes. The beloved lady Peace will be represented by a colossal bust. Her attendants, those spirits of lovely celebration, will be a pair of naked women—played, though (male) scholars often prefer to imagine otherwise, by male actors in appropriately shaped and decorated leotards. And even the central religious sacrifice, of a sheep, never takes place onstage: for Peace, we are told, "abhors bloody sacrifices"; and what is more, "this way, the sheep is saved for the producer."

Now G. M. Sifakis and Kenneth McLeish have argued that this sort of joke is not really a "violation of the dramatic illusion" (for in comedy such an illusion never really existed), but rather a kind of continuing interplay between actors and audience.[30] I would quite agree, and would add that by the *Peace* Aristophanes had developed techniques of interplay with the audience almost to perfection. He holds them in the palm of his hand, from the first warm-up jokes of the prologue to the festive exodos in which they join in singing the refrain of a jolly marriage song for Trygaeus and his bride. The "violations" of what in tragedy would be "dramatic illusion" do make us laugh through their abrupt incongruities. They are a special, very funny kind of joke. But they also keep us more than usually aware that we are watching a play, that the events of the *Peace* are not literally happening. Why does Aristophanes insist on this detachment?

In part (and I shall argue this point at greater length in subsequent chapters), it is because he is an honest magician. Such a one pretends, of course, to work magic; he defies you to see through his tricks; and yet you know, and he himself encourages you to remember, that these *are* tricks of a magician using sleight of hand and various properties, not really working magic. He teases you, showing that "there is nothing up my sleeve," invites you onstage to look more carefully—and let yourself be publicly fooled. And all this is very good fooling, very good entertainment; but it remains honest in a way that fortune-telling and astrology and, I am afraid, a great deal that passes for psychotherapy and even religion these days does not. So with Aristophanes: he is honest, first of all, because he keeps his audience aware of his theatrical art and (in some part) of how it works, or plays. Although he does not quite create illusions, he has acquired the comic poet's art, which is to play upon the hearts and minds of his audience and to bring them through laughter to healing and through relaxation to recovery and recognition. For example, in the *Peace* he brings his audience back to a strong emotional remembrance of the blessings of peace; and once this is done, a number of points can be made clear—among them, that Cleon and other politicians have manipulated the sick, wartime temper of the Athenian people for their own selfish purposes. The gullibility of the Athenians, their deception by Cleon (and before him, by Pericles), are shown up, revealed, made clear by the comic poet's clarification. And yet Aristophanes too is a deceiver when, through his comic art, he persuades his audience to be in better temper and to see all these things with new, happier perception; or rather, he would be a deceiver if he did not, also through his art, maintain our awareness that all this is art and play. He wants, most emphatically, to take the audience with him; but he does not want, in the end, to take them in.

A second aspect of Aristophanes' honesty is that he never for very long forgets, or lets us forget, the recalcitrance of nature, and of human nature, and of history. For if, initially, the holiday humor and escapist strategy of Aristophanes allow us to leave behind ordinary preoccupations about trouble and deprivation and war, still the "flight of the dung beetle" affords a sharper, more realistic look at what has been happening in Athens. Again, Aristophanes conveys this play perspective through joking. Trygaeus, on his "return," tells the audience:

> It was harder than I thought, getting
> through to the gods. Oh, my legs hurt. And
> how small you people were to look at from up
> there. Looking down from heaven, I tell you,
> you seemed a pretty wicked lot. But now,
> from here, you seem—a great deal wickeder. (819–23)

Through all its humor and fantasy, the play makes us more, not less, aware of the real difficulty of securing and keeping peace. The jokes about how the gods went off in anger because the Greeks wouldn't accept Peace when she was offered to them, come close to tragedy. Their idiocy in rejecting peace is just barely made palatable by vulgar joking: they "fingered her down," they "threw out the goddess with pitchfork screams" (more confusion with dung). Aristophanes is frank enough to show the Athenians their folly and tactful enough not to dwell on it. He wants repentance, not remorse. But the play conveys a strong feeling of how contingent peace is, and how much it matters to grasp the right moment, or *kairos*—as in the following exchange between Trygaeus and the chorus:

> *Chor.* Isn't it splendid how
> everything goes the way we want?
> How, when a god wants it so,
> and fortune gets it right,
> one good thing after another
> matches up in the nick of time?
> *Tryg.* Clearly so. Here's our altar waiting for us outdoors.
> *Chor.* So hurry now, while this wind
> sent by the gods is strongly blowing,
> aversative of war;
> evidently, a god is shifting
> all these things to the good. (939–46)

The *kairos* joke refers here to theatrical magic. How convenient that an altar for sacrifice should appear just when you want it! But this same joke reminds us that, outside the theater, good things do not come automatically when you want them; that when they do come, they may be ignored or rejected; that Chance is a powerful goddess; that the winds of fortune veer swiftly and unpredictably. (This last image recurs frequently in Euripides' tragedies and also in Thucydides' history.) A related and very painful idea suggested throughout the *Peace* is that the gods are angry at Athens, that the city is no longer under their loving care and protection. Or have they (a still more alarming thought) withdrawn because modern thought has demythologized them? There is, I think, a paradox here. Only Aristophanes' strong traditional sense of the gods' presence, deeply rooted in comic celebration, allows him to face, and face down, the threatening idea (which again is very prominent in Euripides and Thucydides) that they have departed.

One chief method by which the celebratory and skeptical sides of Aristophanes' vision are held in balance is through teasing. I give two examples from the *Peace*, both about food. The first belongs to the celebration of the return of Peace and the imagined sacrifice in her honor. Trygaeus invokes her blessings; a servant begs her not to behave like an ordinary flirtatious tease playing peekaboo; and then Trygaeus prays that her blessings will continue:

> No, please: but show yourself entirely
> candid and open to your lovers
> who have been languishing for you
> for lo! these thirteen years;

Free us from fights, loose our tensions,
so we can call you Staying Lucy;[31]
make an end to our shrewd suspicions,
    oh-so-clever,
      which we babble against each other;
and mix us Hellenes all together
where we began, with loving-kindness;
cool off our overheated spirits,
    mix in a mellow understanding;
and may our marketplace be filled
    with goods of every kind:
    garlic out of Megara,
    quinces, cukes, and pomegranates,
    [strawberries, bananas, grapes,
    Godiva chocolates, Riviera pears],
    snug little down-coats for the servants;
and then, out of Boeotia, come
    a great parade of food,
geese and ducks, quail and pheasant
    (Oh, how pleasant!),
culminating
    in cartloads of COPAIC EELS,
so we'd all be crowding around,
grocery-shopping, bumping into
Morychos, Elvis Parsley, other
gourmandizers: last would come
Melanthios to the market, late,
and all be sold, and he lament
with an aria out of his *Medea*:
    "O dearest eel,
      I feel I am
      unwived of you,
      deprived of you,
    brought to your bed of ashes
    in a *sauce bonne femme*!"
And all the people will clap and sing,
    "For he's a jolly good—failure!"   (987–1016)

The first request, for Peace to undress fully for her lovers' delight, implies that, outside the theater, she has not yet shown herself fully. There is much more work to be done. Peace is then pictured as a magical cook who will recompound all the people "with a larger mixture of the juices of friendliness and mercy, qualities in which they were deficient" (Platnauer's commentary). Her gentle, beneficent cooking is contrasted with the horrible efforts of the ogre War to pound all Greece into a mixed salad. It is also contrasted with the wretched diet on which Cleon kept the Athenians. And it also suggests the comic playwright's own efforts, as a "good humor man," to put the Athenians into better temper—which is a chief purpose and meaning of this play. Yet all this turns to comic fantasy in the picture of all those good things coming, so abundantly and so effortlessly, into the marketplace: culminating in the famous eels from Lake Copais of which Aristophanes was so fond. The fantasy turns humorous as Aristophanes imagines all of "us" and all the usual gluttons pushing and shoving to get some of those eels, and it reaches a climax in the picture of Melanthios' discomfiture. But why is this? Melanthios' frustration is very funny; it makes other people's happiness seem even better by comparison; also, it may have seemed fitting that a person who wrote bad tragedies should end up enacting one. But the exclusion of Melanthios is apotropaic too. It is the negative side of the old fertility ritual, which balances the invocation of prosperity by the expulsion of blighting influences, of scapegoats. At the same time, the comic disappointment of the glutton Melanthios reminds the audience once more that the blessings of peace are not quite real, or quite secure; that comic fantasy and Athenian history may not altogether coincide.

The point is made even more strongly toward the play's end. As he goes inside to prepare for his wedding, Trygaeus invites the chorus to pitch into their food manfully, and the chorus-leader echoes his appeal:

> We'll see to that ourselves;
>   thanks anyway for telling us.
> Now, people! You were starving before:
>   go for the hare's-meat stew!
> It isn't every day you meet
> with cheesecakes crying "Eat me!" in the street.
> With that in mind, enjoy! Plunge in!
> And eat! Or you'll be sorry.   (1311–15)

Here again the audience are reminded, over the heads of the chorus, that they must grasp the *kairos* this time, must get peace now, and all these good things will follow. Yet there is a teasing unreality about their promise.[32] The hare's-meat stew and fine rolls, mentioned earlier, may be represented by stage props, or they may (very likely) be altogether imaginary. And as for those *plakountes*, those flat, layered cheesecakes with honey poured over them, wandering about in the streets as if to say "Eat Me!": surely they belong to that land of Cockaigne that the comic poets love to describe, where rivers flow with wine or with hot barley soup, and pieces of roasted fowl simply fly into your mouth, each on its own piece of hot buttered toast. We are being teased, even tantalized. But why? Partly, I think, for the old reason, and the old ritual: to keep off evil and the gods' resentment. But partly, to tease us back into Athenian life.

"It isn't everyday," we are reminded, "that you can enjoy the abundant riches of fantasy and the comic stage. So enjoy them while, and as, you may."

Something of this same teasing carries into the last lines of *Peace*:

> So now good-bye, you people, and
> be glad; and if you'll follow me,
> you'll get—cheesecakes soon! (1357–59)

These may still be fairy-tale cheesecakes. And yet the play is a call to real happiness; and if the audience (who are also the voters of Athens) follow the lead of the chorus, and behind them of the comic poet, then they may well achieve peace and very many blessings besides—including good humors, and holidays, and cheesecakes, and many good things that you can see and hear and smell and taste and touch. Even cheesecakes can be real. They may not, to be sure, wander lonely in the streets of Athens. But they are wonderful still, they have a fairy-tale loveliness after the sufferings and deprivations and awful diet of war. Aristophanes thus dismisses us (like the dancing chorus) with well-mixed feelings of joyful hope and skeptical awareness, back into ordinary life. The question remains whether that ordinary life has been, or can be, transformed.

Suppose it cannot. Then we would have to say that Aristophanes writes and sees with a double vision: that with one eye (so to speak) he looks on the world of happiness disclosed by Dionysian revel and holiday and theatrical fantasy, but with the other he looks on ordinary Athenian life, painful, problematical, anxiety-ridden—and ultimately real. By this view, comedy would offer a potent but temporary escape from reality; but outside the theater, outside what Shakespeare would call the "garden gate," time and history wait for us, and all the same old problems are there, and nothing has been changed. But I will not admit that this is (whether in Athens or America) the whole story.

For suppose that there is more to Reality than what might better be called "real life"—the everyday world commonly opposed to fantasy.[33] Suppose that daydreaming and fairy tale and fantasy were a doorway into that larger world of Reality. I have always believed since childhood that they were. You may be skeptical, and rightly so; but if, as the chorus says, you will follow me, then you will enjoy a play perspective (or *theōria*) which is not, in the end, a double vision of things, but rather a single, unified, wholeminded and wholehearted way of looking at the world.

Let me clarify my concept of *theōria* by means of an extended comparison with Shakespeare's *Midsummer Night's Dream*. After that, in the next two sections, I shall conclude this chapter by asking, and tentatively answering, two questions for which the analogies with Shakespeare are remarkably helpful: how are Aristophanes' comedies related to their ancient beginnings in ritual? And how are comedy's laughter and play related to the nature and meaning of the gods?

A *Midsummer Night's Dream* much resembles the *Peace* in its basic pattern of relaxation, recovery, and recognition, and in the structural movement by which that pattern is expressed. In Aristophanes' play we move from Athens to Olympus and back to Athens. In Shakespeare's, we begin at a comic "Athens" with star-crossed lovers and a blocking father; we move with the lovers, and also with the clowns, into the green woods by night; and we return with them to Athens town for the celebration of Theseus' wedding with Hippolyta and for their own nuptials. In the meantime they have been changed. In the woods they encounter not just the fairies' magic but also a more general transforming spell by which things dissolve and melt into one another, perceptions are altered beneath glimmering moonlight or starlight, emotions are transformed. We follow the four lovers through night's confused wanderings, delusions, and terrors into the clarity, warmth, and comfort of a new day. They awaken refreshed, as from a dream from which it is hard to awaken completely; so Hermia says,

> Methinks I see these things with parted eye,
> When everything seems double. (4.1)

Lysander is back in love with her again, and all will be well because Demetrius, his rival, has returned to his older allegiance to Helena. In his case, Puck's magic charm has (without his awareness) acted as a restorative counterspell to the delusion of his love for Hermia:

> To her, my lord,
> was I betrothed ere I saw Hermia,
> but, like a sickness, did I loathe this food;
> but, as in health, come to my natural taste,
> now do I wish it, love it, long for it,
> and will for evermore be true to it. (4.1)

So Aristophanes' Athenians might have said of Peace. Through the illusion of comedy, as through a good dream, harmful delusions are dispelled, a better taste is recovered and enjoyed.

And just as Peace was brought back with her desirable attendants, so fertility, health, and joy are brought back ritually from the woods in *A Midsummer Night's Dream* to be conferred upon the marriage and the house. The pattern of quarrel and reconciliation underlying these gifts also has a ritual, and a comic, quality: for as the quarrel between Oberon and Titania magically disrupts the seasons and course of nature, so their renewed harmony restores nature and gives power to bless human lovers:

> Now thou and I are new in amity,
> And will to-morrow midnight solemnly
> Dance in Duke Theseus' house triumphantly
> And bless it to all fair prosperity. (4.1)

The dancing revel into the house and within it, the exorcising of harm, the evocation of good, all seem to follow in nature as in the rite. And the sense of renewal spills over into Shakespeare's audience, transforming their lives and ours by its theatrical "magic," though it is hard for us, as for Bottom, to say exactly how.

But the comic perspective to which Shakespeare (like Aristophanes) summons us has another side, of skeptical awareness, that we share neither with the confused lovers nor with the hilariously confused clowns. Rather, we look on the lovers' wanderings from a vantage point shared with Oberon and Puck:

> Shall we their fond pageant see?
> Lord, what fools these mortals be! (3.2)

What we see, together with these fairies, is how the lovers fail to see, how their eyes are charmed, how they wander in darkness and confusion. This shared perspective raises us in imagination beyond mortal follies and confusions. It is (as we shall find with Aristophanes' choruses of clouds and birds and initiates) a high, enduring gift of comedy. Similarly, we enjoy watching Bottom, Quince, and their fellows muddle through the rehearsals and performance of that most lamentable comedy, "Pyramus and Thisby." The funniest thing, of course, is their literal-mindedness about the play, their eagerness to bring real moonlight through a casement window, their care to warn the audience, especially the ladies, not to be frightened of the lion. Their performance makes unwitting comedy for the sophisticated lovers' entertainment, and for ours. We are refreshed by their childlike involvement in what they are pretending to be. But we are also made all the more aware that *we* are watching a play, that the fairies (and lovers and clowns) are played by actors, and that the magic of the fairies and the woods is make-believe, theatrical magic that depends on our imagination to render it effective.

To what attitude, then, does the playwright call us? To be detached spectators of human folly? Such a view, satiric and skeptical, is well expounded in Theseus' great speech.

Hippolyta
  'Tis strange, my Theseus, that these lovers speak of.
Theseus
  More strange than true. I never may believe
  These antic fables nor these fairy toys.
  Lovers and madmen have such seething brains,
  Such shaping fantasies, that apprehend

> More than cool reason ever comprehends.
> The lunatic, the lover, and the poet
> are of imagination all compact.
> One sees more devils than vast hell can hold:
> That is the madman. The lover, all as frantic,
> Sees Helen's beauty in a brow of Egypt.
> The poet's eye, in a fine frenzy rolling,
> Doth glance from heaven to earth, from earth to heaven;
> And as imagination bodies forth
> The forms of things unknown, the poet's pen
> Turns them to shapes, and gives to airy nothing
> A local habitation and a name.
> Such tricks hath strong imagination
> That, if it would but apprehend some joy,
> It comprehends some bringer of that joy;
> Or in the night, imagining some fear,
> How easy is a bush supposed a bear!   (5.1)

Certainly, the lovers' frantic behavior supports Theseus' view. In their jealousies and desires, their fears, and their violent shifts of sentiment, they seem (beneath the delusive moon) hardly distinguishable from lunatics. The play demonstrates how susceptible humans are to passion and delusion, to the tricks of strong imagination. And yet our perspective as observers goes beyond that of Theseus here, for we know that (within the play) dream transformations have really occurred. They may be strange, but they are also true. We know also that Theseus the skeptic is himself as much a creation of the poet's wild imagination as the fairies are, or the lovers, or the clowns. He "never may believe" in fairies: that is his business, or his role. But he is scarcely in any position to make a final judgment on the matter; and so his skeptical statement is duly countered by the greater openness of Hippolyta, who has the last word here, to the wonder of things:

> But all the story of the night told over,
> And all their minds transfigured so together,
> More witnesseth than fancy's images
> And grows to something of great constancy;
> But howsoever, strange and admirable.   (5.1)

Later, though, when they watch the clowns performing, it is Theseus whose tolerance, affection, and insight go beyond the easy pose of the detached spectator or satirist, and Hippolyta who remains skeptical: "It must be your imagination, then, and not theirs."

One of the distinguishing marks of great comedy, I think, is that in the end it remains sympathetically involved in the folly of mortals, and even in their pain. And here, in its closeness to tragedy, it runs some risk.

Shakespeare's play, like Aristophanes', brings us back to a strong sense of human limitation. It reminds us of mortality ("But she, being mortal, of that child did die." "So quick bright things come to confusion."). Although the star-crossed lovers escape the tragic fate of Romeo and Juliet, or for that matter, of Pyramus and Thisby, Shakespeare shows us much, here too, of the confusion and uncertainty of lovers, their night terrors. If (with Hippolyta) we watch them sympathetically, we lose the easy advantage of a careless superiority. But we gain something better; we share in their experience of "clarification through release." Even as we remain aware that we are watching a play, and that we are participating in revelry that will have an end (which can also be a tragic perception, as witness *The Tempest*), still we may enjoy most fully, and even ourselves be transformed by, the gift of shaping fantasy.

Aristophanes' chorus, departing, called on the audience to rejoice: "and if you follow along with me, you will eat cakes." Part of this, as said earlier, is teasing; we must watch out for delusion, and for self-delusion; and yet, in the end, the playwright invites us to joy on the other side of delusion, and we assent to this by echoing the old ritual refrain of the marriage song, *Hymēn, Hymenai', o!* In Shakespeare's play Puck is given the last word, after the fairies' ritual dance and blessing. He reminds us that we shall be leaving the theater, now that the play is ending; that we should think of it as of a dream. This likens us to the lovers, awakened yet transformed. And Puck's last lines,

> Give me your hands, if we be friends,
> And Robin shall restore amends,

suggest, even in the traditional request for applause, that we can "give hands" to the players, can join them for a last, sweet moment before the revel ends. For we are participants as well as spectators of this holiday humor. This is the full comic perspective, or *theōria*, into which (and out of which) we have been teased. It includes two ways of looking at the world which we separate, calling them realistic and fantastic. "Methinks I see these things with parted eye, when everything seems double." Yet, as a play perspective, it offers unified vision, the final gift of a shaping fantasy.

4 *Playing Out the Holiday*

"ONCE Shakespeare finds his own distinctive style," writes C. L. Barber,

> he is more Aristophanic than any other great English comic drama-
> tist. . . . The Old Comedy cast of his work results from his partici-
> pation in native saturnalian traditions of the popular theatre and
> the popular holidays. Not that he "wanted art"—including Teren-
> tian art. But he used the resources of a sophisticated theatre to
> express, in his idyllic comedies and in his clowns' ironic misrule,
> the experience of moving to humorous understanding through sat-
> urnalian release.[34]

Barber's work, like Shakespeare's comedy, is two-sided. He shows, on the one hand, how "Shakespeare's festive comedy" is just that: how it draws power and meaning from many play and holiday forms, single or com-bined. For example, in *A Midsummer Night's Dream*, Shakespeare draws largely on the summer revel suggested by the title, and even more on Maying ceremonies in which the vitality of spring is brought in from the green woods to reinvigorate village life. The particulars of such ceremo-nies matter less than the general festive mood, the holiday humor (it need not always be saturnalian) that pervades a Shakespearean comedy, shap-ing its central attitudes and structure, and bringing understanding, or clarification, through release.

All this might apply equally to Aristophanes, and it matters greatly. But it is easier with Shakespeare than with Aristophanes to appreciate the other side of the comic poet's achievement, how he weds play forms and holiday traditions to "the resources of a sophisticated theatre." He integrates them into romantic plots derived from Italian comedy and ultimately from Greek and Roman New Comedy, whether this takes the form of sentimental love comedy or comedy of manners. And he does this with the sureness of a playwright who has gained experience of the stage and has inherited a rich artistic and theatrical tradition. By com-

36

paring simpler festive plays with Shakespeare's comedies, we can see where the latter derive much of their energy and spirit, but we can also measure the degree of their sophistication. With Aristophanes this is not possible. No earlier or even contemporary plays exist to permit comparison. To label his work Old Comedy in contrast with New is greatly misleading, for he came in the third generation of Athenian formal comedy, and long after the informal revel games from which that comedy derived its festive name and significance. It is more accurate, though paradoxical, to speak of Aristophanes' Old-and-New Comedy.

Both Aristophanes and Shakespeare make large use of festive rites, but they do so with an awareness that is far from naive. Since great periods of transition, the old-and-new days of human life and culture, much resemble one another, much that we know about Shakespeare's intermediate position and that of England in his day provides an analogue for Aristophanes and Athens that is worth pursuing further. Here is Barber again:

> During Shakespeare's lifetime, England became conscious of holiday custom as it had not been before, in the very period when in many areas the keeping of holidays was on the decline. Festivals which worked within the rhythm of an agricultural calendar, in village or market town, did not fit the way of living of the urban groups whose energies were beginning to find expression through what Tawney has called the Puritan ethic. The Puritan spokesmen who attacked the holidays looked at them from the outside as people had not had occasion to do before. The effect of the Reformation throughout the Elizabethan church was to discourage festive ceremonials along with ceremonies generally. The traditional saturnalian customs were kept up in the unselfconscious regions of the countryside. But attitudes that meant one thing in the static, monolithic world of village and manor meant other things, more complex and challenging, when continued in the many-minded world of city and court.... Shakespeare, coming up to London from a rich market town, growing up in the relatively unselfconscious 1570's and 80's, and writing his festive plays in the decade of the 90's, when most of the major elements in English society enjoyed a moment of reconcilement, was perfectly situated to express both a countryman's participation in holiday and a city man's consciousness of it.[35]

We saw something of that city man's consciousness played out in *A Midsummer Night's Dream*, in the mocking of naive beliefs and literal-minded play, and especially in the detached observations of the playgoers within the play and in the skeptical attitude of Theseus, who "never may believe / these antic fables nor these fairy toys." Before I return to Aristophanes to drive the analogy home, let me give another illustration of Shakespeare's *theōria*, this time from *The Winter's Tale*.

The sheep-shearing festival in act 4, scene 4 of *The Winter's Tale* represents a popular holiday, a time for dressing up, singing, dancing, laughing. The excuse lies in nature. Sheep-shearing time is a natural occasion to celebrate, to rest, to enjoy the rewards of labor. But since Shakespeare's audience, not being simple rustics, must look on such revels with a certain detachment and ironical humor, their response is itself included in the play, in the comments of the king and Camillo. As disguised spectators, they make snide comments: "This is a brave fellow." As in *A Midsummer Night's Dream*, the naive rustics and clowns, engrossed in their playing, make sport for the more sophisticated onlookers. Yet observe that these same spectators are drawn, significantly, into the revels. Perdita, aware herself of the changing seasons and their shifting proprieties, welcomes them with flowers. Their own masquing reminds us that they too are players—and we know from the first half of the play what dangerous and wicked and very childish playing can take place at court. Even now, the king is a dangerous spy, and a potential spoilsport; but at least he perceives the holiday games as refreshing:

> *Shepherd* Away! We'll none on't. Here has been
> too much homely foolery already. I know,
> sir, we weary you.
> *Polyxenes* You weary those that refresh us. Pray,
> let's see these four threes of herdsmen.

He is right. The rough dance of the "saltiers" gives pleasure to the onlooker, reviving his spirits. In the end it brings recovery.

The old shepherd's tactful concern for his guests is outdone in delicacy and grace by Perdita herself:

> But that our feasts
> in every mess have folly, and the feeders
> digest it with a custom, I should blush
> to see you so attired, swoon, I think,
> to show myself a glass.

Even as Perdita plays, she remains aware that her play is folly and make-believe, that it is opposed to everyday, sensible behavior, and that it belongs to a festive tradition that gives it license. Again, even without a glass, she watches herself play:

> Methinks I play as I have seen them do
> in Whitsun pastorals. Sure this robe of mine
> doth change my disposition.

Here Perdita alludes to another form of holiday play, to the plays or morris dances presented around Whitsun, in mid- to later spring. And here again, the holiday gives refreshment and renewal. Perdita remains aware of how playing, putting on a costume (mask, role, disguise) can change the way we feel and think. Her words remind us that we are watching actors in a play. At the same time, since Perdita is (within the larger play) a genuine princess, her words convey a reality beyond her own awareness. The fairy tale restoration of innocence and joy, through grace and repentance, in the play's second half is as right and true a sequel to the insanities of the first half as spring is to winter. We accept both as true in nature. At the same time, we remain aware that this is "a winter's tale." We are refreshed by it and renewed as by nature herself, but we are not deceived. Nor need we strain after a holiday perspective more complex than Perdita's. "Sure this play of ours . . . doth change our disposition."

If I have lingered on Shakespeare, it was in order to return to Aristophanes with renewed appreciation of festive elements and meanings in his comedies. And here I want to express a longtime debt to F. M. Cornford's book *The Origin of Attic Comedy* (1934). In its basic features, Cornford argued, Aristophanic comedy reproduces the "canonical" elements of an old ritual plot involving the struggle (*agōn*) of the year-god against his enemies, his death and resurrection, and the culmination or celebration of the latter in a revel and sacred marriage (*kōmos* and *gamos*). Cornford uses anthropological parallels, many of them taken from Frazer's *Golden Bough*, to illustrate various ritual ceremonies and forms that, he argues, underlie the repeated patterns of action and song in Aristophanes' plays. Prominent among these are the induction of spring, the combat of winter and summer, and the casting out of a scapegoat. Cornford believed that Aristophanic comedy was derived from ritual by way of a "degenerate folk play," which he describes, and that, like Greek tragedy (for whose development Gilbert Murray had a parallel theory), it retains much power and meaning from that ritual origin.

Cornford's book, though still widely read by scholars in other fields, is generally disregarded by classicists. This is partly because the Cambridge Anthropologists are unfashionable nowadays; people who treat the Raw and the Cooked, or the Deep Structure, with reverent seriousness still tend to laugh at the *Eniautos Daimōn* (or Year Spirit) and all his works. But there are other reasons than mere fashion why scholars do not take Cornford's theory seriously.[36] It does not fit Aristophanes' plays, and it does not explain in a convincing way how Greek comedy developed out of ritual. Let me, because I care about Cornford, expand these criticisms before coming to his defense.

The most obvious weakness of the book was its Procrustean effort to make Aristophanes' surviving plays (which are all we have of Old Comedy except for a few bushels of fragments) fit the imagined structure of that old archetypal ritual plot. The *Knights* and *Birds* came closest;

but generally things kept happening in the wrong order (for example, the parabasis came before the agon, not after), or else a key element like the Marriage appeared to be missing. I would add, as a second serious criticism, that Cornford's scheme failed to do justice, not merely to Aristophanes' variety and art, but also to the self-awareness of his comic muse, the way old ritual patterns and play-forms have been integrated into sophisticated comedies with the help of a long literary and theatrical tradition—in short, just what Barber has demonstrated in the case of Shakespeare.

The third serious criticism of Cornford's theory concerns his hypothetical ritual drama and "degenerate folk play." For although Dionysus' violent birth is prominent in Greek myth, and a tale of his death and dismemberment (from which the human race sprang) is centrally important in the Orphic mysteries, it is not clear either that the latter version had any widespread influence or that Bacchic initiations, which were more popular than Orphic ones, put any such stress on a death-and-resurrection myth—although the initiates' experience through ecstatic worship of communion with the god may have encouraged their hope of some kind of salvation in the afterlife. It remains true that the usual emphasis in Dionysian myth and cult, as we know it from literature and art, is on release, transformation, and renewal of spirit, but not on death and resurrection. It is misleading, though Dionysus is a vegetation god, to compare him with Near Eastern vegetation deities like Tammuz or Adonis who die and are reborn, so that the worshipers mourn for them and then rejoice. The initiates of Demeter seem to have participated more clearly in such a pattern, but it did not lead to drama. Nor can we show that "carnival plays" grew out of Dionysian worship as, in medieval Europe, they did out of Christian worship—or better, attached themselves to it and were transformed by it. Comparisons to such rudimentary folk dramas as the Plough plays, the Saint George plays, and the Thracian Mummers' play are misleading. In fact we know very little about the evolution of ancient Greek comedy from festive play forms. In the Appendix of this book, I give my own reconstruction of what probably happened. In so doing, I have emphasized the great distance between the old seasonal revelry and fertility magic on the one hand and Aristophanic comedy—which is a very late form of the "old comedy"—on the other. But still more, I have argued that Cornford was basically right: that the older structural units of Old Comedy like the parabasis and the agon grew out of ritual, and that the old festive meanings, derived from ancient ritual and magic, and transformed but also heightened by Dionysian worship, are the lifeblood of Aristophanic comedy. Without these, it would not have nearly the cathartic power and the life-enhancing spirit that it has.

Of Cornford's basic insights, which are always on the side of the comic angels, the most important is his sense of a balance between positive and negative elements in the parabasis and elsewhere. He traces this balance back to the two complementary aspects of agricultural or preagricultural fertility rites: to evoke the blessings of prosperity and increase, and to expel or avert any bad influences that might harm the people or the animals or blight the crops. Such a balance is most apparent in the old ABAB structure of the parabasis, where choral odes that hymn the gods or ask blessings for Athens are followed by epirrhemes, passages of recitative like patter songs, in which the chorus make satirical or teasing comments about individuals, or Athenian politics or culture, or the behavior of the audience.[37] This combination is one of the oldest, most stable parts of comedy (the other is the formal agon). It brings us close to the rudimentary *kōmos* or "revel" from which comedy grew. What is more important is that this balance between positive and negative elements, more than anything else, keeps us from confusing the wholeness of comedy with the partiality of satire. Aristophanes may satirize individuals like Cleon or institutions like the Athenian law courts, and he may comment negatively or critically on many aspects of contemporary life, but that satire or criticism is never central to an Aristophanic comedy. It is one aspect only: the negative side of festive celebration.

Cornford's second great contribution, I think, was to bring out a strong sense of ritual conflict between Old and New in the different comedies, and especially in the agon. To be sure, it is harder to show the ritual background here for Aristophanes than for Shakespeare, who could draw on a long-established popular tradition of combats between Winter and Summer, or between Carnival and Lent. Ancient Greek tradition affords many examples of ritual combats, of choric team versus choric team, or leader versus leader, or leader versus chorus; but Cornford had to rely on a wealth of outside material, mostly taken from *The Golden Bough*, and on analogy and inference to support his view that a basic conflict between Old and New (whether in the form of kings, years, or gods) underlay Aristophanes' comedies and gave them their special shape and meaning. Sometimes these comparisons and analogies apply only feebly to the plays we have. Nor is Cornford very convincing when he attempts to link these conflicts with a basic myth of Dionysus' death and resurrection. All the same, the persistent conflict between Old and New in Aristophanes' plays, and their constant insistence on renewal, seems best understood, and most meaningful, against such a ritual and festive background. And this, again, may deter critics from their contagious bad habit of reading certain comedies in too negative a manner, as though it were comedy's way (as it sometimes is tragedy's) to lament the decline of the Old rather than to welcome, with great rejoicing, the triumph of the New—or better (what some of us prefer) the rejuvenation, hence ultimate triumph of the Old.

Cornford's third great contribution was to show how various characters take on a larger-than-life meaning in their festive roles. The value of his specific theories depends, of course, on how well they suit the individual plays. I have found it very helpful, over the years of reading and teaching Aristophanes, to think of the Paphlagonian in the *Knights* as a Scapegoat; of the sausage-seller in that play as a Magic Cook; of Euripides and Socrates, in the *Acharnians* and *Clouds* respectively, as related subtypes of the Learned Doctor. And (to anticipate discussion of that problem play, the *Clouds*, in a later volume) Cornford's view of this Socrates as an Antagonist and Imposter seems absolutely right. It suggests the creation of a dominant secondary figure, rather like Shylock or Falstaff, who has captured the attention of later generations of audiences and readers, and who continues to fascinate us, and trouble our minds, because he came to exist on so large a scale.

If I were revising Cornford's book today, I would put more weight on a fourth feature of Old Comedy: the ritual (and Dionysian) significance of the fat and phallic hero, especially once he gets something to drink. And a fifth (no pun intended) might be the importance of the violent confrontation between the chorus and an individual whom they pursue, try to stone to death, and so forth. This pursuit goes far back in ancient ritual, and through its expression of anger, hostility, and violence it contributes much to the cathartic effect of Old Comedy. I would also put more emphasis than Cornford did on the celebratory sacrifice and feast, which the various imposters interrupt, and somewhat less on the final *kōmos* and *gamos* (which is not always there). But these revisions, and others that might be suggested, seem minor when they are compared with Cornford's main achievement. This was, in sum, to bring out the celebratory nature of comedy—which is where I began this chapter, with the *Peace*, and where I shall now return.

At the center of the *Peace*, which more than any other Aristophanic play expresses this playful spirit, there is, instead of the usual alternation of odes and epirrhemes, a single ode, triumphantly gay. I paraphrase it briefly:

A Appeal to the Muse: repel enemies and dance
  with me, your friend; celebrate (as of old)
  the joys of gods and men;
B rejecting Carcinus and his dwarfish dancer sons.
A Such things the fair Graces teach, and the good
  poet sings, in spring, when the swallow calls
B and when Morsimos and Melanthios (those vile
  tragic poets) get no chorus; spit on them,
  goddess Muse, and
A "play out the holiday with me" (*sympaisde tēn heortēn*).

I have noted the balance of positive and negative elements by the letters A and B, as images of music, poetry, and festive celebration are balanced by the teasing rejection of "bad spirits"—in the persons of two contem-

porary poets, brothers, gourmands, and writers of bad tragedy. It is the
old ritual balance of hymn and invective, invocation and casting out. It is
playful at heart, a self-conscious part of "playing out the holiday." And
so is the whole second part of the *Peace* that follows this parabasis. Its
positive celebration of peace in feasting, sacrifice, and prayer is balanced
by a group of comic scenes in which intruders are routed: first the oracle-
monger Hierocles, who claims that making peace with Sparta is unnatural, and that you can't change human nature; and then, various weapon-
sellers who have perverted nature, and whose implements are converted
to more peaceable and natural purposes and effectively recycled. The
play thus moves to its climax in Trygaeus' wedding to Opora—an unusually clear example of Cornford's *kōmos* and *gamos*. The comic hero,
who is master of ceremonies as well as bridegroom, leads the final
prayer, an old, simple prayer for prosperity:

> Attention, please! And watch your words:
> it's time to escort the bride outdoors,
> time to carry the bridal torches,
> time for the folk to join together,
> singing the glad refrain;
> and time to carry our props and clothing
> back to the country where they go,
> once we have danced and said our grace
> and driven out old Evilface:
> Once we've prayed to the gods
> to grant the Hellenes riches,
> so we create and procreate
> in barleycorns and wine;
> prayed that we bite our figs,
> prayed that our wives give birth,
> prayed to get back, like days of old,
> all the good things we lost before,
> and make an end to the swordplay.　　(1316–28)

And after that, the chorus, and presumably the audience, join in to sing
the wedding song, which stands also for their larger participation in the
recovering, and celebrating, of Peace and of all the good things that come
with Peace.

The Greek words for play, *paisdein* and *paidia*, are derived from the
word for child, *pais*; and in order to appreciate the *Peace* and "play out
the holiday" with Aristophanes, one must become a child again. I am
reminded here of Groucho Marx, leafing through a pile of state documents in *Duck Soup*. "Why, a four-year-old child could understand this
report," he exclaims. And then, after a pause: "Run out and find me a
four-year-old child." It may be significant that small children do turn up
in the *Peace*, in unusual numbers.[38] In the prologue, Trygaeus' child tries

to dissuade him from his mad venture (this is parody of Euripidean tragedy); toward the end, two children come outdoors, to "strike up" some tunes in practice and (the two are punningly connected) to urinate; they turn out, comically, to be the sons of Lamachus and Cleonymus, the warmonger and the—coward. However differently they are used, all these children appeal to the child in us who knows how to "play out the holiday." I have also in front of me a modern Greek version of the *Peace* for children, by Sophia Zarabouka.[39] The drawings are warm and colorful; on the cover the lady Eirene flies toward the reader, smiling and waving her hand in greeting; she is dressed in blue, with flowers in her hair, and she carries a green olive branch and is attended (of course!) by white doves. My first thought on seeing this book in an Athenian bookshop was to wonder what the author had done with all the dirty jokes. Would it be the same play at all? But over time I have become convinced that this child's version of the *Peace* as a fairy tale catches what is most essential to it. The comic heroism of good, stout Trygaeus, the wickedness of the ogre War, the loveliness of Peace and the joy of her recovery, as it is celebrated in feasting (fowl turning on a spit) and finally in dancing and singing—all are here. Perhaps one of the ironies of the *Peace* is that, after complexity and struggle, things are really very simple after all. Even a four-year-old child can understand and join in the play. The grown-ups will enjoy the sex jokes too, but not, for all the philological notes, unless they perceive them as part of the general atmosphere of play and celebration.

And yet while we may be children in heart or may return temporarily (given the right circumstances) to such a state, we cannot return fully to where we were—to the old play and the old beliefs. We are too conscious of the distance traveled, the length of the return. We are called back, with Aristophanes' chorus (and audience) "to the country"; but in mind and spirit we are no longer simple countrypeople. Hence, when Aristophanes celebrates country joys in a second parabasis in the *Peace*, he does so with an ironic distancing that looks forward to Hellenistic mime and, even more, to Hellenistic pastoral.[40] The chorus sing an easygoing song of winter and summer pleasures. They bring us back to the seasons, to the processes of nature and agriculture where comedy has its roots. The sowing is done; rain is falling; call in your neighbor Comarchides (the name suggests Master of the Country Revel) to eat and drink generously, in gratitude for "the god's doing well by us." The details are humorous and folksy ("There used to be cream cheese inside, and maybe a brace of rabbits / unless the pussycat got loose and dragged them out last evening."). And Aristophanes uses this folksiness deliberately, to bring us back into the slow, natural rhythm of the country, where the returning season brings the returning opportunity to celebrate the accomplishment of tasks, the goodness and cooperativeness of nature, and the helpfulness of familiar, even neighborly gods. It is the peasant's world, right out of

Hesiod. It is the old world from which play and comedy spring—where peace can be grasped and appreciated. It is the world to which Aristophanes leads his audience back as they "play out the holiday" with him.

And yet Aristophanes' audience are no more identical with these simpleminded peasants, chattering about their cream cheese and their bunnies, than Shakespeare's disguised courtiers, or courtly audiences, are with the shepherds in his Forest of Arden or at the sheep-shearing festival in *The Winter's Tale*. The familiar little world of country work, country belief, and (even) country holiday has become a little distant, a little strange. It evokes nostalgia but also amusement. And what of the gods whose worship underlies the festive rites of comedy? In 421 B.C. neither Aristophanes nor his audience believed easily and unselfconsciously in beneficent Olympian gods' presiding over the incalculable forces of human life. Indeed, the *Peace* plays largely on popular anxieties about the gods, the fear that they are angry at the Greeks or have withdrawn somehow from things (the play puts both fears together, suggesting that the gods have withdrawn from things because they are angry). Now all this is in place in Old Comedy. The light treatment of the gods (and of anxieties about the gods) is familiar fooling, part of the license of comedy, the gift of Dionysus. To play out his holiday is to return to the good old festive rites—to Cornford's world, so to speak—just as one returns to those good tastes and smells that have been missing for so long a time. But are those festivities, and those festive meanings, and those gods behind them who sanction comedy's play still efficacious, and still real?

5   *Play and the Gods: Sacred Laughter*

L E T me turn briefly to the *Acharnians*. The first thing
that Dicaeopolis does after negotiating his private peace with the Peloponnesians is to celebrate the Rural Dionysia. The chorus of Acharnians,
fierce old charcoal-burners and veterans of Marathon, hurry into the
orchestra in pursuit of the "traitor," to stone him to death, and arrive
just in time to witness his private religious celebration:

> *Dic.* Attention, please! No ill-omened words, now.
>   Basket-bearer, move a little forward.
>   Xanthias' job is, hold the phallus high,
>   keep it erect. Now daughter, set the basket
>   down. It's time to make our offering.
> *Girl* Mother dear, would you bring the ladle out?
>   My piece of cake's exposed. It wants some topping.
> *Dic.* All's well so far. Dionysus, patron,
>   grant that my sacrifice and my procession
>   meet with your favor: may my folks and I
>   conduct this country Dionysia
>   to a prosperous conclusion, now I'm freed
>   from military service. Make this peace
>   go well for me, my peace of thirty years.
>   Now daughter, see you bear the basket nicely.
>   Put on your formal debutante expression,
>   sour and snooty. (Happy the husband who
>   beds you and gets a lot of farting kiddies.)
>   Now, forward step. Be careful, or some guy
>   will nibble off your jewelry in the crowd.
>   Xanthias! *Will* you hold the phallus straight?
>   Keep it erect, behind the basket-bearer.

I'll keep you pace, singing the phallic hymn.
Wife, you watch from the roof. Now: forward, march.
Phales, Dionysus' friend,
revel-companion, wanderer
at night, seducer, hot for boys:
I greet you again—it's been five years—
now that I've made my private peace,
freed from troubles, freed from cussed
war and Lamachusses now:
for Phales, Phales! It's really much more fun
to catch a thieving servant-maid,
   her bundle all undone,
   who pinched some of my goods,
   on her way back from the woods—
grab her and lift her and throw her down
and send my old grapepicker into the town—
   O Phales, Phales!
   Drink with us today—
     no matter if you're hung over tomorrow!
I'm sure a bowl of good peace soup
   will cure your headache's sorrow.
As for our shield, we'll simply leave
   it hanging in the smoke—
we'll simply leave it hanging in the smoke!   (241–79)

It is a playful, make-believe version of a real ceremony. Dicaeopolis invokes Dionysus; then he leads forth a *pompē* or religious procession in which the phallus is prominently displayed and a comic little hymn is sung to the god Phales. The erected phallus is a sign of hope and vitality: it suits Dicaeopolis' revived fortunes, and it embodies the Dionysian energy that pervades Old Comedy. The playful little revel shows how much Dicaeopolis is on the side of life, and vice versa. *In hoc signo vinces.* It also draws on comedy's own roots: for even if the phallic procession is not, as Aristotle suggests, *the* direct ancestor of Athenian comedy, it clearly embodies one of the oldest, most basic meanings taken up in the later development of the comic genre.

We may imagine the pleasure of Aristophanes' audience as they participate vicariously in Dicaeopolis' phallic celebration. It raises one's spirits—O Phales, Phales! Yet this encouragement goes with a playful awareness that all this is make-believe and play, an awareness stimulated partly by jokes about the theater and still more by the incongruity between what Dicaeopolis is doing and what usually happens at a Rural Dionysia. For how can you "go inside" in the city (as represented here) and "lead a rural Dionysia"?[41] And for that matter, how can a single household conduct a public ceremony? It is all as ridiculous as a one-family Fourth of July parade with fife and drum. The humor is partly satirical, demonstrating the isolation of the "fair-minded," sensible man from the larger community that has been given over to folly and war. His triumph, like his commonsensical vision of things earlier, must remain private and unshared. Yet the incongruity suggests something more. Religious meanings have been uprooted from the country along with the country people who lived by them, people like Dicaeopolis, who "looks away toward the country, is in love with peace, loathes the town, desires his own deme with great longing." We might recall Thucydides' description of the uprooting of the people of Attica. Their migration into the crowded city, by Pericles' policy, was very painful, and not just because of material losses and personal inconvenience.

> The uprooting (*anastasis*) proved painful to them because most of them had lived, at any given time, in the country. . . . (2.14.2)

> It gave them pain, and they took it hard: to be leaving their homes and the shrines that had been theirs, their ancestral shrines, from the time of the most ancient settlement, and to be preparing to alter their whole way of life, and for each person to be leaving what was, really, his own polis. (2.16.1)

Notice the intimate association of home, countryside, and religion here. To leave one's country deme was like being exiled from one's polis; it was also to be uprooted from ancestral worship that had been continuous, had given meaning to life. It was a kind of cultural death. And, as Dicaeopolis' "rural Dionysia" reminds us, it raised severe problems for comedy's own power and significance.

For it was, after all, the gods' presence in festival that comedy celebrated, and it was the gods' power that made holidays possible, and holiday play. That is why Josef Pieper chose as the epigraph for his book *Leisure: The Basis of Culture* a quotation from Plato's *Laws*:

> But the Gods, taking pity on mankind, born to work, laid down the succession of recurring Feasts to restore them from their fatigue, and gave them the Muses, and Apollo their leader, and Dionysus, as companions in their Feasts, so that nourishing themselves in festive companionship with the Gods, they should again stand upright and erect. (2.653c–d)[42]

When we think about religion and comedy, we are apt to think of holiday *license*, the way that disgraceful words, gestures, and actions are sanctioned by religious tradition in the theater of Dionysus. But although this *aischrologia* is a basic, much-loved component of Old Comedy, what is still more basic—and what lies behind Dicaeopolis' Phales song—is the affirmation of life, the sense of something to celebrate. And that is precisely what is threatened by cultural dislocation, whether in Athens or in America. For if holiday is play time, is even a doorway into a timeless present in which life's goodness may be perceived and enjoyed and played out in games and in art—a doorway into a different time, and a different world, into which we escape from the weary and anxious routines of ordinary living, yet from which we return transformed, with renewed perspective, so that the ordinary world is extraordinarily transformed along with us—yet it remains true that holidays, even Dionysian holidays, are also created in time and that they are subject to political, social, cultural, and even economical realities. Indeed much of Pieper's book (to which I owe my own best idea of scholarship) is taken up with the threat to holiday meanings, and hence to leisure and contemplation, in an increasingly secular and work-oriented world. Even now, I might add, holidays in America are losing their spirit and meaning, are becoming adjuncts to the weekend. People are fooling around with the calendar, as Aristophanes' cloud chorus complained long ago (on behalf of the Moon). I must write my congressman about this shortly.

The gods, after all, can only do so much. They can present us with old, familiar holidays: but what if we choose, or are compelled, to abandon the culture and traditions of our ancestors? What if we leave the country for the city? If we have war instead of peace? Moreover, if those very gods are being outdated and demythologized, how shall we keep the holiday?

In Sophocles' *Oedipus Tyrannus*, the chorus of old men of Thebes react with strong concern, in the second stasimon, to the scene in which Jocasta encourages Oedipus to disregard the oracles about his parentage: for prophets, she argues, have no sure knowledge of things. She is not (to her mind) ruling out the gods. She is only discrediting alleged intermediaries between gods and men. But the chorus, who (in their way) sometimes see deeply into things, are terrified. They invoke piety and the gods' eternal law; they warn of the steep fall of insolence; they pray that irreverent evildoers may be punished: "Or else, if such acts are held in honor, why should I dance?" They go on to ask Zeus to vindicate Apollo's oracles, for "the things of God are passing" (*errei de ta theia*). The sequel more than justifies their prayer. The oracles are "proved to fit," though with terrifying results from which the chorus, and the audience, must avert their eyes. But go back, and notice how the chorus stepped out of role in that earlier ode. Not old Thebans but Athenian *choreutai* ask, "Why should I dance?" If religion is passing, why have tragedy at all? Or (for that matter) why have comedy? Who, or what, is left for the players to celebrate? Any answer we give—and I am thinking now of comedy—must be bound up with the mystery of play and of sacred and healing laughter.[43]

For if festivals of the gods provide time and place for play, yet play and laughter have their own ancient privilege of recreating festive meanings and of renewing even the gods. I am not thinking here of the Olympians' boisterous laughter in Homer, as, for example, when they laugh at the lame Hephaestus bustling about with a tray of drinks—laughter of the "easy-living gods" that resolves their tensions and conflicts (as those of humans cannot be resolved) into an easy harmony. I am thinking rather of that moment in the Hymn to Demeter where Iambe leads the Mother of Sorrows to "smile and laugh and have a merry heart." The hymn has described the rape of Persephone and Demeter's grief. In pain, anger, and deep mourning she has roamed the world in search of her daughter; she has not eaten or drunk or bathed. On learning the truth from Helios, she withdraws further; she wanders over the earth and finally comes to Eleusis, where (as in fairy tale) the royal family welcomes her in disguise. She comes to the palace, but she stands majestically upon the threshold and won't take a chair (192–205):

> But Demeter, bringer of seasons, giver of brilliant gifts, was unwilling to sit down on a shining chair. She waited, silent, her fair eyes cast down, until Iambe, clever girl, set before her a fashioned seat (covering it with a silvery fleece). Long she sat there, in silence, grieved to the heart. She greeted no one there in word or act, but without laughter, fasting from food and drink, she sat, pining in grief for her deep-girdled daughter, until Iambe, clever girl, by teasing her with many playful jests, turned the holy Lady to smile, and laugh, and have a merry heart. (And in aftertime, she often gave her pleasure.)

Observe the natural sequence of events. First Demeter is induced to accept a chair, to relax a little physically. Then Iambe's jesting relaxes her mind, teasing her back into cheerfulness of spirit. The joking that restores her is here described with epic decorum; in a more primitive version of the story, a woman named Baubo makes Demeter laugh by exposing herself suddenly—a very basic comic gesture. Iambe's jokes may have been obscene too; we shall never know. Her name is derived from *iambisdein*, "to lampoon in verse." What matters more is that Iambe personifies the healing nature of laughter, which refreshes Demeter even in her deepest mourning and brings her back to herself.[44] After she laughs, she breaks her fast by drinking the *kykeōn*. Then she enters into the royal household as Demophoon's nurse.

In his fine commentary on the hymn, N. J. Richardson suggests that Iambe's jesting and Demeter's drinking of the *kykeōn* (a strengthening potion) reflect key moments in Eleusinian ritual and in the initiates' psychological experience.[45] The scene gives an aetiological model for several ritual elements: the preliminary purification; the fasting and abstention from wine; the ritual jesting, or *aischrologia*; the drinking of the *kykeōn*. Among the parallels for this jesting that Richardson cites, the best known is the *gephyrismos*, or "joking from the bridge," on the way to Eleusis. It seems that play and worship are close friends. All genuine religious ceremonies offer some opportunity for happy and creative play, some recognition of our animal spirits; otherwise, worship would be a tense, forced, stunted thing. And bawdy stories have a more than historical or psychological place on the road to Eleusis, or to Canterbury. They anticipate the joy of arrival. They also ensure that those who arrive to worship are whole people, for wholeness is a companion of holiness.

Yet even as we recognize the aetiological nature of these mythic elements and the psychological significance of what they represent, we are in some danger of reducing the meanings of myth and ritual, and especially, in the Iambe scene, of losing the all-important sense of the sacredness of laughter. It is more than healing; it is sacramental.

Northrop Frye has treated comedy as reflecting a "myth of spring";[46] and here, in the Homeric Hymn, we find such a myth in which laughter plays a part. Persephone, playing and laughing among the flowers in childish innocence, was carried off by Hades, and Demeter's grief seems irreconcilable; indeed, even after her nursing of Demophoon is broken off by his mother's folly, she orders a temple built at Eleusis and stays there, wasting away (again) with longing for her daughter, and wasting the crops, whose seed she hides away in the earth. It is a terrible year. But Aidoneus, god of the underworld, is persuaded finally to let Persephone go, though (by his trick) she must remain underground four months of every year; and so the hymn moves to the joyful reunion of Demeter and Persephone, to the restoration of the earth's fertility, and to Demeter's teaching the holy rites of her mysteries to the princes of Eleusis. In a way, the heartwarming mutual joy of mother and daughter, and the springing forth of leaves and flowers out of deadness, bring us back to that springtime of innocence and play where the hymn began. (The verb for "warmed each other's hearts" is *iainon*, recalling Iambe; and among Persephone's playmates were Ianthe, Iache, and Ianeira.) On this level the myth portrays the rebirth of innocence, of the child's power to laugh and play that seemed dead forever. Iambe's jesting shares in advance in that rebirth. Yet the hymn goes deeper. Not only must Persephone spend each winter underground, but humankind, with the infant Demophoon, has lost that perfect nursing care, that chance at agelessness and immortality. The loss, though gently told, is very sad. The baby (like Demeter in her sorrow) refuses to be consoled. Instead, by way of recompense (to her? to us?), Demeter institutes her holy Mysteries, whose experience offers utmost hope. The initiate's hope was not spelled out in articles of belief. It was gained by a "revelation," as of a sheaf of wheat shown forth in a great blaze of light out of the darkness. It was the joy of the dead earth flowering, the seed reborn, nature restored, deepest life renewed. We need such experience of joy—as at an Easter vigil, when the new fire leaps out of darkness, and new-lit candles are carried in procession into the darkened church—if we are to comprehend the full meaning, and the full power, of play and laughter.

In the hymn, Iambe's jesting anticipated Demeter's recovery of joy. The joking of the initiates relaxed their spirits for worship but also pre-empted some joy and meaning of that worship. Laughter is sacramental, and it is sacred. It is occasioned by festive joy, but it is also co-equal with festival, whose deepest meanings it can re-create—much as Iambe's jesting renewed Demeter's spirit. Holiday, festival, comedy, play, are the gods' gifts to us. But play—the play of holiday, of festival, of comedy—also gives us back the gods.

Why then, and how, and for whom (to return to Aristophanes) may the comic chorus dance? Any answer we give must be provisional, and had best be playful. I began this chapter with the farmers' dance in the *Peace*, that wild pre-celebration of a peace not yet actually recovered. Celebrate first, plan afterwards, is the comic prescription! Comedy brings a healing perspective that helps restore peace; Peace brings Theoria, including the *theōria* of comedy, in her festive train. The comic chorus dances madly because there is really a time to dance. Their dance is ancient, it is sacred, it honors Dionysus—whose gifts of wine and release are closely akin to Demeter's gifts of corn and renewal, and whose joyful mysteries overlap very much (and not least in jesting) with those of the Mother. To follow Dionysus in dance is always somewhat mad, though this madness may avert larger insanity. And the dance of the comic chorus may have seemed more than somewhat mad at a transitional time in Greek culture when the older mythology was being overthrown, the Olympians demythologized. At such a time, I want to argue, comedy's laughter may play out a rite of passage from one world to another. But also, at such a time, sacred laughter still recreates (or re-creates) the gods; comedy dances in the shadow not just of death, but of meaninglessness; and comedy's play draws, as it must, on the deepest sources of joy and hope and meaning. Which is really what this book is all about.

Chapter Two

Desire with Hope

Children playing at Dionysian procession, with "Dionysus" and his bride, later fifth century B.C., *miniature Attic red-figure* chous. *Courtesy Metropolitan Museum of Art, New York (no. 24.97.34).*

6   *Release of Inhibition*

I began with the gods, and with festival: not just from courtesy, but because play gets meaning and sanction from holiday. All the more does it seem right to have postponed the question of comedy's psychological effects, and especially of the "catharsis" that it provides; for the great exponents of catharsis, notably Aristotle and Freud, need to be placed in a larger perspective than their own if their teachings are not to prove limiting, or even tyrannical. Let me briefly illustrate this point.

Freud (to begin with the more available, explicit theory) teaches us much about the nature of laughter and the circumstances, both external and internal, that produce it.[1] Like his teaching on dreams, his argument about jokes and joking is confirmed by our daily experience: we recognize that release of inhibited psychic energy, expressed in an explosion of sudden laughter; and we sense that the more powerful were the inhibited *Tendenzen* of obscene and aggressive feelings (or, we might add, of repressed anxieties), the greater and more satisfying is the release. Freud reminds us, too, of many ways in which adults recover childish sources of pleasure through joking and nonsense. Again and again I find myself invoking Freud to explain the force of Aristophanic jokes. Such psychological explanations can be supported by the text, for Aristophanes is aware of the cathartic nature of his comedy, and he plays suggestively on the very connections between jokes and dreams, comic symbolism and dream symbolism, that interested Freud.[2] Psychological explanations have the additional merit of fixing our attention on the reaction of a living audience to a play. And yet, import too much Freudian seriousness, too much psychological explanation, and you kill the spirit of the comedy that you are trying to describe.

The problem is not merely that the treatment of early twentieth-century neurosis on the couch scarcely resembles the holiday enjoyment of an Athenian audience in the theater of Dionysus—though Viennese psychoanalysis needs to be supplemented here by the physical excess and psychic exuberance of carnival. It is quite helpful to emphasize the emotional release, the lifting of inhibitions (especially those regarding sex and hostility) through jokes and comedy. But it is wrong, in approaching Aristophanic comedy, to make this release a beginning, or an end, in itself. The gift of release is derived from holiday, from celebration of life's goodness. And although the vicarious expression in comedy of feelings of indecency and aggressiveness provides much enjoyment, much recovery of pleasure and energy, a great comic poet like Aristophanes does not stop there but draws his audience into further recognitions, into a larger perspective on human life. The release of strong inhibited feelings in laughter thus forms what we should call a *preliminary* catharsis, not a final one. It is a catalyst. It fuels a further, more significant process of comic combustion.

While I remain much indebted to Freud, the term *catharsis* recalls my other extensive debt, to Aristotle.[3] He seems to have started with a bold analogy: the heightening of strong emotion in the theater to a point of release is compared to the familiar medical process of "purgation" that relieves the body of excessive humors or of some imbalance and hence brings back health. In response to Plato, who had criticized tragedy and comedy for releasing powerful and dangerous emotions from the necessary control of reason, Aristotle seems to have argued that people will be healthier psychologically, will lead happier and better lives, if strong emotions like grief and anger can be ventilated from time to time. His insight, that the theater furnishes such occasions, may have come from personal observation and experience; it was also a truism that crying and laughing make people feel better. Aristotle's purgation theory owed something to rudimentary Greek psychiatry, to an awareness of how some disturbing excess of emotion in "excitable" or "enthusiastic" people could be drawn off and, as it were, "purged" by exciting musical harmonies and rhythms. For ordinary people, who were less seriously disturbed, something of the sort happened in the theater of Dionysus, under religious auspices, so that it could be considered a species of "purification"—though in the religious, not the moral (and certainly not the Puritan), sense of the word.

It seems likely that Aristotle went beyond this purgation theory, which was a first line of defense against Plato's criticisms of tragedy and comedy, to a more subtle and complex "clarification theory" emphasizing the structural elements in drama by which the fullest pleasure of "catharsis" was attained and the rational and aesthetic meanings of that experience thereby acquired. Aristotle only briefly indicates the concept of catharsis in his formalist analysis of tragedy in his (surviving) *Poetics*; he uses it very little; there is no reason to think that he would have said much more about catharsis in comedy. He may take the idea for granted. Certainly he is much more concerned with the play's overall structure and coherence. Aristotle leads us, rightly, to consider the effect of the play as a whole. Unfortunately, in doing so, he makes us readers more than spectators, and he plays down the power and immediacy of our emotional response in time, movement by movement, scene by scene. The children of Aristotle disregard what the children of Freud most stress, and vice versa. Or might we say that the term *catharsis*, with all its rich Greek connotations, points to a fuller critical perspective that subsumes both points of view? Thus it seems right, and important, to speak of Sophoclean tragedy or Aristophanic comedy as offering an emotional "purgation"—or better, a purgation and purification—through tears and laughter arising out of the vicarious emotional experience, and the emotional response to this, of the Greek audience. But it also seems right, and important, as well as Aristotelian, to say that the great tragic and comic playwrights move beyond and through this emotional release to a fuller "clarification" of mind and spirit arising from the fuller experience of the play.

Earlier, when describing Aristophanes' *Peace,* I adduced a sequence of relaxation, recovery, recognition. This sequence is most helpful for analysis, and I use it often in this book. Yet the three experiences described by relaxation, recovery, and recognition occur almost simultaneously, and they belong to a larger unity of emotional and intellectual experience that the Greek term *catharsis* beautifully and richly suggests. My present chapter centers on emotional release and hence is somewhat purgation-centered and Freudian. Yet it forms only part of a larger, progressive account of Aristophanic catharsis that occupies my first four chapters, in which I try to construct, and to maintain, a perspective within which the special insights of Aristotle and Freud, and of their followers and critics, may be used most fruitfully for the enjoyment and understanding of Aristophanes' comedies. My own account of the psychology of comic release begins, not with Aristotle, or even with Freud, but with Plato, whose criticisms of drama stimulated the one and anticipate, often quite remarkably, the insights of the other.

In Book 3 of his *Republic,* Plato first criticizes artistic *mimēsis* for its variety and instability. To play several parts, to represent several persons, runs contrary to that earliest, most fundamental axiom of the new state, that each person shall "do his own thing" and not someone else's, shall play one role and one role only. The simplicity of one undivided personality is required within the soul and within the state. But since the multiform "representations" of myth, music, and culture enter into the mind and soul of a developing person and shape his or her character for good or ill, Plato must insist on complete control of the cultural environment, which includes, among other things, the complete censorship of literature and drama. Indeed his postsophistic awareness of the way education works, of the effects of environment and associations, and, above all, of the many ways in which character can be corrupted and spoiled (*diaphtheiresthai*), shows him the necessity of a cultural indoctrination so thorough that it will resist the dye of any later, alien influence. If Homer smuggles in any intellectual or emotional messages other than those that have received the seal of the philosopher's approval, why, then, Homer—and Pindar, and Sappho, and Sophocles, and certainly Aristophanes—will have to go.

Among other things Plato stresses the importance of giving people the right role models, in fiction as in life. He says that to represent gods and heroes as subject to strong emotions—as grieving, or quarreling, or passionately in love—offends against piety and the true nature of things. What may matter more is the example for good or bad. How can we lead harmonious lives if we model ourselves after the Homeric gods? Or how can we practice self-control if the great heroes, like Achilles or Theseus or Heracles, fall into outbursts of anger or grief? It is obvious, too, that the censor will disapprove of the Old Comedy:

> We shall not, then, have any representations of base people, of low and cowardly types, and of people . . . who revile each other, and satirize each other, and cast invective at each other, whether drunk or sober; and we shall not have any representations of all the faults that such people are constantly committing, in word or in act, against themselves and (at the same time) against one another. (395e–96a)

Plato uses three overlapping terms that clearly refer to the practices of Old Comedy. The first verb, *katēgoreō*, denotes insult generally; the second, *kōmōideō*, has become restricted to personal abuse and invective, or what we might call "satirizing" (rather than "comodizing"); the third, *aischrologeō*, refers to the mixture of indecency, obscenity, and invective that constitutes such abuse. To laugh at these clowns is to take something of their low behavior—their cowardice, scurrility, and lewdness—into ourselves. It is to admit Falstaff as our tutor. But the sensible person, Plato insists, will "feel shame" and resist. His intellectual and moral upbringing will lead him to feel disgust at such representations, and not to yield to their promptings for a moment and so shape himself into the mold of baser types—except occasionally for the sake of play and recreation. This last may be an escape clause. Plato does not develop it, but Aristotle does; indeed, he justifies most of culture under the umbrella of relaxation and play, which must be part of an educated person's life.

In Book 10 Plato returns to his criticism of *mimēsis* and sets it on a firmer epistemological and psychological foundation. Having explained his theory of Forms, he can now assert that artistic representations are merely "imitations," at three degrees of removal from reality and truth. Furthermore, having elaborated his theory of psychology and education in the state and in the individual soul, he can explain more precisely than before just how tragedy and comedy undermine people's self-control. When, for example, we take pleasure in the representation of grieving by

Homer or a tragic poet, our "surrender of ourselves" and our "sympathizing" with fictional characters who grieve, in the song or on the stage, militates against our usual, responsible effort to maintain order and calm and self-control in our own lives. We fail, dangerously, to realize what is happening to us at such times.

> But the best part of our nature, from being inadequately trained in theory and habit, relaxes its guard (*aniēsi tēn phylakēn*) over this grief-loving part, on the excuse that it is only being a spectator of other people's sufferings and passions, and that it acquires no disgrace in giving assent and pity to another man who, claiming to be virtuous, grieves beyond what is fitting and right. (606a–b)

Observe the careful psychology. We are, says Plato, ordinarily self-controlled; our reason keeps guard on dangerous passions; education strengthens that guard. For example, in facing misfortune, we have been brought up to display fortitude, not give way to lamentation. And yet the tragic poet creates fictional situations that evoke, for instance, strong pity. We are seduced into weeping: for Oedipus, for Hecuba, for Iphigenia. We thereby "let down our guard" without realizing it. And afterward, being morally weaker, we are more inclined to weep for other people in real life, for our friends or relatives—or for ourselves.

The same would be true for fear or for other strong emotions aroused in tragedy. I turn now, with Plato, to comedy:

> For the comic, too (*peri tou geloiou*), doesn't just the same theory hold? There are certain kinds of clowning and buffoonery that you would be ashamed to indulge in personally; but if, when these are represented on the comic stage, or displayed in private joking, you take extreme delight in them and do not reject them as vile and hateful—then isn't it the same as with pity? For again you let go, and you release that something in yourself that wants to fool around (*gelōtopoein*: literally, to make laughter), that you used to restrain and control through reason, being afraid of getting a reputation for scurrility and clowning. You let go, then and there, and act like a child, and so you don't realize it, but gradually you are induced to become a comedian in your own private life as well. (606c)

This is, I think, a brilliant and accurate account of the psychological effect of comedy, whether on a Greek or a modern, post-Freudian audience. Let me develop it in some detail.

(1) One of the main inducements to good behavior in any civilized society is the sense of shame with which people are brought up. This includes a strong sense of aversion to behavior, whether in others or (especially) in oneself, that is "ugly and shameful," *aischron*. We begin, of course, by being ashamed before other people, afraid of what they will

think of us, or say about us, or do to us. Although we first feel shame before parents and relatives, the feeling is soon extended to society at large, and it lasts through life; thus Aristotle, in his *Rhetoric*, describes shame as a painful emotion, a constant fear of having one's reputation injured or impaired.[4] People are afraid of losing face, getting a bad reputation, becoming victims of slander. Hence they must keep a close watch over their words and actions. There are exceptions. A friend, says Aristotle, is someone to whom you may let your *phaula*, your "no account" thoughts and actions, and your low tendencies, become known; for the shame we feel before our friends is not for reputation, but for reality, for the genuine faults in how we live. For the most part, however, Aristotle's account of shame shows people living in a narrow, judgmental society in which they must constantly be on their guard lest their faults and weaknesses be revealed.

All this is traditional, outer-directed. Yet we may imagine that shame, for the Greeks as for ourselves, had a more inward aspect. Here the sense of "ugliness" in *aischron* is particularly important. Besides the fear of getting an ugly reputation, shame included, as it still includes, an inward fear of acquiring ugliness in oneself; this fear reinforced a strong, instinctive aversion to certain words, actions, thoughts and feelings. There is every reason to think that the Greeks were "inhibited" in sexual matters: not so desperately, to be sure, as Freud's patients and many of his contemporaries, but a good deal more than most Americans today.[5] This inhibition was painful, then as now; it was also necessary, then as now, to the life of a sane and civilized society. The child had his tutor, who could punish him. The adult had an inner guardian—the introjected superego, we might say—to deter him from ugly-and-shameful behavior, even if this was not seen and condemned by the fearful judgment of society.

(2) Yet there were moments of release, as in the theater. Plato describes these in language that remarkably anticipates Freud. When the normally inhibited person listens to a vulgar or scurrilous joke, he is induced to "let down the guard" of the moral and rational censorship, to admit something of the clown or joker into his soul. Still more, when he enjoys the invective and obscenity of the comic stage, does he relax the inward censorship of shame and turn "comedian." Plato would agree with Freud about the delightfulness of this relaxation of inhibition, the way it is manifested in strong and sudden laughter. Unlike Freud, however, he condemns all such psychic relaxation as subversive, to the soul as to the state: for if the good life, in the soul as in the state, consists in the rule of reason over emotion, and in the strict regulation of thought, feeling, and behavior in accordance with fixed and unchanging norms, then even the briefest relaxation of control, the most momentary "letting down one's guard," may lead to revolution. Such letting go might be welcomed, in traditional Greek thought, as a gift of Dionysus, of holiday, of the the-

ater; but it was the very thing that Plato, by temperament and conviction, most dreaded and denounced.

(3) The passage quoted from *Republic* 10 carries a further valuable suggestion, that joking and comedy help people recover the pleasure of childish play. (The word *neanikon* also denotes the *energy* of active young people, hence the psychic energy released when inhibitions are relaxed.)[6] To Plato, as to most classical moralists, it seemed that the main business of children was to grow quickly and efficiently into responsible adults. Play (*paidia*) should always serve education (*paideia*). And yet one of the joys of comedy is that it brings us back to the play and nonsense of childhood, to pleasures that we often forget, but that may still contribute largely to our happiness as adults.

Let me support this point with certain recollections of my own childhood. When I was eleven and my brother Philip was seven, we were sent to bed much too early, so we stayed awake telling stories to each other about imaginary countries. Both Kajir and Philidonia (the Blue and the Red Country) were orderly, efficient, and powerful realms. But we also created a Yellow Country of laughter and silliness, which "belonged" to our maternal grandfather. If our father was strict, autocratic, puritanical, the very embodiment of social inhibition and constraint, then Grandpa was the opposite: funny, laughter-loving, fond of sports, but somehow weak and ineffectual—the *senex lenis*, in fact. His Yellow Country, then, gave space to play and nonsense bordering on anarchy. Indecencies, normally unthinkable, were at home there—much as Grandpa had been at home in "speakeasies" during the time of Prohibition. Within the safe bounds of the Yellow Country, we enjoyed bathroom humor, enjoyed long, fantastic tales of sex. We also made up comic adventures in which ordinary social roles were turned topsy-turvy, in which adults who had caused us grief or annoyance were humiliated and punished. Had a psychiatrist eavesdropped on our stories, he might have said that the Yellow Country provided an excuse for the release of pent-up feelings about sex, family, and society, for the expression of aggressive tendencies, for the playing out of deep anxieties about life and death. He might also have treated our fantasies as compensating for the feelings of powerlessness of two children brought up under more than usual constraint. He would be right, in part; yet the Yellow Country had more to it than psychiatry could explain. It celebrated the comic side of life. Like Grandpa's sense of humor, it was a true part of our inheritance. And it conveyed, without our knowing it, something of myth, something of the Golden Age ruled over by old Kronos before Zeus, the strict father figure, brought in his harsher regime. It exhibited, in comic and mythic form, the reality of joy.

I want, therefore, to use a personal shorthand and argue that the comic stage of Dionysus provided its audience with a reentry into the Yellow Country. Plato would have agreed; for he appreciated, more than

Aristotle did, the pleasures of relief from inhibition offered by the theater—though he preferred to forget that these pleasures were a god's gift, sacred as well as healing for the theatergoers. The thing to remember is that many of comedy's special attributes belong to this more general experience of release. The indecency, the aggressive violence, the waiving of anxiety and sadness, all explain the enormous appeal of comedy, but they should not be taken, even together, as exhausting its purpose and its meaning. For comedy is the place where all these good things are free to happen. It is a wildlife preserve, a god-given refuge from civilization and its discontents—through which, however, civilization is greatly strengthened. It is also a place where the "pursuit of happiness" can be played out and clarified, for Athens or for America. Its characteristic movement, from release to clarification, conveys the full range and power and meaning of the comic catharsis, providing the critic with a good entry into Aristophanes' plays and their interpretation while keeping fresh the feelings of relaxation, recovery of joy, and recognition that lie at their heart.

7   *Clowning as Reassurance: Preliminary Catharsis*

A person comes onstage. His face is hidden by a large grotesque comic mask. He looks fat. Over his tights, which are padded to produce a big belly and big buttocks, and which show a phallus, modestly coiled up for the present, he wears a short chiton and a himation. He comes forward and speaks:

> Oh, slings and arrows of outrageous fortune!
> So many heartaches, so few happy moments!
> So few, so very few. Exactly four.
> But heartaches, plenty, sand-grain-zillions of them.
> Let's see. What did I like worth real rejoicement?
> I know—it really warmed my heart—it was
> when Cleon coughed up half a million dollars.
> Oh, that was great. I'm grateful to the knights
> for that day's work. O, patriotic deed!
> But what a pain I had, what a tragic pain,
> when I sat there gaping, waiting for Aeschylus,
> and the man announced, "Bring on your troupe, Theognis!"
>
>   (*Acharnians* 1–12)

The modern reader or critic begins with these lines. He will be plunged into Aristophanic jokes, changing levels of diction, topical allusions; he will be caught up in the play's momentum. But he will largely miss the experience of pleasure, relaxation, and reassurance that the Athenian audience had when this figure first came into sight. Even before being identified as "Dicaeopolis," he is The Clown. He is cousin to Charlie Chaplin and Harpo Marx. It is good to see him again. Indeed, even before he appears, it is good to sit in Dionysus' theater on holiday, expecting a comic performance. Even the wartime audience of 425 B.C. will laugh in anticipation of good things.

Why should this person with the odd costume and daemonic mask give instant reassurance? It happens through conventions that differ from our own; I use the term "clown" to bridge the gap. And conventions take getting used to. Without habituation, they might be terrifying or absurd. Not long ago, when I was showing two young friends around Greek vases in the Boston Museum, they were baffled and mystified by the Pan Painter's two red-figured scenes. On one side there was Artemis (to be identified), a youth, and some stylized hounds; it required much explanation, much setting of scene and mood, before my friends could respond to a depiction of the Actaeon story with appropriate sentiments of pity and fear. On the other side, there was the goat-headed Pan, pursuing a shepherd boy with intent to rape; he has a great erection, as has the pleased herm looking on.[7] It had not occurred to me that anybody might be appalled by the scene. *I* find it funny; but then, I am used to associating ithyphallic figures on vase paintings, especially satyrs, with Dionysus' gifts of liberation, energy, and joy. What might appall now reassures instead. And so with Old Comedy: a great variety of conventions, of mask and costume, language and gesture, music and dance and song, join within familiar play forms to create and sustain the constant reassurance that makes comedy effective.

It is hard for me, an American scholar, fully to appreciate the clown who will be Dicaeopolis; harder still to explain him to others who find such distance between Greek reassurances and their own. I may use a modern clown, Charlie Chaplin perhaps, for comparison; but how would I ever *explain* Charlie Chaplin to an ancient Athenian? Let me try, using notes I made several years ago after seeing a revival of *Modern Times* and *The Great Dictator* with Philip and our children (it was his birthday, so we had cheeseburgers before the movies and chocolate cake afterwards)—but will these notes mean very much except to the already converted?

> Charlie Chaplin makes us laugh, makes us feel good from his first appearance on screen. He is a very ordinary type, the "little tramp," a perpetual underdog and friend of other underdogs, society's waifs and strays; small, often timid and helpless, so a test case for the strength that lies hidden in human beings. He is often a victim and scapegoat; he gets pushed around a lot by bullies and officials and policemen. But he is resilient; he bounces back from defeat and tries something new; he is energetic and resourceful in getting around obstacles toward what he wants (and sometimes fortune helps him in remarkable ways). Above all, he survives. He has what we might call the great clown's virtue of survivability. After all the vicissitudes of *Modern Times*, all the frustrations and disappointments and defeats snatched from the jaws of victory, he is *not* defeated; he can still make the gamin smile; and saying to

her, "We'll get along," he walks side by side with her down the middle of life's highway, in his pathetic yet jaunty way. So there is hope for all of us yet.

Charlie has a mix of qualities that makes him hard to define morally and spiritually, yet which helps guarantee his full appeal to us—to our own mixed condition of id, ego, and superego, which he helps us to accept and integrate. He is very naive and childlike: quick to be taken in, but quick also to enjoy what the present moment offers—a friend's kindness, a quiet time of repose on someone's lawn (before the policeman comes), or even in a comfortable jail cell; quick also to go after what he wants energetically and wholeheartedly (as most of us are too worldly wise to do); naive too in the sense of childlike wonder that makes life perpetually fascinating. Yet he can be very clever and cunning too, can combine his dove's innocence with some measure of the prudence of serpents. He is vulgar in his way of attending to life's basic necessities; he scratches when he itches; but his vulgarity (which has a daintiness about it) is of the type that survives humiliation—another great comic power. He can be very naughty (which is the child's version of bad); he can take and use what isn't his; he can be destructive to property, insulting to dignity, greedy and foolish in the pursuit of good food and comfort; yet these selfish qualities are indistinguishably mixed with unusual kindness, decency, chivalry, and self-sacrificing generosity. Charlie's behavior reassures us, deep down, that we can be acceptable even with our silly and bad qualities; and at the same time, it gives kindness and decency a good name. Most of his comedies are not morally instructive in any obvious way. Yet his naughtiness, his mischievous clowning, are clearly on the side of the angels (or vice versa). He makes us feel better: and perhaps we are.

Clearly it is harder for a grown-up to explain Charlie Chaplin than for a child to enjoy him; and this should give us pause before attempting to describe a comic figure like Dicaeopolis. For Aristophanes' characters can be paradoxical figures both in their nature and in the kinds of laughter that they elicit. Thus, we laugh at Dicaeopolis (1) because he is *like ourselves*, reflecting our common pleasures and pains and our common feelings; (2) because he is *lower* than we are, more vulgar and shameless and naive, so that we laugh with superiority and sometimes with scorn; and yet (3) from very shamelessness and lack of inhibition he attains a strength and effectiveness *greater than ours*, which is admirable, borders on the heroic, and reassures us deeply about our own nature and possibilities.[8] Let me illustrate this paradox in some detail.

First, Dicaeopolis is like ourselves. He is not a tragic hero, or meant to be. Often his rhetoric approaches the tragic, or borrows from it—indeed his first line could have been spoken by a tragic hero out of Euripides (and perhaps was)—but as he descends to his catalogue of the pleasures and pains that comic flesh is heir to, it becomes clear that he is comically "bugged," not tragically stung, by life. The difference is enormous. Dicaeopolis does not draw us into the familiar mythic world of tragedy where high and noble actions, choices, and sufferings evoke pity and fear. As a man like ourselves, who would sit passively (it seems at first) in the Assembly, a victim of scheming politicians and incomprehensible foreign policy, and of the displacements and discomforts of an idiotically self-prolonging war, Dicaeopolis begins by reflecting our everyday experience, not at Argos or Thebes or Troy, but at Athens in 425 B.C. We enjoy the mention of familiar people, places, things on the comic stage. We take pleasure in shared recognitions and shared responses. We like hearing about the ordinary pleasures and pains that, to tell the truth, occupy most of our life and thought.

But, second, we laugh not just with Dicaeopolis, but at him, because his behavior is so far inferior to our own. He is, from the first, wonderfully indecent. Like the famous Belle of old Natchez "who said, when ah itchez, ah scratchez," he describes how he groans, yawns, stretches, and farts out of boredom and irritation at the Assembly's sluggishness; and undoubtedly he suits the gestures and actions to the words. He is quite shameless and uninhibited. We have to laugh at this silly person who farts, who admits to farting, in public. We laugh from superiority as he is shushed in the Assembly, then as he is set upon by 'a company of Thracian mercenaries with enormous phalluses, robbed of his garlic, and symbolically shafted. We enjoy his humiliation (though it is also our own) with the natural cruelty or *Schadenfreude* of grown children. But we also laugh with relief as Dicaeopolis' clowning leads us to lay aside our inhibitions, to revel in low and basic fun. It is good to be back in a world where eating, vomiting, farting, and sex (though rather passive sex to begin with) take center stage. As Plato would say, it is great fun to relax, to let down our guard.

But, thirdly, there is more. If we laugh at Dicaeopolis for his ridiculous behavior, yet he is stronger than we are, for he cannot be shamed or humiliated or kept down for long.[9] His very shamelessness carries him forward at the Assembly, to speak for peace, to expose the frauds and imposters who prey upon Athens; it carries him forward to make, defend, and enjoy a separate peace. He dares to speak out, like the child who cries that the emperor has no clothes. He dares to confront public opinion (the chorus of old Marathon-fighters), to beard Euripides in his tragic den, and even—like the Euripidean beggar-hero Telephus facing the Achaean princes—to plead the unpopular cause of peace and international justice before the angry chorus, and the angry audience. Even the braggart Lamachus, the personification of militaristic ambition and the idiocy of war, has to yield to his scurrilous honesty. Dicaeopolis wins a full victory over his enemies, over the forces of misery and destruction. Dionysus has watched over him. But even if this victory were denied him, still the clown's shamelessness, his energy, and his sheer survivability would be, like Charlie Chaplin's, a sign of hope for us, and a kind of triumph.

Indeed this triumph of Dicaeopolis is twice democratic: first, because it gives voice to the ordinary Athenian's feelings, his frustrations with civic life, his resentment of officials, and his wish to overcome nuisances and enemies generally; but second, because it affirms the lower part of human nature, the desires that Plato would suppress, and especially the ugly-and-shameful (*aischra*) or "no-account" (*phaula*) parts of psychic life. It is the reverse of how Homer treats Thersites in *Iliad* 2. This man, we are told, was the most ugly-and-shameful man who came to Troy. He was bandy-legged, lame in one foot, round-shouldered, pointy-headed, nearly bald; and his character matched his appearance. He behaved and spoke in a disorderly way, knew no right measure, railed at the chieftains, and did everything he could to make the Achaeans laugh. He was, in fact, a primitive satirist. Thus he showered insult on Achilles, Odysseus, and Agamemnon; but Homer makes it clear that the army disliked his behavior: "They felt great resentment and blamed him in their hearts." Odysseus, however, scolded and threatened him: "If I catch you playing the fool like this again, I'll strip off your cloak and tunic that cover your genitals, and I'll beat you and send you home crying, with unseemly blows." And he did beat him, with Agamemnon's scepter. Thersites was hurt; he cried; he sat down again in fright and was silent. And the Achaeans, though much grieved by their misfortunes (which *were* the fault of Achilles and Agamemnon, if not of Odysseus), yet laughed heartily at Thersites' discomfiture and joked with one another: this was Odysseus' greatest feat, to shut up this mocker. Now he wouldn't rail at the princes again.

Like the Hephaestus scene that ends *Iliad* 1, this Thersites scene provides comic relief and contrast amid conflict, distress, and suffering. Its humor is brutal and primitive. The ugly-and-shameful Thersites becomes a scapegoat, to carry off the bad feelings of the army. We laugh, as they do, with pure *Schadenfreude* to see him mocked and beaten; since he mocked others, the reversal is especially agreeable. Yet Homer subordinates the comic scene to serious ends. In *Iliad* 2, military and social order are reestablished after their large-scale breakdown in *Iliad* 1; thus the army is marshaled in good order, hierarchy is reasserted, discipline is reaffirmed. The comic exposure of Thersites therefore does more than provide comic relief: it vindicates the usual social and psychological controls suggested by words like *kalos* ("fine," "beautiful"), *aretē* ("excellence"), and *aidōs* and *nemesis* ("shame" and "blame"), and inversely by *aischros* ("ugly-and-shameful"). Satire may reinforce social mores but may also turn individualistic and critical; thus Archilochus' iambic poetry will contain much of Thersites. But Homer's strong laughter is conservative and antisatirical here, confirming the social and moral status quo.

But Dicaeopolis, the comic hero, succeeds where Thersites failed. An expert at indecent exposure, he uses it to unmask and discredit the real enemy, who are the frauds, the corrupt politicians, and the war profiteers of Athens. The free speech (*parrhēsia*) with which he, and Aristophanes behind him, beards officials and authorities and inhibiting people generally, is very democratic, a gift of the Athenian democracy as well as of Dionysus. But comedy's *aischrologia*, the mix of invective with obscenity that was characteristic of Old Comedy, also gives democratic expression and release to that lower part of ourselves that is ordinarily shushed like Thersites, and especially to what we feel to be ugly-and-shameful in ourselves. All this gives great pleasure, through mechanisms and for reasons that Plato indicates and Freud largely explains. It affords much "purgation," much healing laughter. But it is still where Aristophanes begins, not ends.

Where he takes us can be described in different ways. One is recognition; I suggested earlier, in discussing the *Peace*, that Aristophanes brought his audience through a recovery of good feeling to a play perspective in which they could "recognize" themselves and their situation. But this recognition involves some degree of conflict and pain. Worries, as about war and politics, were put aside at the theater's entrance, but they are reviewed in the light of comedy. Conflicts, sometimes insoluble ones, are played out in the comic *agōn*. Above all, Aristophanes comes to grips with deep anxieties of his time, anxieties about change and the death of known, trusted meanings and beliefs. In all this, he draws close to the brink of tragedy, like all great comic playwrights—and like his hero Dicaeopolis, who assumes the pathetic rags of Telephus, only to throw them off in good time: for he is not Prince Telephus, nor was meant to be.[10] Yet he came close, and we with him. At times we are just barely saved by the net of comic language, comic gesture, comic convention, from falling into the abyss of tragedy. Hence we emerge, I think, from the comic theater not just cheered up, but somehow changed, and seeing the world as changed with us. We are reminded that life is good, that willful, "Euripidean" indulgence in misery is bad. We are ourselves again; and although conflicts remain, both internal and external, and always will, they are not now the same necessities they seemed before.

To illustrate the larger recognitions to which Aristophanes brings us will require several chapters and a more detailed analysis of several plays than is desirable here. For now, I only want to suggest two things: first, that the release of strong feelings of indecency and aggressiveness in healing laughter is and must remain a primary aim of Aristophanes' comedies, always to be enjoyed, and never to be neglected by the critic; but second, that this kind of release, like the warm-up jokes of the prologue, yet constitutes only a preliminary catharsis, releasing energies that the poet uses to build a larger comic explosion, a further catharsis, arising from nothing less than the total comedy. To this final achievement, and this final satisfaction, the liberating sex jokes and hostility jokes are merely foreplay. Even Freud turns fraudulent if he and his *Schadenfreud-e* prevent us, as critics, from going all the way.

Yet the feelings evoked by comedy need further exploration before we turn to a fuller account, in chapters 3 and 4, of comedy of ideas and comic recognitions. For we have not exhausted the healing possibilities of this Yellow Country. Laughter makes many good things happen; not least among these, it revives our power of wishing and hoping. Once more I turn to Plato for his strong insight into comedy. The myth that he puts into Aristophanes' mouth in the *Symposium* is a marvelous tribute from one artist to another. It also brings us, through much comic foreplay, to just those erotic feelings that Aristophanes was at pains, I think, to bring about in his audience. In the remainder of this chapter, I shall follow Plato's lead and describe some ways in which Aristophanes' plays provide a clarification of wishing and hoping that follows on, and is made possible by, recovery and release.

8   *Aristophanes' Speech in Plato's* Symposium

ARISTOPHANES plays a strong competitive part in the drama or agon of Plato's *Symposium*.[11] Like the dramatic contest it commemorates, which Agathon had won, this symposium is a contest in erotic speeches and mastery of life, which Socrates must win. His speech outshines the others; he is symbolically crowned by Alcibiades, on Dionysus' behalf; he outdrinks the comic and tragic poets, Aristophanes and Agathon. Yet these are strong antagonists: no straw men, but outstanding representatives of their craft.

Well before his speech, Aristophanes appears as a strong and dangerous competitor. Ordinarily, we learn, he would have been one of the most vigorous drinkers. His staged hiccups give comic relief, but he uses them to jockey for position (after the doctor, Eryximachus, whose speech he wants to parody), and he announces his intention to avoid, not making people laugh, "for that would be sheer gain, my Muse's own turf," but making himself ridiculous. He will use laughter to come out on top. This little skirmish with the doctor is like a proagon, a preliminary contest, in an Aristophanic play.

Plato, of course, is the controlling dramatist this time, and he means to use Aristophanes as a fictional character for his own purposes. The comic poet's humor will clear the air of much abstraction and pretense inherent in the previous speeches, yet will also, like Agathon's speech, be a foil to Socrates'. Again, as with the others, part of Aristophanes' account will be used and redirected by Socrates, but will be rejected. Aristophanes tries afterwards to reply, but he gets no chance. A band of revelers bursts in, led by the drunken Alcibiades. It is a fitting punishment for the comic poet who had maligned Socrates in his *Clouds*, that wine and revelry (*kōmos*) should keep him from having the last word.

But Plato also pays high tribute to Aristophanes (as also to Agathon) in his dialogue. Part of this is emulation, since the myth put in Aristophanes' mouth is, of course, Plato's own *mimēsis*. Among the comic techniques that he borrows and exhibits are lampooning of individuals and types; parody of literary genres; plays on words; buffoonery; mock didacticism; parodic use of scientific, technical, and conceptual language; straight-faced telling of nonsense; wild fantasy; ridiculous explanations of things; irreverence toward the gods; comic moralizing; mixture of colloquial and "high" language; funny images and comparisons; sexual humor; topical reference; anachronism; and delight in bodily functions and circular motion. At least one joke, on homosexual politicians, is lifted directly from the *Knights* or *Clouds*. What is, however, still more Aristophanic is the way that this laughter-making is used: first, to clear the air, or the *erōs*, of much cloudy abstraction and pretense, generated by the intellectual fog-machines of the sophist and the doctor; and second, to bring about in their place a fresh atmosphere of erotic feeling, of wishing and hoping. Let me take these in turn.

Eros is, says Aristophanes,

> a doctor, a healer of those ills whose cure would bring the utmost happiness to the human race. I shall attempt to give a full explanation of his power for you people; you in turn will instruct the outside world. But first you must grasp the pathologies of human nature. For of old our basic nature was not the same as it is now, but different. For in the beginning, the human race was divided not into two species, male and female (as it is now), but into *three.* . . . (189d)

Aristophanes shows up the previous speakers as inadequate by outrunning them in fantasy and at the same time undercutting their pedantic concepts through constant recollection of the low, real world in which people live. Pausanias himself had criticized Phaedrus' praise of Eros as an ancient, mighty divinity. Such a view, he said, was simpleminded. His own sophistic analysis revealed the existence of two Erotes, one worthy to be gratified (being educational and conducive to virtue), one not; Eryximachus essentially accepted the division and extended it into every area of experience, from medicine to farming, music, and astronomy: everywhere the skilled practitioner found a healthier Eros to gratify, a right balance of disparate elements to establish through the appropriate scientific technique. And Aristophanes? He goes beyond the dualists: "There were, you must know, *three* kinds of people!" It seems things must break up further before they can begin to come together again. Aristophanes' straight-faced didactic manner of telling his wild and woolly story parodies the professors and indicates that they too need not be taken very seriously. At the same time, curiously, his fantasy brings us back to earth, our own earth, after their abstract flights. Hence the comic "comparisons" from low-life occupations. When, for example, Aristophanes tells how Zeus sliced the Wholepeople in half and Apollo sewed and patched up the separate halves and smoothed out the wrinkles, like a skilled leatherworker, he is not just being funny, or mocking the learned doctor by describing a "sawbones." He is also bringing us home to our own bodies and the feelings associated with them. His special interest, of course, is human sexuality.

Most obviously, he takes us downward from the head to (of course!) the genitals. As he does so, with the shamelessness of a Dicaeopolis or a Trygaeus, we realize that the previous speakers had quite ignored these parts, as though sexuality was all in the mind (or was their argument a cover for certain lower pleasures that a gentleman or sophist preferred not to mention?). But Aristophanes puts sex where it belongs. Zeus had the brilliant idea of turning the genitals to the outside of each half-person, so they could have sexual intercourse with each other and gain some respite from the fierce craving for reunion with the lost other half. At the same time we are reminded of the variety of sexual experience, homo- and heterosexual. The joke about Pausanias and Agathon as homosexual lovers, offspring of the whole-male, is typical comic lampooning, but it also brings out what Pausanias himself had so skillfully concealed: that bodies were involved as well as arguments, and that the latter should, finally, bear some real relation to the former. As so often in Aristophanes' plays, the joking implies an acceptance, indeed a hearty celebration of bodily functions, and hence of ourselves as sharing fully in the human condition—which is where any adequate investigation of Eros must begin.

Begin, not end; for the comic spotlighting of the genitals and their varied and delightful modes of behavior is only part of a larger rediscovery of human sexuality, which involves personal feeling, desire, and passion.[12] Pausanias and Eryximachus had not only taken an intellectual, or clinical, approach to sex. They had depersonalized it in their businesslike way, had treated it as a matter of technique, of achieving the same kind of homeostasis in human relations as the growing of crops might require, or musical harmonies, or the complex interrelations of the heavenly bodies. It is all a question of indoctrinating people (or plants) with appropriate habits of preference—and the skilled technician, whether physician or farmer or prophet, holds the keys to the requisite maintenance of balance and control in all these various "erotic" areas. Now while Aristophanes would probably concur that sexual intercourse provides an agreeable release from tension, he refuses to define human sexuality in mechanistic terms as part of a general system of "repletion and evacuation." If one part of being human is to have bodies, and bodies which do quite delightful things, the other is to have personal desires that are not satisfied in so easy or mechanical or technologically viable a manner. When Aristophanes makes Hephaestus stand over the two lovers, tools in hand, and ask them (ever so kindly) what it is that they really want, the implication is clearly that human sexuality is more than sex, more than a restoration of homeostasis or, in modern terms, the right management of "outlets" or "orgasms." There is the desire we have for a special beloved person; beyond that there is some further insatiable desire, best expressed in myth. What we want, says Aristophanes, is to be reunited with our lost other half, to recover the blissful existence of the Wholepeople we once were. "Love therefore is the name we give to the desire and pursuit of the whole."

Notice the combination, desire *and* pursuit. The nostalgic wish begets positive forward motion, which is evidence of divine grace as well as human initiative: for if we are not just helpless victims of an unfortunate situation, pining away for the unattainable, it is because the same gods who earlier punished our overexuberant vitality now conspire to help us recover our long-lost wholeness and joy.

In general the critics (Simone Weil is a notable exception) have ignored the religious dimension of Aristophanes' myth.[13] Were they confusing irreverence with skepticism? Naturally, Aristophanes is irreverent; that is one side of comedy, to ventilate negative feelings of hostility and doubt, whether about the gods or about anything else imaginable—and of course, all this wild commentary is sanctioned by religious tradition and the very gods in question! It is, so to speak, all in the family. Plato's earlier statement, that Aristophanes' entire concern is with Dionysus and Aphrodite, is suggestive here, less for its joking implication that the comic poet spends his energies on drink and sex than for the strong bond it implies between him and the Olympian gods. By contrast the previous speakers paid only lip service to religion. Pausanias "divided" Aphrodite and Eros, stripping away their mystery and power and replacing them, to all practical purposes, with a dubious utilitarian theory of erotic relativism and education; and Eryximachus, though he introduced significant notions that Socrates would pick up later, of prophecy and the daemonic, tended obviously to see religion as one more area of specialization to be mastered by a competent professional. His world picture was very scientific, very serious, and very secular—all, of course, a foil for Aristophanes.

One curious feature of the comic myth is its stress (modified as we shall see) on human sinfulness. It is a variant of Hesiod's account of the loss of the Golden Age. Like Hesiod, Aristophanes looks back nostalgically to a time when nature provided mankind with utter happiness; only he is closer to Freud than Hesiod was, and his magnificent Wholepeople with their rounded shapes and redoubled limbs are no more innocent than real children are:

So they were mighty in strength and energy, and they had lofty thoughts as well: they actually attacked the gods; in fact, what Homer says of Ephialtes and Otos is meant of them, that they tried to build up a ladder to heaven to make war on the gods. (190b)

They have, in other words, the *normal* excessiveness of children, or perhaps adolescents. Their punishment plays on the fear of castration—with apologies, not to Freud, but to Empedocles, whose fantastic cosmogony and zoogony included the splitting up of Wholenatures under the growing rule of Strife, and at another stage, their coming together again from scattered limbs under the growing rule of Love.[14] In Empedocles' scientific poem, the processes of separation and recombination repeated themselves endlessly; wherever we come in the process (and the question is hotly debated by scholars), it hardly seems encouraging. Aristophanes' myth is less cyclical. It presents a one-time fall, as from some remembered or intuited childhood bliss. Aristophanes explains this fall in comic, yet religious terms, as the punishment (how could it be otherwise?) for our normal hybris, our human sinfulness. Yet reassurance quickly follows. Punishment is followed by healing, by a beginning of recovery. The new invention of genital sexuality is a splendid "contrivance," a sign of hope. We lose, but also we gain. It is like growing up.

Aristophanes concludes with a comic warning against further misbehavior, which might lead to further "slicing," and with an injunction and encouragement:

No: everybody should be told to show piety toward the gods, so that we may escape those ills and obtain those blessings, with Love as our leader and our general. Let no one go against Love (only god-forsaken people do that); for by becoming reconciled to the god, as friends, we shall do what few people do in these days: we shall discover and meet up with our own (lost) loves. Now I don't want Eryximachus to make fun of my speech and say that I'm referring to Pausanias and Agathon here. It may be, of course, that they are such a pair, halves of the all-male and meant for one another. But I am referring to *all* men and women, and I am saying, that this is the way for our race to become utterly happy (*eudaimōn*), by each person's bringing his love to fulfillment, gaining his own lover, and thus returning to his ancient constitution, his old way of living. This is the best thing. But if it is, then what comes nearest to it is the best thing under present circumstances: and this is, to find a lover who is naturally congenial to oneself. We would do right to praise Love as the god responsible for this: Love, who at present helps us most, by guiding each to his own, and who moreover provides us with very great hopes for the future—hopes that, if we act reverently toward the gods, he will restore us to our oldtime nature, and will heal our wounds, and will make us utterly happy and blessed. (193a–d)

How hopeful, really, is this ending? Is there a suggestion that, in real life, we have to settle for second best—that we shall never get, or recover, what we really want? That would be very painful. It would, and surely does, reinforce Plato's own view that this approach fails in the end. He means to use the soul's powerful nostalgia for lost wholeness, but he will insist, through Socrates and "Diotima," that this nostalgia is finally for the Good, and that the way to the Good is the Socratic way, the way of the philosopher or lover of wisdom, who rejects images and practices the Way of Renunciation. For such a person—for Plato's true lover—anything resembling ordinary sexual love can only be an ironic masquerade, a way of enticing people into the deeper love of reality. As we look back from that final initiation of love over which Diotima presides, and to which the Socratic catharsis leads, we must see Aristophanes as a kind of pagan prophet, whose half-divine comic inspiration pointed to more than he could ever realize, or understand.[15]

It is my wish, however, to let Aristophanes have the last word. The end of his speech strikes a beautiful balance between acceptance and longing, acceptance of present reality and hope that goes beyond that reality. The combination is playful, touching, and (I think) genuinely Aristophanic. And it suggests something at the psychological heart of his comedies that I mean, with love, to pursue: a "clarification" of wishing and hoping that brings healing with it, and also understanding. Fairy tale, not fable, gives the best analogue today.

9   *Wishing, Hoping, and Fairy Tale*

SUPERFICIALLY Aristophanes' myth in the *Symposium* resembles fable.[16] It has the same casualness of structure and diction, the same lighthearted, irreverent treatment of the gods, the same "Just So Story" quality that we find in many fables of the Aesopic collection—fables that Aristophanes knew and sometimes used in constructing his comic fantasies. Yet these fables lack the basic hopefulness of the myth. They are, for the most part, cautionary tales about human life and human nature, under a humorous animal disguise; and usually they point a moral (which eventually became attached to the tale, or passed into a proverb), like our own "Look before you leap," or "From the frying pan into the fire," or "Stick to your own trade" (or, to your own nature), or "Don't count your chickens before they're hatched." Many of the stories warn against wanting too much, or trying for too much, which so often leads to being cheated or disappointed. It is as though the light-soaring hopes of Greek children and adults alike needed, like great gas balloons, to be pricked gently and guided back to solid earth. For what, in the end, do these fables teach us? To be careful, in the first place, and practical, and more than a little tricky; and only secondly, to be good, fair, and honest. Not that goodness is not frequently rewarded in fables: for wickedness tends to outsmart itself, and the cheater is often cheated in turn, and the villain is foiled, or beaten, or killed; but it is shrewdness, not goodness, that generally takes the prize.

Aesopic fable conveys, on a simple level, the same warning against excessiveness, and especially against excessive wishes and aspirations, that is often found in Greek epic, lyric, and tragic poetry; only in these, folly and sinfulness are closely intertwined, and they lead to disasters that no one could laugh at. Hope, *elpis*, may be described as a foolish optimism about life, or as a characteristic of light-minded youth, unaware of life's difficulties; but hope can also take on a more daemonic aspect, as an infatuation that grips the mind, distorts the judgment, and drives people into irretrievable ruin.[17] When Theognis speaks of Hope and Risk as "dangerous *daemones*," he is not just using personification. As E. R. Dodds says, "they are endowed with a life and energy of their own, and so can force a man, as it were from the outside, into conduct foreign to him."[18] Such a view recurs frequently in Pindar and Aeschylus, Sophocles and Herodotus. Thus, in the great ode on *Atē* in the *Antigone*, the chorus sing of how "Hope, much beaten back, is an aid to many men, but to many it is a deception of light-minded passions." Here, as often, *elpis* shares in the ambivalence of *erōs* itself, which so often turns destructive or self-destructive in tragedy.

Hesiod's evaluation of hope in his *Works and Days* is less sinister, yet remains predominantly negative. He tells with scorn what happens to a lazy man who will not work but lives on hopes:

> The man who doesn't work, who waits upon idle hope,
> wanting the stuff of life, tells over many troubles:
> hope's not a good resource for a needy man to get,
> sitting upon his bed, whose livelihood is lacking.[19]
>
> (498–501)

It is like the story of the Ant and the Grasshopper. What is the use of daydreaming, of waiting for something to turn up, when you lacked the discipline earlier, and the foresight, to raise sufficient crops? Now it is too late. In such a realistic context, hope becomes "empty," a distraction from the real business of life. And yet Hesiod hints at a more positive evaluation of hope in his Pandora myth. There, Hope remains "by the will of Zeus" beneath the lid of the jar after all the troubles of life, and all the diseases, have flown forth.[20] Hope may still be delusory. Often it is. But life without hope (as Hesiod seems to have known) would be unbearable.

If, given this background of warnings about the delusiveness of hope, we return to Aristophanes' myth in the *Symposium*, we find there what seems to me a remarkable hopefulness. Plato catches brilliantly the way Aristophanes builds with laughter, the way he uses different kinds of joking and comic reassurance—what I call the "preliminary catharsis"—to create a lovely story of recovery through grace and will and the leadership of Love. The myth, like Hephaestus' question posed to the lovers as they lie entwined together—"What is it you people *really* want?"—stirs something very deep, an erotic longing that we need to recognize, and to deal with, if we are to feel truly hopeful about life. But to put it differently: it would be a cruel and painful thing to arouse, and to experience, this kind of erotic longing without the accompanying hopefulness that is present in the myth, and that Plato recognized, so perceptively, in Aristophanic comedy.

Although Aristophanes' fable retains the outward trappings of the fable or "Just So Story," at heart it has less in common with the realistic, cautionary Aesopic fable than with something very different: the fairy tale. Since the point matters, I shall explain what I mean by fairy tale, using modern examples, before returning to the Greeks and to Aristophanes. To make a few summary points:

(1) The term *fairy tale* is somewhat misleading, since few of these stories are about fairies. I use it as a lame, though emotionally evocative, English variant of the German word *Märchen*, which Bolte and Polivka define as

> a tale created out of poetic fantasy, especially one from the realm of enchantment, a tale of wonder that is not tied to the conditions of real life, which is enjoyed by high and low, even though they find it unbelievable.[21]

And similarly, Stith Thompson:

> A Märchen is a tale of some length involving a succession of motifs or episodes. It moves in an unreal world without definite locality or definite characters and is filled with the marvellous. In this never-never-land humble heroes kill adversaries, succeed to kingdoms, and marry princesses.[22]

The best-known collection of fairy tales, by the Brothers Grimm, also includes some other types of story, like the animal tale (which is close to fable), the religious legend, and the joking tale—what the Germans call a *Schwank*. For the most part, though, they are tales of wonder, peril, and enchantment, in which the normal laws of logic and causation are suspended. A princess sleeps for a hundred years, and all the castle with her, until her prince passes through the hedge (the thorns turn to bright roses) and awakens her. An ugly little importunate frog turns out to be an enchanted prince. Fairy tales are full of talking birds and animals who give good advice and help the hero or heroine carry out what seem impossible tasks. At the same time fairy tales always describe the ordinary things of our experience: bread and milk, stones and trees, pots and pans, geese and sheep. They are often told in a very simple, natural manner; they are clear, exact, positive, and precise.[23] Good and evil are clearly distinguished in fairy tale, as they are not in ordinary life; emotions are externalized and simplified, so that a child or a simple person can understand them; and through various stylistic traits like repetition, the fairy tale conveys its reassuring sense of a harmoniousness, an orderliness beneath the perils and vicissitudes of life. To old as well as young, it gives what J. R. R. Tolkien has called the gift of *recovery*, restoring the freshness and color beneath what seemed ordinary, familiar, and drab.[24] It also helps us recover that lost sense of oneness with nature that our primitive ancestors once had and that we, when we lived in the animistic world of childhood, still largely enjoyed.

(2) Fairy tales generally move to a happy ending. Cinderella marries her prince; so does the goose girl, who is restored to her rightful station; Hansel and Gretel kill the witch and return home with the riches they have acquired. Yet the road to that final happiness is long and difficult; it takes us through a world of pain and grief and loneliness and suffering, a world in which children may be lost, and lovers separated, and people we love are exposed to sickness, or to crippling transformations, or to death. To the vague terrors from which children suffer so much, fairy tales give a local habitation and a name. Since these terrors are, in the end, about real possibilities and experiences of life, and since people cannot grow up without meeting and overcoming them, fairy tales should not altogether be regarded as "escapist." Yet usually (though not always) in fairy tales, the great good wishes for joy and love and victory prove more than a match for the great fears. The witch is killed, the way out of the forest is found, the evil spell is broken, the lovers are reunited, the true identity of the dragon-slayer is revealed, the imposter is found out and punished. Tolkien speaks of the "eucatastrophe" of fairy tales, the wonderful turning point toward happiness. He describes how they give, not just "recovery," but consolation and joy.

Psychologists have variously tried to account for the ways in which fairy tales seem to nurture and encourage right human growth. In *The Uses of Enchantment* Bruno Bettelheim gives a modified Freudian interpretation of many familiar stories, emphasizing how they encourage ego integration and the overcoming of Oedipal problems.[25] Working along the same lines, my colleagues Max Steele, who teaches creative writing, and Jeffrey Andresen, a psychiatrist, have produced a collaborative essay on "Hansel and Gretel" that explains much of the psychological insight and power of that story without losing sight of its beauty, charm, and art. I think myself that Jungian interpretations, such as those by Jung's disciple Marie-Louise von Franz, bring out the extraordinary psychological insights conveyed through fairy tales still better than Freudian interpretations.[26] Much of what I have learned about the power and meaning of fairy tale—and about the psyche—comes from von Franz. Yet differences of psychological interpretation and language are not all that great. The essential points remain: that fairy tales bring healing, that they bring reassurance about life, and that they bring growth. The three go together.

(3) Max Lüthi has said that fairy tales are "unreal but not untrue,"[27] and so has Bettelheim:

> The child intuitively comprehends that although these stories are *unreal*, they are not *untrue*; that while what these stories tell about does not happen in fact, it must happen as inner experience and personal development; that fairy tales depict in imaginary and sym-

bolic form the essential steps in growing up and achieving an independent existence.[28]

Let me postpone to a later time discussion of the question, Do these stories describe only "inner experience and personal development"? For now, I want to emphasize that, however "escapist" fairy tales may be, they are invariably marked out today as fictions. Their beginning formulas take us into a world that is not our own, that cannot possibly be confused with the world of ordinary, "real" life. "Once upon a time," begin the fairy tales. "Once upon a time, and a very good time it was, though it wasn't in my time, nor in your time, nor anyone else's time. . . ." Or again: "In olden times when wishing still helped, there lived a king whose daughters were all beautiful, but the youngest was so beautiful that the sun itself, which has seen so much, was astonished whenever it shone in her face." Sometimes the beginning employs a comic impossibility, or *adynaton*—"When hens had teeth"—to mark off the world of the fairy tale even more emphatically from our own. And the same is true of the endings.[29] The fairy tale brings the hero or heroine to entire happiness and content, but the storyteller, often by a wry last comment, reminds us that he is just that, a storyteller, and that his own lot, and ours, must be very different. He got some presents, he may say, but he lost them all. Or he may ask for money now. Or he may tease: "Now I'll wish a beautiful piece of cake into my hand, and for you—a beautiful stalk of straw into yours!" One way or another, this teasing marks but also eases what might otherwise have been a difficult and painful transition back into ordinary life. Fact and fiction, everyday world and fairy-tale world, are sharply distinguished from one another, so that not even a young child could be confused.

Yet the distinctions that folklorists so much emphasize, between myth, legend or saga, and fairy tale, are differentiations that came about relatively late in human culture, and only in some parts of the world at that. Even in *Grimm's Fairy Tales* a number of pious legends are included that evoke, or at least once evoked, a curious mixture of belief and humorous disbelief. In many ways fairy tales gain sustenance from primitive and childish beliefs the world over. Twentieth-century Westerners are still somewhat parochial in time and space; our confident assurance (which may not always be so very confident) that the dead do not return, that the old woman next door is not a witch, that the odd-looking fellow coming down the street does not sometimes turn himself into a werewolf—all these assumptions are modern, and local, and cannot everywhere be taken for granted. (Conversely, to the primitive mind today, the airplane and telephone are magical things.) In medieval Europe, fairies and witches were not so far away; pious legends, other popular legends, and fairy tales coexisted more closely. Much of the charm of Arthurian story, of Chaucer's tales, of Shakespeare's plays, comes from their inhabiting that yet uncertain borderland between magic and history, pagan and Christian. It was only in the later seventeenth century that the fairies, themselves once frightening, were frightened away from western Europe. In some places—in parts of Germany, for example—the world became disenchanted much later. By compensation, many Romantics came to think of childhood as a privileged time when fairy tales, which had been relegated to the nursery, could still be believed in and enjoyed.

Let me add one more, provisional note before returning to the Greeks, and to Aristophanes. While Schiller could feel that there was "deeper meaning" in fairy tales than in "the truth that life teaches," that

> Tiefere Bedeutung
> Liegt in dem Märchen meiner Kinderjahre
> Als in der Wahrheit, die das Leben lehrt,[30]

he—like most other Romantics—had no doubt about the clear line separating the world of reality from the world of fairy tale; he just (sometimes) preferred the latter and felt it in his heart to be more meaningful. But today things have somewhat changed. For one thing, we have come to enjoy as everyday occurrences the ease and freedom and mobility that, in more stable communities, were the stuff of fairy tale. As Max Lüthi says:

> We often refer to our present-day world as a modern fairy-tale, and this is indeed so: not only in the sense that nowadays doors open by themselves when we wish to enter a shop, that music comes forth at the touch of a button, that distant forms appear on a screen as they once did in a magic looking-glass, and that we can be carried through the air faster than a thief of Baghdad ever was on his flying carpet. Our world is a modern fairy tale also in a more fundamental, deeper sense: modern man has become so wholly mobile, he breaks away so easily from his accustomed environment, goes to faraway places and is prepared for whatever he may encounter; his existence is like that which, for centuries, only fairy-tale figures enjoyed.[31]

That is one reason why the once clear boundaries between fact and fiction, real life and fairy tale, have begun to blur a little. We look, seriously, to science fiction to catch glimpses of what future history may bring. Another reason for the blurring comes from modern science. For today's physicists, space and time behave in very strange ways indeed, and laws that once seemed inexorably true—for example, the Law of Contradiction—seem less so in an age when light may be described as consisting *either* of waves *or* of particles, and when the nature of what is observed changes with the observer. Science seems closer to mythology today than it did in the eighteenth and nineteenth centuries; and perhaps, the fairies may be coming closer again. It seems a good time to return to the richness of Chaucer's world, or Shakespeare's. Or, for that matter, to the world of Aristophanes.

The Greeks had fairy tales, as they have today (although no connection can be established); only these were not written down and hence did not survive in the simple form in which nurses or old grand-mothers told them to children.[32] Plato and other writers give us some idea of the impact of such stories on the imagination of the growing child. The word they use is *mythoi*, "stories." The term seems undifferentiated, like the Latin *fabula*; it must have covered myth, legend, some history, fairy tale, and fable. In an early reference, in Aristophanes' *Wasps*, the puritan son instructs his father to tell some polite anecdotes at a dinner party; the father immediately thinks of a story about Lamia, the man-eating witch and shape-shifter, or about talking animals: "Once there was a cat and a mouse." The latter may have been an instructive fable, or it may have come closer to fairy tale; we cannot tell. The point is that the old man's mind quickly reverts to a childish level where he feels comfortable—as he does not in the polite society of his son's friends.

Scholars in search of Greek fairy tales have found their motifs and types embedded in heroic legends as these are represented in epic, lyric, and tragedy. I shall come to these shortly. The greatest fairy tale from antiquity comes late, and stands alone: the story of Cupid and Psyche in Apuleius' *Metamorphoses*. It is rich and meaningful; many leading analysts have treated it in recent years. Curiously, the most complete isolated fairy tale from classical Greece is the story of Gyges told in Plato's *Republic*:

> Gyges . . . was a shepherd who served the king of Lydia. One day there was an earthquake, and a great chasm opened in the earth. He went down, and saw a great bronze horse with windows in it, and a huge naked corpse inside it; on the dead man's finger was a golden ring. Gyges took the ring and fled. By accident, and then by experiment, he found that turning the ring a certain way made him invisible. After ascertaining that the ring really had this power, he arranged to be sent to court, where he used the ring to sleep with the queen and murder the king: so the shepherd Gyges became king of Lydia. (359d–60b)

This story, which has undergone much literary stylization in Plato's retelling, reminds us more of the Thousand and One Nights than of Grimm's fairy tales, or Andersen's. Indeed it contradicts everything Bettelheim says about fairy tale, for in it the Oedipal wish is almost undisguised and is intentionally acted out. Glaucon tells the story to support his argument that most people accept justice as a compromise; for if they had Gyges' ring and could act unjustly without being observed, then surely they would. Actually Glaucon is playing devil's advocate here. He has a good moral nature, and he wants to prod Socrates into establishing the intrinsic value of justice apart from its appearance or its accidental benefits. It may be too that Plato is using this story to convey the deep psychological horror of injustice in the soul, much as he does later in depicting the tyrant whose life becomes a living nightmare of blood, sex, war, and terror. It is interesting, however, to see how the story of the magic ring raises the question again: what is it that people really want? There may be, there often is, a contradiction between the sentiments that people usually profess and the unexamined wishes that they nurture in their hearts. "What would you do if you had Gyges' ring?" It is the question that fairy tale raises over and over, clarifying our wishes for us. Plato's answer is grim, and it explains much about Plato, his psychology, and his politics; but it is no more final than his Gyges story is typical of fairy tale, ancient or modern.

As a more cheerful alternative to Plato, I want to offer two stories from the Aesopic collection that may well go back to classical Greece. The first is The Cat and Aphrodite:

> A cat fell in love with a handsome youth and prayed to Aphrodite to change her into a woman. And the goddess, feeling pity for her love, turned her into a lovely woman. So the youth saw her, fell in love with her, and brought her home to where he lived. But when they were sitting together in the bedroom Aphrodite wanted to find out whether the cat had changed her nature together with her outward shape, so she sent in a mouse. Now the woman all at once forgot her present circumstances: she jumped up from the bed and went after the mouse to catch and eat it. Aphrodite, feeling quite disgusted, changed her back to her former shape. (Hausrath no. 50)

Is this a fable or a fairy tale? The moral is familiar from many fables: people do not easily change their true nature, nor can it be disguised from the perceptive. Yet the intervention of Aphrodite and the magic transformation of the cat into a woman are the stuff of fairy tale, and they might easily have had a happy ending.

By contrast, here is The Woodcutter and Hermes:

> A man who was cutting wood beside a stream happened to drop his ax, and the stream whirled it away; so he sat on the bank, lamenting his fate, until Hermes took pity and came to him. "Why are you crying?" he asked. When he learned why, he went down into the water and brought him up a golden ax, and asked if it was his. When the man said it was not, Hermes went down a second time

and brought up a silver ax, and asked if this was the one he had lost. Again he said no. The third time, Hermes brought him his own ax, which he said was his. But the god, delighted with the man's honesty, gave him all three. So he took them home and, when he saw his friends, he told them everything that had happened. But one of them envied his fortune greatly and decided to get the same things for himself. So he took up an ax, went to the same stream, and while he was cutting wood, he dropped it on purpose into the current, and then he sat down and cried. When Hermes appeared and asked him what had happened, he said that he had lost his ax. Then Hermes brought up the golden ax and asked, was this the one he had lost? And the man, becoming excited in his greed, said that it was. And not only did Hermes not give him that ax, but he did not even give him back his own ax, that he had lost. (Hausrath no. 183)

There is a moral, of course, that has become attached to this story in the Aesopic collection: the gods oppose the unjust as much as they cooperate with the just. Yet the rest is fairy tale. The good are rewarded with a magic gift of riches; the bad are punished for their envy and greed, and they end up worse than before. The story of Mother Holle in the Grimms' collection is very like this, and many others too. Of course, they satisfy the child's desire for justice. It matters that the good should be rewarded and the bad punished; and, as often, the punishment fits the crime very nicely. But the magic gift bestowed on the woodman is surprising and wonderful. And the giver is the god Hermes: a familiar and easygoing god, to be sure, and often brought into humorous stories, but a god all the same. If the story borders on fable, it also borders on legend. It shows very nicely, I think, a form that Greek fairy tales could take when the nurses who told them were not frightening their young charges with goblin or Lamia stories, or when they were not telling the legends of the great heroes—in which the fairy tale elements remain very striking. From many possible examples, I shall limit myself to two: the story of Odysseus in Homer's epic, and the story of Bellerophon as it is seen through epic, lyric, and tragedy.

Many elements of fairy tale are incorporated into the *Odyssey*, preserved within its epic structure and adapted to its epic values and epic meanings. Athena appears, like a good fairy, to send Telemachus on a journey in search of news of his father, so he will grow into a man. Menelaus has ventured into realms of fairy tale: the old man of the sea, when captured by craft, gives him saving advice. And Odysseus himself tarries long in those same realms, where he is almost, but for Athena's help and his own indomitable will, forever lost. When I was six and first read the *Odyssey*, it seemed, in the parts I liked best, just like other fairy tales, such as "Jack and the Beanstalk," or "Hansel and Gretel." Today I know better. When, for example, I read or teach the Cyclops episode, I am conscious of Homer's artistry, his elaboration of the simple tale, his use of preparation and suspense, of irony, humor, even pathos. I am also aware of the larger implications of this episode. Odysseus' rashness, his taunting of the Cyclops, brings on Poseidon's wrath, and hence later grief. More deeply, it shows the egotism of the merely "achieving" warrior out of which Odysseus must grow into greater humanity and wisdom, and more genuine success. All this matters greatly. Yet all this is joined with older, simpler truths that a six-year-old can understand: that human wit is stronger (sometimes) than monstrous violence; and that, through wit, courage, and a measure of grace, a person can overcome great peril, no matter whether he is a hero on a journey or a boy faced with the perennial problems of growing up.

So too with Circe. Here the fairy-tale elements are even stronger, as Odysseus' companions wander through the wood, come to the witch's house, and are turned into swine; and as Odysseus, coming after them, receives the magic antidote from Hermes, so that he may resist Circe's spell, save himself, and save his comrades. It was, when I was six, a fascinating and strangely reassuring story. Today, again, I know more. I am more aware of the sexual element in the story, the threat that Circe will unman Odysseus. A Freudian interpreter might say, without much distortion of the evidence, that the story is about the attractive and dangerous power of sex—about seductive mother figures, or overwhelming Oedipal desire, or the male's fear of women. Yet if we follow the story, we know (as the six-year-old did not) that Odysseus sleeps with Circe and that, in the end, it is Circe's wise counsel that enables Odysseus to steer a safe course through later perils like the Sirens and Scylla and Charybdis, if not the Isle of the Sun. It is also Circe who sends him to the underworld to learn about death and life. I am tempted, therefore, to give Circe a more Jungian interpretation today, to say that she represents an erotic force with which we must come to terms if we are to succeed, or else (the two come close) represents the mysterious anima that must be integrated into the male psyche as a wise and helpful component. But again: although my reading of the Circe episode has grown much more sophisticated and self-conscious over the years, and much more aware of the significance of Circe within the artistic economy of the *Odyssey* as a whole, it still remains consonant with the child's instinctive reading. To overcome witches, as to overcome giants, remains what it always was, a good, and a useful, and a hopeful thing.

Still more does the larger movement of the *Odyssey*, through adventure and peril towards "eucatastrophe" and a happy ending, justify comparison with fairy tale. It suggests that wishes may ultimately come true, even though we, like Penelope, need to be somewhat cautious and skeptical about this. Yet the *Odyssey* joins fairy tale with epic themes and meanings that may, in the end, be less hopeful. Homer insists that joy is mixed with sorrow, that no gain comes without loss, that growing up is painful, and that homecoming requires a knowledge and acceptance of one's mortality. Odysseus had the chance to deny mortality, to forget his humanness in Calypso's overwhelming embrace. Yet he chose to return to Penelope, to Ithaca, to mortality. The fantastic narrative of Books 5 to 13 not only illustrates this moral and rational choice, but also brings Odysseus back, out of fantasy, by way of the half-magical land of the Phaeacians, to ordinary human existence on Ithaca. I believe that one of the greatest gifts of fantasy and fairy tale is to teach us how to make this journey. Stories in which wishes and hopes come true teach us better to understand, and to judge, our human wishes and our human hopes. Yet they are not simply about what people call "acceptance of reality." Odysseus brings back fairy-tale treasures from Scheria on the Phaeacians' magic ship, which bears him home untiringly, without a pilot's guidance; and with Athena's help, he hides them in the misty cave on Ithaca. Reality, in this view, is not exclusive of fantasy, not identical with "real life" in the usual limited sense of that phrase; which is why, if the *Odyssey* teaches awareness and acceptance (as most good fairy tales do), it also teaches the rightness of wishing and hoping.

Our *Odyssey* may have been unusual, not so much for the fairy-tale motifs that it incorporates as for the happy ending toward which the story moves with such assurance. Wolf Aly reminds us of other stories, now lost, with strong aspects of fairy tale, like those of Melampus and Polyidos: heroes who learned the language of birds and beasts and, through their help, became great healers.[33] There are isolated motifs that still give pleasure, like the magic horn of the goat Amalthea, a horn of plenty, which passed into proverb, or the cap of Hades, which Perseus (among others) used to make himself invisible. The Greeks also had stories of silly heroes, like the German *Schwanken*; Margites, whom Aristotle makes the ancestor of the comic hero, is one such idiot. For the most part, however, these fairy-tale motifs are carried in heroic legends that move, in the forms given them by lyric poetry or tragedy, to a grim ending. This goes against the nature of fairy tale, often turning it into something quite different: a cautionary tale about human limits, and the rightness of accepting these, and the vicissitudes of life; or a depiction of the real struggles that even a mortal hero out of fairy tale must undergo, and to which he often must succumb in the end.

The case of Bellerophon's story is typical, as it is shaped and reshaped in epic, lyric, and tragedy.[34] Through all these, we perceive the clear outline of a fairy tale with numerous parallels in many cultures:

1. A youth travels to a king's court, where the queen falls in love with him and tries to seduce him. When he refuses her advances, she makes up a lying story about him for the king.

2. The king sends him away, to the court of another king, bearing a letter whose secret instructions are to put him to death.

3. This king welcomes Bellerophon at first, but on reading the letter, sets him three impossible tasks (which, if completed, will bring him the hand of the princess and half the kingdom). These are to kill the fire-breathing Chimaera, to defeat the Solymi, and to conquer the Amazons.

4. Bellerophon sets off, with the usual uncertainty. He finds the winged horse Pegasus but cannot catch or tame him. But Athena comes and gives him a magic golden bridle, with which he tames Pegasus and rides him aloft, to overcome all his obstacles from the air. He kills the Chimaera, defeats the Solymi (whoever *they* are), and overcomes the Amazons—the fiercest enemy perhaps saved for the end.

5. On Bellerophon's return, the king is unwilling to keep his promise. He sets an ambush, but his warriors are all killed by Bellerophon, to whom he then awards his daughter and half the kingdom.

The story may not end here: but so much, which is pure fairy tale, can be put together from Homer's account in *Iliad* 6 and Pindar's in *Olympian* 13. Yet the differences of tone and emphasis are striking. In Homer, Glaucus is describing the nobility of his lineage. He is descended from the hero Bellerophon, hence is fully worthy to meet Diomedes in combat. (It turns out, amusingly, that the two are cousins and hence exchange presents instead of fighting.) Homer brings out the dark encounter with the seductive mother figure (many of these stories suggest a boy's struggle with Oedipal feelings), the honorable behavior of Bellerophon, and his heroic triumph almost alone—for Pegasus is not mentioned here—against all obstacles. But he goes on. Bellerophon has three sons by the princess. One is hated by the gods and becomes a wanderer; another is killed by Ares as he fights with the Solymi. Of the third, nothing is said except that he is the speaker's father, who taught him to seek honor. So here, with utter suitability to the epic, fairy-tale achievement shines out from, and is again submerged in, the struggle of human life—from which the Lycian heroes Glaucus and Sarpedon try once more to emerge with honor and glory.

In *Olympian* 13 Pindar focuses more closely on the fairy-tale beauty of the central story. He tells how Athena came to Bellerophon in a dream-vision, bringing him the magic golden bridle, when he was unable to catch the winged horse; how, by a seer's advice, he sacrificed to Poseidon and promised a shrine to Athena Hippias (so we realize that the gods are deservedly on his side); and then how he joyfully mounts Pegasus and "from the frigid folds of the high empty air" darts down upon his enemies and overcomes them. Pindar adds:

His destiny I shall keep silent;
but Zeus's ancient stalls on Olympus
receive the horse.

It is a touching conclusion. Pindar reminds his Corinthian audience, as they celebrate the athletic victory that recalls ancestral glories, of how Bellerophon came to a bad end. But by not telling that end, by keeping the "bright side outward" in this tale, Pindar stays closer than Homer did to the bright, promising spirit of fairy tale; he also reminds us that his tale of Bellerophon is a fiction that he has shaped himself, in his own way—though a fiction that reveals things that are, as the bright gold suggests, imperishably true.

But the ending, outside of this ode and outside Homer's account, was grim, and it came early to constitute a warning against overstepping mortal limits. Bellerophon tried to ride Pegasus to Olympus; he was struck down by Zeus and fell to the earth, a cripple and wanderer. It was probably Euripides who gave the story the tragic cast that it has since retained.[35] In one play, *Stheneboia*, he set his young hero against the dangerous older woman passionately in love. The play was shocking and offensive, very like the first *Hippolytus*, and it ended with something like general consternation after the youth returned and hurled Stheneboia to her death from the winged horse. This cannot have been a very comforting ending. The Bellerophon of *Stheneboia* returns to the Oedipal shadow and deals with it in the worst way—much as if Hamlet had killed Gertrude. Differently, in Euripides' *Bellerophon*, the hero decides to go to Olympus, perhaps to face the gods directly (in the manner of Job) with the question, Why do the good suffer, and the evil prosper? He crashes, of course (offstage), and later reappears as a very pitiable creature, crippled and in rags. Again, we may gather from Aristophanes, the audience was shocked.

Basically, Euripides had three ways of turning fairy tale into tragedy. The first and most striking was to take the fairy-tale hero a further step forward, or backward, into ruin. An even better example than Bellerophon is Jason, the middle-aged sometime hero who "forgets" the princess who saved him—a common fairy-tale motif, but here given realistic Athenian overtones—and is utterly destroyed by her passion. It is hard, after Euripides' *Medea*, ever again to think of Jason as a hero. Secondly, Euripides may preserve the happy picture of fairy tale, but only as a foil to the suffering and evil of human life. Thus the bright story of Perseus is made to contrast in *Electra* with the "real" tragedy at Argos, where Orestes' killing of his wicked mother is itself a very wicked deed, not at all like Perseus' killing of the Gorgon (to which it is compared). If there is a moral, it is that real life is not made up of distinguishable good and evil like fairy tale. A third, more confusing arrangement is represented by *Alcestis*. Here, while keeping his fairy-tale plot, Euripides treats it with a sometimes shocking realism that makes us see it very differently. It is hard, as with Shakespeare's problem plays, to know how far we should accept, and rejoice in, the happy ending. In other plays, however—*Ion, Helen, Iphigenia among the Taurians*—the fairy tale ending is presented less ambiguously, and it is so completely integrated into the play that we may accept it wholeheartedly: much as we did the end of the *Odyssey*, which foreshadows (or better, forelightens) all these plays; or as we shall accept the happy endings of New Comedy, often derived from Euripidean melodrama, or the end of Shakespeare's *Winter's Tale*. It works both ways. Euripides and Shakespeare consciously give us happy-ending plays that are the stuff of fairy tale. At the same time, fairy tale becomes a metaphor of some deeper grace that works to the good in human life, is blest by the gods, and—sometimes—wins out after all.

I come now to my own hypothesis: that Aristophanes' comedies convey to their adult audience at Athens much of the wisdom and healing power that fairy tales have always exercised, then as now. The idea is not new, though it has sunk into disuse and needs refurbishing. Almost a century ago Theodor Zielinski wrote his monograph *Die Märchenkomödie in Athen*.[36] Nobody reads it today except as a curiosity, and its scholarship is very dubious indeed, for Zielinski used modern Greek fairy tales, in the absence of ancient ones, to support his assertion that Aristophanes and his rivals wrote "fairy tale comedies." It is not safe to reason backward from modern Greek tales to the existence of ancient ones like them, even though other evidence (not adduced by Zielinski) encourages such a conclusion, and studies of modern Greek folklore—like those of many other primitive cultures—generally sharpen our sensitivity to how ordinary Greek peasants may have thought and acted in the old days.[37] Yet I think that, for all its circular reasoning, its inadequacies of scholarship and critical perspective, Zielinski's argument is fundamentally right: much as Cornford, for all his mistakes and misinterpretations, was fundamentally right in arguing that the power and meaning of Old Comedy were derived from ritual. Let us not throw away the baby—the right instinct for what is there—with the bath water of rejected argumentation.

Zielinski's two main instances of fairy tale motifs in Old Comedy show the weakness, but also the great strength, of his approach. First, he derives the *Birds* from two common motifs of fairy tale: the Animal Kinsman, with the closely related motifs of people learning bird language and the assembly of birds; and the Animal King's Wooing, which regularly includes building a wall or castle and marrying a princess. Now all this does little to explain the genesis or structure of Aristophanes' *Birds*, let alone its meaning. Whatever motifs Aristophanes used or drew inspiration from, he built an enormously complex and subtle structure that dwarfs interpretation, and was meant to. I reserve my attempt until later. But what Zielinski makes us realize is how much man's isolation is broken down in Old Comedy, where, as in fairy tale, he converses with birds or beasts or even trees, or with supernatural beings. That is, he rediscovers his place in nature, in that green world from which the development of consciousness had cut him off, and to which—because of that conscious self-awareness, which comedy also promotes—he cannot return except in imagination. Or by Dionysus' gift.

Zielinski finds the second great influence of fairy tale in the motif of magical abundance. He cites the fragments of "Schlaraffenland" fantasies, mostly preserved by Athenaeus, in which rivers run with wine or barley-soup, and hot rolls float up into your waiting hands, or pieces of hot roast quail float into your mouth, or cheesecakes jostle one another in their eagerness to be consumed (rather like Al Capp's cute little Schmoos).[38] Zielinski is right: these wish-fulfillment fantasies are the stuff of fairy tale, with its magic purses that never run out, its wishing rings, and its tables that cover themselves with abundant food and drink ("Tischlein, deck dich!"). What we do not know, and what makes a great difference to any interpretation, is the context from which the fragments have been torn away. Was Crates, for example, satirizing utopian speculations, with a dig at mystic vegetarianism, when he pictured a Golden Age world restored in which animals were better off: a world with no animal sacrifices, but with many wonderful things to eat, and with no need for slaves, since tables would set themselves for feasts? The very term *Schlaraffenland* suggests a problem. Taken precisely, it refers to a special kind of tale that is very silly, where everything is done topsy-turvy: something between a fairy tale and a *Schwank*. Such stories appeal less to wish fulfillment than to the hearer's pleasure in incongruity and silliness, which has to comment, "How ridiculous that is." They are tall tales—*very* tall tales. But how the comic poets used such motifs, and what they came to mean, is another, very complicated question.

Let me take an example from a play we have. The *Plutus* begins with the troubles of ordinary Athenians (in 388 B.C.: it is Aristophanes' latest extant play). Wealth is blind; the unjust prosper. But Chremylus, the hero, moves toward a solution. He seeks the Oracle's advice, finds a blind old man, and brings him home. The old man turns out to be the god Wealth; he is healed of his blindness in the temple of Asclepius; and once he regains his sight, the good are rewarded and the bad punished as in fairy tale. Here is the account given by Carion the slave of the sudden new prosperity of Chremylus' household:

> How sweet it is, guys, to be perfectly happy,
> with no effort or contribution of your own.
> Look at how this precious pile of riches

has broken into our house,
>   even without a search warrant.
How sweet it is to be rich.
Our shelves are stocked with cookie-rolls and sugar,
the cellar's full of whisky and champagne;
all the pots and pans in the cabinet
are stuffed to the brim with thousand-dollar bills.
You'd be amazed. We've got our own oil well
in the back yard. Sweetly perfumed soap
in all the bathrooms. Oranges in the attic.
The dishes, cups, and saucers all have turned
to sterling silver. And the paper plates
to plātinum, with diamonds. See for yourselves!
We've even got an automatic oven
inlaid in tortoiseshell and ivory.
As for ourselves? What do we servants do?
We go on playing craps, as usual,
only we play for jackpots of gold coins.
And when we wipe ourselves—it's not with just
plain toilet paper now. We use the best
imported silk. A happy shit-uation.
Well. The master's put on a garland now,
to sacrifice a pig and a goat and a ram.
I came out because I couldn't stand the smoke.
I tell you, it really hurt my eyes.   (802–22)

It is hard to convey the special flavor of these comic daydreams, with their mix of splendor and silliness. There has been such a growth of material consumption and expectations since Aristophanes' time that I have had to alter several images to keep up with the inflation of day-dreams. Hence I added diamonds to gold and silver. The paper plates were changed to plāt-inum by the internal logic of the wordplay, in which Aristophanes revels, and which later explains his scatological joke. It is strange how the wish-fulfillment dream of one age can, in fact, become the accustomed reality of another. Zielinski mentions a lost play of Eupolis, in which someone describes how hot water is piped into private houses so that people can enjoy abundant and luxurious hot baths.[39] We do just that; indeed I recently installed a solar hot-water heating system, for producing abundant, but also energy-efficient, hot showers; so, I suppose, the next thing is to go after the rivers of hot barley-soup—and social justice, and a lasting peace.

I am teasing now, as the comic poets tease us when they frame their grandiose images of hope. In part, they are being satirical: for in these comic daydreams, we are brought to realize the childish greed and silli-ness of our inner wishes, and also the greed and silliness of a highly materialistic society. Who needs an ivory oven (I added the tortoiseshell), or silk for toilet paper? It is like the silver chamber pot that Trimalchio's slave carries around for him, always ready for use. The *Plutus* (to which I shall return in chapter 5) is in many ways a satirical play, one that makes us think about the power of money in relation to the structure of society, the work ethic, and the nature of moral and religious values. The fantasy of abundance plays out these questions in a new light, just as it plays out the nature and the meaning of human wishes. Perhaps the very silliness of Carion's report helps bring us back to reality, helps us accept the normal human condition, which is one in which smoke gets in your eyes. Yet the fairy-tale plot with its magical transformations conveys a hopefulness about human life and its real riches that stirs the heart and will, and that arises (like that "oil well"?) out of a deep intuition about life that the comic poets transmit.

But there is more. If comedy resembles fairy tale, if it draws on what Zielinski calls "die alte, treuherzige Märchenweisheit" about wishing and hoping,[40] all this takes on a different and fuller meaning in the theater of Dionysus, the god of transformation and release. In the next section, I return to Aristophanes' *Peace*, retelling it as a fairy tale and then asking how faithful that interpretation is to the spirit and meaning of the comedy. Then, after reviewing the effect of mask and costume, the carnival spirit of festival, and the nature of the god who presides over these rites and these comedies, I complete my argument that Aristophanes' plays are a kind of "Dionysian fairy tale," bringing (in Tolkien's terms) escape, recovery, consolation, and joy.

10   *Dionysian Fairy Tales*

ONCE upon a time, when wishing still did some good, there was a farmer named Trygaeus who lived in the Attic countryside with his two small children. He was a quiet, peace-loving man who hated war because it ruined the countryside and killed the farmers. "Where is Peace?" he would ask his friends and neighbors. "I want to find Peace." But no one could tell him, and after a while, most people thought he was crazy to keep on asking for Peace, so they paid no attention to him.

Still, Trygaeus was a sturdy fellow who didn't give up easily. He decided in the end to go up to Heaven personally and ask God what had happened to Peace. So first he built a great ladder and tried to climb to Heaven, but it didn't work. He came crashing down on his head—*ouch!* Then he had a better idea. He found a great Moon Moth and fattened it up until it was big and strong enough to carry him to Heaven. Then he climbed on its back, and he flew away.

Pretty soon he found himself flying over a beautiful country with fields and streams and hills and high mountains. One mountain was higher than all the rest, rising high into the clouds, and on its very highest peak was a shining golden castle. "That must be God's home," Trygaeus said to himself. So he had the moth land on the mountaintop, and he let it pasture there while he himself marched right through the great golden gates and into the golden castle. Once inside, though, he found the castle lonely and empty. You could see that God and his Saints hadn't lived there for a long time. There were cobwebs all over the golden chairs and the golden couches and the great golden dining-room table where the Saints used to hold their parties. Trygaeus walked about from room to room, looking for some sign of life. At last he found Saint Peter quietly smoking a pipe in God's study. You can imagine how surprised Saint Peter was to see the visitor. "Where do *you* come from?" he asked. "What is your name? And what are you doing here?"

"I've come here on a Moon Moth," answered Trygaeus, politely. "My name is Trygaeus. And I've come to ask God what has happened to Peace."

Saint Peter seemed angry at first, but after a while he calmed down; and after Trygaeus gave him a present of some good Athenian pipe-tobacco that was in his pocket, he became positively friendly. Little by little, as he smoked away in great contentment, he told Trygaeus the story. It seems that Peace was a beautiful princess whom everybody loved. For a long time she had lived in the golden castle, cheering up the Saints and watching over people on earth, whom she protected from the hardships and dangers of war. In the last years, however, the people hadn't seemed grateful any longer for the kindnesses of Peace and her many good deeds on their behalf. They insisted on fighting with each other instead and having terrible wars that went on and on although they could perfectly well be stopped if people had any sense. So in the end, God had thrown up his hands in disgust, and he and the Saints had gone off for a long vacation to the other side of Heaven, very far away from the Earth, leaving only Saint Peter behind to look after the castle (which he didn't much like doing, since the place seemed cold and lonely); and what was worse, God had let War, who was a great villainous ogre, take charge of human affairs. In fact, War had shut the beautiful princess Peace into a cave, from which he boasted he would never let her out again.

No sooner had Saint Peter finished this tale than Trygaeus heard a great series of thuds coming near. It was the ogre approaching. He was carrying an enormous wooden mortar and singing to himself in a voice that would knock you silly:

> Fe, Fi, Fo, Fum,
> I smell the blood of a Greekish bum.
> I'll pound their cities, heart and soul,
> to go inside my salad bowl.

Trygaeus was terrified to see the ogre and hear his dreadful words. Luckily, though, the ogre couldn't find the pestle that he used for grinding up salad ingredients. So he went away again, to borrow a pestle from another ogre, called Devastation, who lived in a town fifty leagues away. How happy Trygaeus was when the sound of the ogre's footsteps faded away in the distance!

"Now's your chance, man," said the now helpful Saint Peter; and Trygaeus wasn't a person who would miss a good chance when it offered itself. So he called around and found a whole crowd of farmers like himself who were prisoners of the ogre but really wanted Peace back. They didn't all speak the same language, but they certainly all wanted the same thing; and so, when Trygaeus gave them some orders, they hurried and found some hammers and crowbars and a lot of rope, and before you could say Jack Robinson or some other silly thing, they had knocked down the walls of the cave where Peace was hidden and pulled the beautiful princess out, and also her two companions, Thanksgiving and Holiday, who had been shut up with her in the dark cave.

You have probably never seen anything as beautiful as the lovely princess after she came out of the cave. She was wearing an emerald green gown, with a silver belt, and her dark hair shimmered in the sunlight. Quick as a wink, Trygaeus put her and her two companions on the back of the moth, and he waved good-bye and thank you to Saint Peter and the farmers, and then, before the ogre could return, they flew off, for Earth. (But I am told that Saint Peter and the farmers went off too, so that War never found out what had actually happened. He just sat there stupidly and grumbled to himself; and for all I know, he may be grumbling there still.)

But back on Earth, everything was just fine. Trygaeus' friends and children had been afraid that they would never see him again: but suddenly, they heard a great whirring of wings, and the great moth flew down and landed right in front of their eyes. How they all clapped their hands and shouted with joy when they saw the beautiful Peace, and Thanksgiving and Holiday with her. Peace came forward and made them a little speech in which she said that she'd never leave them again. Now all the people were sorry that they'd ever been impolite to Peace and forgotten about her kindnesses to them and let her go; but they were very joyful all the same because she had come back. "Don't ever leave us again," they all cried; and Peace said that she wouldn't ever leave them again. So they all cried and laughed and hugged each other and were very happy. In the end they decided to have a big party to celebrate Peace's return and also in honor of Trygaeus, who had brought her back. So they had a wonderful party, with cakes and wine and dancing and red and green balloons. And Trygaeus (whose own wife had died years before) married the lady Thanksgiving, and Holiday often came to visit them and play with their children, and if I'm not mistaken, the party is going on still. I can't be quite sure, because I wasn't invited; I just peeked in through a window.

Obviously, I have made several changes in retelling Aristophanes' *Peace*. Some are small ones, like the balloons and pipe tobacco. These are anachronisms, but they are quite in the spirit of Aristophanes, and they keep the story on a level that children, or childlike grown-ups, can appreciate. I also changed Zeus and Hermes to God and Saint Peter, and the other gods to Saints, and Olympus to Heaven:[41] first, so that a child could grasp the story without explanations; second, for the cheerful irreverence, which is characteristic of many folktales; and third, to suggest the anxieties about war and peace and divine providence or its absence that shadow Aristophanes' play and are greatly relieved through it. Details of description are borrowed from fairy tales that I loved as a child—from Dr. Doolittle, from the Oz books. I did not, however, need to borrow anything of the basic pattern, which Aristophanes gives in complete form.[42] A brave and foolhardy person, of no great consequence, sets out on a quest, to recover something or someone that is lost; he travels over great distances, risking life and limb; he arrives in a strange and wonderful land; he confronts difficulty and danger (the ogre), which he overcomes by his cleverness, together with some help or advice from others; he finds the princess (Peace) and some magical treasures (here, Thanksgiving and Holiday), and he returns home to a general celebration, often including a marriage. I have no intention of trying to show that this generalized fairy tale plot underlies every surviving play of Aristophanes. That would be nonsensical. I *am* arguing that, despite the differences, Aristophanic comedy has much the same emotional power and significance as a good fairy tale, and that it gives a very similar kind of pleasure, and of encouragement.

Let me go further. Three years ago, in Athens, I picked up a modern Greek version of the *Peace*, rewritten for children and much simplified, by Sophia Zarabouka.[43] My first impulse was to ask, how was this possible? What could she have done about all the sex in Aristophanes' plays, and the scatology? (She has also done versions of *Birds* and *Lysistrata*.) Of course, they are gone, and many jokes with them; but what is remarkable is how much of Aristophanes' spirit is preserved in this story for children. The portly but intrepid hero, who with serious concentration feeds up his Beetle (on some unspecified round, brown, cake-like substances) and flies it to Olympus; the suspicious god Hermes, who is won over; the hideous Polemos, who mashes up towns made up of little, toy-like houses and temples in his bowl; the friendly, cooperative farmers; the beautiful Eirene, who dances through the air, smiling and bringing joy; the feasting with roast chicken, and drinking; the welcoming of a sickle-seller and the brusque rejection of arms salesmen with their wretched cannons and other instruments of war—all this brings Aristophanes' play back to life in a convincingly Greek manner. And in the end, when the children wave green branches and dance a round dance with Peace, as white doves fly above, I came to feel that in what mattered most Aristophanes *did* write for children after all, that his play was meant to bring us all back from the self-perpetuating madness of spears or cannons or bombs to the sane outlook of ordinary children who know how to love and cherish the gifts of Peace. Or: as so often in children's stories, the ordinary, recovered happiness of life takes on a fairy-tale loveliness, with all the colors of remembered joy.

But what of the differences between my fairy-tale narrative, or Sophia Zarabouka's, and Aristophanes' play? First, and most obviously, many of the dirty and indecent parts have been left out. Trygaeus' steed was a giant dung beetle. It is, though highly magnified, the same creature of fable that flew to Olympus and deposited a dung-ball in Zeus' lap, causing him to leap up and spill the eagle's eggs—by which event justice was served, retribution brought about. The dung beetle stands, or flies, for the triumph of the underdog, for ordinary people like ourselves. It also vindicates our animal nature, which is taken up whole, and shamelessly, into that same triumph. Yet, although the language and stage action sink to a lower level here than is usual in fairy tale, still the underlying note of reassurance about the body and the "lower" instincts, and indeed, the underlying sense that these need to be valued and integrated into our lives if any real victory is to take place, belong regularly to the world of fairy tale, with its helpful horses and birds, its powerful transformed frogs and bears, its transforming toads. Again, if I have left out most of the sex, which Aristophanes celebrates with such great metaphorical inventiveness and fun, this too belongs to that sensual but also very playful and spontaneous world of fun that the child in the grown-up best understands.

My second, very considerable omission was, of course, Athenian politics. For even if the dung beetle amounts to more than an allegorical dig at the late Cleon, still the *Peace* takes place, not "once upon a time," but at a special, critical moment during the Peloponnesian War, when very particular peace negotiations between Athens and Sparta are in question. The mislaid pestles of War are Cleon and the Spartan Brasidas, both happily removed. The chorus, we must imagine, consists of Greek farmers; but still more, they stand for the Athenians present in the theater of Dionysus, who must all pull together and recover Peace here and now. Hence the play is, like all the others, a present to the polis. It is not, despite teasing hints, a political allegory or a fable, but it is something like a comic and political fairy tale for grown-up Athenians.

I may seem to have made a third omission, of theatrical self-awareness, when I translated the *Peace* into a fairy-tale narrative. For the marvelous travels and transformations that fairy tales report and the child's imagination accepts, must be undermined by the realities of stage production. The dung beetle (to take the most obvious example) was a large wooden contraption, swung by a crane, controlled by a crane-operator, and "ridden" by an actor who expressed, as a kind of footnote to his portrayal of Trygaeus, his own "real" nervousness about the proceedings and called attention to the mechanisms that were being used— as Euripides, portraying Bellerophon's ride on Pegasus, would not have done. I argued earlier that this was more than a violation of the comic illusion. It was a reminder that, in comedy, the illusion is not and should never be complete. When we watch comedy, we play at make-believe; the

pleasure of self-awareness joins with the pleasure of imaginative participation in the events enacted before us. Since Aristophanes' stage, like
Shakespeare's, was largely bare of scenery, his audience, like Shakespeare's, had the duty and the pleasure of piecing out these imperfections
with their thoughts, of imagining that Trygaeus was flying to Olympus,
and even of seeing, in the colossal bust of Peace, the beautiful figure
whom their hearts desired. All this fun, and all this comic realism, may
seem far removed from narrated fairy tale, just as *Lamb's Tales* seem far
removed from actual performances of Shakespeare. But is the child's
imagination, as he or she hears (or reads) fairy tale, so very different
from the spectator's at a comedy? For the child does not literally believe
in the truth of the story that is being told. Rather, he or she moves with
some suspension of disbelief, but also with some awareness of playing at
make-believe, into the wonderland whose laws differ from those of ordinary reality.

The normal structure of fairy tales, which I have imitated, marks the
transition between worlds. The beginning, "Once upon a time, when
wishing still did some good," brings us to Othertime and Otherplace and
intimates the distance to be traveled between that world and ours. And
the ending, "and if I'm not mistaken, the party is going on still. I can't be
quite sure, because I wasn't invited; I just peeked in through a window,"
brings us back teasingly from the trip. With a smile, instead of a painful
letdown, we are brought back to everyday reality; we have, as it were,
peeked through a window at marvels about whose reality it would be
foolish to be "quite sure." We can't stay at the party: we have to leave it,
in the company of the narrator and guide; yet we have the consolation of
imagining, that somewhere, and in some time, it may be going on still. It
is of the essence of really good fairy tales to release us, easily and joyfully
(though with a little pain), back into ordinary life—which yet seems
altered by the journey. Yet Aristophanes' comedies, and Shakespeare's,
do the same thing. They tease us out of ordinary thought and care into a
green world where things are marvelously transformed, and we with
them; and then, at the end, they tease us back again out of fantasy, but
bringing our new insights and new selves with us—much as Odysseus
brings Phaeacian treasures to Ithaca, to hide in that misty cave, by Athena's guidance. The realities to which we return, or are released, are realities that (in some small way at least) have been changed, because we
ourselves have been changed. I know this to be true from my own experience. How much more would Athenian realities have been changed for
an Athenian audience by the transforming powers of theater, of festive
revelry, of Dionysus? Let us consider these in turn.

To begin with theater: even a tragic actor may, by donning the appropriate mask and costume, become a hero or a god or an old nurse; and
while we remember, with an underlying awareness, that we are watching
the actor perform a part, yet habit, convention, and the power of imagi-

nation lead us quickly to see "Oedipus" or "Phaedra" before us, to become emotionally involved in their actions and in their sufferings. In comedy, the role-playing is more various, and we forget less easily that we are watching a play. Actors appear in the very transparent guise of dogs and cheese-graters, hoopoes and barbarian gods. Choruses of clouds, birds, or frogs sing and dance and join in the action. Part of comedy's delight is therefore, as Plato noticed, the vicarious liberation it provides from our ordinary roles in life that nature and society join to enforce, firmly distinguishing female from male, human from beast, animate from inanimate nature. For a brief time, the barriers are broken down. We can be children once more. We can "be" dogs, or frogs, or birds. We can relapse into an animistic frame of mind in which we are no longer isolated from the rest of nature, but enjoy communion with birds and beasts, and trees, and even gods. It is extraordinary what power costume has to effect these changes in thought and feeling. Still more, the mask has its own daemonic power to return us to a primitive, irrational world, and to conjure up dangerous energies that lie beneath the surface of ordinary, civilized life—energies that quickly turn destructive, so are best played out during the festival of a controlling god. Comedy draws on these energies for its fun, its excitement, and its significance; and if they are watered down or forgotten, comedy becomes trivialized.

Again: many fairy-tale transformations in Old Comedy take force and meaning from the revelry (*kōmos*) and carnival atmosphere to which comedy belongs. What is essential to the revelry of carnival is that roles should be reversed, habits and institutions turned topsy-turvy. People enter, for a limited time, into a nonsense world, a *monde renversé*, a *verkehrte Welt*. At such a time, superior and inferior roles are exchanged: a fool may become king, or a boy, bishop; men and women may change clothing; slaves may enjoy a Saturnalian liberty of speech and equality with their masters; and there is a general atmosphere of unrestricted eating, drinking, and sexual indulgence. Naturally, then, the plots and conventions of comedy reflect these carnival practices. Often a low character, like the sausage-seller of the *Knights*, is raised to high office and dignity (a change that, to be sure, may reflect a conservative view of democratic usage); or again, women may dominate men, and may take over the conduct of public affairs, as in the *Lysistrata* and *Ecclesiazusae*. Such reversals, naturally, are a major source of comic incongruity. Think of Praxagora and her followers in men's costume, with beards (which they manage with great difficulty) and staves, and of poor Blepyrus coming outdoors in his wife's nightie to do his business (luckily, it's dark, and he's all alone!). These travesties, these farcical scenes, draw on ancient play forms that can always be counted on to make people laugh. They have in them a strong component of child's play, which carnival helps grown-ups to recover. At the same time, however, carnival releases dangerous, even daemonic energies. With its license, its masking, its sexual travesties, it breaks down accustomed roles and habits, and it flirts dangerously with the breakdown of the individual personality, and the society. Indeed it plays its games in an in-between time, of temporary chaos and anarchy, between winter and spring, between Christmas and Lent, between the old year and the new: which is why, in the end, King Carnival has to be dethroned, or killed, or sent away (like Falstaff), even in comedy. Otherwise, the excessive vitality manifested in comedy would prove murderous and destructive, like the death that seems its opposite. Hence the limits of anarchy, the *temporary* chaos.

I am suggesting that the fairy-tale transformations of Old Comedy are, in part, manifestations of powerful, even daemonic energies that are implicit in play and masking, inherent in carnival, and released, but also finally controlled, by the worship of Dionysus. If it is the god's energy that gives release and joy and rejuvenation and that breaks down the barriers of social roles and human isolation, yet it is equally the god's saving power that wards off the possible destructive consequences of these same released energies. Let me illustrate this point from Dionysian myth and cult before returning to the kinship, now seen within this context, between fairy tale and comedy.

(1) At Dionysus' epiphany, the regular laws of nature are waived, and wonderful things happen. For example, the daughters of Minyas, who resisted the new god, are working at the loom: but suddenly, that loom becomes overspread with ivy and grapevines, and milk and wine trickle from the ceiling. This miracle, which is typical of Dionysus, reminds us of how close delight comes to horror: for although, in picturing such a change, we are delighted by the image of release from ordinary work, and ordinary burdens, that is the god's gift to man- and womankind through wine and dance and festival, yet it is terrifying that things should lose their identity, should melt together, should change into one another. The daughters of Minyas were driven mad. Lycurgus, Pentheus, all the god's enemies who failed to acknowledge his power were plunged into living nightmare, and into madness. And so would *I* be if the power I am describing, at my desk, suddenly manifested itself: if this typewriter became overspread with ivy and grapevines, and the ink in my fountain pen turned to purple wine.

(2) Dionysus' irruption into human life breaks down social and natural barriers, sabotages ordinary relations of authority. Powerful rulers are brought low; ordinary men and women, even weak ones, are endowed with superhuman strength. Prison gates open; palaces collapse; iron chains snap asunder; the thyrsus proves stronger than the iron-tipped spear. All this seems like nature's revenge on the social edifices and constraints that hem her in. At the same time, Dionysus' worshipers (whether as a gift, or as a punishment) plunge back into a state of nature: running on the mountaintops, sleeping in the woods, leaping and dancing like fawns or lynxes, suckling young animals at their breasts, or

else tearing them to pieces. They are brought forcefully out of their ordinary human isolation, which is also the isolation of the human and rational mind, into communion with the god, and with the beasts, and with the two at once—with a god who manifests himself in bestial form.

(3) Dionysus infuses enormous creative and recreative energy into vegetable, animal, and human life. He works especially in moist things; he gives the great gift of wine; in his miracles, people strike the earth and bring forth water, milk, honey, and wine in streams and fountains. He makes things swell and grow in reckless exuberance. Often this swelling takes a sexual form: the personified phallus, Phales, is Dionysus' companion, and satyrs prance around him with great erections; but all this sexual invigoration—which comedy largely celebrates in its obscene jokes and gestures and in the motif of rejuvenation—is only one special aspect of the general burgeoning of nature at the god's coming. He gives energy, vitality, in every form.

(4) One way, again, of bringing together these diverse manifestations is to say that Dionysus is the god of liberation, and of escape. He brings liberation from social and rational constraints, and even from the iron laws of nature. The gifts of Dionysus the Liberator can (let me repeat it) destroy. Wine can lead to drunkenness, superabundant energy to rioting and murder. Victims of the god are driven mad, or torn to pieces, or both. Yet the same god's gift of release, whether it comes through wine-drinking, or the dance, or the ecstatic plunge back into animal nature, yet brings a joy to the heart, and a spring to the tired mind and the tired limbs, without which life would hardly seem worth living.

I would argue, then, that the fairy tale motifs that Zielinski and others have found in Old Comedy, such as talking birds and tables that set themselves with bountiful food and drink, take on special force, and special meaning, from the worship of Dionysus and from the revelry of his festival.[44] They express, in comic and popular form, an ancient awareness of a divine energy that irrupts into the world and transforms it: an energy that, if not divine in nature, and divinely controlled, would be demonic. Let me illustrate the difference by comparing two modern fairy tales, *Alice in Wonderland* and *Mary Poppins*, in which the sense of transformation is especially strong.

In *Alice* Lewis Carroll (who is the nonrespectable side of the mathematician Charles Dodgson) takes us into a world of astonishing, often frightening transformations. Like shifting dream images, Alice's adventures depict the fearful realities of power and passion that the civilized Victorian world conspired to conceal. They show a world in which growth is sudden and terrifying, things and people disappear and reappear without warning, people turn into animals, and totally rude, totally irrational behavior is covered only by the thinnest pretense of education, reason, and logic. It is the dream of a world that appears sane on the surface but is really quite mad—as the Mad Hatter's tea party is mad, and the Queen's croquet game, and the trial of the Knave of Hearts. Yet through his art Lewis Carroll imposes language and structure on this dream, and he catches the shifting transformations within formal game patterns, within the rules of language, or logic, or cards, or chess, that the human mind has created. He struggles, through the logic of nonsense, to ward off chaos, especially emotional chaos—to impose some sort of order on a world that threatens nightmare and madness.[45] It is hard for a grown-up, at least, to feel that he altogether succeeds.

Let me now set against *Alice* one of the Mary Poppins stories, "Full Moon."[46] It is, in many ways, typical of that collection, written by a woman who welcomes, yet duly reveres, the power of Dionysus—or something very like it—in the world. (I paraphrase and quote at some length because the Mary Poppins stories are little read in these degenerate days.)

After Jane and Michael Banks are put to bed, and perhaps sleep, a voice summons them. They follow the voice, out of bed, out of their house, through the streets, until they find themselves at the familiar entrance of the Zoo. A full moon is shining. A Brown Bear welcomes them and gives them tickets. Once inside, they find various animals—wolves and a stork, a beaver and an American vulture—deep in conversation, apparently discussing somebody's Birthday; and there are other strange occurrences:

> Just by the Elephant Stand a very large, very fat old gentleman was walking up and down on all fours, and on his back, on two small parallel seats, were eight monkeys going for a ride.
>
> "Why, it's all upside down!" exclaimed Jane.
>
> The old gentleman gave her an angry look as he went past.
>
> "Upside down!" he snorted. "Me! Upside down? Certainly not. Gross insult!" The eight monkeys laughed rudely.
>
> "Oh, please—I didn't mean you—but the whole thing," explained Jane, hurrying after him to apologize. "On ordinary days the animals carry human beings and now there's a human being carrying the animals. That's what I meant."
>
> But the old gentleman, shuffling and panting, insisted that he had been insulted, and hurried away with the monkeys screaming on his back.

Later on, escorted by a great Lion, the children see humans in cages at their feeding time:

> Jane and Michael had a good view of what was happening, through a gap between a panther and a dingo. Bottles of milk were being thrown in to the babies, who made soft little grabs with their hands and clutched them greedily. The older children snatched sponge-cakes and dough-nuts from the forks and began to eat rav-

enously. Plates of thin bread-and-butter and wholemeal scones were provided for the ladies in galoshes, and the gentlemen in top-hats had lamb cutlets and custard in glasses. These, as they received their food, took it away into a corner, spread handkerchiefs over their striped trousers and began to eat.

It turns out, when they reach the Snake House, and see Mary Poppins, and meet the Hamadryad (who is very old, and very wise, and very dangerous), that all these reversals of nature are taking place because it is one of the very special times when Mary Poppins' birthday coincides with the full moon. The Hamadryad gives her a present of his old skin, which he shrugs off, for a belt. The climax of the festivities is a dance, the Great Chain, in which all the creatures join hands, or paws, or wings, in an experience of oneness, of which the Hamadryad speaks:

> "We are all made of the same stuff, remember, we of the Jungle, you of the City. The same substance composes us—the tree over-head, the stone beneath us, the bird, the beast, the star—we are all one, all moving to the same end. Remember that when you no longer remember me, my child."

As the dance moves, and the whole world seems to rock around them, Jane and Michael (by another imperceptible transition) find themselves in bed. When they awaken the next morning, they wonder whether they have dreamt it all: certainly, they have had the same dream, down to every detail. Mary Poppins, on being questioned, is very indignant at the very suggestion that *she* could have been seen at the Zoo, and at night too! But the children notice, quietly, that

> Round her waist Mary Poppins was wearing a belt made of golden scaly snake-skin, and on it was written in curving, snaky writing:

> "A Present From the Zoo."

I have described this story partly out of gratitude, since my own appreciation of comedy, and of life, is derived in large part from *Mary Poppins*, and partly because these stories include and illustrate two key aspects of "Dionysian fairy tale." The first is that, with Mary Poppins, a wonderful transforming energy breaks through into ordinary life, so that the Banks children find themselves soaring through the air with balloons, or having tea parties (with plenty of bread and jam and cake) on the ceiling, or communing with dangerous and powerful personages—with hamadryads and with stars. The stories bring us, delightfully, out of ordinary custom and routine (which nonetheless remain extremely important) into a world of magic where the laws of nature are suspended and normal relations are changed (though kindness and decency count for much, and you must exhibit good manners at tea, even on the ceiling). Part of the fun consists, naturally, of recognizing familiar people and things in such strange and wonderful surroundings. Still more comes through surprise, incongruity, and reversal, as with the monkeys riding the old gentleman, or the people in cages being fed. The fantasies are rich and fulfilling. They abound in delighted laughter, of release. But they are also (and this is their second key aspect) reassuring, ultimately safe. Daemonic energies sometimes get loose, and they are very dangerous, as children well know; but they are always brought back under control by the protecting figure of Mary Poppins, who is surrounded by the magic and excitement that she helps generate, but never really affected or altered by it. She always guides the children home again, back to the bedroom (did they dream it all?), back to safe and known reality— though some piece of that other world can still be glimpsed and its associated memories enjoyed. The world has been transformed a little, and the children, and we, with it. That is why we can laugh so richly, and so well, after reading and rereading these stories.

Even if I were not aware that P. L. Travers was, and is, a serious student of mythology, folklore, and anthropology, and something of a mystic, I would be justified in speaking of the *Mary Poppins* stories as Dionysian.[47] What I really want, though, is to reverse the proposition, to argue that Aristophanes' Dionysian comedies are like fairy tales. To be sure, they are fairy tales for grown-ups, and for Athenians; they are full of sex and scatology and politics (the last two are connected); and they show, like Shakespeare's festive comedies, a sophisticated awareness of their own conventions and of their religious derivations. Yet in the wonderful energy of their transformations, and in the hopefulness and joy that accompany that energy and release, they are best seen as a gift of Dionysus, a part of his revel, his festive celebration.

It may be that these Dionysian meanings, and this fairy tale quality, can be seen in a simpler, more naive form in the satyr play. Although we only have one wholly surviving satyr play, Euripides' *Cyclops*, Dana Sutton has shown how often fairy tale plots, including the use of magical instruments, can be found in the remains of satyr plays.[48] Comparison of the *Cyclops* with plays like the *Peace*, or the *Birds*, or even the *Plutus*, brings out very strikingly the sophistication of Aristophanic comedy, but it also reminds us of the Dionysian meanings, and the Dionysian power, that the two play forms have in common. In my next section, on wine-drinking, I compare the two, pay tribute to Dionysus (wine being his special sacrament), and reintroduce a comic perspective that is at once realistic and hopeful about life's transformations. Then, in the last section of this chapter, I give an interpretation of the *Knights* as a Dionysian fairy tale for Athenians.

11   *Wine-drinking and Recovery:
            Euripides'* Cyclops *and
            Aristophanes'* Knights

SATYR play is a country cousin of comedy; and, being
more primitive than comedy, it shows the family traits of Dionysian fairy
tale in a simpler, more obvious form.[49] Our one surviving satyr play,
Euripides' *Cyclops*, may not have been typical in all respects.[50] It must
have been typical in its playfulness: for, in essence, it is less a mythological burlesque than a satyr *play*, this time involving the Cyclops and
Odysseus, out of Homer. It should really be called *The Satyrs Meet
the Cyclops*, on much the same principle as *Abbott and Costello Meet
Frankenstein*. Its spirit remains (as comedy's mythological burlesque
does not) naively true to Dionysian worship. Indeed the reason why the
satyrs have been shipwrecked on the Cyclops' coast near Etna, and become his prisoners, is that they were sailing in search of their leader,
Dionysus, after he was carried off by pirates. This reference is to a powerful myth of Dionysian capture, transformation, and escape. The present drama, which represents the satyrs' escape from slavery and their
recovery of joy by the implicit help of Dionysus, forms a companion
piece to the great myth, but in a lower key, a simple and much-loved
popular form. It is a little like the *Second Shepherd's Play*.

The term "Dionysian fairy tale" may seem inappropriate at first because of the play's vulgarity and especially the sexual references (though
these are scarce, and real European fairy tales, before they are prettied
up for polite society, have a great deal more vulgarity than most people realize). Yet Euripides here simplifies Homer's Cyclops episode into
something much closer to its beginnings, closer to Jack and the Beanstalk. The clever hero outwits the foolish giant and gets away. Odysseus
is somewhat tricky; he has moments of fifth-century sophistication; but,
unlike his usual self in Euripidean tragedy, he turns out to be a basically
good person who won't leave without taking his companions, and who

takes Silenus and the satyrs with him when he escapes. There is no shadow of *hybris* here, or genuine moral complexity.

The Cyclops too is simplified. He becomes, first of all, a spoilsport taskmaster who makes the satyrs buckle down to their bucolic chores and gets angry when they take time off to play, as almost any adult would if faced with such a pack of noisy, irresponsible children: for although the satyrs are played as adult, somewhat daemonic figures, akin to the beasts they care for, yet they remain at heart playful, irrepressible children.[51] They are called, appropriately, children (*paides*) of Dionysus, and their real business is to play (*paisdein*), to fool around. Secondly, of course, the Cyclops remains Homer's cannibal giant who bashes men's brains out and eats them for breakfast, lunch, and dinner: but he is stupider now, and more gross, and more the Bad Giant Cook who seems to be an archetypal figure in children's stories. He is a close relative of the ogre in Aristophanes' *Peace*, War with his giant mortar, ready to pound the Greek cities into a mixed salad. But whereas Aristophanes plays with personification and puns, and always keeps the real nature of war before his audience's imagination, the details here reported by Odysseus are delightful and engrossing in themselves, and need no outside reference. I am reminded of Tolkien's description of the three trolls in *The Hobbit*, whose brutish words and actions horrified but also entertained me when I was eight. Notice what care Polyphemus exercises in his cooking. He cuts strips of manflesh off the bodies with his great butcher's knife, and roasts these; other parts he throws into a great cauldron to boil. That is how these things are done: and we are reminded, not just that Euripides is burlesquing heroic epic, but that Homer, and the tradition behind Homer, had greatly refined the folktales here used in order to maintain the epic's loftier tone. We come back, with this satyr play, to the level of a young child's imagination, where life seems very much a question of eat or be eaten, and villains, whether ogres or witches or wolves, constantly try to eat you up.

But what gives this *Cyclops* its special Dionysian flavor is the wine. Here again the contrast with Homer is telling. In the *Odyssey*, and after careful preparation by Homer, Polyphemus is made drunk on unmixed wine, and his brains are fuddled; so also here. But Euripides also makes a more positive use of wine, connecting it with central Dionysian motifs of recovery, encouragement, and celebration.

The satyrs, in their entrance song, playfully address a ram and a ewe, with whom they are quite at home. They also sing of the difference between slavery and freedom, and of how they miss their Bacchic dances, the sounds of frenzied drumming, the splashing of wine, the singing and dancing with nymphs, and the pursuit of Aphrodite. Accordingly, after Odysseus brings wine (which he will exchange for meat and cheese), old Silenus' wine-drinking becomes a ceremony of restoration. "Splash it out," cries Silenus, "so that I may drink, and may *remember*." He knows what they have been missing; yet only the real smell, the real taste of the wine will bring that full knowledge and enjoyment back. Even before seeing the wine, he is overcome by delight at its smell; and when he actually tastes it, the wine goes straightway to the very tip of his toes, and the god, Bacchios, calls on him forcefully to sing and dance. This little celebration is an end in itself, a rite of Dionysus, an affirmation of life's goodness.[52] It also revives the will to action. "To Hell with this stupid Cyclops," cries Silenus: surely the right attitude, although he is intimidated by the returning giant and tries to blame Odysseus for everything. Perhaps this sneaky behavior justifies his disaster later when the Cyclops hauls him off to the cave, drunkenly seeing in him a new, more beautiful Ganymede. But the escape plot moves forward. Odysseus gets the Cyclops drunk and helps everybody get away. As if to mark the contrast, he asks the satyrs whether they really *want* to escape from the giant and dwell in the halls of Bacchios, with river nymphs, instead. Silenus, the old wretch, is bird-limed by his cups:

> but you, who are young and vigorous,
> come and be saved along with me,
> and take back your old friend Dionysus,
> who is nothing like a Cyclops. (434–36)

They *will*, of course: will escape, will help Odysseus. And so they do.

This last statement should, however, be qualified in terms of the tone and meaning of satyr play. For the satyr chorus only help Odysseus insofar as a group of silly, playful, basically irresponsible children might help a grown-up. What do they actually accomplish? First, they play out a *kōmos*, or revel, with the drunken giant. He is here the comic butt, the stupid lout who needs to be "educated" (*paideuein*, here related to *paisdein*) in partying and revelry, and whose drunken, off-key roaring is the comic counterpoint to the singing of the chorus. Part of the point of this is to redirect him back into the cave, so that he won't go and join the other Cyclopes, and spoil the plot; but this remains an incidental excuse for the revel itself, which is the real center of the play's energy and movement. The real way that the satyrs help anyone is through celebrating. They are, very like the farmers in Aristophanes' *Peace*, terribly excited and happy at the idea of escaping, and Odysseus, as the grown-up here, has to quiet them down; but when the time comes to act, they prove too cowardly to take part in the actual blinding. That is in character—and it leaves Homer's story intact. But they do sing encouragement to Odysseus and his men; and after the Cyclops is blinded, they tease the great brute with misdirections, as in a game of blind man's buff, until everyone has escaped. Then, like happy children, they dance out, to sail home with Odysseus.

It is hard, with our present lack of evidence, to judge how much satyr plays had in common. The audience must have expected a chorus of satyrs who would sing and dance, and prance around, and make rude jokes; must have expected to see their Papa Silenus, the fat old drunken coward; must have expected a simple plot taken from myth or legend, lowered in style, with much burlesque and vulgarity, but essentially (I suspect) unaltered. Evidently the satyr plays gave relief to the audience after tragedy. They must also have given relief to the tragic poet after *writing* the requisite three tragedies! They remained popular, partly because they were so funny, and so lighthearted; but partly too because they retained basic elements of Dionysian celebration in a simpler, more archaic form than was possible in the more sophisticated genres of tragedy or comedy.

Dana Sutton, to whom I am very grateful for pointing out the fairy-tale motifs in satyr play (including a good deal of magic) and the "child-like view of life" that goes with these motifs, has argued that only one side of comedy, the low, vulgar, farcical side, resembles satyr play, while the more sophisticated comedy of ideas is far removed from it.[53] I do not altogether agree. It is true that, as I have already suggested, comparison of, say, the giant scenes in Euripides' *Cyclops* and Aristophanes' *Peace* brings out the far greater artistry, thoughtfulness, and self-aware dramatic play of the latter. In many ways comedy has changed, and grown older and wiser, as its country cousin has not. Yet the family resemblances, and the shared Dionysian meanings, still go deep. Comedy shares with satyr play, not just superficial motifs like the dangerous cannibal giant, but the permanently underlying pattern of escape, recovery, and joy, that characterizes Dionysian fairy tale generally. Let me now illustrate this from a different Aristophanic play, the *Knights*. I begin with a wine-drinking scene that shows the difference between comedy and satyr play, and, beyond difference, the deeper similarity.

The background, related in the prologue of the *Knights*, is typically one of trouble and oppression. Two unnamed slaves come out and complain. They have been beaten; they cry; they are afraid; they joke about the possibility of running away, or "getting off." Then, for the audience, one of them explains. A new slave, a monstrous Paphlagonian, has won their master Demos over and gained absolute control of the household. All this, of course, has a second meaning, political and satiric, that the audience will readily grasp. The old householder, Demos, is also the Sovereign People of Athens—themselves. The Paphlagonian is the blustering demagogue Cleon; the slaves are two generals, Nicias and Demosthenes, whom Cleon slanders, and whose achievements he steals and serves up as his own.[54] In many ways, therefore, the play is presented as a satirical fable about Athenian politics, whose secret mechanisms of deception and gullibility it brilliantly reveals. At the same time, however, allegorical fable is subordinated to fairy tale, and the Athenian meanings are brought within the scope of a basic Dionysian movement of escape, recovery, and joy.

The theme of escape is introduced almost immediately, as one slave tells another that they shouldn't just cry there, helplessly: they should have been seeking *sōtēria*, a way of being saved. The first idea one of them has is literally to run away, as slaves do. The second is to commit suicide, which might be the tragic response to such a situation. But, by a splendid transition, their thoughts are diverted to wine-drinking, and from there to hope and purposiveness:

> X Best thing for us is to drink bull's blood.
> Die like Themistocles. That's my first choice.
> Y To drink, you say? Let's have straight whisky, then,
> for luck. And find ourselves some useful plan.
> X "Straight whisky, then?" You've got your mind on booze.
> How can a drunkard find a useful plan?
> Y What do you mean, you teetotal idiot?
> Insulting booze? I tell you, *drinking* straight
> means *thinking* straight. You get a tip from tippling.
> Anyway, what's more practical than whisky?
> Dewar's White Label, spells out do-ers. Look:
> when people drink, then right away they're rich,
> captains of enterprise, successful lawyers;
> their life is perfect, and they help their friends.
> No: fetch me forth a fifth of whisky straight
> so I can wet my wits, and then confabulate.
> X Oh, dear. Now how will this affect our state?
> Y Just fine. Just fetch it out. I'll rest the while;
> once I get drunk, I'll throw up a great pile
> of dreams and schemes in systematic style.   (83–96)

For two battered slaves, this discussion is strangely philosophical. It brings out, on the one hand, the delusive power of imagination stimulated by wine-drinking: for we know that drinking does *not*, in actuality, make a person suddenly rich, or a captain of industry, or a champion of the law courts. All this is what the Greek proverb calls "dream riches," *onar ploutein*. For life suddenly and magically to turn perfect is an illusion. And yet it is in the nature of illusions to act upon life, to create their own reality. And drinking can indeed bring relaxation of care, warm the heart, stimulate the brain to new ideas and new resolutions. The prologue to the *Knights* makes me think of that marvelous scene in Verdi's *Falstaff* in which, from the cold and damp, and from defeat, and from chilling thoughts of old age and mortality,

> Va, vecchio John, va per la tua via;
>   cammina
> finche tu moiiia . . . ,

the comic hero is revived by the power of good sack:

Versiamo un po' di vino nell'acqua del Tamigi.

.   .   .   .

Dolce cosa! Il buon vino spende le tetre fole
dello sconforto, accende l'occhio e il pensier,
    dal labbro
sale al cervel . . . ,

so that, with Bacchic inspiration, underscored by Verdi's joyfully rising
strains, Falstaff is himself again. He will fall again, too. The plot demands it. He has to be tricked and deluded, to satisfy morality—and
delight the audience. But his spirits cannot (as this drinking scene su-
perbly reminds us) be kept down.

Aristophanes raises the question of the meaning and value, not just of
wine-drinking, but of the human imagination with it, and the nature of
hope. He warns, as always, of the tricks of "strong imagination." He also
suggests that relaxation, such as wine confers, brings a hopefulness, a
power of conception, that is an absolute prerequisite to successful action
and the "carrying through of affairs." Such a connection between wish
and will is regularly suggested in Greek by the close verbal relationship
between *boulomai*, "to wish," and *bouleuō*, "to plan."[55] You begin by
wishing, by forming a picture of what you really want, and you go
on from there to develop an intelligent plan of action. Aristophanes
strengthens the connection with a wordplay on *pinein*, "drink," and
epinoia, "idea," which I have overtranslated by "drinking . . . thinking"
and "tip from tippling." The pun supplies a comic proof that good
imaginative thinking has to begin with wine, with relaxation, with a
certain basic hopefulness about oneself and the world. In comedy, as in
satyr play, the act of drinking is a focus of Dionysian meanings, of
recovery and escape: for it stirs wish and will, encourages us to act, and
provides the idea, or plan, out of which successful action may (despite all
the risks of delusion, of which comedy makes us aware) be developed.

Indeed within the *Knights* wine-drinking proves altogether justified.
One thing leads to another, with marvelous results. After slave Y drinks
the stolen wine, he conceives the idea of stealing the Paphlagonian's
oracles. When this is done (by X, of course), the secret of the Paphlagonian's downfall is discovered: he is fated to be overcome by a person
still more vile than himself, a sausage-seller. No sooner said than done:
the sausage-seller enters on cue, and the great struggle, or series of contests, begins. Evidently the gods cooperate with our wishes, and the
"good luck" drink implies the positive intervention of a helpful *daimon*.
It is all, so to speak, a question of good spirits.

We remain aware, through all this, that we are watching a play, that
the plot springs from a conception (*epinoia!*) of the playwright and is
brought to life by actors and a stage manager. If anyone waves a magic

wand, it is the playwright and director. Indeed the two slaves, being actors, get some of their encouragement from the audience:

> Let's just ask them to show us,
> by their expressions,
> whether they really like the things we're saying and doing.
>
> (37–39)

At this point the audience applauds (it is like a stage direction). They are, if anything, part of the play. But conversely, the encouragement imaged in wine-drinking and played out onstage has a strange power to transform Athenian life even outside the theater: for what people called, and still call, "real life" is shot through with illusion. For example, a blustering demagogue like Cleon may, through the spellbinding power of oratory in collusion with the everlasting gullibility of his audience, obtain a strange hold on Athenian politics very like the giant's evil power over his captives in fairy tale. People see him as enormous and terrible; and since they do, he is. They also become intimidated and slavish, feeling themselves too weak, too small, to do anything about him. But Aristophanes' comedy does more than reveal, as it satirizes, Cleon's demagogic methods and the popular gullibility on which they play. It conveys what the wine-drinking scene describes, a power of creative wishing that empowers will and resolution, good planning and good action. It fosters a genuine, and very right, escape movement: for the dreamer *can* become a man of affairs, *can* win contests, *can* carry things through to the finish, and win happiness.

A contrast with Lucian will bring out the difference that I am arguing between Aristophanes' comic fantasy, *in* and *by which* life is wonderfully transformed, and the ordinary kind of castle-building fancy that merely diverts people from toil, weariness, and the real pressures of life. In Lucian's *The Cock*, a poor man, Micyllus, is wakened abruptly from a dream of abundance—of food, drink, and gold. He longs, pathetically, to dream again. Lucian's point is that the fantasy-writer or poet or rhetorician gives people as splendid an imaginary treat as the dream of riches that was dispelled by the cock's crowing: "I don't know which I would prefer, for your narrative is twin brother to the most charming hallucination and delusion. I hold you and that so luxurious dream in equal honor and respect."[56]

Lucian's perspective here is aesthetic, and it is skeptical. For him the story, and implicitly all art, is only a higher kind of illusion that consoles and diverts us momentarily without effecting any real change in our circumstances, any more than would a lovely wish-fulfilment dream. But Aristophanes would go further. He knows, as well as anybody, the power of delusion, and of self-delusion, and the treachery of the human heart that gives people like Cleon their really monstrous power over others. Yet still more deeply and centrally he celebrates the healing and transforming power of human imagination, including his own, as it is stirred by Dionysian festival rites and given shape through art and theatrical convention, conscious always of its own playing and illusion, and conscious of its interplay with the imaginations of an Athenian audience. We are never, as we sit in that audience, asked to give literal credence to the devices of Aristophanes. That would make him as bad as his antagonist Cleon. We *are* asked to enjoy the play, and to encourage the actors (even as they encourage us), and to join in the contest, and to bring about the victory of Aristophanes, which is also (like the sausage-seller's victory) our own. From the first, our enjoyment of Aristophanes' comedy makes us, not just skeptical observers who increasingly see through the delusions of Athenian politics, and of human life (for the two go closely together), but also self-aware participants in a Dionysian fairy tale by which our politics and life are momentarily—and perhaps more than momentarily—transformed.

12   *Magic Cooking in the* Knights

T H E *Knights* is usually read as satire, on Athenian politics generally and on Cleon in particular.[57] He is obviously the evil "Paphlagonian" slave (the word combines "bluster" with barbarism) who has captured the old Demos with shameless flattery, scared off the other slaves (generals and such), and, without being subject to account, taken control of the state.[58] But this vile creature, against whom good people are helpless, is beaten by the still viler sausage-seller in one agon after another—in contests of shamelessness, bribery, flattery, oracle-mongering, and sheer present-giving—until Demos hands himself over to the sausage-seller's tutelage and is transformed by him into the energetic Athenian People of old. The Paphlagonian, like a ritual scapegoat, is banished to the lowest place. He will stuff dubious sausages at the gates. But the sausage-seller, now Agoracritus, will dine in the Prytaneion.

Certainly, this *is* effective satire: at Cleon's demagogic style and methods, so comically overtrumped by the shameless sausage-seller; at the foolish old Demos who lets himself be taken in by such monkey tricks. Yet if the play were no more than satire, we would end up with a taste of irony and a sense of ultimate frustration, a feeling that nothing can really be done about Cleon or about the problems of Athens that give him power—problems of irresponsible politics, economic bribery, class conflict, terrorist accusations, and the power of sophisticated oratory to sway men's judgment. By this reading, the play would speak, finally, for the hopelessness of moderate and sane Athenians. Its ridiculous outcome would mean that the problems are insoluble and fatal. And yet the play is more than a satire. It is a comedy; it embodies the spirit of hopeful wishing and acting, from the drinking scene described earlier, through the series of contests, to the happy and successful outcome. It also moves to a comic recognition (*anagnōrisis*) and reversal (*peripeteia*), marked by oracles coming true, in a nice inversion of the complex tragic plot admired by Aristotle.[59] Only the wretched Paphlagonian is doomed; for everyone else, things work out magnificently. Human wishing and initia-

tive join with providential help to produce a fairy-tale movement and a
fairy-tale ending.

One reason why scholars read the play as satire, not comedy, is that
they fail to appreciate, and to identify with, the sausage-seller. They miss
the relaxation of inhibition with which comic catharsis begins, the delightfulness of reentry into a childish world where normal restrictions
and laws do not hold. It is the *monde renversé* of carnival, where "the
powerful are put down from their seat, and the humble are exalted"
(*deposuit potentes de sede et exultavit humiles*, as people chanted at the
medieval Feast of Fools). What may have begun in Aristophanes' mind as
a satiric idea, at the expense of the vulgar "tanner," Cleon, is taken up
into a comic fable that reaches deep into human nature and human
wishes. The sausage-seller who climbs from nowhere to the top of the
greasy pole has much in common with those lucky tricksters of fairy tale
Dick Whittington, who became thrice Lord Mayor of London, and the
master of Puss in Boots, who married the princess; only, since this is a
comic fairy tale for grown-ups, he also incorporates, and brings to ad-
vancement, the genuinely low aspects of our human nature that are ordinarily hidden or kept down: the greed, lust, and violence; the eating and
drinking, evacuating and regurgitating, and all the shameless words, gestures, and actions that go with these. Some of this, naturally, reflects
Cleon's vulgarity; but, still more, it looks to a lost wholeness of human
nature, and of Athens. The alliance here formed between the sausage-
seller and the aristocratic young knights (and all the clever people in the
audience) is not just paradoxical; for there is, in reality as in fairy tale, a
curious alliance between the lower and the higher parts of our human
nature, and it is only through such an alliance that people find the force
to move forward, to combat enemies like Cleon, and to gain (so to
speak) the princess and the kingdom. In private life, the healing of inner
divisions brings growth and mastery of things. So too in public life:
hence Aristophanes' lyrical evocation, throughout the *Knights*, of a *joining together* of ships and horses, sailors and knights, old and young men,
Athena and Poseidon; hence, too, his insistence on a shared victory that
will be, at one and the same time, a victory of Athens over external and
internal enemies, of the demos over deception, and of Aristophanes over
his less adequate rivals. All this—the sense of hopefulness, the affirmation of human nature, the care for democracy and drive toward a shared
victory—elevates the *Knights* from what might have been merely a political satire, though a great one, into a genuine comedy.

Let me now illustrate this difference between comedy and satire by
turning to food, in which we are all vitally interested. It is always funny
when complex political and economic issues are reduced to questions of
food, drink, and sex. In the next chapter I discuss Dicaeopolis' account,
in the *Acharnians*, of the causes of the Peloponnesian War, the Cucumber

Caper and the Tart-Stealing Affair, which remind one of how Swift cari-
catures wars over differences of religious doctrine in his account of the
strife between the Big- and Little-Endians—over how you open your
breakfast egg. Perhaps one way of describing the difference between Aristophanes and Swift is to say that Aristophanes would be more concerned
with eggs: with their uses, their taste, their high metaphysical significance. For him, the metaphorical examination of politics in terms of
food is not just comic reduction (though that is there), but a way of
regaining a common human perspective on things. It is good to come
down to food and drink because they are a lowest common denominator
of human experience, transcending personal, social, and national barriers. "Even revolutionaries like chocolate chip cookies," as a *Doonesbury* cartoon has it. I have always been impressed by a story told by
Maxim Gorky, of how Chekhov dealt with three society women who
visited him and "put questions" about the Greco-Turkish war, in which
they were obviously not at all interested:

> Anton Pavlovitch looked at her kindly, and answered with a
> meek smile: "I love candied fruits . . . don't you?"
> "Very much," the lady exclaimed gaily.
> "Especially Abrikossov's," the second added solidly.
> And the third, half closing her eyes, added with relish: "It smells
> so good."
> And all three began to talk with vivacity, revealing on the subject
> of candied fruit great erudition and subtle knowledge. It was obvi-
> ous that they were happy at not having to strain their minds and
> pretend to be seriously interested in Turks and Greeks, to whom up
> to that moment they had not given a thought.[60]

A stronger conversationalist and philosopher—Socrates, perhaps, or
Samuel Johnson—might not have given up so easily. He might have led
the ladies' minds by stages from candied fruit to other, more serious
issues. But Aristophanes would do better. He would explain the war, or
the political situation, or the question of modern tragedy, in terms of
candied fruit that everyone, from the society ladies to their probably
starving coachman, could clearly understand. As his comedy sinks beneath satire, to a level of delight in bodily processes like eating and
evacuating, so it also rises above satire to a grand vision of what might
be called the redemption of the body politic, a vision as hopeful as it is
also realistic.

We should begin, then, with Aristophanes, on the lowest level of
things. Perhaps it is better not to talk about the "sausage-seller" unless
that image is reinforced by clear, sensual memories from our childhood,
of hotdog sellers on street corners, or perhaps of the "good humor man,"
whose tinkling bell and white wagon announced wonders of vanilla and

chocolate ice cream—better to forget the term "sausage-seller" for now, despite its connotations of low retail fraud, so very like demagoguery, and see him instead as the Butcher. He was, after all, a butcher's or cook's apprentice. Now, as the Butcher, he is a vital and dangerous figure, armed with a *machairos*, or butcher's knife, that is virtually a short sword. He has the right tools to deal with the Paphlagonian, and the right aggressiveness of temper. He plays rough and fights dirty. But as a butcher, too, he has nurturing possibilities that the evil tanner lacks. He can cut enemies into shreds, like him, but he can also prepare and carve the meat. He is, potentially, the Cook: an archetypal figure of comedy who is solidly on the side of life, and of celebration.[61]

Often (to come to a second level of meaning without losing sight, or taste, of the first) Aristophanes' satirical scenes point beyond themselves, to something larger. Take the reported conflict of the sausage-seller and the Paphlagonian before the Council. The latter storms in with his usual stock-in-trade, his denunciations and slanders (in the style of Joe McCarthy), but the butcher undercuts him with a quasi-official announcement that the price of anchovies has fallen, overbids his proposed hecatomb of thanksgiving by proposing a double-hecatomb-plus-a-thousand-kid sacrifice, and—as the councilors leap over their railings, to go after the cheap anchovies—seals his victory by presenting them with free coriander seed and leeks for seasoning their fish. It is a terribly funny report, with touches of *Alice in Wonderland*. In an odd, even pathetic way, it shows the impact of wartime austerity, deprivation, and inflation on the Athenian temper. It exposes, of course, the effectiveness of economic bribery as a political weapon; it also hints at a deeper-going change in Athens, from a unified polis to a new, divided state where people's governing interest is economic, based on prices and wages in an increasingly limited market. It is this new bourgeois state that is so easily exploited by demagogues like Cleon, since it increasingly lacks any higher sense of unity or pride or purpose. Yet the point of this scene is not just critical and negative. Much as, in the *Acharnians*, roast fowl proves better than ostrich plumes, and real pleasure than empty boasting, so here in the *Knights* the good life is more easily founded on honest anchovies (with an occasional big meat sacrifice) than on slanders about subversion. Cooking may be a potent metaphor for political flattery and manipulation (and so Plato will develop it, in his *Gorgias*, in a critique of Athenian democracy and its leaders); but the cook can also be a figure for the good statesman, the good public servant in a democracy, like Themistocles:

> Do *you* dare to compare yourself with Themistocles? *He* filled our city like a cup, to the brim; *he* kneaded in the Piraeus, for breakfast; *he* served up new fish courses, without abolishing the good old dishes—while *you*, with all your fortifying and all your oracle-

mongering, *you* tried to turn Athens into a nation of—shopkeepers.
(813–16)

In a democracy, the public must be the final arbiter of what is good for it.
(Plato, of course, would disagree.) The proof of the pudding is not in the
cooking but in the eating. And the would-be statesman must learn to be
an imaginative caterer, a skillful butcher and baker, and a generous steward, if he is to do the job: in short, must learn to be a good public
servant.

This Cleon/Paphlagonian is not. He is more concerned with eating
than with serving food, and that is his downfall: for in the final agon, the
Demos-pampering Contest, which is a kind of potato race with presents
of food, the Paphlagonian is not only beaten at his own game of bribery
and cheating but is revealed as a fraud who kept most of the cake for
himself. This is the unforgivable sin. The Paphlagonian is dismissed from
office ("Thou shalt be steward no longer!"), and the sausage-seller takes
his place, with magnificent results.

The satire is partly at the greedy, embezzling Cleon, and partly at the
Athenians who, despite their native shrewdness, are taken in by his
tricks. It is all a question, Aristophanes suggests, of who is fooling
whom. But what goes deeper than satire is the comic poet's demonstration of why Cleon succeeds, why the demos is taken in. What makes him
vulnerable is, ultimately, his own power of wishing. He wants (as which
of us does not?) to be petted and pampered and fed full, like a great big
baby; he wants all the good things of life to be brought to him without
his having to make any effort: and something like this can indeed be
accomplished in the "welfare state," but you cannot remain that pampered, and that passive, without relinquishing control of things. In the
end the baby is a helpless, dependent creature. It is true that, as the
Greek proverb says, "old men are twice children," but that does not
mean that they should hurry, or be hurried, into a second infancy!
Demos' tendency to feelings of infantile omnipotence also makes him
vulnerable to people who sell daydreams of power and glory. He loves to
hear the prophecy of how he will "become an eagle in the skies." Nothing could be sillier; nothing so well conveys the aspiration, which we all
share, to transcend human limits. It is a hard dream for the sausage-seller
to combat.

> Pa. I have an oracle that tells, on wings unfurled,
> thou shalt become an eagle, and rule o'er all the world.
> S.S. I have one too. The Earth *and* the Red Sea.
> "In furthest Ecbatana shalt thou rest thy bones,
> Holding thy court, and eating chocolate ice cream cones."
> Pa. But I had a dream. I saw the Goddess herself
> pouring out health and happiness over the city.

S.S. I had one too. I saw the Goddess herself
   come from the citadel, with an owl upon her head,
   and she came and poured heavenly milk and honey
   over your head. Pickle-juice over *his.*   (1086–95)

For us, as we read the play, the new oracles of "Fakis" mock those of Bakis by going them one step further in their union of low creature comforts and high-soaring fantasy. To rule the world, eating ice cream the while—it is so clearly a child's daydream. So too the alleged vision of Athena shows up the silliness of the delusions of grandeur that oracle-mongers fostered, and politicians played on, during the war. That the goddess "holds her hand over the city" was a matter of ancient faith and pride—but with a soup ladle? And pickle-juice? All the same, there is something very comforting, as well as satiric, in this grotesque picture. Athens *is* cared for, somehow. And old Demos has to be won over, finally, on the level of wish and dream: not through disillusionment, though this is necessary, but through a sense of hope and promise that goes deeper than disillusionment and the showing-up of vice and folly.

"I give myself over to you," says Demos—though this decision is delayed, until the last game has been played out—"give myself over to you, to care for and reeducate in my old age," *gerontagōgein k'anapaideuein palin.* The wordplay is important. Old Demos has been governed and "led around" (*gerontagōgein*) much as children are governed and led around by their "pedagogues." The second verb, *anapaideuein,* "to reeducate," also hints at "making a child again" out of old Demos; but in anticipating his rejuvenation it implicitly contrasts the aims and methods of the sausage-seller, and (I think) of Aristophanes, with those of the Paphlagonian/Cleon. Through his welfare state, the latter had succeeded in reducing Demos to a second childhood. He was turning infantile and impotent. By contrast, the magic cooking of the sausage-seller restores Demos to the youthful energy and vitality of the "old Athens" of Themistocles' day, providing a rejuvenation for which all the babying and pampering in the world could only be a miserable substitute. Nor does life only consist of eating. There is also sex. As the rejuvenated Demos prepares to enjoy the favors of two beautiful females representing Peace, not to mention some pederasty on the side, the fairy-tale ending in the comic mode becomes complete, down to the little, teasing touch of self-mockery: "What joy! It's back to the good old days!"

Reeducation follows, not precedes, rejuvenation. In the final scene Demos realizes, with some pain and embarrassment, how foolish he has been. This recognition is an important and necessary part of the full comic catharsis, the clarification of wishing and hoping to which Aristophanes means to bring his audience. Yet political reeducation can only come through, and after, the more basic psychological experience of revival and restoration. As the sausage-seller says earlier, once Demos goes back into the country, and spends some time in peace, tasting oatmeal, warming his heart, listening to the grapevine, then he will realize how many blessings your social security cheated him out of; he'll go for you like a fierce farmer tracking down some vicious— vote. That's why you fool him, and cheat him, and make up foolish dreams about him. (805–9)

It is all (as later, in the *Peace*) a matter of recovery, of getting back your natural good taste. But that is the gift of the sausage-seller, and of the comic poet, and, behind them both, of Dionysus.

It may seem strange, and even paradoxical, that the low sausage-seller should be transformed at the play's end into the noble Agoracritus. We cannot help wondering whether he was in disguise the whole time, an aristocrat assuming base manners in order to get control of Demos. But this is to ignore the fairy-tale movement by which the sausage-seller is changed, providentially, and also with human help, from a nobody into a great Somebody. It is also to exaggerate the change in him. His new name is ambiguous. It can mean "Chosen in Assembly" but also "Chosen in the Market" (with overtones of market-brawling).[62] What is more, he has not really changed his trade, but has risen from a low butcher's apprentice, and then a butcher, to the height of that profession, which is to be a Magic Cook. This last is an archetypal figure of comedy, as Cornford has shown.[63] He is like a fairy godmother, only he wields a butcher's knife, or a soup ladle, in place of a magic wand. His destructive power, to cut up meat, or people, into shreds, here implies (as the Paphlagonian/Cleon's leatherwork does not) a nurturing and recreative power as well. In later Greek comedy, the cook is a familiar, reassuring figure: he introduces low kitchen humor into Menander's sentimental plays, and as caterer, he is happily associated with the wedding feast and the spirit of celebration. In Aristophanes, however, he is something more. He retains something of the ancient *mageiros*, the sacrificial cook, from whom the more specialized and secularized trades of butcher and caterer are derived. It is a high calling, assumed by Trygaeus in the *Peace*, and by Peisetairus in the *Birds*, but most fully and satisfactorily by the sausage-seller in the *Knights*, a play in which ritual meanings (as Cornford points out) and fairy-tale motifs are especially strong.

We saw how the sausage-seller takes on the mantle of Themistocles, that great *chef d'état* who "kneaded in the Piraeus" and "served up new fishes" without depriving Athens of her good old courses—a lovely picture of moderation in statesmanship. He is also related to the *comic poet as cook*. In the parabasis (537–39), Crates, the old comic poet, is described as enduring the whims and buffets of the public, "Crates, who . . . breakfasted you at small expense, cooking up delectable plots and masterpieces of dry wit for you." The point is that to be a comic poet is as risky, difficult, and often ungrateful a business as to be a cook.

More likely than not, you fail to please and get buffeted around. But this analogy is especially suggestive in a play in which salvation comes through right cooking. The cook, the statesman, and the comic poet are three of a kind. It is all a question of feeding people imaginatively and well, and of holding out in spite of difficulties.

In the end, I think, this sausage-seller turned magic cook is a disguise of Aristophanes himself. As ever, he is the "good humor man" who brings his audience to a revival of energy, hope, and good spirits, and to a clarification of wishing and hoping that includes, but goes beyond, disillusionment and undeception. His fairy-tale plot is deeply hopeful. It embraces but transcends much satire, both political and psychological. It also, unlike the deceptions practiced by the politicians, shows *itself* up clearly as illusion, as stage magic, as fairy tale. The early praise of wine, which may give hope and confidence, but may also foster delusion, frames the subsequent action with a reminder that we are going to watch, and to experience, a comedy, that we are invited (as old Demos within the story cannot be) to a comic perspective, or *theōria*, that combines enjoyment with awareness. Only in this way—and because he experiences the same Dionysian revival of spirit that he shares with us—can Aristophanes remain what he is: a good steward, a nurturing cook, an honest public servant.

Chapter Three

Comic Ideas and

Comic Transformations

Dionysus and Ariadne with actors of tragedy and satyr play, with Pronomos the flute-player and (bottom left) the seated poet Demetrios holding a script (bookroll), from an Attic red-figure volute krater by the Pronomos Painter, ca. 400 B.C. Courtesy Museo Nazionale Archeologico, Naples (no. H 3240); photo by Studio Foglia.

13   From Idea to Performance: The Uncertain Stage

THE comparison just cited, of the comic poet to a gifted chef, belongs to the parabasis of the *Knights*. After the sausage-seller goes in to fight with the Paphlagonian in the Council, the chorus of knights turn to the audience, and, as usual, the chorus leader speaks on the poet's behalf.

If any of the old comic poet-directors had asked us to come forward and address the theater-public in the parabasis, he'd not have obtained this favor easily. But OUR POET deserves it, because (1) he hates the same individuals we do, (2) he speaks out bravely for Right and Justice, and also (3) he marches as to war against the Spyclone and the Worrycane. Now, for the thing you keep coming up and asking, like an exam: why didn't he apply for a chorus in his own name? He wanted us to explain. What he says is, he used delaying tactics not without purpose. No, it was his belief that putting comedy onstage (*kōmōidodidaskalia*) was the hardest thing you could do. Many people knocked at the door, few were allowed inside.[1] He also recognized how very fickle you people were, how you betrayed and abandoned the earlier poets after they got old. Take, for example, what happened to old Magnes after his grey hairs came. How many times he had put his comic rivals to flight, using

> every voice that could be tried,
> every shape that could be seen,
> stringing it, winging it, Lydianizing
> and fruit-fig-flyzing
> and dyeing himself frog-green—

Not even Magnes could make it to the end. He was kicked out when he was old and tired and couldn't keep it up. The jokes were gone. And take Cratinus. The paragon of praise, he'd rush over the

fields like a Russian torrent, ripping up oak trees, plane trees, enemies all from the roots. At parties people sang,
> "Sing a song of Doro,
> my sweet in-former love,"

or

> "You who belong
> to the building-trade of song . . ."

Those were the days. He really flourished then; but now he's senile,
and you've no pity, when

> his guts are gone,
> his pick is broken,
> no pitch, no tone,
> just food for jokin'—

Why, you let him bum around like old Con-ass, a dried-up singer,
wearing a withered crown, dying of thirst—a man whose earlier
wins should have entitled him to *drink* in the town hall, and not to
play the fool, but to watch plays as a senior citizen, next to Dionysus. And then Crates. What bad-tempered buffets you gave him, a
man who'd send you off with a nice cheap lunch, whose elegant
lips would shape the most refined conceptions (*mattōn asteiotatas
epinoias*): sometimes he'd fall, sometimes stand his ground: and he
was the only man who finished the course. Our poet looked, and
shuddered, and took his time. "Better the oar," he said, "before the
tiller: row first, watch at the bow, and only then steer your own
ship." So, people, just because he didn't plunge in stupidly and
flounder,

> raise him a mighty surge of applause
> with all eleven oars (or *ause*),
> whom so proudly you'll hail
> with his forehead
> > bright-gleaming.   (507–50)

Even without the jokes (and there are many), Aristophanes' audience
would hardly have taken these remarks at face value. The poet's self-
praise is expected, and it is exaggerated. As usual, he boasts of his honesty and valor. He has spoken out for the right, against terrible odds; he
has fought against monstrous forces of evil (namely Cleon). As usual,
too, he boasts of his superior artistic merit. His plays display ingenuity
and true wit; those of his competitors are unimaginative, unoriginal, and
just plain vulgar. With marvelous effrontery, he writes off his rival
Cratinus as a has-been. Cratinus' garland has dried up, like a last year's
fertility wreath; it is obviously time for the amiable but incompetent old
drunkard to be pensioned off, to be rewarded with free, um, *drinks* at
the Prytaneion, and with a good front seat at the theater—the better to
enjoy Aristophanes' plays!

It would be nice to know what Cratinus said about Aristophanes in *his* parabasis the next year, when his *Wineflask* took first place and the *Clouds* took third. The continuing *agōn*, or self-advertising competition, must have been vigorous. Let me turn, however, to those theatrical facts of life into which the jokes in the parabasis give us glimpses, beginning with the pressure of competition and the demands faced by the *didaskalos*, or poet-director.

Aristophanes stresses, first, the importance of winning. Only first place counts in the comic poets' competition. If we look, though, at the statistics that Carlo Russo has collected, we see how difficult victory was, for Aristophanes belonged to an emerging generation of comic poets who had to compete, in the 420s, both with successful older poets and with one another; at the same time, the number of comedies performed in Athenian festivals was cut from ten to six because of the war.[2] We might think that to have one's play accepted for performance was already a considerable achievement; still, Aristophanes makes it clear that in the theater, as in sports, only winning counts. To take less than first prize is to "take a fall," as even great Crates sometimes did. To win, on a great surge of applause (which must influence the judges in their voting), means to depart in a blaze of glory, "with forehead bright-gleaming."[3] The joke (Aristophanes was prematurely bald) will amuse the audience and placate the envious gods; but still, these anapests show the young playwright at a peak of confidence, fresh from one victory at the Lenaea and pressing for another, which he in fact obtained.

Secondly, Aristophanes indicates the importance of "learning the ropes" in theater. If thousands of people have (naturally) been coming up to this brilliant young poet and asking why he did not "apply for a chorus"—that is, produce and direct a comedy—under his own name, the answer is that producing comedy for the stage (*kōmōidodidaskalia*) is extremely difficult, like piloting a ship, and even the most brilliant of comic playwrights has to pass through a gradual apprenticeship. This was because the poet's work ordinarily did not end, as it does today, with writing a play. Rather, after he "created" it (the Greek term is *poiein*, "to make," not *graphein*, "to write"), he was expected to "teach" or "direct" it, *didaskein*. The comic poet or playwright must therefore become a poet-director.[4] His responsibilities included the training of the actors, in tone, gesture, delivery, movement, grouping, and comic business; the training of the chorus in song and dance—*after* he had composed the music and arranged the choreography; and the organizing of every aspect of stage production from masks, costumes, and props to the use of stage machinery, the manipulation of time and space, and the relation of the actors to the (expected) audience. How many poets today, even with the resources and manpower of the modern theater, would take on such responsibilities?

Aristophanes tells us that he felt unready to produce and direct his earliest comedies. (He later compares himself to a modest girl who finds herself pregnant and is unprepared to bring up the child herself.)[5] So he gave over the producer-director's responsibility to other men, Callistratus and (later) Philonides, who became the official *didaskaloi*. This made Aristophanes' life easier, and may have been something of a novelty, anticipating later specialization of functions in the theater.[6] We should pause here to think gratefully of these shadowy figures, otherwise unknown, who brought many plays of Aristophanes to birth, or berth, on the comic stage. They should be enrolled in some theatrical hall of fame, together with producers like the generous Lucius Ambivius Turpio who rescued Terence from disaster.[7] Yet the victories won through Callistratus' efforts were chalked up to Aristophanes' account. Callistratus produced the *Acharnians* of 425, as he had produced the *Babylonians* of 426, but it was Aristophanes whom Cleon hauled before the Council on a charge of maligning the polis in the presence of foreigners, at the Dionysia of 426; in the parabasis of the *Acharnians*, Aristophanes gives himself full credit for services rendered to the polis; and so forth. His work as poet was not disguised. How could it have been? He wrote early, and he wrote well. It took a while longer to master the stage, to produce and direct the theatrical "event," as Aristophanes first did with his *Knights* in 424.

The problems of performance are interesting, and I shall return to them after raising another major question suggested by the parabasis of the *Knights*: namely, what is the comedy of ideas? Aristophanes praises the comic poet who feasts his audience on new ideas, new sallies of wit, much as, elsewhere, he praises himself for introducing clever new ideas (*epinoiai*) into his plays and for not relying, as some people do, on the tired old jokes, the old slapstick, the old vulgarities. But what is a comic idea? Where does it come from, and how does it work? And how is it connected with other comic ideas, or with serious concerns that the poet may have had in mind when he was writing the play?

Most people who speak of Aristophanes' comic ideas really mean the *organizing ideas* of his plays, which seem to spring in full battle dress from the poet's teeming brain. For example: a man is frustrated by war; no public peace treaty is forthcoming; so he makes a private peace for himself and his family (*Acharnians*). Or a woman is frustrated by war . . . so she organizes an international sex strike, thus forcing the men, who *ought* to feel extreme frustration, to capitulate and make peace (*Lysistrata*). Or on a different but related subject: Athenian politics are controlled by persuasive scoundrels, notably Cleon; men of taste and judgment cannot get elected to public office; so an ultrapersuasive superscoundrel must be found to oust Cleon, seize the reins of power—and be transformed into a noble democratic statesman. Now these are, to be sure, great and funny ideas, but they are neither isolated nor static. The organizing idea (*epinoia*)—and there may have been more than one—

grows into the play, and grows with it, and changes as it grows. Nor can it be defined in maturity by any hypothetical first intention of its maker. It may, like a child, have begun as a gleam in the poet's eye; but as it takes form and grows, it surprises and delights its parent. Scholars all too often put asunder what the poet has joined together. They isolate comic ideas for analysis, divorcing them from other comic ideas to which they are joined inseparably by language and staging. Above all, they forget that Aristophanes' comic ideas are ideas-in-action, ideas that must take on flesh and blood in order to be realized in the theater, before a living audience. Tom Stoppard, stressing the importance of performance, has often contrasted "the event and the text" in public lectures; but he has sometimes added a corollary, that in his plays the word becomes an "event." And so it does for Aristophanes.

Two comic ideas from the present passage illustrate my point. The first is embodied in the very phrase *mattōn asteiotatas epinoias*, "kneading most urbane ideas." In witty metaphorical language, Aristophanes portrays comic ideas as tasty tidbits and the comic playwright as a skilled chef who feasts his audience at small expense. Food and thought are linked here, in a pleasant metaphor; for Aristophanes, all good things are interchangeable. But the witty little phrase also links up with the main thematic images of cooking and eating throughout the *Knights*, and especially with the picture of Demos as a great pampered baby, the way to whose heart is (mainly) through his stomach, and whose constant question, "What have you done for me lately?" has to be met with instantaneous gratifications like cushions and warm sweaters, hare's-meat stew (what counts is not who made it, but who serves it up) and cake. It is no longer sufficient to be a farsighted statesman like Themistocles, who "kneaded in the Piraeus" and "served up new fishes" as well, "without taking away any of the older courses" (815–16). He was, as said earlier, a great *chef d'état*; and even the low sausage-seller breaks out of character to praise his merits, to which the Paphlagonian arrogantly and stupidly aspires. Although this passage appears after the parabasis, it may have been written earlier; the point is, that the conception of Crates as a great food-poet exactly matches that of Themistocles as a great food-statesman. The difficulties that poet and statesman face, the skill they require, the degree and kind of achievement possible for them, are very much the same.

This little *epinoia*, then, does not exist in isolation. The image it contains is, first of all, comic and celebratory; it affirms a richness, a delightfulness in things, in which the comic poet lets us share. Second, the metaphors of cooking, serving, eating, and digesting food serve a dramatic and a unifying purpose. Out of them passages and scenes are created; and they link these passages and scenes together to make a poetically and dramatically satisfying whole. But third: the creative images and metaphors are also exploratory. Their meaning is not given in advance, as in simple allegory or fable. Rather, they are a means of investigating new relationships, discovering new meanings in things. The first person to be delighted and instructed by Aristophanes' comic inventions was Aristophanes.

Another typically rich *epinoia* comes in the picture discussed just now, of "learning the ropes" of theater. Greek literature is filled with metaphors of rowing or steering ships, metaphors that express the difficulty, and the need for care and skill, in managing anything from politics (the "ship of state") to poetry-writing. And once again, the metaphors of sailing, steering, and naval warfare are integrated into the fabric of the *Knights*, connecting diverse ideas and concerns with one another. Most obviously the Paphlagonian and sausage-seller maneuver in their arguments like ship's captains opposed in war, or like pilots trying to outrun a great storm. There are many references to the actual Athenian navy, its value to Athens, and the urgency of paying the sailors what is owed them—as the Paphlagonian (Cleon) has not done. The poetic association of ships and horses is striking. As the aristocratic knights become allied with the low sausage-seller to defeat their common enemy, so horses, maintained by the rich, are linked imagistically with ships, rowed by the poor. In the ode shortly following the passage given above, Poseidon, the sea god, is invoked as lord of horses and patron of the knights; the delight of racing chariots is described, and of racing ships. In the comical antepirrheme, the knights praise their horses for leaping "manfully" into their ships and sailing off to attack Corinth. No doubt the amphibious operation, with its massive horse transport, was impressive in real life. Still more, these wonderful sailing horses who shout "Hippapai!" at the oars are a fairy-tale image of the political unity of Athens, in which Aristophanes deeply believes, and which it is his comic business to rediscover. But they are a new invention, a *found image* uniquely suited to this play.

And there is more. The "surge of applause," a metaphor taken from the dip and splash of oars in the sea, will be the confirming sign of Aristophanes' own victory over his competitors. He wants this victory badly, however much he may joke about his bright-gleaming forehead. But he means it to be a shared victory, on many levels: of himself over his opponents; of the sausage-seller over the Paphlagonian; of the Athenians over their military foes; and of the better judgment of the demos, in all three instances together, over the worse. A little "confirmatory" pun brings ships and theater, naval and dramatic victory together. The word *Lēnaïtēn*, combining "Lenaean" and "naval" in portmanteau fashion, confirms the relation between the two and drives the point home. Typically, Aristophanes does not just use these metaphors of sailing and naval warfare as humorous illustrations of preconceived conceptions or attitudes. They have a poetic life of their own, flashing like oars as they dip in the sea; and they are linked with other images and metaphors, such as horses and riding, to create new associations and explore new meanings. The result, as with the food, is an unexpected present: from the comic Muse to Aristophanes, from the poet to his audience. The unity, harmony, and reconciliation of opposites that he wanted for Athens had first to be found in his own comic imagination as he set about creating, through words, gestures, actions, and stage conventions, the living world of his play.

Let me defer, for later discussion, two major questions suggested by the parabasis of the *Knights*: the place of Aristophanes' comedy of ideas in the development of Greek comedy, and the relation of the imaginary world created by this "comic teacher" to the real world of Athens. For now, I want to concentrate on the working playwright, whose efforts may be divided into two stages of activity, both badly attested, both requiring much speculation.[8] He had, first, to create a play and to present it, in some form, to the archon for acceptance. This was called, "applying for a chorus." Then, once the play was accepted, he had to prepare it for production, "teaching" the chorus and the actors (or having them taught) what was necessary. This second stage culminated in the single performance, at the Lenaea or the Dionysia, and was quickly over—at which point the comic poet probably began thinking about his next play.

We begin, for the first stage of production, by working backward from the unknown date or dates on which the playwright had to present his work to the archon: to the "king," if he meant it for the older, more traditionally sacred Lenaea; to the eponymous archon for the newer and grander City Dionysia. This must have happened (1) after the new magistrates took office in July (Hecatombaion), at the beginning of the official calendar year, and (2) in time for several months of organizing and rehearsing. For the Lenaea, in later January, we would expect a play to be submitted and accepted in July or August; perhaps this might happen a month or two later for the March Dionysia, although the more important festival might require longer preparation. We do not know. And that, already, hampers our understanding of how a play came into being and in what ways it might have been influenced by current events.

Nor do we know in what form a new play was submitted to the archon (and perhaps to a committee of experts who assisted him in selecting plays). Did Aristophanes supply the archon with a finished script?[9] Or the committee with several copies? It seems improbable. What is more likely is that he presented himself in person, outlined the plot of, say, the *Knights*, and read (or better, delivered) some scenes, or passages from scenes, that would illustrate the new play's excitement, fun, and brilliance, as well as give an idea of what surprises, difficulties, and expenses

the production would involve. The main thing, since this was a preliminary competition, was to convince the archon that the festivalgoers,
those ordinary Athenian citizens and voters, would be delighted with the
performance. The playwright's earlier successes, naturally, would make
the point more effectively than almost any presentation. But all this,
again, is speculative.

Let us assume, then (working backwards), that Aristophanes completed a good working script of plays for the Lenaea at least by August of
the preceding year, and for the Dionysia at least by October. Of the
surviving plays, the *Acharnians*, *Knights*, *Wasps*, *Lysistrata* (?), *Frogs*,
Ecclesiazusae, and *Plutus* were performed at the Lenaea; the *Clouds*,
Peace, *Birds*, and *Thesmophoriazusae* (?) at the Dionysia. But these,
taken alone, give a misleading impression of leisure. Aristophanes often
wrote two plays a year; in the active period between 427 and 421, when
he was breaking into the theater, he wrote twelve plays; and in 423/22,
in a frenzy of writing brought on by the defeat of the *Clouds* in 423, he
apparently wrote *two* plays to be performed at the Lenaea of 422![10] But
when did he begin to write? Or better, to daydream about future plays?

A year ahead, we might guess; Cratinus boasted about one play at least
that cost him two years' hard labor,[11] and the comic poets may sometimes have looked further ahead than that. Can we be more precise? A
side reference in 425 by the chorus of angry Acharnians,

> I hate you even more than Cleon,
> and I'll cut *him* up into leather strips for the knights,
>
> (300–301)

may look forward to Aristophanes' own intended attack on Cleon in his
satirical *Knights* of 424 (where the knights would form the angry chorus).[12] We cannot be sure.

Even when specific evidence for such plans is lacking, we can see ways
in which one performance pointed to, or stimulated, the next. The *Wasps*
is like a sequel to the *Clouds* (which itself, as Aristophanes says, took up
the theme of education from his well-received *Banqueters* of 427). It
deals with fathers and sons, again; deals with the same dialectical issues
of nature and education, but in reverse; and its parabasis responds so
directly to the defeat of the *Clouds* by bad judges—and its plot is *about*
bad judges—that we can imagine Aristophanes turning immediately to
work on it, for consolation and revenge. Often, comic poets must have
been stimulated directly by one another's work, if not by one another's
insults. After Aristophanes satirized Cratinus in his *Knights* as a senile
drunkard, the older poet came back with what must have been a hilarious play about himself, his mistress Strong Drink, and his jealous wife
Comedy—surely making the Aristophanic point that drinking and creativity go together. Often, too, the comic poets must have parodied new
(as well as old) tragic plays, drawing on their plots, or characters, or

striking features of production. After Euripides' delightful production of his *Andromeda* and his "new *Helen*" at the Dionysia of 412, Aristophanes must have started work (did he borrow copies of the plays?) on the *Thesmophoriazusae* of 411.

What scholars, especially historians using literary sources, neglect at their peril is this same uncertain matter of timing, for the events and impressions most reflected in comedy are those of the previous spring and summer, not those of the time when the plays were actually performed. To appreciate the *Acharnians* of 425, for example, it is helpful to reread Thucydides and review the major events of winter 427/26 and (especially) summer 426. But how much does this help us with the beginning of the *Acharnians*, where Dicaeopolis, the average citizen (and spectator), reviews some things that he liked or didn't like from the preceding year? I give the passage again:

> Oh, slings and arrows of outrageous fortune!
> So many heartaches, so few happy moments!
> So few, so very few. Exactly four.
> But heartaches, plenty, sand-grain-zillions of them.
> Let's see. What did I like worth real rejoicement?
> I know—it really warmed my heart—it was
> when Cleon coughed up half a million dollars.
> Oh, that was great. I'm grateful to the knights
> for that day's work. O, patriotic deed!
> But what a pain I had, what a tragic pain,
> when I sat there gaping, waiting for Aeschylus,
> and the man announced, "Bring on your troupe, Theognis!"
> Don't you believe that made my stomach queasy?
> I liked it, though, the time when, after Moschos,
> Dexitheos came on, to do a Boeotian song.
> But just this year it killed me—I couldn't believe it—
> When Chaeris snuck in to play the Battle Hymn.   (1–16)

A center of national activity, Athens in the 420s was still a small enough world that allusions to local events, to minor personalities and foibles, could be recognized quickly and enjoyed by all. We know about Cleon, of course, but not about the half a million dollars (literally, five talents). Was it a real-life defeat or one presented in comedy, perhaps in Aristophanes' *Babylonians* of 426—in which case the year's greatest pleasure was (of course!) watching a comedy by Aristophanes? We do not know.[13] Nor do we know about Theognis, Moschos, Dexitheos, and Chaeris except from the scanty footnotes of ancient and modern scholars. Like the modern satirist or nightclub comedian who works with newspaper sometimes literally in hand, Aristophanes exploits recent events, joining small things with great, and often with fine incongruity. Our newspapers do the same, but with less artistry of (intended) juxtaposition. In the

Chapel Hill Newspaper of 9 March 1984 (note the date) an account of
the latest gunfire in Lebanon follows one about the restoration of a
symbolic and highly controversial star to the dome of our local planetar-
ium. Aristophanes would care about the star, as I do, because small,
local, everyday things matter to him; in this respect he speaks for his
audience. He also, as a comic poet, enjoys the incongruous juxtaposition
of small things and great. But even more, he has a genius for connecting
things as disparate as bad tragedy and war propaganda (in the *Acharnians*) or Athenian foreign policy and the price of anchovies (in the
Knights)—and he could easily have risen to the challenge and written a
stellar comedy in which the military and diplomatic mess in Lebanon
was clarified, or further confused, through the perspective of the Christmas Star. The wonder is, that so many matters of local, family fun are
made as available to us in Aristophanes' comedies as they are: that not
only tragedy but Old Comedy too is, in Aristotle's terms, "more philosophical than history." (History too is sometimes more philosophical
than history, but that is another matter.)

Problems still remain, many of them caused by the topicality of Old
Comedy.[14] We do not know who most of the minor figures are, or why
they are funny, or why, in some way or another, it matters. We may
gather from the plays that Cleonymus was a fat coward, and Theorus a
toady, and that both were associated with Cleon (which damns them
forever); but we cannot really know why Aristophanes made them his
continual butts, and the audience enjoyed Cleonymus jokes and Theorus
jokes, until these took on a life of their own as running gags. What
matters more is that we cannot recover, with all the help of scholarship,
anything of the fun and force and meaning of a single throwaway Cleonymus joke. Time and again, we are defeated, as time carries these things
away.

I have often found it helpful, when teaching Aristophanes (and especially in translation), to use modern analogies; but time has had its way
with my analogies too. A funny thing happened to me on the way to
writing this section for the last (?) time. In April 1976, when I delivered
a lecture on Aristophanes and Athenian politics in connection with our
nation's approaching Bicentennial celebrations, I could illustrate my
points with the recent case of Wayne Hays. This man (how many readers
will even faintly remember the name alone?) had been the powerful
chairman of the Administration Committee of the U.S. House of Representatives. It turned out that he had hired his girlfriend, Elizabeth Ray, as
a secretary, though she could only type twelve words a minute; a scandal
ensued, and Hays was forced to resign his position as chairman; later he
failed to be reelected to the House. At the time it made for splendid
laughter. There were many good jokes and cartoons, long since forgotten. Secretaries all over the country wore buttons proclaiming that they
could really type. The sex scandal in Washington made for comic relief in

a troubled year. It seemed instantly comprehensible, a simple case of naked corruption. It also appealed to the age-old need, which is very strong in America, to find a scapegoat from time to time who can be loaded with colorful sins, preferably of a sexual nature, and expelled amid general rejoicing. All this may seem self-righteous and hypocritical, and often it is. But to those who (as I did) believed him to be an unscrupulous man—he was said to be a bully and a tyrant, not only to elevator men and waitresses in the Capitol, but even on the floor of the House itself—his fall was more than satisfying: it was absolutely right. Our *Schadenfreude* was justified. The jokes had redeeming social value. In short, the fall of Hays was exactly the stuff (I almost said, the *type*) of Aristophanic comedy. It goes with Cleon vomiting out those five talents.

In 1976, when I discussed Hays's predicament as a modern example of satire, I illustrated the transience of political humor by recalling the case of Wilbur Mills and his "Argentine firecracker" two years earlier. Mills had been another powerful chairman, of the House Ways and Means Committee. A strict-living man (as it seemed), and a good one (as I still believe), he took to drink and became infatuated with a striptease dancer who precipitated his downfall by diving one night, drunk and fully dressed, into the Tidal Basin. That time too the jokes had burst out like fireworks. Lascivious delight joined with moral self-satisfaction. A certain malicious *Schadenfreude* had its moment, and so, then too, did the sense of relief we all feel when life seems stripped down to its ordinary, understandable self. But by April 1976 Mills had been forgiven, and largely forgotten, and it was Hays's turn to be exposed.

But there is more. Sometime later, in May 1983, I wrote:

> The irony, of course, is that today, as I write, the Wayne Hays affair has in turn been forgotten, and requires footnoting. The force of that 1976 laughter cannot be recovered unless, for the sake of analogy, some comparable scandal breaks upon us soon, producing a new display of dirty linen from official briefcases. Very likely these words will prove prophetic. How delighted I would be personally if James Watt (to name an obnoxious name) could be laughed out of office. But as a scholar, my present business is to note the power of time to shroud once-topical jokes in learned footnotes.

Just so. Ten months later, as I was writing this chapter, James Watt passed from the scene, cast out by public odium and, not least, by his unfortunate joke about women, Jews, blacks, and cripples. There is justice in things. And now, what if—? But I stop here; time cannot be arrested in his flight.

The scholar can explain jokes but not revive them. It is one thing to identify people, places, and things, to reconstruct a context, to uncover plays of language, and to recreate what we can of ancient traditions of funmaking: for example, the habit of attacking the government, which is quite familiar to anybody who keeps up with political cartoons; or the remarkable deployment of obscenity, which (on the whole) we have lost. Surely all this matters, we insist. Surely it justifies the sums of money we are paid. But what we cannot do, for all our educational magic, is to recover the lost moment of delighted recognition and raucous laughter that gave Old Comedy its oldest and strongest life. All annotation of comedy is damning, even the most expert. And if Old Comedy lost its savor by the fourth century, it was not just because of a change of taste (to which I shall return), not just because the old jokes seemed hurtful or obscene; it was because they seemed pointless. The plays most read and taught in Byzantium were those that treated broader social and educational issues: the *Clouds*, the *Frogs*, and especially the *Plutus*. And today, if you teach Aristophanes in translation, you had better start with the *Birds* and the *Lysistrata*: not, surely, because they are very moral or very clean, but because, over the years, they have remained accessible.

To Aristophanes, who was not (especially) writing for posterity, time posed a more immediate threat. A year's history could outrun his comedy, at best spoiling occasional jokes, at worst reducing the larger plot to ineffectuality. For each comedy was committed to production by autumn, to appear in spring. It is possible, indeed probable, that a playwright could make small changes up to the last minute, especially in the iambic portions where characters comment on recent events[15]—much as Garry Trudeau, I am told, continued to update his musical comedy *Doonesbury* by inserting last-minute references to the Reagan administration, and so forth. But major changes were not possible; so Aristophanes needed luck as well as foresight if he was to succeed.

Once, at least, he was lucky. Although the *Peace* was produced at the Dionysia in March 421, just a few days before the peace treaty with Sparta was actually signed, any celebration of peace must have seemed premature back in spring 422, when Aristophanes began drafting the play. It was, to be sure, a comparatively relaxed time, when farmers could revisit their wasted lands; but a definite peace, a lasting return to the country, must have seemed dangerously unreliable.[16] I argued earlier that the *Peace* self-consciously pre-celebrates the hoped-for peace, irrationally at bottom, yet stirring the real will to succeed. It must have seemed a great stroke of luck, then, when Cleon and Brasidas, the two great movers of war, died in October—and died, I think, just in time for Aristophanes to revise the scene where War, the great ogre, can't find a pestle to grind all of Greece into his crazy salad. The death of Brasidas, the death (how wonderfully satisfying!) of Cleon, the growing confidence that a peace treaty would actually be signed—all these things must have exhilarated Aristophanes and his company as the Dionysia drew nearer, lending a livelier skip to their dancing; but they reinforced, not created, the meaning and force of the play.

Aristophanes was lucky with the *Peace*; everything came together at the right time, the *kairos*. Was he equally lucky with the *Frogs*? He probably began that play under the immediate impression of Euripides' death in 407/6. The idea was that Dionysus should miss Euripides, should travel to Hades to find him, and should witness a great contest between Aeschylus and Euripides—the old tragedy and the new—for the Chair of Tragedy in the underworld. But then Sophocles died too, in 406/5, probably after the *Frogs* was well under way. It may have been an embarrassment. Sophocles had to be written into Hades but not really used. And a few verses, praising Aeschylus' lyrics as "the best to date" may have turned offensive in view of Sophocles' recent death, so much so that Aristophanes seems to have substituted new verses for them. (The original ones are still preserved, alongside the new ones, in the manuscripts.)[17] Still, despite some awkwardness, I doubt that Sophocles' death led, or could have led, to any major revision of the plot. It was too late for that. Rather, it must have deepened Aristophanes' already very strong feeling, communicated to and through his players, of the death of tragedy, of the passing of an older Athenian spirit (which may, on reflection, have been lost much earlier), and of the paradox, which is central to the *Frogs*, that this spirit remains more alive among the dead than among the "living."

One insertion, at least, must have been made at the last moment. Toward the end of the *Ecclesiazusae*, the chorus turn to the judges and appeal for proper consideration:

> I want to give the judges a small piece of advice. To the shrewd ones: remember my shrewd ideas, and vote for me. To the laughter-loving ones: I gave you laughs, so vote for me. To everybody, in short: you'd really better vote for me. And I don't want us to get into trouble because I drew first go; see that your memory stays clear; don't break your oaths, but keep on voting honestly; and don't you act like the lower sort of call girls in whose remembrance only the latest customer can stick.[18] (1154–62)

The plea sounds familiar. In the parabasis of the *Knights*, the Athenian audience was described as forgetful of old benefits, attending only to the gratifications of the present year. Now things are worse, for the audience has to be warned not to forget the first day's comedy when it watches the third. The joke about call girls, while enlivening the plea, may convey the playwright's indignation at those same old Athenians who are always hypnotized by the latest words, in entertainment as in politics (the latter is a major theme of the *Ecclesiazusae*). "What have you done for us lately?" But my point is that Aristophanes used these verses because his play was allotted the first position among the competing three. We don't know when the lots were drawn. The verses were probably ready long in advance; Aristophanes may have prepared alternate remarks to use in the event of a different draw. However that may be, they were used in the actual performance of 392, and it is a sense of that performance, that moment of uncertainty and appeal *before* the judges' verdict, that our text conveys.

All the poet's efforts led to a single performance of his play.[19] There were, with one known exception (the *Frogs*), no repeat performances at Athens, although the poet might be invited to tour the local theaters of Attica for off-season festivals.[20] The play's success could not, therefore, be judged by the length of its "run" at Athens or by the box office receipts, as in Shakespeare's time or ours.[21] Instead, it would resemble the success of a television special that is watched for three hours one weekday evening by sixty million people, whose choice to tune in and watch justifies the weeks and months of arduous preparations, and is soon over. But we would do better to think of an Olympic chariot- or footrace or wrestling contest such as Pindar celebrates in his victory odes. The athlete's preparations, his long training and toil (*ponos*), lead over months and years to the one crucial moment of testing (*kairos*) that passes so swiftly; and lead, at best, to that moment of crowning glory that Pindar celebrates, and whose remembered brilliance may last a life-time and even longer. Similarly the long preparations of poet and actors culminate in a brief performance, a momentary testing, that may be crowned with victory in the competition, celebrated with a feast. So too, today, every great dramatic performance is unique, even if it has a "run," and there is a poignant sadness as well as relief when it is over. But the religious occasion makes a difference. A Greek comic performance, like a chariot-race at Olympia and Delphi, belonged to the enactment of festi-val in a god's honor; it was caught up in the gods' timeless world; so that to lament that Aristophanes' *Acharnians* or *Knights* or *Peace* enjoyed only a single performance is to miss the point.

Still, granted the meaningfulness and satisfaction of performance, we shudder to think of the length and complexity of the preparations. What happens after the chorus is "granted" by the magistrate, and after the poet (we hope) is paid something in advance? As earlier, we discern the outlines, but we remain uncertain about the timing and the details of preparation between acceptance and performance.

(1) A *chorēgos* is officially assigned: not a "producer" in the modern sense, but rather a sponsor or "angel," a citizen of means who will pay for the training and outfitting of the chorus and for the provision of miscellaneous charges ranging from the props to the cast party. Why did rich and prominent citizens such as Pericles accept the *chorēgia*? They were lovers of art; they were public-spirited; they found it helpful in politics to show a record of public-spiritedness; and it must have been

fun to be associated with successful, well-remembered plays, which could (increasingly, in the next century) be commemorated by public "choregic" monuments. If there was glory, the *chorēgos* certainly shared in it. But he must have provided, not only some necessary money, but also some needed moral support and encouragement (as well as unwanted advice?) for the struggling poet.

(2) The training of the duly paid chorus would proceed under the direction of the *didaskalos* or director, normally the poet himself. Although an assistant director (*hypodidaskalos*) might be hired to supervise the singing and dancing of the chorus in rehearsals, the poet-director created the songs ("music" as well as "book"), planned the choreography, and saw to the integration of everything the chorus did into the larger scenic organization of the play.

(3) The actors were assigned by the archon and paid by the state. In tragedy the chief actors, the *prōtagōnistai*, were assigned by lot for each set of three tragedies and a satyr play, thus presumably insuring the fairness of the competition. Was it the same for comedy, or could a comic poet develop his personal company? It would be nice to think that Aristophanes could count sometimes on using a specific actor, so that, for example, the hilarious portrayal of "Euripides" in the *Acharnians* of 425 would encourage Aristophanes to conceive and develop his comic "Socrates" in the *Clouds* of 423. But we know almost nothing about fifth-century actors. In the fourth century, with all its tragic revivals, the actors became predominant and had their own competitions and prizes. In the fifth, was there more a sense of the company? The star system and teamwork seldom go well together, especially in comedy.

What were rehearsals like, and how did the poet-director work with his cast? There are no certain representations of comic performances, let alone rehearsals, on fifth-century vases. The poet's presence, however, is suggested by the Pronomos Vase, depicting a satyr play being performed or, more likely, rehearsed.

> The upper portion shows Dionysus, the god being celebrated. He is assisted by Paideia, the personification of the scenic games, who sits at the end of the divine couch holding a mask in her hands. They are surrounded by masked figures: not real portraits of actors, but the idealised figures of the myth. In the lower portion, a satyric chorus is represented, precisely evoking a theatrical scene. In this zone of reality, parallel to that of myth, the artisans of the victory are represented: Demetrius the poet and Pronomos the flute-player. The latter occupies the place of honor, just below the god.[22]

The juxtaposition, I would argue, of mythic and everyday figures is significant, for Dionysus and his entourage are not just decorative; rather, the players embody their spirit, carry out a revel-performance in their honor and under their present inspiration. Surely the same holds for comedy (and for tragedy). The mask, we are reminded, is a Dionysian emblem; it carries the power that transforms ordinary people into figures of myth and legend. At the same time, the incarnation of the Dionysian spirit is conveyed by ordinary people, for a limited performance in space and time. The music, represented by the flute-player, has a central role—and we know that flute-players were highly paid and honored. But the poet is emphatically present, though at one side. His visible instrument is the bookroll, or script, from which he "teaches." He has not, like most modern playwrights, retired from the scene, handing over his play to a director's rough care (and many changes). Even if, as sometimes happened, Aristophanes was not himself the *didaskalos*, we must imagine him as constantly present at rehearsals, "learning the ropes" of directing and producing a play, but also, surely, conveying to the chorus and the actors his sense of how the comedy was meant to work, and to be played.

We should not, I think, exaggerate the importance of the script.[23] Because we ourselves depend so heavily on the written word, we assume that Aristophanes' actors, like those today, were given scripts from which to learn their parts and their cues, and even some stage business; yet it seems likely that this instruction was conducted orally and with demonstrations by the poet-director. It may be that the poet had, and sometimes referred to, his own master script, incorporating changes in it when they seemed desirable or necessary, and perhaps allowing copies to be made; we need that master script as the archetype of the copies of the play that were transmitted to posterity. But the playwright, like the orator, still lived and taught in a mainly oral environment. From earliest childhood he and his actors and choristers had learned from the spoken (or recited, or sung), not the written word. W. B. Stanford has argued recently for some advantages of this method.[24] Delivery of speeches in plays, as in assemblies or law courts (the term, *hypocrisis*, is the same), requires the right use of qualities like rhythm, volume, and voice quality, "a kind of sub-musical accompaniment to the conceptual meaning of the words."[25] It would be advantageous if all these things could be "taught" simultaneously with the words, learned correctly the first time—and, for comedy, learned in connection with all those gestures, actions, and other effects that should accompany them.

Aristotle says that if a poet wants to convey emotion, he should first feel it himself, should adopt the poses of his own characters as he writes—or, as we would say, should feel himself into the parts.[26] This "method writing" was discussed, and practiced, in the fifth century, and already Aristophanes makes fun of it: in his Euripides of the *Acharnians*, who puts on rags and writes with his feet high up, and so creates a flock of crippled beggar-heroes; and in his Agathon, in the *Thesmophoriazusae*, who wears women's clothes in order to create effective female characters (or so he says). But the poet who creates these parts feelingly will also convey them feelingly to his actors. If Aristophanes did not, as has been suggested, play his own comic hero Dicaeopolis in the *Acharnians*, still he must have played him in rehearsals for the first actor's benefit. Not just the words, but the burps and farts, the comic groans, the vulgar and extravagant gestures and all the comic business—all had to be created by the poet, communicated by the poet and/or the director, and conveyed, with care and precision, to a final Athenian audience.

We can only imagine the effort and near chaos of the last days of rehearsal, when (as now) costumes and props were finally fitted and arranged and used, and when the play was moved into the actual theater (though still without a live audience).²⁷ There is, however, a scene in Aristophanes' *Ecclesiazusae* that may give us a closer view of the director's efforts, fears, and frustrations. Praxagora's women have come together before dawn to take over the Assembly by a revolutionary coup; they have, as was arranged, put on their husbands' suits and shoes, and carry staves, and have brought false beards to wear; and there is just time for Praxagora to give them one last run-through before the actual Assembly meets.

Woman I'm not sure. Lack of experience is frightening.
Prax.   Isn't that just why we're gathered here, so we can practice in advance the things we have to say? Won't you hurry up and get your beard adjusted—and the rest of you women, too, who have learned your parts for speaking? (115–19)

Like a good director, Praxagora worries about everything going wrong; she fusses about the way the costumes hang and the beards fit; she insists that mistakes in diction are really serious:

Woman Oh, by Apollo—
Prax.   Just stop right there. I wouldn't think of taking a single step towards the Assembly if you don't get these things *exactly right*.
Woman Give me the garland. I'll try it again; I'm sure I've learned it properly this time. . . . (160–64)

The scene is hilarious, with the women making mistake after mistake, and Praxagora becoming exasperated as she tries to keep things under control. Aristophanes' point is, not least, that the business of everyday politics at Athens is a sort of playacting; the orator who knows his (or her) business will carry everything before him, regardless of the true merit or idiocy of his advice. Yet, as often in later comedy, much of the fun is derived from theatrical experience. The women taught, with such exaggerated effort, to play men's roles were themselves played, of course, by male actors who were taught, with some real effort, to play women playing men. And Aristophanes, the experienced director, must have conveyed to and through "Praxagora" something of the anxiety that directors and producers feel as the time of the actual performance draws near.

It must have happened fast. It always does. The poet-director led his actors forward and presented them to the festival audience, naming the play that they would perform. Lots were drawn, for order of presentation. The time came at last; the play was given; it was quickly over. There was, we hope, a huge surge of applause at the end, so that the judges would be moved to vote Aristophanes' play the first prize. There was a cast party, with plenty of food and drink, given (as his last contribution) by the *chorēgos*. And that was that—unless Aristophanes had the pleasure of hearing a song or two from his play sung by people at symposia, or decided, on request, to take the play into the provinces later on.[28]

The modern philologist's interest begins, curiously, where Aristophanes' ends. He wants to know about the text, not the performance. What "clean copy" was it taken from, in the first place, before it was published?[29] (D. L. Page identifies this with the prompter's copy, but for the fifth century both "prompter" and "copy" are objects of speculation; there is only that uncertain bookroll in the poet's hand.) Then, when the play was published, how many copies were circulated? And was a master copy kept? For philologists studying the transmission of texts, the darkest period is that between a fifth-century play's production and the decree of Lycurgus in 330 B.C., establishing or reestablishing an official text to be kept in the archives, with which actors of old tragedies must compare their scripts. Only from then can we speak of an "authentic" text, after the damage was done—after actors had cut, added, explained, and embellished the poet's verses for about a century. Presumably, official texts of the Old Comedy writers were established in 330 also. Alexandrian scholarship soon followed, and then Byzantine. We owe an enormous debt to all those editors, commentators, and schoolmasters for what we call, and rightly, the survival of Aristophanes' plays; yet we must realize that to their author, that literary survival would have seemed a shady afterlife indeed. It was a joke for him, even in 405, that people could read his comedies and appreciate their subtleties. And he was touched, perhaps, by the spirit of life lingering in those texts, much as his comic hero Dionysus finds himself on shipboard reading a copy of Euripides' *Andromeda* and conceives such a nostalgic passion for the dead Euripides that he goes down to Hades to bring him back.[30] Yet Aristophanes implied, in that same play, that "revival" on the stage gives old tragedies a kind of continuing or new life that no reading can bestow. A play's life is what lights up the stage—although, by a paradox central to the *Frogs* (and in Eliot's words),

> the communication
> of the dead is tongued with fire beyond
> the language of the living.[31]

So I teach, or write, with this same paradox in mind. On the one hand, the Budé text of Aristophanes in my hands seems crammed with brilliance and vitality; on the other, it remains a dead thing to which only the reader's imagination, nourished on live performances, can give life; so that the scholar of ancient comedy much resembles Horace's mad Argive who used to sit in an empty theater, watching and applauding imaginary performances of plays—until, to his great sadness, he was "cured."[32]

I must write, then, with much gratitude for the text and for the tradition behind it, on which the survival of Aristophanes depends, but still more with nostalgia (*pothos*) for the living performance and with an acute sense of that missing third dimension of theater. For without the music, the songs and dances, the bright costumes, the props, the comic business, and even the way the words are spoken, we scarcely "have" the plays. I am afraid of becoming a bore on this subject, of what is missing. It is like Oscar Wilde's tour through the South in 1891, when people kept telling him, as he praised a house or town or landscape, that he should have seen it before the war; so that in the end he hesitated to admire a full moon, lest someone should say, "Ah, but you should have seen it before the war!" Still, I *would* like to have seen Atlanta (or Munich) before the war, and I *would* like to have sat among Aristophanes' audience at a live play; but as things stand, I must try to read the text, and write about it, with a strong sense of what is missing—much as my wife (not I) can read the blueprint of a house.

It is some help, and consolation, to have worked with revivals. From directing and acting in Roman comedies, at Harvard and in Chapel Hill, I have learned much about what works and does not work, what can and cannot be done, on the comic stage. It was my experience of directing Aristophanes' *Clouds* at Harvard in 1959 that, more than anything, convinced me that most criticism of that play was ridiculously off base. Reading in depth is hard, and takes training, but it need not be very complicated: indeed even a slight sense of performance brings out the many simple and obvious things about a comic (or tragic) performance that the sophisticated critic so often ignores. When Tom Stoppard lectures on "the event and the text," he prefaces his remarks by telling of an experience in California, when he told an audience of university professors that he did not write his plays to be studied. The professors looked absolutely appalled, and he realized that what was unimportant to him—studying the plays—was in fact their justification for existing.[33]

My account, therefore, of some of Aristophanes' comic ideas in the following chapters (and in volume 2, where I shall treat the *Clouds* at length) must remain subject to, and be tested against, that sense of lost performance. The "text," though priceless, will be ancillary to the "event." And that includes (although we cannot be part of it) the sense of an audience in whose presence the play most fully lives; for the actors on the (I think) slightly raised *logeion*, the dancers in the orchestra, and the spectators on their benches overlooking both, are all together part of the theatrical event, especially in comedy.

The point is not just that Aristophanes made jokes about public officials who, he knew, would be occupying the front seats, thus drawing them into the area of his comedies. It is rather that comedy, even more than tragedy, requires a constant interplay with an audience—as though, until they take their seats, some of the actors are missing. I have often experienced this sensation when directing comedies, and I was reminded of it a few years back when watching Lili Bita, a modern Greek actress, give a performance in Gainesville, Florida. She regularly gives three scenes, in English translation: Clytemnestra's speech, after she kills Agamemnon; Medea's speech to Jason; and Lysistrata's speech to her female co-conspirators. The tragic scenes from Aeschylus and Euripides were received with silence and awe. It was as though frightening secrets of sexual conflict, pain, and murder had been brought out from beneath the surface of our ordinary lives. But when Lili Bita removed her black robe and put on a countrywoman's headscarf to go with her bright blouse, to do Lysistrata, she urged the women in the audience to join in, and the men too. We were to play out a contest with her, dividing into teams (males versus females), calling out encouragement or rebuke, and laughing in different ways, yet laughing together, at the old familiar jokes about figs and bananas. Under her leadership, we brought something of *Lysistrata* back to life. For what matters most in the end is not the politics of that play, or the uses of obscenity, but the sense of play by which sex and politics together are defined, and we are liberated. There is a great deal of child's play in *Lysistrata*; but it takes the child in us—preferably watching a performance, if only in his or her mind's eye—to get the point.

14   *The Creative Playwright:*
From Stoppard to Aristophanes

IT was good to hear Tom Stoppard's voice on a tape
that a friend sent me, speaking informally about *Rosencrantz and Guildenstern Are Dead.*[34] It was the voice of a craftsman who enjoys his art,
who is proud of it, who is constantly learning about it, and who doesn't
mind sharing something of this with the public. "The main preoccupation of a man writing a play," he says, "is to keep the theatrical interest
high." This can be hard work. Stoppard speaks of the "nuts and bolts of
dramatic necessity": for example, the business of the substituted letter,
which had to be worked out onstage. The playwright contrives many
details. But we also hear his excitement, his delight in the creative process. Writing is an adventure for him, like "exploring." His plays grow
like "live organisms." He speaks of the delight he felt when the idea
came to him of beginning act 3 in the dark, on the boat; the end of act 1
came to him "like a Christmas present." The playwright labors, but
he also enjoys a special serendipity. And little things keep turning up,
unlooked-for and beautiful. An actor, by chance, brought out the latent
silliness in the phrase "toenails on the other hand." It was not planned or
intended; it just happened. They used it, since it worked.

Rosencrantz and Guildenstern Are Dead was first produced in 1967,
when Stoppard was thirty. A black comedy, it shows an irrational, deadly
world as it might be viewed by those very unimportant characters in
Hamlet if they came center stage. They are fumbling and foolish, and at
sea—literally at sea, in act 3—and all their clever talk is whistling in the
dark; but they have a certain dignity, as doomed human beings, and we
are made to feel for them as we would for ourselves. It is a brilliant play,
in conception and in execution. Although it parodies *Hamlet* and makes
that troubled prince and all the court look extremely silly, as they must
look in a modern realistic light, it succeeds in bringing alive the pain and
terror of *Hamlet*, the sense of meaninglessness and the chill of death,

which have been obscured for us by the familiar beauty of Shakespeare's lines, by their being taught in schools, which gives them a meretricious nostalgic appeal, and by their being, as the lady complained, "so full of clichés." I thought, after seeing *Rosencrantz and Guildenstern*, how much this shift of emphasis was like Euripides' procedure in writing his *Electra*. That play too comes nearer black comedy than tragedy. It includes much parody of Aeschylus, whose noble prince and princess become a pair of paranoid killers, wild and decadent aristocrats wholly misplaced against a background of normal life in the country. Euripides makes us feel, in that play, what an ugly thing murder is, and especially matricide. It is not heroic, and it is not excusable; if Apollo ordered it, then Apollo was clearly wrong. All this runs counter to the Aeschylean theodicy. It does, however, bring back for a modern audience the pity and terror that Aeschylus once inspired, before he became a familiar classic, a monument of Athenian culture to be quoted at table and in the schools.

From *Rosencrantz and Guildenstern* I came to *Jumpers* (1972). Imagine my pleasure when, after years and years of maintaining the excellence of Aristophanes' *Clouds* against opposition, both ignorant and learned, I came across a modern play that makes fun of professors, that explores complex questions of religion, morality, and ethics, and yet retains its farcical nature with slapstick, puns, music, song, acrobatics, and naked women. The two sides are married in a thoroughly successful comedy of ideas, much as the hero, George Moore, the absent-minded moral philosopher, is married to Dottie, the lovely music-hall singer, whose mind snapped when the first men landed on the moon, and who (though neither realizes this) is joined with George in a sort of complementary lunacy. All this is enormously encouraging to a lover of the *Clouds*. The point is not that Aristophanes influenced Stoppard (though he might have), but rather that intelligence and theater can still coexist so wonderfully. The old comedy of ideas is still alive and kicking. Thanks be to— Dionysus.

I have, since *Jumpers*, become a Stoppard-watcher: partly for sheer pleasure, and partly to remind myself what comedy is like, how it works on the stage. There is so much to see and hear that we miss in an Aristophanic text. As you watch, you become aware of Stoppard's mastery of juxtaposition. While George is dictating his fumbling but brave draft for a lecture on God, Dottie is undressing in the bedroom, on the other side of the stage, so that the audience's attention is somewhat less focused on George's monologue than the reader's will be. (The juxtaposition of study and bedroom is not just good theater: it brings out, in a comic, touching, and sometimes pathetic way, the distance between the husband and wife that cannot be overcome.) As you watch, you become aware of these contrasts. You also notice how much props matter, like George's bow and arrow, and the tortoise he holds in his hand (trying to demonstrate the fallacy of Zeno's paradoxes, though his hare, Thumper, has been mislaid); and you notice so many other things: the lighting, the music, the acrobatics, the statements made by costume (and lack of costume), the exits and entrances, and all the subtle interplay between actors and audience that makes for good theater. The actor playing George is trying to catch and keep *our* attention. I talked with one such actor after the performance. He told me what a challenging part it was, what demands Stoppard makes on his actors, and how much mental preparation the play required (he studied philosophy for months in order to understand what he was saying).[35] He also described the thin line separating farce from tragedy. When, at the end of act 2, George pulls down the arrow with which he has accidentally shot Thumper atop the bookshelf, steps back in anguish, and treads heavily on Pat, the tortoise, killing him, the moment is excruciatingly funny and painful at one and the same time. My actor friend (also called Pat) said that the play tended more toward farce or toward tragedy on different evenings, depending on the audience. Would I have been mistaken, then, to decide for one or the other on the basis of a careful reading? I pride myself on being a skillful reader of plays, but again and again I find, on seeing a performance, that I have missed a great deal in reading, and sometimes that my interpretations of tone and effect have been quite wrong.

Stoppard is ambitious: he makes things work, like long monologues, that you would not expect to work. Speed is essential, and split-second timing, and such devices (again, not easily imagined from reading his plays) as a blink of the lights or the striking of a cuckoo clock. Stoppard visualized, and counted on, these stage effects when he wrote. He also counted on skilled actors, like John Wood, who played Carr in *Travesties*: "I wrote *Travesties* for John. It's hard not to write a play for him. I write plays for somebody who can speak speeches quickly. With long syllables."[36] The point is exaggerated but real. Stoppard has regularly taken risks that other writers have not, partly from genius, but partly because he could count on support. And sometimes one success must have led to another. After Michael Hordern played George Riley, the fumbling, absentminded, self-deceiving, yet strangely dignified and engaging hero of the farcical play *Enter a Free Man*, Stoppard must have been emboldened to create the much more difficult part of George Moore in *Jumpers* for Hordern to play. Perhaps the element of George (Riley) in George (Moore) is one of those serendipitous inside jokes that the creative playwright relishes.

In connection with *Jumpers*, may I tell a joke on myself? I had hoped to use this play as evidence that a comedy of ideas very like Aristophanes' *Clouds* could succeed with a general audience; but after winning rave reviews in London and in Washington, *Jumpers* did not survive long enough in New York for me to see it. The people there thought it too intellectual. By contrast, some years later *Dirty Linen* ran for months on

Broadway and made thousands of dollars. This was a little sex farce that Stoppard tossed off in a few hours, to benefit a friend; it depends largely on double entendres and on incongruity, like dignified politicians pulling lace panties out of their (of course!) brief-cases. It is, actually, a good sex farce. On a small scale it illustrates how a comic idea works: in this case, a dramatization of "dirty linen in public." Aristophanes would have enjoyed it. But, I think, the failure of *Jumpers* in New York nicely suggests what may have happened to the *Clouds* in Athens, and it lends Aristophanes credibility when he states that the *Clouds* was an excellent play, his best to date, and that the judges were altogether wrong.

The critic of modern drama, to be sure, has enormous advantages over that of ancient. Not only can he test his impressions against actual performances, he can also qualify or reinforce them with information gained from reviews, letters, pictures, interviews with the author, and so forth. In addition to the taped comments mentioned earlier, I have twice heard Stoppard lecture in person on "the event and the text." Naturally, not everything in interviews or public lectures can be taken at face value. Stoppard enjoys irony, self-irony, and comic exaggeration, rather like Aristophanes in the parabases of his plays. All the same, and perhaps because he was a newspaper critic earlier, and interviewed people, Stoppard has been very open and forthcoming about the business of being a playwright—the kind of thing we would give our eyeteeth to know about Aristophanes. And even the simple biographical facts (are they ever simple?) Stoppard gives us steady our judgments and bring us back to the plays with, I think, renewed interest and appreciation.

To begin with, we know a good deal about Stoppard's life. His birth in Czechoslovakia (he describes himself as a "bounced Czech"), his childhood uprooting, his coming to Singapore and India, the loss of his father in the war, his being brought to England by a British stepfather, and changing his name from Straussler to Stoppard, his schooling, his work as a newspaper reviewer of plays and films, the progress of his own dramatic writing, and his great success—all these do not explain his creative genius, but they give a context for it. I give two examples, both minor, but again with an eye to what we are missing with Aristophanes. In *The Real Inspector Hound* Stoppard makes fun of the critical jargon used by reviewers; when they make quasi-official pronouncements, they are pompous and silly. Of course the satire is especially effective when it is partly self-satire, coming from a former theater critic who knows these pretensions from the inside. All the more does the play turn funny and frightening when the theater critics are precipitated into the action, of a murder mystery, that they have been watching. Observers become participants, and victims. This happens often in Stoppard's plays and is highly effective as drama, a way of vicariously involving the audience in the confusion of things that drama can represent. But it is the more moving, and the more humane, for its inwardness: the author's identification of himself with these people who try to control things, and to remain aloof, but are drawn into the maelstrom of life and death.

A second biographical item has seemed to me happily suggestive for Aristophanes. As Socrates in the *Clouds* combines two aspects of philosophy—its absentminded impracticality and irrelevance to ordinary life, and its threat to traditionally held religious and moral values—so in *Jumpers* philosophy is split into the comically ineffectual and the (somewhat less) comically villainous. On the one side, there is the bumbling, absentminded, and self-defeating hero, George Moore, who is ultimately fighting for the moral order and for truth; on the other, there are the "Jumpers" of the play's title, intellectual acrobats of a logical positivism that is shown to lead, through moral relativism and an opportunistic pragmatism in politics and in daily life, to casual murder and the totalitarian state. Their leader is Sir Archie Jumper, a professor of philosophy and vice-chancellor (note the *vice*) of the University, who is also a doctor, a psychiatrist, a lawyer, a gymnast, and the head of the Radical-Liberal Party that has just, as the play begins, taken over England. To a large extent Stoppard's portrayal of both aspects of philosophy, the impractical and the sinister, was based on the style and writings of a well-known philosopher, Professor (later Sir) Alfred J. Ayer. What is interesting is that Ayer saw the play and enjoyed it greatly. Later on, he reviewed it, explaining in print why George's arguments on behalf of God and morality wouldn't do. And eventually he invited Stoppard to a fine dinner at New College, a feast of food, wine, and ideas. Not that Ayer and Stoppard became close friends; but they do seem to have enjoyed each other's company, as great-hearted rivals may, and found it stimulating.[37] Would it be fanciful to imagine that a similar relationship existed between Aristophanes and Socrates? The latter, we know, was slandered mightily in the *Clouds*. He was made into one of the great archvillains of comedy. Yet an anecdote suggests that he enjoyed the play, rising in the audience so that strangers might compare him with "Socrates" onstage;[38] and Plato, who was devoted to Socrates and appalled by his condemnation (on false charges arising out of slander) and his death, could still, in his *Symposium*, picture a splendid dinner party held seven years after the play, at which Aristophanes and Socrates compete as brilliant, funny, great-hearted rivals. We cannot, this time, recover the facts; but the fiction gives us what we might, really, have imagined to be true.

Let me turn to a more complex question, of Stoppard's relation to politics. In three recent plays, *Professional Foul*, *Every Good Boy Deserves Favor*, and *Dogg's Hamlet, Cahoot's Macbeth*, he has dealt with the repression of artists and intellectuals in Russia and Czechoslovakia. His anger and concern are evident from these plays, and they are confirmed by his writings for the press, his personal interest in individual Czech dissidents, and his attempts to intervene on their behalf. Yet his passionate concern nowhere detracts from the intellectual and artistic integrity of his plays. In the first place, he refuses (unlike some of his contemporaries) to make art serve purposes other than its own, of political statement or reformist propaganda. The play's final meaning arises out of its play with language, character, and idea, not vice versa. Second, Stoppard is, and remains, fiercely given to exposing the subtle and diverse forms of nonintegrity shown by people like himself—by artists, professors, journalists, and intellectuals generally. (His recent and brilliant play *The Real Thing* emphatically adds playwrights to the list.) And third, while he has always believed passionately in human freedom and worth and individuality, in ways that could be labeled bourgeois-intellectual or conservative, he has consistently seen artistic and intellectual freedom and integrity as the best sign, and guarantee, of a free society. To subordinate art to politics, to expose less than the whole, many-sided truth, would seem a betrayal. What is also interesting, though, is that in time an artist may become sure enough of his integrity to put a larger measure of concern and passion into his plays, and to make, through his characters, increasingly clear and direct statements of what he stands for personally, and stands against. Yet he remains a great comic playwright who has not been trapped, whether by zeal or by fashion, into expressing any serious message that is less, finally, than the whole, never quite serious (though often very painful) truth.

If the known biographical context for Stoppard's writing is steadying to critics, though never wholly reliable as a guide, we benefit still more from other known and shared contexts, especially literary ones, that are painfully absent to the reader of Aristophanes. It helps, naturally, to be Stoppard's contemporary. He describes our own world; we have seen it, or heard about it; so it does not require elaborate footnotes that get between us and the belly laugh, or the grimace of pain. We also know, at first hand, the conventions of the modern theater, the devices of nonrealistic drama that give play to Stoppard's vivid, contrapuntal imagination. We know what he shares, or does not share, with contemporaries like Harold Pinter. We know much about earlier playwrights whose vision and techniques influenced his: Pirandello, Wilde, Shaw, Brecht, and (especially) Samuel Beckett. Precise information is helpful here, and sometimes indispensable, as Stoppard lavishly and unashamedly builds his cloud-capped towers of wordplay and action upon the inventions of other writers. The best example of this is Wilde. Stoppard loved his plays, which he first saw and reviewed in his Bristol days; his own wit was stimulated by Wilde's, and the earlier writer became for him a consummate figure of style, of the aesthetic impulse triumphing (for a time) in all its glory and pride, high above ordinary passions and disturbances. One part of Stoppard, epigrammatic and aloof, emulated Wilde. Another part was not able, or willing, to "withdraw with style from the chaos" of human life;[39] it kept being drawn in, with tragic or comic consequences;

but the conflict of the two could still be depicted, in play after play, with a craftsman's care and a brilliance of style over which Wilde's genius continues to preside. *Travesties* borrows extensively and wonderfully from *The Importance of Being Earnest*. You really have to know the one in order to appreciate the other; fortunately, the two are sometimes played together in repertory today, for our greater understanding and delight.[40]

More obviously, Stoppard has drawn on Shakespeare throughout his career, with love and admiration. He treats his plays, especially *Hamlet* and *Macbeth*, as a common mythology (perhaps the only one left) from which to work—and even so, he sometimes needs to remind the audience of what is being parodied. Shakespeare seems inexhaustible as a source. He is also a touchstone of art, and of meaning, in a shifting universe. In *Dogg's Hamlet* there is a hilarious, fifteen-minute version of *Hamlet*—followed by a ninety-second, instant replay of that!—as if to say, "This is what a modern audience wants, and this is what it will get." It is indescribably funny. (I laughed so hard that it hurt.) But the second play of the pair, *Cahoot's Macbeth*, gives a different, and strangely moving, travesty of *Macbeth*. Shakespeare's play, as it turns out, is being performed secretly, in a private house in Czechoslovakia; it is interrupted, and finally stopped, by a sinister Inspector; and by degrees, the familiar condition of Scotland, bleeding under Macbeth's tyranny, becomes the Communist tyranny in Czechoslovakia that has to stop performances of *Macbeth*. The parody goes on brilliantly. It is very funny and very painful at the same time. Although *Dogg's Hamlet, Cahoot's Macbeth* is not widely known, I suspect that Stoppard was experimenting with new techniques of parody, confusion of levels, and audience involvement that are not easily mastered, but that point to some masterpiece of comedy yet to come. My immediate point is that Stoppard is most creative when he draws most richly from Shakespeare and from other sources; and that, though he is a gifted entertainer and never a pedant, the more we know about literature and drama, the more we can enjoy, and be moved by, his plays.

But what I find most instructive in Stoppard-watching is to catch glimpses of how a play grows from seminal images or ideas to its final realization on the contemporary stage. "You start off," he says, "with a kind of half-baked idea for a play and tend to work it out."[41] From this comes a "ground plan" of a play, and later a first draft, which may pass through several very different incarnations before things become settled. Let me use, as examples, what I have gleaned about *Rosencrantz and Guildenstern Are Dead* and *Jumpers*. (A more extensive account of *Travesties*, in section 15, leads back to Aristophanes.)

The conception of *Rosencrantz and Guildenstern* seems to have started with a casual suggestion that Stoppard's literary agent, Kenneth Ewing, made to him in a taxicab, early in 1964: that if Rosencrantz and

Guildenstern arrived in England according to plan, they might well have found themselves at the court of—King Lear.[42] This is evidently the sort of thing that tickles a comic playwright's imagination. It gave him a title, "Rosencrantz and Guildenstern at the Court of King Lear." And that turned, eventually, into a full-length prose comedy, under its present title, that received an amateur performance in Edinburgh in 1966 and—just barely catching on—a professional one in London, at the Old Vic, in 1967. It then, to everyone's surprise, including Stoppard's, became an enormous success. I myself have taught it in class, together with Euripides, Shakespeare, and Chekhov; and two of my sons have studied it in English courses and have been examined on its content and meaning. (For that matter, Stoppard mentions that his son was examined on *Professional Foul* for O-levels. "He received a C.")

It is typical of the struggling playwright that during rehearsals in London he was still fiddling with the play and improving it—still finding out what worked, or did not work, on the actual stage. He describes how he becomes totally involved in rehearsals, even accompanying a new play from London to Washington or New York, to make sure that the production works. The technical difficulties can be considerable—something of which literary critics (who seldom go to plays) seem to have little idea— and there is the constant struggle to keep the attention and interest of a real audience. But Stoppard submits to criticism, and even accepts drastic changes, so long as he keeps some sense of control over what happens to his ideas.

> I'm very free about that sort of thing as long as I'm there, and pretty rigid about it if I'm not. I think of rehearsal as being a very important part of getting the play right. I had very good rapport with Robert Chetwyn, and with Peter Wood, and that is the main thing—it's not that somebody is born to direct your plays, or that they particularly understand them. I always feel it's like what Evelyn Waugh said about the Second World War, that the great thing was to spend it among friends. Getting a play on is so awful, the important thing is to spend it among friends.[43]

Sometimes, too, Stoppard explains to his actors what is going on, in case it isn't clear (even with the many stage directions included in the script). The split between poet and director (*didaskalos*) is reassuringly incomplete.

To return to the earlier question of where plays come from: it would be a mistake to think that Stoppard, or any other playwright, begins with a single isolated idea, for as *Jumpers* illustrates, other ideas, images, and concerns are always waiting in the wings. Stoppard has said that *Jumpers* grew out of an image, suggested in *Rosencrantz and Guildenstern*, of a pyramid of acrobats—with one man blown out of it. He adds, however, that at the same time, there's more than one point of origin for a play, and the only useful metaphor I can think of for the way I think I write my plays is convergences of different threads. . . . One of the threads was the entirely visual image of the pyramid of acrobats, but while thinking of that pyramid, I knew that I wanted to write a play about a professor of moral philosophy. . . . There was a metaphor at work in the play already between acrobatics and mental acrobatics, and so on.[44]

Somehow the idea worked. It suggested other comic ideas, like the University gymnasium with stained glass windows. It became associated with the way relativists (and playwrights) are always taking off in new directions, like people bouncing on a trampoline, or with the "leap of faith" that the old-fashioned champion of God and morality must make. Or it joined, in a more complex manner, with older images, ideas, and preoccupations about the moon, about the word *moon*, and about the consequences of landing on the moon. Since these associations, which are brilliant and poetic, are also very difficult to do justice to, let me end these remarks by pointing to a simpler comic idea that is important in *Jumpers* and, in its way, is very moving: the man with the bow and arrow.[45]

At one point in *Jumpers* an inspector comes to the door to inquire about a murder. What he finds is a man (George) with shaving cream on his face, a bow and arrow in one hand, and a tortoise in another. It all has a logical explanation. George has been shaving absentmindedly while preparing his lecture, "Is God?" The bow and arrow are meant to illustrate the fallacy of one of Zeno's paradoxes; the tortoise (together with the missing hare) points to another. One of Stoppard's favorite theatrical devices is to produce a wildly improbable combination of things from what turns out to be a comprehensible sequence of natural causes. But this particular combination seems to have arisen from a true story about a man Stoppard knew who was seen running outdoors in his pajamas, his face covered with shaving cream, and a peacock (which he had just retrieved) under his arm. Just what, Stoppard asked himself, would a passerby have made of this? What, for that matter, would he think he had seen? There are several variations of this in Stoppard's farce *After Magritte*, in which natural events combine to produce absurd tableaux; by the time he wrote *Jumpers*, Stoppard had fully mastered the technique of building to a wild, hilarious moment on the stage.

And he had learned to do something more. If George is a ludicrous and helpless figure of a man, yet he is also, in his way, a warrior for the good, an archer sent into combat with Archie the archvillain. "Bring me my bow of burning gold," cries William Blake, "bring me my arrows of desire." A heaven-sent warrior like the prophets of old, he will rebuild Jerusalem "in England's green and pleasant land," as every British schoolboy knows. The comic hero has a less glorious panoply. He means to be a warrior, but his bow misfires—horribly—the one time he uses it. He "will not cease from mental fight," but he isn't very good at it, and besides, he has shaving cream all over his face. He is not a hero, or a prophet. He is like the rest of us, only sillier, because he takes on a hero- or prophet-sized job. We have to laugh at his foolishness, his incompetence, his lost grip on things. Still, for all that, he is on the side of the angels (if there are any), and so is the poet who created him, bow and arrows, tortoise, shaving cream, and all.

15   *Comic Ideas in Action: Stoppard's* Travesties

THE comic idea, or *epinoia*, underlying *Travesties* results from the typically Stoppardian combination of two sets of facts. One was that Lenin, James Joyce, and a Dadaist named Tristan Tzara all lived in Zurich during the First World War and hence might have known each other. To the comic playwright who revels in incongruity, who delights in discovering relationships between seemingly incompatible things, the facts must have seemed a gift and a challenge. In April 1972 Stoppard was thinking of playing Lenin off against Tzara (he had not yet discovered that Joyce too was in Zurich): "I think it might be nice to do a two-act thing, with one act a Dadaist play on Communist ideology and the other an ideological functional drama about Dadaists."[46] In *Artist Descending a Staircase*, which was produced later that year, two artists casually recall how Tzara, first misremembered as "Tarzan" (a primitive type?), and Lenin both lived in Zurich in 1915.[47] A joke about "*Tsar Nicholas*" suggests a playful connection between them that Stoppard might have exploited. Instead he added Joyce, and he found (in Ellmann's biography of the novelist) the second piece of trivia that fired his imagination. Joyce had been the business manager of the English Players in Zurich. Their first performance was Wilde's *Importance of Being Earnest*. Joyce found a minor consular official named Henry Carr to play the role of Algernon, but afterwards Carr quarreled with Joyce, who underpaid him and then had the nerve to ask for money for tickets that Carr had allegedly sold. As Ellmann tells it,

> Carr said he had not yet received the money, and in any case had had to buy a new pair of trousers for the part. He called Joyce "cad" and "swindler" and threatened to throw him down the stairs. Joyce objected primly to this language . . . and went straight to a lawyer. He sued Carr for the tickets, Carr countersued for his

trousers; Joyce added a second suit for libel. The first suit was won by Joyce, the second, with costs, by Carr.[48]

Joyce had the last word, however, since he was able to put Carr into *Ulysses* as a brutish soldier.

Stoppard's idea, arising from these facts, was complex and brilliant. He would bring Lenin, Joyce, and Tzara together; he would filter the imaginary events he wanted through the unreliable memory of Carr as an old man; and in so doing, he would make all these characters behave as though they were acting out parts from *Earnest*. As it works out, Gwendolyn and Cecily are directly imported from Wilde's play, the former to be Carr's sister, the latter as a librarian. Tzara is Tristan (his real name) with Gwendolyn, but he pretends to be Jack, Tristan's politically conscious brother, when he is in the library under Cecily's eyes.[49] Carr, falling in love with Cecily, and also wishing to spy on Lenin (for he is now the British consul, and his government wishes Lenin to be prevented from returning to Russia), pretends to her that he is Jack's irresponsible Dadaist brother Tristan. In the end Lenin returns to Russia, Joyce gets on with *Ulysses*, the lovers are reunited, after quarreling, in a Wildean tour de force—and in what may be Stoppard's bow to historical reality, Old Cecily, long since married to Old Carr, has to remind him that most of what he thinks he remembers never happened at all.

But if we want to understand how the playwright's imagination works, we must look at subsidiary comic ideas that reinforce the principal ones and make them go. I give two examples of wordplay that seem to confirm Stoppard in his purpose. The first concerns Joyce, whom Tzara describes to Carr as follows:

> No, no, Mr. Joyce, Irish writer, mostly of limericks, christened James Augustine, though registered, due to a clerical error, as James Augusta, a little known fact.[50]

Why is this brought in? Stoppard likes to ridicule the pedants, from whose *obscura diligentia* he and his plays must sometimes have suffered. (In *Travesties* he makes fun of the copyright protection of sources from which he wants to quote liberally.) Often, however, the unconsidered trifles that he snaps up prove to be suggestive links between different levels of meaning, or of dramatic action. Stoppard associates Lenin, to a small extent, with Miss Prism, for both of them give Cecily rather boring lessons in "political economy." More extensively, he gives Joyce something of the role of chaperone, and something more of Lady Bracknell's role of a person in (moral) authority over Gwendolyn. That is, Joyce plays—Aunt *Augusta*.

We should not think of these comic relationships as simply being contrived. It is rather as though Stoppard discovered them, by free association, to his delight and ours. Minor connections reinforce the basic conception but also in a sense prove its rightness, like pieces fitting into a jigsaw puzzle. Take Stoppard's use of "Dada," which is more thematic than the "Augusta" joke. Dada is a nonsense word, the emblem of a nihilistic movement in modern art that rejected traditional forms and meanings ("My art belongs to Dada"). It is also baby talk, such as lovers use:

> *Tzara*: Have you ever seen my magazine "Dada," darling?
> *Gwen*: Never, da-da-darling!

But *da* is also the Russian word for "yes." Lenin's wife, Nadya, uses it emphatically to announce the Tsar's abdication, and Stoppard, to mark a turning point in history: "Da, da, da!" There may be a suggestion here that Lenin will introduce total conformity into Russia, and that the Russians will be reduced under communism to using a kind of political babytalk. There will be no room for "no" in Russia, or for "anti" ("auntie"), or for what Stoppard elsewhere calls "the yes-noes of yesteryear"; nor will there be room for the genuine art that produces Molly Bloom's "yes, I said yes." This constantly amusing wordplay helps prove the rightness of Stoppard's major premise, that all the revolutions that the play explores, in art, literature, and politics, must somehow, and significantly, be connected.

It would be fun to make a fuller study of the function of free association and wordplay in the creation of a Stoppard comedy, as in that of a witty dream. More could be done, for example, with the nonsense-link between "Tsar" and "Tzara." Let me turn instead to more central associations, of trousers and hats. The play's title, *Travesties*, indicates the burlesquing of serious ideas, or serious people, or both. It implies the pastiche of Wilde's own comedy. And its literal meaning—"changes of clothing"—refers to an age-old component of all drama, and especially of comedy, with its many disguises and impersonations. Let us see, before coming to the play's central confrontations, how different meanings emerge through the use and the misuse of clothing.

From reading about Carr's silly lawsuit (or law-*suit*) with Joyce, Stoppard conceived the idea of a character whose mind becomes increasingly obsessed with trousers. Of the war, Carr says:

> You forget that I was there, in the mud and blood of a foreign field, unmatched by anything in the whole history of human carnage. Ruined several pairs of trousers. Nobody who has not been in the trenches can have the faintest conception of the horror of it. I had hardly set foot in France before I sank in up to the knees in a pair of twill jodhpurs with pigskin straps handstitched by Ramidge and Hawkes . . .

I think the travesty works two ways here. On the one hand, everything that is false in the rhetoric of patriotism is undercut, partly by the use of clichés, and still more by the inevitable return of Carr's mind to the great matter of trousers—which seems to have become his King Charles's head. It is as though the whole wretchedness of war had become concentrated in a malevolent personal attack on those splendid trousers. On the other hand, the release of laughter allows us, for a moment, to see some serious things. One is that patriotism and duty exist, and that they matter. Tzara and Joyce, in their different ways, ridicule patriotism; Lenin will undermine it (for the Germans allow his return, precisely, because it will spoil the Russian war effort); so only Carr, in his foolish yet decent way, goes off to fight for whatever it is—for those "brave little Belgians" and "saucy little Serbians." It seems clear that Stoppard likes him for it. Another thing that emerges is the horror of war, conveyed less by words like "horror" or tragic images than by our sense of war's effect on the mind of Carr, which flees violently and eccentrically from its memories. He was a shell-shocked victim; he needed the somewhat unreal peace and calm of Switzerland—and of art—to recover. The third thing that Stoppard makes us perceive, though not for long, is the huge distance between Flanders and England, between trench warfare and civilized life. In their silly way, good trousers are an emblem of civilization, as of high art. They give a rare aesthetic pleasure to the wearer and the beholder. In wartime, in the trenches, they have no place—and neither do the frivolities of art and society that can (sometimes) make civilized life such fun, and even worth fighting to preserve.

Let me move on, with Stoppard, to higher things like coats and hats. Tzara, the careless aesthete, wears colorful flannels and a straw boater, right out of Wilde's second act; so too does Carr when he plays the no-good brother. Joyce wears mismatched coats and trousers, partly from absentmindedness, partly out of a wish to be different and a liking (which does wonders in his art) for incongruity. But it is the hats that become a dramatic metaphor of good and bad art. As the play opens, Tzara is pulling words out of a hat at random, in the library. This reflects his nonsense principles and was the actual practice of Dadaist poets—though it is typical of Stoppard's inside jokes that the sequence of English nonsense words forms what is in fact a French limerick. There is sense to his nonsense. Later, Tzara tears a Shakespearean sonnet into pieces, throwing the separate words into Joyce's hat (which he borrows for the purpose). Gwen sadly recites the lost sonnet, "Shall I compare thee to a summer's day?" (an example, incidentally, of Stoppard's way of reminding us of what is being parodied), and then she pulls out a random sequence of words, and reads them aloud. The result is oddly obscene—another parlor trick of the comic playwright.

There may be a suggestion here that Tzara is a feeble imitator of genuinely revolutionary art, such as Joyce is currently about in his *Ulysses*. (People wonder what Joyce is doing, reading Homer together with the Dublin street directory for 1904. "I admit it's an unusual combination of sources," says Carr, "but not wholly without possibilities.") Tzara makes fun of Joyce's poems as "old hat." But Joyce does better. Even as he catechizes Tzara, "Is it the case that within a remarkably short time performances of this kind made Dada in general and Tzara in particular names to conjure with wherever art was discussed?" he pulls a white carnation, apparently made from the bits of paper, out of his hat. This is followed by colored handkerchiefs, by the flags of several countries, and—after Joyce describes the real artist as a "magician put among men to gratify, capriciously, their urge for immortality"—by a rabbit. The point is not, of course, that Joyce can really do magic. Neither, for that matter, can the actor, upon whom Stoppard makes rather large demands. The point is rather that the genuinely creative artist gives real pleasure to people, like a magician or entertainer who seems to bring something out of nothing. He is a creator, though still a bit of a trickster—unlike Tzara, who ends up breaking pots. Joyce will give new immortality to Homer's life-giving epic from a world that is all too easily reduced to fragments, to broken pots. He raises imposture to art as one might turn bits of paper in a hat into a white carnation. It is a trick, but a *good* trick.

If there is one serious problem underlying *Travesties*, it is the question, "What is the artist's responsibility to society?" It has come up in other plays of Stoppard's, most notably in *Artist Descending a Staircase*; it is asked about related occupations like that of the journalist or reviewer (*The Real Inspector Hound, Night and Day*), or the professor (*Jumpers, Professional Foul*). Stoppard evidently knows from the inside how much pleasure the artist has, or the aesthete, or the professor, in escaping from the usual confusion of things into a world of calm, order, and logical structure. Often he portrays a sensitive person overcome by life—by what he feels to be its crowded, messy, threatening, and emotionally overwhelming nature—who wants to take refuge at the feet of a great egotistic aesthete (*Lord Malquist and Mr. Moon*), or in a hospital where he will be wholly cared for (*A Separate Peace*), or in a steady, unending routine of ordered work (*If You're Glad, I'll Be Frank, Albert's Bridge*). There must be something of Stoppard himself in all of these gentle lunatics, as well as in the aesthete who controls his existence with style, both of language and of dress. In *Travesties* Switzerland itself seems a magical refuge, with its peace and its regularity of existence: not only for wandering artists, pretenders, spies, and other riffraff, but for a normal person like Carr who has gone through war. We all need to escape. Some of us need it more than others. But the real demands of life, of history, of passion—the chaos of things—are heard all the more clearly for the quiet, and they make a memorable claim.

Stoppard's own feelings are much involved in the question of the artist's responsibility, and he has evolved certain convictions about life and art that come out, again and again, in his plays, as well as (increasingly) in statements outside the theater. He is very critical (not least from personal experience and from self-knowledge) of the behavior of artists and intellectuals, of the claims they make, the privileges they demand, and the irresponsible way in which they often behave, which may connive at evil or help to bring it about.[51] At the same time, he is thoroughly opposed to the coercion of artists and intellectuals and their unjust treatment when they speak out, by totalitarian governments. His plays seldom make a simple statement about things. Often they show contradictions. Logic matters, but professional logicians are useless, or worse. Freedom of the press is necessary, but it can be betrayed by British journalists, readers, and union leaders, as well as by cynical African dictators. And art—there is no simple answer here either. Stoppard's comedies are exploratory, not didactic; he writes plays not least to find out what he thinks.[52] He has a gift of bringing out relations between different things, different sides of life, through techniques like wordplay and associative metaphors: trousers, hats, and "Dada." But meanings tend to be opened up, not foreclosed. Above all, they are explored through the agon technique, of confrontation between characters who set each other off with their different personalities, convictions, and ideas. Let me summarize three such agons from *Travesties*.

(1) *Carr versus Tzara*. Under a superficial veneer of friendship out of Wilde, the two fight bitterly, especially over war and patriotism. Carr is a British gentleman, bourgeois, snobbish, provincial, something of a philistine in artistic manners; what he really likes is Gilbert and Sullivan (which is to his credit), and he is only drawn into playing Algernon in Wilde's comedy by the possibilities of dressing up that it will offer him. At the same time, as we saw, Carr is a decent person. He is moral and patriotic, though he tends to think, as he speaks, largely through clichés; he is not and cannot be very reflective. Tzara shows up Carr's patriotism as, it seems, absurd by demonstrating the irrational nature of war in general and the First World War in particular. He is very likely right. In turn Carr denounces the privileged, irresponsible position of the artist. What a wonderful thing it is—how did he ever come by it? And he too seems right—the more so because Tzara is delighted to display his own self-negating program of decadent nihilism. It is all nonsense (though it is such delightful nonsense, with comically redeeming wit out of Wilde and others). What Tzara has, finally, against contemporary society is that it has room for a person like himself. (This is like Groucho Marx's statement that he "wouldn't belong to a club that would have me.")

(2) *Joyce versus Carr and Tzara*. As a man, Joyce resembles Tzara in being something of a fraud. He is (but this is filtered through old Carr's obsessive memories of litigation and trousers) a parasite and a sponge, living off other people's money, always borrowing a pound or two, and building up library fines on someone else's ticket. In appearance, in

speech, he is a self-dramatizing poseur—and perhaps a less honest one than Tzara. Yet he is genuinely creative, where Tzara is not. He does have a contagious wit and sense of style. His personal borrowings may be shabby, but his literary borrowings and recombinations are quite splendid. His *Ulysses* is a great work, worth the cost. He shirks normal duties, like going to war, and makes fun of patriotism, but his cultural efforts, of putting on Wilde and other plays, do redound to the credit of Great Britain; and to the question, "What did you do during the Great War?" the answer, "I wrote Ulysses," is not a bad one after all. Joyce is an irresponsible man, but a good artist.

(3) *Lenin versus the artists.* This is a different kind of confrontation, for after Lenin reaches Russia, he is represented as being completely in charge, and he speaks through monologues; his wife makes personal observations in between. Notice that he has abandoned the bowler hat that he wore earlier; he is dressed conservatively in a three-piece suit, but a famous photograph is shown in which he grips a worker's cloth cap in his right hand while he speaks. (This picks up Tzara's comment that "history comes out of a hat, too.") Lenin insists on the artist's complete responsibility to society, and hence on society's total control of art. He points out, in a letter to Gorky, that artists tend to be irresponsible: Gorky himself said once that "We artists are irresponsible," and now he is complaining about a few bourgeois intellectuals who have been thrown in jail. (This looks forward to the modern injustices by which Stoppard is disturbed.) Evidently Lenin has decided to be ruthless about artistic freedom. Institutions too, like libraries, are to be controlled (it was in the library, of course, that Lenin built his ideas, together with Joyce and, to some extent, Tzara). Yet there is a price to be paid. Lenin's wife comments, sadly, on how Lenin really preferred bourgeois literature like Pushkin to the trash that passes itself off as revolutionary. He was moved, too, by Beethoven—but he could not afford to let himself be moved. There is a sad contradiction here, as well as a reminder that great art, which is universally recognizable, helps to make life interesting, worthwhile, and fully human.

What, then, is Stoppard's conclusion about the artist's responsibility to society? It would be the neatest trick of the week if he came up with a clear and simple answer; it would also go against the play's trend, which is to expose the relation between things but also their complexity. Artists are irresponsible people; that seems necessary, if they are to maintain their artistic integrity, and the only real alternative is art in the service of the state; but Tzara, the fully irresponsible artist, seems to deny art in practice as much as Lenin does in theory. Perhaps the better artists, however irresponsible their personal lives are, still serve society by making human life richer through their art, and can do so because, in their art, they are responsible to something genuine: to style, wit, intellect, self-honesty. This is the case with Joyce. It is presumably the case with Wilde, and with Stoppard. It is, all the same, not a simple answer to the question, as old Carr's closing remarks might remind us:

> I learned three things in Zurich during the war. I wrote them down. Firstly, you're either a revolutionary or you're not, and if you're not you might as well be an artist as anything else. Secondly, if you can't be an artist, you might as well be a revolutionary . . . I forget the third thing.
>
> (BLACKOUT.)

We are all a little like old Carr. Our thought and experience over the years seem to yield great insights, only these don't sound right in the end, or else they disappear. Perhaps Stoppard is telling us not to try to draw a moral from the play. It does, I think, clear the mind about life and art. And it exemplifies the power of good art that Joyce defends, of enriching human life and making it meaningful.

Several months after writing the above, I had the fortune to see a superb performance of *Travesties* by our local repertory company.[53] It was the more enjoyable because they did a fine *Earnest* two weeks before, and they built on it for *Travesties*, even using some of the same sets and props and comic business. It was an exhilarating evening. The singing and dancing, the vaudeville turns, the self-parodying comic movements, brought out much fun that Stoppard intended for his play, or would have welcomed. The theatrical magic was there, and it worked, all the way through. Even Cecily's very long lecture about Lenin worked, despite the obvious risk (which Stoppard intentionally took) of boring the audience. Just how it worked would be hard to explain. A comic episode, with the disguised Carr, helped to break it up; a memorable striptease by Cecily (all in Carr's mind, and doubtless of great symbolic value, like the trousers, coats, and hats) followed and balanced it. We could say that Stoppard took the risk (an academic lecture? on Lenin?) and carried it off, just for the fun of it; but in retrospect the overall balance of characters, ideas, and moods seems more than clever. It is oddly moving, and it goes deeply into modern life.

Stoppard flirts with tragedy, as great comic poets will. In the second act we feel the enormous shadow of the totalitarian state stretching out over art and thought and human life. If Lenin's triumphant return to Russia, as narrated by Nadya, begins with the (historic) consideration of various disguises that he might try and proceeds through a dramatic train journey to an even more dramatic arrival, we are reminded that history itself, as enacted and (still more) as remembered, is very like theater; but this recognition, which borders on the comic or the absurd, is tempered by the painful human situation of Lenin himself, who must give up his personal feelings, his own artistic preferences and tastes, in the interest of an increasingly barren revolution. Art is swallowed up in political revolution, and humanity, it seems, is swallowed up with it. The play becomes frightening, and sad. But then Lenin and his wife disappear from the stage, and the wild world of comedy returns for a Wildean resolution, with song and dance and a double marriage. In one sense the escape seems quite unreal. In another sense it is an escape into a world of art, humanity, and joy that is *more* real (as well as brighter) than Lenin's Russia. The play is exhilarating because it is a good and true escape: and that, perhaps, is as much as can be said for any comedy.

16   Acharnians, *I:* The Creative Word

LIKE *Travesties*, the *Acharnians* has two interwoven comic ideas, superimposing art on politics.[54] The more obvious of the two is "the separate peace." This plot has the easily recognizable structure of what I have called "Dionysian fairy tale."

(1) The hero, Dicaeopolis, is frustrated and discomfited by a bad situation, the misery of continuing war, which is abetted by politicians and trickster-diplomats both domestic and foreign. He stands for the common man, but is more daring. At first his courage in speaking out, in demanding peace, in exposing imposters (like the child who proclaims, "The emperor has no clothes"), exposes him to more than usual rebuffs and humiliations—which the audience will enjoy. But he is not downed, and his indomitable will meets with supernatural help. He takes advantage of a godsent opportunity, the appearance of a "half-divine" Amphitheos empowered by the gods to make peace; but since Amphitheos is, naturally, rejected by the mad Assembly, Dicaeopolis, who now embodies the "just city" in his private person, commissions Amphitheos to make a private peace for himself and his family alone. Amphitheos goes off; he returns shortly afterwards with magical *spondai*, "libations," that are also, by a wordplay, "peace treaties." Dicaeopolis savors them, finds them good, and prepares to celebrate, and to savor, the joys of peace.

(2) But the peace is challenged by the angry chorus of old Marathon veterans. They want to stone Dicaeopolis to death as a traitor. He eludes their anger, first by melodramatic tricks out of tragedy, together with commonsensical arguments, then by what amounts to another sort of magic: borrowing a tragic beggar's costume from Euripides' rag-and-bone shop of the soul, which fills him with contagious sophistic argumentation to win his case before the chorus-as-jury. He not only defends himself but justifies making peace with Sparta. The chorus is half convinced; half, still opposed, call in the braggart captain Lamachus as their

champion; but that imposter is put down by Dicaeopolis, partly with argument, partly with buffoonery. This completes the agon, or loose series of contests, in which Dicaeopolis fights for the peace that he has achieved.

(3) Dicaeopolis now enjoys his just deserts, or desserts. He enjoys, as in a wish-fulfillment dream or fairy tale, a private market in which all good things come to him effortlessly: a Megarian with "piggies" for sale (these are actually his daughters), a Theban with all manner of fish, flesh, and fowl, culminating in a delectable Copaic Eel. Sycophants and other imposters are beaten away; Dicaeopolis keeps the drops of peace (which, from being a magic drink, has now turned into a healing ointment) mainly to himself; the rest have not earned it and will not enjoy it. This is fairy-tale justice. The chorus admire his triumph, which is also set against the mishaps of the hero-manqué Lamachus. "Thou preparest a table for me / in the presence of mine enemies." The play reaches a climax in two scenes of counterpoint. Dicaeopolis, called to feast with the priest of Dionysus, prepares his picnic basket with all the accoutrements of eating; Lamachus, called to a frontier skirmish in the snow, prepares his knapsack and arms for battle. Later, after the comic version of a messenger's speech, Lamachus returns, hobbling, with a broken ankle and so forth, upheld by two servants, while Dicaeopolis returns from the feast, reveling, upheld by two whores. His victory, which is a victory of Dionysus over the war god, is now complete.

Critics have sometimes complained that the play's later scenes are anticlimactic, episodic. One could reply, as Douglass Parker has done in a book, as yet unpublished, on the unity of the *Acharnians*, both that the scenes are carefully contrived and balanced, and that they are required, in detail, by the play's movement from misery to happiness, from frustration to success, and, in very concrete terms, from a meager diet of garlic (and even *that* is threatened by war) to a superabundance of good food, wine, and sex. I would add that this comedy, like the *Peace*, not only plays out a recovery of the good things of peace in a teasing manner before the audience (as also, in the *Acharnians*, before the envious chorus), but gives them an experience of recovery, of participation in the delights of peace, that must remind them feelingly of what they have lost. I give one example where the sensuality of the language is especially important, a comparison between shadow and substance, from the double "arming" scene:

Lam. Bring me hither my plumes, my helmet's plumes!
Dic. Bring me hither my ducks. My thrushes also.
Lam. How lovely, fair, and white is the ostrich plume!
Dic. How lovely, warm, and brown is the roasted duckling!

Actually, Dicaeopolis uses a word, *phatta*, that the dictionary translates as "wild pigeon" or "ringdove." Roast ringdove may be delicious, as quail is said to be, but it is out of my experience; roast duck has more general appeal today, while still remaining fowl. If I were rewriting the *Acharnians*, I would develop my own thematic contrast between the turkey and the bald eagle: for roast turkey, with mashed or sweet potatoes, and cranberry jelly, and rolls, and rich hot gravy, and apple pie and pumpkin pie, would surely be the right Thanksgiving meal for an American equivalent of Dicaeopolis to celebrate with; the bald eagle, that fierce emblem of national pride, remains inedible. (It is a crime to kill, let alone eat, a bald eagle. Benjamin Franklin was surely right when he proposed that the wild turkey, not the eagle, should be the national bird.) Anyway, real nourishment wins out in comedy. Lamachus' plumes, waving proudly from his helmet, are good for nothing in real human terms; nobody ever dined well on "boastrich plumes." It is time that Athens went on a better diet.

Notice that the image of feathers has, characteristically for comedy—I am thinking of those hats in *Travesties*—a life of its own.[55] "He has winged himself for the dinner," sing the admiring chorus, of Dicaeopolis. "He has high, confident thoughts. As emblem of his way of life, he has scattered these feathers before his door." They refer to, as it were, turkey feathers, contrasting these with Lamachus' gorgeous but unavailing plumage. But while Lamachus' plumes are discredited—and will, shortly, be brought quite literally to the dust—Dicaeopolis becomes metaphorically "winged." The verb, *epterōtai* ("he has become winged"), is a figurative word for mental excitement. It also has a sexual meaning, implying erection, that will be manifested in the last scene. But there is more. For the comic hero's triumph to be complete, he must take wing from sullen earth. Eating and drinking lead to sex; one recovery leads to further aspiration. By a logic of their own—and the turkey feathers are an example of a minor comic idea, supporting a larger one—the feathers do more than embody a thematic victory of fowl that is really fair over seeming-fair that is foul in its consequences. They point to the essence of the comic hero. He is fat, and heavy, and knows the true value of good food and drink—and he will fly. Nothing less than a total reversal of the laws of ordinary life will do. Admiringly, like the chorus, we recognize that this outrageous happiness is what we really want. It is the comic playwright's business to bring us back to that recognition. What we do afterwards, outside the theater, is not, in the same way, his affair.

I could comment further on other images and comic ideas employed by Aristophanes to flesh out and unify his play of "the separate peace." The *Acharnians*, though the earliest comedy of Aristophanes extant, shows mastery of the techniques of what Aristophanes might have called the old comedy: it also rehearses themes, like the unmasking of deception, the recovery of peace, and the transformation of poverty into plenty and weariness into rejuvenation, that recur throughout his plays and belong generally to "Dionysian fairy tale." Yet let me backtrack. The *Acharnians* is not as simple an "old comedy" as it seems. There are odd contradictions in it: a man called "Just City" who acts apart from the city; a fair-minded man who is intensely selfish; a common man who masters sophisticated pleading. And all this is bound up with a second comic idea, the parodying of Euripides' *Telephus*. The figures of this comedy find themselves reenacting parts in *Telephus* much as Stoppard's characters play parts out of *The Importance of Being Earnest*.[56] Dicaeopolis plays the beggar-hero, Prince Telephus: first in melodramatic fashion, snatching up a coal scuttle as hostage (their coal being very "dear" to the Acharnians), as Telephus seems to have snatched up the baby Orestes, to save his life and get a hearing; then, explicitly, going to Euripides' house for the complete Telephus costume, in which he makes a Euripidean plea before the chorus. These, the old Acharnians, by a wordplay become the Ach-aeans. And Lamachus, when he appears, seems to be Achilles. The parody moves in and out, sporadically, but is not forgotten; it reaches its climax in a comic version of the tragic messenger's speech, in which the hero Lamachus' feather is broken and dies, but the man survives to run, ignominiously, into a spear—which is where Telephus started.[57]

Why all this parody? And what has it all to do with the comic plot of "a separate peace"? I want, in the next sections, to give a detailed analysis of Dicaeopolis' Telephus speech, the speech in rags, which works on several levels at once, joining serious meanings with comic incongruities that remind us not to take statements at face value; and then, to look at Aristophanes' comedy against its tragic background. But first I want to pursue the matter of wordplay. It is easy to see that Aristophanes is very fond of puns, which he uses constantly to amuse his audience. But the pun, in Aristophanes, is more than casual fun, and more than the comic reinforcement of a preconceived idea: it is itself a comic idea, or *epinoia*, with which the poet thinks, builds, and connects.[58] There is nothing like wordplay for leading us into the creative process by which comic ideas are joined together and a play is built. I shall give six examples. Two are "confirming" puns; three are puns that take on dramatic life, helping to create scenes. The sixth pun is seminal, creative on a larger scale, part of the comic idea on which the *Acharnians* is constructed and from which other, lesser ideas and images are derived. It is an *epinoia* par excellence.

Let us begin the account of puns by relaxing. The analysis of a comic plot and the relation of its parts to one another requires a certain attention; now it is time for the thought-wearied mind (mine and yours) to relax, to rest a little in fooling around. Aristophanes likes to use familiar puns, old chestnuts, to relax and warm up his audience, especially in his prologues, much as Shakespeare falls back on wordplays with "angel" or "crown," or with "sole" and "soul." And one of the simplest, most childish sorts of wordplay is the pun on proper names. Dicaeopolis' foil is called Lamachus. That was the name of a real-life military personage. We cannot know whether the historic Lamachus ever met Aristophanes, or whether he was pompous in real life; the point is rather that *this* Lamachus is chosen for his name, which includes the root of "battle," *mach-*. He was destined, it seems, to embody the pretensions of the military mind and the miseries of war.[59] We must not forget how much pleasure Aristophanes took in this way of thinking, to which wordplay constitutes a type of proof, nails a point home. Dada, dada, dada!

The translator, or adapter, of Aristophanes works creatively with words, and he catches, if he is successful, some of the comic poet's original pleasure in creating and shaping an imaginary world by the power of words and the relationships discovered through them. It is good to realize something of this pleasure. The comic poet is lord and sovereign of an imaginary country, a person of godlike power, long before his play reaches the stage for which it is intended. I shared some of that pleasure when I wrote a very free adaptation of the *Acharnians* called "Drum and Guitar" in 1967. It was intended to reach Broadway and help end the Vietnam war—but no matter. The villain was General Winmoreland (a close associate of General Dynamics and other Generals, like Motors and Electric, who made up the military-industrial complex). It is curious how dated the play seems today (much more so than the *Acharnians*), and how jokes on names that gave me such pleasure then, like General Winmoreland, and the militaristic Cardinal Spellbinder, and (by contrast) the effete cult leader Timofey Weary, would require explanatory footnotes today. But the point remains, that *I* had great pleasure in constructing that imaginary world, in weaving those names into a pattern of comic action in which everything seemed somehow to fit.

There were good moments in my play, like the time when my hero required a magic wand in order to turn the leader of the militant local DAR chapter into the young and beautiful Miss Columbia. He did it simply by calling to the stage manager to bring him a "real magic wand." (There was some dubious byplay with the audience, along the lines of, "Do you believe in fairies? If you believe, clap your hands"—from *Peter Pan*.) I mention all this because it gives me pleasure; and that pleasure in the free play of fantasy, bordering on paranoia, is very much to the point.

I was *not* able to do justice to one of the best wordplays in the *Acharnians*. Dicaeopolis is enlisting the chorus on his side through a shared indignation that old men (like them) remain in the ranks, while young swells dodge the draft and are paid, overly paid, for missions of alleged diplomacy:

> Some are in Thrace, earning a hundred dollars per diem;
> some are with Chares, some among the Chaonians,
> and some in Camarina and in Gela and in Catagela.
>
> (602, 604, 606)

Behind the joke, which unfortunately must be footnoted today, lie current anxieties. Aristophanes ties these up playfully with his major satiric theme, of gullibility and deception. His point is that the Athenians have lost sight of the real, tangible benefits of ending the war and making peace, partly through their justified but unproductive anger at Sparta, but also because they are continually tricked by foreign governments, and by their own boondoggling diplomats, into hoping for some grand but unlikely (or risky) alliance, or else for some grand (but even more risky) extension of their sphere of power and influence in the western Mediterranean, in southern Italy and Sicily. Two jokes clinch the point. First, the name "Chaonians," the name of a real tribe in northern Greece, suggests at once the chaos of Athenian foreign policy and foreign involvements (my own effort was, "in Cambodia, and Laos, and—Chaos") and also the deceptiveness of politicians: for words involving the root *cha-*, "to gape wide," are used throughout this play, and also throughout the *Knights*, to denote stupid and dangerous gullibility. The Athenians sit openmouthed, taken in by flattery and falsehood. Again, they are mocked (*gelaō* means "to laugh," *katagelaō* "to mock" someone) by the imposters, domestic and foreign, who take advantage of them. Gela is a real Sicilian town. So is Catana, the name we expect to follow. But Catagela is a marvelous invention that proves Aristophanes' point, binding up the connections between gullibility, deception, and foreign policy (or lack of policy). It exemplifies the comic logic, the discovery of play relationships, that gave Aristophanes such great pleasure. But more than that, it achieves a momentary and sparkling existence of its own.[60] It is a kind of Platonic Form, an eternal Mocksville. As a symbolic triumph, a shaping of order out of chaos, it points ahead to the larger victory of Dicaeopolis; for only by recovering our playful, imaginative, reordering powers can we overcome political deception and turn the mockery against our enemies. The wordplay, like the wine-drinking, is a Dionysian sacrament of release, a turning point at which defeat is reversed into victory.

In a different way wordplays can become actors, generating comic scenes around themselves. As said earlier, *spondai* can mean "libations" but also "peace treaty"; so Dicaeopolis secures a private peace treaty by obtaining and quaffing the right, magical drinks of wine.[61] The value of this wordplay is tested and confirmed by further correspondences during the wine-tasting scene: for example, the newer, five-year wine (= shorter-term treaty) smells of pitch (or recent bottling = ship-outfitting for new naval engagements). The political point is clear. Only a genuine long-term agreement will do; otherwise the war will only be delayed, the arms race encouraged. Yet the political meaning of the *spondai* is not primary. Drinking is an end, not a means. Dicaeopolis' reception of the *spondai* embodies Dionysian release and recovery, which are at the heart of the play, and anticipates the full, explicitly Dionysian celebration with which the play will end. War is a wretched business all around; in comedy it is seen as an interruption of the feast—as by people who get drunk and quarrelsome and smash things. The point is to restore life's proper business, which is feasting. (One might say of war what Wilde said of work, that it is the curse of the drinking classes.) It is an axiom of Aristophanes' that all good things are integrally connected, including food, drink, sex, country, peace, theater, and holiday. A nodal pun like *spondai*, linking wine and peace (and by implication Dionysus), is partly confirmatory for Aristophanes of life's comic unity, though here it has a creative role in building a simple scene and advancing the plot of "the separate peace."

A later scene is built on a pun on the word *choiros*, which means "pig" but is also a slang word, "cunt"; a Megarian comes to Dicaeopolis' private market, to sell his two girls disguised as "mystery piggies."[62] (In my "Drum and Guitar" I tried a comparable scene, about "pussy from Vietnam," but it remained an academic exercise: the life wasn't there.) Aristophanes vivifies the basic obscene joke with dialect humor, which is itself a kind of half-disguise, enabling the audience to laugh at a silly foreigner while also playing a guessing game, of seeing through word-disguises; he uses subsidiary jokes, variations on the basic food-and-sex motif, that must have been accompanied by a good deal of comic business, especially gesturing. Thus the mystery piggies will be sacrificed later on, to Aphrodite; their meat will taste most succulent when it is placed on the spit; and so forth. It is coarse, old-style buffoonery. In fact it is what the Athenians, with their superior wit, might have called "Megarian humor."[63] (They told Megarian jokes when they weren't telling Boeotian jokes.) Behind the jokes are painful glimpses of history and the wretchedness of war. Shortly before, in Dicaeopolis' speech, Aristophanes traced the war back to Pericles' embargo on Megarian goods, the famous "Megarian Decree" that brought that city to starvation, so that, naturally, it appealed to the Peloponnesians for help.[64] Starvation is not funny, nor prostitution born of war. There is a real sense of pain here. Comedy borders on tragedy. But what keeps the scene comic is the figure of the Megarian father. He is shameless, the embodiment of that vulgar "Megarian humor." He is also immoral and opportunistic, like Jeeter Lester in *Tobacco Farm* or some of Steinbeck's funny poor, or Flannery O'Connor's; and he gets what he wants, even though Dicaeopolis isn't really taken in (the two play along together as in a vaudeville bit), and all he gets is, touchingly, the very ordinary salt and garlic—the simple essentials—that Megara used to produce. The Megarian is partly a scapegoat who takes on, as Lamachus will later, the misery that was Dicaeopolis' lot. He also shows, in his grotesque way, that the human spirit can survive catastrophe; perhaps also, that in a more festive world this backwards transformation of people into animals need never have happened.

I shall return to the Megarian scene, which still makes me uncomfortable; but since my present concern is with the comic ideas, I want to suggest some ways in which the *choiros* pun and scene link up with others to form an artistic whole.

They fall, first of all, into a larger pattern of transformations. Things are always turning into one another, metaphorically and dramatically, in this play; it is a little like *Alice.* A coal scuttle may be seized and taken hostage like a baby, for the Acharnians depend on charcoal for their meager living, which has worsened under pressure of war. In Megara, not only do girls become meat, but bread becomes divinity: isn't it "dear as the gods"? In the next scenes, Dicaeopolis will welcome an eel from Lake Copais, much as a husband in tragedy might welcome a long-lost wife, or a father his daughter, and a nasty little sycophant will be packed up like pottery and exported to Thebes (he is, after all, a crackpot). But how are all these transformations connected? Most of them seem to reflect the unnaturalness of war, its power to pervert ordinary feelings and values. At the same time, they seem expressive of Dicaeopolis' increasing mastery of things, and of the transforming power of Dionysus that makes his victory possible.

There is, second, an imaginative link between the Megarian scene and the two sycophant scenes. This is supported by still another wordplay. The word *sycophantēs*, which came to mean "informer" and then, more generally, any shyster, trickster, or flatterer, originally had the literal meaning of "one who shows up figs." The connection came about because, when foreign produce was contraband, a breed of self-appointed informers came forward to denounce the illegal products—and make a tidy profit for themselves. (I remember how a tough, though not profiteering, group went around American supermarkets in the 1950s denouncing Polish ham as part of the international communist conspiracy.) Aristophanes has Dicaeopolis argue earlier that these sycophants helped bring on the war by enforcing the Megarian embargo, which never should have been promulgated in the first place, let alone put into practice. But there is another connection with the scene of "Megarian humor," for "figs" are also slang for male or female genitalia.[65] "Would you eat figs?" asks Dicaeopolis, and the piggies oink enthusiastically. No wonder the first sycophant appears to "show" the piggies as contraband. His business is quite literally obscene. It is also, in a sense, not altogether different from the business of the dirty-minded Old Comedy writer, who

likes his Megarian humor and knows its value to the overall comedy—
yet who, as *his* name, *Aristo-phanēs*, implies, wants ultimately to "show
the best" to his audience.

There is a third, inverse imaginative link, between the piggies and the
eel, as Dicaeopolis moves from simple sexual enjoyment to a higher,
more lyrical and erotic experience. As he sits in his private agora, all
good things come to him of their own accord, as in a wish-fulfillment
dream or a return of the Golden Age of old. Earlier, it was the Megarian
with the piggies; now it is a splendid procession from Boeotia, which is
enemy territory but the home of many good things to eat, fish, flesh, and
fowl. The procession enters, to the clamor of Theban bagpipes. We savor
its approach. The good things from Boeotia are listed, in an incongruous
but mouth-watering catalogue; and they find their climax in the epiphany of an eel from Lake Copais, a supreme delicacy, whom Dicaeopolis
welcomes as a long-lost love out of a recognition scene in tragedy.

> O dearest one, O long-desired lady,
> How we poor players have longed for your return;
> Morychus also. Servants, kindly produce
> brazier and bellows for the barbecue.
> My boys, behold the noblest-born of eels
> (almost six years we've spent in yearning for her);
> Address her, children. I will even provide you
> with charcoal for the stranger-lady's sake.
> But lead her in.
>   Oh, never, not even dying, ma'am,
> may I be separated from you—in your sauce *bonne femme*.
>   (885–94)

It is splendid fun: the parody of Euripides, the alternation of tragic and
everyday diction, the juxtaposition of a sentimental family reunion (and
what could be more poignant than a recognition scene out of Euripides?)
with references to a good fish fry and to the notorious gourmand Mory-
chus. Yet the comic address is more than parody. It is curiously moving,
lyrical in its own right. Why is the fusion of eel and lady so convincing?[66]
Partly it is because, as said earlier, Aristophanes perceives all good things
in terms of one another: food, drink, sex, country, holiday, peace, theater. Comic joy is polymorphous and synaesthetic. Partly, too, we come
to accept the recurrent transformation pattern. If wartime turns girls into
meat, the process is neatly reversed when peace transforms an eel into a
beautiful lady. That is just what we expect from Dionysian fairy tale. But
it is the feeling of *pothos*, yearning, that marks the scene as special for us.
Aristophanes may begin with the lowest common denominator of human needs, for food, drink, and sex; but what is especially human is to
desire, not just anything to eat, not just any old fish, but something
special: the Copaic Eel. (An equivalent today might be *pothos* for a good

Havana cigar.) Human wishes may begin low, but they end high; they become invested (as animal needs do not) with erotic fantasy; and they embrace, in a juxtaposition that is comical but also true and beautiful, the ridiculous and the sublime. The scene of the Copaic Eel is not just parody. It *is* a recognition scene, the high point of the experience of recovery and recognition—of peace, joy, what we really want—that the play provides. To remember, in war and misery, what peace is, and joy, and the richness of things: *that* is the real recognition that Aristophanes gives us, in this Dionysian comedy. It can transform us, and the world around us, if we let it. Peace is like a fairy tale come true.

I may seem to have wandered far from a simple consideration of puns as fundamental comic ideas. If I have, it was not from willfulness, for the nature of an Aristophanic pun is to be creative, to link up with other puns, and the nature of a comic idea in Aristophanes is to link up with other comic ideas, not to exist in isolation. Lamachus and Catagela, *spondai* and *choiros* and *sycophantēs*, all conspire to play together imaginatively, to shape a comedy in words, images, and actions. The ultimate comic idea is the play itself, the sum of all the rest, brought to creation on the stage before a living, appreciative audience who take pleasure in it.

But this brings me to my last pun, which involves, precisely, pleasure and pain. It is on the *Acharnēs*, the charcoal-burning mountaineers who suffered especially from the early years of the war, and who give the play its title. Douglass Parker, that supreme master of wordplay, points out that by a recurrent suggestion in the play, they are the "joyless people," the *a-char-nēs*. (The root meaning "joy" is *-char*.) Their dramatic role is to oppose Dicaeopolis and to reject peace, and hence to reject the possibility of joy. But the poet's imagination also transforms them into the *Achaioi* or "Achaeans," the people whom Prince Telephus must confront in Euripides' tragedy. These too chose war, to everyone's sorrow. They are, so to speak, the well-grieved Ache-aeans. The play on *Acharnēs/Achaioi* helps establish the parody.[67] It also leads, through parody, to an exploration of rhetoric and tragedy, and especially tragic rhetoric, in relation to the real nature of human life. Through parody and self-parody, and many disguises, it moves toward an unmasking of the truth.

17   Acharnians, *II:*
The See-through Rags

IN Euripides' *Telephus*, as best we can reconstruct its
action, the Mysian prince Telephus arrives at Argos disguised in beggar's
rags.[68] He has been wounded by Achilles' spear in a pre-Trojan skirmish,
and an oracle has foretold that he can only be healed by that same spear.
He perhaps confides in Clytemnestra, who gives him advice. Later on, he
listens to a council of war, and he joins in, giving a dangerous speech in
which he defends the absent "Telephus" for fighting the Greeks and
criticizes the war against Troy as unjust—waged for Menelaus' bad wife.
The council is disturbed; Menelaus and Agamemnon may argue; Odysseus arrives, announces the presence of a spy; and after a search, Telephus is discovered. At this point he may seize the baby Orestes and make
a further, personal plea. The Greeks eventually accept him (though
Achilles, coming in late, may be displeased), promise him healing, and in
return are promised that he will lead them to Troy, though not fight
there. He turns out, by a last irony, to be Greek-born, not an alien after
all.

This reconstruction is speculative; and since it is supported in part by
Aristophanes' two parodies of the *Telephus*, in the *Acharnians* and again
in the *Thesmophoriazusae*, we run some risk of circular argument when
we try to describe how Aristophanes' parody works. If only we had
Telephus, as we have *Earnest*! Still, the hypothetical reconstruction is
backed by enough evidence outside comedy to let us see what Aristophanes makes of Telephus' beggar-disguise and his speech to the Achar-
nians/Achaeans.

In the *Acharnians* the search for the spy is shifted to an earlier time:
the angry chorus of old Marathon fighters, now charcoal-burners and
(usually) weary old men, enter in pursuit of the traitor, to stone him.
Dicaeopolis tries to reason with them, to calm them down. Telephus had
spoken proudly, in Euripides' play:

> Agamemnon, not even if a man holding an ax
> were about to bring it down upon my neck,
> will I keep silent, having a just reply.[69]

The comic hero more modestly proposes to speak with his head over a chopping block "in case what I say isn't right, and doesn't seem so to the majority." The audience will catch the silliness, if not the specific parody—the more so, when Dicaeopolis catches up a coal scuttle as hostage. (It is like those great moments in Gilbert and Sullivan operas: as when the pirates, called upon to surrender in Queen Victoria's name, do so instantly because, being gentlemanly pirates, they "love our Queen.") The Acharnians are thrown into consternation. They plead with him; he secures his hearing; everything is ready for the main speech—but the action veers off in a surprising direction.

> *Dic.* Lo, and behold! Here is the chopping block,
> and here's the speaker. Not a very big one;
> still, I won't hide beneath my shield; no, I
> will speak my piece about the Spartan Question.
> And yet, what frightens me, I am familiar
> with country folk. It makes them mighty proud
> when they and Athens get impressive strokes
> from some imposter (whether or not it's true);
> they're sold, and paid for, and they never know it.
> I am also
> familiar with our senior citizens.
> "Off with his head!" That's all they want for lunch.
> And I am familiar, of course, with my own case,
> to wit, what a bad time I had with Cleon
> after the comedy I gave last year.
> He hauled me off into the Council chamber,
> and slandered me, went down on me with lies,
> and covered me with a flood of filthy language—
> I almost suffocated from the crap.
> Wherefore, kindly indulge my oratoric passion;
> let me prepare myself
>   in most pathetic fashion.
> *Chor.* What wrestling tricks
>   are these you play?
> What artful dodges? What delay?
> You can go to Hieronymus
>   for all I care,
> and ask for (something like
>   his facial hair)
> a magic cap

> to make you disappear:
> pull out your tricks (like Sisyphus),
> of almost any shape:
> this is a fight you're simply never
> going to escape.

Dic. It's time to get a persevering soul?
Why then, *Euripides* must be my goal.
[*He goes over to Euripides' house.*]
Knock, Knock. (366–94)

Dicaeopolis had proposed earlier that the Spartans were not altogether to blame. It is a dangerous thesis to argue before countrymen who love patriotic blarney and old men whose temper is normally fierce and bitter, and who snack on voting pebbles. (This looks to the *Wasps*.) But now, abruptly, the speaker turns into Aristophanes, who attacked Cleon in last year's *Babylonians* and was brought by him before the Council on the charge of ridiculing the demos, and in the presence of foreigners.[70] The tongue-lashing was probably accompanied by threats. ("If you do this again . . . !") Aristophanes seems to have submitted quietly—and to have thought about material for later plays. Perhaps, for an Athenian and a comic poet, humiliation was threat enough; perhaps there was a chance that Cleon would reimpose, or try to reimpose, an earlier censorship law restricting the free speech of comedy. Still, even without exaggerating the real danger to Aristophanes or to comedy, we may believe that it *did* take courage: (1) for Aristophanes to speak out before an Athenian audience, including Cleon, and argue that Athens was not necessarily or always right; (2) for Dicaeopolis to speak out before the Acharnian lynch mob, his head over the chopping block, and argue that the war was not entirely the Spartans' fault (a conviction evidently held by Aristophanes); and (3) as it turns out, for Telephus to speak before the warlike Achaeans on behalf of "Telephus" and the Trojans, who had some justice on their side too. The three dangerous speeches will become confused, in comic fashion. But first (this is the surprise) Dicaeopolis/Aristophanes breaks off his plea, asking the chorus to let him prepare himself by dressing up as pitifully as possible. They agree, and he goes to Euripides' house (this being comedy, it is next door)[71] to procure a suitable costume and, with it, a "persevering soul" for the occasion.

The chorus, and the audience with them, wonder what Dicaeopolis will do. They guess, appropriately, that he will use some magical device out of folklore, like the helmet of Hades that makes people invisible. The immediate joke is on Hieronymus, whose long, thick, shaggy hair makes him virtually invisible, but the idea of the magic cap looks forward to the next scene, where Dicaeopolis' Telephus costume will produce a magical effect both on himself, as an inspired speaker, and on his audience. We are warned, also, that this *is* a device. "Use all the tricks you can," say the chorus, "and see if you can fool *us*!" Dicaeopolis will do just that. And so will Aristophanes, whose comic business is to do such tricks and provide such illusions as can be seen through, like Telephus' rags. For if he unmasks others, and unmasks the ingenious devices of tragedy or rhetoric or tragical rhetoric, he also means, in the end, to unmask himself.

The Euripides scene is superb. Dicaeopolis knocks; a haughty intellectual servant tells him that Euripides is busy composing tragedy, but he insists, so the great man is wheeled out on the *ekkyklēma*, the movable platform used to make indoor scenes visible outdoors.[72] The poet is seated aloft, on a high couch, dressed in tragic rags like his own characters'; he is practicing an empathetic "method writing." Dicaeopolis approaches him humbly and begs for a rag from the old play,

> for I must give a long set speech to the chorus;
> if spoken badly, the penalty is death.   (416–17)

(Notice, again, the breaking of what might have been a dramatic illusion if this were not comedy. Dicaeopolis has an actor's work before him, and he thinks of the Acharnians as "the chorus.") "Which rags?" asks Euripides. There are so many ill-dressed heroes in his plays, so many people reduced to utter misery: is it Oeneus? The blind Phoenix? Philoctetes (of the wounded foot)? The crippled Bellerophon? "No, someone much more miserable," says Dicaeopolis each time. The man he wants was "a cripple, a pushy beggar, a great chatterbox." This turns out, of course, to be the Mysian or Mys-erable Telephus, and Euripides directs a servant to give Dicaeopolis the Telephus costume, which is stored between Thyestes' filthy rags and Ino's.[73] Dicaeopolis is delighted, puts on the ragged costume, and instantly asks for more.

> *Dic.* Great Zeus, who *wholly* seest through all things,
>   grant me to dress in most pathetic fashion.
>   Euripides, now that you've made me a present
>   of these fine—rags, give me what goes with them,
>   the little Mysian bonnet, for my head?
>   For I this day must seem a beggar, yet
>   remain myself, and yet seem not to be;
>   and the audience must know just who I am,
>   but the chorus-men must stand there, looking stupid,
>   so I can flick them with my clever phrases.
> *Eur.* Granted. I see your shrewd mind is shaping
>   elegant plans.
> *Dic.*   God bless you, my dear man,
>   "and God bring Telephus—what I have in mind."
>   That's great! I'm filling up with clever sayings!
>   Oh—but I need the stick a beggar carries.

> *Eur.* Take it, and depart the rock-hewed dwelling.
> *Dic.* O, soul! You see my *soulitary* rout
> *sans* many implements and props; now turn
> pleading and wheedling and importunate.
> Euripides,
> give me a little basket? With burned edges?   (435–53)

The joke is that Dicaeopolis, as he takes on the Telephus costume and props, is gradually transformed into that tragic personage out of Euripides, taking on his persistence and his nerve. He becomes as importunate as a child teasing a grown-up, refusing to stop the game. With relentless comic logic, he begs, and begs, and begs. He asks for, and gets, a little cracked cup, a little broken soup pot with a bit of sponge for a stopper, and some inedible green stuff. "You'll be the death of me," cries Euripides. "Here, take it. Gone, all gone, are my dramas." Dicaeopolis starts off, again, but has to turn back one last time and ask for the most important prop of all: "some chervil, from your mother?" It is the final insult. The palace gates are closed (that is, Euripides and his tragedy-factory are wheeled back in). Dicaeopolis must do without the chervil. He returns now to the fray, giving tragic injunctions to his soul to fare forward fiercely. It is time to give the great set speech that will confuse everybody, baffling the chorus members, if not (we hope) the audience.

The Euripides scene is not just a side-thrust at contemporary tragedy in a political comedy. On the contrary: the *Acharnians* has been concerned with theater from the very beginning; it is about art as well as politics, and the two are mixed and juxtaposed in a number of suggestive ways. The state of tragedy will be a recurrent issue in Aristophanes' plays, reaching its climax in the Aeschylus–Euripides contest in the *Frogs*. The present scene is an early skirmish on that front. Although Aristophanes cannot resist the old chervil joke—it must have been a comic trademark for Euripides, like leather for Cleon or bare feet for Socrates—his satire is carefully worked out. He presents Euripides as an intellectual, proud, absentminded, aloof from ordinary people and concerns. This is not just casual slander (nor will it be in the similar case of Socrates, as depicted in the *Clouds*): it suggests that the modern tragedian has put himself outside society or, as he thinks, above it.

He is also shown up as a fraud who plays upon the tear ducts of a sentimental audience. He uses obvious pathetic effects—effects that one should readily "see through"—to evoke pity and make people cry; take away the rags and other props, and you have, quite literally, taken away his tragedies. Now it is true that Euripides had, and still has, a remarkable ability to induce fear and (especially) pity in his audience. I have seen a hardboiled New York audience weeping buckets at an adaptation of *Iphigenia at Aulis*, not least when the little baby Orestes was carried onstage in Clytemnestra's arms! Euripides is always bringing little children on, to break down the audience. And he was always, it seemed, bringing on pathetic figures in rags, heroes fallen on evil days. But the point is not just that Euripides uses pathetic, cheap tricks that amount to a regular fraud. It is more that he has injured tragedy itself. We expect, and need, representations of heroes and heroines who are stronger, more noble than ourselves. The fine costumes of kings and queens proclaim outward nobility, the high good fortune from which these heroes or heroines may fall, but they also suggest an inward nobility and greatness, larger than life, from which these exemplary characters cannot fall, even in stark misfortune: they remain *great*, whether for good or for ill, and we in the audience catch something of that greatness and nobility to ourselves. But Euripides took away the inward nobility of his kings and queens even as he dressed them in old rags. He made them people like ourselves. This was more than pathetic: it was demoralizing. Heroic endurance was replaced by unheroic scheming. Heroic action was replaced by melodrama, as people were blown about by meaningless winds of chance. There were, in fact, no longer any heroes and heroines, just pathetic people in rags who made you cry. As Dicaeopolis said, though in different words, in the first lines of the *Acharnians*: you don't get good tragedy anymore. You don't get Aeschylus, you get Theognis. Or, we might add, Euripides.

If costume counts for much in tragedy, to set, maintain, or alter a mood, it is exploited in comedy with far greater variety and freedom.[74] Splendid costuming is a mark of Old Comedy and of the generosity of rich Athenian *chorēgoi*. The brilliant outfit of a bird chorus gave, and still gives, immediate pleasure, such indeed as we gain from watching colorful birds. It is not that the illusion is complete, that the *choreutai* have really been transformed into birds; but mask and costume work upon the faculty, which we have possessed since childhood, of make-believe, so that in watching the bird chorus sing and dance we gain some vicarious pleasure of sharing in the life of birds. Similarly the strong transvestite tradition in comedy, which is rooted in ritual, in magical ideas, and in simple play, permits the pleasant vicarious experience of leaving traditional roles and limits behind, as women dress up as men, and men as women. The scenes in the *Thesmophoriazusae*, in which Euripides' cousin Mnesilochus is dressed up as a woman, to spy on a women's festive assembly, and in the *Ecclesiazusae*, where Praxagora and her women dress in their husbands' clothes and, wearing beards and carrying staves, take over the Assembly—all these are perennial fun, with their reversal jokes and sexual humor. But together with creative role-playing, comedy uses costume for effects of surprise, embarrassment, and humiliation. One of the nuisances of the *Birds*, a pompous, greedy priest, is stripped of his himation and chiton, which are bestowed upon a shivering lyric poet (whose only merit seems to be that his profession comes close to Aristophanes'). Praxagora's husband, Blepyrus, comes onstage in his wife's nightgown (he was in a hurry and couldn't find anything else to wear). Many people in his place might die of embarrassment, but he survives. In the *Thesmophoriazusae*, in a second parody of *Telephus*, Cleisthenes (for Odysseus?) runs in to tell the women that there is a spy among them: a frantic search ensues and Mnesilochus is discovered, quite literally. He has no breasts; he does have—a phallus that plays hide-and-seek. The play goes on, after this indecent exposure, to further travesties: Mnesilochus playing Andromeda to Euripides' Perseus and Echo; Mnesilochus playing the "new Helen"—the only Euripidean parody where we have the original for comparison—to Euripides' Menelaus. All this is great fun, exploiting the tricks of modern Euripidean melodrama for comic purposes, while commenting subtly on the nature and meaning of Euripides' art.

One of comedy's gifts is to restore to us what we enjoyed in childhood, a sense of trying on roles and experimenting with them much as we try on clothes. The masked and costumed actor suggests possibilities of our freedom. A second gift is the recognition that we habitually play roles without being conscious of them: husband and wife, father and son, lawyer or professor or king. If tragedy strips away such roles, literally or metaphorically, from its heroes like Oedipus or Lear, to show human beings in their essential nakedness and exposure to the storms of life, comedy likewise strips away roles with costumes, only to expose a free, lively, and vigorous human nature underneath. The exposed phallus is the sign of our vitality. Hence the comic masquerade succeeds both when it works and, better still, when it is discovered and unmasked.

To return to the *Acharnians*: the theme of exposure of fraud and deception is programmatic in this play. It is set forth most visibly in the first of the paired Assembly scenes. A magnificently robed Persian official is introduced, accompanied by two eunuchs. He is the "King's Eye," an official appellation, but one that struck Aristophanes' funny bone, for the man is gotten up as one enormous eye. Underneath his pseudo-Persian we can make out some plain Greek: the Athenians are gullible idiots (literally, "gaping assholes") if they think they will get gold from the king. What is more, the Eye and his eunuchs understand Greek perfectly well. This is, in part, because they are Greek *actors*. But also, Dicaeopolis "unmasks" the eunuchs.[75] One is Cleisthenes, an ordinary Athenian pervert, who has been "gotten up as a eunuch" (the language is that of costuming for a play). The other is Strato, another such type. Fraud tends to take a sexual form, but the Thracians, in the next scene, are quite undisguised: their great uncircumcised phalluses are their own indecent exposure, needing no outside help. Anyone can see what is going on, how the Athenians are fooled or, as the case may be, "shafted." (Sex is used as a metaphor of falsehood and victimization in this part of the play.) But the Assembly won't stop being fooled, despite Dicaeopolis' efforts; he gives up in disgust and makes his separate peace.

What, then, of Dicaeopolis' own masquerade as the Euripidean Telephus? First, we note a difference. In Euripides' play, Telephus entered in disguise as a beggar; in Aristophanes', we *see* Dicaeopolis borrow the rags and costume himself as Telephus-as-a-beggar. Second, and more important, we can literally "see through" the great holes in the Telephus costume to the comic costume beneath, the short chiton over body padding (of belly and buttocks, with a coiled but still visible phallus). The inadequacy of the costume is typical of comedy: "Nay, you must name his name, and half his face must be seen through the lion's neck." So, Dicaeopolis will "disfigure or present" the role of Telephus in a manner that will make the audience laugh: partly at the incongruity of these mixed-up roles, but partly with a sense of superiority at being able to see through them, for they are the only observers who are not supposed to be fooled. Even the *choreutai* will become confused! And no wonder, when we have an actor (who might be Aristophanes)[76] who is playing a comic figure, Dicaeopolis, surnamed "Just City," who is playing the Mysian prince Telephus, who is pretending to be a Greek beggar in order to argue his own (Telephus') case before the members of a comic chorus who are playing old Acharnian charcoal-burners who are now going to be treated as Achaean dignitaries— If all this doesn't teach the audience to become aware of role-playing and deception, then what will? And not just aware of role-playing, but also of rhetoric.

Oratory was nothing very new in Greece. Even Homeric heroes valued it; Achilles was brought up to be "a speaker of words and a doer of deeds." What was new in the later fifth century was that the art of persuasion began to become a professional technique, perfected by professional teachers and writers, like Gorgias of Leontini, and taught to young Athenians who could pay and who had the leisure to devote time to serious study.[77] The practical rewards were immense. A convincing speaker could win lawsuits, which were multiplying in litigious Athens; the complaint of the old men of Aristophanes' chorus, that bright young speakers run circles around them in court, is humorous in its pathos but conveys also the pain and urgency of a serious problem. On a more ambitious scale, a good speaker could influence political decisions in the Assembly. The term *rhētor*, often used disparagingly, became like our "politician." To understand the force of the new technique, we should look at the role of advertising in political campaigns today, especially television advertising. Successful candidates for the very highest offices are "packaged" with a good "image" and sold to the electorate by the same people who sell soap, soft drinks, candy, new cars, and toilet paper. It is alarming to anyone who cares about democracy—not least because the people with the most money can buy the most television time and hire the slickest packagers to sell their product. (As I write, Jesse Helms and Jim Hunt are spending around $25 million on a slanderous race, mostly via television, for a U.S. Senate seat from North Carolina.) Like radio before it, television exercises a power of propaganda that reasonable people must find appalling.

Marshall McLuhan has written eloquently, even prophetically, about the power of a new medium to enthrall and hypnotize the mind.[78] For us that medium may be electronic, like radio and (now) television; but earlier it was print, the spell cast, for example, in Cervantes' time by novels about chivalry. The words used by McLuhan, like "enthrall," "hypnotize," "trance," "spell," all suggest that the new, unfamiliar medium exercises a subliminal power of persuasion on its audience that is, to the popular mind, very like magic. I suggest that the rhetorical technique of persuasion in Aristophanes' time had the same mysterious power and was seen in the same manner. Thus Gorgias, in his Encomium of Helen, praises the power of the *logos* to change the mind. The spoken word can excite or allay emotion, as in the theater. It can bring healing, as "incantations" do:

> For inspired incantations by means of words are conducive of pleasure and extrusive of pain; for when the power of the incantation is brought together with the soul's opinion, it charms and persuades and transforms it by sorcery. And two techniques of sorcery and magic have been discovered, these being mistakings of the soul and deceptions of opinion.[79]

After citing several examples of the power of persuasion, as it is exercised by scientists, speakers in public debates, and philosophers, Gorgias compared the psychological effect of persuasion to the physiological workings of powerful drugs, for good or ill:

> For just as different drugs draw different kinds of moisture out of the body, and some make an end of disease, but others of life, so with words: some give pain, some pleasure; some frighten the hearers, others bring them into a state of confidence; and still others, with a certain evil persuasion, drug and enchant the soul.

The metaphor of sorcery should not be taken lightly. It conveys an irrational power in oratory that mysteriously, suddenly, and powerfully changes the constitution of the psyche. To "change someone's mind" may seem an ordinary occurrence, but it is really a remarkable phenomenon, a sort of wizardry. It is true that when he presents himself as an enchanter with words, Gorgias has his tongue in his cheek. He is playing with the audience, advertising the power of a technique that is not altogether mysterious but can be taught for pay. Yet its moral ambiguity remains. Rhetoric is a dangerous weapon for good or ill. And Plato would claim, with some reason, that Gorgias himself never understood the nature of the human soul or the meaning and purpose of the art, which (Plato argues) only philosophy can teach.

Aristophanes, who was as skeptical about philosophy as he was about

rhetoric, demonstrates the power of rhetoric in still another way by letting us see, from a comic perspective, how it works. For him, too, it is
like magic. In a world filled with deception, where people are always
practicing on public opinion, deceiving the polis about war, diplomacy,
and politics and concealing their own basic greed and ambition, Dicaeopolis cannot uphold a right and just (*dikaion*) position without external
help. He needs, as the chorus saw, something like a magic cap of invisibility—which is exactly what rhetoric can be, in unscrupulous hands. Yet
his own borrowed rhetoric, like the borrowed Telephus rags, will be such
that one can see through it. The antidote to the spell of the new medium
is somehow to perceive it differently, from outside. That is what Aristophanes' travesty, his mix-up of roles and costumes, enables us to do.
He too is a magician, a creative conjurer; but like a good magician he
defies us to see through his tricks, to figure out how they are done—not
to believe literally in their delightful magic.

In order to convey Aristophanes' confusion of levels of meaning, his
rhetorical skill in argument, and his comic art of showing up that skill,
let me translate Dicaeopolis' speech section by section. The technical
arrangement and devices are clearly marked. The speech actually combines features of two usually distinct oratorical genres: the juridical, for
use in court (as, here, in the defense of Telephus-Dicaeopolis-Aristoph-
anes); and the deliberative, for advising a course of action (for instance,
peace with the Trojans/Spartans) in an assembly.[80]

> PROEM
> Gentlemen of the—audience:
> I must ask you not to feel resentment
> if I, a beggar, dare to discuss the polis
> among Athenians, doing a comic play:
> your comic writer, too, can be right-minded,
> and what I'll say, although it may shock you,
> will still be absolutely right and just.
> You can be sure Cleon won't hurt me this time
> with his monstrous allegations that I
> impugn the polis when foreigners are present:
> we're by ourselves this time; our competition
> is the Lenaion's; no strangers are here yet
> representing their towns or bringing tribute;
> we're winnowed clean of all those foreign chaffs.
> (Our bran-new resident aliens don't count.)
>
> (496–508)

Out of the confusion of roles—a confusion that shapes Dicaeopolis'
speech in a playful manner, calling attention, like his costume, to the
elements of disguise, pretense, and make-believe—emerges the persona
of the honest comic poet, defending his own integrity and that of

comedy. The beggar is now Aristophanes, his subject is the polis, his audience is—the audience. Earlier Cleon had slandered him, saying that he defamed the polis in the presence of foreigners. Now he defends himself (notice the suggestion again that Aristophanes is under attack, not just Dicaeopolis and Telephus), though ironically: there aren't any foreigners around this time! What he says will be *deina*, things surprising and (for the speaker?) dangerous. They will also be *dikaia*, right and just. Aristophanes merges here with his character Dicaeopolis, or "Just City." His speech could be a charade on that name. Another made-up word, *trygōidia*, brilliantly sums up the situation.[81] It is a cross between *tragōidia* ("tragedy," derived from "goat-song") and *tryx*, which means "wine lees," implying comedy's basic association with Dionysus, drunkenness, and vintage celebration. The new-coined word suggests how comedy flirts with tragedy, parodies tragedy (the *Telephus*, of course), even rivals tragedy, but remains itself. "We comic *tryg*-sters also know"—as tragic players do—"what is right and just."

> NARRATIO (Account of the Facts)
> First: for my part, I really hate those Spartans.
> I hope Poseidon, god of Taenarum,
> will shake and quake and blow their houses down!
> I've had my vines cut down, like all the rest.
> And yet, my friends (for I may call you friends),
> why do we blame these things all on the Spartans?
> It was men from here—I'm not saying, the polis;
> don't get me wrong, *I'm not saying the polis*—
> but nasty little people like fake coins
> who'd never got a decent mark in their lives,
> but were shyster lawyers, insisted on proclaiming
> cut-rate suits. "That comes from Megara!"
> And if they saw a cucumber, or hare,
> or garlic clove, or a pig, or a bunch of salt,
> "That comes from Megara!" Confiscated. Sold.
> Well, so far, these are your *local incidents*;
> but then, a stupid bunch of drunken cowboys
> stole Simaetha the whore from Megara.
> Then the Megarians, hard up and lonely,
> stole in return two of Aspasia's *whores*,
> and *whar* broke out all over the Greek *whorld*
> —all from three girls who liked to use their tongues.
> And the result? Great Pericles, enraged,
> thundered and lightened out of high Olympus,
> drafting decrees that read like drinking songs:
> > "Megarians, don't cross the ocean,
> > don't linger on land or on sea;

you'd better not take any notion
to deal with my markets or me."
And the result? After starvation (slowly)
settled at Megara, they asked Sparta: could you
get the decree removed (the one that came
straight from the whores' own mouths)? But we refused,
though they asked us politely, many times.
And the result? Why, shield was clashed on shield.

(509–39)

The speaker is very clever. He could be a pupil of Gorgias. The immediate problem to deal with is the anger of his audience, which he defuses by identifying with it and giving it strong expression. "I hate those goddam Spartans as much as you do!" He means it too; he is really angry about people who cut down vines. But then, comically anxious to have the audience remember that he is *not* attacking the polis, he explains the genesis and development of the war in terms of food and sex that anyone can understand. It is all quite ridiculous; it also suggests the absurdity of making war when one could have peace. Behind this parodic account of the Cucumber Crisis and the Whore-stealing Caper, we catch an ironic glimpse of the actual process of history, much as Thucydides describes it: the outbreak of a great action from small immediate causes, or "pretexts"; the quick escalation of hostilities through action and counteraction; the role of a powerful individual, Pericles, in forcing the issue; but still more, the dominance of irrational forces by which the great powers are caught up, beyond their control, in apparently irreversible conflict. Aristophanes, of course, makes it sound silly. It all comes down to selfishness and greed. At the same time, the comic reduction of high diplomatic complications to simple matters of food and sex brings out, once again, the great theme of this play, that the pleasures of peace are a great deal nicer, and more fun, than the pains of war. Roast duck is better than ostrich plumes; the sausage—or the Phallus—is mightier than the spear. It is all a question, so to speak, of making love or war—of being Dicaeopolis or Lamachus, of choosing joy or (in the Euripidean style) misery. Is there really any choice?

The account of the whore-stealing competition parodies the famous passage in which Herodotus traces the conflict between East and West back to the (legendary) stealing of four women: Io; Europa and Medea; and Helen. Herodotus gave these incidents in chiastic and escalating form in order to convey the mutuality of guilt incurred through transgressing boundaries, both geographical and moral; he also brought out the difficulty of ascertaining final human responsibility for the outcome. Thucydides, though not a moralist, would agree that it is hard to fix responsibility for a war; and so would Aristophanes. At the same time, the parody recalls the old poetic insight that made Helen's beauty the cause of the Trojan War, which is the mythical paradigm of all wars. Homer makes Helen an unhappy instrument of fate and the gods' will. "We cannot blame the Trojans and the well-greaved Achaeans for fighting over such a woman," say the admiring Trojan elders on the wall. Beauty, for them, and for Homer, has its overriding privilege; it is integrally bound up with the call to heroism. But Euripides, in play after play, gives a different, postheroic picture. Helen now becomes an image of some vanity for which men throw away life and happiness. Real beauty, decency, the loveliness of civilized life, all are thrown away in war. It seems that Telephus, in that play, spoke against the folly of a war fought to recover Helen for Menelaus. His argument, echoed in later plays, gains increasing force and pathos during the Peloponnesian War. Here, it is parodied; it loses its pathos; we are kept aware of the conflated levels of disguise, imposture, and sheer confusion; but the pain is still close. That is part of Aristophanes' greatness as a comic writer.

> ARGUMENTATIO (with "Proofs")
> Of course,
> someone might say, they shouldn't have done those things.
> Tell me, how do you think they *should* have acted?
> Suppose a Spartan took a little sailboat
> and confiscated *one* Seriphian puppy,
> would *you* have sat quiet at home? Far from it:
> straightway you would have launched three hundred ships;
> the city would be crammed with screaming soldiers,
> calls for the trirarch, wages being paid,
> gilding of figureheads, shops in an uproar,
> foodstuffs measured out, oarloops, wineskins,
> water pails procured, sardines, bouquets,
> plenty of blue-eyed girls—and black-eyed sailors;
> then at the shipyards: flattening of oars,
> clattering, hammering, anything but boring—
> piping and griping, and whistle while you work.   (540–56)

This magnificent account of the Puppy Dog Incident is based on a frequently used argument designed to win the jury's sympathy for a defendant: "What would *you* have done in such a situation?" It is wild and funny, and it brings out what history books usually ignore, the tumult and confusion inherent in any great military enterprise. Once again we are reminded of how a very small incident may trigger a major conflict. (The shooting of the Archduke Franz Ferdinand comes to mind. I think Aristophanes would have enjoyed citing the War of Jenkins' Ear, a conflict whose origin seemed terribly funny to me when I was a schoolboy because our grave headmaster happened to be named Mr. Jenkins.) Still more, Aristophanes' description beautifully conveys the hysteria of war, the superheated exaltation with which people plunge into war.

There is something like this in the Marx Brothers movie *Duck Soup*, when, after war becomes inevitable (because of sheer human perversity), everybody joins in the great production number, "Freedonia's Going to War!" We are meant to enjoy the wonderful madness, the hysterical Freedonian (American) patriotism, even as we laugh at its idiocy. Still more, in Aristophanes, we find a final *admiration* of the prodigious energy of Athens, the way in which the great war machine swings into action on a moment's notice, the way Athens goes all out—city and Piraeus totally committed—to get back the little stolen Seriphian puppy. It is, after all, a matter of National Pride. Such things usually are. We begin to look forward to the supreme madness of the *Birds*.

> PERORATIO
> You'd have done it, I know. And Telephus:
> you think *he* wouldn't? Then you've got no sense.
>
> (555–56)

We return to where we started, to the mix-up of identities. It is "Telephus" who has been speaking all this time: to the Achaeans, or the Acharnians, or the Athenian audience. It was parody, and it was imposture. However effective Telephus' begging was, however right and just Dicaeopolis' plea, however honest and just the plea of the comic playwright, still we are meant to see through all of them, as we see through Telephus' costume, and learn, perhaps for the first time, not to be taken in.

There is, I suggest, a great dramatic moment in the next scene that we may miss for lack of a specific stage direction. The chorus, half convinced, half not, has become divided against itself; the hostile half has called in its champion, Lamachus; and Dicaeopolis, refusing to be intimidated by that officer, has laughed at his boasting and his fine feathers, treating him scurrilously. Lamachus is indignant.

> *Lam.* Do you, a beggar, say these things of the general?
> *Dic.* You think I'm really a beggar?
> *Lam.*   Who are you then?
> *Dic.* Who am I? An honest citizen. . . .

Things are still mixed up. Lamachus, a captain, has taken on the rank of general; probably, he is playing the role of Menelaus or Agamemnon (who would be given that anachronistic title in Euripidean tragedy).[82] In the *Telephus*, an argument seems to have broken out, when Odysseus entered to report the presence of a spy; he eventually discovered Telephus and revealed his identity. Aristophanes has Dicaeopolis reveal his own identity. He is not a beggar—not Prince Telephus, nor meant to be. I suggest that he throws off his Telephus disguise with a grand gesture recalling the climactic moment in the *Odyssey* when Odysseus throws off his beggar's rags and reveals himself as king and hero. So Dicaeopolis here: he won't masquerade as a beggar anymore, or as a prince pretending to be a beggar. His business is to be a comic hero, not a tragic one. Put differently: he will win the victory as himself.

The masquerade continues, of course. Aristophanes is still playing Dicaeopolis, playing the "just citizen"; we shall follow his imposture into the parabasis. Looking back, however, we can see that the multiple imposture of the speech in rags has enabled Aristophanes to do many things at once: to mix things up hilariously; to make fun of Euripides; to make a personal "just plea" about the war; to show up the delusory power of all modern rhetoric, *including* his own; and to provide an account of war that is not propaganda, and in which such usually antithetical elements as grief and laughter, parody and seriousness, pity, horror, and admiration are extraordinarily joined. This is a great tribute to the power of comedy, its vision, and its uncompromised integrity.

18   Acharnians, *III:* Comic Integrity

THE comic poet's integrity can be illustrated further, from the parabasis of the *Acharnians*, and from the continuing rejection of Euripidean tragedy. It may be described negatively if we say what Aristophanes is not. He is not a propagandist or a moralist. And he is not, finally, a tragic poet.

The parabasis, which may contain the original nucleus of Old Comedy, shared with the agon, or contest, the enormous advantage for the writer of being a highly stylized, highly playful form.[83] It provides a break in the play when the actors, especially the protagonist, may rest; the chorus strip off their outer costume and "come forward" to the audience, to speak, sing, and dance. We are especially concerned here with the first part of the parabasis, in which the chorus leader comes forward and recites in some long meter, usually anapests, a patter song on behalf of the playwright. It is a chance to editorialize on social, political, and literary subjects. Extrapolating from what we have, we may say that a comic poet was expected to speak on one or more of the following topics.

1. "My Value to the Community." The poet champions Right, combats Wrong, unmasks Deception, speaks for Truth and Justice and the Athenian Way of Life, and battles daringly against Wickedness and Folly.
2. "My Superiority to my Rivals." The poet has refined and perfected the comic art. He does not rely, as others do, on low, vulgar ploys to hold his audience's attention, nor does he plagiarize good jokes and run them into the ground. Instead he has created witty and delightful plays for an intelligent audience who will naturally award him the first prize.
3. "My Nobility and Integrity." The poet is a good man and a good citizen. He does not give himself airs, despite his great (and de-

served) successes, or try to seduce the young, but throughout his life and art he exemplifies all the traditional virtues. In sum— combining (1), (2), and (3)—he should be acknowledged as a Chief National Asset, the pride of Athens, who will guide his people to victory over their enemies and his, and over every kind of fraud, deception, difficulty, anxiety, or despair.

Now all these claims are made by Aristophanes, and they represent his genuine conviction. He knew his value: as a creative poet, as a spokes- man for many good qualities in life and in art, and as a playwright equipped with unusual faculties for exposing sham. To an extent it is right to take the claims of the parabasis seriously. We can still hear the poet speaking through them to his audience, even to us today. At the same time, Aristophanes' exaggerations, together with the conventions of the form, make us aware that all of these claims are playful as well as serious, and that the poet has adopted a self-advertising persona in order to put them forth. The chorus members may strip off their disguise, or some part of it, when they "come forward" to the audience.[84] Indeed the parabasis was probably derived from the very old portion of the *kōmos*, or comic revel, when the masked revelers, after making fun of each other and of the bystanders, showed their faces. It remained, symbolically, a time of unmasking. And yet Aristophanes does not come forward in his own person. We do not see his face, nor do we perceive his full mind. The striptease of the parabasis does not show us everything we want to see, or know, any more than does that earlier moment in the *Acharnians* when Dicaeopolis, like a new Odysseus, throws off his Telephus rags and reveals himself—as "Dicaeopolis," a comic character in the basic cos- tume and mask.[85] The analogy is striking, so much so that we might see the parabasis of the *Acharnians* as a further experiment in self-exposure and (to state a paradox) in comic honesty. Since the details matter, I give it in full (626–64):

> Our man wins the discussion, folks;
>   he showed the people they were wrong
> about the Peace. So toss off cloaks
>   and start the anapestic song.

During all the time that our teacher (*didaskalos*) has been in charge of comic productions (*choroisin trygikois*), he has never once come forward to the audience to boast about his intelligence; but now, seeing that his enemies are slandering him among the swift-deciding Athenians as a man who makes fun of the polis and insults the people, he requests an opportunity to give his response before the quickly-mind-changing Athenians.

Our Poet declares that he has done you much good, for he stopped you from being imposed on (excessively) by the speeches of foreigners, and from being made happy victims of flattery, Citizens of the Open-Gape Policy. But previously—why, the ambassadors would come from the various towns to fool you, and first of all, they'd call you "violet-crowned," and the moment they did, right away you people would sit up on the tip of your seats, because of those crowns. And then, if the man soaped you up with "Glistening Athens," he'd get everything he wanted because of that "Glistening"—a good epithet for sardines.

In this way (he says), he has become your great benefactor, and also because he showed the people in the various towns what a democratic government they were provided with. Which, you see, is precisely why they will eagerly come bringing you tribute: because they are eager to behold this best (*ariston*) of poets, the one who risked speaking out for Right and Justice among the Athenians. Indeed his reputation for daring has traveled so far abroad that when the Persian king was examining the ambassadors from Sparta, he put only two questions to them: (1) who had the best navy, Athens or Sparta? and (2) which of the two powers was lambasted the worst by Our Poet? For that side, clearly, would have improved the most, and would easily win out, since they had *him* as their cabinet adviser.

And this, you can see, is why the Spartans make peace-offers to you, and why they ask for Aegina back.[86] Not that they care about that island: they just want to abscond with your Poet. But you must resolve never to let him go. Right and Justice, you may be sure, will always be the object of his comedy. Furthermore, he promises that he will instruct you in many good things, so that you will attain utter and complete happiness: not by flattering you, or by sticking you with welfare plans, or by taking you in—no snow-job or blow-your-trumpets job—but rather, by providing the very best in *continuing education.*

> So, bearing this in mind,
> let mighty Cleon find
>   new schemes so facile.
> Justice will side with me;
> you may deride with me
>   him who takes pride to be
>   Coward and Asshole.

Notice, first, the parallels. This is a speech for the defense; Aristophanes has been attacked by his enemies, on slanderous charges of defaming the polis and insulting the demos: we might add, "in the presence of foreigners," for this passage picks up what was said earlier by Dicaeopolis about Cleon's attack on "me, myself." Cleon's name is held in reserve, for the final thrust, but everyone will know who is meant. The Athenians, always quick to judgment, were ready to condemn Aristophanes, much as the Acharnians were ready to stone Dicaeopolis to death as a traitor, and the Achaeans to condemn Telephus without a hearing; but they are mutable, quick to change their minds—or to have their minds changed for them by the power of oratory.

Aristophanes' first claim in self-defense (and we feel that if there had not been an accuser, he would have had to invent one) is that he unmasks deception and flattery. The Assembly scene in the *Acharnians* illustrates the point, for there Aristophanes gives a comic demonstration of how the Assembly is taken in by self-seeking politicians and fraudulent allies or hoped-for allies.[87] The diplomats enjoy continuing pay, foreign travel, and luxurious living, which would all come to an end if negotiations were completed: but fortunately for them, the Persian king has no intention of reinforcing Athens, nor has the Thracian king Sitalces, however much his son may be said to "adore" Athens. The term *chaunopolitas*, "gaping citizens," picks up two ideas from earlier in the play. One is that people get their way by successful boasting, or brag. The other is a low metaphor of gullibility. The "gape-mouthed" or "gape-assed" Athenians are vulnerable to deception as to a sexual attack on their persons. They are helpless, delighted victims of every kind of flattery and fraud that can be practiced on them. Only the comic poet tells them the truth.

Secondly (the two go together), Aristophanes argues that the very freedom of his comedy provides an example of democracy in action.[88] Far from denigrating Athens in the presence of foreigners, it will impress them, will remind the allies of how they are led by a truly democratic city. It will show, not Athens' weakness, but her real security and strength. How much risk, we wonder, was Aristophanes taking? Probably there *was* risk in attacking Cleon once again, a risk that links Aristophanes' defense with those of Dicaeopolis and Telephus. All are (tricky) speakers for truth and justice. Aristophanes goes on to suggest what later became a truism, that your severest critic may be your truest friend, because he shows you the weaknesses and faults by which you are endangered; your flatterer, who glosses these over, or promotes them, is your real enemy. This applies to a state as well as to an individual. But at this point Aristophanes soars out of seriousness (was he afraid of being too serious?) into high fantastic posing. He becomes a Chief National Asset, admired by Persia, coveted by Sparta; for, taken together, ship- and poet-power are unbeatable.

Aristophanes concludes these claims with paradox and pun. The phrase *kōmōidēsei ta dikaia* ought here to mean that his comedy will voice what is just; its literal meaning is that he will travesty, or make fun out of, what is just. We think again of Dicaeopolis, the clown who represents "Just City" but in a wholly selfish and individualistic manner, to which I shall return shortly. There is also a play on the word *didaskalos*, which usually means "teacher" but also, in a theatrical context, signifies the poet and/or director. It was a commonplace for orators to claim that they would "instruct" their audience in the facts of the situation. That is exactly the kind of deception of which Aristophanes is claiming to make his audience aware. Orators deceive you; comic poets, of course, tell the truth.

It hardly seems appropriate, under the circumstances, to speak of Aristophanes' sincerity. Great poets are not exactly sincere, any more than they are transparent. But they are, in their way, remarkably honest. The more we read Aristophanes' plays, the more we become convinced both of the fullness and intelligence of his perceptions and of the strength of his basic loyalties: to laughter, to truth, to Athens, to humanity. I shall say more about these loyalties in a later chapter. For now, I support his claim. In a world shot through with gullibility and deception, the comic poet may prove, paradoxically, to be the best teacher, because his comedy unmasks its own potential fraud and deception as well as that of others. If Aristophanes is honest, it is because he uses a see-through disguise, and because people know better than to take comic statements at face value. Besides, Aristophanes' claim is proved by still another pun. His name tells us that he is the "best showman," or simply, as stated in this parabasis, "the best." What truth, we might ask, could be more transparent?

Earlier I mentioned the artistry and humor of the scenes of Dicaeopolis' triumph after the parabasis:

A1 Megarian comes with piggies.
B1 Sycophant interrupts, is beaten off.
A2 Theban comes with various goodies.
B2 Sycophant interrupts, is packed off like pottery.

But something is missing. My students' dislike for the "piggies" scene (read, to be sure, not seen) nags at my conscience. Is it so funny after all? I have argued, bringing critical defenses to bear on the scene, that it marks the reversal in Dicaeopolis' fortunes; that it fits into a larger transformation pattern; that the characterization of the Megarian as an old fraud, a low trickster who does a vaudeville turn with Dicaeopolis, makes this business comic.[89] Still, granted all this, the scene comes painfully close to the real misery and degradation of war. How can comedy, even great comedy, touch on such things and still remain itself, not turn into tragedy instead?

But it can, it does: and not least, by flirting with, and rejecting, the pathetic tragedy it is tempted to become. Before returning to Aristophanes and Euripides, may I suggest two helpful analogies for the piggie scene, from recent times? The first is a famous scene from Charlie Chaplin's film *The Gold Rush*. Walter Kerr gives the background:

In his autobiography Chaplin has explained the origins of some of the principal comic images in *The Gold Rush*. He had been reading a history of the Donner party, that unlucky band of pioneers who had lost their way to Oregon and become snowbound in the mountains. One hundred and sixty were trapped; eighteen survived. "Some resorted to cannibalism, eating their dead, others roasted their moccasins to relieve their hunger." From one of the most horrifying accidents of American history, Chaplin derived—by a mere trick of the light—a scene in which he boiled and ate a shoe and another in which his companion began to mistake him for an enormous chicken.[90]

In the movie Charlie treats the shoe with finesse. Carefully, delicately, he prepares it, pours boiling water over it (like gravy), coils up the shoelaces like spaghetti, munches on a nail as if it were a bone. But this pretense leads into the next scene. How, Chaplin must have asked himself, can humans practice cannibalism? The comic imagination supplies an answer. The man ("Big Jim") must have been hallucinating, must have thought he saw, not Charlie, but an enormous rooster before him. The movie camera does the rest. This being comedy, they survive and get rich together; but we have looked hunger in the face and seen its menace. So too, I think, in Aristophanes, though his comic reaction to pain is to turn it into still another species of fraud to be disclosed. The results of war, for him, are like the causes, and the answer to starvation is good eating—to choose the breast of chicken over the ostrich plume.

My second analogy resists paraphrase. It is the series of cartoons that Garry Trudeau produced about the Vietnam war. I think especially of how B. D., the superpatriot American, is captured by the terrorist Phred in the jungle and, to the amazement of both, makes friends with him as they drink beer and listen to pop tunes on the radio. Amid all the desolation and war propaganda, beer and music give a lowest common denominator of what human beings still can share, a reminder of their common humanity and even, through this, a hope for a better future. Yet the comic strip comes close to pain, close to tragedy. In a later series the bombings of Vietnam are seen through B. D.'s eyes as he nostalgically returns after his tour of duty and is shown the sights, such as a ruined schoolhouse, by Phred. For a moment, in the next two strips, horror takes over; there is nothing left to laugh at. But Phred survives. He is shrewd and tenacious. He becomes a top-quality terrorist, indeed becomes overpriced and is traded to the Pathet Lao. Becoming tired of the desolation of Laos, he takes a package tour to Cambodia, only to find that the lovely old temples he hoped to see have all been shelled. Horror and grief are expressed under the guise of a tourist's frustration. But Phred is not daunted. He thinks up a new scheme, to bring three hundred refugees to Washington to lobby for help. They are packed up in crates like empty Coca-Cola bottles and flown to Washington, where rich society ladies dote over them; they are given consolation prizes at congressional hearings much as people are rewarded on game shows. The incongruity, between normal American behavior and what is happening in Cambodia, is appalling, but it is also very funny. The satire is strong, but universal; the society ladies and senators may be frauds, but so, to the best of their ability, are the refugees led by Phred. We are all in it together.

It is obvious that Trudeau cares about human suffering. He makes us think about what usually resists thought: the massive ruin and misery brought about by war. Yet he remains tough-minded; he does not fall, or let us fall, into a false sentimentalism or into fraudulent or ineffective guilt feelings; and he gives us a reassuring sense that humans are tough also (as well as fraudulent) and will survive. If part of Trudeau's gift is a strong sense of humanity, of shared pleasure and pain—I think of the wonderful comment "Even revolutionaries like chocolate chip cookies"—and a strong sense of caring that goes with this, the other part is something vital and hopeful that makes for comedy, not just satire; a sense of humor, even in the worst times (like 1969 and 1970); a pleasure in incongruity; an insistence on unmasking pretense and phoniness, especially in oneself; the openness always to what laughter and fun and joy can be found, in small things as well as great; and deep down, a hopefulness about people, and about life. All this seems Aristophanic, but as Trudeau himself has said, it does not always come easy to him:

> As many of the cartoons in this collection amply demonstrate, there are myriad places to go wrong. In what is unavoidably a chronicle of one's own personal maturation, self-indulgence and contrivance abound. And in the pursuit of tomfoolery the desire to join battle sometimes overwhelms. Yet, in more thoughtful moments, I have tried to observe Kelly's famous advice of almost twenty years ago: "There is no need to sally forth, for it remains true that those things which make us human are, curiously enough, always close at hand. Resolve, then, that on this very ground, with small flags waving, and tiny blasts of tinny trumpets, we have met the enemy, and not only may he be ours, he may be us."[91]

As Trudeau here suggests, the "desire to join battle" with vice and folly sometimes overwhelms, and often threatens to overwhelm, the comic spirit. What is needed is, not least, a self-conquest, an insistence on the realization that the enemy (of life, joy, comedy) "may be us." May I draw a similar inference about Aristophanes? I suggest that the man, behind all the masks, felt angry and upset about the waste and misery of the war and the difficulty of ending it. He may have started to write an antiwar play of the type that most critics, mistakenly, have imagined the *Acharnians* to be: a satiric attack on war, a plea for peace. But whatever he first intended, he ended up writing something very different once Euripides came into it. Why did he, really? And what does the *Telephus* parody mean?

On the one hand, the tragic parody gave Aristophanes a chance to exorcise his own grief and anger about the war, which led him close to writing tragedy himself. On the other, Euripides was, in his way, as much of a problem for Aristophanes as was the war. He not only disappointed a theatergoer who expected better, more traditional tragedy: he typified cultural revolution. With him, as with Socrates later, Aristophanes' jokes go beneath the surface of popular prejudice. He must have watched Euripides very closely. He was fascinated by the new tragedy: by its ironic, subtle plots, its beautiful lyrics, its clever set speeches, its lively melodrama; all this he parodies, and continues to parody, with affection. But he perceived the power and the threat of a new tragic vision lying behind these changes: a sense of meaninglessness in the world, of the disappearance of trusted values, of the loss of decency, nobility, and heroism. The "kings in rags" were not just instruments of theatrical pathos; they exemplified a fall from greatness. The seizing of babies as hostages and the other melodramatic scurrying and posturing all belonged to an absurdist view of history. Tragedy no longer consoled by showing that suffering, or its endurance, might be meaningful; it no longer taught courage and dignity by providing high exemplars of these virtues. Instead it gave images of demoralization that reflected, not improved on, what seemed to be happening in the world outside.

We should not forget that what happens to tragedy must also affect comedy. Aristophanes' concern about Euripidean tragedy went beyond aesthetic and moral prejudice; his own world—of the theater, as much as the polis—was shaken by the revolution in tragedy. And comedy was challenged. In the past things had been simpler. The high actions, characters, and language of tragedy—of Aeschylus' *Persians* and *Oresteia*, of Sophocles' *Ajax* or *Antigone* or (more recently) *Oedipus the King*—had provided a regular, dignified background against which the clowns of comedy could perform. In Aristotle's terms, the "no-account" things, *phaula*, were set against the "serious" ones, *spoudaia*. But now the seriousness, dignity, lofty style, and nobility of character were going out of tragedy. Worse still, by bringing its characters and actions down to an everyday level, tragedy was invading the province of comedy, providing what must have seemed a parody of itself. What remained for comedy to do? If tragedy lost its identity, how could comedy recover its own? It must have been a strong temptation for Aristophanes to invade, in his turn, the province of tragedy: not just to parody the new form, but to make his own serious, perhaps tragic statement about the meaning of things, the dignity of human life.

There is (if I may return to Stoppard one last time) a striking parallel today. In accepting and promulgating an absurdist view of the world and of human endeavor, many gifted and influential writers from Pirandello to Ionesco and Beckett have produced, not tragedy, but tragicomedy. Playwrights use farcical techniques to convey their sense of meaninglessness. The silly actions, the aimless talk, the insults, pratfalls, and repetitions that are the stuff of comedy are transferred to a new playground that claims quasi-metaphysical significance. A true comedian like Stoppard must know this material well, feel its powerful attraction, and respond to it as to a challenge. Through parody, he can show up what seems fraudulent and pretentious behind absurdist tragedy. Comedy can always drive silliness a step further, to make us laugh. Stoppard flirts with the theater of the absurd, enjoys and imitates its techniques, but goes beyond it to launch a series of valiant comic attacks—definitely attacks, but still triumphantly comic—on the absurdist and revolutionary world views, with all their implications for art but also for morals and the quality of life. He is valiant but retains his comic integrity, like the man with the bow and arrow, the tortoise, and the shaving cream. Perhaps, increasingly, he can address serious and painful issues, like the persecution of artists and intellectuals behind the Iron Curtain, because he has established, to his own satisfaction and to ours, his integrity as a comic playwright and continues to establish it in each new play.

Charles Segal has argued, in an outstanding essay on the *Frogs*, that one theme of that play is the comic Dionysus' recovery of his identity.[92] If he begins, seeking nostalgically for Euripides, and dressed in a wildly mixed costume of Heracles-Dionysus (the lionskin over the saffron dress and tragic buskin, suggesting a confusion about identity and purpose that is further complicated by exchanges of role and costume with the slave Xanthias), yet he moves towards his own reestablishment, in the underworld, as god of theater and judge, and he rejects Euripides and chooses Aeschylus. I suggest that twenty years earlier, in the *Acharnians*, Aristophanes not only parodied Euripides and rejected his tragedy, but affirmed his own comic integrity for the first time. Dicaeopolis pretends to be Telephus playing the beggar, but we see through his disguise and his rhetoric, and eventually he throws them off. In a similar way, I think, Aristophanes was tempted to play Euripides, to use his theatrical tricks for ulterior purposes, and perhaps even to succumb to his view of things; but like his hero, he lets us see through the disguise, and finally he throws it off and remains himself: a comic poet, at the feast of Dionysus.

And this self-definition of the playwright affects his hero's behavior. People have sometimes been troubled by an inconsistency between the "honest" Dicaeopolis of the play's first half, who fights for truth and justice, and the ultraselfish individual of the second half, who refuses to share his gains with anybody. We can say that he alone fought for peace, and he alone deserves the benefits of peace; but that is not enough. Dicaeopolis throws off sentimentality because comedy is tough-minded. He throws off moral earnestness because of the final importance of being frivolous, of giving full attention to matters of food, sex, and celebration. Comedy cannot serve a serious purpose except temporarily and in a self-exposing manner. It is rather the business of seriousness—Euripides and all—to make comedy possible. What war means is, finally, a wretched interruption of the feast.

It is fitting, then, that Dicaeopolis should refuse to spend a drop of peace, now a magic ointment, on the weeping eyes of a farmer whose oxen were stolen by the enemy. The comic hero is "not a public doctor." There will be no more confusion of roles. Euripidean tragedy, that mixture of fraud and misery, is now for Lamachus to play out. He chose war, so he must get misery, must be called to fight on the snowy frontier with a band of brigands. Being a Euripidean type of hero, not an old-fashioned one, he cannot even die a heroic death; instead, he is wounded (fittingly) by a vine-pole while leaping over a ditch, sprains his ankle, breaks the Great Feather (which bids a tearful farewell to life), and runs into a spear. This last is where Telephus started, and it is clear that if anyone is to play the miserable Telephus, Lamachus is the man. The scapegoat takes on the role rejected by the comic hero. But Dicaeopolis, supported by the two whores, seizes the drinking prize and leads the chorus off in triumph. I like to think that Aristophanes was playing Dicaeopolis and that, at this climactic moment, he too claimed the prize of Dionysus that, in being true to comedy, he had fairly won.[93]

19   *Transformations of Reality*

THIS chapter has dealt mainly with transformations. The poet's imagination, first, transmutes everyday concerns, anxieties, and experiences into comic ideas, into wordplays, images, metaphors, personifications, arguments, speeches, and wish-fulfillment scenes that live most fully upon the stage. For Aristophanes writes, not with the pure liberty of a lyric poet, but with the impure liberty of a comic playwright building toward performance. What his imagination provides, the director must take in hand.

If great comedy has the gift, and the power, to alter our awareness of reality while removing us, temporarily, from ordinary preoccupations of life, this accomplishment must begin with the submission of poet and actor to a Dionysian world. First the poet undergoes the same sequence of relaxation, recovery, and recognition that he hopes to bestow upon his audience. Like a dreamer (the analogy will be developed in the *Wasps*), the comic poet allows the daytime worries of Aristophanes and Athens to be drawn into a different, more fluid and magical world, of the creative unconscious, and of the Dionysian spirit, where they are dissolved and merged and changed into strange new forms. It is these gifts that the poet now reorganizes under Apollo's guidance, with hard work and with literary and dramatic art. Similarly the actor submits himself to Dionysus' inspiration and shares in his transforming power. He contemplates his mask with a kind of devotion as he thinks himself into a role; he puts it on reverently; he is transformed into another person. A vase painting described by Ghiron-Bistagne brings out the force of this experience, which laymen tend to ignore.[94] It shows an ugly, anxious, very ordinary little man holding the mask of an idealized older man, some high tragic figure whom he will, for the time, become. (Just so, in *The Dresser*, a recent play and movie, we see how a selfish, egotistic, and absolutely bewildered old actor is changed almost hieratically into the noble Lear as he puts on makeup, the king's robe, and the wig.) Might we imagine a similar change for comedy? The magic is still perceptible today as clowns put on makeup, are changed before our eyes. Still more, with the ancient costume—the padding of belly and buttocks, the obvious (but mostly unobtrusive) phallus[95]—comic actors took on the clown's fun and shamelessness, the inverted power of a "Dicaeopolis" to act upon the world. And as Plato noted with dismay, something of that same liberating and transforming power is conveyed, vicariously, to the theater audience as they watch the clown's antics and laugh at the playwright's jokes.

Most scholars and critics have distinguished two worlds in Aristophanes' plays. There is the real world of Athens, in which the playwright and his audience live and breathe, and from which the raw material of the comedies is necessarily drawn; and there is the unreal world of wish and fantasy—in which, to be sure, so much of Athenian reality is incongruously mixed up. My own view, which I have been developing cautiously, is that we must get beyond this dichotomy if we are to appreciate the full recognitions to which Aristophanes' transforming comedies can bring us. Let me illustrate it by reviewing the different worlds shown us in the *Acharnians*.

The first world we see is that of "Athens," but the word must be set in quotes, for the Athenians are presented with an absurd, distorted, grotesque version of their "real" world.[96] And through this distorting mirror they are shown themselves. Ordinarily, when the Assembly convened on the Pnyx, the masses assembled on the hill from below, streaming up from the agora; they looked up, literally, to the presiding officers, who descended from above, and to the speakers who harangued them from the *bēma*. Conversely, the spectators in the theater of Dionysus could observe their own political behavior and that of their leaders from a superior vantage point. They need not be intimated by magistrates and policemen, or by official procedures, or by impressive foreign embassies, or by manipulative local politicians. They could see for themselves through carefully staged deceptions, could see how Athenian politics, the "real" and everyday business of Athens, had become a farce.

Naturally, Aristophanes has distorted this picture of Athenian politics, using familiar techniques of "uglification and derision." Such satire was expected. What is more remarkable, I think, is his genius for displaying the underlying queerness and unreality of what passes for normal Athenian life. He shows us a world like that of *Alice*, where all the actors (one or two excepted) commit their usual absurdities with all the trappings of reason, logic, consistency, and right-sounding arguments; only the sum total is mad. Yet this goes beyond satire, for Aristophanes sees, enjoys, and celebrates the wild and extraordinary adventure that ordinary life, taken for granted, really is. Not that this sense of the strangeness beneath the familiar is a new subject for a Greek poet. There is much about it in Homer, in Sappho, in Euripides. But Aristophanes anticipates what, after G. K. Chesterton, we might call the "mooreeffoc" effect,[97] of looking at

the familiar from the other side, and seeing its queerness; and he anticipates Chesterton—and Shakespeare, and Rabelais, and Molière, and (especially) Dickens, and Joyce, and many others—in the exuberance of his
comic delight in that perceived queerness of familiar things and familiar
people. And that delight, which is celebratory, helps us distinguish the
wholeness of comedy from the partiality of satire.

Still, the chief thing that Aristophanes brings out about the "real
world" of Athenian politics is its basic unreality. It is a world of gulls and
knaves, of delusion and self-delusion, where the greatest decisions, of
war and peace, are made on the basis of persuasive images, rhetoric, and
propaganda. To draw parallels from modern life is tempting but super-
fluous. Therefore I shall not comment on how a well-known actor, using
the right makeup and projecting the right image, has been conducting, or
failing to conduct, the American presidency; nor shall I mention how one
of his would-be political opponents just recently borrowed an advertising
slogan—"Where's the Beef?"—from a hamburger ad on television. (Aristophanes could say more about bad cooking, bad politics, and the stuff-
ing of sausages, if not hamburger buns; Stoppard might say more about
"Bunbury" politics.) The point is that what my benighted university
students regularly refer to as the "real world," of business or law or
politics, is shot through with unreality and always has been. Only the
electronic circuitry is new.

From this first world, of "Athens," the comic hero escapes into Aristophanes' second world, of wish-fulfillment. His entrance ticket is, appropriately, a magical drink of wine. It would be easy to say that Dicaeopolis' entrance into his separate peace simply reflects the instinct of any
sensible person, to withdraw from the problems, tensions, and confusions of the "real world" into a world of private fantasy. Aristophanes
himself may have begun with such a flight from reality. And yet what his
hero wants, and goes after, is real enough: the tangible pleasures of food
and drink and sex and country living. The people who are out of touch
with reality are Lamachus, the high-plumed officer, and the politicians
(though they eat well enough), and the folk who listen to them. It is
Dicaeopolis, the rebel and near outcast, who correctly demonstrates that
roast turkey is more real, and satisfying, than the great white boastrich
plume. At the same time, Dicaeopolis recreates and rediscovers the gods'
festivals that give life meaning. His wine-drinking, a Dionysian act, leads
directly to his re-creation of the country Dionysia; and he is crowned
with final victory after he wins the drinking contest at the Choes, the
Feast of Tankards belonging to the (also Dionysian) Anthesteria. What
seemed a private, even solipsistic retreat thus becomes a return to, and
re-creation of, the deepest foundations of Athenian religious and political life.

We have, then, a version of the "real world" of Athens that is extremely unreal, and a version of the "unreal world" that seems remark-

ably down-to-earth. But there is also a third world that includes and reconciles the other two. This is the world of the comic theater of Dionysus, which embraces the actors, the chorus, and the audience all within the god's precinct. I described it earlier, in chapter 1, as the world of *theōria* that joins skeptical awareness with holiday participation. On the one hand, with Euripidean ingenuity, Aristophanes shows us a world that is unmasked symbolically and stripped to its bare essentials; he strips away the rags and props of Euripides' own theatrical deceptions; and he even shows up his own comic and theatrical pretensions by performing a striptease himself. It is true that like a good striptease artist Aristophanes does not show us everything; there is always another layer of irony; but still the process stimulates reflection on the part of the audience. They are meant to remain alert, unlike their usual selves in the Assembly, and to remain aware always that they are watching a play. On the other hand, the illusionary transformations that they watch and enjoy have their root and final meaning and justification in the god's festival, which they are presently celebrating. "This play," Dicaeopolis asserts, "is for the Lenaion." His immediate point is that no foreigners are present and hence Cleon cannot attack "me" (Aristophanes) for slandering the city in public. The levels of meaning, and implication, are wonderfully mixed up. It is enough to make even an Athenian pay attention. But if Dionysian festival makes it possible, within the play, for Dicaeopolis' choice of life over death to find its joyful origin and its joyful consummation, Dionysian festival, in the form of the Lenaea, also supplies Aristophanes from outside with a time and place for joy, and for play, and for celebration.

The comic theater of Aristophanes mediates between the skeptical awareness of realities, including those of theatrical performance, and their joyful transcendence. If its symbol in the *Peace* is that wonderful contraption the flying wooden dung beetle, perhaps in the *Acharnians* it should be the Copaic Eel. This is, I suspect, something fishy, a "beautiful naked woman," probably in transvestite quotes, to balance the "piggies" earlier. He, she, or it embodies the luxurious but very real delights of which the Athenians have been deprived by war, and by meretricious sadness. But the beloved, long-lost eel takes on the wonder and glory also of the heart's desire, and the gods' gift, as she comes onstage from over the border, not just of Attica, but of known reality.

It is time to pay tribute to the scholars who, over the centuries, have elucidated those ordinary Athenian realities among which Aristophanes lives, about which he jokes, and which he transforms through comic fantasy. All these words, all these *things*, baffle the novice. Jokes grow dim when they need footnotes. Lack of information about Athenian politics and personalities, about Aristophanes' career, about Euripides' lost plays (the *Telephus* especially) impairs our ability to laugh at the *Acharnians*, let alone interpret it; but even the ordinary little things in this play are unfamiliar to us. It is hard, already, to appreciate *Travesties* without knowing *Earnest*; but an educated reader from the distant future might feel like a schoolchild faced with a hard quiz:

1. What is a teapot? How do people drink tea? And what is the social and aesthetic importance of tea-drinking?
2. What is a butler expected to do, or not to do? Answer with special reference to champagne.
3. Describe the texture, appearance, and social significance of (a) tailor-made trousers, (b) mismatched suits, and (c) a bowler hat.
4. How is a public library organized? And how are people expected to behave in one (especially librarians)?

No doubt, all this could be explained in A.D. 4500 with the help of newspaper clippings, magazine photographs, and interviews with butlers and librarians (each an extinct species) on ancient videotapes; but the absence of immediate recognition would, to say the least, delay the laughter.

And so with Aristophanes: I am grateful for the hard work of copyists and editors that has resulted in my Budé and other printed texts of Aristophanes' surviving plays; and grateful too for the elucidation of references to people, places, and things, and of the meaning of odd words, that was begun by Hellenistic scholars and is summed up today in commentaries like those of Starkie or Rogers on the *Acharnians*. It has helped to assimilate, over the years, what they could tell me about *kribanos, larkos, pilidion, skandika, epanthrakides* dipped in *Thasia*, and so forth. It would be better still if we had an illustrated lexicon for Aristophanes. Brian Sparkes, who has done wonders with the Greek kitchen, might yet produce one,[98] and Mark Davies, whose keen knowledge of vase painting has helped me often, plans an illustrated commentary on the *Wasps* at least; but even clear visual impressions leave us uncertain about things. Just how was a "coal scuttle" (*larkos*) handled? And what did a "loose felt cap with flaps coming over the ear" (*pilidion*) feel like? And how did the Athenian nose, tongue, and palate react to those little fish dipped into shiny pickle-sauce (*epanthrakides, Thasia*) and broiled over a charcoal fire? And so on, and so forth.

A larger contribution of what I would call the older scholarship, from 300 B.C. to, say, A.D. 1945, has been to recreate the *climate of concern* in which Aristophanes wrote, and his audience received, the plays. It helps especially to read Thucydides, though again, there is notoriously much information that we lack, as about the Megarian decree. Specific details of a year's events and pressures must often be inferred from scattered references; it is ironic that historians have mined Aristophanes' plays for many of these references, and for a sense of how ordinary people lived, worked, and ate, or did not eat.[99] Perhaps the long and patient work of scholarship is best summed up in the encyclopedic article of W. Schmid (1945), running to over four hundred pages, and written against the background of the collapse of European civilization. Earlier Wilamowitz and Jaeger wrote, with great sensitivity, about the political but also spiritual crisis of fifth-century Athens against which Aristophanes' plays are set. We cannot, as Wilamowitz wished, put ourselves in the place of a fifth-century Athenian audience. (I envy my colleague James Peacock his ability to study the Javanese *ludruk* performances at first hand, music, singing, audience reaction, and all, and to bring back tapes.) But still we can do much, leaning on the older scholarship, to recreate that first "real world" of Athens on which Aristophanes drew, and which his comedy so wonderfully transforms.

But gratitude aside, the older scholarship had and still has serious weaknesses, which are derived mainly from its single-minded concentration on reconstructing the one "real world" of fifth-century Athens. Hence the general tendency to read Aristophanes' comedies as fixed and transparent allegories with a satirical and critical purpose. The comic poet, by this view, is primarily a critic. He exposes vice and folly, using satiric techniques; he demonstrates the need for moral and social reforms that may or may not be possible. Although his power of fantasy and his ability as a popular entertainer are great and admirable, each "comic theme" that he invents (to borrow a more recent distinction by K.-D. Koch) remains in the service of some "critical idea" earlier held by the poet.[100] Thus he is against Cleon, Euripides, Socrates. He is against the warmongers, the dishonest politicians, the sophists who corrupt Athenian youth. Although his comedy rises above party politics, it is generally conservative and traditionalist. The plays were, and are still, remarkably funny, though one could wish to be spared the many vulgarities thrown out to amuse the groundlings; but it is, in the end, Aristophanes' passionate seriousness, his concern for Athens, and his success (all joking aside) as a moral educator of the polis, that raises his plays above the Old Comic norm and gives them immortality.

Let me, without (I hope) seeming ungrateful, illustrate three weaknesses of the older scholarship, using the *Acharnians* as a reference point.

First, people have had trouble appreciating the play's second half: in part because it seemed "episodic," a relapse into scenes and songs of traditional vaudeville entertainment, but of no special merit; and in part because the serious component of the play seemed over and done with, and all that remained was fun and games. The embarrassment or dislike of scholars for obscenity, which they never could translate adequately, or explain, let alone integrate into the imaginative fabric of comedy—I think especially of Gilbert Murray—largely accounts for their failure to appreciate the second half of the *Acharnians*.[101] But still more fundamentally, they failed to see how, for Aristophanes, celebration is the alpha and omega of comedy, the whole of which satiric criticism is merely the part.

Second, people have tended to isolate the "critical idea" behind each play, separating it even from other "critical ideas." Thus the *Acharnians*, being a play against war, only incidentally makes fun of Euripides, as a representative of the new culture that elsewhere is singled out for attack. But what people have tended to miss—even Jaeger, with his sense of the overriding importance of cultural and spiritual change at Athens[102]—is the way that Aristophanes interweaves art and politics, tragedy and war, and explores them poetically and dramatically in terms of one another: a brilliant tour de force, like Stoppard's method in *Travesties*, but also (and again like *Travesties*) a remarkable way of reflecting on the whole connected world of Athens.

And third, people have ignored the exploratory nature of Aristophanes' comedies, which they share with all great poetry, and their special power of transforming real-life experience. For all those Athenian facts that are the end point of traditional scholarly investigation—the facts of tragedy, inflation, political corruption, self-seeking ambition, and the self-perpetuating war—are the material that suffers a sea change into comic images and ideas, out of which new insights and complex recognitions may come, for the poet himself and then for his audience, ancient or modern.

One of the best restatements of what I would call, very generally, the older scholarly viewpoint, was made by Thomas Gelzer in 1979:

> All these different elements of fantasy have one thing in common: they transfer the action of the comedy into the "Other World." There, comedy takes up its position outside of everyday reality, which however remains the central object of its concern. From there it exercises its criticism; from there it projects its traditional standards and value-judgements onto the politics of the Demos. For this purpose, Aristophanes deploys his fantastic inventions: they allow him to shed light, from varying perspectives, on the reality that is being criticized.[103]

Gelzer is surely correct when he argues that Aristophanes enjoys, and makes use of, a critical perspective from "outside." But I think he curtails Aristophanes' intention, method, and accomplishment, so that what emerges is not quite Old Comedy, but something more like the satire of Jonathan Swift. From the fantasy perspective of Lilliput, of Brobdingnag, of the Houyhnhnms, Swift dissects the corruption and folly of British institutions with a savage and imaginative brilliance that has never been surpassed; but what he saw, and found fault with, remained the same from beginning to end (unless we add his ironic picture of himself as would-be reformer). By contrast, Aristophanes surprises us, and I think surprised himself, with unexpected turns and unexpected recognitions. What he shows from his fantasy perspective is different from what he started with. Perhaps he intended originally to write a satirical play about war and Athenian politics; but once he has entered into Dionysus' realm—and once he has played with all the unmasking, and the connecting, and the exploring of paradox—the final recognition that emerges from the *Acharnians* is not just that war is bad (though it is), or that politicians are corrupt, or that Euripidean tragedy trivializes life. It is, if anything, that joy is not to be blackmailed—that water, as Chesterton said, is all right, provided it doesn't get into the wine.[104] But the production, the taste, and the celebration of good wine is what, in the end, the *Acharnians* is all about.

By 1965 critical assumptions about Aristophanes had shifted.[105] Books by Otto Seel and Cedric Whitman and translations by William Arrowsmith and Douglass Parker conveyed and fostered a new sense of delight in Aristophanes as a creative poet. One side of the "new criticism" just now catching up with Aristophanes was the appreciation of his plays as poetic worlds or heterocosms[106] with their own internal coherence and unity.[107] These worlds were made up wonderfully from words, from puns and images and metaphors whose perceptible continuity gave artistic coherence to the plays. If the new critics and translators were sensitive to tone, and especially to rhetorical effects and parody, they also had a robust enjoyment of food, drink, and sex, not only acknowledging and translating obscenities, but bringing out that union of delicacy and grossness, the lyrical and the grotesque, that is especially Aristophanic. At the same time, these writers brought a new tolerance of ambiguity in Aristophanes, of the balanced play of thesis and antithesis, and of shifting viewpoints; for example, the way that a seeming solution may be abandoned, or not work out, or backfire, or lead to absurd results. The comedies were (for the most part) great fun; they combined splendidly low humor with splendidly high flights of poetic fantasy; and they were, at the same time, plays of ideas that could lead an audience to think.

Whitman's book, more than any other, brought an appreciation of Aristophanes' poetic creativity as something good and beautiful in itself, not just a means of scoring political or social points or of "purging" the community in any obvious way.[108] Thus Whitman differs with Jaeger, as the new criticism, generally, has differed with the old:

> [Jaeger's view] places the fantastic aspect of comedy in the service of the critical, a fact emphasized by the word "allegorical." To

reverse this order, and to see the fantasy itself as the primary mode, to which satire and critical observation are foils, perhaps comes closer to identifying Aristophanes as an artist.[109]

Whitman revels in Aristophanes' creative power and fun. He describes wonderfully the play of metaphor, the life of dramatic images (or people as images), and the power of the grotesque, with its fusion of god–man– beast, on which the playwright especially draws in creating his comic heroes. Whitman appreciates, more than others before him, the degree to which the world of comedy, as a poetic heterocosm, is satisfying in itself, as opposed to being merely "significant" in relation to the ordinary, problematic world in which we live. And he sees its creation as answering, like the comic hero's actions, to the deep-set human impulse to create a world of one's own choice and to live in it: a world, this time, not of tragic struggle and grandeur, but of comic victory over things and people (not least, through the art of *ponēria*), and of sheer enjoyment.

All this seems fair, and rich, and the best antidote I know to the usual tyranny of the "critical idea" over the "comic theme." I must confess to feeling a strong *pothos* for Cedric Whitman as I reread his book. Wherever that brave spirit is—perhaps conducting an *agōn* with old-fashioned classicists in heaven—I miss his wit and verve, his critical intransigence, and his insistence on absolutes never allowing of compromise, in Aristophanes as in Sophocles or Homer. Still, particular points of agreement or disagreement aside, I think that Whitman's approach shows two faults that were typical of the wild Sixties. It stresses the pure charm of poetry as against the impure charm of theater. And it rests, beneath all the fun, on a world view that, at bottom, is existentialist and despairing.

First, Whitman largely ignores the limitations placed on fantasy by actual performance, and the playful ways in which the poet both acknowledges and overrides those same obstacles—for example, in the "flight" of the dung beetle, which is a cumbersome wooden contraption as well as a grotesque, half-mythical fusion of the earthy and the sublime. And although Whitman shows how well Aristophanes fuses Athenian realities with creations of the imagination, he tends to lose sight of the Athenian audience, both as living people with real, immediate concerns to which comedy must respond, and as a part of the theater, with whom, as well as about whom, Aristophanes means to play.

My second difficulty with Whitman's reading is that it is not only set against, but founded upon, a modern existentialist theory of the absurd. Just as tragedy presupposes such a theory, with its implications for heroic isolation and responsibility, so too, in Whitman's view, does comedy—although it superimposes its own vision of a larger, more structured, more satisfying absurdity upon the other. The supreme example of this for Whitman is the *Birds*, with its gorgeous palaces built in midair upon the nonfoundations of Gorgias' rhetorical and philosophical metaphysics. My own view, by contrast, would found Aristophanes' heterocosms on a more popular, traditional, and religious foundation. In its appreciation of nonsense, it comes close to Whitman; but as I wrote him back in 1960, I think that existentialist philosophers like Heidegger, whom he so much admired, would have been kicked out from the sacrifice and feast like so many imposters and frauds. For their view of life is too sophisticated, too serious, and in the end, too sad.

In Seel's book, too, which I greatly admire, there is an underlying sense of darkness. Seel writes movingly about the deep sadness he finds in Aristophanes, like the deep joy he perceives beneath Sophocles' tragedies; comedy and tragedy come close to one another in laying bare the roots of what is human. Throughout the book, Seel credits Aristophanes with the discovery of problems, especially human ones, as against the giving of solutions. In his penultimate chapter, "The Absurd as Way Out," he sees the world as something that cannot be healed, for all comedy's efforts. What comedy offers, then, is an escape into the freer, more joyful world of poetry and imagination. Seel's absurdist vision is not so fixed as Whitman's. In his last chapter he praises the transcendent quality of laughter and play. But he leaves us with a painful sense of the gap between the world we want, which is reflected in comedy, and the world doomed to failure and pain, in which we really have to live.[110]

Seel has, at the same time, a strong sense of Aristophanes' comedies as theater. He writes with unusual perception about how Aristophanes plays with theatrical illusion, employing technical devices and tricks that, at the same time, he unmasks. Seel also suggests how much we have lost, as in the music and the dance. And he feels the interest and the power of translations and of modern revivals. His main emphasis, however, is on how much of Aristophanes is lost to us past recovery. What we are left with is the written text.

I look back, then, to the 1960s as a time when in Aristophanic criticism as in other, perhaps larger questions, the bridges between fantasy and reality had broken down. For the appreciation of Aristophanes' plays as fun and fantasy, it was a glorious time. The single play came into its own as a complex, yet integrated and somehow poetically unified creation of fantasy. It was a work of art, self-contained and self-explanatory, a thing of beauty and joy forever—like the image of Cloudcuckooland itself, built out of wordplay in midair, or like a great technicolored bubble that rises and bursts upon the murky waters in which, like frogs, we humans dwell. Yet the bridges were down. There were, for the newer critics, no means of return from fantasy to Athenian reality. There were no diplomatic relations (to borrow a phrase from K. K. Ruthven) between art and life.[111] It was all like my first and favorite heterocosm, the Land of Oz, when its creator, by a magic spell, cut it off from communication with the United States of America and the rest of the world. That the critic of Aristophanes, at once confined to the text and assured of its artistic integrity, could escape into the contemplation of comic art with only a careless regard for the problems of Athens and the real-life situation of an Athenian audience—or even an Athenian poet—seemed then, to me and to many others, at once a gift of freedom and a powerful consolation for the sadness felt at the heart of things.

In A.D. 2005 we shall know better what gains were made in Aristophanes criticism between 1965 and 1985—and what losses were taken. But I feel confident that our renewed sense of theater will prove a lasting gain.

What we don't know about Aristophanes' stage—and what, infuriatingly, a single performance in 425 B.C. could have showed us—is still considerable. Take the *Acharnians*. How many doors were there in the *skēnē*?[112] How was the *ekkyklēma* used, and what furnishings, in the Euripides scene, were actually brought out on it? To what extent did the actors, especially Dicaeopolis, interact with the chorus in the orchestra? It hurts to think that we shall never know for sure. We can only make educated guesses. But if hard-core scholarship continues to remind us of how little we can ascertain about Greek stage action, we have at least gained the courage to reply that the older positivistic assumptions of scholarship will no longer do: that we *must* recreate somehow in our mind's eye and ear the way the music and dancing worked, and the costumes and props, the gestures and movements and comic business. Without these we have only a poor, mutilated sort of libretto: a worthy object, certainly, of scholarly interest, but not much resembling a comic play.

Yet the case for reconstruction is by no means desperate. Oliver Taplin has shown how, for Greek tragedy, most of the stage directions that mattered were written into the script, and can still be found there.[113] This seems largely true for comedy, also, although much of the farcical stage business must have been prompted by the actor's experience and the advice of the poet-director.[114] Furthermore, as Taplin points out, what the audience actually saw onstage was only part of what the dramatist meant them to "see":

> Theatre history has concerned itself with what happened and what was seen in the "real" world of the Theatre of Dionysus, the actors, and the *mēchanopoios*: dramatic criticism, however, considers what happens in the created world of the play in performance, and what is "seen" by the sensibility of a captivated audience.[115]

It follows that, if Taplin is right, we can bring ourselves through sensitive reading to see much of what Aristophanes' original audience "saw" in the magical theater of Dionysus.

Our awareness, too, of dramatic conventions and their effect has grown much in the last decades. I think of such long and careful studies, building on earlier scholarship and often correcting it, as Thomas Gelzer's book on the epirrhematic agon, or Paul Händel's *Formen und Darstellungsweise* (a masterful treatment of many formal aspects of Aristophanes' comedy, from prologue to exodos), or Manfred Landfester's close analysis of the techniques of building and resolving a suspenseful plot. The better we understand these inherited dramatic forms and techniques, the better we can appreciate the artistic mastery and sophistication with which Aristophanes deploys them and integrates them in his comic action—much as we are coming to see how Homer deploys inherited techniques of "oral composition" with its formulas and themes in the service of a new and powerful poetic vision, or how Pindar carries out a traditional and necessary "Programm" while making poetic statements and exploring a poetic vision that is highly individual and new. The inherited forms and techniques do not, of themselves, create the resulting works of art. They are, rather, the instruments on which the masters play; only, unlike musical instruments, they are transformed in the playing, as an old genre changes into something new.

All too often, unfortunately, the sophisticated appreciation of forms, details, and techniques hinders, not helps, our enjoyment of the song, the poem, the play. And all too often critical analysis resembles the wicked maidservant of fairy tale who usurps her mistress's rightful place. Cleverness is not enough. We need to be receptive, and we need, sometimes, to be simple. If this holds true of reading Greek tragedy, where the impact of the immediate scene is too easily forgotten, or played down, as we attend to overall patterns of image, idea, and action, it is even more true of Old Comedy that analysis should wait upon enjoyment, and should serve laughter.

Consider, for example, the unembarrassed freedom with which Aristophanes organizes time, space, and personal motion.[116] The very "Inkonsequenz" that used to trouble scholars at their desks today appears as one of the basic techniques, and one of the joys, of Old Comedy. In the *Peace*, as we saw, Trygaeus travels from Athens to Olympus and back again: first by dung beetle, then on foot—and with no change of scenery. In the *Acharnians*, after achieving his separate peace, Dicaeopolis decides to celebrate the Country Dionysia; he does this, as though transported into the countryside, where the angry chorus of Acharnians discover him; and shortly thereafter, he is back in town, before his own house, and next door to Euripides' house—which later on (I think) becomes the house of Lamachus. With comic lightness, with almost magical ease, the comic hero moves back and forth between houses, between town and country, and even, like the comic playwright himself, between different levels of reality.[117]

We realize, more and more (here is another gain), that Old Comedy, unlike New, involves a continual interplay with the audience from beginning to end. Since it never sustains a convincing illusion, we should not assume "violation of the dramatic illusion" as a regular comic effect.[118] Sometimes, to be sure, the hero assumes a tragic pose, or tragic diction, only to throw these off, descending to words, gestures, or actions that would never do in tragedy; and sometimes Aristophanes seems to connive with the audience at creating a fairly realistic situation onstage, only to have someone break through the "fourth wall" by addressing the audience directly, or reminding them, by calling attention to theatrical mechanisms, that this is a play. Aristophanes does this especially in his treatment of Euripides, who experimented with introducing a number of realistic elements into his plays.[119] The more Euripides tries to justify, and render more natural, the depiction of an "indoors" scene by using the *ekkyklēma*, the more insistently Aristophanes calls attention to the machinery and to the confusion (which he increases) of indoors and outdoors. The more naturalism Euripides employs in using a central altar as a "tomb," the more Aristophanes makes the whole business ridiculous. One implication is that tragedy was never meant to be realistic. What is more important is that, after Aristophanes bursts the tragic bubble with his own very "realistic" vulgarity, his comedy relaxes into its own special playfulness and imaginative freedom. As Peter Arnott says, "This is the make-believe not of elaborate scenic illusion but, something we have almost completely lost in our own theatre, of the child who will in his games make a castle from a chair and a forest from a carpet."[120]

Arnott is right about make-believe: but doesn't the modern theater delight in it, and teach us equally to take delight? From Brecht on, playwrights have invited their audiences to join in the business of creating and dismantling illusions. Seeing a Stoppard play like *Travesties* is like being invited to take part in a good romp. And Shakespeare's plays move again today as they were meant to, without embarrassment. When I was twelve, and my father took me to see Margaret Webster's beautiful *Tempest*, there were (I thought) long waits between scenes, and great creakings and groanings behind the curtain, while the stage sets were rearranged; but today, not only do producers use superb stage machinery like the turntable, but also actors improvise many stage effects, like the changing of scenes, with casual make-believe in which the audience is invited to join. That is one reason why a live play, even with second-rate actors, is so much more fun than a production by experts seen on television. Two years ago, in our local Paul Green Theater, we could imagine the Forest of Arden all around us as leaves showered down upon a bare stage and actors brought in baskets of bright red apples in the warm, friendly, comfortable glow of red and yellow lights (in contrast to the "cold" scenes earlier of the evil court, all in black and white). It seemed—and I am susceptible to these things—an enchanted moment when Orlando, weak and discouraged, came upon this Arden. Shakespeare would surely have been pleased. By contrast, the BBC production of *As You Like It*, with its camera eye roaming over vistas of stately oaks in a real English forest (as if, without these vistas, Shakespeare's wit and poetry could never hold a living-room audience), left us cold.

Although conditions have changed—although we enjoy the magic of the turntable and artificial lighting—modern theatrical performances are more faithful to the play, and fun, and make-believe of comedy than were the eighteenth- and nineteenth-century productions on which so many scholars of the ancient theater were nourished. The lightness, the ease, the play and fun of theater have reawakened as from a long and heavy sleep. The necessary thing is not to maintain an effortful illusion. Ariel may be played, and very well, as a self-confident black equerry with a flywhisk. What magic is needed, the audience will supply. But the place where the magic happens, where it works, is still the theater; and the controlling magician, behind Prospero (or Dicaeopolis), is the poet-director himself.

Before I make my last comments on this magic art, I want to express my hope that late twentieth-century theatrical criticism may combine the best features of the older scholarship and of the new. For the comic theater is a place where the different realities that are the proper object of these studies still remarkably embrace. We cannot, if we care, know too much—we are grateful for the smallest tidbits of information—about the Athenian spectators sitting on the benches of Dionysus' theater in all the accumulated heaviness of their historical experience and their personal concerns. But neither, I think, can we appreciate too much the lightness and ease of comedy's play, the irresistible levity with which it releases the audience from the bonds and bounds of "real life" and transports them, vicariously, into a world that answers more to the heart's desire. Where the lightness and heaviness meet is the theater. It is a privileged place, and one where, in our directed escape from gravity, we are brought to a more than usual awareness of what is real, even in ordinary life, and what is not. Hence the very full perspective that I have described as *theōria*. If the old-and-new theatrical criticism of comedy knows its place and knows its purpose, this is, I think, in the end to show something of that perspective, in which the heaviness of earth and the lightness of heaven are balanced, and, with the healing laughter of recognition, to let it be enjoyed.

If the comic poet-director is an honest magician and a successful cathartist, that is, I think, not least because he recognizes his own limits and those of his art. Although I am tempted here to describe still another Stoppard play, *The Real Thing*, in which a playwright-hero confronts the world of political action and, still more, the world of private emotion (including his own), and carries it off in great style,[121] I prefer to return to Shakespeare, to two moments in *The Tempest* when the poet, bidding farewell to his art, marks out its limitations and its scope. These comments will, in turn, suggest some last considerations about Aristophanes as a poet of the theater.

I begin with Prospero's speech to Ferdinand, which can be read on several levels:

> Our revels now are ended. These our actors,
> As I foretold you, were all spirits, and
> Are melted into air, into thin air:
> And, like the baseless fabric of this vision,
> The cloud-capp'd towers, the gorgeous palaces,
> The solemn temples, the great globe itself,
> Yea, all which it inherit, shall dissolve,
> And, like this insubstantial pageant faded,
> Leave not a rack behind. We are such stuff
> As dreams are made on; and our little life
> Is rounded with a sleep.[122]

Prospero comments, most immediately, on the masque just now performed, a little play within the play, in which Ceres, Iris, and Juno arrived to honor the betrothal of Ferdinand and Miranda and to shower blessings on them, and nymphs and country swains danced in their honor. After Prospero breaks off the "revels" abruptly, remembering Caliban's plot, and shows himself angry and troubled, he reassures Ferdinand. There is no need to worry. The actors were all "spirits," were all under Prospero's control. It is really all right.

But what disturbed Prospero so? There is Caliban, but he can be dealt with, and he will. Then too, it required effort and concentration to control the spirit-actors and keep them on course, to bring the little play (or the larger one) to a successful conclusion. Prospero's outburst partly indicates the strain. He feels the nervous relief of a poet-director whose show is just now over. But also, I think, his momentary disquiet shows regret: for he must surrender his magic art shortly, and return to the real-life management of Milan; and behind him, Shakespeare too is moving toward retirement from the theater, with mixed feelings, surely, of relief and regret.

The masque conveys in miniature something of the larger play that Prospero has enacted on his magic isle by means of his art, with the dainty spirit Ariel as his chief instrument (or head actor). The visible symbols of his art are his magic cloak and his staff, with which he controls people's waking and sleeping, or their movements; in the background there is his magic book (corresponding to the playwright's directorial script); but the fullest expression of art and magic in the play is the controlling music throughout.[123] The play, as Prospero creates it, moves from the creation of the tempest itself to the submission of Prospero's enemies, the restoration of his ducal power, and the happy betrothal of Miranda and Ferdinand. With this goes the inner change that the characters undergo, a two-part catharsis of mind and spirit; the villains especially, Alonso, Sebastian, and Antonio, are brought to a pitch of confusion and guilt bordering on madness—symbolized by confused noises and roarings—and then, by healing music, into a state of mental and spiritual clarity not before possessed by them. And it may be (but Shakespeare makes us wonder) that even Caliban, who represents intractible human nature, is brought to a degree of moral sense where he will "sue for grace." The healing process on the isle seems complete, and we are to imagine (but is this delusion?) that it will carry over to Milan, where Prospero, now retired from the uses of magic, will practice the art of rational and moral government (and self-government not least) that he has learned, and rehearsed successfully, upon the isle.

If Prospero's play brings his visitors, together with himself, to a state of moral clarity and spiritual awareness beyond the usual delusions and self-delusions of greed and lust, Shakespeare's larger play shows up other delusions with penetrating realism. It is well known that the fancies of old Gonzalo about the "golden world" reflect the powerful hopes of sixteenth- and seventeenth-century Europeans that the New World, just then discovered and colonized, might preserve an Eden-like innocence. Of course Gonzalo is confused about all this, as about geography. As the mocking courtiers point out, "the latter end of his commonwealth forgets its beginning." (He would have no sovereignty, yet imagines himself as an all-powerful, all-benevolent king.) The presence of Caliban in the play belies the dream of natural innocence, for Caliban is naturally brutish, lustful, and murderous and has resisted moral and spiritual education. That he is exploited as a slave, however, and corrupted by Trinculo and Stephano, the Europeans who get him drunk, is a further, unhappy comment on the myth of the noble savage and on Gonzalo's hopes for his brave new world. Yet it is significant that the sophisticated courtiers who mock Gonzalo are not only more vicious than Caliban but ultimately, in their way, as self-deluded and foolish as he is. Their cynicism finds expression (as such people's will) in a series of silly remarks and trivial jokes. And the parallelism of the two "conspirator" plots, with their parallel imagery of delusion and self-delusion, suggests that the sophisticated, worldly, very "realistic" strivings of Antonio and Sebastian after power and pleasure are not, at bottom, very different from those of the clowns who would take over Prospero's power—and who are fascinated and snared by the "trumpery" of fine costumes. Both villains and clowns are tricked by fancies and images, of crowns or riches dropping on their heads; and even Caliban, who cries on wakening from his dreams of glory, knows better than that. He learns that he was foolish to serve a drunkard as a god. Will Antonio and Sebastian realize that they were just as foolish?

What realizations do come, together with catharsis, occur within the larger illusion of Shakespeare's play, where (as in fairy tale) crowns drop down from heaven upon the good, deserving people. Prospero regains his duchy, Ferdinand regains his father, Miranda finds a husband and will become a princess. All this is the stuff of fairy tale, and Shakespeare knows it, and means us to know it. And yet life itself, which we take to be real and solid, is the stuff that dreams are made of, or clouds, or cloud-castles. Our little world of life ends suddenly in death, as a waking dream might end; and the greater world, the "great globe itself"— which is at once the charmed world of theater and the universe itself— will equally dissolve into the elements from which it came, or into nothingness.

The comic catharsis works, for Shakespeare, as for Prospero. We are brought to a perspective in which we see our lives as illusory, yet as belonging to that greater illusion within which human hopes and desires are clarified and lesser delusions and self-delusions may be recognized for what they are. Yet completion and success bring pain with them, as Prospero makes ready to dismiss Ariel from his service once his work, like an actor's, is rightly "discharg'd"; as he discards the instruments of his art, with its magical control over things (the cloak, the staff, the book); and as he prepares to leave his charmed island for the more real, more problematic world of fifteenth-century Milan. And there is something sad when the actor who played Prospero now speaks the epilogue in his own person:

> Now my charms are all o'erthrown,
> And what strength I have's mine own,
> Which is most faint: now, 'tis true,
> I must be here confin'd by you,
> Or sent to Naples. Let me not,
> Since I have my dukedom got,
> And pardon'd the deceiver, dwell
> In this bare island by your spell;
> But release me from my bands
> With the help of your good hands:
> Gentle breath of yours my sails
> Must fill, or else my project fails,
> Which was to please. Now I want
> Spirits to enforce, Art to enchant;
> And my ending is despair,
> Unless I be reliev'd by prayer,
> Which pierces so, that it assaults

Mercy itself, and frees all faults.
As you from crimes would pardon'd be,
Let your indulgence set me free.

Like the earlier speech, this works on several levels. It reminds us, first, that the "magic" that will transport Prospero to Naples, and then to Milan, is the magic of the audience's imagination, working in sympathy with Shakespeare's own. Second, their applause will conclude the play, "releasing" the actor, like Ariel, from his bond of service and also ratifying the success of Shakespeare's project, which was to offer a pleasing entertainment (like Prospero's masque earlier). Only with the final applause does this success, and the play's completion, become quite real. But there is more. The actor, and the poet-director, is vulnerable outside the charmed circle of his theatrical performance. Once outside, he lacks control over things; he is exposed to danger and death, and tempted to despair. And precisely now, in his human nakedness, the support and prayers of other people are absolutely necessary to him—as they were to Prospero set adrift with his infant daughter. The actor, and the playwright behind him, begs forgiveness for any faults that may have marred the play's effect, which was meant to be beautiful and healing. But this looks further, to the human and divine forgiveness that everyone requires: for in the end people must rely on mercy, and on grace. Human forgiveness has been exemplified by Prospero, within the play. It is healing, as revenge cannot be, and it brings blessings. But Shakespeare must look finally to God's mercy and grace as he steps outside the charmed circle of theater, and as he thinks of his mortality, like ducal Prospero back in Milan, "where / Every third thought shall be my grave."

Returning now to Aristophanes: we may be sure that he (and Callistratus) felt the same tension about their project that Prospero/Shakespeare felt, and the same sense of relief, tinged with regret, after it came to a successful completion. Aristophanes, of course, differs from the aging magician, in his youth, his relative inexperience of theater, and his hopefulness. The "surge of applause" that ratified the success of the *Acharnians* swept him onward to new efforts, as poet-director now, and to new accomplishments. Despite all the grief and worry of plague, war, and incipient exhaustion at Athens, it must have been, for the young playwright, an exhilarating time to be alive.

Like Shakespeare after him, Aristophanes through his art enacts a rite of comic catharsis, through which human wishes and desires are clarified and delusions and self-delusions are shown up for what they are. An honest magician, he calls attention to his own theatrical sleight of hand, as well as to the easily seen-through tricks of contemporary tragedy and oratory. He is already, in the *Acharnians*, a master showman, an *aristophanēs*. In spite of, and through, his many disguises, he is the most honest person around.

And one side of this honesty is his refusal (I think again of Stoppard) to make comedy serve any lesser purpose, of moral instruction or reformist propaganda, than its own. It is true that outside Dionysus' theater and precinct Athens continued on her wretched course. We cannot point to any practical result that Aristophanes as Dicaeopolis, spokesman for the "just city," may have gained: for the war went on, the politicians (notably Cleon) went on, the new culture went on; there is no evidence of moral regeneration, or of reform. Whatever dismay or indignation Aristophanes may have felt at his incorrigible fellow citizens went into later comedies, like the *Knights*, the *Wasps* (where Bdelycleon's attempts at moral reform are quite exploded), and the *Birds*, becoming the stuff of great-hearted laughter, not least at himself. But Aristophanes never succumbs to weariness, or to cynicism, or (finally) to despair.

Is this so, I wonder, because of his relation to Dionysus? We saw how Shakespeare, like Prospero, moved outside the charmed circle of his art, to the "Milan" or England where he was only a man, dependent on mercy and grace for his survival. But for Aristophanes, I think, the bounds of "inside" and "outside" were less clear. In one sense Athens, in the form of thirteen thousand spectators, came within the charmed circle, the precinct and theater of Dionysus, and could be changed: not by the pretend magic that Aristophanes renounces, but by the real magic of Dionysus working behind and through that renunciation. For in 425 B.C. the god's transforming presence could still be perceived through his plays, and most of all through comedy, bringing release and joy. The *Acharnians* communicates that joy, shows it to be real, and refuses to let it be blackmailed by war, or by existentialist despair, or by any other prevailing fashion. Joy irrupts into life and here it is. We greet it, despite everything, with irresistible levity: not because it will improve the morale of Athens (though surely it will, it does), but because there is a time to laugh and rejoice and celebrate, and the time is now. "Hurray for the Victor!" sing the chorus. The victor is Dicaeopolis: he is Aristophanes (with Callistratus' help); and he is Dionysus.

Chapter Four

Dream Transformations

and Comic Recognitions:

Wasps

Dionysus and Ariadne in their chariot, in a magically transformed world, from the Phineus cup, ca. 520 B.C., black figure. Photo courtesy of David Mitten and the Fogg Museum, Harvard University, reproduced by permission of Bruckmann Verlag from A. Furtwangler and K. Reinhold, Griechische Vasenmalerei.

20   *Dream-interpreting*
           and Comedy

THE *Wasps* begins, like the *Knights*, with a dialogue
scene between two slaves.[1] I give it in full, since the details matter.[2]

Sosias   Hey, there, Xanthias. What's got into you?
Xanthias I'm practicing . . . letting down my guard duty.
So.   The master's stick will get practice, I can see.
         Don't you know what a monster we've been guarding?
Xa.   Of course. I was only casting off some cares.
So.   Go ahead. Good luck. I myself do feel
         a drowsy numbness over my eyelids steal.
Xa.   You out of your mind? Or practicing TM?
So.   I gave in to sleep. A potent spirit sent it.
Xa.   You're serving the same potent spirits I am.
         Just a moment ago, the old Sandman
         made a nodding campaign against—my eyelids.
         A wonderful dream came to me just now.
So.   Came to me too, like nothing you ever saw.
         But you tell your dream first.
Xa.   A great big eagle
         I saw flying into the marketplace;
         it grabbed a brazen *aspis* [snake, or shield]
         and carried it high into the heavens,
         and then—Cleonymus threw it away.
So.   Well, your Cleonymus is like a riddle.
Xa.   How's that?
So.   Someone could put it, at a party:
         What creature is it that, on land, on sea,
         and in the air, still throws away its shield?
Xa.   Oh, me. What trouble's lying in wait for me,
         seeing a dream like that?

So.	Don't be anxious.
	It's nothing terrible, I swear it's not.
Xa.	Doesn't it seem terrible to you
	that a man should throw away his whole—equipment?
	Well. Your turn now.
So.	I dreamed—a biggie.
	It was about the entire ship of state.
Xa.	Well, that's a lot of ship. Go ahead, tell it.
So.	I'd just fallen asleep; I dreamed a flock
	of sheep were sitting on Assembly Hill,
	carrying staffs and wearing little coats.
	And then, I thought, there spouted forth to them
	a great haranguing demagogic whale
	that takes in everything. Rather like "Jaws,"
	only it shrieked like a hog that's being singed.
Xa.	Yuck, Yuck!
So.	What is it?
Xa.	Better stop right there.
	Your dream stinks horribly, like rotten leather.
So.	Next thing the damn whale did, was weigh out fractions
	of suet on the scales.
Xa.	That's very bad.
	He means to divide the people into factions.
So.	And then, I saw Theorus sitting down
	beside him, with a man's body and a rook's head.
	And Alcibiades said, in his lisping way,
	"I weally think Theowuth ith a *cwook*."
Xa.	Well, Althibiadethe got it wight that time.
So.	Isn't it queer, though, having Theorus turn
	into a rook?
Xa.	Best thing could happen.
So.	Why?
Xa.	You're asking why? Man turns into a rook;
	The symbolism's absolutely clear:
	he'll be a *rookie* on the devil's team.
So.	Isn't that something? I should get ten bucks
	and put this analyst on a retainer.

(1–53)

This whole dream section is usually passed over by the critics with little attention, as though its chief function were "to provide a string of jokes to get the audience warmed up."[3] True enough: these are warmup jokes. They seduce the audience into a relaxed but attentive state of mind. They are old lampooning, conveyed with new art; they introduce a political comedy (we shall hear more about Cleon and Co. in this play); and they provide what I have called a "preliminary catharsis," fueling the audience's receptivity to the larger healing experience, of the play as a whole. At the same time, the dialogue points in a self-reflexive way to a series of important affinities between dreams and dream-interpreting on the one hand and jokes, riddles, comedy, and comedy-interpreting on the other. All these involve psychic relaxation; all introduce us to a nonsense world of absurd and fantastic combinations and transformations; and all, when rightly taken, bring a healing catharsis and a series of ultimately joyful recognitions. But this is to anticipate much. Let us begin where Aristophanes does, with relaxation.

The two weary slaves guarding Philocleon nod off and dream. Through relaxation not just the slaves, but the audience with them, pass over a bridge from everyday anxieties to the world of transforming fantasy. Hence the appropriateness of the joke *phylakēn katalyein*, which Douglass Parker translates, "I'm studyin'. How to Relieve the Watch. One easy lesson." The word *phylakē*, which will recur, suggests both the "guard duty" that the slaves elude through sleep and the "watchfulness" of our waking consciousness, that tiresome policeman from whose Argus-like supervision we are delivered in sleep—and also in comedy.[4] The slaves guide us, succumbing to a "sleep from Sabazios." They have been drinking, of course: it is like the prologue of the *Knights*, where two slaves (generals) turn from defeatist thoughts of suicide to the happier, escapist joys of drinking, which lead in turn to new confidence and hope and to the oracle-stealing plan that sets the plot in motion. Hope thus mobilizes will, and wine is the Dionysian sacrament of hope. Similarly, by the gift of Sabazios (a new, imported version of Dionysus), the slaves in the *Wasps* fall asleep and dream, and their dreams, which are also jokes, begin the catharsis movement of the play.

In the first discussion, of Xanthias' eagle-and-snake dream, the idea of relieving anxiety is prominent. In this dream, an eagle flies into the agora carrying an *aspis* (asp); but right away, before we can ask whether this portent heralds good or ill, it clarifies its own meaning. The *aspis* turns punningly into a brazen shield that is thrown away by—Cleonymus. In short: our attention was engaged, only to be discharged in laughter at a familiar Aristophanic joke. "Oh, he's making fun of Cleonymus again!" Sosias makes the point differently, comparing Cleonymus to a riddle such as people pose at drinking parties, a riddle that required a punning shortcut answer.[5] Anyone whose children go in for riddles, as mine do— elephant and pickle jokes, say, or monster jokes—can vouch for the way they relieve the atmosphere, discharging it of tensions. So with the Cleonymus snake-shield; but Xanthias insistently recalls the thought of anxiety and fear. He is alarmed, as people are by strange dreams. Does it portend some dreadful consequence? Not so, says Sosias as dream-interpreter and therapist: don't be anxious! But Xanthias has the last word, explaining his anxiety with a joke that in fact interprets the dream finally and solves the riddle. Since the phrase *apobalein hopla* is equivocal, meaning to "throw away arms" or to "lose one's testicles," the dream turns out to be a comic dramatization of a very basic sexual anxiety. What seemed a simple joke builds to stronger laughter, greater relief of pent-up feelings and anxieties: in small, yet programmatically, to a healing catharsis.

Yet Xanthias' model dream is only a preliminary: the "big" dream of Sosias that follows is more complex and more significant, for it concerns the entire ship of state. Sosias has dreamed of an assembly of sheep on the Pnyx, each with its mantle and staff; they were being harangued by a monstrous whale. The audience will be ready for political satire; they are accustomed to the use of comic "likenings" as a basic form of insult; a series of hints leads unmistakably—especially if one knows Aristophanes and remembers the *Knights*—to the identification of the whale as the corrupt, bellowing demagogue Cleon; and to drive the point home, Xanthias anticipates the audience's happy recognition ("He's talking about *Cleon!*") by an indirection or disguise so transparent that it can *only* point to Cleon: "Your dream stinks horribly, like rotten leather." The allusion is a comic trademark. Leather goes with the tanner Cleon just as chervil goes with Euripides' greengrocer mother. It is a symbol that the audience cannot fail to grasp. By now, without being told explicitly, they have "gotten" the joke and interpreted the dream. Next the riddling image of the whale-monster "weighing beef-fat" is interpreted by Xanthias as a wordplay, on *histē dēmon/dēmon diistanai*, "to weigh the suet"/"split the people." Again the underlying concern, this time about political disunity at Athens, has been transformed by means of a wordplay into an absurd dream image. Since this joke is familiar from the *Knights*, the audience can enjoy the relief of discovering the usual sort of satire on Cleon beneath the new fantasy disguise, much as Sosias, alarmed by the strangeness of his confused dream, is relieved and reassured by Xanthias' interpretations. They get the joke, solve the riddle, interpret the dream, and receive the catharsis, at one and the same time—the slaves helping each other by turns, and the audience as they collaborate with Aristophanes.

The same holds for the next dream fragment, added for separate analysis. Theorus sits on the ground beside Cleon; he has a crow's head (*kephalēn korakos ekhōn*). This time the dream gives its own punning answer in the lisping words of Alcibiades: "*holas? Theōlos tēn kephalēn kolakos ekhei.*" Theorus has, literally, a flatterer's head. It is a beautifully roundabout way of scoring a point against one of Cleon's creatures. But Sosias is still anxious because of the "peculiar" (*allokoton*) dream transformation; he needs further reassurance, and he gets it. It is a *very good dream*, says Xanthias, for it shows that Theorus will "go to the crows"— that is, go to Hell. It is all a roundabout way of making the simplest, most obvious of comments: "To Hell with Theorus!"

As said earlier, Aristophanes is warming to larger political themes, and he is entertaining the audience by putting them in a happy and receptive mood; but the connections implied in this scene between jokes, riddles, dreams, and comedy are worth dwelling on further, since they affect the interpretation of the *Wasps* in particular and Aristophanes' comedy in general.

(1) Aristophanes' scene makes us realize that jokes and dreams share a common mechanism of disguise and discovery, buildup and resolution, absurd surface appearance and revelation of some latent idea or meaning. Freud has of course provided further insight into the connections here intimated by Aristophanes.[6] He has illuminated the role of the unconscious in jokes, as in dreams, though without by any means exhausting the nature and meaning of their relationship. He has shown how strong emotional "tendencies," aggressive and/or obscene, elude the conscious censorship (which is like Aristophanes' *phylakē*) and emerge from hiding in jokes, as in dreams; and he has magnificently described the parallel formation of jokes and dreams through techniques devised by the unconscious: with superficial absurdity, pivoting of meanings through wordplay, condensation, displacement, and substitute-formation, and masking and disguise. In all this an admirable comic artistry is revealed. I shall give examples shortly from my own dream notebooks. But the pleasure of dream-interpreting is in large part an intellectual one, like that of solving riddles. Freud himself often spoke of the "detective work" of psychoanalysis. A recent novel, *The Seven-Percent Solution*, very nicely made him a colleague of Sherlock Holmes. To "get" a joke, to solve a riddle, shows us in miniature what it is to interpret a dream of complex symbolism—or a comedy.[7]

(2) Aristophanes brings out the feeling of anxiety that is aroused by certain dreams and dispelled by right interpretation. Xanthias is worried by his peculiar dream; he wonders what it portends; he requires reassurance. The experience must have been common. Although Artemidorus' dream book, the fullest extant ancient treatment of dream symbolism, was written centuries later, three important conclusions can be read back into the fifth century B.C. without anachronism: first, that many dreams arouse anxiety and dread because of their baffling form and uncanny nature; second, that some dreams are significant, foretelling the future, and not just rehashing the day's "residue"; and third, that their "allegorical" (riddling or symbolic) form can be deciphered by a good dream-interpreter, an *oneirokritēs*. The dream-interpreter thus (1) relieves anxiety, (2) distinguishes "projective" from "residual" dreams, and (3) explicates dream symbolism.[8] In a comic way Xanthias does all this. Aristophanes may be laughing at the two-bit dream-interpreters of his time, who belong in the same category as oracle-mongers and other itinerant fortune-tellers. There is always some fakery in the business of psychotherapy. We are to remember that. But there is also some genuine healing. That possibility is crucial in the *Wasps*.

(3) Aristophanes introduces the idea of a public dream, one that concerns the "hull" of the state. An oracle, or an omen like the eagle holding a snake (if not a shield), would naturally concern the welfare of the state. Similarly, many private dreams have public significance. As Aristophanes' comedy moves back and forth, in its characteristic manner, between feelings, attitudes, and actions of private and of public life, it may provide something analogous to a political dream, significant for the future, conveyed through riddling symbolism that requires skillful interpretation.

(4) The dreaming and dream-interpreting of the prologue is quite specifically connected with the plot of the *Wasps* and with the poet's intention toward his audience, for Xanthias, who played dream-interpreter, goes on to guide the expectations of that audience. Before giving the background of the plot, he comments generally on the nature of the play. What will it be? On the one hand, nothing too "big" (*mega*) for them; on the other, no tired clowning, no "Mega-rian" vulgarity:

> we have a little story with a point,
> no more intelligent than you yourselves,
> but wittier than vulgar comedy.   (64–66)

What is a "little story with a point" (*logidion gnōmēn ekhōn*)? The phrase suggests something like a fable of Aesop with its accompanying moral, or inherent lesson; and since it will not be too intellectual or complicated for the audience, they are expected to succeed in "getting the point"—as they did not last year, with the *Clouds*. Aristophanes will complain of that failure in the parabasis. For now, as though to forestall a repetition of disaster, he has Xanthias take the audience with him step by careful step. The father of his *sleeping* master has a peculiar (*allokoton*) disease that they can only "get" and "interpret" (*gnoiē, ksymbaloi*) correctly with his guidance (71–73). Although the guessing game that follows provides more audience involvement, as well as a pretext for a new string of personal jokes (is the father addicted to dice-playing, like Amynias over there?[9] or to drinking, like Sosias and Dercylus?), it also connects dream-interpreting with watching and grasping comic ideas and comic action. The implication, I think, is that the main action of the *Wasps* will resemble a significant public dream in its peculiar manifestations and transformations, and one that, if it is rightly received and understood, will give great pleasure, and great healing.

(5) But, finally, this very question, of psychological healing, becomes a central plot element of the *Wasps*. It turns out that the father (whose name is Philocleon, "Love-Cleon") has a manic obsession with the jury court. He can think of nothing else, do nothing else, be drawn nowhere else. His son, Bdelycleon ("Hate-Cleon"), has tried various forms of therapy, which all failed. He tried (1) persuasion, (2) ritual catharsis-and-washing, (3) Corybantic treatment, and (4) incubation in the temple of

Asclepius—but every time, Philocleon bounced right back into the jury court. The image is a comic one and will recur. At present (Xanthias explains) Bdelycleon has given up on therapy and turned to simple force, shutting up the old man in the house so he cannot go to court. He will try to escape, of course. That is a basic Dionysian theme, and it will provide the outer and inner action of the play, which might be called "Philocleon's Escape."

The fourth therapy, incubation in Asclepius' temple, nicely connects our scenes, for had it worked, it might have done so by means of a healing dream. In a dream, or in a dreamlike vision, Asclepius himself might have made an epiphany, or his ministers or health-giving snakes might have appeared, or in some similar way a health-giving prescription might have been revealed to the sick man's relaxed and receptive mind. Yet this attempt at psychotherapy failed with Philocleon, as the others had, and as (to anticipate) Bdelycleon's subsequent, most imaginative efforts must also fail. But what (again to anticipate) of Aristophanes' own comparable attempt? Will he succeed where Bdelycleon fails? Will his audience get the point this time, learn the lesson, receive the healing catharsis? The answer, I want to suggest, is ambiguous. Insofar as Aristophanes, like Bdelycleon, tries to manipulate and control his audience, or simply to reform them, he is bound to fail. Dionysus looses, not binds. Yet this very failure, which is the essence of the plot and the only real "point" it has, provides a still better catharsis, a deeper, more comic recognition, and—to pursue our analogy—something like the best, most hopeful interpretation of a very significant dream.

I want now, before continuing with the *Wasps*, to follow Aristophanes' lead and pursue the analogy between dream and comedy, their experience and interpretation, in greater detail. This may seem a digression, but it offers several advantages. For one thing, most people are not familiar with the process of comedy-writing, but they are gifted, witty, highly creative artists when it comes to producing dreams. Although I draw here on years of recording certain of my own dreams in red, green, and yellow notebooks, and of interpreting them, with the help of Freud and Jung, but also through my professional ability as a literary critic, I have reason to think that my experience is fairly typical and that my conclusions have a broad general application. For another thing, I have increasingly become convinced that our understanding of comedy (as also of tragedy) is badly hampered by a one-sided intellectual approach to its "problems." Many scholars, like many lawyers or doctors or businesspeople, have developed their critical and analytical faculties at the expense of other capabilities, especially that of feeling; but in our dreams, as these draw richly and colorfully from the unconscious and from repressed aspects of the personality, we compensate for that very one-sidedness, and we may learn, if we respect our dreams and listen to them, to become more complete people. This is good in itself; it is also true that people in touch with their feelings will respond more fully, and more appropriately, to comedy and tragedy than people who are not. At the same time, an interest in dreams is not, as might be feared, an invitation to pure, unmediated Dionysian experience. Far from it. Dreams require good interpretation for the completion of their meaning, and of their healing power: this means a cooperation between Dionysus and Apollo. Dreams well up from the unconscious; that gives them their richness, and their fullness of insight into our private and even public lives. But to examine them at all and learn from them, we must recall them when waking, write down what we remember (which will only be part of what we dreamt), and reflect on them, perhaps communicate them to others. Only by this full process does what was unconscious emerge into the light of conscious recognition.[10]

The basic pattern, then, that I am describing for dream and comedy may be summed up, this time as *relaxation, transformation,* and *recognition.* It has, again, the advantage of balancing Apollo with Dionysus, and vice versa. In comedy, as in dream interpretation, we recognize the familiar and known beneath strange disguises and masks, and this is an intellectual pleasure; we also recognize integral relationships between images and actions that would ordinarily seem widely disparate. But there are also emotional recognitions, as we are brought (in dreams, as in comedy) to remember feelings, and even parts of ourselves, that we had forgotten on the conscious level. In the healing catharsis that dreams and comedy bring, both kinds of recognition are important, and they are complementary. That is why my account of comic catharsis has been incomplete up to now. In the first two chapters I have stressed the Dionysian experience, both festive and psychological, of release, and of recovery of good feeling: here catharsis was tentatively defined as "clarification through release." But even then I have emphasized the two-sidedness of *theōria,* as it combined participation in the Dionysian revel with the critical awareness of a spectator in the Dionysian theater; and in the third chapter I gave more attention to the place of language, form, and theatrical art in shaping the meaning of Aristophanic comedy. His oldest extant play, the *Acharnians,* provides recognitions that are sometimes simple and sensuous (roast turkey is better than ostrich plumes), but also sometimes complex, sophisticated, and self-aware (there is a man behind the mask behind the mask behind the mask . . .). It is very hard to describe a comic catharsis that so greatly appeals to, and affects, the deeper human emotions and the critical intelligence at one and the same time, and most accounts of catharsis have failed, precisely, to keep a balance between the two sides of our experience. All the more reason to pursue the analogy of dreaming and dream-interpreting as it keeps them both in play.

I begin once more with *relaxation*. The muscles of my body relax in the later evening, especially if I have gone swimming during the day. The mind relaxes, too: not all at once, if it has cares and preoccupations (such as preparing a series of lectures, or reorganizing a section of a book on Aristophanes); I may need to unwind, with milk or crème de menthe, and a detective story by Dorothy Sayers; and before I actually fall asleep, I may catch fragments of disjointed phrases or images floating through my brain or associating themselves into nonsense patterns like films of Lucretian atoms.

Sometimes my dreams only give back images of my waking concerns or activities of the past days. For some people, this kind of dream is the most common: hence the simplest explanation of dreams as reflections of everyday life. At other times I may have trivial wish-fulfillment or anxiety-dreams, or dreams that let me go on sleeping by incorporating some outside stimulus, like dogs barking and cars honking, that might interrupt my sleep. (A thirsty person dreams of drinking water, and so forth. At one stage, when I was regularly writing down my dreams, I would sometimes dream that I was writing them down, and go on sleeping—an example, perhaps, of the inner censor at work as well as the guardian of the gates of sleep!) But sometimes, especially when I am on vacation, and body, mind, and spirit are all relaxed in a friend's comfortable house, I may dream a more significant dream, one with colorful feelings and symbolism, that takes me deep into what seems a nonsense world. It is this kind of dream that can best be compared with Aristophanic comedy.

This dream world, with which we are all familiar, *transforms* ordinary life into fantasy: not least, by relaxing the usual laws of science, logic, and propriety under which we live, or choose to live, most of our waking lives. Thus, in dreams, I fly through the air; I converse with my dead father, or the pope, or Mel Brooks, or the queen of England; I "am" Aeneas, or Lancelot, or Henry VIII, or Frodo Baggins; I walk down surrealistic streets, past strange and inviting shops, in New York or Cambridge; or I meet my younger self back at school. I battle against Nazis, witches, gigantic swollen wasps. I attend a respectable dinner party, wearing only my pajamas. I rampage through (excuse me) unmentionable sex scenes. I speak, hear, or think of strange and significant phrases: "the Roman Daedalus," "*lōroth*," "Eden Lane," "telephone tokens," "cowardly rose"; "The Hawthorne and the Hay"; "Among the cold *hic iacets* of the dead." People, places, and scenes shift or merge without warning. Pleasures turn into panic and disaster. Seemingly unrelated incidents and scenes follow one another—though Freud and his detective agency know better.

Let me note here that certain figures from my dreams, and certain episodes, have close affinities with comedy. I give one curious example, of the drunken policeman. A recurrent figure, he seems to be a father- or authority-figure rendered ineffective by a kind of wish fulfillment. In one of my most colorful dreams, "Cakes and Confession," I was arrested for public indecency but treated very kindly by the drunken old police chief at the station, who gave me a party at the end. The dream reminded me, in turn, of a comic play that my friend Smith and I invented when we were schoolboys of twelve (the dialogue became fixed as we recited it back and forth over lunch). In general outline:

> Our English teacher, Mr. Edwards, is harassed: first by a dumb pupil named Lewis, then by an organ grinder playing outside his window. He appeals for help, first to a group of unhelpful janitors, and then to three crazy policemen, one Irish, one German, and one Russian. Of these latter, the first two insult him, but the third is drunk and gets him drunk, and in the end, everybody goes off happily to "The Russian Bear."

The triumph of nonsense over logic in our "Eddy Game," and of indecorum and chaos over discipline and order, is a schoolboy's wish-fulfillment daydream, and it incorporates many comic elements that recur in dreams. What is curious is that it also shows, in miniature, just the sort of basic ritual plot that Cornford posited as underlying Old Comedy. But Smith and I had not been reading comedy or recalling rituals. If our "Eddy Game" was Dionysian, it sprang fully organized from our unconscious. Whether or not we can speak of comic archetypes, the drunken policeman epitomizes very nicely the spirit of release from inhibition and repression that dreams and comedy so often share.

But such specific links aside, the interpretation of dreams has general features that bear strongly on the meaning, and the pleasure, of comic *recognition*. For, as suggested earlier, the analysis of dreams is a kind of detective process in which seemingly irrational factors are explained, and significant connections are made, by the tracing of small but meaningful clues and by the re-creation of an underlying pattern of feelings, motives, actions, and events. Freud and his school have illustrated, not the whole meaning of our dreams, but something of the process by which the "latent dream thoughts" are shaped into the mystifying and nonsensical "manifest dream content."[11] Prominent among the techniques of transformation are condensation, displacement, and substitute-formation; masking and disguise; the pivoting of meanings through wordplay; and the use of symbols. The interpreter must break down the dream scenes into parts and inquire into the meaning of their details, perhaps by inviting free association, or perhaps by a less arbitrary process of personal amplification; later, in good time, the different parts of the picture may be put together in a coherent and meaningful fashion. What is remarkable here, even when the dream material and its implications are personally painful, is the variety of *pleasures* that we obtain, analyst and patient together, through the detective process: pleasure in identifying people and things, in unmasking disguises, in tracking down relationships, in unfolding puns and allusions, and in the play of association by which all this is done. Let me give some concrete examples from my dream notebooks.

(1) A disguise is unmasked. Behind all those strange female figures— Queen Elizabeth, the Queen of Hearts, Mrs. Robinson—is (at least) my mother. I am amused to catch the connection. "Why didn't I see that earlier?" It is like solving a riddle, or getting the point of a joke.

(2) A verbal joke, or pun, is explained. I am tried and condemned "in the old city of Peking"—no doubt for childish voyeurism, or "peeking." I am the father of "Prue Hoffman," an actual student's name, but also a pun on *hoffen*, "to hope"; I am hopeful about a daughter, and the more I read Freud, the more I pun in German in my dreams. It is a compliment to the master. One afternoon a friend gives me pills for seasickness before a trip. That night I dream that she has given me pills for "mal di mère"—the sort of brilliantly suggestive wordplay that my conscious mind never produces, turning seasickness into "mother-distress." (The second word is not bad French, but an allusion to another friend, called Dee. I spare you the interpretation. The issues are painful, but their expression remains very witty indeed.)

(3) Sometimes the dream pun operates through a pictorial image or a dramatic representation of some common phrase or saying. This is like a rebus or the game of charades. Thus, Queen Elizabeth serves me rolls (roles). Or a friend shows me how to *hang up* a raincoat. Or my car becomes stuck on Park Avenue and can't get off the old *block*. At other times a phrase or line comes into my head later, explaining part of a dream or even the underlying relation between different parts. Thus, in a dream, I find a blue suit of my father's in a closet. Later it comes into my mind that a life like my father's would *suit* me very well indeed. Even now, as I write this, I laugh: partly with the satisfaction of being a good detective, of "discovering the riddle" (as Lewis Carroll has it); but also, with the pleasure of some psychological release from inhibition or anxiety, or the lifting of some repression, that the playful disguise mechanism, once it is interpreted, has made possible for me.

(4) Freud encourages us to track down allusions that lie behind an image or a phrase, and he has made us especially aware of sexual symbolism. This awareness too can be funny, like perceiving double entendres in comedy. Thus, at one moment in a dream, I poke a boy with a large black umbrella, and everyone knows what *that* means. Or does everyone? The dream alluded to a performance of Plautus' *Mostellaria* in which I played the old man, the blocking character, and poked a *puer* (the word means "boy" or "slave") with just such an anachronistic umbrella; but I would add, that the image of the Child, or Puer Aeternus, together with Jung's interpretation of that archetypal image, has an importance in my psychic life, my reading, and my teaching, that goes well

beyond the sexual implications of the umbrella business.[12] It is a question, for me, of staying young in heart, though old in mind. Although we may enjoy sexual symbolism, as Freud detects it, and learn much from it, we should not let it dominate our interpretation to the exclusion of other symbolic meanings or associations. To dream of swimming, for example, may refer to the pleasurable desire to return to the womb, for which we are all nostalgic; but for me, swimming implies a confidence and a hopefulness about life that I occasionally feel deep down in my being. Someone who learns to swim not only masters a new skill but entrusts himself or herself to a new, strange element. A third possibility of interpretation is that I regress, with pleasure, but in order more successfully to move forward through life, as through a strange element. A good symbolic action deserves more interpretation, not less—though the interpreter should always be guided by a strong sense of context, in life as in literature.

(5) At the same time, there is a danger of overinterpreting symbolism. In one cheerful dream, my wife and I offer chicken Florentine to F. (my former teacher). The immediate stimulus was from waking life (we were planning to offer this dish to another older professor); there was also an allusion to the Florentine poet Dante, whom I was then reading and teaching, and hence to the underworld scenes in Virgil and Dante, to the psychiatric ("underworld") process, and ultimately, to the meaning of life and death. That is all well and good: but it should not detract from the real and immediate pleasure of prospectively sharing this excellent chicken-and-spinach dish with friends. Chicken Florentine is good and significant in itself. It becomes, with the further associations, an image of hope, such as Aristophanes would have enjoyed. It unites the sublime with the sensual in the manner of comedy. Other dreams may benefit from more elaborate interpretation. When I dreamt of looking out a window and seeing beautiful large birds descending, with green and red tail-feathers and little riders on their backs, I sensed that I was in the world of Jungian archetypes; that this was some stage in the adventure of the spirit that the Wise have already mapped. It may be so. It may also be that the image was suggested by some fairy tale read long ago (and Jungian analysts have established many connections between dream symbolism and that of fairy tales). My point is, more simply, that this dream came like a gift, bringing encouragement out of some deep (or high) place of the spirit. It gave hope, and it gave healing.

I suggest that Aristophanes and his age already knew much about dreams, their symbolism, and their significance, that modern psychologists have laboriously relearned and put into words; and that the analogy he draws, and indeed plays out, in the *Wasps* between dream and comedy gives us important clues to the manner in which we should receive, and interpret, an Aristophanic comedy.

In the preceding discussion I have emphasized the intellectual side of interpretation, together with the pleasure that it gives. By processes of analysis and synthesis reinforced by free association, we not only unmask disguises of the "dream work," interpret symbolic objects and actions, clarify wordplays, and discover underground connections between elements of the dream fantasy and the underlying feelings or thoughts or attitudes, some of them deeply buried in the unconscious, that gave rise to these: also, by relating these to one another, we establish thematic connections between diverse episodes or scenes in our dreams, and we may even arrive at an overall interpretation, or "meaning." Sometimes this meaning is caught in a statement or quotation or phrase that seems to sum it up neatly and explain it, like the answer to a riddle. More often we sense an underlying unity of feeling and perception that is harder to put into words. In either case, to arrive at a coherent interpretation is deeply satisfying. It gives a pleasure like that which my mother found in her favorite game of "Concentration" on television, in which, little by little, fragments of words and images were revealed to the contestants, until enough of the puzzle was shown that the rebus (a sentence made out of letters and images) could be guessed, and the prize won.

Just so: the gifts of understanding and healing that good dreams bring are best realized when the dream fantasies are well interpreted. Yet they would be worth little if interpretation only gave us back what we already knew about—our ordinary concerns and experience, from everyday life. It is only when the recent stimuli of events and cares and impressions trigger deeper-lying feelings and concerns that something important can be drawn up from the dream transformations, bringing a healing clarification to our hearts. Unconscious inspiration and the reflective consciousness, Dionysus and Apollo, still work in concert. The art of interpretation, receptive to feeling as to idea, still responds to the poetic artistry of dreaming. Or of comedy.

Let me conclude with a bit of play that came to me, once more, as an unsolicited gift. In the paragraph just above I avoided using the term *catharsis*, a key concept for me and one whose meaning has been much disputed. Twice in the last few years I have had riddling dreams on this very point. One, which I have entitled "Doing my Duty," was simply scatological. It had me sitting on the toilet—which, I think, is precisely where Aristophanes would send intellectuals who worry about the precise meaning of critical concepts. It illustrated, in a way that Freud would have found highly appropriate, the simplest, most basic aspect of release and relief that the term *catharsis* implies. It was also a warning not to go too high and lose ourselves in laxative metaphysics. My second dream had a more self-reflexive and riddling quality. I dreamed that I had to teach a class about comedy, but I was not yet fully awake and decided to go in search of a cup of coffee: "so," says my account in my dream notebook, "I tell the students about 'comedy' and 'coffee,' writing these words on the board, and I ask them to think of a third word beginning with *c*, meaning 'effect of comedy,' while I'm gone. . . ." In this dream, which was largely about my search for personal warmth and refreshment, the dream-artist played with me, setting me a riddle. Only after waking did I realize that the missing word was—of course!—*catharsis*, the very concept that has caused me much waking anxiety in the attempt to describe it adequately, and which my dream had taken up and transformed in its own playful and emotionally clarifying and healing manner, into a form of release.

Here, then, is a proof—to be sure, an Aristophanic kind of proof—that the catharsis received from comedy, if it is rightly received and understood, is precisely analogous to the catharsis afforded by a good dream that is well received and well interpreted. For comedy, just as dream, works through relaxation, transformation, and recognition. It takes up the everyday concerns and the recent events of our lives, which the satirist or the nightclub entertainer would only scoff at and give us back unchanged; and by the transforming magic of poetry, imagination, and unconscious wit, it turns these concerns into comic *epinoiai*, into absurd and funny phrases, ideas, and actions, in the relaxed nonsense world of comic fantasy; and this, in turn, offers a series of recognitions, some simple, some complex, to the receptive heart and the observant mind. The meaning, or meanings, of a play by Aristophanes wait upon our experience and enjoyment of the play; even the author could not fully appreciate the meaning of his own conceptions until these were brought to birth in the theater of Dionysus. This meaning, we must insist, is never the same as some preconceived idea or attitude with which Aristophanes began. That war is undesirable, Cleon vicious, politics confused, the jury courts a mess—all these are starting points for comedy, but the *end* of comedy is never dogmatic statement or propaganda. It is, rather, *theōria* and catharsis: a deeper understanding, a more joyful perspective, a personal and social renewal, a clarification at once of heart, mind, and spirit effected by the Dionysian release of comic fantasy through the shaping of art. Or, to quote one last time from my red dream notebook: "The overall feeling . . . is one of comfort and support, a movement backwards into childish happiness so that I feel somehow more willing to go *forwards*."

21   *Getting the Point:*
        Symbolism of the Wasp's Sting

THE action of the *Wasps*, its prologue suggests, will
resemble a dream filled with strange symbolic creatures and happenings
(such as a flock of humanized sheep in assembly, a haranguing whale, a
crow-headed attendant) that has large public significance and deserves
careful, reassuring interpretation. And we are not disappointed. The play
presents a chorus of jurymen-as-wasps. After farcical scenes of struggle
and debate, a dog will be prosecuted by another dog for stealing cheese,
with a cheese grater and other household implements giving testimony.
The scene borders on fable and political allegory, but also on dream and
fairy tale. We are invited to experience something like a strange dream,
but at the same time to interpret it, and to share in the discovery of a
solution, and the perception of a cathartic process, that will not be complete until the play's end.

In my own interpretation, I shall move slowly, giving attention to
qualities of feeling associated with the action and brought out by it. The
present section centers on an obvious symbolic component of the dream
play, the "stings" carried by the chorus of jurymen-wasps. Aristophanes
teases us to guess the meaning of these wasps and their stings. He gives
hints, as we shall see; and in the parabasis, the wasps explain themselves
to the audience, as if to make sure that they do not, again this year, fail to
get the point and enjoy the comedy. But this does not mean that we
should jump to conclusions, or take what the wasps say at face value.
Aristophanes liked, in his own time, to baffle intellectuals who prided
themselves on their skill as literary critics.[13] Let us then go slowly; and
instead of explaining the "symbolism of the wasps" in isolation, let us
reconnect their antics with those of Philocleon, in the emotional counterpoint that the play's action provides.

From the slaves' first description of Philocleon's jury-obsession and
Bdelycleon's attempts to cure it by persuasion, psychotherapy, and even-

tually constraint, the prologue opens into a farcical scene rather like a game of peekaboo or tag. The basic movement is ridiculous in the manner that Henri Bergson has described: a human behaves in a mechanical manner, like an object; the more he is pressed down or in, the more he springs back up or out.[14] That Philocleon cannot, will not, be suppressed is a basic theme of the play, here played out in advance. The way the old man keeps popping out, by window or roof, must have been hilarious. He is, from the first, a very energetic old man. His efforts are associated with different creatures (who may, as in dream or fairy tale, embody lower instincts): he hops up a wall like a jackdaw, moves about through cracks like a mouse, and tries to fly away from the roof, like a sparrow. But his special affinity is with the donkey. In a burlesque of Odysseus' escape under the great ram from the Cyclops' cave, Philocleon tries to escape under a donkey. Unfortunately, he gets himself under the wrong end of the beast. He is also caught and shoved back inside, together with the donkey; he is not Odysseus, nor meant to be. We laugh at the silliness of his attempts, and at their frustration. All this gives the pleasure of a children's game. Yet the theme here dramatized, of "escape from confinement," has only just begun, and it has strong Dionysian associations, for the god of escape-artistry must be on the old man's side. The son may be a therapist, and his good intentions may parallel those of a reformist poet: but what we feel, and what must matter more, is that he is a jailer. We have to be—with Dionysus—on the father's side.

When the chorus of old jurymen arrive (and I shall turn to them shortly), Philocleon has subsided, significantly, into passivity. He does not, for a time, look out or speak. He needs (as we all do) to be encouraged, to have his energies aroused again by the cheerful songs of the chorus. They look to him as their hero, as the roughest, toughest juryman of all; but when he reappears, he behaves like a Euripidean heroine who is sadly and hopelessly in love—like Phaedra or Stheneboia, perhaps, or like Danae locked in her tower. The tragic parody is very funny.[15] What could be less like a heroine pining away for lovesickness than the stout old Philocleon? After a long silence, signifying his utter tragic distress, he finally speaks, or "sings":

> I'm wasting away,
> simply wasting away,
> hearing your voice, my friends,
>   but I am una-
>   ble—to sing!

Much as a tragic heroine longs for her beloved, Philocleon's lyrics express a deep and passionate longing for his jury court. Live or die, he desires only to be there. As always, the parody reassures us that this is comedy, not tragedy; that clowns survive defeat and humiliation; that the emotions of pity or terror evoked by tragedy will not be required on this occasion. This will be important, since Philocleon will come very near in this play to a tragic hero's experience of death in life. At the same time, the parody brings out a genuine, if perverse, erotic quality in Philocleon's jurymania. It is silly, of course, that he should "love" the jury court in such a literal way; we would say that he had "fetishized" the voting urns and pebbles and the entire court apparatus. It is all rather kinky. Yet as will become increasingly clear, Philocleon's emotional life, his feelings of vitality and self, are all bound up with the jury life. "What life is there . . . ?" (to paraphrase a famous poem of Mimnermus on the sadness and emptiness of old age without Aphrodite) if you take this away from him? Escape and *erōs* go together.

Philocleon's eroticism is played off against, but also reflected in, the behavior of the chorus. These are described as wasps in advance of their appearance, when Bdelycleon tells Xanthias not to trifle with them:

> No, you're a fool. If anybody gets
> the tribe of old men angry, it's like a wasp's nest.
> They have a sting (*kentron*) projecting from the hip;
> it's very sharp, for stinging. And they scream
> and leap and dart about like sparks of fire. (223–27)

Their entrance onstage, however, is far from wasplike. Old, slow, tired, muffled in mantles, they enter chanting some rather silly verses about their own slowness and tiredness, and how they miss their naughty youth. Nostalgia will be their leitmotif. They used to be in the army, and they look back to vigorous exploits on campaign, which all turn out (like the reminiscences of Justices Shallow and Silence) to be foolish capers having little to do with actual warfare. Now they press on in the mud and darkness toward the courts. Jury duty replaces the old military campaigns. They are led by boys with lamps, figures of playful youth who show them no respect. It is clear that they look to Philocleon as someone who exhibits the youthful vitality and toughness that command respect. He is their hero, champion, and leader; and he will be a test case for the meaning of their lives.

They succeed in rousing the old lover, and they encourage him to try another plan of escape, letting himself down as from the walls of a city under siege; but once more Bdelycleon starts to beat him back, with farcical countermaneuvers executed with the help of his slaves. He calls for help, and now the chorus go into action. "Why wait any longer," they cry, "to set our anger in motion, the anger we feel when our wasps' nest is attacked? Now it comes, now it comes, now the sharp sting with which we punish is extended!" They strip for action, giving their cloaks to their boy-attendants and revealing a wasp costume underneath. Each old jury-man is now wearing a black and yellow tunic, narrowly wasp-waisted, with a large "sting" extending from the hip. Raising these stings to the ready, like swords, they advance to the attack.

Remember that we are not watching a chorus of "wasps" but a chorus of "old jurymen" partly outfitted as wasps.[16] It is a mixed disguise, and it calls for a mixed reaction. On the one hand, the "wasps" carry some of the old dangerousness, even the daemonic force, of an animal chorus. We are virtually confronted with anger itself. This reminds us of comedy's ancient power to exorcise demonic forces by playing them out in the animal masquerade and dance. The chorus's attack on the isolated individual, as a scapegoat, may also go back to the beginnings of comedy in fertility ritual; it can be seen in the similar attack movements in the *Acharnians*, the *Knights*, and especially the *Birds*. It is a wild and dangerous moment. At the same time, the "wasps" are partly recognized as old-jurymen-being-wasps. The choristers, that is, are imitating old men who have now taken on some semblance of the angry, rapid, darting movement of wasps. We recognize that they embody the angry traits of jurors, the bad temper heard in the actual "buzzing" of a packed court, which issues in the stinging condemnation of defendants. At the same time, the dance movements of the chorus imitate military maneuvers, reminding us that the old jurymen are (as they keep recalling) proud veterans of the Persian Wars: they fought at Marathon, and some of their old valor can still be seen in their present aggressiveness as jurymen-wasps.

All three—soldier, juryman, and wasp—are sharp-tempered and carry a sting. The soldier brandishes a spear (and so, later, will Philocleon carry a sword); the equivalent for the juryman is his *enkentris*, the stylus with which he draws the long penalty-line on the voting tablet. At the same time (and here we return to dream symbolism), the wasp-sting is unmistakably phallic. The word for "sting," *kentron*, also means a point or goad, and it is regularly used in Aristophanes' plays to indicate the phallus. So does the verb *ek-teinō*, "to extend," and so, surely, do the movements suggested by the chorus's self-encouragement: "Erect stings! Attack the enemy in the rear!" This is not to say that, as some have thought, the wasp-sting projects from the groin. It seems likely that the chorus wore the usual, comparatively innocuous curled-up phalluses, not the "vulgar" long, dangling type or the erect type. The "sting" projected, rather, from the hip, close to the hindquarters (as it does with actual wasps, if one gets to look carefully). But the sting is still very evidently phallic, and the contrast between it and the little curled-up phallus is very much to the point.

For what the old men really want (and here the strange antics of the chorus merge symbolically with the impossible behavior of Philocleon) is the experience of sexual potency that makes them feel really alive. What has happened as they grew old is, first, that frustrated sexuality has turned into a habitual feeling of anger and, second, that the exercise of their power in court has taken on, as sadism will, a perverted yet still strongly erotic quality. The pen-alty stylus is not only like a sword: it is the only functioning instrument of potency that they have left. We see this as in a charade being acted out. In a queer way, Philocleon *is* their erotic champion, a Don Juan of the jury courts. He is the test case for their vitality as they grow old. Remove him from the court, take away his "sting," and you take away his life—and all their lives.

In the following scenes, the chorus quiet down and Bdelycleon becomes engaged in single combat with his father: first, in the formal agon; then, vicariously, in the Trial of the Dog. I shall consider these scenes separately, as they come, but I want to jump forward momentarily to the parabasis, where Aristophanes again guides our thoughts toward interpretation. The parabasis comes directly after the defendant dog is acquitted, which is a defeat for Philocleon, coming very close to a tragic death. After that (and the themes are closely interwoven), Aristophanes praises himself in the "anapests" as a brave reformer and cathartic healer, and then the wasps are given a chance to speak for and about themselves.

They begin with nostalgia, but also with reassertion. "Of old," they proclaim, "we were valiant: in dancing, in war, and most of all, in *this* respect" (pointing to their little phalluses). Now their hair is gray,

> and yet, out of these remnants,
> > we must find some youthful strength:
> for I think, my old age
> > is stronger and better
> than all the curls and posturing
> > and queer-assed talent of your youth today.

Which leads them, precisely, to explain the "idea of the stinger," *epinoia tēs enkentridos*, in case anyone in the audience has been wondering about it. Aristophanes has just described how he "broke his *epinoia*" in the ambitious *Clouds* the previous year, because many people failed to get the joke. This time he will spell it out. The chorus of wasps carefully explain their own meaning, point by analogical point. They are (they explain) very courageous beings; when the barbarian came with fire and smoke to loot their hives, they flew out angrily, fought, stung, and conquered him. And still today, as jurors, they exhibit the same temper; they "swarm" into various courts; they provide a livelihood for themselves by "stinging" (meaning voting to condemn); and they resent those stingless drones, or parasites, who have no *kentron*, that is, never served in the army, yet share their privileges and their fees.

The point is clear enough, despite Aristophanes' casual way of confusing wasp traits with those of bees or hornets. The wasps are jurymen and veterans. Once they pursued invaders with anger and spears; now they "pursue" defendants (Aristophanes is playing, as often, on the literal and figurative senses of *diōkō*, "to chase/prosecute," and *pheugō*, "to run away/be a defendant") with the same anger and the penalty-stylus. Would the audience get the further implication that for these old men jury duty is a kind of surrogate warfare? Not very consciously, perhaps; but the point has still been made, that the aggressiveness that Bdelycleon has been trying to mitigate, or to exorcise, is the same quality of temper that saved Athens in her hour of need.

But what the wasp-chorus have *not* explained is something that, I think, stood out quite clearly: the sexual nature of the wasp-sting. Aristophanes is still playing with the audience, waiting for them to get the point, much as one might interpret the symbolism of a colorful, significant dream.

Let us imagine, again, the process by which Aristophanes wrote a comedy. He began with personal anxiety and concern: about Athenian politics and politicians, about the new welfare state, about the power and irresponsible behavior of the jury courts—especially as those were controlled by irresponsible politicians like Cleon. He also disliked Cleon personally. More important, it was time to write a new comedy, and one that would (more anxiety here) be more successful than last year's *Clouds*. Aristophanes may have thought of writing a satirical comedy about Cleon and the jury courts. It would have been what the prologue announces, something like an allegorical fable, "a little story with a point." But when his concerns underwent a creative transformation that resembles the production of a dream, with a chorus of jurymen-as-wasps, and an escapist hero, who struggles against a spoilsport son (who, as it turns out, has traits of the sensible, reformist poet, and is even called "Hate-Cleon"), what emerged upon interpretation was—and is—very different from a simple satire. The comedy, like a good dream, brings out a number of very strong emotions. It brings out anger; it brings out *erōs* lying behind the anger. Its manifest story is of a man trying to escape from physical, or psychological, confinement. The two, we may say, go together: the expression of erotic feeling and vitality marks a successful escape from the confining limitations of old age and human weakness. The result of the comedy, as of a good dream, is surprising—perhaps it was even to its creator. It describes the failure of political reform and therapy; even, as we shall see, the failure of play-and comic therapy. This is a joke on the reformist playwright. But Philocleon's escape is still more deeply comic, and Dionysian. It is, in the last interpretation, a vindication of *erōs* and a sign of hope.

22   *The Comic Agon*

ARISTOPHANES brings out strong emotions that can
be painful; he shows them working under the surface of society, driving
people to strange or harmful forms of behavior. If we draw back a little,
though, we notice that these emotions are played out within a definite
and familiar structure provided by Old Comedy.[17] Tension builds up,
and it breaks out in combat. There is a mimed combat on the physical
level, often between the chorus and one of the characters; here, it is
between the wasp-jurymen, rescuing Philocleon, and the slaves helping
Bdelycleon restrain his father. This combat is farcical but inconclusive. It
leads to a heated verbal exchange: here, between the chorus and Bdelycleon, and then between Philocleon and Bdelycleon; and this in turn
leads to the formal agon between father and son. The two agree to turn
the dispute over to the judgment of "these people": the chorus, or perhaps the audience. Accordingly, the slaves release Philocleon; he asks for
a sword, to kill himself (in tragic fashion) if, as is unthinkable, he loses;[18]
and if he fails to abide by the arrangement, he swears—never to drink
unmixed wine again.

In all this we sense that the comic tradition has contributed its own
superb mechanism for dealing with feelings of anger and playing them
out to a satisfying resolution. What may have originated in the ritual
hunting or casting-out of a scapegoat by a lynch mob has long since
become a stylized "attack" danced out by a comic chorus: the Acharnians hurrying to stone Dicaeopolis, the Knights charging at Cleon, our
jurymen-wasps attacking, the angry Birds repelling two Athenian travel-
ers. Physical violence turns to farce; it is followed by verbal violence, the
exchange of screams, complaints, insults, and challenges; and in good
time, this preliminary verbal skirmish is followed by the most formal
contest of all, the so-called epirrhematic agon, with its very pronounced
formal structure:[19]

A1	Ode	A2	Antode
B1	Katakeleusmos	B2	Antikatakeleusmos

C1	Epirrheme	C2	Antepirrheme
D1	Pnigos	D2	Antipnigos

The names, used only by scholars, are somewhat ridiculous. All the better, to mark the conventionality of the agon, with its clearly delimited sections and its precise responsions as each side comes up to bat. All this gives aesthetic pleasure, but it reminds us, still more, that we are watching a *game*. In their little preliminary verses (A1, A2) the chorus may bring out the seriousness of the issue, the magnitude of what will be at stake in this dispute (Is Philocleon a king or a slave? What is the value of an old man's—hide?); but even more than being concerned wasp-jurymen, they become cheerleaders whose principal function is to proclaim the agon and stimulate each side to do its best. This leads to B1 and B2, two long verses each of "exhortation" and "counterexhortation." The two speeches of C1 and C2, which may variously be broken up, are in the long verses of a patter song; and lest we might still take them too seriously, they end in D1 and D2, a very fast "choker" and "counterchoker" of shorter verses rattled off as fast as possible. However serious the issues of the agon, however painful their emotional content might threaten to become, they are still cast in a recognizable and reassuring play form that the audience must have looked forward to—almost as if someone had cried, "It's time for the agon now! Everybody up for the agon!" They know, once more, that this is comedy, that they are in good hands.

Often the cheerleading chorus or the contestants introduce the debate, or parts of it, with terms referring to sports. In the first version of the *Clouds*, the two rival Arguments, the *logoi*, were apparently gotten up as fighting cocks; their dispute over ethics and education was marked as a cockfight of the mind. Most pairs of debaters must have squared off in some less obvious but still suggestive manner. Thus the wasp-chorus encourage the "man from our gymnasium" to speak effectively; and Philocleon, as he begins, speaks like an eager runner launching himself "from the starting line." The metaphors remind us how much the Athenians enjoyed intellectual as well as physical contests. They had a strong competitive nature, and their forms of discourse, whether social, political, or philosophical, fell naturally into an agonistic form. At the same time, the comparison with sports reminds us that this, too, is only a game. Let me enlarge on this idea, since it is crucial to comedy.

The term *agōn* denotes a contest or struggle, often of a violent sort: hence our word "agony," which casts a backward shadow on the Greek word. Gilbert Murray and others have associated it with the struggle of a tragic hero against his enemies, and against suffering and death: rightly so, and the comic *agōn* should be seen against the background of the tragic one. But the translation "game," or "sport," or "play-contest," gives the comic *agōn* its special connotation of nonfatality. Games, and especially sports, may always have had their "agonizing" side. My athletic sons set their teeth in pain as they compete in half-mile runs or in crew races. Greek athletic competitions were painful, full of effort (*ponos*), first in long training, then in the culminating struggle at Olympia or Delphi. Boxing, wrestling, the *pankration*, meant taking and inflicting pain. Chariot-racing was the more exciting because it was dangerous. Athletics have always involved, and appealed to, a basic brutality in human nature: think of football, lacrosse, and ice hockey today, which come close to warfare. The difference remains, that they are played within tightly fixed rules—in short, that they are *played*.[20]

I give the example of a tennis game, which gives me personal pleasure. How silly it seems, and how arbitrary, viewed from the outside, that grown men and women should put on a special costume, of white shirts and shorts (or skirts) and sneakers, and should "serve" or "return" balls across the net, trying to stay within white lines on a court, and having umpires call their shots "in" or "out." Game, set, and match: these are played with as much effort and concentration as people might expend in business or law, in making money or in gaining political power. Sweat pours down the face. The arm, the shoulder, the leg muscles ache. Indeed the effort and discipline of tennis, as of other sports, is a model for any hard and successful effort. Yet even when I lose, I smile and congratulate my victorious younger brother. I may even leap over the net to shake hands with him. It has been fun. Besides cheating, which is unthinkable, the great sin in tennis is to be a bad sport, to take the game too seriously, to forget that in the end, no matter how hard we play, it is only a game.

Although sports have always been good training for business, or for war (which long ago stopped being a game), and the battle of Waterloo may have been won on the playing fields of Eton, yet sports are also a model of the civilized life. They teach people to live by rules, to compete within fixed limits, and not to cheat. Passionate involvement is called for, and strong competition, in business or in politics, as in sports; but the penalty calls in sports when competitive energy passes its rightful bounds are a model for what should be the enforcing of just limits in real-life conduct. Sports show the positive grace, not just the protective cover, of law, order, and justice. The medieval tournament provided a model for chivalry as well as an alternative to war. The Olympic and other great public games in Greece gave order and beauty to the competition between states; they were strengthened in so doing by the play forms of religious ritual and holiday. To go back still further: in Homer, the funeral games for Patroclus reconcile the living not just with the dead but with the living. The games help to restore the basic order of things that the quarrel between Agamemnon and Achilles had disrupted. They include, to be sure, a certain amount of cheating by competitors, and of what we would call cheating interference by partisan gods; still, all in all, as Achilles presides and gives out prizes, their outcome seems generous, fair, and right. What could, outside the ring, have been murderous passions are controlled inside it, played out in the service of a reconciling social and cosmic order. Thus the *Iliad* moves back from conflict to a peaceful close.

In his book *Homo Ludens* Johan Huizinga has shown brilliantly that much of Western culture evolved from play forms. In the law court, for example, people came to settle disputes according to fixed, solemn rules. And this is something to be grateful for. Aeschylus, in his *Eumenides*, celebrated the passage from blood revenge to rational justice and due process of law as a glory of Athenian civilization, fostered by the evolutionary gods themselves. Written law, and equal treatment before the law (*isonomia*), are foundations of the Athenian democracy, long antedating the more specifically "demo-cratic" institution of the popular jury courts that are the focus of Aristophanes' *Wasps*. And still today, despite the law's delays, despite the ineptitude of judges and juries and the vicious complexities and abuses of litigation, the system of law still protects us, by its fixed rules and procedures, from falling back into the old bloodshed, or vendetta. Yet custom, inhibition, and self-interest shield us from noticing, or calling attention to, the ultimately arbitrary nature of the rules of law, which are the rules of a highly civilized and civilizing game. The courtroom is a special kind of playground. The judge's robe, the usher's "Oyez, oyez, oyez," the calling of decisions ("Objection overruled!"), all belong to the world of game and play. The rules of law are very rational in their regard for precedent, their concern for reasonable argument, and their insistence on certain kinds of proof, but at bottom they rest on no more finally solid foundations than do, say, the systems of chess, or geometry, or Thomistic theology, or symbolic logic. It is alarming to think that a system as basic and necessary to our lives as law is "only a game." The idea breeds anarchy, or confusion. I shall return to it in section 23, on the Trial of the Dog, for it is a major theme in the *Wasps*. For the moment, I think, we may take comedy's usual view, that to break or bypass the law is spoilsport behavior—that it literally spoils the sport, or the play, by which we become most civilized, most human, and most truly free in life. It is like upsetting the pieces of the game, or breaking your racquet and walking off the court.

The Athenians watching Aristophanes' *Wasps* would not, by and large, have thought of law as "only a game"; but they did look on oratorical displays and debates as entertainments. Indeed, such "musical" or cultural competitions were added to athletic programs at Olympia and elsewhere. The century from 450 to 350 B.C. is a high water mark of Athenian fascination with oratory, of its regularization in theory and teaching, and of its importance in everyday life. "Orator" became synonymous with politician. Gorgias speaks of the "necessary *agōn*s through arguments" that were conducted, at high stakes, in the jury courts and popular assembly;[21] the skillful speaker might escape danger in the courts, and he might capture economic and political power in both areas. At the same time, the Athenians' pride in their intellectual abilities to follow a speaker, and even anticipate his arguments, were joined with gullibility. The new medium of professionally shaped oratory was more than enjoyable: it was positively hypnotic. If Pericles praised the Athenians for the value they put on rational deliberation, Cleon brought out the shadow side of their nature when (himself practicing a trite demagoguery) he rebuked them for being "spectators of words and auditors of deeds."[22]

Through various poetic and theatrical devices, the comic playwright encourages his audience to enjoy the play of argument, much as one might watch tennis balls flying back and forth across the net: with no expectation of serious consequences to the players or oneself. Nobody is really hurt in comedy. It is not like tragedy, where the agon usually results in some painful decision, or loss, or suffering, or humiliation, or suicide, or murder, to all of which we respond as if they were real, with pity and terror. Still less is it like real life, where people's life and property, or a nation's security, may ride on the success or failure of arguments in the law court or assembly. The safety net of play is always there. We see through the imagined agon to comedy's own fixed rules of play, which remain as visible as they are arbitrary. We may even remember, or be reminded, that Aristophanes' play is itself part of a contest. He competes for first prize, against rivals; he campaigns, like a politician (but making his intentions transparent), for the support of the audience, on which the decision of the official judges must largely depend. Indeed, their last year's misjudgment, when they gave the *Clouds* only third prize, enters into the subject matter of this year's comedy.

But the comic agon does more than enable the audience to enjoy the play of argument without serious consequences to themselves or others. It also makes possible a complex series of recognitions. We are made aware on several levels of "the games people play." It is one thing to show up corrupt politicians like Cleon who trick ordinary people like ourselves and take advantage of them for selfish ends. Such are the usual, the proper butts of comedy. But Aristophanes goes further. He makes us recognize the games that *we* play, like old Philocleon, in our ordinary lives. It is not just that we are gullible, or misled, or victimized (though we usually are); it is more that we *want* to be deceived, that we play along with our deceivers because they hold out the fantasy promise of happiness. In real life, to be disabused of such illusions is like a kind of death. In comedy, one survives. Philocleon will not fall upon his sword. (If he does, it will turn out to be made of plaster.) The audience will see their illusions as in a mirror; but like Perseus looking at Medusa in the mirroring shield, they will not be turned to stone. Their hopefulness will grow, even when the games they play are shown up. This is, not least, because the comic poet shows up his own trickery too as "only a game." The framework of comedy, with all its accumulated devices and conventions, supports a surprising number of recognitions that, outside that charmed circle, might be intensely painful, disorienting, even life-killing. In comedy's playground, its dancing place in the theater, in the holy precinct of Dionysus, the recognitions can bring not only honesty, but healing. They are therapeutic, like a good dream rightly interpreted. They effect catharsis.

Before coming to the actual agon between Philocleon and Bdelycleon, I want to recall a cathartic process set earlier in train, in the proagon, or preliminary skirmish.[23] The chorus have been crying out angrily against Bdelycleon as a subverter of the democracy, a conspirator who would bring back tyranny. He deals with Sparta, he wears a fringed cloak, he lets his hair grow long! Notice how their prejudice already makes itself ridiculous by dwelling on externals, as though woolen fringes, or long hair, or a long, untrimmed beard prove conclusively that a person has dealings with the enemy. Bdelycleon develops the point, and Xanthias caps it off:

Bd. Every other word you speak is "tyranny," "conspirators."
　　No matter what the argument, it's "tyranny, conspirators."
　　I never even *heard* the name of "tyranny" these fifty years:
　　now it's more common than sardines, it rolls around the
　　　　marketplace.
　　Say a man buys shrimps or flounder, passing up the anchovies:
　　right away the man who's selling cheap salt fish denounces him.
　　"You see? That swell's getting a party ready—towards a tyranny!"
　　Or he buys expensive mushrooms, just to liven up the shrimp:
　　then the woman who sells the beans and lettuce from her own
　　　　backyard
　　comments darkly: "See, this thing's mushrooming into tyranny.
　　We don't want to have a man for all seasonings here at Athens!"
Xa. You're so-o-o right. Only yesterday I was feeling lazy in a brothel
　　and I asked my hooker, would she mind taking the galloping
　　　　position?
　　Oh, she got mad. "You're getting up a Gallop poll for
　　　　tyranny!"　　　　　　　　　　　　　　　　　　　　　(488–502)

The last joke, literally on *hippos* ("horse") and the name Hippias, makes a fine punch line, but the whole passage is splendid in its idiocy. It is also typical of the way Aristophanes flirts with paranoia and takes it as far as it will go, to expose its inherent absurdity. We are caught up in a wild and crazy vision of conspiracy that moves with relentless logic through the fish stalls, through the vegetable stalls, and finally through the brothels, seizing on unmistakable signs that the enemies of democracy are at work. And what would these subversives be plotting but to restore the tyranny of Hippias—the last tyrant of Athens, who was expelled in 510 B.C. and whom the Persians had tried unsuccessfully to bring back as an old man in 490, sixty-eight years before this play?

Tension is dispelled in laughter. The chorus quiet down. Even Philocleon quiets down, at least to the point of expressing more lucidly what is at stake for him in his struggle with his son. For Bdelycleon sees his efforts as sensible and kind: he wants to free his father of his "earlyrising-sycophantic-lawsuit-effortful habits" so that he will enjoy a more comfortable and gentlemanly life of leisure. But Philocleon won't trade his jury life for any degree of promised comfort:

> Subversive boy! You promise birds' milk,
> pie in the sky, and endless play,
> but all I want is my jury life
> that *you* keep trying to take away.
> It isn't lobster, it isn't sole
> my soul is pining for to get:
> Only a saucy little lawsuit,
> piping hot, served *en brochette.*   (508–11)

He cannot be bribed, not by eels (as the Greek has it), not even by birds' milk, the ultimate in fantasy riches. But he is shaken by Bdelycleon's claim that he is really a dupe and a slave, not an omnipotent ruler. Hence he agrees to the formal debate.

Philocleon's main speech (C1; I skip the preliminaries to this formal agon) is splendidly naive in its account of the pleasures and the sense of power that the jury court provides him. It also reveals a fantastic self-inflation amounting to megalomania. For Philocleon, who now identifies himself with the entire jury, enjoying its sovereign power of life and death, describes how rich and important people defer to him out of fear, flatter him, play up to him. So, for that matter, do the politicians: Cleonymus, Cleon, Theorus (the same gang who appeared in the joke-and-dream prologue, even in the same order). When he comes home, his jury pay wins him respect and independence. When he is in court, he feels—and this is the climax of his statement, the rattled-off *pnigos,* D1—that he is like Zeus himself, lightning and thundering. It is an experience of sheer potency. To have everyone afraid of him: what more, what better could life have to offer?

If Philocleon's speech as a whole reveals his delusions of grandeur, the great bubble of self-inflating fantasy that his more realistic son will

prick, its exaggerated details still bring out some of the emotional gratifications a real juryman might enjoy. Defendants do anything and everything to appeal to his pity. They even trot out their little boys and girls, to
soften his anger. Or they tell jokes: "Some tell us stories, or something
funny from Aesop, or they make jokes, so I will laugh and put down my
temper (*katathōmai*)" (566–67). Here Aristophanes is making several
comic points at once. Through his naive speaker he makes us realize the
extent to which the courtroom has become a place of entertainment.[24] It
offers various pleasures: some comparatively harmless, like being told
jokes; some more harmful, like "interfering with a maiden's will" (there
are more sex jokes here, reminding us of Philocleon's warped erotic
nature); but perhaps the most telling point is that the jury court has
merged with the theater. A fantastic sequence of vignettes confirms the
point. If a good tragic actor is on trial, he must recite a famous speech
from Aeschylus' *Niobe*. If a piper wins his case, he must pipe the jurymen off with a good tune. All this goes to show, in its ridiculous way,
that the jurymen are paid off, or manipulated, with emotional satisfac-
tions all too much like those offered by the theater. They attend the court
for a good cry, or a good laugh. They like having their emotions played
upon by clever speakers; they feel that they control the situation, that
they remain aware of what is going on, and that they remain free to act
just as they please, regardless of speeches, or justice, or anything else that
might get in their way.

But the comparison between court and theater cuts two ways. The
comic poet himself may use humor to dispel the fumes of anger, to
promote good feeling and clarity, to effect a catharsis. We just saw an
example of this in the Hippias joke. Is the comic poet, then, a manipulator of people's emotions, like the sophisticated orator? The idea is suggestive and complex. The fullest extant ancient account of the nature of
the emotions comes in the second book of Aristotle's *Rhetoric*. It includes, among other things, a full description of the motives of anger,
and of pity. This might remind us that the great advances in Greek
psychological understanding arose largely from the needs, and the labo-
ratory experience, of the law courts. It may even be that this in turn
influenced Aristotle's concept of the tragic or comic catharsis experienced in the theater. I shall return to the connections later on. What
matters for now is that humor—the telling of a joke, a fable, a funny
story—can be, precisely, a means of getting other people to do what one
wants. Which usually means, to dispel or "put down" their anger.

Aristotle says that anger is caused, among other things, by the thought
that you have not been treated with proper respect.[25] And through
Philocleon's description of his life at home, where his jury pay com-
mands respect and a show of affection, and gives him a happy feeling of
independence, we gain a momentary glimpse into a situation that must

often have been very different: of men falling into weakness and dependency as they grow old, being treated without much respect, and building up a sense of frustration and anger that becomes habitual. But we have seen these old men already, in the entrance of the old jurymen led by boys. If for them, as for their champion Philocleon, the jury court provides not just entertainment but a feeling of really being alive and of having some measure of control over their environment (even if they don't approach the condition of thundering Zeus)—then what will it mean to take that existence away from them, whether by persuasion, or by bribery, or by a comic catharsis within which both bribery and persuasion might be subsumed?[26]

The chorus sing (B1) of how impressed they were by Philocleon's speech. They seemed to grow bigger as they listened, even to be—*judging* in the Isles of the Blest. The incongruous image suggests the power of delusion working upon the mind. But they have also come to see Bdelycleon as a defendant. To get off, he must soothe and soften their temper. Just let him try! As jurymen, they resist; but also they wait to be amused and placated. As chorus, they egg Bdelycleon on (B1 and B2) to great efforts. What can he possibly have up his sleeve?

He will have much; but first, in a conventional disavowal of oratorical ability, he lets the mask slip a little: "It is hard: it takes a fearful intelligence, and more than lies in comic players (*trygōidoi*), to cure a disease long ingrown in the polis" (650–51). It is like Dicaeopolis' speech in rags, when the persona of the comic hero (playing a tragic hero, who is playing a beggar) is dropped momentarily, to reveal—the persona of the comic playwright. Dicaeopolis' defense mirrored that of Aristophanes, but the audience were meant to see through both, as through the Telephus rags themselves. So too here: Bdelycleon momentarily turns into "Aristophanes," the comic playwright as therapist, who would use the techniques of comedy to perform, if possible, a healing catharsis of the body politic. It may be possible, or it may not. But "Aristophanes" gives us fair warning that behind and through the persona of Bdelycleon, he is going to try.

We might also have been warned by Bdelycleon's behavior before and during Philocleon's speech. Not only is he calm and collected, like a lawyer sure of his case: he calls for his briefcase, takes out writing materials, and makes notes of important points while Philocleon is speaking. To us this would seem quite normal behavior. To the Greek audience it would have seemed peculiar, and very funny, much as today if a lawyer for the defense brought a computer into court and used it, with audible clickings and whirrings and other odd noises, to program his defense.

The point is that Bdelycleon has mastered the latest technology. His rhetorical tricks are made visible. We are also reminded that this is all a game.

In the best manner, recommended by teachers of rhetoric, Bdelycleon takes the points made by his father and turns them around. Often he uses the same words. Like a "teacher" rehearsing the simple facts, he gives what seems a rational argument based on statistics out of his notebook:

National income: two thousand talents a year;
Jury pay: (obtained by multiplying three obols per diem when court is in session by six thousand jurymen, gives you—roughly) one hundred fifty talents a year;
Which is: less than one tenth!

Philocleon is shocked, and not for the last time. Where has all the money gone? To the same old gang, his son replies. It is they who are really feared, who are given all manner of wonderful bribes, and who have the real power; while you get little, you are pushed around by petty officials and bureaucrats, and you are kept poor on purpose like a half-starved mongrel dog who is meant to leap savagely at enemies when the master whistles. Your bad temper is an instrument in their hands. It helps them blackmail rich opponents—and get those beautiful bribes all for themselves.

It may be true. But it is also sleight of hand, and so is the subsequent picture that Bdelycleon draws, of the riches that the jurymen ought to gain from the Athenian empire. Take the tribute-paying cities, about one thousand of them; assign twenty jurymen to each: presto! that would maintain twenty thousand jurymen "in hare's-meat stew, golden crowns, cream, and cream cheese." It is a beautiful, silly picture of the Schlaraffenland kind so prominent in Old Comedy. Just think of all those jurymen wearing golden crowns—and swimming in cream cheese! If anyone in the audience was quick at math, he might have noticed how Bdelycleon's "reliable statistics" shift around. The six thousand jurymen have become twenty thousand. What is more important is that Bdelycleon uses fantasy as a weapon to counter fantasy. He matches a delusion of power with one of riches. (It may be that the riches were there; but they were hardly so available in wartime, and only a fool would spend them like this. Anyway, there were *not* one thousand tribute-paying cities.) He adds (D2) that he personally will give Philocleon anything he wants, if he will stay out of court. Anything, that is, except—"paymaster's milk!"

We are meant, as an audience, to be carried along by the force of the argument. We are also meant to realize how tricky it is, and to see what it does to old Philocleon. His reactions are melodramatic, in the grand style. He is "stirred up from the depths" (696), his mind is "transported," he "doesn't know what is happening to him" (697). And later, after the revelation of the great riches he might have had,

> Oh, me. What torpor is this, that steals
>   over my (voting) hand?
> My sword I can no longer hold upright.
>   I am weak and soft. (713–14)

The sword that Philocleon lets droop from his nerveless fingers is a sign
of potency. It recalls the proud military past of the old jurymen. It is also
a phallic symbol (the more so, if Philocleon held it up, then let it droop,
the way I would have suggested had I been directing the play); like the
wasp sting to which it corresponds, it is an image of the compensation
for lost erotic vitality that the courts have given to the old man. To let it
drop is a tragic gesture, of defeat.

And it is followed by a tragic silence. While the chorus describe how
impressed they were by Bdelycleon's speech, and call on Philocleon to
yield, and praise his son as a thoughtful, kind, and generous benefactor,
and appeal to him to be reasonable and take this good advice when it is
offered, and while, moreover, Bdelycleon continues to promise a string
of comforts appropriate to his father's old age (some of which sound
pleasant, and nearly all of which sound condescending), Philocleon himself remains in a state of collapse, unreplying. Then, like a tragic hero or
heroine fallen into some great passion or distress, he finally breaks silence with a cry of utter pain, and with an aria that rises from the depths
of his laden heart:

> *Ph.* Oh, me! Alas! Oh, I!
> *Bd.* You there, why do you cry?
> *Ph.* Promise me none of these things, you.
>   I want to be where the skies are blue,
>   where the herald cries,
>   "Who hasn't voted? Let him rise!"
>   In juryland I'll take my stand,
>   holding on high my voting hand.—
>   Hasten, o soul divine!
>   Where *is* that soul of mine?
>   Swing low, sweet—bird thou never wort.
>   *Oh*, how I'll clean out Cleon, the old thief,
>   if I get him into court! (750–59)

How ridiculous this is. The crusty old juryman was simply not meant to
be Euripides' Phaedra. He didn't die of lovesickness before, and he won't
now. And yet how very painful it is to be stripped of an illusion of power
and glory and plunged back into the real, the ordinary world of old age.
It is like losing one's soul. Aristophanes may sympathize with the old
scoundrel more than we realized. Certainly the state of mind that he
portrays, in this tragic parody, comes very close to tragedy. The escape
into comedy is a very narrow one. But it is suggested, also, by the end of

the song, where (in very tragic fashion) passive grief shifts into active and savage anger, against Cleon. This is exactly what Bdelycleon intended, and "Aristophanes" with him. In riddling fashion, the last three words, *kleptonta Kleōna laboimi,* anticipate what will be staged in the next scene, the Trial of the Dog.

23   *Bdelycleon's Game:*
The Trial of the Dog

As a compensation for the loss of his life in court, Bdelycleon provides his father with a luxurious substitute: he will judge at home. The following scene has a strong feeling of wish fulfillment about it, like Dicaeopolis' private market in the *Acharnians*, or the Demos-pampering scene in the *Knights*. The idea is that Philocleon will enjoy the excitement of jury trials together with the ease and comfort of staying home. If the sun shines, he will judge outdoors; if it rains, he will stay in. If the jury (namely, Philocleon) feels hungry, there is hot soup ready, on the fire; wretches need not "hang, that jurymen may dine"; and besides, since this is all improvisation, the soup cups will double as voting urns. Likewise, a chamber pot hangs ready, in case the jury needs to piss. By the same economy of ways and means, the chamber pot will serve as a timepiece (*clepsydra*, a water clock; literally, "water-stealer").

The fantasy is ridiculous, but it is also gratifying. As often, we miss much of the vicarious pleasure today because we live in a world where science has already supplied most of the marvels of the Golden Age. We can watch a football or baseball game on television, seeing the details of play up close, without having to fight for tickets, drive to a distant stadium, worry about rain, or struggle for Coca-Cola and hot dogs; we can sit indoors in a comfortable chair, with cold beer from the refrigerator and a bathroom close by and uncrowded. Soon, I suppose, we shall shop and "go to the office" from home also; and before very long, the inconvenient business of being called to jury duty will be dealt with via two-way television. Not much, in this science-fiction world, is left for the comic poet's imagination to perform except to remind us that we are being bribed by "bread and circuses" into forgetting who we are.

In the game provided for old Philocleon by his son, and for the audience by Aristophanes, the images of comfort and luxury are still extremely gratifying. Their first business is to give pleasure, and laughter.

But the Trial of the Dog also invites critical observation and reflection. It is a play within a play. As we watch it and (with Philocleon) enjoy it, we become aware on several levels of "the games people play," how they are constructed, what rules they do or do not follow, and what kinds of deception or self-deception they involve. In the process almost everybody and everything is shown up as fraudulent: the court system; Cleon and Laches; Bdelycleon, and the moralizing or reformist "Aristophanes" behind him. And the playing out of the trial as a multifaceted game of deception and undeception almost, but not quite, puts an end to play itself.

We see, first, how the "jury court at home" is set up as a sort of game. This is the more evident because the actors manage with just a few props and a largely bare stage, so that the audience must, as ever, use their imaginations to fill in what is lacking. When the father, son, and slave set things up, they are rather like children playing a game of let's-pretend. (Compare the little children on those squat, red-figured Athenian *choes* who dress up as grown-ups and pretend that they are having a parade.) They are also like actors performing a scene under the playwright's direction, working out stage business as they go. There may even be moments, which we miss, when actual directions to the actors are incorporated in the dialogue between characters: a nice economy, again, of ways and means. At first, it is primarily Bdelycleon who organizes the let's-pretend game. With the assistance of his slaves/stagehands, he produces: (1) the pisspot, symbol of primary satisfaction; (2) the brazier and soup kettle with soup bowls; and (3) a rooster to keep the jury awake. For (4) the statue of the hero Lycus, he passes off an available substitute.[27] At this point, Philocleon joins actively in the game. It is he who missed the statue; he also misses (5) the railings setting off the court from the general public, but this time he goes off himself and returns with a pigpen as a substitute. After that Bdelycleon decides that the soup cups will serve as (6) voting urns and the pisspot as (7) clepsydra. The game of Courtroom is coming along well. When the slave Xanthias rushes in to present what will be the first (and only) case—the dog Labes got into the kitchen and bolted down a whole Sicilian cheese, and another dog says he will prosecute—we are halfway ready to believe that this was not planned, but a happy surprise. It is also like entering into a dream, but one, again, that can be interpreted, that provides a whole series of recognitions. Let me, before presenting the dog's trial, sketch out the various levels on which these can occur.

(1) We see, from a play perspective, how an Athenian law court works. Part of the fun is being able to observe and even join in the action of a jury trial without the real-life inconveniences of the jury court. Philocleon is spared the difficulties of rising early, of following official directions, of depending on chance for the number of cases (if any) on which he will sit, of waiting in line for his pay—which, as he points out, is split

inconveniently between pairs of jurors. All this is easy now. The welfare state, which might be thought to have grown from Pericles' institution of two obols for jury pay, which Cleon increased to three—a very "democratic" idea, but also a political bribe if there ever was one—has now expanded to its logical limits. In normal life, too, the procedures of the jury court are psychologically inhibiting as well as physically inconvenient. Most people would have felt constrained by the religious and legal procedures, the proclamations ("Order in the Court!"), the powerful politicians, the ever-present petty officials. From all this Philocleon is freed, and the audience with him. And as a result they are free to realize, more than ever before, that trial by jury is a game. Set off from the profane world by a set of railings (or, as the case may be, a pigpen), and set off from ordinary existence by special rituals involving prayer, the jury court becomes a playground, with its own special space and time, within which play is free but also ordered by certain arbitrary rules. The Greek terms, on which Aristophanes constantly plays, *diōkō* and *pheugō*, "to pursue" and "to flee," help to make the trial like an athletic contest, a special kind of race in which the prosecutor tries to catch up, the defendant to get home safe. So the jury trial, with all its excitement but also with its normally grave consequences, is shown to be only a game. And we watch, carefully, with relaxed attention, to see how it is played.

(2) We see, or see through, Cleon's game; for it is ridiculously easy to recognize Cleon beneath the very incomplete disguise of the prosecuting, loud-barking dog. On this level the trial is a transparent political satire, representing and commenting on an actual or projected prosecution of Laches by Cleon.[28] This piece of satire is not the same as Aristophanes' comic idea, but it may be the kernel from which it grew; we should never underestimate his joy in exposing Cleon as the cheat, fraud, and blusterer that he apparently was. Not that Laches comes off so well in the present analogue; but Cleon is clearly the greater villain of the two. The revelation of his bullying tactics is meant as an edifying lesson for Philocleon ("Cleon-Lover"), who has been led around by the nose by that demagogue. It is equally intended by Aristophanes, Cleon's erstwhile victim, as a useful lesson for his own captive audience, bribed into relaxed attention by an entertainment precisely analogous to that offered to Philocleon by his manipulative son.

(3) Which brings us to Bdelycleon's game. We see that, although he is the law-enforcing, presiding magistrate, he also enters into the trial and influences its outcome in a cheating manner. He is quite as much a cheat here as the villainous Cleon or the dumb, guilty Laches. But this overt manipulation of the trial-game points to a still more significant manipulation behind the scenes, for Bdelycleon uses the trial, and the whole "jury court at home," both as a substitution-bribe, to keep Philocleon away from the actual courts, and still more, as a kind of play therapy, to

exorcise his father's bad temper in a harmless manner and change his character for the better. The lawyer for the defense, struggling for an acquittal, here coincides with the son struggling to reform his perverse old father. A vote for acquittal would signify that both aims had been achieved. The parody of the usual ceremonial prayer reveals Bdelycleon's intention:

> O Lord Apollo, street-wise god,
>> before my gates who art enshrined,
> accept this novel sacrament
>> we offer up for Daddy's mind,
> and make his tough and stubborn ways,
>> which are excessive, now to cease:
> turn down the fire beneath his heart
>> and stir in sugar, milk, and peace.
> Let him be gentle from now on
>> and feel for people facing trial,
> so, when they cry,
> he'll wipe his eye
>> and change his angry temper—for a smile.   (875–90)

The metaphor of the "sacrament" or initiation rite suggests some kind of quasi-religious fraud. It may recall the "false initiation" offered by Socrates in last year's comedy, the *Clouds*. What is more important, it is linked with the earlier report of Bdelycleon's attempts to heal his father's obsession by various kinds of therapy. He had tried persuasion (*anepeithen*, a word that recurs significantly in this play in its other sense, "bribe"). He had tried religious purification, and then Corybantic music: both were forms of catharsis, of religious and psychological healing (the two go closely together), and both could therefore be summed up under Xanthias' term *teletai*, "ceremonies" or "rites" of purification. Incubation in Asclepius' temple followed, then downright physical constraint. Bdelycleon failed before; but in attempting a new "rite" he is attempting a new kind of therapy, related basically to the old ones, but with overtones now of fraud. This is play therapy, or comic catharsis.

(4) But this in turn brings us to see, and to see through, the game of "Aristophanes," for in many ways Bdelycleon ("Hate-Cleon") personifies the aims and methods of the comic poet, who hates Cleon and wants to teach his audience a moral and political lesson by putting them in good humor.[29] We saw earlier that defendants in court used jokes, fables, and funny stories as a means of dispelling the jury's anger and prejudice against them. Humor could be, indeed was, a rhetorical weapon. By analogy Aristophanes' present play, "a little story with a point," could resemble an Aesopic fable, humorously conveying a moral and educational lesson to its hearers. We saw also that Bdelycleon's mask slipped

when he spoke of the difficulty of healing, not his old father, but a disease long engrained in the polis. If Bdelycleon is a fraud and a manipulator, then it is very likely that "Aristophanes" is one also. The situation will resemble that of Dicaeopolis' speech in rags, with the Telephus mask slipping to reveal Dicaeopolis and the Dicaeopolis mask slipping to reveal Aristophanes. There is the same comic joy in mixing up levels, and the same joy in unmasking fraud and pretense, including one's own. In Bdelycleon's prayer the metaphor of a new rite, suggesting religious therapy but also religious fakery, shifts to another, equally ambivalent metaphor, of the magic cook. In the *Knights*, this became finally a very positive self-representation of the comic poet; but before that, cooking was closely linked with flattery, bribery, deception, fraud, and demagoguery—of someone who would outdo Cleon at his own methods.[30] In the passage here, this suggestion of fraud comes uppermost in connection with Bdelycleon and with the reformist "Aristophanes" behind him. Hence it is appropriate that the chorus, joining in Bdelycleon's prayer and praising his efforts as very patriotic, very people-loving, should end with the word *neōterōn*. That is, Bdelycleon is best of the "younger people," the moderns, but also—a second meaning—of the "revolutionaries." What he is attempting is, at bottom, subversive, conspiratorial, and antidemocratic. He is really trying to set up a tyranny after all. And "Aristophanes," if we are really seeing through his game too, is not much better.

(5) There is, of course, yet another game: the game of the comic poet, the play that includes, and lets us see through, all the other games. We shall understand it better at the end, after "Aristophanes" has professed himself a champion therapist or *kathartēs*, in the parabasis, and after Bdelycleon's efforts at moral and psychological reformation have altogether failed, and those of "Aristophanes," by extension, with them. But this is to anticipate much. Let us return to the Trial of the Dog. I give it whole, as a complete and hilarious play within a play. It is less important to keep my levels of interpretation in mind than to follow the little play as the audience would have followed it, with enjoyment. Still, along with that enjoyment, Aristophanes draws his audience toward certain recognitions. Through game and riddle he teases them into awareness, as into joining in the interpretation of a queer but significant dream.

THE TRIAL OF THE DOG

Bd. Order in the court! The jury will take their seats.
Nobody will be seated after the picture—
I mean, after the trial has begun.
Ph. Who's on trial? *He* won't get away!
Bd. I shall read the formal accusation.

The case of Mr. Dog, of Berkshire County,
versus J. Paul Getty, of Huntington.
Defendant is charged with slurping down a bowl
of caviar from Iran. All by himself.
Suggested penalty: ring around the collar.

Ph. Impounded to a pulp, if *I* catch him!

Bd. And here now's the defendant. J. Paul Getty.

Ph. Gotcha, you villain! What a mug-shot face!
Thinks he can fool me, making up to me?
Where's the prosecutor, Mr. Dog?

Dog. Arf, arf!

Bd. Accounted for.

Ph. Why, it's another Getty, just good for barking.
And licking food off plates.

Bd. Silence in court! The jury *will* be seated.
You there, you take the stand, and prosecute.

Ph. (Meanwhile, I'll pour myself this onion soup and slurp it down.)

Dog. Gentlemen of the jury. Give this charge
your full attention. He has Done Us Dirt,
me most of all, and then the *hoi polloi.*
What has he done, you ask? Why, he sneaked
into the pantry, grabbed some caviar
fresh from Iran, and ran away with it,
and filled his lousy belly in the dark.

Ph. Just what I thought. First time he opened his mouth,
I knew it was a case of—*caviar emptor.*

Dog. And after that, he didn't give *me* a share.
How can anyone go into public service
if he doesn't serve me first? I WANT MY CUT!

Ph. He sure didn't serve the public. Which is *me.*
I think the prosecutor's getting hot
just like this soup.

Bd. Good god, Daddy! Don't decide the case
till you've heard both sides give their evidence.

Ph. The situation's clear. It—*shrieks* for itself.

Dog. Don't let him home free. Of all living men,
he's the most dog-gone solitary glutton.
Think how he circumnavigated all
the pantry shelves, and skimmed off all the dough.
Of all the thieving dogs—he takes the cake.

Ph. Egg-sactly. Every time we get doughnuts, he
eats all the rest. And I'm left with the hole.

Dog. You've got to punish him. You know the proverb:
two early rob-bers never get the worm.

Don't leave me barking up the wrong tree,
or else I'll go on strike—won't bark at all!

Ph.　Ohboyohboy!
What a neat case! It's tidier than Swiss cheese—
it's got no holes in it. Man *looks* like a thief,
man *is* a thief! Don't you think so, rooster?
He really does, he cocked an eye at me.
Where's the manager gone? I want my pisspot.

Bd.　Get it yourself. It's witness time. I call
the witnesses for Getty to come forward.
Mortimer Pestle. Holly Cheesegrater.
Mistah fender. Messy: pots and pans.
—Must you go on pissing? Won't you be seated?

Ph.　I'll make *him* s-it. In his pants, he'll be so frightened.

Bd.　Why don't you let up on the macho bit?
Why do you get so angry at defendants?
Now, Getty. Take the stand. Make your defense.
What's wrong now? Can't you speak? Dog got your tongue?

Ph.　Somebody hasn't got a leg to stand on.

Bd.　Not so. Same thing happened to him just now
that happened when old T. C. was on trial.
The poor man got a seizure. Of the tongue.
Out of the way. I'll give the defense myself.
GENTLEMEN OF THE JURY: It's no easy matter
to answer all the slanderous charges made
against this man. But still, I'll do it, for
he's a very decent dog. He chases wolves.

Ph.　But I say he's a thief. And a subversive!

Bd.　He's nothing of the sort. As sheepdogs go,
I'd say he was a Champion First Class.

Ph.　What's the good of that, if he gulps down caviar?

Bd.　What's the good? He fights; he guards your door.
Haven't you heard of "caviare to the general"?
Forgive his faults; he never finished high school.

Ph.　I wish he'd never finished the first grade:
then he wouldn't be making this defense.

Bd.　Please calm yourself. Here are the witnesses.
Cheese-grater, take the stand. And see you speak
in a grate-big voice. Tell us: were the soldiers
grateful recipients of all the spoils?
—He says they were.

Ph.　　　　　　　　　　He *says*. Of course, he's lying.

Bd.　My dear, deluded Dad. Have mercy on
poor Getty here. He lives on bread and water;

he never spends the night in the same—kitchen.
And look at the other. He's what you call a lapdog:
just laps up lunch. Or else he yaps and yaps.

Ph. Oh, me. What fatal weakness
    comes upon me from behind?
Some evil overtakes me:
    I begin to change my mind.

Bd. I beg you, Daddy, pity the poor dog,
don't ruin him. Where did those children go?
Take the stand, little puppies. Just look cute
and make pathetic little whimpering sounds.

Ph. Get down. Get down. Get down. Get down.

Bd.   I'm getting down,
only that phrase, "get down," has gotten a lot
of decent people down. Still, I'll get down.

Ph. Why the hell did I slurp that onion soup?
Look at me, crying my whole mind away,
and all for nothing. All for onion soup.

Bd. Doesn't he get off then?

Ph.   Hard to be sure.

Bd. Come on, Daddy. Display your nicer side.
Just take this ballot, and go drop it in
Bowl Number Two, and let him off. *Please*, Daddy?

Ph. I can't do it. I never finished high school.

Bd. Let me lead you around, the shortest way.

Ph. This is Bowl Number One?

Bd.   It is.

Ph.   Well, here's my vote.

Bd. (Fooled him! His verdict is Not Guilty, but
he doesn't know it yet!) Let's count the votes.

Ph. How did we do? How has the contest gone?

Bd. Hard to be sure. —Getty, you've GOTTEN OFF!
—Daddy, daddy! What's happened? Help! Some water!
Won't you lift up your head?

Ph.   Tell me one thing.
Did he really get off?

Bd.   He did.

Ph.   Then I'm done for!

Bd. Don't worry. It's all right. Just please get up.

Ph. How can I have this sin upon my conscience?
Let a defendant off! What will I do?
God in heaven, grant a poor sinner mercy!
I didn't mean to do it. It's not my style.

Bd. It's all right, Dad. Don't carry on like that.

> I'll look after you, see to your every need,
> take you to dinner parties, and on cruises—
> you can have fun all the rest of your life,
> and lots of *rest*,
> and you won't be bothered with a single pest.
> But let's go in.

Ph. All right, if that's what you think best.

Again (the reader should be warned) I have introduced my own jokes, substituting Iranian caviar for the satiric business about the Sicilian cheese that Labes gulped down (= money that Laches, as general in Sicily, allegedly embezzled). I tried to be faithful to the various dog jokes and metaphors, and the mix-up of canine and human descriptions; and I thought that J. Paul Getty, as the rather funny name of a billionaire, would do nicely for the Labes/Laches joke. What I have not done, for reasons of space, is to give full stage directions. These can be supplied from Aristophanes' text without much difficulty, and embellished with music, pageantry, and slapstick. The parade of witnesses must have been, and could still be, a great comic spectacle. To my mind one of the finest, and lowest, moments in the scene comes when Bdelycleon looks for water to revive his fainting father. Just visualize the stage setting and ask yourself what "water" will be available to throw on the old man. It is a final manifestation of the *clepsydra*, the water clock.

As well as being a recognizable satiric skit, the trial takes on features of a dream scene like those mentioned in the prologue. There we heard of a whale haranguing a flock of sheep, while a crow-headed man sat nearby. Now, one dog, played as a dog-headed man, prosecutes another such creature in domestic court; kitchen utensils appear in procession, a cheese-grater takes the stand, and whining little puppies beg for clemency. Also, a rooster, barely mentioned in the text but prominent on-stage, crows from time to time to keep the jury awake. But how should this dream scene be interpreted? What recognitions would the audience have enjoyed?

First and foremost, they cannot have missed the satire against Cleon. It seems likely that *Kyōn*, "Mr. Dog," combined features of a Cleon portrait mask with features of a dog.[31] Nor was the dog comparison new, for in the *Knights* Aristophanes had already described Cleon as a villainous hound. Had Cleon claimed in real life to be a "watchdog of the people"?[32] Probably he had, and this struck Aristophanes' funny bone; certainly it is demolished by the sausage-seller in his counter-oracle:

> Beware the Cerberus-hound, my son,
> that takes you in with a fawning gait:
> the moment you turn your eyes away,
> it steals the food right off your plate.

> The brute will sneak into your kitchen, still unseen,
> and lick your dinner dishes—and the Islands—clean.
>
> *(Knights* 1030–34)

The wordplay that Aristophanes exploits here, between *kyōn* ("dog") and *Kleōn*, may by this time have become a satiric commonplace at Athens, almost like a cartoon. The same may be true of the Cerberus comparison. In the *Wasps* Aristophanes dramatizes the comparison and takes the wordplay further. He makes *Kleōn* a riddling amalgam of *kyōn* with *kleptō*, "to steal"; thus his name may be interpreted meaningfully as "Stealing Dog."[33] Philocleon's angry wish quoted earlier, *kleptonta Kleōna laboimi*, "May I catch Cleon stealing!" anticipates the essential elements of the dog trial: the stealing, Cleon, and also Labes—the latter being an amalgam of General Laches, Cleon's enemy, and the root *lab-*, to "get" or "grab."

Aristophanes clearly meant his audience to enjoy themselves as they followed the clues that point to his attack on Cleon. He pretends earlier to put them off the track, saying (through Xanthias the slave) that he won't resort to the old tired ploy of chopping Cleon into mincemeat; but much of the fun of the play comes from the way Cleon keeps coming in, one way or another, like an obsession. The dreams point to Cleon; the protagonists' names mean Love Cleon and Loathe Cleon; people keep mentioning Cleon; and sooner or later—sooner, if they are quick to pick up hints, but later in any event—the audience are provided with the happy recognition of Cleon and Laches behind the dog trial: the familiar beneath the absurd.

Nobody in the audience would have missed the point that Aristophanes was getting at Cleon, that in his view Cleon was much guiltier than Laches or anyone else, for that matter, who might be put on trial. They probably *did* miss the broader suggestion that most everybody steals at some point or other, that the jurymen and Philocleon have stolen (when they were young and strong), and that, in fact, the entire courtroom is pervaded by the atmosphere of deception and fraud symbolized by the controlling *klepsydra*, the "water-stealer." It may be, as said earlier, that Aristophanes had thought of writing a satire on Cleon and the jury courts. What is remarkable is how the present comedy has grown beyond such a limited satire, both in its fun and in the recognitions that it makes available to the audience. The Trial of the Dog, embodying that satiric kernel of the play, has now become a play within a play. More than the dog-mischief of Cleon, it exhibits the tricks of the defense; and behind these, it shows up the manipulative behavior of Bdelycleon as he tries to control and reform his mischievous old father. We also watch Philocleon's defeat, and his near-tragic collapse as a person.

Bdelycleon intervenes to speak for "Labes" because the poor hound is terrified by the thundering denunciations of the prosecuting dog and the strong anger awakened in the jury. There is, of course, a theatrical joke here. Labes has to be "struck dumb" because he is played by a nonspeaking actor; the three speaking parts are for Philocleon, Bdelycleon, and Kyon. Normally, of course, defendants spoke for themselves in Athenian courts. If they were rich or influential, a friend or (increasingly) a rhetorician might write out the defense plea for them to learn. But here, the presiding judge and "lawgiver" (*nomothetēs*) steps into the trial like a *deus ex machina*, to force an acquittal. He tries, obviously, to get around the issue of Labes' theft of the cheese, or embezzlement of public funds. He argues (1) that Labes is a good watchdog, (2) that he didn't know better, (3) that he divided the spoils with his soldiers, as the witnesses attest; and (4) that while Labes does all the hard work, the other dog stays home and practices blackmail. On the political level, much of this can be recognized as holding true of Laches and Cleon. On the juridical level, it is largely irrelevant—the usual throwing of dust in the jurymen's eyes. The climax comes when Bdelycleon calls up the poor little whining puppies, to awaken the jury's pity—the last recourse of a guilty party in many trials (and one of the concessions that Socrates refused to make to the expectations of his jury). It almost works. Philocleon actually cries, though he blames it on the hot soup. But he recovers his will to condemn, so that only the overt lie of Bdelycleon tricks him into voting for acquittal. The behavior of the defense, and of the presiding magistrate, can only be described as a steal.

Throughout the scene the audience could see themselves in Philocleon as he watched, and commented on, the trial. The question whether Labes is or is not guilty yields to a more basic question: how the jury (Philocleon) *feels* about his guilt or, put differently, whether Philocleon can be seduced by pity into acquitting a defendant and, by pleasure in this substitute-court play, into relinquishing his old lifestyle. Will he acquit Labes? Will the play therapy do its job?

He will, it seems, acquit Labes, and this will signify the end of his former lifestyle. But the feeling is one of defeat, not accomplishment. It is marked, as in the previous agon, by melodramatic words, gestures, and actions that parody the collapse of a tragic hero when he recognizes his true situation. Thus Philocleon describes his sense that a terrible weakness is coming over him. The word he uses, *malattomai*, means "to be softened," recalling the wish of Bdelycleon to remove the hardness from his father's temper; but it also means "to sicken," and we are reminded of the first presentation of Philocleon, as a lovesick heroine out of Euripides. For him, to be persuaded (or bribed) to change his mind is like a grievous sickness, almost a kind of death. Then, when he is tricked into acquitting a defendant, he faints dead away. He feels utterly defeated. He can only be raised with difficulty from a state of total collapse. Of course it is utterly ridiculous that a person should collapse because he has acquitted a defendant. One would think that he had killed his father and married his mother. We sense too that Philocleon will survive this defeat and this distress. Still, his last words are poignant as he gives in to Bdelycleon's renewed offer of a comfortable retirement: "All right, if that's what you think best." These words are not mock-tragic. They are the language of the despair that ordinary people feel offstage when some hope or illusion falls through, and they are left to live each day as best they can, to grow old, and to die.

I think of a comparable moment in Shakespeare's *Henry IV*, Part 2. Falstaff, the old rogue, has heard of Henry IV's death and has ridden to London posthaste to watch Prince Hal's coronation, not even stopping to change his clothes. His mind is full of dreams of glory, of how, with his protégé on the throne, he will have full license at last to reward his friends, get back at his enemies, trample down law and justice, do everything he wants. So he rides to London, with the old justice, to whom he owes money, in his wake. But he is too late. Everything has changed. His boy has become King Henry V, and he will not—he cannot let himself—recognize his old tutor in folly. He rejects him in some of the cruelest lines in comedy. And Falstaff, after a pause, turns to his companion and remarks, "Master Shallow, I owe you a thousand pound" (5.5). That is all. The old man's heart is broken. We see the sequel in *Henry V*, when Falstaff dies.

In ritual terms, it is fitting that Falstaff should be rejected, and even killed. It is like Carnival giving way at last to Lent. Even more, it is like a Saturnalian interregnum, a time of misrule and license, being brought to an end by the arrival of the new or renewed order of things. Falstaff, the inverter of all honest values, can have no place in the new order. That stands to reason. But to banish Jack Falstaff is, in a sense, to "banish all the world." It is like doing away with comedy itself.

So too, I think, with Philocleon. Despite the melodrama and mock tragedy, there is something very painful and, for a bitter moment, uncomic about Philocleon's surrender. Earlier it seemed reasonable that Bdelycleon should try to reform his father, winning him away from his accustomed vice and folly (which all go with "loving Cleon") and his bad temper; but now, as he gives up, we perceive how a man feels when his illusion has been taken away. His jury life was a game, but one that gave him a sense of really living. It raised him above the long defeat of growing old. It was what a modern psychologist calls the *causa sui* project, the self-chosen activity by which one tries to give meaning and value to one's life and to raise it above mere human existence.[34] What Bdelycleon has done is to spoil his game, to take away his illusion. Behind his play therapy, he is really a puritan and a spoilsport. And although the chorus proceed into their usual "Go ye rejoicing" song, we are left with the impression more of failure than of success—of a therapy that has led to a loss of self, a psychological death.

24   *Game, Dream, or Nightmare?*

THE modern phrase "games people play" brings us near the heart of Aristophanes' *Wasps*. It also includes positive and negative connotations of "game" and "play" that need distinguishing.[35] What do we mean by saying that something is "only a game"?

Even to think about games gives pleasure, relaxes the mind, bridges the sometimes hostile worlds of work and play. For games are, in a sense, hard work. Card games like bridge, and chess, no less than soccer or tennis, require concentration and intense involvement, if you are not to fail, and fail badly, or perhaps let your partner down; and their challenge may be heightened if you play for money, or for master points: but still, the heightened attention they require differs from that of, say, a business or political conference, or a meeting to revise the college curriculum. It is likely that bridge and tennis prepare us for playing the game of business, or of politics, with skill, care, enjoyment, even a certain grace. Yet these games belong to a different, a more privileged world where we can make mistakes with impunity, where it does not really matter in the end whether we win or lose. The basic pleasure is still there. And if it is not, then the game has stopped being a game.

One reason why games give such pleasure, as well as serving as paradigms of social interaction and fair competition in the "real world," is that they combine great freedom with great order. All games have rules. Indeed a game is defined by its set of rules, as these control the various moves and choices that make up play. In chess, I move when my turn comes; I have to move; and my choices are limited by where my pieces, and my opponent's pieces, are placed on the board, and what they variously can or cannot do. In tennis, I serve or return the ball only at certain times and (if I am to win) within certain boundaries marked out by white lines. The special freedom we experience in games depends on these rules and limits. Without them—without the white lines and the net—we would never have the enormous satisfaction of making, even of watching, a good shot. And our opponent's skill gives *almost* as much pleasure as our own. At the same time, our pleasure is vastly increased by that other freedom of knowing that this is "only a game," that it is not "for real." This means (and I am obviously not speaking of professional sports, whose spirit is easily corrupted) that we can exert ourselves to the limit of our powers without fear of final humiliation or disgrace. We can accept defeat and still be pleased.

Outside the charmed playground, in the world of "real life," thoughts of games and of game-playing can be liberating to the spirit and of much practical value to the mind. My father, an anxious businessman pressed by competitors, could still relax briefly and smile at the thought that this was *like* a tennis game—although the money at stake was very real. And so, today, when I become discouraged by the burden of scholarship, the sheer number of problems to be solved and details to be worked out, I encourage myself with the thought that, after all, scholarship is a freely chosen pursuit and something very like a game. At heart it may even *be* a game. That is what Hermann Hesse perceived and wrote about in his brilliant novel *The Glass Bead Game* (*Das Glasperlenspiel*).[36] The great Game of Castalia, played out every year with great ceremony, is a metaphor for the intellectual play, the delight in discovering relationships between different fields of study, that underlies the activities of the mind and brings them together in momentary, symbolic unity and harmony. Hesse's book pays beautiful tribute to that spirit of play, which not only enriches and revives what we call the academic world but, paradoxically, keeps it honest—keeps it from becoming a practical appendage to business and politics. On the other hand Hesse reminds us through the experience of his protagonist, Joseph Knecht, that this is "only a game." On the further side of the walls of Castalia there is the world of history, of ordinary struggle and ordinary suffering. And Joseph, the Magister Ludi, who achieves the highest intellectual and spiritual rank and plays out the great Game, is also the person whose sensitivity, intelligence, and sense of self lead him to perceive the borders of the play world and, in the end, to transcend them. He renounces his position with humility and self-sacrifice, but also with a strange excitement, a feeling of freedom and adventure. And shortly afterwards, he dies.

But all this is somewhat pretentious. *Revenons à nos moutons*. Much as I am encouraged in my scholarly work by making comparisons with play and games, I must admit that I find it painful to be told that my writing is "only a game." Is it possible that something I put so much time, thought, and effort into is not quite serious? Or quite real? Do I write, after all, as my mother played golf: to amuse and challenge herself, to relieve her aggressions, to find companionship, to pass the time? Is my choice of activity arbitrary? Does it matter? And what, then, of all my other beliefs, and principles, and rules of life—all those white lines within which I live and work and make my customary moves?

I think of an Epistle of Horace (1.18) in which he advises a young literary friend about the day-to-day difficulties of getting along with a patron. Some are really painful, and even dangerous; others are less serious than you may think. For example: your "powerful friend" may ask you to go hunting when you feel like writing poetry; it is a nuisance, of course; but isn't poetry-writing really as much of a game (*lusus, nugae*) as hunting? Play along with his game, Horace suggests, and he will play along with yours. It is good advice. But there is an undertone of bitter self-irony, that poetry should be "only a game," like hunting, in the end.

Horace takes this idea further in *Epistle* 2.2.[37] After describing some practical obstacles to writing poetry, he asks, ironically, whether having (as he has) a strict critical judgment is worth the cost. Wouldn't it be better to live in a world of self-delusion where everything you did seemed fine, just fine? He illustrates the point with a story, of the mad Argive:

> There was, one time, a gentleman of Argos who used (he thought) to watch wondrous performers, sat, laughed, and clapped—all in an empty theater. Otherwise he was perfectly well adjusted: nice to his neighbors, amiable with friends, sweet to his wife—he could pardon his slaves and not go mad over the *cork au vin*—watched out for rocks, avoided gaping pits. But when, by his relations' care and wealth, his brain was washed [hemlock served as a kind of shock treatment], and he came to himself, "You've killed me, people, not delivered me," he said. "My greatest treat's taken away, the trick of mind that once made me so happy."

The Argive is a Dickensian figure. His eccentricity was harmless, and it helped him fulfill the normal obligations of life with unusual sweetness and goodwill. What was gained by destroying his illusion?

In its immediate context the anecdote supports Horace's ironic point about criticism, and self-criticism. Why work so hard, when ignorance is bliss? Why have "good taste—and bad temper"? But behind the irony, a further question arises. In a world where awareness is painful—where philosophy means acceptance of reality, and poetry-writing means hard work without illusions in conformity with that same reality—wouldn't it really be better to be self-deluded? To live, like that harmless Argive, in a world of illusion? Horace does not, in the end, think so. For a poet, as for a person, it is better finally to be sane than insane; but part of that sanity, for him, involves the recognition that his poetry-writing has been "fooling around," a kind of playing (*ludicra*). Much of the playful illusion, hence much of the pleasure, departs from this as we get older and more self-aware. Horace may have become "better," like good wine, as he got older—may have become a better poet, and a better person. But that does not mean that he became a happier one.

If now we compare Philocleon with Horace's Argive, the differences are striking. For Philocleon's illusion did not produce gentle, kindly, sociable behavior. On the contrary: the angry old juryman was a menace to society. His game, as it is exposed in the *Wasps*, turns out to be thoroughly vicious and arbitrary; it is self-indulgent; it serves the purposes of corrupt bosses, notably Cleon; in short, it is a game that disregards the basic rules of law and justice on which the law courts were established. Hence it is right and proper, from any morally or rationally or socially responsible viewpoint, that Philocleon should lose his game and that his manic illusion should be stripped away by his son's clever therapy. All the same, we are made to feel for the old scoundrel. He is, like Horace's Argive, "killed, not cured" by the therapy he has received.[38] He feels reduced to nothingness, to being "nobody," *outis*. The word gains impact from a famous episode in the *Odyssey* where Odysseus tricks the Cyclops, in part, by withholding his name and calling himself *Outis*, "Nobody." The punch line comes after the Cyclops is blinded, when he shouts out to the other Cyclopes that "Nobody has blinded me! Nobody has done me harm!"—to which they answer that, if nobody did it, it must have been the gods. Odysseus gets away, returns home, and recovers his kingdom. He makes a successful transition from realms of fantasy back to the real world of Ithaca, of hearth and home. Hence the *Odyssey*, like a good fairy tale, reconciles us to the limitations of our humanity. But Philocleon is far from being Odysseus. We saw that truth played out earlier, in the abortive escape effort with the donkey. He cannot outwit his son as Odysseus outwitted the captor Cyclops. And when he is reduced to being "nobody," it is (at least for the moment) painful. There is also, as we saw, a suggestion that Philocleon is like a wasp whose sting has been drawn, who can only die.

At this point it is worth remembering Aristophanes' claim in the prologue that his comedy is like a dream that alleviates anxiety and brings healing, providing that it is rightly taken, rightly interpreted. Is this really true? If we sympathize with old Philocleon, or see ourselves in his place, then the comedy should leave us with a sense of powerlessness; but this is a feeling characteristic of nightmare. Often, in nightmare, our normal powers of speaking, walking, or running seem to fail, people and places we thought familiar become confused, and we are carried along helplessly through a stream of queer circumstances altogether beyond our control. The truth is that much of human life really has such a nightmarish quality, especially when we or those we love grow sick or old, or both. But what could be more painful than such frailty when one is stripped of the illusion of exercising any control over one's own life, or the lives of others? That comes close to tragedy—to *Richard II*, to *Lear*. Take away my game, and you take away my life, you plunge me into nightmare.

Am I exaggerating? The sense of emptiness and defeat that I have been describing may have seemed to Aristophanes' audience only a shadow that passes over the stage and is quickly gone. And, as we shall see, the *Wasps* moves quickly, through the parabasis, to its farcical conclusion. Yet the threat is there, and Aristophanes is sensitive to it. He had to confront the anxiety of death and also the anxiety of meaninglessness as his comedy stripped away the veneer of human lives, the tricks of rhetoric, and the games that people play. But how does his comedy outface the tragic implications of all this? By what comic conventions, or playfulness, or hopeful vision, does Aristophanes avert that final sense of nightmare in the *Wasps*, and elsewhere?

I want now to enlarge this question by using a somewhat extensive comparison with *Alice in Wonderland*, which has superficial resemblances to what I have termed Dionysian fairy tale but is, in the end, something quite different. In Lewis Carroll's story, we are taken into a dream world whose swift changes, substitutions, and fusions border on nightmare—and suggest a nightmare reality beneath the placid surface of our ordinary conscious life and that of society. Yet the controlling sense of a game, of order and meaning imposed on chaos by language and logic, is so strong, and so reassuring, that it dispels the anxiety of meaninglessness in things and the nightmarish feeling of terror that this anxiety can bring.

I begin with another mistrial. The trial of the Knave of Hearts, with which *Alice in Wonderland* ends, combines parody of a real courtroom scene with the absurdity characteristic of a dream. The question at stake is a nonsense issue out of a nursery rhyme: Who stole the tarts? The jury, made up of assorted creatures, shows itself stupid and confused throughout the proceedings; the witnesses are useless; the evidence is nonsensical; the judge is the incompetent and ineffectual King of Hearts (whose furious Queen presses for a sentence first and a verdict afterwards); and all this is further thrown into confusion by Alice's sudden, alarming growth. "Who cares for *you*?" she cries, as the Queen calls for her beheading. "You're nothing but a pack of cards." At this, they all fling themselves upon her, and she wakes up.

This court scene can be enjoyed as comedy, since it offers the reader an escape from the intimidation normally associated with the law and felt most oppressively in the courtroom. Ordinarily a judge is intimidating, and a jury, and the official language of the court, and the strict procedures by which evidence is heard and a verdict arrived at. Perhaps the poor Hatter, who stands trembling there with his teacup and his slice of bread and butter, reminds us of that ordinary feeling of anxiety and fear in the face of the apparatus of law and justice. Yet in Carroll's scene that apparatus is reduced to silliness. Everybody is incompetent, including the judge and the jury. Even the Queen, who keeps crying out "Off with his head!" is somewhat less frightening now, to us, as to Alice, because we know by now that despite her threats, people's heads usually stay on their shoulders after all. So we should not be intimidated. We need only remind ourselves, like a dreamer beginning to be conscious that she is dreaming, that they are "nothing but a pack of cards."

But, again as in comedy, this perception of "only a game" has its dangerous side. For the world in which we live is held together by beliefs and institutions, among which justice and the law hold a high place: and what would happen if these turned out to be mere conventions, as arbitrary in their way as the made-up rules of a game? Earlier in *Alice*, the Mouse told his horrifying story about the behavior of the all-powerful Cat. "I'll be judge, I'll be jury, said cunning old Fury; I'll try the whole cause, and condemn you to death." It is like one of those fables in which might makes right, and nature—animal nature, which is the mirror of our own—is red in tooth and claw. The social institutions of law and justice protect us from the rule of the stronger, from the unlimited violence, cruelty, and oppression that come so easily to human, as to animal nature; but what if the restraints of law have no real validity in nature? What if everything is arbitrary, and nothing is real? We may be liberated from inhibition, and from the threat of condemnation, by the comic anarchy of the trial of the Knave of Hearts: but what use is this if it plunges us into the larger threat, of meaninglessness? For Carroll, I think, we may give an answer on three levels.

(1) We may say that the mistrial serves to remind us of what a trial should be like, and that we may take pleasure in our ability to make the comparison. We know better, that is. We know how a trial should be conducted. We know that a judge should enforce right procedure, that a jury should be attentive, that witnesses should be called to bring in proper evidence, reasonably treated, and reasonably examined. In making the comparison we enjoy the self-satisfaction of an intelligent child (like Carroll's first audience) who knows how these things are done, how they should be done. It is like recognizing the serious moral verses behind all those nonsense parodies.[39] We may compare the game of croquet, with and without those flamingos as mallets, those curled-up hedgehogs as balls, and those soldiers who arch themselves as wickets, when they aren't off somewhere else. All this nonsense may strengthen our sense of how things are normally done, and should be done: how games, whether croquet or courtroom, should be played strictly according to the rules.

(2) And since Carroll's wonderland is presented in the form of a dream, it is possible to escape from it by waking up if the sense of emotional turmoil, of the threat of things falling into dissolution, becomes too great. From the confusion of the trial, Alice awakens to a

gentle afternoon on the riverbank. The cards become drifting leaves. Alice runs in to her tea—which will *not* be like the Mad Hatter's tea party. Meanwhile her older sister enjoys a reverie, half drifting into Alice's enchanted world, half wakeful and conscious of the real autumn afternoon. It may be that Carroll meant, in the end, to invite us to share that double vision of the adult, which resembles what I earlier called *theōria*. It is a way to enjoy the pleasures of fantasy without the sense of threat, or of nightmare.

(3) But Carroll's greatest gift is to catch disorder, emotion, and potential chaos in the net of language, nonsense logic, and art. The form he uses is so ridiculous on its surface that it gives the lie to what sometimes seems desperately serious in the emotions hidden beneath. The breakdown of justice uncovered through the Mouse's tale, for instance, is covered again by an auditory and even visual pun, for the "tale" turns out to be a poetic narrative in the shape of a "tail," trailing off to nothing. Its content cannot be taken with final seriousness. Alice grows literally up and down, but what is more important, she grows in the ability to accept, and adapt herself to, queer and unfamiliar situations, as though she were learning strange new games: like croquet with flamingos and hedgehogs, or some giant game of cards. These cards, even the face cards, shrink to manageable size as she grows accustomed to their nonsense games. Still more, in *Alice through the Looking-Glass*, the structure of a chess game played out according to rules gives controlling shape to the strange, dream-like adventures and transformations through which Alice moves; and her growing up, again, from pawn to queen gives an image of the control that we may obtain if we name, describe, and learn the rules of the game we are playing, however odd they may sometimes seem.

For the wonderful secret of the nonsense world is that it has its own internal logic, which is revealed through language as in the solving of a riddle. Under the sea, Alice learns, boots and shoes are done with whiting (not blacking), and they are made of soles and eels. That is all quite logical, part of an extended system in which every word has its special purpose, or porpoise. Again, Alice hears how the Mock Turtle's education included reeling and writhing, ambition, distraction, uglification, and derision, and so forth. Everything in our world has its precise nonsense equivalent in that other world. It all fits, which constitutes a sort of proof that the system works. And "reeling and writhing" are not just dizzy parodies of reading and writing: they belong to a dance pattern that we, together with Alice, are just beginning to appreciate, and that will find its climax in the description of the great Lobster Quadrille. What is so satisfying is the sense we find in nonsense, the meanings drawn from absurdity. Thus the Gryphon explains how he hadn't time to learn Fainting in Coils:

"Hadn't time," said the Gryphon: "I went to the Classical master, though. He was an old crab, *he* was."

"I never went to him," the Mock Turtle said with a sigh. "He taught Laughing and Grief, they used to say."

"So he did, so he did," said the Gryphon, sighing in his turn; and both creatures hid their faces in their paws.

The nonsense joke again constitutes a sort of proof, like the answer to a riddle. And sense moves into nonsense, and back again. In our world many a classical teacher is, figuratively, an old crab; under the sea, he is literally one. Yet beneath the protective layer of language there are strong feelings, and beneath the surface of Latin and Greek a person may teach, or learn, "laughing and grief." This is one of the jokes that comes very close to reality. Perhaps that is why Carroll backs off again, as the creatures hide their faces in their paws. For the world of nonsense that they inhabit is meant to give us the laughing without the grief. All the same, it is the half-submerged sense of grief and terror just barely averted by nonsense language and nonsense logic, and by the nonsense game and the game of art, that gives the laughing its special power. We have the relief of skirting many emotional dangers from which we are just barely saved. That may, in the end, be the point of Carroll's dizzy game.

It may seem that in opposition to the academic and mathematician Charles Dodgson of Christ Church, Oxford, the dreamer and nonsense-writer Lewis Carroll inhabits, and opens up, a Dionysian world of confusion and madness. Not only do Alice's Adventures Underground (the original title of the story) have a markedly Freudian character, which has invited and received a great deal of Freudian analysis, they seem, still more, to lay bare all the disorderly feelings and wishes and fears that lay beneath the highly ordered surface of Victorian society. The violence of the dialogue and actions in which these feelings are played out in *Alice* seems in proportion to their repression in ordinary family and social life. Yet one feels that the writer feared more than welcomed the Dionysian element in himself and in nature. His art is really more Apollonian, a way of containing in language, logic, and game-structures all those wishes and fears and confused feelings that threatened to get out of hand. In the end, as Elizabeth Sewell has shown, Carroll's nonsense was a defense against emotional chaos.[40] It is a good and brave defense, and a very funny one, and we are lucky that Charles Dodgson did *not* go to a Freudian psychoanalyst to be relieved of the pressure of his unconscious anxieties and his neurotic way of life, but wrote *Alice* instead.

Returning now to Aristophanes, we may ask: what is *his* game? How does he transcend those painful feelings of loss, disillusionment, and emptiness that he knew from tragedy, and surely also from life, and that emerge as one aspect of his comedy?

In part he does this through the inherited conventions of comedy, and especially through comedy's ways of reminding us of its own fictionality. When we watch tragedy, we are drawn into sympathy with Oedipus or Hecuba and hence into an imaginative sharing of their grief and pain, which subsume our own. But comedy half-preserves our detachment, giving us the pleasure of looking on pain like distant gods. We recognize Philocleon's pain and grief, but we still laugh at it: partly from malice and a sense of superiority, partly because Philocleon is not really a tragic hero (or heroine) out of Euripides but is his own tough self underneath, and will endure; but even more because we are reminded that this is a play written for our amusement and performed by actors—among them, the protagonist playing Philocleon. From experience of comic conventions, we know that Philocleon will survive; from common sense, we know that the actor will survive—not to mention the playwright. All of which encourages us to think that we can too.

Another way of putting it is that Aristophanes, as a sophisticated playwright, draws us into realizing that we are watching a game within a game within a game. It is true, and painful, that Philocleon's game has been lost, his illusion dispelled. But we see also that this is Bdelycleon's game, to control his father's actions through successful therapy. First he counters his father's delusion through imaginative persuasion, using all the latest tricks of argumentation; then he uses a form of play therapy to bring the old man to his senses. But we see through his game, as Philocleon does not. It too is deception and cheating, displayed under the "stealing" sign of the clepsydra. And behind Bdelycleon's game we are brought to see the game of "Aristophanes" insofar as he is, or rather has taken on the persona of, a young reactionary and would-be moral reformer who employs the techniques of play therapy for his predetermined educational purposes. His game will be exposed further in the parabasis. It will also fail, like Bdelycleon's; but this is to look forward to the play's ending. What matters for the moment is the sense of games within games. In an ever-expanding field of play, the loss of any one game, like Philocleon's—though it may not be lost for good—cannot be taken with final seriousness, or grief.

In the end, too, Aristophanes' *Wasps* has a Dionysian movement that *Alice* lacks. The wonders and terrors of Wonderland may be entrancing, but they have to be kept at a distance through nonsense language and nonsense logic and the sense of art as a final controlling game. It is significant that Alice's adventures are presented as dream adventures from which, as they become too alarming, she may wake up. But if Aristophanes' *Wasps*, up to the parabasis, is rather like a dream that has not given the encouragement it should, or the sense of hope, but has somewhat approached nightmare, Aristophanes' answer is to plunge back into it after the parabasis, as we may plunge back into dreaming, to see if the dream can work out better this time. And, in very Dionysian fashion, it does.

25   *Philocleon's Escape*

IT is exciting to find Aristophanes himself playing on the idea of catharsis in the parabasis of the *Wasps*. I have already used the phrase "comic catharsis" to cover a broad range of meanings, which I may be suspected of smuggling back from Aristotle and his interpreters into the fifth century: but here is Aristophanes using the term as a watchword of his intentions in writing comedy. Right away, the wasp leader, speaking for Aristophanes, asks the audience to pay attention "if you love something *katharon*." He means, or seems to mean, a good "clean" comedy unpolluted by worn-out vulgarisms; the idea of "cleansing" is still latent. Then Aristophanes presents his formal complaint, as in court. The audience, as judges, did him wrong. Despite his multiple benefactions, some surreptitious (as a ventriloquist speaks through other people's bellies), and some open (*phaneros*), on his own responsibility; despite the fact that he was not puffed up by his enormous and highly deserved successes, but demonstrated high moral conduct and never prostituted his Muse to obtain personal ends; and despite, finally, his conspicuous valor in attacking from the very beginning no ordinary opponents but a certain appalling and hideous and ferocious monster, not to mention lesser "shivers and fevers" that preyed on simple folk: still, Aristophanes' audience betrayed him, they let him down:

> Though you found such a cleansing hero to ward off evil from the land (*alexikakon . . . katharten*), yet you betrayed him last year when he sowed a crop of very new ideas. Because you didn't *get them clearly* (*gnōnai katharōs*), you rendered them ineffective. (1043–45)

And yet it (the *Clouds* of 423) was an excellent play. By Dionysus, it was! Those who failed to "get" it then should be ashamed of themselves—not the playwright, whom the "clever people" commend for his unusually daring effort.[41] What remains is for the audience to make amends by cherishing original poets in the future; that way, if they store up their clever ideas, the clothing of the Athenians will smell sweetly of—cleverness, all the year long.

I have paraphrased at length because the anapests as a whole constitute a complex definition of the terms *kathairein* and *katharos* as Aristophanes means us to understand them. Most obviously, he compares his services to those of Heracles' "cleansing" Greece of monsters. With Heraclean temper, Aristophanes faced up to a monster that combined the worst features of many horrible creatures, including the Hydra *and the dog Cerberus* (a reference that must be clear by now even to the meanest intellect); he did not cower, did not stoop to taking bribes, but fought, and still fights, for his ungrateful public. As said earlier, all this self-praise was traditional and expected. Aristophanes must have enjoyed posing as a champion, a hero, and a National Asset, much as Picasso in his later years liked to portray himself in such various and splendid roles as hero, warrior, Olympic victor, lover, and bullfighter. What is new and subtle is the way Aristophanes combines the political claim, to be a public benefactor, with the literary one, to be writing a new, improved, clever, and daring sort of comedy whose success depends on the audience's "getting it clearly" (*gnōnai katharōs*). Combine the two ideas, and Aristophanes is offering his comedy to the public both as "good clean fun" and as healing therapy.

This double claim must wait until the end of the play to be evaluated properly, for, as often, the parabasis occupies an ironic position *within* the play's development; it is not an independent statement sent from on high. For the present, however, we may summarize the connections by now established between "Aristophanes" and Bdelycleon:

1. Bdelycleon tried various forms of therapy, including literal *catharsis* (both as religious purification, and as a washing-out of impurities from the body) on his father. Aristophanes, through his comedy, performs an analogous "cleansing" of the land.
2. Bdelycleon's function, given in his name, is to "loathe Cleon," and to fight Cleon's influence on his father. Aristophanes fights the Cleon-monster—not least, by lampooning him as a ferocious, Cerberus-like hound—much as Heracles "cleansed" Greece of monsters (and incidentally, overcame Cerberus and brought him up from the underworld).
3. Bdelycleon's mask slips in the first agon, revealing "Aristophanes" in his role of would-be healer of the disease under which Athens labors. This is analogous to Bdelycleon's continued efforts to practice a healing therapy on his father, dispelling his obsession.
4. Bdelycleon employs play therapy to amuse his father, compensate him for staying away from the law courts, and change his temper for the better. This is like the way defendants tell jokes, fables, and

funny stories to entertain the jury and, in the process, mitigate their dangerous anger. (The two intentions merge as Bdelycleon speaks for the defense in the Trial of the Dog.) But this is also an image of how "Aristophanes" may be using comedy to amuse but also reform his audience, by putting them in better temper. His intentions, of course, are thoroughly laudable. He says so himself. But his methods—and especially the comic catharsis that he practices—are quite as suspect as anyone else's, and may be as fraudulent in the end. Let us wait and see.

5. There will be still another connection, after the parabasis. Aristophanes has been trying to reform and refine the Athenians' taste in comedy as well as politics. Teaching them to "get" his clever ideas this year, as they did not the year before, he wishes to guide them to an appreciation of "clean" comedy, "clearly" perceived and with "cleansing and clarifying" results. But this effort will itself be the occasion of slapstick humor when Bdelycleon is shown teaching his old father to behave like a gentleman, telling polite and witty stories. When he fails—and he *will* fail, disastrously—the joke will be on Bdelycleon, but by implication, it will also be on "Aristophanes" the reformer of comedy, the master of clever ideas and comic catharsis.

All these analogies between Bdelycleon and "Aristophanes" are focused in the anapests of the parabasis. Here the playwright, in praising himself, seems to put his cards on the table, to show up his own intentions and his own trickery. But in doing so, he also transcends them. "Aristophanes" the reformer, the heroic cleanser, the monster-slayer, is himself only a persona for the playwright behind the scenes, who continues to re-create himself as a person and an artist as he plays out these different parts through his comedy.

It is also worth remembering (before we come to the dénouement) that the parabasis goes on, beyond these anapests, to the wasp-songs and statements discussed earlier. And we are now in a position to see these in full perspective. The wasps explain their own symbolism, the connections between their military temper in the past and their jury life in the present, so clearly that the audience can make no mistake this year. (The leader of last year's cloud chorus should evidently have done something of the kind.) Yet two things are odd. One is that Aristophanes is disingenuous about the symbolism of the wasp stings. Perhaps he wants to tease his audience into getting the rather obvious point, the phallic symbolism, on their own. The other odd thing is that *erōs* has been opposed to *catharsis* all along, and it is still. Bdelycleon has wanted to cure his father's sadistic but still very erotic passion for the jury courts; but rather than heal the old man, his attempts at therapy only render him feeble and faint, if not at death's door. The cure, from an erotic viewpoint, is much worse than the disease. Philocleon's vitality also made him the champion of the tired old jurors, a test case for their life's meaning. When he lets his sword fall, when he collapses to the ground, when he tamely lets Bdelycleon lead him into the house, his defeat and failure imply theirs also. And conversely: when the jurymen-wasps boast of their ancient temper and renown, and especially when they call for a recovery of their strength—

> And yet, out of these remnants,
> we must find some youthful strength:
> for, I think, my old age
> is stronger and better
> than all the curls and posturing
> and queer-assed talent of your youth today—
>
> (1066–70)

their "and yet" is a rebuke to weakness, a challenge in the face of the evidence that life and the play thus far have offered. The facts seem to add up to weakness, defeat, and loss. It is time, then, to defy the facts. The scenes following the parabasis give the lie to the therapeutic efforts of Bdelycleon and the reformer "Aristophanes," but they also respond to that brave challenge offered by the wasps. There must (they are right) be more to life than this.

In the first scene after the parabasis, Bdelycleon dresses his father in new clothes, much as he would like to dress him in new, polite habits to consort with "gentlemen" at a party. It is an uproarious scene of trying to improve human nature. There are many borrowings from the *Clouds*, from scenes of Socrates trying to teach Strepsiades (who resisted with a kind of saving stupidity); and there are many ironies pointing to Bdelycleon's managerial tendencies, his resemblance to Cleon himself (do you become like the enemy whose weapons you adopt?), and the essential bankruptcy of his bourgeois aims—to get his father into the country club. The metaphor of cooking recurs: Philocleon almost melts away in the furnace of his new clothes; he begs Bdelycleon to get a meathook ready to pull him out. So too does the idea of sleeping and dreaming: Philocleon is led to the "couch" and, as he says, given not a real feast but a "dream dinner." But once again, it is the spring mechanism at work. The more Philocleon's nature is restrained, the more violently it will break forth. When Philocleon goes to the party, gets roaring drunk, makes an ass of himself, insults everybody, steals a flute girl, and comes reveling home with her, knocking things over on the way, stealing food, and beating up tradespeople—this is the breakout that we have somehow been expecting all along. For the son it is utter disaster; for the father, a final escape from manipulation and control, yet with a fully appropriate excuse: "You *told* me I shouldn't think about lawsuits any more!"[42]

Still another strong irony is the way the fable or funny story backfires. Bdelycleon had instructed his father in polite conversation (*logoi semnoi*) befitting clever people (*dexioi*). His idea of civilized conversation includes edifying stories and anecdotes (provided, we might say, they get past the censor); and later on, when Philocleon worries rather prophetically that he might get drunk and offend people, his son reassures him: in polite society, you can always soothe ruffled feelings by means of a funny story or a fable:

> Not if you spend your time with gentlemen.
> *They* can always placate offended parties;
> or else, *you* can relate some witty tale,
> an Aesop's fable, or a Sybaris joke
> you heard at the dinner party. The whole case
> will be dissolved in laughter. You'll get off.   (1256–61)

"Well, I'd better learn a lot of stories," says Philocleon, who (again very like Strepsiades) is pleased by the idea of doing mischief with impunity. Presumably, if he took this advice, Philocleon would succeed like one of the defendants he described earlier, who regaled the jury with jokes and funny stories. It would put the others in a serviceable good humor. What actually happens is that Philocleon reverts when drunk to the lowest, most primitive type of humor, the derogatory comparison or *eikōn*.[43] He tells jokes and stories, to be sure, but they are all vulgar and quite pointless:

> So, he insulted them all around the table,
> cracking his country jokes, and telling tales
> like an utter fool. They had no point at all.
>
> (1319–21)

All this was reported, but shortly it appears onstage. When a bread-seller comes in, complaining of damages, Philocleon tells his son (mimicking his earlier advice) that "clever tales will settle everything." It is true: humor relieves tension, reconciles disputes. But the "Aesopic" fable that Philocleon starts to tell adds insult to injury. It is (of course!) about a dog, and it provides an excuse for him to shout "You stupid bitch!" in the woman's face. Another story ends up with what sounds like a moral or proverb: "I don't care!" Now a second person enters to summon Philocleon on a charge of assault and battery. Philocleon offers to be reconciled; he wanders into a "Sybarite" story about a man who fell out of a chariot and broke his head, ending in the familiar moral, "Everyone should stick to his own trade"; and presumably he beats him offstage while going on about a Sybarite woman and a "hedgehog." The comic genres are becoming confused. As he raves on about Aesop and the Delphians and something about a beetle, his long-suffering son carries him bodily into the house—at which disastrous point the chorus sing a mocking little song praising Bdelycleon for his *cleverness* and his success—so far as it goes—in reforming his father's character and bringing him to a new and very civilized style of life.

The joke is on Bdelycleon, whose instruction and therapy have backfired. But it is equally on Aristophanes; hence, I think, the special emphasis on funny stories and fables that don't work out the way they should. We should remember that Aristophanes claimed to be a *kathartēs* in both the social and the literary realm. We could say, he claimed to cleanse Athens of its faults and demons, and comedy of its tired vulgarities and ploys. And yet, just as the reformation of Philocleon explodes into ruins, failing very much like an experiment *in a fable*, where some creature reverts suddenly to its former nature, or some disguise is stripped off, or someone's attempt at a new way of life fails, prompting the moral, "Stick to your own trade" (or nature)[44]—at the same instant, Aristophanes' *Wasps* relapses into the old vulgarities that constitute the old self of Old Comedy. What Xanthias announced would be a "little story with a point," cleverer than most, but not too clever for the audience, turns into beating and screaming and running and knockabout farce and some wonderfully obscene byplay about a torch that is really a naked flute girl. Bdelycleon is knocked down, in a true-life boxing story; Aristophanes' chariot of reform crashes again. And we are glad. Shut up again in the house, the irresponsible Philocleon reemerges finally to perform a joyful, drunken, and triumphant dance.[45] "An impossible business, by Dionysus!" cries Xanthias the would-be warder. Precisely: it *is* an impossible business to reform human or Athenian nature; and (by Dionysus!) comedy in the end must be about human freedom, which now includes the freedom not to be reeducated or reformed or brainwashed or made the involuntary object of a catharsis—even a comic catharsis. The greater the constraint of attempted reform, the wilder the escape, the more manic the final dance. The old man is mad, and Athens is mad, and nothing can be done about it ("Drink hellebore!" cries the helpless Xanthias); and if there is a victor in the end, it is the god of madness, Dionysus himself.

 I want now to borrow the Aristophanic freedom to reverse myself and ask whether the *Wasps* does not offer a healing catharsis after all, albeit a different one from the kind we have been discussing. It is, after all, the nature of Dionysian religion to provide that temporary abandonment of self-possession that enables people to escape the greater insanity to which the self-willed rationalist like Pentheus may or must succumb. And although the wild ending of the *Wasps* is a tribute to Dionysus and a reaffirmation of the primitive and irrational, whether in human nature or in comedy, yet even Philocleon's clownish dancing and joking are planned by Aristophanes as part of the total play. A larger catharsis is intended and achieved, under the auspices of Apollo and Dionysus, than either Bdelycleon within the plot, or Aristophanes-as-Bdelycleon, might have desired or even imagined.

Let me return, one last time, to the idea of dreaming and dream interpretation. In the prologue Aristophanes set up important analogies between dreams and jokes or riddles, between interpreting a dream and understanding a comedy. He invited the audience to join his troupe in interpreting the play's action as if it were a strange yet favorable dream. To do this we must now look beyond all the strange dream-creatures, the dogs in court and the dancing wasps, and concentrate on the single, unifying image of *escape*. This is more metaphor than symbol: it is conveyed more in feeling and action than in words; but it is crucial to the final and very positive interpretation that this dream-like play calls for. For although we have stressed Bdelycleon's failure, the play can more justly be entitled "Philocleon's Escape."

The basic pattern was played out in the slapstick scenes before and after the entrance of the chorus: Philocleon is shut up within the house and tries to escape, is pushed in, pops out again, and so forth. Similarly Bdelycleon's efforts to reeducate and reform his father are attempts to confine him, to keep him in. Bdelycleon is a spoilsport and a jailer, though with the best intentions. Will the old man elude the "watch"? Will he make his escape somehow, like Odysseus from the Cyclops' cave? Again and again he is foiled; he seems to be "nobody" more than Odysseus; yet in the end he escapes, by the implied help of Dionysus the looser of bonds, into unregenerate animal nature and drunken revelry.[46] It is a final dramatization of the idea *apopheugein*, used throughout the play of defendants trying to "get off free," now transferred at the end to the runaway Philocleon himself. His final dance signifies happiness and victory, not unlike Alexander the Great's famous dream of a dancing satyr.[47]

What kind of recognition goes with this dominant escape theme? This time, I think, it is a recognition less of the mind than of the heart: not satirical like the dog allegory, or thought-provoking like the wasps' symbolism, but recognition as the *recovery* of an energy we once possessed, which (under various pressures) we had forgotten, and which, now rediscovered, promises a more confident and vital way of life. The plea and affirmation of the wasp-chorus, given earlier, is answered by the recovery of their champion Philocleon. An ironic recovery, to be sure, as he plays the ardent lover wishing to escape the constraints of paternal domination—"I am a minor and watched very closely . . . he's afraid I may be corrupted, for you see, I'm his only—father!"—but the paradoxical truth is that Philocleon *is* more youthful, passionate, and energetic than his anxious son, who is old and crusty before his time. His recovery is the playwright's final healing gift to the chorus, who go out dancing, and behind them, to the Athenian people: for if Philocleon's defeat and disillusionment point to the need of accepting reality, as intelligent and sane people must accept it, yet Philocleon's successful rebellion and escape demonstrate the energy and erotic passion and hopefulness—those very Athenian traits—that make living in the real world not just tolerable, but deeply worthwhile.

If I am right, then Aristophanes has presented Athens after all with a healing catharsis. It has many features in common with the forms of psychotherapy attempted by Bdelycleon: the therapy of the word, the purification rites, the Corybantic music and dance, the Asclepian incubation. As the *Frogs* later attests, Aristophanes regarded the experience of producing or watching comedies as participation in a Dionysian rite; and it is above all Dionysus who presides over and guarantees the catharsis shaped by comedy: through the relaxation of tension, through the dream-like experience of a fluid world in which things turn into each other and the normal laws of scientific and critical thought are relaxed, and through the various recognitions, emotional as well as intellectual, that arise out of the experience of that transformed and transforming dream world. Such a comic catharsis is a magnificent gift. What Aristophanes says in the parabasis is true. Yet his truthfulness is guaranteed by the way he exposes every single trace of fraud or deception or coercion, *even by himself*, that might accompany the desired catharsis. Bdelycleon is a shadow of Aristophanes: he is what Aristophanes either was, or might have been; for just as Bdelycleon, the would-be reformer, adopts his enemies' tricks and becomes like them in the end, so comedy itself could become manipulative, could use its devices of joke and fable and play for uncomic purposes of behavior modification and propaganda. The path to demagoguery is paved with good intentions. Yet in the end Aristophanes' play is noncoercive and it is honest: noncoercive like a dream that on being rightly interpreted brings out its own true story from our unconscious feelings and thoughts; and honest, because it includes the exposure of its own shadow side, its inherent dishonesty.

In thus exposing and renouncing the art of brainwashing the public, Aristophanes pays high tribute to honesty and also to personal and political freedom. Not that the *Wasps*, any more than other comedies, shows very much confidence in the intelligent judgment of the Athenian people, whether in court or elsewhere: but it does seem to cast a vote against oligarchy, against turning over the management of affairs to clever people like Bdelycleon—or Aristophanes himself. The play is deeply prodemocratic. I cannot think of another play that better exemplifies the value of Old Comedy as a watchdog of Athenian democratic freedom. At the same time, the *Wasps* reaffirms the fundamental unity of

Old Comedy and of its audience. To be sure, the prologue and parabasis of this play seem to show a widening gap between Aristophanes' new comedy of ideas and the old vulgar farce, and also between the "clever people" in the audience who can "get" the poet's clever ideas and those others who do not—as with the *Clouds* the previous year. Such a division threatens unity, much as the Cleon-whale "divides the people" in Sosias' dream. But does Aristophanes accept this division? At first he seems to; when he suggests that the audience are "clever" (*dexioi*) and so will be able, at least with his guidance, to follow the new comedy, he seems insultingly condescending; yet he gives enormous weight to the ridiculing of cleverness and clever people in the last part of the *Wasps*. The chorus make fun of Bdelycleon, who turns out to be rather silly after all. They also lampoon various "clever people" who turn out to be idiots and perverts—ingenious perverts, to be sure. (One of these is, not coincidentally, a comic poet.)[48] Yet it would be wrong to read the end of the *Wasps* as an unequivocal rejection of intellect. The last scenes, vulgarity and all, belong to an integrated comedy that can appeal to its varied audience on several levels of thought and feeling at one and the same time. Aristophanes succeeds in reintegrating his own comedy even as he succeeds in reaffirming the basic unity of the Athenian people. And we may suspect that he accomplishes this because he has first, through the comic spirit, achieved a corresponding reintegration within himself. His comedy brings much wholeness, many kinds of healing.

I want finally to suggest that the positive themes of escape and recovery for which I have been arguing in the *Wasps* can be found, spelled out in much more explicit terms, in the next year's play. In the *Peace*, Athens returns to health, together with the rest of Hellas. The Athenian people have been sick with a war neurosis whose symptoms are suspiciousness, litigiousness, and bad temper generally; but now, restored to the blessings of peace, leisure, and the countryside, they recover their earlier good humor, their enjoyment of life, and the sane perspective that accompanies such enjoyment. Rejuvenation and reform thus go together in *Peace* as they could not in *Wasps*. The roughness of bad-tempered jurors will be sloughed off, to everybody's gain including their own; they will turn youthful again, sleek, and tender—but clearly with no loss of sexual potency! On careful study, the *Peace* is filled with motifs taken from *Wasps* but inverted, much as *Wasps* inverted so many motifs from *Clouds*. Thus the magic cooking works this time: Peace will "compound better humors" in the Greek peoples and will "mix them together" in friendship as in a good sauce (996–99). (This is much nicer than the crazy salad that War makes of cities, using such ingredients as Sicilian cheese and Attic honey.) A "demon hard to purge" (*ō dyskatharte daimon,* 1250) is transferred from the hero to a nuisance type, a scapegoat; for Trygaeus himself is not insane, as people think, but rather a master of that creative madness that bypasses the limits of feasibility and accomplishes what we all want done. This time, too, the fable works for progress. Trygaeus borrows something like Aesop's beetle (which we remember from Philocleon's drunken scene) and rides it in comic and fabulous fashion to Olympus. Conversely, the negative warnings, so often found in fable and proverb, that you can't change human nature are used this time by Trygaeus, with comic inversion, against the religious imposter who cited them as a necessary obstacle to peace. "You won't make the crab walk straight," proclaimed Hierocles; "you can't make the rough hedgehog smooth" (1083, 1086). And so Trygaeus, excluding Hierocles from the sacrificial feast, answers his protests with a firm reminder: "You won't make the rough hedgehog smooth" (1114).

It seems strange in retrospect that although the crab proverb was never quoted in the *Wasps*, still that play ended with a dance of the "crabs," tiny spinning children of Carcinus the old king crab himself. It is a wonderful nonsense dance, delightful in its own right like the Lobster Quadrille in *Alice* or Edward Lear's owl and pussycat dancing to the light of the moon. Could it also be a riddling, dramatic embodiment of that same unmentioned proverb, "You won't make the crab walk straight"? That was the point: nobody, not even a comic poet, can straighten out Philocleon or the Athenian jury system or human nature itself. And yet, even if crabs won't walk straight, these crabs at least can evidently dance—and what could be more fun, or a better symbol of energy, excitement, and very hope, than their spinning dance?

Chapter Five

Aristophanic Loyalties

Dionysus Reclining, from the East Pediment of the Parthenon. Courtesy Department of Greek and Roman Antiquities, the British Museum, London.

26   *Loyalties of a* Kōmōidodidaskalos

I F I deferred until now the question of Aristophanes' political attitudes, it was not for lack of interest, but to gain time. For it takes time to establish a right comic perspective within which political and social issues may be worked out or, better, played out, and newly understood; and it takes time to establish the difference between comedy seen as a jolly means of conveying previously held "critical ideas" and comedy seen as a transforming, even philosophical process through which new recognitions are created, and new understanding gained, about human nature, society, and politics. The distinction is crucial. If we look back at the *Acharnians*, we see that the brief for peace with which Aristophanes may have started becomes joined with the showing-up of pathos and propaganda, including the poet's own. If we look back at the *Wasps*, we see that although Aristophanes may have originally intended to satirize Cleon and the jury courts, he ended by writing a comedy that ridicules any lesser intention, any would-be reform of litera-ture and politics. For the *Wasps* is not, as it pretends, a simple fable with a moral. It is not a political allegory like Orwell's *Animal Farm*. It is more like the end of *Gulliver's Travels* in the way it turns laughter against the author's own wish that humans might be as virtuous and rational as his Houyhnhnms; but where Swift's laughter is bitter, ex-pressing frustration and scorn, Aristophanes' laughter is magnanimous, encouraging and even liberating, as we all (would-be educators included) share vicariously in the triumph of Philocleon's escape.

Although modern critical readings of Aristophanes' plays differ in de-tail and emphasis, they tend alike to discredit the two basic assumptions prevailing before 1945: that Aristophanes' political attitudes could easily be abstracted from his plays, and that these could be described ade-quately by terms like "conservative" and "educational."[1] The poet, it was generally agreed, stands for common sense and tradition; for peace, as against war; for the farmers, as against city types; for the old religion, as against sophistic questioning; for the old education, the old music, the old tragedy, as against the new; for the older, more moderate democracy, as against the new radical politicians, their imperialism, and their abuse of democratic institutions such as the assembly and the jury courts: in sum, he is patriotic, concerned for Athens' good, loyal to her established ways, and prepared to fight for them through his comedies. His basic critical purpose, of attacking vice and folly, is made acceptable to his popular audience through the funny devices and curiously permitted licenses of the Old Comedy.

Critical readings since 1945 have made us more skeptical. We would hesitate now to commit Aristophanes to *any* clear attitude or belief, let alone any intention to influence his audience in this or that direction (except, possibly, toward peace). Instead we have become aware of his remarkable tolerance of contradiction and paradox. Not only do his actors and singers express conflicting attitudes about things—delight in military victories alongside pleas for peace, delight in modern cleverness alongside dismay at sophistic corruption, reliance on the basic good sense and intelligence of the demos alongside exposure of its everlasting idiocy and gullibility: not only that, but contradictions seem enshrined in the very heart of the plays. Thus, in the *Acharnians*, the spokesman for civic morality is a relentlessly self-seeking individual; in the *Knights*, corruption is only defeated by worse corruption; in the *Wasps*, the reformer ends up looking like the enemy. (I pass over the attack on Socrates in the *Clouds*, which more than anything else has scandalized Aristophanes' readers over the centuries.) But not only does the poet tolerate contradictions that undermine his hypothetical (and very proper) stances; he also distances himself, with irony and self-irony, from the very attitudes and judgments that we want to pin down. His own incipient attitudes become personae like "Dicaeopolis" or "Bdelycleon," with laughter's searchlight full upon them. His showing up of all deceptions, including his own, is praiseworthy as well as funny, convincing us of the great honesty of his plays; but still, it inhibits us from asking (let alone trying to answer) the old questions. What does Aristophanes believe in? What does he have to say to his captive audience? And to us today?

Let me begin (since I want to be positive, despite the prevailing skepticism) with something I think self-evident. This is Aristophanes' passionate concern for Athens and for her good. "We must look every day," Pericles proclaimed, "upon the power and the greatness of Athens, and we must become her lovers."[2] Aristophanes looks on these, and he looks on the weakness and confusion of post-Periclean Athens, battered by war, plague, inflation, dissension, and cultural change; and through all this, he shows the lover's steadfast care. His patriotism is critical, but it has staying power. I think, if he were interviewed today, he would avoid slogans like "My country right or wrong" (a claim easily misunderstood)

and would prefer to sing the moving but self-mocking verses out of
Pinafore,

> but in spite of all temptations
> to belong to other nations,
> he remains an Englishman.

So Aristophanes "remains an Atheni-*an*," continuing his struggle with
the beloved and maddening city. In doing so he avoids the two pitfalls by
which lovers and patriots are generally tempted. One is to become partisan, to throw oneself altogether into the cause of, say, political reform.
The problem of the activist is that despite his excellent intentions, he all
too easily loses perspective, uses any means to victory, even turns propagandist. It can happen to good poets. Bernard Shaw, whom Gilbert Murray compared to Aristophanes, shows the danger, for all his wit, of
harnessing the comic muse to the chariot of philosophical statement
and social reform. When this happens, comedy loses its power to explore, and to rediscover, the truths about human nature that govern
political life and can sometimes refresh it; instead of which, comedy
becomes a means of sugar-coating those truths about man, woman, and
the universe that the dramatist previously grasped as a philosopher and
prophet. Which is to say, not just that Shaw belongs in some Aristophanic comedy, together with Socrates and Euripides, but that the very
greatest comedies do not allow their meanings to be planned in advance,
or stated easily—least of all, by the author himself in a critical preface.

If one temptation of the patriot or poet is to throw himself into a
cause, risking loss of perspective and even loss of honesty, the other is to
withdraw from active concern because of disillusionment or discouragement. Athenians, of course, could choose exile. Alcibiades, leaving Athens for Sparta, justified himself in the mood and language of a rejected
lover turned cynic: the Athens he left was not *his* Athens, it was no
longer the city he knew and loved and served.[3] Other, less selfish Athenians might have said the same. Euripides went to the court of Macedon
to spend his last few years in comfort. He was thought to be peculiar,
antisocial, and antidemocratic; more probably he felt emotionally over-
whelmed by Athens in her last wild decade of struggle. Aristophanes'
Birds, of 414 B.C., initially shows two ordinary Athenians, conservative
types, who just want peace and quiet. The great imperial city created by
Pericles has become too much for them. They have become alienated,
have taken to flight. I have a strong feeling that these would-be fugitives
embody the poet's own wish (in Stoppard's phrase) to "withdraw in style
from the confusion," to seek refuge in the aesthetic realm, the world of
self-contained fantasy. Viewed politically, this is a cop-out. Viewed hu-
manly and psychologically, it tends to schizophrenia.

My argument so far (analysis of the *Birds* will test it further) is that
Aristophanes' comedies are indeed escapist, but that in their escape art-

istry they lose neither perspective nor commitment. Unlike the political activist or the literary propagandist, Aristophanes takes himself and his audience on the escape route to an otherworld from which Athens and the problems of Athens may be perceived in a new and different light. Unlike the alienated man who withdraws literally or else emotionally, seeking through drugs or cultivated isolation to maintain some lasting detachment from human and political concerns, Aristophanes remains passionately and insistently concerned with Athens. Amid the imagined delights of food, drink, and sex, and the fantastic paraphernalia of personal fulfillment, even from comic Heaven and comic Hell we hear the same question passionately and insistently repeated: how is Athens to be saved? The everyday Athenian concerns are left behind at first, by comedy's gift and that of Dionysus; but they are left behind only to be rediscovered, or recognized, in that otherworld's queer light. Instead, therefore, of demanding, "What did Aristophanes think about X and Y?" I have put more open-ended questions to each comedy: "To what recognitions do you bring us, play?" "And to what recognitions did you bring the Athenians when they were spectator/participants (*theatai*) in the theater of Dionysus?"

If the recognitions for which I have argued so far are subtle, many-layered, and sometimes paradoxical, I can only say that this is where reading and rereading Aristophanes (as his original audience never did) has brought me. He has an unusual gift of relating one concern to another in the transforming light of comic fantasy; an unusual gift, too, of relating problems of social and political behavior to other, even more basic human problems and human emotions. He is, despite or rather through the conventions of his genre, as complex and sophisticated a thinker as Euripides or Thucydides. And yet, now that I have paid my tribute to complexity in Aristophanes' plays, using modern techniques of analysis and influenced by the modern critical bias toward irony, ambiguity, paradox, and critical distancing (both as found in literature and as exhibited toward it), I want to step back and speak more naively and more positively about Aristophanes and Athens. If his basic "attitudes" have disappeared under scrutiny—if we cannot simply know what he thinks about things because he never thinks quite simply about anything—then can we speak instead about his basic *loyalties* as these are glimpsed through and behind the plays? I think that we can, and that we should. Aristophanes is loyal, first, to what I would call the whole and comic truth; second, to human nature in all its diversity and its creative possibilities (both aspects being very democratic, and very Athenian); and third, to what anthropologists call *communitas*, which is something like experiencing the polis behind the polis. I shall try now to describe these loyalties, illustrating them briefly from the *Lysistrata* and *Thesmophoriazusae*. In sections 28 through 31 I shall discuss Aristophanes' "allegiance to Utopia," which comes close to the other three loyalties; the

Birds will be a test case, then the late *Ecclesiazusae* and *Plutus*. There remains, I think, a still more basic loyalty underlying the rest, to the affirmation and celebration of life itself. This ultimately religious loyalty will continue to be assumed and to be illustrated, but not defined, through the remainder of my argument.

Aristophanes' first loyalty is to the whole and comic truth. His business is to make laughter, to strip away pretense or abstraction, to practice indecent exposure on a universal scale. We recognize his honesty: not because he tells us, in so many parabases, that he is an honest poet, but because he successfully exposes his own pretenses along with others'. If he uses rhetoric, it is transparent, like Dicaeopolis' rags. If he attempts comic catharsis, he shows us all the tricks that "Bdelycleon" uses. The masks, the names just cited, represent Aristophanes' lesser purposes, educational or moralistic or reforming; they do not define the comic poet or "confine him any finer" than he is. Hence we come to trust the comic poet behind the masks and scenes. And once having come to trust him, from a full reading of his plays, we may be justified in returning to his claims of artistic and moral integrity and, despite their self-exaggerations (and also, in a sense, because of these), in taking them seriously.

Great comedy requires talent, tradition, and high moral and artistic standards. That is why we miss it so today. It is true that Old Comedy enjoyed an unusual degree of external freedom in matters of insult and invective, and later ages of critics focused their attention on this licensed play, or *libertas*—much as one might look, bemused, at a naked three-year-old running around a living room. Aristophanes' fun and wit owe much to the absence, and something to the threat, of censorial restraint. He enjoys abusing his enemies with new and grotesque flights of "uglification and derision." He enjoys pushing criticism, not just of politicians but of the Athenian people themselves in action, about as far as law and custom allowed it to go, and perhaps a little further.[4] Yet this external freedom, though essential, is not enough. In the late 1960s Barbara Gerson's *MacBird* won high praise from critics (who should have known better), because it made savage fun of an American president, Lyndon Johnson, during the Vietnam war; but *MacBird* was neither intelligent nor funny. Nor does the use of four-letter words, *in itself*, amount to free speech. Insult and indecency are splendid resources for comedy, but they need to be exploited with economy and taste. Their effectiveness depends, finally, on their subordination to larger aims than scoring fast points off opponents, or on the laugh meter. For great comedy, an inner standard of freedom is required, an almost philosophical loyalty to truth-seeking and the larger view. To settle for less, merely to satisfy audience expectations or gain some limited effect of propaganda or airing of bias, is not enough.

Let me illustrate the problem of comic standards by a modern example and then work back to Aristophanes. In Trevor Griffiths's play *Comedians* a retired nightclub comedian named Eddie Waters is lecturing some students, explaining why a nasty limerick just won't do:

> It's not the jokes. It's not the jokes. It's what lies behind 'em. It's the attitude. A real comedian—that's a daring man. He *dares* to see what his listeners shy away from, fear to express. And what he sees is a sort of truth about people, and about their situation, about what hurts or terrifies them, about what's hard, above all, about what they *want*. A joke relieves the tension, says the unsayable, any joke pretty well. But a true joke, a comedian's joke, has to do more than release tension, it has to *liberate* the will and the desire, it has to *change the situation*. (Pause.) There's very little won't take a joke. But when a joke bases itself upon a distortion . . .—a "stereotype" perhaps—and gives the lie to the truth so as to win a laugh and stay in favor, we've moved away from a comic art and into the world of "entertainment" and slick success.[5]

The real comedian, Eddie is saying, must first have insight into the truths of human life and human nature. He must then have the courage to face these truths (some of them very painful) and carry them into his work. For his business is to make people laugh, but it cannot stop there. Many kinds of jokes, like the limerick in question, seem to release tension, but in fact they only trap it, leaving things the way they are; while a good comedian, by "liberating" will and desire, somehow makes a change in things. It is true, that people out there normally expect to hear what they already are used to hearing: to laugh at the old Irish jokes, the old Jewish jokes, the old mother-in-law jokes, and so forth. Eddie does not say (though he evidently thinks) that some such jokes should be ruled out because they are basically hostile and cruel. He argues, rather, that they are untrue because they appeal to stereotypes; because they relate, not what the comedian sees, but what the audience expects. The implication, though, is that artistic and moral standards for comedy are ultimately one and the same. To use merely the old, trite, hurtful jokes is a kind of betrayal, at once of comedy and of one's own human nature and human responsibilities.

Eddie's statement goes far, yet falls short of what Trevor Griffiths sees. It is troubling that, within the play, nightclub acts are allotted by men like the crass Challoner, who is "looking for someone who sees what the people want and knows how to give it them";[6] troubling, that the two men ultimately hired take his advice, betraying Eddie's standards; and even more troubling, that the best comic performance in the tryout springs from ice-cold hatred. It is brilliantly done, as Eddie himself admits. It is also truthful, though lacking in human warmth and in the hope, to which Eddie clings, of changing the world a little for the better.

Now, I have been arguing all along that Aristophanes' jokes do more than "relieve the tension," though that is where they start; that he is concerned "to liberate the will and desire . . . to change the situation." I have also been arguing that Aristophanes' hope "to change the situation" never betrays him into concealing his deeper insights into human nature and politics. The frauds, pretenses, and deceptions that he exposes include his own, or what were (potentially) his own; the *sycophantēs*, or irresponsible paid informer, is the shadow of what *Aristophanēs*, that best comic poet or expert at indecent exposure, might have been. His self-mocking but serious claims in the various parabases—to speak for what is right, without fear or favor; to attack, not just the usual small fry of politics, but really dangerous people (notably Cleon); to abandon insults once they become mindless and trite; and not to employ the power of insult and invective for some kind of blackmail—all these claims, taken together, amount to a statement of moral and artistic integrity that can be believed. It is, for the comic poet, equivalent to the praise of the good statesman that Thucydides accords Pericles: that he had insight into things, and the ability to convey that insight; that he was patriotic and could not be bribed.

The freedom of Old Comedy is somewhat ambiguous, like that of the "free press" today. The term first suggests freedom from external interference, censorship, and control. We laugh when the dictator of a small African country boasts, in Tom Stoppard's *Night and Day*, of allowing "a relatively free press"—which turns out to mean "a press controlled by my relatives."[7] Yet Stoppard also raises the question of whether the newspapers back home in Britain are truly free, given the power of greed and ambition, advertising and public demand, bureaucracy and pettiness and labor strife. The final suggestion is that they too are only "relatively free," in Grimsby as in Kambawe.

The comparison is relevant because Old Comedy somewhat occupied the place, and enjoyed the privileges, of the free press in a modern democracy where its rights are guaranteed by law; but scholars have usually paid attention to the external, not the internal freedom of the comic poets. Hellenistic, Roman, and Byzantine scholars tried to understand where that curious impunity, that *ius nocendi* ("right of injuring"), had come from, and how and why it had eventually been removed. Aetiological stories were passed down, like the tale of the poor countrymen who came into the city by night, their faces disguised with wine lees, and sang lampoons against their rich and powerful oppressors: the precedent was found to be socially useful, and masked invective became an accepted tradition.[8] It made some sense to later ages that the unusual license of Old Comedy, to practice insult and invective, should have been granted and maintained for social ends, but also that eventually the *ius nocendi* had to be withdrawn, when the Athenian democracy ended, or else when the attacks of comedy went beyond any reasonable limit or restraint.

Writing probably in the mid-420s, the "Old Oligarch," an antidemocratic pamphleteer, tried to explain comedy's freedom, together with the limits of that freedom, in his own logical way:

> They do not allow comedians to attack the people so that they may not be abused themselves; they encourage personal attacks if anyone wishes, knowing that the butts of comedy are not for the most part from the common people nor from the masses, but rich or noble or powerful.[9]

(In this argument "they" refers to the tyrannous democratic majority who arranged everything in their own interest. The writer gives them credit for intelligence and consistency, though hardly for moral wisdom or patriotic sense.) The prohibition mentioned here implies that past a certain point, the comic poet could be regarded as attacking the democratic constitution of the polis. This is borne out by Cleon's attack on Aristophanes after his *Babylonians*, of 426 B.C., which dealt with Cleon's corrupt methods and with the mistreatment of the subject allies. We do not know exactly what happened.[10] It seems, from Aristophanes' defense in the *Acharnians* and from his rueful comments there and elsewhere, that Cleon hauled him before the Boule on some dangerous charge, like making fun or speaking ill of the polis and insulting the people in the presence of foreigners. The charges seem to have been dropped after Aristophanes "played the monkey," apologizing in comic or not-so-comic fashion. People thought it was very funny when Cleon made him squirm![11] It may be that in his attempt to muzzle Aristophanes, Cleon appealed to existing laws of a very general nature. People could be brought to trial on criminal indictments (*graphai*) of "wrongdoing against the demos" and of "verbal assault." But what matters is that Aristophanes went right back afterwards, to his attack on Cleon and his criticism of the Athenian people as stupid and gullible (though not, to be sure, in the presence of foreigners at the Great Dionysia). Even more significantly, comedy's freedom of personal attack was not restrained by any law of censorship, except during the brief period of 440–437, after the Samian War: not after the outbreak of the Peloponnesian War, nor even in the panic and dismay of the 410s and after. The force of religious and popular tradition was too strong.

Yet Aristophanes cannot have counted on continuing immunity in his litigious Athens, and his claim to courage has much to recommend it. It must have taken courage to face up to the intimidation and mudslinging of the Cleon-monster; it may have taken still more courage to bring Demos himself onstage as a stupid, gullible, and thoroughly incompetent old man. It is true that, as K. J. Dover points out, such criticisms were common in Athenian oratory.[12] (Even Cleon is depicted by Thucydides as using them.) It is also true that Aristophanes criticizes, not the basic constitution of the democracy, but the leading astray of the people by the politicians, in assembly or council or jury courts—that he appeals from Demos deluded to Demos aware. All the same, his claim to courage in the *Acharnians* and elsewhere seems justified. It cannot have been easy to speak out against the wrongdoing of the sovereign people, as honesty and fair play (*ta dikaia*) demanded. Aristophanes makes the point, in his own defense, that the flatterers who confirm the public in delusion are their dangerous enemies, while the comic poet who tells the truth in "speaking ill" of them is their real friend—in fact, a great and envied national resource! The claim here given is exaggerated in comic fashion, and self-parodying, as if to warn the poor old gullible public against still another kind of delusion practiced upon them. At bottom, though, it is sincere, and it is justified. And I very much wish that we had Aristophanes in the president's cabinet today.

Another claim, not to rely on stereotypes, bears on Aristophanes' loyalty to what I am calling the whole and comic truth. Of course he uses the old comic bits that he makes fun of, but he joins them with new, witty ideas, and he builds from the lesser preliminary release through joking to the larger comic recognitions. Other poets, he says, take good political jokes (namely his own, like the comparison of Cleon to an eel-fisherman muddying the waters) and run them into the ground.[13] This may have been true; we cannot know. But we do know that Aristophanes opens up ideas and perceptions that are far from trite.

Lastly, there is Aristophanes' claim that he never abuses his comic license for unworthy personal ends:

> And although our poet was elevated and honored more than any man before him, he never became carried away by this, or got a swelled head, or reveled around the wrestling schools, trying to pick up boys. For that matter: whenever some resentful lover wanted to have his former love publicly lampooned, our poet insists that he never agreed to this. For he thought, quite reasonably, that the lady Muses with whom he was engaged ought never to be found in the procuring business. (*Wasps* 1023–28)

The picture is very funny. We are to imagine an Aristophanes so carried away by his enormous accomplishments, his unheard-of theatrical triumphs, his universally acknowledged superiority to all other poets, that he "revels" drunkenly (and by daylight) around all the gyms, trying to seduce boys! But is the idea merely ridiculous? Success, and artistic success not least, has always tempted people to *hybris* and disorder. I think of Dylan Thomas's drunken poetry readings on American campuses, and of the many female students who collected his sexual autograph after those readings. This sort of thing, Aristophanes suggests, is like returning to the original "revel" from which comedy started. In actuality an Athenian comic poet might easily have been tempted to satirize some individual, if not from personal spite (or even blackmail), then to comply, as here suggested, with a friend's request. It may be that the joke refers to some rival poet's behavior, in which case the satirist is indirectly satirized. Yet this commonplace kind of corruption is made to stand for a larger and more serious "prostitution of the Muse" that Aristophanes rejects: the temptation to make his comedy serve any lesser purpose than the discovery of the whole and comic truth. He is (to keep up the sexual metaphor) a master of indecent exposure, but this has to be universal—has to include the comic poet's own prejudices and pretenses. Which leads me, by a train of thought that will become obvious, to his second great loyalty, to human nature: in its common ridiculousness, its diversity, and its creative possibilities.

In *Orthodoxy* G. K. Chesterton states as the first principle underlying his liberal and democratic beliefs the proposition that

> the things common to all men are more important than the things peculiar to any man. Ordinary things are more valuable than extraordinary things; nay, they are more extraordinary. Man is something more awful than men; something more strange. The sense of the miracle of humanity itself should be always more vivid to us than any marvels of power, intellect, art, or civilization. The mere man on two legs, as such, should be felt as something more heartbreaking than any music and more startling than any caricature. Death is more tragic even than death by starvation. Having a nose is more comic even than having a Norman nose.[14]

The thought of the things "common to all men" brings us first to tragedy. Once the gifts of fortune and trappings of rank are stripped away, men are "poor naked wretches," the storms of life beating down on their unprotected bodies. In Sophocles' *Antigone*, where the naked, unburied corpse of Polyneices is a central image, the chorus in their Ode on Man find humankind to be "wonderful and terrible" (*deina*): not so much, as the sophists believed, for their high accomplishments—Chesterton's "marvels of power, intellect, art, or civilization"—as for the contrast between these same high endowments and accomplishments on the one hand and the uncertainty of good or evil on the other, toward which they move, together with the certainty (still) of death. Tragedy is democratic and leveling because life and death are. It brings us, through the vicarious sufferings that evoke pity and terror, to a renewed sense of our shared humanity. But comedy, with its shared laughter, is even more deeply democratic, since it acknowledges the lower side of human life that tragedy, with its heroic aspirations, must largely ignore: the everyday business of eating and drinking, of sex and evacuation. Comedy brings us back relentlessly to the lower bodily self as the lowest common denominator of social and political experience. Comedy strips away pretense, cuts through abstractions, unmasks the rhetorical slogans by which we so often live or die. But this same stripping away of status and pretense, rhetoric and abstraction, also exposes, with its wonderful indecency, that basic shared humanity, that common experience and feeling and common sense, on which any good, true, and humane politics must be founded.

I give three examples from the *Lysistrata*, beginning with the most obvious form of indecent exposure in that play. The great erect phalluses worn onstage make their bearers perfectly ridiculous. (Much of the effect can be reproduced today with loaves of French bread or with elongated balloons attached to actors' costumes; I recommend an all-female *Lysistrata* to bring out the basic fun and silliness with which sex is treated in this play.) In the plot, of course, these great erections demonstrate that the women's sex strike has made its effects felt. Like a contagious disease, these effects spread to include all the men of Greece impartially, soldiers and officials, Athenians and Spartans; so they are brought to the negotiating table by a common and pressing need—led, as Lysistrata says, if not by the hand, then by the handle.[15] It is thematically appropriate that the men, who have ignored and violated the ordinary concerns of domestic life, should be brought to their knees (so to speak) by such very ordinary accoutrements of domestic life as diaphanous slips and nightgowns. Beyond that, the phalluses point to a basic, overwhelming, and universal need in the public as well as the pubic realm. Behind the scenes—hardly mentioned, because they are so very painful, but the very silence produces a deeply tragic effect in the midst of comedy[16]—we feel the defeat of the Sicilian expedition, the loss of so many soldiers and ships, the scarcity of funds, the defection of subject allies, the overall weariness and demoralization of Athens and of the rest of the Greek world. If recovery is possible, it must begin with the recognition of a common need, almost (but this is comedy) of a common helplessness. Pretenses of personal or national dignity can only impede such realization.[17] The great phalluses, more than anything else, indicate that common need and near-helplessness, but they are also a sign of vigor and energy, insisting on a solution that can and must be found.

My second example also involves sexual indecency of word and gesture. The chorus of the *Lysistrata* is divided into two semichoruses, of old men and old women, who engage in playful, ritualistic combat until they become reconciled and reunited in a single singing and dancing chorus. At one point the old men angrily strip for action, removing their mantles and then their tunics, and their actions are matched, as in a comic ballet, by the old women; but eventually, after the several exchanges of angry but increasingly playful abuse and the miming of kicks, punches, and the like, the old women take the initiative in setting things right by dressing the old men again and caring for them gently and tenderly. It is very touching: as though, in comedy's view, one must lose one's dignity in order to find it. Like the young men with their great phalluses, the old men without (really) much to show are perfectly ridiculous—and this is their own silly fault. They shouldn't have been so pigheaded. But their nadir of indecency, while funny in itself, also looks toward the truly human society needing to be restored, much as (to follow Lysistrata's own illustration of women's skill and patience in handling things) a woolen cloak comes into being through the several processes of shearing, wool-gathering, cleaning, carding, spinning, and weaving, so that in the end human nakedness may be clothed with some measure of protection, dignity, and grace.

My third example involves drinking. Toward the end of the *Lysistrata*, two men praise the spirit of the drinking party that the Athenian and Spartan representatives have just now been enjoying, within the Acropolis:

> *A* I have never seen such a nice drinking party.
> The Spartans were so agreeable; and we,
> once in our cups, seemed so intelligent.
> *B* It figures. When we're sober, we're no good;
> in fact, if my proposal makes it through,
> I'll have our diplomats be *always* drunk.
> For now, what happens? The moment we get to Sparta,
> sober, we look for ways to stir up trouble;
> whatever they say, we never pay attention;
> and what they don't, we read between the lines;
> everything we report is inconsistent.
> But this time—
> there we were, in full agreement.   (1225–36)

The reversal is striking. In sober daylight, diplomatic relations were always a disaster, since the Athenian negotiators were so busy looking for trouble, reading between the lines, and entertaining shrewd suspicions of their opponents that they simply were unable to hear, let alone report, what the Spartans had to say. They might have been drinking that wonderful coffee described by Pope, "which makes the Politician wise / and see thro' all things with his half-closed Eyes."[18] Such subtlety, or oversubtlety, may seem clever, but its results—the never-ending war, the frustration, the loss of men and resources—prove its real stupidity. Conversely, when the Athenians and Spartans get drunk together in this play, they behave in a more open, more agreeable and friendly way. It is a truism that as men drink, they open up their inmost thoughts, and so can be trusted. It follows that drunken diplomacy is the best kind because it breaks through barriers, building on the exposed helplessness, but also on the shared goodwill and resourcefulness, of our common nature. (Our son Joe writes me that he met a young Russian in Bulgaria. "He spoke no English, but we drank vodka together, and he made a toast to peace. Peace is a good thing; we made many toasts.") In a different context, to be sure, a drunken brawl might have occurred, and even a small-scale war; but this time Dionysus' gift of wine proves reconciling and good.[19]

The comic hero is a paradoxical and parodic figure. He is also that shared human nature writ large. An easygoing, low-minded person, he rushes into situations where tragic heroes or wise statesmen fail, and he sweeps everything before him by imagination, shamelessness, and the ability, which so many heroes and statesmen lack, to survive humiliation. In some ways the comic poet seems to lend to characters like Dicaeopolis, the sausage-seller, Trygaeus, Peisetairus, Lysistrata, and Praxagora the power of his own unlimited comic and poetic imagination, which triumphs over all obstacles; but sometimes the reverse seems true, and his characters lend him in return that comic shamelessness, that acceptance of the sheer fun and messiness of living in a body, that fuels their (and his) remarkable success.

Dicaeopolis and the rest are democratic figures, standing for the lower bodily nature shared by everybody at Athens, and for the heroic spirit too that ordinary people possess, far removed though they may seem from Oedipus or Antigone, or from Pericles. They are also democratic in exemplifying, however grotesquely, the Athenian tenet that ordinary people are capable of carrying responsibility for public affairs, in the assembly or council or the jury courts, and even of running themselves for office and becoming magistrates. As the *Knights* suggests, there is something very wrong when a Cleon comes from nowhere to seize highest power; but behind that misfortune is something else that is even more right, a fairy-tale adventure that democracy has realized in fact. What is even more democratic is Aristophanes' acceptance and enjoyment of diversity, built also on comedy's sense of shared human nature. Partly, of course, he enjoys the great parade of city types whose colorfulness is the stuff of comedy. He *needs* them all, needs the "politicians, perverts, panders, poets, pickle-sellers, oracle-sellers, decree-sellers, fortune-tellers, fortune-seekers, fortune-wasters, emissaries, commissaries, cut-purses, cowards, harp players, harbor-masters, harlots, tax-collectors, informers, Euripides, fakes, fools, foreigners, fishmongers, and philosophers—all the riffraff."[20]

The list (Cedric Whitman's) is Aristophanic in its nonsensicalness, its pleasure in extravagant and incongruous listing—which is akin, however, to the pleasure of seeing all these different faces and types in the hustle and bustle of a modern city. The sensible man, the moralist, the social or intellectual snob, would have felt appalled by the spectacle, reduced to helplessness or to merely satirical protest. That is the reaction of the Old

Oligarch, always drawing his line between that "riffraff" and respectable people like his intelligent, moral, and well-brought-up self. My own view is that by gift of the comic Muse and of his own uninhibited characters like the sausage-seller, Aristophanes learned early on not to be a snob, not to be a "Bdelycleon." He enjoys the great parade of types, not in the manner of the detached, alienated satirist, but with a comic magnanimity that looks forward to Chaucer, Rabelais, Shakespeare, and Dickens. But at the heart of that comic magnanimity is the acceptance and enjoyment of shared humanity, the sense of kinship with all those knaves and fools who populate the world, who are all together with us in the same leaky boat.

This sense of kinship, more easily felt than expressed, takes various forms. The frauds and confidence men and social parasites who live by their wits are like cousins of the comic hero (and of the poet behind him), to be acknowledged with a wink before they are kicked offstage. Lesser villains like sycophants embody the shadow side of the comic poet, his role merely as "informer," satirist, or policeman. The greater villain (Cleon, of course) is what the comic poet as reformer might have become if he had surrendered to his own power of rhetorical manipulation, albeit with the best intentions. "We have met the enemy, and . . . he may be us." The massed opponents of peace and sanity at Athens, the old Marathon fighters who form the chorus of the *Acharnians* and *Wasps*, are driven at heart by human needs, and human wishes, with which the comic poet has to identify more deeply than with any more superficial, less human effort at reforming the state and "cleaning things up." This is not to say that the frauds, villains, and opponents are not, in their different ways, dangerous nuisances who need to have something done about them. They are, and they do. What is required, indeed, is the comic hero's sure response: to discommode the parasites, overcome the villains, and convert the opposition—but all this done with a power that emerges from total acceptance and enjoyment of human nature, one's own and others'. The sausage-seller's victory over the Paphlagonian, Dicaeopolis' victory over Lamachus (and Euripides), Philocleon's escape—all these, in their different ways, reflect the comic poet's own rediscovered vitality, his achieved triumph over the spoilsport and snob in himself, and his loyalty, beyond any lesser informing or reforming aims, to human nature in all its variety, its fun, and its democratic confusion.

In his Funeral Oration Pericles says that tolerance of diversity is a feature of the Athenian system.

> We practice freedom in our public structures; and in private, too, we do not dislike a person for his personal lifestyle, or condemn him by our suspiciousness and by the burden of hostile looks.

Although the point is made negatively, being about tolerance of individual differences, Pericles sees variety, together with openness, discussion, and culture, as itself a good thing—though all this needs to be balanced by discipline, restraint, obedience to laws and magistrates, and the readiness to exert oneself for the public good. But he also implies that the Athenians may pride themselves on an *inner* diversity:

> In sum, I say that our city, taken as a whole, is the school of Hellas; and taken individually, I think each Athenian could show himself most independent, meeting different occasions with the greatest versatility and grace.[21]

In his reaction later to the excesses of Athenian democracy and to the instability that they showed, Plato would object to the inner diversity as well as the outer. In his ideal society, each person would serve just one (needed) function. Specialization would be "justice." But, equally important, the soul's right order and virgin simplicity would not be violated by the dangerous multiplicity of role-playing, of experimenting with a variety of lifestyles, jobs, and beliefs, as one might go from booth to booth at a great fair, sampling the different wares—or as a playwright might create, and an actor play, many different parts.[22]

But this is just what the comic hero does in Aristophanes' plays. He tries on new costumes, new ways of behavior, as a means of acting on the world around him. He is equally ready to throw off a costume or a role when the time comes. To overmatch the world's pretenses, Dicaeopolis borrows and uses Euripides' Telephus costume. His control of the borrowed sophistication and art, as a sort of magic, is impressive; still more, is his ability to throw it off and reveal his comic "self" at the right time.

The creative possibilities of role-playing are wonderfully explored in the *Thesmophoriazusae*, a play full of literary parody but by no means restricted to aesthetic concerns. There an unnamed relative of Euripides agrees to spy in female disguise on the women's secret gathering. He gives himself away, in the debate over the "Euripides question," by confessions about women's life and behavior that out-misogynize the alleged misogynist; is revealed, in a great scene of indecent exposure, to be a man with a phallus that refuses to be kept down or concealed; is seized, humiliated, and kept under guard. But that is only the beginning, an excuse for trying out a great number and variety of theatrical devices from Euripidean tragedy. The man plays Palamedes, wildly throwing out oar-blades with messages on them. He plays Andromeda to Euripides' Echo and Perseus. He plays the "new Helen" to Euripides' Menelaus. Then, after all these tragic ploys fail, he is let off the hook by Euripides' compromise with the women and by a simple, old-fashioned comic trick played on the Scythian guard. The parody is brilliant and appreciative. It comments variously on Euripides' new romantic tragedies, as well as on some old melodramatic devices that Euripides continued to use. But beneath the parody, this play breathes encouragement. It suggests that Athenians can play many parts, can survive humiliation and defeat, can find a way out of seemingly hopeless difficulties. The poet who most fully exposes, most fully accepts human nature as it is—that roving phallus again—is also the poet who most enjoys, and most believes in, the diverse possibilities of a creative and various polis. No role is final, and no situation, if you are irrepressible like Euripides' relative. There is always another role to play.[23] And the next role, the next disguise—or its stripping off—may show you, and show the polis, the real way out.

27   *Loyalty to* Communitas: Lysistrata, Thesmophoriazusae

ARISTOPHANES' third loyalty, to *communitas*, is less to an idea than to an experience of closeness, equality, and fellow-feeling that recurs at certain privileged times in the life of a society. As Victor Turner has described it in his books and essays, *communitas* may arise spontaneously on such occasions as a good party or a shipboard voyage, or may be created on a grander scale by a massive breakdown in social structures; but most often it comes about at regularly organized occasions in the individual life cycle or the social year when the normal systems of role, status, and hierarchy are temporarily laid aside.[24] For example, young men undergoing initiation experience *communitas* when they enter into the in-between or liminal state. They are cast out from earlier attachments and life structures; spend a transitional period, which takes on an aspect of timelessness, in undergoing initiatory experiences and learning secrets of tribal wisdom and behavior and of cosmic meanings; and then, when they are ready, are brought back and reintegrated into their society. The experience of *communitas*—of being in a closely united group temporarily freed from divisions of role and status—belongs to the in-between, liminal state. Similarly, a group of people on pilgrimage, coming from diverse backgrounds, occupations, and states of life, become joined together in the free, close, and equal associations of *communitas* as they make their way together toward a religious goal. One way or another, the temporary withdrawal of people from their usual social structures and bonds revives the sense of coherence and vitality on which those same structures depend. Society needs structures, but it also needs the periodic nurture of *communitas* to be most healthily and wholly itself.

Certain experiences of *communitas* described by Turner are especially relevant to comedy and to the rituals underlying comedy. In a Ndembu "rite of elevation," a man chosen to be chief is reviled and humiliated by the whole village.[25] Together with his wife, he is pushed around, pelted with dirt, and grossly insulted—all this as a kind of initiation, a preparation for assuming the dignity and responsibility of the chieftainship. We might explain this psychologically today, might say that the chief will rule more effectively once bad feelings have been aired, or that the good chief will always remember that at bottom, beneath the trappings of office, he is one of the tribe. There is an apotropaic element too. Yet the Ndembu rite seems to have its own deeper wisdom. The permitted outbreak of insult and violence, contained within a larger ritual order and control, brings the people together in a special closeness and ease, a brief playtime that makes the ordinary structures more workable and more real.

We can see how comedy grows, together with *communitas*, from what Turner calls "rites of status reversal," like the Apo ceremony of the Ashanti. A Dutch historian described this in 1705 as

> a Feast of eight days accompanied with all manner of Singing, Skipping, Dancing, Mirth, and Jollity; in which time a perfect lampooning liberty is allowed, and Scandal so highly exalted, that they may freely say of all Faults, Villainies, and Frauds of their Superiours, as well as Inferiours, without Punishment.[26]

R. S. Rattray, an anthropologist writing in 1923, quoted an old priest's explanation of how the Apo ceremony benefits the soul. People hurt each other, and they bear grudges, so that the soul (*sunsum*) frets and sickens:

> Our forebears knew this to be the case, and so they ordained a time, once every year, when every man and woman, free man and slave, should have freedom to speak out just what was in their head, to tell their neighbors just what they thought of them, and of their actions, and not only to their neighbors, but also the king or chief. When a man has spoken freely thus, he will feel his *sunsum* cool and quieted, and the *sunsum* of the other person against whom he has now openly spoken will be quieted also.[27]

Evidently holiday rites like the Apo ceremony have a healing effect on whole societies, not just on the individuals concerned. They provide a periodic catharsis, clearing the air of much bad feeling and resentment caused by the daily friction of ordinary social roles and actions. But the effect of these rites of reversal is not just negative. They provide an experience of *communitas*: that is, of society "as an undifferentiated, homogeneous whole, in which individuals confront one another integrally, and not as 'segmentalized' into statuses and roles."[28] From such experiences a primitive society like the Ashanti gains a sense of its own inner being, and a feeling of revitalization, that our own society sorely lacks today.

In discussing such rites of reversal, or forms of carnival play or "the world turned upside down" in relation to political stability and change, anthropologists and sociologists bring out a curious ambivalence that should guide our interpretation of Old Comedy. On the one hand, these play forms act as a safety valve for existing social structures and institutions by affording a temporary respite from their pressures. Thus the Saturnalian custom that masters wait on slaves once a year—a custom that has persisted in master-servant and officer-subaltern relations the world over—underscores, in its holiday humor, the real subordination and constraint that must prevail for the rest of the year. Similarly, occasional festivities of sexual inversion, of "women on top," may even reinforce a regular subordination of women to men in marriage or in society. All rites of reversal, after all, point up the precise system of hierarchy and classification that is abandoned temporarily, mixed up, or put upside down. All this strengthens the status quo. And yet the opposite is also true: all these rites allow the temporary emergence of a different kind of society, a rearrangement of roles and powers that at least remains vivid to the imagination and at most spills over into revolt, into the active attempt to change social laws and institutions. The carnival experience of "women on top," for example, may give women a clearer picture of the real power to which they are entitled, which they may reach out sometime and grasp.[29] The festive reversal by which commoners dress up, drink, and push their social superiors around may provide an imaginative model for a full-scale revolt of the masses. Rites of status reversal or carnival may therefore take on a radical or anarchic meaning as well as a conservative one. They may threaten the status quo as well as support it. In the end their political significance is ambivalent because they are beyond or behind politics rather than part of them. If they revitalize but soothe political life by a kind of catharsis, they also judge it, freely and uncompromisingly, from a point outside the system. And this, as lawgivers, magistrates, and policemen know, is always dangerous.

All this bears closely on comedy, which is born of festive rites and inherits from them its licensed insults and indecencies (*aischrologia*). To quote Turner again:

> If the liminality of life-crisis rites may be, perhaps audaciously, compared to tragedy—for both imply humbling, stripping, and pain—the liminality of status reversal may be compared to comedy, for both involve mockery and inversion, but not destruction, of structural rules and overzealous adherents to them.[30]

The metaphor of "stripping" is apt. Tragedy strips its kings of their outward dignity and authority to bring out the poor, bare, forked creatures beneath—who may or may not be reclothed in dignity and grace. In a similar way, comedy strips away outward differences of role, status, and hierarchy, and the pretenses that accompany these, to reveal the nakedness (humiliating, funny, potent, and fruitful) that people have in common. Comedy is a great leveler. It revels in festive reversals: in the exaltation of nobodies to supreme power and authority; in the merry-making (and peacemaking, and new-world-making) of "women on top." Magistrates and ordinary citizens, elders and youths, notables and no-bodies, men and women—all come together through comedy's laughter into the joyful reexperience of unity, equality, and shared feelings. They reenter, one might say, the polis *behind* the polis, enjoying the unstruc-tured *communitas* from which the ordinary structured society draws so much of its vitality and its inner meaning. For comedy's privilege, derived from ancient rites and festivals, is to draw us all back into the green world, from which we emerge, individually and as a society, renewed in spirit and more fully ourselves.

Hence, again, the remarkable position of Aristophanes as the *kōmōi-dodidaskalos*, the "comedy director" or "comic poet as teacher" who plays out his comedy before thirteen thousand Athenians.[31] Insofar as the theater audience is *not* a real and serious political assembly, Aris-tophanes can make fun of politics, but can also speak the truth, as a licensed fool and jester, in a way that few or no politicians can. But there is something else. As *kōmōidodidaskalos* Aristophanes re-creates a fes-tive audience, calls back the Athenian people into *communitas*.[32] His criticism or advice about actual politics is only secondary, a by-product of that recreated spirit of *communitas*, of the polis behind the polis—or better, of the whole, united, and happy polis behind the divided, sick, and neurotic one. Recovery of health, recovery of vision, recovery of a sense of self, personal and communal: that is what comedy is about. It would be nice if all the rest went well, the votes and elections, the politi-cal decisions—and it would be nice (Aristophanes would say) if we could drink birds' milk and find cheesecakes running to meet us in the street. But to touch base again, to remember who we are, is at least a beginning.

The spirit of *communitas*, strongly evoked in all Aris-tophanes' comedies, seems especially relevant in the *Lysistrata* and *Thes-mophoriazusae*, of 411 B.C., plays that respond not only to defeat and near-exhaustion of men, money, and morale, but to the growing threat of dissension, even revolutionary division (*stasis*) from within.[33] In retro-spect we see that the threat was real. The activity of oligarchic clubs and politicians like Peisander resulted in formal negotiations with Alcibiades and the Persians and eventually in the modification of the democratic constitution in the "revolution" of 411. Although we cannot pinpoint political references in the two comedies (the *Lysistrata* was produced probably at the Lenaea in February, the *Thesmophoriazusae* at the Di-onysia in April, and Aristophanes wrote the plays several months earlier), is it a coincidence that plot and conspiracy bulk so large in both? In the *Lysistrata*, the women "swear together" to abide by the sex strike. When the old men assert that

> something big is in the air;
> I seem to smell some great affair;
> I think I catch the scent
> of Hippias' tyranny, (616–19)

that old ridiculous suspicion, that a long-dead tyrant might be restored to power, seems more relevant than usual after the women have (within the play) seized the Acropolis as part of their international conspiracy. The Persians had tried, within the old men's alleged memory, to bring Hippias back, and agreement with the Persians now might well bring Alcibiades back from exile. That the game is sexual and its aim peace with Sparta does not quite remove the sense of danger. In the *Thesmophoriazusae*, the tension grows, the feeling of danger and justified suspicion seems more acute. After invoking the Olympian gods and (with nonsexist emphasis) the Olympian goddesses generally, the presiding woman official invokes a curse on

> any person who is plotting evil against the demos of the women; or who is entering into negotiations with Euripides and with the Medes on conditions that are harmful to the women, or who plans to have a tyrant's rule or bring the tyrant back again, or who gave report of a suppositious child. (335–40)

The teasing is remarkable. Aristophanes hints at the real danger of negotiating with the Persians and Alcibiades to the detriment of the Athenian democracy, then falls back into the safe comic context of the women's world—of adultery, suppositious children, serious drinking.[34] Again, in the following ode, the chorus denounces all the women who (1) deceive, (2) violate established oaths, (3) try to change and replace laws and decrees, (4) reveal secrets to the enemy, or (5) bring in the Medes—for all these acts are impious and harm the polis. All this comes very close to the growing political crisis at Athens. As it turns out, the feeling of threat proves justified within the play: for there *is* a plot against the women, a spy who would betray the secrets of their sacred assembly, who will shortly be denounced, searched out, and exposed. We could say that here, as in the *Lysistrata*, the conspiracy is grounded harmlessly in laughter. Yet the chorus's plea to the gods to "stand by" seems more than usually heartfelt. The tension, the fear, the threat of conspiracy, amount to more than an ordinary comic joke.

In response most of all to the threat of disunity, both plays use role reversal, the "fruitful conflict of the sexes," and the magic of sexual withdrawal and exchange of clothing to evoke a model of *communitas*.

In both plays, symbolic tensions are focused and played out and reconciliation won: for men with women, for Athens with Sparta, and (more centrally, I would argue) for Athens with herself.

In the *Lysistrata*, the heroine brings about a dissolution (*lysis*) of war's accumulated tensions and miseries by a kind of homeopathic magic. The women's sex strike concentrates tension, focusing it on the men's most universally vulnerable spot, so that from sheer urgency they cut through all the impossible complications of diplomacy and make peace. As in genuine fertility rites like the Thesmophoria, the temporary sexual withdrawal of the women contributes to the betterment of marriage and child-rearing. At the same time, the temporary inversion of male and female roles reinforces social harmony, as Lysistrata hints when she urges her women-followers to persevere:

> *Lys.*   For there's an oracle that says we'll win
> if we avoid dissension. It's right here.
> *Woman* What does it say? Tell us.
> *Lys.*   Be quiet, then.
> "Whenas the swallows shall be assembled to one place,
> and flee the hoopoes, and keep away from phalluses,
> respite from ills shall come, and high-thundering
> Zeus turn things top to bottom—"
> *Woman*   So *we'll* be put on top?
> *Lys.*   "—but should those swallows not stand together,
> but each one swing
> away on her private wing, then everyone will sing,
> 'Feature for feature,
> there's no more stuck-up creature
> than women—I mean, swallows—in the entire world.'"
>
> (767–76)

If the women remain united, says Lysistrata, they will come out on top. We could reverse the proposition and say that the topsy-turviness of the play's action, its *hypertera nertera*, re-creates the spirit of *communitas* by which dissension in the actual society (*stasis*, *diastēnai*) is overcome. If the citizens of Athens remain united—if they do not, like those lascivious women-followers, try to "run off" against their oaths—then Athens will prevail. The war must be ended, and not least because of its demoralizing and disuniting effects at home; but the inner recovery, more urgent than ever before, cannot wait (as in earlier plays) for the attainment of that external peace. It must come first.

Again, the conflict in Athenian society is played out suggestively in the sexual maneuvers and battles of the old men and women described earlier. The chorus, when first seen, have experienced *stasis*; they are divided into two symbolically warring parties. The old men attack the

Acropolis (to save it) like an invading army, with logs and fire; the old women defend it with pitchers of water; they exchange taunts and insult-songs, mimed kicks and blows, in the oldest agonistic tradition of Old Comedy; and when, touchingly, they make peace at last and come together as one united chorus, the audience enjoy a vicarious sense of reunion and new harmony. And this is further emphasized in what the newly united chorus sing:

> Please do not think
>   that it is our intention
> anything bad about
>   a fellow citizen to mention:
> rather, we want to say and do
>   only what is kind.
> The troubles we've already got
>   are quite enough, you'll find.   (1043–48)

They will not indulge in personal satire, which, albeit expected, might prove divisive. Instead they join in a childlike game, promising their listeners all kinds of wonderful blessings—which won't come about. The teasing is, as ever, apotropaic. It also reminds the Athenian audience, as ever, that happiness is not so easily won offstage as on. Yet the medium, of harmony without divisiveness, is the message that Aristophanes offers and that needs most urgently to be taken in.[35]

Throughout the *Lysistrata*, comic techniques and forms are modified to proclaim the politics of harmony, *eunoia*.[36] Instead of the usual agon, Lysistrata asserts first that things are in a mess and, second, that the women (who share no responsibility for the mess, or involvement in it) will set things right; but she avoids specific personal criticisms, and her own proposed program is very general, based on wool-working and the preparation of clothing. The polis has only to follow women's example. (1) As women wash dirt out of wool, beat out offending particles, and pull out burrs, so the polis should wash out its filth, beat out evildoers, and "comb out" people who club together unlawfully for political purposes. And (2) as separate bits of wool are joined in a common basket for spinning into yarn, so all the scattered people—public debtors, metics, colonists—should be joined in a skein of goodwill (*koinēn eunoian*) from which a great cloak can be woven for the people. As throughout the play, the women's domestic wisdom invades and transforms public affairs. The audience will laugh at the wool-gathering as the *proboulos* does: what possible connection could it have with the real world of Athenian and international politics? But Lysistrata evokes the sense of shared unity and purpose on which successful politics depend. Its image is the woven cloak, bringing dignity and protection. Without social unity people make themselves pathetically helpless in their anger, their suspicions, and their quarreling, like the old men in the following scene who strip, not for the usual parabasis, but for a mock-fight with their other halves that they cannot possibly win.

The old men are angry but impotent, like the old jurymen of the *Wasps* but older, wearier, more confused. They want rejuvenation but have no idea how to go about it. The old women, by contrast, are clear-minded and vigorous. As evidence for their involvement with, and right to speak for, the polis they adduce the religious duties they performed as girls and young women. They were the sacred Carriers, Mill-girls, Bears, Basket-bearers. As Helene Foley has shown, they represent the symbolic and ritual power that women traditionally exercise for the good of the polis.[37] Their efforts bring the fertility and rejuvenation that it needs, as imaged earlier in the casting-out of the *proboulos*, or special commissioner (who is given women's clothes and attributes, then prepared for burial) and in the phallic renascence of subsequent scenes. Male vigor and assertiveness are desirable, but they cannot—as Myrrhene's strip-tease reminds us—be an end in themselves.

Still working through sex, Lysistrata brings the Athenian and Spartan diplomats to terms by keeping the naked personification of *Diallagē*, or Reconciliation, before their eager eyes. It is sleight of hand, but it fits the comic moral: remember what you really want and go after it! In keeping with the spirit of reconciliation Lysistrata refuses to make particular criticisms, which would mire her in the hopeless old question "Who was to blame?" She emphasizes the positive. Athens and Sparta worship the same gods at the same international festivals. They have received common benefits: Sparta from Athens (tactfully, for the audience, this is put first), and Athens from Sparta, when the "friends of Hippias" were cast down and the "cloak of freedom" was restored. Here the spirit of Panhellenic unity strengthens, not weakens, the vigor and unity of the Athenian democracy at home. Conversely, the recovery of internal harmony will enable the Athenians to deal more vigorously, lucidly, and confidently with foreign affairs. The result is a general rejuvenation. Even the old men and women of the chorus disappear, to be replaced by the Athenians and Spartans who tipsily emerge from the Acropolis, now turned dining hall, to sing and dance in the exodos to the Olympian gods.[38]

We feel, indeed, throughout the play how strongly Aristophanes is appealing to those same gods for the salvation of Athens and of Greece. If the play is about sex, it is also about religion; the one still implies the other; and it is, curiously, the modern sophisticated reader who is too distracted by the sexual jokes and the stripteases to feel the force of the connection. I return to Lysistrata, the dignified and serious mover of all this commotion—and comedy's answer, incidentally, to all the violent, passionate, and demoralized "heroines" of Euripidean tragedy.[39] Lysistrata combines the comic authority of the "woman on top" in the topsy-turvy world with the more serious authority reserved to women in rituals of sex and marriage and in religious worship generally. Indeed it seems likely that Lysistrata is modeled partly on Lysimache, a priestess of Athena Polias.[40] Her namesake speaks for the spirit of *communitas* evoked by the topsy-turvy world, but she also represents the goddess who joins male and female attributes, who embodies the strength and unity of Athens ("holding her hand over the beloved city still," as Solon said), and whose celebration in song and dance exemplifies the bond of common worship that can reunite even the wartorn states of Greece. It is as if, here and in the *Thesmophoriazusae* (and later in the *Frogs*), the urgencies of a demoralized time impelled Aristophanes not merely to proclaim comedy's usual message of recovery and hope, but to look through and behind comedy to the gods themselves who resolve tensions, who foster *communitas*. Dionysus is there in the last hymn, but he does not stand out. With Zeus and Hera, the sacred married pair, he is placed between Artemis and Aphrodite, polar divinities of female life, here invoked as working in unison. It is the women of Athens and Greece, and Lysistrata (or Lysimache) behind them, and the goddesses behind her—Athena, Artemis, Aphrodite—who have that final power to save, to which even Dionysus seems to defer in the present play. In the *Thesmophoriazusae*, it will be the great goddesses, Demeter and Persephone, together with Athena.

Although the *Thesmophoriazusae* is about literature, not politics, its comic and religious strategies much resemble those of the *Lysistrata*. Again the women secede; only this time their secession reflects the actual Thesmophoria, when women abandon household structures, responsibilities, and divisions of role and family so that the fertility and wellbeing of Athens may be furthered by the old agricultural magic.[41] And again, the women take on a festive independence. They form a counterassembly with its own agenda: namely, what to do about Euripides and his attacks on women? This becomes the excuse, again, for playing out the "fruitful conflict of the sexes" as sexual antagonism is expressed and the male intruder is hunted down, exposed, and punished. I suggested earlier that Aristophanes uses the transvestite play, with its old magic and fun, to convey new possibilities of role-playing and action for the democratic polis. When things seems hopeless you can always try a new play and a new part! Acting becomes itself an image of successful escape. But still more significantly, the war between the women and Euripides moves through conflict to reconciliation. An agreement is reached. Euripides will stop slandering women, and they will release his battered relative. It is as though, this time, the spirit of reconciliation needed in Athenian life could best be discovered through the world of play, where nothing, not even threats of torture and death, need be taken with final seriousness.

The parallel with Euripides' tragedies is more than superficially important. We see it best in the "new *Helen*," wonderfully parodied here in a confused, speeded-up version with comic interruptions by a literal-minded old woman guarding her prisoner. As ever, Aristophanes is showing up the tricks of Euripidean melodrama, the sentimentality (a little too neat?) of those recurrent scenes of recognition and rescue. He may sense too that Euripides is intruding on comedy's turf.[42] And he suggests that Euripides, while seeming to sympathize with women's psychology and social condition, has produced images of women that, in the end, are worse than ever. And yet Aristophanes sees something new and pays comic tribute to it. In his escape plays, *Iphigenia among the Taurians* and *Helen* (both probably produced in 412 B.C.; we are missing the *Andromeda*), Euripides presents the weary, demoralized Athenians with fairy-tale images of recovery. He shows them reunion, with a lost brother or sister, husband or wife; rescue and return from a distant land; recovery of a sense of identity, out of confusion, deception, and isolation; and best of all, forgiveness after intolerable wrongdoing and a new, childlike innocence reborn out of guilt, suffering, and loss. Like Shakespeare's *Winter's Tale*, these plays are tragedies of grace. They draw, like comedy, on the myth of spring—Persephone restored to her mother and the upper world. Aristophanes appreciates all this, as well, perhaps, as Euripides' new, more genuinely positive image of woman.[43] All the same, he insists that escape is comedy's affair. What works finally in his play is not one of Euripides' untiring devices, but a bit of comic burlesque, a sex trick of the oldest, most obvious kind practiced on the stupid Scythian policeman. It is the striptease-and-run all over again. But what works finally outside the play is reconciliation, based again on the shared experience of festive *communitas* that comedy evokes but that, behind comedy, is the god's gift.

It is no accident that the gods are addressed so directly in this play, their presence invoked and celebrated in song and dance. For at heart the play is about the overwhelming necessity of that felt presence and of the gifts it brings of reconciliation, release, and joy. Play itself (*paisdein*) is celebrated as an attribute of the Thesmophoria, the festival reflected here. We feel it equally as the god's gift in and through the Dionysia in which the festive audience is presently participating. Here, as later in the *Frogs*, Aristophanes seems to search, behind comedy, for the sources of comedy's freedom, play, and joy, and to find these not so much directly in the worship of Dionysus as indirectly in the worship of Demeter and Persephone, to which the Dionysian is so closely akin. It is as if Aristophanes himself went on holiday, like the women in his story, to rediscover the powers of *communitas* and play—as if he, like Euripides' relative, were a disguised participant in their rites. Something like this is conveyed in the last beautiful hymn of the chorus:

Pallas, who care for choruses, by custom I invite you to our choral dance. Virgin unwedded who hold our city, manifest in strength, holder of the keys: appear before us, Lady, who hate tyrants. It is right.

The women in community invite you: come to us, bringing holiday-loving peace.

Benignly, graciously, Queens of Power, come to our grove where holy rites are revealed by you that men cannot behold, by light of torches, solemn and immortal sight.

Come now, join our worship, we pray you, Thesmophorian Queens of Power. If ever before you heard our prayer and came, then we cry to you, come, be with us now. (1136–59)

Pallas Athena is called on, confidently, to preserve the city. She "hates tyrants": that says enough about the present threat. Behind her, supporting her civic spirit, come the great goddesses, their saving power imaged in the bright flame of torches. By a logic inherent in the play, Euripides' proffer of reconciliation, the women's acceptance of this, and the relative's escape follow immediately on this hymn. It is as if the gods' felt presence that gives holiday its meaning and power, and play its point, had now to be called on directly to provide reconciliation, harmony, and escape from troubles—all intimated by the experience of *communitas* that comedy, even more than late Euripidean tragedy, evoked for the Athenian people.

I return to this subject in chapter 6, in connection with the *Frogs.* For the present I want to deal with comic utopias as a special mythic instance of *communitas.* Aristophanes' "loyalty to Utopia," expressed so grandly in the *Birds* and persevering, beyond Athens' fall, in the *Ecclesiazusae* and the *Plutus*, will be a test case for the other loyalties that I have been describing: to the whole and comic truth; to human nature in its diversity and its creative possibilities; and, especially, to *communitas.*

28   *Allegiance to Utopia*

THE title is paradoxical, and meant to be. I could have used "loyalty to creative fantasy," but that sounds too subjective and too abstract. The term *utopia* has two meanings, both intended by Sir Thomas More. One is derived from the Greek *eu-topia*: the great and good place where people lead happy and contented lives. The other, more familiar, comes from *ou-topia*: the nowhere or never-never-land where such happiness exists. Either meaning would seem incompatible with the ordinary conception of "loyalty," for the world of pleasure and freedom transcends that of normal duties and obligations, and the heart's desire for a nowhere land lessens ordinary local and patriotic allegiances. But is this necessarily true? Or can *eu-* and *ou-topias* nourish those other loyalties of a more delimited and responsible kind? I shall argue that they can, and that they do.

For, first, Utopia (as *eu-topia*) is the place where human needs not only are satisfied, but also are reconciled with each other and with the needs of society in a harmonious and satisfying way. In ordinary experience, naturally, instinct wars against regulation, the "pleasure principle" against the "reality principle"; we surrender a large measure of personal freedom and happiness in order to enjoy the benefits of civilized and social life; and different needs—play and work, enjoyment and planning, liberty and obedience—seem at worst to destroy one another, and at best to coexist in a precarious, often painful tension. In Utopia, however, individual happiness is reconciled with public order. In Plato's Republic (though many today would find this a bad place, or *dystopia*), the individual soul is happiest when the community is best served. In More's Utopia, the monastic asceticism to which More felt personally drawn is joined with the humanistic social organization that fosters the best life for all.

Secondly, Utopia (as *ou-topia*) remains in dialogue with the world as we know it. (This is, along with scope and viability, one of the virtues of a well-constructed "secondary world.")[44] Most often this dialogue takes

the form of a powerful contrast. Plato makes the instability and dishar-
mony of Athenian culture and politics into a foil for his ideal Republic;
similarly, the first book of More's *Utopia*, by concentrating on contemporary English economic and social ills, points up by contrast the desirability of Utopia—and perhaps its unattainability. This last is crucial. If,
through inspiration, leadership, effort, and the course of time, our world
may be brought nearer to Utopia, then we may feel more hopeful; but if,
on the contrary, something perverse in the world's nature or our own
holds us back from real progress, or drags us back- and downwards,
then the contrast of Utopian virtue and happiness with our own habitual
folly and wretchedness gives scope to satire—and to bitter anger or despair. Read Book 4 of *Gulliver's Travels* and you feel, with Swift, that
humans are hopelessly alienated from the happiness of rational living.
Read Edward Bellamy's *Looking Backward* and you feel that life can
become better, happier, and more just; it is only a matter of time—and of
technological and moral progress. Often versions of Utopia are like pipe
dreams from which we reawaken to a stronger, harsher awareness of
psychological and social limitations and of the iron laws of historical
reality. Is it altogether an illusion if, at other times, the Utopian vision
brings desire with hope, so that the bonds seem looser, and the prison
walls less strong?

Before returning to ancient Greece and to Aristophanes, let me illustrate the power, the relevance, and the hopefulness of Utopia by lingering
a while (this will be my last personal digression) on thoughts of Oz. For
the Oz books of L. Frank Baum, written between 1900 and 1919, con-
jured up the first great secondary world on which my imagination was
nourished. I still feel a "loyalty" to Oz today, which may illustrate the
point I am making in this section—the more so, because Oz is unusual in
being an American utopia. In the following discussion I shall be concerned not with the *Wizard of Oz* movie, in which Oz is only (to the
approval of psychologists and educators) a beautiful dream, but with
Baum's fourteen Oz books, in which Oz is quite as real as America, and
Dorothy returns there, with her aunt and uncle, to take up permanent
citizenship—as who would not?[45]

Oz begins, significantly, by being uncivilized. As the Good Witch of
the North explains to Dorothy, "In the civilized countries I believe there
are no witches left. . . . But, you see, the Land of Oz has never been
civilized, for we are cut off from all the rest of the world. Therefore we
still have wizards and witches among us."[46] This distinction is basic,
and, as Dorothy finds, both the loveliness and the dangerousness of
living in Oz follow from it. But gradually (in the later books) a civilized
order develops within this magical land. The fairy princess Ozma is
made ruler of Oz after the wicked witches are defeated. As she maintains
her rule, by a strict control of the technology (that is, magic), peace and

security fan out from Ozma's palace at the center, through the Emerald City and the surrounding farmlands, into more distant regions of the four countries of Oz. Dark corners remain, to challenge peace and order; but gradually they are explored and subdued to Ozma's rule. The regular Oz book pattern is one of adventure and return: of an exciting and perilous journey among strange peoples (who may be friendly or hostile, amusing or frightening, or a mixture of these), but always followed by a return to the peaceful, ordered, ultimately civilized life at the center of things, in the Emerald City.

Why was Oz so satisfying when I was a boy? It was, of course, pure escape. From the demands of family, the pressures of school, and all the anxieties of growing up, it brought me into a world of unparalleled comfort and ease scarcely further away than my green armchair: a world where handkerchiefs grow into well-furnished tents; where lunchboxes and dinner-pails grow on trees, ready for the plucking; where animals can talk and inanimate objects can be brought to life; and where, if there is no party or celebration going on, then someone is probably planning one. Anyone would have wanted to escape into such a world—the more so because Baum's art made it unusually accessible and familiar and complete. But there was more. On reflection I see how much Oz helped me to reconcile such disparate things as law and freedom, duty and pleasure, work and play. Ozma's laws are always there, few but firm; the overriding principle is the Law of Love, rather dimly and sentimentally expressed, to be sure, yet successful in maintaining a charmed community where kindness, tolerance, and contentment are leading virtues, and where pride, jealousy, competitiveness, and hostility have no place. Again, the voice of duty is strong in Oz, calling people (and not least, Ozma herself) to effort and risk; yet the dutiful journey is followed by the happy return, culminating in a party or celebration that seems an end in itself. Similarly, work is not only balanced by play, but it exists for good purposes: to make people feel useful and fulfilled, to make life more comfortable or beautiful for others. In short, as I look back, I think that the Oz books gave virtue, duty, effort, and responsibility a good name.[47] They suggested that being good was not only morally better than being bad, but also more interesting and a great deal more fun. They drew me into a world where nature and civilization met on friendly terms, and what we want to do coincided with what we ought.

And yet for all its moral and educational implications, Oz remains a child's world where people need not grow old or die. Dorothy stays around ten. Ozma, a few years older, is not too old for children's games. It seems paradoxical: but Ozma and her friends and counselors combine the seriousness, dignity, and responsibility of grown-ups with the freshness, openness, and spontaneity of children, so that they are *childlike* in the best sense of the word; whereas villains like the Nome King, superficially grown-up, are transparently *childish* in their greed, their self-centeredness, and their temper tantrums. The contrast is ironic, but real enough to us as we grow older. Oz, because it preserves children's best life, teaches us (outside Oz) to be ourselves. A privileged world, enriched from the world of fairies above and of beasts below—the Cowardly Lion and Hungry Tiger beside Ozma's throne—it reconciles us with ourselves, with being human, even in an unenchanted world.

It would be mistaken to search for a political or social program in the Oz books, even if they have sometimes been taken as expressions of nineteenth-century populism or of the economic principles of William Jennings Bryan. Such efforts at definition are tempting because Oz, as will be seen, is a very American utopia; but they run quickly into contradictions. Thus food, clothing, and tools are shared out in Oz in a somewhat communistic manner, "from each according to his ability, to each according to his need"; but all this takes place under the rule of an arbitrary though benevolent monarch. Baum provides female role models, albeit young ones, but makes fun of feminists (like his mother-in-law); he makes fun of the military and essentially does away with it—but he also makes one realize how defenseless the good and innocent people can be. I never mistook Oz for the model of a workable society in real life. Yet if I have a conservative temperament, a liberal voting record, and a hippie heart—if I am, in Robert Frost's words, "not confused, only well mixed"—I owe this largely to the Oz books. More than that, Oz strengthened in me what I have been describing as the principal loyalties of Aristophanic comedy: to laughter and freedom, to the enjoyment of human diversity, to a sense of *communitas* underlying (if somewhat reversing) the social structure. The first is embodied in the figure of Scraps, the Patchwork Girl, one of Baum's finest creations. Intended to be a servant, Scraps received an overdose of cleverness, wit, and poesy. Her jokes and comic verses disrupt solemnity and are restrained with difficulty; her mischievousness and high spirits assert themselves as an essential, irrepressible feature of life in the Emerald City. I think that my own sense of laughter as anarchic at bottom, and as setting a limit to order and seriousness even of the best kind, owes much to Scraps, that uninhibited clown, maker of playful verses, turner of unending cartwheels and somersaults.

My second loyalty was also nurtured by Oz, where so many queer people, even downright misfits, are made welcome (though in limited numbers) at Ozma's palace. I think of Tik-Tok the mechanical man, or the conceited Frogman, or the irresponsible Shaggy Man, or Professor H. M. Wogglebug, T.E. The last is one of Baum's best satiric creations. Pompous as only a "thoroughly educated" professor can be, he heads a college that is almost entirely concerned with athletics; indeed he invents pills that provide instant learning of algebra, geography, elocution, and so forth, so that the students can give almost all their time and attention to sports. (Professor Wogglebug went on, significantly, to invent Square

Meal Tablets, but this time the students rebelled and threw the learned professor in the lake.) The satire is splendid. It is very American, very up-to-date. Yet Professor Wogglebug, for all his conceit, becomes one of Ozma's chief advisers. He adds, in his way, to the fun and diversity of things. With typical American humor Baum makes fun of the pretenses of intellect and formal education; but, as always in the Oz books, comedy with its human acceptance and inclusiveness proves more important than satire with its rejections. Such tolerance and enjoyment of diversity, as belonging to human nature, is deeply democratic, not just in the social but in the psychological sense; for it is our own various qualities and instincts that are drawn together, and accepted, and invited to the great banquets and feasts together with all those animals and all those queer people in the Emerald City.

My third loyalty, to *communitas*, is exemplified by what I have been saying all along. *Communitas* is created by the shared experience of a paradoxical world: the world of carnival or role reversal where things are turned upside down and nonsense and anarchy have their day. And Oz, despite its high civilization, is founded on such a reversal, by which the grown-ups withdraw and the believing child is made ruler of things. The magic of Oz is the magic of a child's imagination made effective in an otherworld. Its experience is reflected in the International Wizard of Oz Club, to which I belong: a motley collection of some two thousand Oz enthusiasts from a wide diversity of regions, professions, ages, and political and religious beliefs, who share still more basic loyalties to play, laughter, creativity, fantasy, and the unforgotten dream of that rich, beautiful, and happy place.[48]

All this is escape, from modern civilization and from America; but it is an escape from which we may move into a deeper acceptance of civilization, as suggested earlier, and also of America. When Edward Wagenknecht called Oz a "Utopia Americana," that title indicated some special qualities of the Oz books that link them with reality.[49] Wagenknecht praised Baum for having "enlarged the resources of fairyland" by drawing on new American materials instead of just relying on the traditional plots and characters of European fairy tale. The Scarecrow, the Tin Woodman, the Wizard himself, are peculiarly American types; the common sense, practicality, and cheerfulness that they share are peculiarly American virtues. Above all, as Roger Sale has shown, Dorothy herself has a remarkable and very American gift (shared by Baum himself) for taking each situation as it comes and making the most of it.[50] It is fitting that she become a princess of Oz: this otherworld is a place in which American traits are easily and fully assimilated and reach an exemplary perfection.

But there is more. The movement between Oz and America goes both ways. "All the magic isn't in fairyland," says one of Baum's characters to another; "There's lots of magic in all Nature, and you may see it as well in the United States, where you and I once lived, as you can here." The examples given are the growth of a flower and the turning of electricity into light.[51] If Baum lived today, he would surely be delighted, and surely alarmed, but probably much surprised at how many of his magical inventions (for example, Ozma's Magic Picture) have been replicated by science and engineering. He would respond with delight to the wonders of modern life; only, he might feel nostalgia (or noztalgia), as we do, not so much for the magic of Oz, as for the secure and satisfying life that the technology of magic (like the magic of technology) there supports.

I want finally to suggest that the "Ozian perspective," which I am using as a personal shorthand for the Utopian, involves a mix of skepticism and hope that helps remarkably in the ordinary business of living. An Ozian loyalist, so to speak, believes that brains are very important, but not that they are easily acquired or that they are more important than the heart. An Ozian loyalist is skeptical of all modern "wizards," such as psychiatrists and cult leaders, who promise, or are imagined to promise, what they cannot perform; yet he remembers how the Wizard of Oz, once unmasked as a humbug, later returned to Oz to learn real magic from Glinda the Good. Ought a therapist, or a teacher, to aspire to less? Again, an Ozian loyalist will be suspicious or critical of the various utopian schemes offered on today's market. This one, he will observe, requires the user to wear green spectacles. That one falls short of what is wanted—the beauty, comfort, and happiness of Oz. He will be quick to sympathize with the appeal of such things—"Ah yes, that is a little like Oz!"—but quick also to perceive what is fashionable fakery, like the so-called Greening of America.[52] In short, he will hold out for the Emerald City. Only such a complete vision, answering to the heart's desire, can give us the power to test other utopian visions and find them wanting, yet not be cut off from hope and fall into despair.

In the Greek mythic imagination, the world of utter happiness was a world that humankind had forfeited or lost. Hesiod's myth of the Four Ages, or Races, gave it lasting shape.[53] The Golden Race had led peaceful, effortless lives; they neither sowed nor plowed, but the bountiful earth gave them all good things, of its own accord; even death for them was like a gentle sleep—and they became beneficent wealth-giving spirits, *daimones ploutodotai*, beneath the earth. Unhappily, later ages became progressively estranged from the gods, from nature, and from one another. Impious, ungrateful, and fiercely competitive, they turned to war and struggled to survive, and life became more and more disorderly and brutal, reaching its nadir in the Iron Race—and (for Hesiod) in the present age. Against this background of loss, Hesiod preaches his gospel of work and justice. These bring their rewards: people and livestock flourish under just princes, and the hard-working peasant, his barns deservedly full, finds relief from toil in those times of rest and refreshment that the turning seasons regularly provide. Yet there is no suggestion that those grain-filled barns or those cups of sweet wine drunk with friends really compensate for that first remembered happiness, where nature pampered the human race in its first childhood, like an all-loving, all-nurturing mother. Nor would Hesiod's peasants have time to cultivate nostalgia. The way through their troubles is forward: to give up idle dreams; to accept reality, and to manage it as best one can.

There is a close resemblance between Hesiod's myth of the Ages and the account of the loss of Eden in *Genesis*. In both versions man was meant to be happy but through some fault in him, or in her (Pandora later, and Eve), or in the world, could not continue in that blissful state but became an exile. Presumably the tales draw on common Near Eastern sources. They also reflect, and appeal to, the universal psychological experience of growing up from early childhood, and perhaps from that pre-Oedipal state where the universe seemed to revolve around one's infantile demands. Yet the difference between Greek and Hebrew tradition is striking. A promise of restoration runs through the Biblical literature and tradition, as it does not through Greek myth and thought. The Messianic prophecies and promises tell of a New Jerusalem, a renewed and joyful city favored by the Lord, whose glory will be in her midst. For Christians later, this New Jerusalem lying ahead, as Eden lay behind, was an image of the Kingdom of Heaven to which the faithful were called. Like pilgrims on life's journey, they moved through toils and dangers toward their real home, toward that city set with precious stones that blazed forth in the light of God's all-redeeming presence. As Dante looks back from his privileged place at the old tales of the Golden Age in the "pagan scriptures," he sees that the ancient poets were singing about Eden and its loss, but singing in a way that was prophetic of its true recovery.[54] Above all others, Virgil was the poet of "desire without hope"; yet his prophecy of the return of the Golden Age, *redeunt Saturnia regna*, was true beyond his knowing. Nostalgia was a clue, return a trusted promise.

A very few notes of something like this eschatological hope can be overheard in Greek mystical writings, especially fifth-century ones tinged by Orphic influence. Empedocles depicted a unified, harmonious state of the world under the rule of love, symbolized by Queen Kypris. The world in its motions moves away from that perfect unity and joy, but then at the fated time moves back again; and the soul's return to its pristine heavenly state, by way of purifications and magical charms (*katharmoi*), after its initial fall from grace, must have borne some analogy to the larger, cosmic return to unity and perfection. The Pythagorean communities practiced similar "purifications" aiming at the soul's redemption and return to a heavenly state: the language of salvation is there, but a gnostic spirit, contemptuous of the body, separates these sectarian groups from anything like the shared joy and hope of a recovered Golden Age. An ode of Pindar is brighter and happier in its imagery of salvation. In somewhat Orphic, mystical language, it indicates rewards and punishments after death, and the recurrent cycles of the soul's existence; but certain souls,

> as many as waiting thrice on either side dare keep the soul entirely from injustice, complete the road of Zeus to Kronos' tower. There around the island of the blest winds, daughters of the ocean, breathe. Golden flowers blaze, some landward from glorious trees, and water nurtures others, with fronds of which they wreath their arms and crown their heads, in Rhadamanthus' upright sway.[55]

Hesiod had exempted a race of heroes from his downward movement, assigning them to an afterlife in the Islands of the Blest. In Pindar's fantasy (which is self-consciously poetic, yet closely aligned with the deep beliefs about gods and men depicted in the victory odes) every good soul—not just some ascetic or intellectual elite—has a chance to return to that heavenly joy, symbolized once again by gold and, beyond Zeus, by the reign of Kronos. This comes as near to *redeunt Saturnia regna* as the Greek imagination—with one exception, to be noted later—could get. But such images of salvation drift apart from the mainstream of Greek thinking and practice.

In his book *The Liberal Temper in Greek Politics* Eric Havelock contrasts the regressive myth of the Golden Age with the progressive scheme generally agreed on by thinkers like Democritus and Protagoras, according to which the human race moved gradually upward from primitive beginnings that were "nasty, brutish and short."[56] The mastery of technology by trial and error, the gradual acquisition of family and social ties, the building of communities, the creation of laws, and the enjoyment of artistic pleasures: all this was a success story, and, by virtue of man's own intelligence and effort (rather than the gods' gift), one that showed signs of continuing. Here is where utopian thinking enters in for the secular mind. If custom-and-law (*nomos*) builds on nature (*physis*)—on the common nature that we share with the beasts, and on the special human traits of mind and hand—then one might hope for continued improvement until human society and life attain their ultimate rational perfection.

Of this dream too we catch only fragments. I think of Democritus' statements on child-rearing and adoption: how the latter is a human improvement on our common animal endowment, and how the selection process might be carried further until everyone has a child "after his own heart" (the viewpoint, naturally, is the male's) and no one would be stuck any longer with a natural but unsatisfactory child.[57] We may be skeptical. Would unwanted children have been traded around like unwanted cards in the game of Hearts? Yet Democritus' confidence in human society and institutions is impressive. It typifies the optimistic spirit of the 440s and 430s at Athens, when many incentives to utopian thinking coincided. The democratic Athenian experience suggested how easily laws and customs could be improved over the course of time. Comparative ethnography stressed the universal importance of *nomos*, but also it offered a wide gallery of possible lifestyles different from one's own and sometimes temptingly better. Again, the experience of founding new colonies like Thurii gave occasion for experimenting, in theory and in fact. Could a new city be created without the known faults of the old? Hippodamus and others circulated pamphlets on town planning. Radical ideas were in the air: of the rights of women, of children, of slaves; of the brotherhood of peoples and nations across political boundaries. Would it be difficult to construct new states in which freedom, equality, justice, and happiness might flourish as never before, by virtue of the triumph of human reason and invention?[58]

It is generally believed by scholars that this utopian confidence failed for historical reasons at Athens. War, plague, and eventual defeat brought with them uprooting from the land, crowding in the city, economic scarcity, a widening gap between rich and poor, disruption of family life, internal factionalism and distrust, the breakdown of an older democratic consensus, the undermining of religious traditions and institutions—all tending toward panic and eroding built-up confidence in reason, human nature, and the democratic and political life. It seems appropriate to speak of a sense of weariness and failure, or of a "failure of nerve."[59] Although Athens made a remarkable comeback, that earlier confidence was gone forever. We might ask, however, whether it did not carry the seeds of its own intellectual destruction. If the older sophists believed in the perfectibility of human laws and institutions building on nature, their more radical successors tended rather to place *nomos* in opposition to *physis*, as mere convention versus reality, or as oppressive law versus the needs and instinctive wishes of human nature. The first antithetical stance is represented by the "enlightened" young radicals who disregarded the laws as nonbinding, or attempted freely to subvert them. Their utopian dreams, which Plato so well exposes after the fact in figures like "Callicles" or "Thrasymachus," were dreams of tyranny, of unlimited self-assertion, rather than reform—albeit "return to the ancestral constitution" was a convenient mask to wear. The second stance, not altogether different, is exemplified by Antiphon the Sophist. In his penetrating and thorough critique of human laws and institutions, such as family and the law court, Antiphon exposes these as being oppressive, troublesome, and anxiety-forming; everywhere *nomos* is opposed to the freedom, happiness, and self-fulfillment for which human nature instinctively strives and to which it is entitled. Here the utopian vision is of what we want to do but never can. "Man is born free, but everywhere he is in chains." (And so is *she*, Euripides' Medea adds.) Antiphon is said to have been a practicing psychiatrist. He seems less to have hoped for institutional reform than to have felt the sheer weight of institutions as such, as though anticipating Freud's analysis of civilization and its discontents.

"Things ought to be different." In a chapter on utopian thinking in the later fifth century, Friedrich Solmsen cites a number of variations on this theme, especially from the plays of Euripides.[60] The key word is *chrēn*: people *ought* to have two voices, one to pretend (as they generally do), the other to refute that voice by telling the truth; people *ought* to set up sperm banks so that they could buy children in temples and avoid the use of women altogether. And so forth. These contrary-to-fact wishes of course reflect the character and mood of the speakers (not unlike self-refuting voices): the consternation and anger of Hippolytus against the nurse, Phaedra, and all women; the consternation and anger of Theseus against Hippolytus. But they also reflect a feeling of frustration in the age. Something is deeply wrong in human nature, or in human institutions, or in history; what the heart of man requires can only be expressed in the language of the impossible dream. Nowhere is the poignancy of this feeling stronger than in Euripides' *Hippolytus*, of 428, which reflects the plague and war, the death of Pericles and of all the liberal, rational aspirations with him. "Would that I could become a bird," sing the chorus, "and could fly over the ocean . . . to the garden of the Hesperides." They are reacting to Phaedra's fate, to the loss of innocence in things; the ode, as it continues, also reflects Phaedra's death wish. She will find escape from life's bondage—in the hanging knot.[61] The singers (like Euripides?) will find escape only in music, in the image of that enchanted garden in the West, in Never-never-land. It is very sad, and very moving, and very much like "Somewhere Over the Rainbow" as Dorothy sings it,

> Birds fly over the rainbow;
> why then, oh why, can't I?[62]

and as Judy Garland sang it, years before she died from an overdose of sleeping pills.

In Euripides' play these lovely lyrics seem to mark the death of older utopian hopes in the fifth century. What is left behind is merely private and fanciful, the aesthetic enjoyment of an escapist, fairy-tale vision as it is embodied in music or in art, or in literature. This is, I think, one of three manifestations of the decline of utopian vision at Athens. The second is political, the reaction of certain Athenian groups against the very excesses of Athenian freedom and opportunity that they themselves had enjoyed. In bright, sophist-trained young men, especially, the wish mentioned earlier, to subvert the existing laws and become tyrants, was joined with the quite different wish to live in a simpler, more ordered, more understandable world like Sparta, where all aspects of private and public life were controlled by tradition and strict authority. The revolutionary spirit was wed to the reactionary. In psychological terms, the radical son, rebelling against the weak, liberal father, yearned for the strong, controlling, authoritarian father he never had (Maoist radicals offer a recent parallel); or, to paraphrase the old joke, "I wouldn't live in a city that would have *me!*" Critias and the Thirty Tyrants are the end product of this revolt. And so, in a different way, is Plato's *Republic*.

The third form taken by the decline of Utopia, and equally influencing Plato, was not so much antidemocratic as antipolitical. It was to seek happiness or salvation in a small, independent community, shaped perhaps on the Pythagorean or the "Socratic" model. In one form or another, the watchword of all these communities was "Live according to Nature." The fourth-century Cynics were especially inventive in trying new lifestyles, like modern groups living in experimental communes. Men and women lived on equal terms; some tried open marriage; Crates wrote poetically of the Land of Knapsack whose citizens were self-sufficient and happy. In their less dramatic ways the later schools, Stoic and Epicurean, experimented with communal living; they helped individuals to lead meaningful lives of reason and virtue in an expanding, cosmopolitan world, and they exercised a leavening influence on Greek and, later, Roman society; but their utopian visions seem shrunk and compromised by force of time, reduced to the maintenance of an adequate private world amid the confusion of things. The dream of the Golden World is replaced by the image of the Stoic sage, perfect in wisdom and self-control, or of the Epicurean friends in their undisturbed Garden. For utter joy, now read tranquility—of the happy few.

The reactionary and philosophical tendencies of "Utopia limited," which I have gone forward to sketch, meet in Plato's *Republic*. In scope, in imagination, in artistic structure, in the power of relating and harmonizing disparate aspects of individual and social experience, Plato's creation is one of the greatest products of the fifth-century Athenian culture that he sees as having failed, and on which he turns his back. It still has an enormous (and I think insidious) charm today; it still overshadows all the modern utopias that are its descendants. What is sad is the way liberal Athenian dreams are perfected, only to be harnessed to reactionary aims. Women receive equal educational and job opportunities, at last; but the family is dissolved, and sex becomes an instrument of state policy. Or again: the highest cultural and philosophical education—an extension of Plato's own?—goes into the making of a rigid ruling elite. In the end the appeal of Plato's *Republic* lies in the simplicity and order that it provides. The world is once more stable, and everyone knows his place in it. The moral and cultural simplicities mislaid in fifth-century Athens are here regained, and one of the greatest, most universal human needs— for simplicity and order—is most fully satisfied, but at an enormous cost.

Many people today would call Plato's state a *dystopia*—like Aldous Huxley's *Brave New World*, which was so intended, or B. F. Skinner's *Walden Two*—where indeed Western civilization may be headed.

I suggested earlier that Utopia should be for the future what Eden was in the past. What has happened, with Plato, to the nostalgia for the Golden Age? The answer is that it has been compromised away.[63] Plato accepts the primitive beginnings of human society much as the naturalists had imagined them, only he combines their dour life with an imagined moral simplicity and piety, an early closeness, later lost, to nature and the gods. This is the "hard Golden Age" that Varro and Virgil will place in the Roman countryside, where the hard-working farmer most closely retains the old-time virtue and the old-time happiness of the *Saturnia regna*. The idea, from Plato to Virgil, is very moving; it suggests to what degree, in the real world, Eden may be recovered. But this is not (as Virgil also shows) at all the same thing as recovering the remembered ease and comfort and joy of the lost Golden Age. The mind accepts our state of exile and makes the best of it, though the heart rebels, still wishing to fly like a bird to those fabled islands in the utter West.

If there is one place remaining where the soft Golden Age continues to be depicted as a region of the heart's desire, it is Old Comedy. I give three fragments to indicate the persistence, fun, and variety of the Schlaraffenland or Cockaigne convention in the later fifth century. In the first, taken from Telecleides' *Amphiktyones*, old Kronos himself seems to praise the blessings he provided in the good old days. He begins in conservative fashion, with commonplaces of old-time happiness out of Hesiod.

> I shall now describe the life that I provided for mortals from the very beginning. First and foremost, there was universal peace—like water over the hands; then the earth brought forth no dread, no diseases, but all one needed came forth of its own accord (*automata*);

But at line 4 the scene goes mad with magical abundance:

> All the gullies were awash with good red wine. Loaves of French and Italian bread would compete with one another: "Eat me," each one would say. "My content's most refined!" Filets of sole would march on home, broil themselves, and lay themselves out on the table. Veritable rivers of scotch broth would surge alongside the couches, carrying steak- and veal-tips high among the waves . . . and there were deep-dish apple pies flavored with cinnamon. And hot roast quails would simply fly down your throat. And there was

a mighty jostling of militant cheesecakes charging at one another around the jawbone. And children would play jacks with turkey wishbones. Oh, people were big in those days, and mighty fat. There was a fine supply of giants.[64]

How would an Athenian audience react to such a description? With sheer delight, I think, first of all; but then, with a sense of being teased, and probably with a feeling of superiority to the child (in other people? in themselves?) who would be so gullible as to be taken in by such promises. It may be, indeed, that Kronos is competing in some contest, trying to win popular favor (for some divine election? or reelection?) by making lavish campaign promises.[65] In any event the exaggeration is ridiculous. It is like watching Charlie Chaplin's daydream in *Modern Times*. Faint from hunger, he imagines that he and the girl are sharing a simple cottage in the country. Grapes and oranges hang from trees outside the window, and he picks some to eat while waiting for dinner (it will be a great roast); then a cow saunters past, stops on command, squirts milk into a pail until Charlie signs to her that there is enough, that she may now move on. (Shortly afterwards he wakes up, to the reality of a policeman moving him on.) We laugh at the child in Charlie, the child in ourselves, who wants so much—not just grapes and oranges, but magically cooperative cows—and who is taken in so easily. We know better, of course. We should not be taken in. We may enjoy the pleasure of the imagined feast, as it appeals to our unconscious wishes, and yet turn to deal (more effectively than Charlie) with everyday realities.

But is that all? Even in Chaplin's movies, the suggestion recurs that the world is really full of riches, like a great department store seen through a child's eyes; only these riches are divided unfairly, or are attainable only through luck, or else, like teasing spirits, they come and go. But in the Telecleides fragment there is something more. The torrents spilling with wine recall Dionysus' miracles. Poets and vase painters elsewhere depict the fountains of wine, or the streams of wine, milk, and honey drawn forth from the earth by the lightest touch of the god's votaries. For all the silliness and teasing, the comic poet still recognizes a rich transforming power beneath the surface of things. The Golden Age riches are remembered nostalgically, yet are not entirely lost.

It seems hopeful in a different way when, in other comic fragments, the dream of plenty is transferred from the Golden Age past to the Utopian future. A passage from Pherecrates' *Persians* looks to the time when rivers of soup with hot rolls, and so forth, will run *automatoi* through the streets, and even Zeus (becoming less puritanical?) will rain down retsina.[66] (One of my favorite "Ozzy" pictures was of a Soup Sea, with hot buttered rolls floating on the surface; another was of a country adjoining Oz where it rained lemonade and snowed popcorn. Needless to say, Baum and Thompson had not been studying fragments of Old

Comedy!) Again, the context is lost; the description may have been connected with the fabled riches of Persia—which ordinary Athenians never quite managed to enjoy. Another fragment, from Crates' *Beasts*, affords a better sense of context:

> *A* Then nobody will own a servant, male or female? Will an old man have to serve himself?
> *B* Not at all. I'll make everything self-mobile.
> *A* So? What will they gain from that?
> *B* Things will come forward right away, whenever anyone calls for them: "Table, lay yourself." "Platter, arrange yourself." "Bread-basket, knead your dough." "Ladle, draw out." "Where's the cup? You, go wash yourself." "Saucepan, put on some beet dressing." "Come on, fish—" *"But I'm not done on one side!"* "Then sprinkle some oil on yourself and some salt, and turn yourself over."
> *A* Well, see if you can match this. I'll bring hot water (like a public aqueduct) running into everyone's own private bathtub. A man will only have to say, "Turn on the water!" And the soapdish will come running up of its own accord, and so will the washcloth and the slippers.[67]

The agonal form suggests competitive promises, as given by politicians. One promises a chicken in every pot (cooking itself, of course); another promises abundant hot water in every private bathroom. Here again, the pictures of magical ease are delightful. (We somewhat lose the fun because we *have* automatic ovens and hot showers, just as we have Baum's Magic Picture right out of Ozma's palace.) Crates' description includes typical fairy-tale motifs, rendered with a homely touch and vivid humor. Again, we may enjoy a sense of superiority to the child in us who is being teased; but there is more. The wonders of "automation" go back to Hephaestus, a close friend of Dionysus'; in *Iliad* 18 Homer describes how the god made magic tripods to help him in the forge, and magic robot-maidens to support him. But technology, of which Hephaestus is the patron together with Athena, is also the result of human effort and experiment in the scientific, non-Hesiodic scheme of things. The two strains meet, as they do in twentieth-century science fiction, where the mechanical figures of *Star Wars*, R2D2 and C3PO, reassure us that the Scarecrow and the Tin Woodman of Oz have not altogether disappeared but are present beneath a new and partly transparent technological guise. The moments when fairy tale and science kiss are few, but they count for much in our troubled age.

Crates' fragment suggests something more: the power of utopian thinking to explore possibilities of social change that ordinarily seem unthinkable. Athenians depended on slavery for what comfort and ease they had, and they accepted slavery without much critical reflection, as a provision of nature. A few liberals may have pleaded for more humane treatment of slaves, and a very few, for regarding them as natural equals; but only the comic poet speaks out for doing away with slavery altogether. The solution, to be sure, lies in the realm of magic—or of future technology. With full automation the services of slaves will no longer be required. This may sound like an *adynaton*, "when the moon turns blue"; still it shows how, if the Golden Age nostalgia is conservative, the utopian fantasy implies possibilities of political and social revolution. It becomes a way of thinking clearly and creatively about the future, where (as in the fairy tales of the dangerous Three Wishes) the thing we deeply want, and ask for, may be the thing we get.

Fragments from the *Ploutoi* of Cratinus suggest how the utopian revolution may have been carried further, on an Athenian and cosmic scale, and how the way forward to Utopia may also be the way backward, to the lost Golden Age.[68] The chorus, entering, explain that they are Ploutoi (spirits of wealth, reminiscent of Hesiod's wealth-giving spirits, *daimones ploutodotai*). They are Titans by birth, like old Kronos, who was dethroned by Zeus; now it appears that Zeus has been dethroned in turn, "and Demos rules." They may be looking for Kronos; they may have come to Athens to bring riches, especially for the good and just. We cannot know. It may be that Cratinus is burlesquing tragedy, and especially Aeschylus' *Prometheus Bound*, where Prometheus holds the secret of Zeus' fate—to be overthrown by a son stronger than himself, if he marries Thetis—and where the chorus of Oceanids, daughters of Prometheus' Titan cousin, come to console him; it may be, too, that Cratinus is satirizing modern democratic politics at Athens. More important, for our purposes, is the comic myth of release and revolution. Zeus, who overcame and "bound" his father Kronos and the Titans, is overcome in turn: here, it would seem, by the Sovereign People of Athens as a new, cosmic superpower; and in Aristophanes' surviving plays, by Dinos (Whirl, or Vortex, or Cosmic Revolution) in the *Clouds*, and by Peisetairus in the *Birds*, and by Ploutos in that play—embodying the power of riches to control and transform the world. New and questionable powers triumph over the older Olympian order; what matters in comedy is that they are in alliance with the still older Kronos and the Titans, who stand for powers of nature but also for the impulses of the uncivilized heart. To "unbind" these daemonic figures is to liberate psychic energies, to reconcile us with ourselves, to make us "rich" and happy. It is a mythic counterpart of the experience of Dionysian release, and a comic analogue of the prophecy *redeunt Saturnia regna*.

Naturally we must use these and other fragments of lost comedies with caution. We almost never know their immediate context, or the plot from which they are taken; so they cannot serve as foils to Aristophanes or as evidence for some imagined essence of Old Comic structure and meaning. We especially miss the ways in which they may have served satiric purposes, as an ironic commentary on contemporary political aims and methods. All the same, I believe that these images of fantastic happiness were at the very heart of Old Comedy, and that (as their persistence confirms) they appealed enormously to the Athenian audience. I have tried to explain this appeal by suggesting that they perform several vital functions, at once psychological and social. First, they look backwards. Through their accumulation of ridiculous, childish, even outrageous pictures of sensual bliss, they evoke our ancient wish for total happiness, a deep nostalgia by which all human beings are united. (Man is an animal that remembers that it once lived in Eden.) In tragedy, as in Euripides' lyrics about birds flying west, or ships sailing over the sea with sails spread wide, this nostalgia forms a painful contrast to the complexities of real life—though the pain is relieved, in "cathartic" fashion, by its expression in beautiful poetry. In comedy, I have been arguing, the nostalgic images of escape are also forward-looking, and they even point to a transformation both of our inner selves and of the outer world:

1. As we take refuge in images of wish fulfillment and regression to the world of our childhood, we find healing from the wounds of growing up, recovery from the stresses and anxieties of life that have dimmed our vision, and increased energy and courage to go on.

2. And as we enjoy a sense of superiority to the child in us or in others who believes literally in those rivers flowing with wine or hot barley soup, and so forth, we are teased into a realization that the Utopia we most deeply want, beneath all surface desires, is that fairy-tale world where our wishes are completely and magically granted, and that this world is Never-never-land (or Oz).

3. And yet the best presentations of this fairy-tale, "nowhere" world retain a curious power to reconcile us with ourselves and with reality, to help us build bridges between the world we want to inhabit and the world we must: between nature and law, freedom and order, wish and will, pleasure and duty, play and work; and they send us back into the real world with fuller zest and greater effectiveness, precisely because we feel not entirely bound to its laws, nor entirely imprisoned by the dilemmas that it poses.

4. Finally, the "real" world must appear, in the end, not simply as something to be adjusted to or compromised with (as we are teased or forced into doing, as we stop being childish), but as something to be transformed, through deep-set magic, into a newer and greener and brighter world more in keeping with those old childlike wishes of ours and of the whole human race. Lesser utopias may rise and fall, and we may smile, or laugh, at their inadequacy. The greater Utopia is still that magical no-place toward which we should be heading. It is the Golden Age restored, the age of Kronos calling out to us, not only from the remembered and longed-for past, but also from the intuited and longed-for future.

All this is a roundabout way of describing what I mean by the paradoxical phrase "loyalty to Utopia." For Aristophanes and for Old Comedy, I have suggested, it was undergirded by the religious experience of Dionysian ritual and celebration. But do Aristophanes' plays, as we read them today, bear these meanings out? Or does the satirical, realistic element in them overcome, in the end, the golden fantasy and dream?

In his important book *Le carnaval et la politique* Jean Claude Carrière argues that it does. He speaks of the failure of Utopia in Aristophanes' time. It loses what he calls its function of mediating effectively between the real city and the idea of an instinctive and immediate happiness. And, as Old Comedy nears its end,

> either Utopia distances itself from the real, or else it is rejoined and destroyed from the inside by reality. From now on, Utopia is incapable of playing a role of reference toward the present or of "moving" it. This failure of Utopia is revealed by a double process: the progressive disconnection of Utopia in relation to reality, and the ironic treatment of Utopia insofar as it remains in relation with reality.[69]

Aristophanes' *Birds*, and his *Ecclesiazusae* and *Plutus*, may serve as test cases. In the former, Carrière argues, Utopia is undercut by a "second-level" satire, as the new, "natural" regime comes to reflect unpleasant realities. In the last plays, Utopia is depicted realistically, and as being unrealizable. I think that many, perhaps most, twentieth-century readers of Aristophanes would agree with Carrière, though they might put the case differently. But I want, in the rest of this chapter, to offer a strong dissent. I do so as an Ozian loyalist, but also as a reader concerned, not with what Aristophanes should realistically and reasonably have said, but with what, unrealistically and unreasonably, he does in fact say.

I argue in section 29 that Aristophanes' *Birds* begins with simple "escapism" of a Euripidean, or conservative, or philosophical kind, and turns it around altogether, to create a Utopia Atheniensis with a great power to reconcile opposites and to look hopefully toward the future—in short, to perform the offices of mediation that Carrière says are no longer possible. The *Birds*' Cloudcuckooland was, and is (not least by general acclamation), one of the most successful of comic utopias; it has the fullness of power of the Old Comedy; it is only matched in richness and depth of comic vision by Rabelais' Abbaye de Thélème and by Prospero's isle in *The Tempest*. That the *Birds*' final reading must be satirical, critical, and realistic, I utterly deny.

Aristophanes' later plays pose different problems, since they somewhat depart from the form and spirit of Old Comedy, in the direction of Middle Comedy, or New. I examine these departures more closely in my final chapter. Tentatively, however, I wish first to reaffirm the predominance of comedy over satire, even in these late plays. I argue, in section

30, that in the *Ecclesiazusae* Aristophanes satirizes a "Utopia limited" of the radical Right and the political philosophers and explodes it into comedy, in ways that recall his older and still enduring utopian loyalties; and, in section 31, that in the *Plutus* he introduces the old Dionysian fantasy, the Golden Age restored, into what is becoming the bourgeois world of later comedy. It is almost as though Old Comedy had outlived itself in order to point the way to its later revival, its reincarnations in Plautus (I think), in Rabelais, and in Shakespeare.

29   *Utopia Unlimited:* Birds

THE plot of the *Birds* carries a more striking reversal than any other Aristophanic comedy.[70] Two refugees from Athens seek the birds' help in locating a quiet town to live in; they end up fortifying a great bird-metropolis, blockading the gods, and winning control of the universe. Initially, the two Athenians seek a *topon apragmona*, a place without busyness and troubles, where they can settle down and lead a quiet, untroubled, comfortable life, as if wrapping themselves in a soft woolly blanket.[71] It's not, says Euelpides (the "Man of Good Hope"), that they hate Athens; not that Athens is not great and rich: only that the legal hassles and financial worries are too much for them. Hence they have decided to consult the birds, via the hoopoe Tereus who is, in myth, an Athenian in-law, a Thracian king transformed into a bird. As the idea begins to work, it escalates. Suggested towns seems unsuitable, for it is hard to escape from Athenian warships and spheres of influence; Euelpides asks about the birds' own life, which sounds idyllic, flitting from seed to seed in the flower gardens; but then, Peisetairus ("Comrade-Persuader") takes over.[72] He perceives a great plan, of "power to the birds." After a farcical agon, Peisetairus persuades the assembled birds, as rightful world rulers, to build and fortify a great bird city between gods and men. It is soon built; it is named Cloudcuckooland, and dedicated with appropriate rituals (and driving-out of intruders); tremendous walls are constructed in midair by technician and worker birds; the Olympians are effectively cut off, by blockade, from their enjoyment of men's sacrifices, as well as from other conveniences; so that in the end, they accede to Peisetairus' full demands that sovereignty be restored to the birds and a heavenly princess be given to Peisetairus, with Zeus' thunderbolt as her dowry.[73] The play closes in celebration as the new king of the universe prepares for his wedding.

The contradictions are striking, and I shall return to them; but we should not lose sight of the recovery gained in this play. We are drawn imaginatively, with the two Athenian escapists, into a lovely, recreative green world; the sights and sounds of nature are played out in poetry and dramatic movement. We hear the *itō, itō* of the birds, the tweeting that (as Cedric Whitman points out) actually means "Come hither" to a Greek ear;[74] the colorful bird costumes, the music and song and dance, revive our spirits, and we are drawn to see the world as the birds do, as an enormous and plentiful garden full of wonderful sights and sounds and colors and smells and tastes. It is a pastoral world, of natural simplicity endowed with the poetic self-consciousness of high art. The initial escape movement recalls the Euripidean nostalgia for a simpler, happier world where innocence and beauty are not destroyed. "Would that I were a bird," sing the chorus of women in *Hippolytus*: "Would that I had wings and could fly . . . over the streams of Ocean . . . into the farthest West, to the Garden of the Hesperides."[75] It is very poignant, like "Somewhere Over the Rainbow":

> birds fly over the rainbow;
> why then, oh why can't I?[76]

The wish to escape from trouble and pain into a happier world is universal. In Euripides' tragedy, and not only in *Hippolytus*, it reflects a feeling of hopelessness about the immediate situation and the general human condition. The best we can do, it tells us, is to fly from pain and sorrow into some never-never-land of art, fantasy, and the heart's desire. Its passion to escape is the measure of actual helplessness and despair. But in comedy, as I argued earlier, despair never wins out, and nostalgia can be transformed to good hope. Even when we first see them, the Athenian escapists are on the move, toward their salvation. It is like the movement in the *Knights* from despair (drinking bull's blood), via refreshment (drinking), to new energy and new action (stealing oracles, welcoming the sausage-seller to combat the Paphlagonian). So too in this play: escape brings recovery, nostalgia is converted into hope. Indeed the significant name "Euelpides" comes very close to "Euripides" but comes to mean "optimist," "man of good hope." It can also, to be sure, suggest gullibility, as Euelpides is drawn into Peisetairus', his "companion-persuader's," great, wild, and mighty schemes; hope may take on aspects of madness, yet the movement of hope is fundamentally right. To envy the birds is a waste of time. The thing to do is to get wings, to build Cloudcuckooland.

As always, the sense of recovery is accompanied, but not negated, by skeptical awareness. "You can get wings," says the play: and sure enough, Peisetairus eats a little magic root and sprouts two wings (one thinks of the peers turned fairies at the end of *Iolanthe*); and his attendants bring out great baskets of wings to supply their ornithomanic Greek visitors. Persuasion and deception play their part in the "winging"; as always in Aristophanes, being taken, or lifted, up into the air is suggestive of gullibility; just so, in the *Knights*, Demos always loved the oracle's dream-promise that he would become "an eagle among the clouds." The clouds, indeed, are symbols of illusion; the cloud city is where idle dreamers build their cloud castles; and as we know, idle philosophers and poets prosper from their exploitation of the midair realm, *ta meteōra*. But our tendency to be deluded through persuasion does not negate our imaginative power, which the *Birds* celebrates, to realize wishes, turn words into acts, and create something out of nothing. Of course, Cloudcuckooland is "constructed" on the comic stage, and largely from the spectators' imaginations. Actors imitate birds who imitate people. Yet their play world has power to convince our imaginations that, beyond delusion, wonderful things can happen; and it reflects the playwright's wonder at how, in the "real" world too, the imagination creates its own reality. He did not need to wait for the airplane to be invented, to prove his point—or for the Eastern Airlines exhibit "Wings of Man" at Disney World, where as the viewers are taken on an imaginary world-flight, great soaring seagulls around them change into sleek jetliners as a great chorus of singers proclaims, "You can have wings!" For the Greeks, it was boats that had "wings" to spread and fly. What mattered was feeling: and every exaltation, every erection of spirit (the sexual image is much to the point, in this play)[77] could be said, in some mysterious and real way, to give people wings—even while wingedness continues to symbolize a longed-for escape from human limitations and failures.

The problem of the *Birds*, then, is not that our imagination is prey to deception and delusion, or that flying is so different from our "real life" experience. That could be said about any play. The problem is rather one of contradiction within the fantasy. For the pastoral world to which the Athenians wish to escape, and which they discover in nature among the birds, offers peace and quiet and refreshment because it is a green, untroubled world; yet almost in the moment that they find it, the strangers disturb and transform it through their unbridled energy and inventiveness. That is, they end up by re-creating just that superbusyness or *polypragmosynē* that they had wished to escape from.[78] So quickly does the tranquil garden become capital of a new world empire.

The contradiction is rooted in human experience, for people often rebound from quiet and rest into great new projects. But it is more particularly rooted in Athenian nature. It depicts that same restlessness of the *daimonion ptoliethron*, the "god-driven city," that had seemed to Pindar, even as he wondered at its resistless energy some thirty years earlier, to be disrupting and perhaps destroying forever the peace and quiet (*hēsychia*) of well-ordered Greek states like Aegina and his own Thebes; and of which the Corinthian spokesman in Thucydides' history says, after describing the resilience, confidence, optimism (*euelpides!*), and revolutionary spirit of the Athenians, that they "neither take any rest themselves nor allow anyone else to rest."[79] You can take Peisetairus and Euelpides out of Athens, but you cannot take Athens out of them. They carry it with them, not unlike the dangerous Alcibiades; and they impose it, rebuild it wherever they go. The reversal is humorous, like one of those fables again, which Aristophanes liked, in which some creature reverts abruptly to its former nature. It is like a true story I heard, of an American businessman who retired to Ceylon to enjoy a simpler life, free of business worries and complications. In the pleasant but hot climate he missed his refrigerator, so he had one sent from America. Some friends admired it, so he sent for three or four more. Before long he had set up a thriving new business, importing and selling refrigerators to the Ceylonese. "Sell on, o ship of state!"

The joke is, that you can't change American, or Athenian, or human nature. The problem is that which pastoral poets, and especially Virgil, were to confront: the disruption of the Garden by the Machine: by history, by energy and power and noise.[80] Beneath the new foundations of the bird city Cloudcuckooland we hear the roar of the machinery of the Athenian empire. The key word for all this is *dynamis*, "power": not static power, but self-increasing, self-endangering power. Thucydides analyzes the nature of power in his *History*. It requires a certain quiet in the beginning, to build up surplus wealth to provide for walls, a secure base for operations, and to invest in ships, the modern armament, bringing in more wealth that can be invested further, but must also be secured further . . . and so forth. The process is dynamic; and to the historian, it is finally destructive. It was the huge growth of Athenian power that, he thought, really brought on the Peloponnesian War, not the specific accidents that merely set the spark to it. But that same Athenian *dynamis* is reflected in Peisetairus' bird empire. Like imperial Athens, he turns allies into subjects, builds walls, enforces tribute, blockades enemies, carries out all the operations of a great war. There are specific references to Athenian warships that go everywhere, to the recent wiping out of Melos; above all, though it is unmentioned, the audience would think of the Sicilian expedition presently going on, which was virtually a bid for world empire. Peisetairus may suggest Alcibiades, who largely rekindled the war—and was now in exile. More obviously his name is a play on Peisistratus, the sixth-century Athenian tyrant. Historically the paradox was that freedom reversed itself into tyranny, that Athens, the citadel of freedom, became a "tyrant city" that enslaved much of Greece. But the "persuasion" in his name is essential too, for in Aristophanes' time, persuasion was the essence of power. It was persuasion that built walls, that sent out ships. Persuasion could confer "tyrannical" power on those who mastered its techniques. The hero of the *Birds* becomes what his name implies, a tyrant of persuasion. His power, like that of comedy itself, springs from recovery and renewal, from the green world of nature and the birds. Is the point of the play that the energies born of recovery destroy their own nurturing environment—that the lovely green world is rediscovered only to be lost again, and perhaps forever?

    As I write, I am looking at a poster called "Building a Rainbow."[81] It is absurd, Aristophanic, reminiscent of the *Birds*. In it hundreds of little people are constructing a great, colorful, overarching rainbow. Evidently their jobs have been organized, divided, and coordinated on sound principles: some mix great pots of reds or greens or purples; others run on catwalks, or climb, or fall off, or ride great hoists and cranes as a massive segment of rainbow is hoisted into place like the crowning block of the St. Louis arch. The poster includes many small-scale satirical vignettes, affording comic recognition of the familiar amid the fantastic. There is, for example, a VIP lounge for company executives. In another place, workers are on strike for better conditions; some carry picket signs. The sense of massive turmoil is Aristophanic. What is odd is that the conflation of ordinary construction procedures with high fantasy on the one hand and common human foibles on the other brings with it such a sense of comfort and reconciliation. The technology and skills on which we pride ourselves (as in the St. Louis arch, or the moon shots), but which, with reason, we also fear, are harmonized with the dream of beauty and redemption symbolized by the rainbow. If the song "Somewhere Over the Rainbow" expresses universal nostalgia, this poster "Building a Rainbow" tells us, in its comic fashion, that scientific and technical skills can still be wedded to human needs and the heart's desire. It helps us transcend the old antithesis of the Garden versus the Machine.

    We might wonder, then, whether the building of the great walls of Cloudcuckooland in midair was not a sign of hope and reconciliation as well as contradiction. Historically, wall-building is central to the dialectic of *dynamis*, of self-expanding power. Walls provide, first of all, security for expansion and war: the rebuilding of the walls of Athens after the Persian Wars (by a trick) marked the renewal of Athenian ambitions in Greece; the building of the Long Walls to the Piraeus gave Athens the security and strength, almost the invulnerability of a great sea power. As it turned out, the amazingly rapid construction of offensive and defensive walls and counterwalls marked decisive turning points in the war in Sicily and hence in the Peloponnesian War (which was to end tragically with the pulling down of Athens' walls to the sound of flutes). Wall-building suggests at once the technological skill of Athens and the realities of power politics in the Greek world. But all this skill is harnessed by Peisetairus to the erection of a super–cloud-castle. It is as though a great steel plant were converted to the manufacture of daydreams, or as though General Foods turned its mighty resources to mass production of pie in the sky. The conversion of energy is accomplished mainly through supporting puns: thus we might say that "ten thousand *cranes* did the lifting" and that "the major dome-effect was planned by *Wren.*" Through wordplay everything is proved, everything falls into place. It may be madness. It may reflect the actual madness of Athenian dreams of world power underlying the Sicilian expedition. It is all tied in with delusion and deception, which are inherent for Aristophanes in the world of clouds and middle-air. But it is a heartening, comforting, even reconciling sort of madness, for all that.

Another, more extensive reconciliation in the *Birds* is between law and nature. It lies in the creation of what I shall call the greenlaw world.[82] Initially the two Athenians are escaping from a world of too much law— of constant, troublesome, expensive litigation—into an easier world, perhaps into a life more in accordance with nature, like the life of the birds. The protest against Athenian litigiousness might sound conservative, since the unpolitical rich seem most to have suffered from it; but the enterprise equally suggests the more modern wish to throw off the shackles of law and custom (*nomos*) and enjoy the freedom of "nature" (*physis*), which our customs and laws and institutions and all the machinery of civilized life so much restrict.[83] Beneath the wish for peace and quiet, then—for a politically more "quiet" constitution—lies that other, potentially unquiet and revolutionary wish to satisfy more fully the instinctive needs and wishes of our human nature. Certainly the heroes escape, and we with them, into a world where these wishes may be recognized and expressed, "clarified through release." We move away from ordinary social and legal constraints into what appears to be a world of utmost natural freedom.[84] But from this a new, enlarged sense of *nomos* emerges. Again, reconciliation comes largely through wordplay and word-exploration, for the Greek word *nomos* means both "custom-and-law" and "strain" or "tune," and, by a shift of accent, "place of pasture." Thus, early in the play, the hoopoe appeals to his mate (*synnome*) to "loose the strains of sacred hymns" (209–10). The first words, *lyson de nomous*, suggest revolutionary activity: "break down the laws" or, better (this is more Dionysian), "dissolve the bonds of law." But the completed movement turns this dissolution into expressive music and song, to be taken up by the very gods on Olympus. The conflation of ideas indicates a movement, very basic to this play, through the release of imaginative freedom to a renewal of the sense of law in a harmonizing greenlaw world of nature, the garden, and the songs and flight of birds.

Since the harmony thus achieved is a comic harmony, it most emphatically must include our lower, nonrespectable wishes along with our higher flights of imaginative aspiration and artistic creation. The heroes seek a place where, so to speak, only wedding invitations will come in the mail ("If you don't come now, I won't call for you when . . . I'm in trouble!"), and where a charming boy's father will scold you ("What? You saw my son after his exercises, and you didn't run up and kiss him . . . and play with his balls?"). In a world where wishes become wings, if not horses, low wishes are played out alongside high ones, the sublime juxtaposed with the ridiculous, as in the alternation of soaring odes and teasing epirrhemes in the main parabasis. Having established, in a great Bird Theogony, their ancientry and power as gods (see below), the birds sum up in the *pnigos*: they won't run away and hide themselves in the clouds like Zeus, but as *present divinities*, will confer

> upon you and your children
> and children's children
> health and wealth
>   and happiness,
> riches and peace,
> youth and laughter,
>   feasting, song and dance,
> and the milk of birds,[85]

to the point, they conclude, of surfeit and exhaustion (729–36). An alternation follows of high song and teasing epirrheme:

Ode A Invocation of the "woodland Muse"; holy *nomoi* of song rise from the birds' throats for the gods and for poets' sweet inspiration.

Epirrheme A Come hither, where all things deemed ugly-and-shameful by law and custom (*nomos*) are fine and beautiful instead, like striking your father in fighting-cock fashion, or becoming a citizen by fowl play.

Ode B The mighty song of the swans. All nature trembles before it; wonder seizes the gods; Graces and Muses cry out a song of joy.

Epirrheme B There's nothing like a pair of wings. Why be bored watching tragedy when you could fly home for lunch and fly back to the theater in time for the comedy? Why not fly off and relieve yourself at need (don't shit in your pants)—or fly off, enjoy a quick fuck, and get back before the lady's husband suspects anything? What a (s)winging life!

The birds are teasing us, of course; it will turn out later that the father-beater has no place in this bird community. Nature's laws are more complex than at first appears. But there is a wonderful release in this expression of low and childish wishes. It is like Mozart's inclusion of the sensual Papageno alongside the prince in *The Magic Flute*, as though salvation would be incomplete and unsatisfying if it didn't include our lower selves, and especially our wish for sexual freedom, instinctive satisfaction. The odes and epirrhemes set each other off, by strongest contrast: spirit and flesh, art and passion, gods and ordinary people, high-rising immortal hymns and low, teasing invitations to immorality. Sublime and ridiculous are strikingly juxtaposed. But somehow (and this happens often in Aristophanes), the hymns are more sublime and beautiful, not less, alongside the low joking; and together (as in Mozart) the two encompass the full range of human wishing in a larger, reconciling set of *nomoi* dissolved and "released." We are welcomed, teasingly, into the greenlaw world.

The new laws are not defined, but they are played out in a series of traditional farcical scenes in which intruders are expelled from Peisetairus' sacrifice and feast for the founding of Cloudcuckooland. The first group of imposters consists mainly of bureaucrats and lawyers who would reintroduce the very complications of life from which the heroes were trying to escape. These include a long-winded, officious priest, with all his religious forms and formulas; a poet for all celebratory occasions (who, though a greedy and importunate beggar, is treated nicely because, after all, he is a distant cousin of the playwright); a fraudulent oracle-monger; a geometrician and town planner, who wants everything laid out in regular, scientific fashion; a public inspector; and a decree-seller, who is largely concerned with standardization of weights and measures. All these people must be kicked out because they complicate life (to their own profit), because they are parasites on civilization (like bugs on plants), and most of all, perhaps, because they want to define and confine human freedom to their own constricting measures and rules. Their expulsion therefore confirms the freedom, the naturalness of the new greenlaw world.

On the other hand the order and harmony of that world, indeed its *nomos* quality, is borne out by the redirection and expulsion of three other characters who come to Cloudcuckooland in search of wings and of the freedom (proclaimed earlier by the teasing chorus) to do whatever they want. The first is, precisely, the son who wants to strike his father.[86] His mistake is, not to want freedom, but to want to select one of nature's laws and reject another: for animal behavior is as varied and complex as it is natural; and if fighting cocks strike their fathers, yet the storks support theirs in their old age. Hence Peisetairus redirects the youth's energies into military service on the frontier. Then Cinesias, an airy-fairy poet, enters to exploit Cloudcuckooland for dithyrambic material; he is ridiculed, but again (being a relative?) is spun off harmlessly like a whirling top. The third intruder, a sycophant and outright villain (though a comic one in his shamelessness: "I won't betray my father's trade!") is turned into a *whipping* top and spun off more painfully. Apparently, Cloudcuckooland has no fixed procedures for law and order. Each case is dealt with, fairly and arbitrarily, as it appears.

Here, though, the paradox of play and power reasserts itself. For though Peisetairus' decisions seem fair and right, embodying a comic justice and establishing a middle landscape between too much law and too little, they are nonetheless the arbitrary decisions of a supremely powerful and irresponsible autocrat. In this they resemble the judgments of Azdak, the revolutionary judge in Brecht's *Caucasian Chalk Circle*. The greenlaw judgments are dealt out by a *tyrannos* who has placed himself above all laws. Indeed Peisetairus' progress marks the extreme freedom of wish fulfillment, for it embodies our fullest and final human wish, which is for nothing less than everything. It is like the fairy tale of the fisherman and his wife. Granted wishes by a magic fish, the fisherman asks for everything his wife demands, and gets it: from cottage to castle, from her being king to emperor to pope; only, when she wants to take God's place in ordering the movements of sun and moon, she and he are sent back to where they started—living in the pot. The fairy tale recognizes the unlimited nature of childish wishing but teaches the necessity of limit. Not so the *Birds*: Peisetairus gets what he wants, which is (in the end) to rule the universe in Zeus' place. So the lovely redefinition of *nomos*, the discovery of the greenlaw world, which somewhat anticipates the rediscovery in the fourth century B.C. of the idea of natural law, is made effective within the context of autocracy and world empire, which contradicts every sense of *nomos*. Here is where the *Birds* parts company with, say, such comedies as *As You Like It* or (if I may call it a comedy) *The Tempest*, plays that better fit Northrop Frye's formula for comedy in his "myth of spring": a movement from the gray world, of harsh or unnatural laws, into the green world, and back again, where law and society are renewed.[87]

We seem to have moved again from reconciliation to contradiction. Freedom turns into power; power maintains and establishes freedom. Is this an ironic comment on human aspirations toward natural law and freedom? Or is it a satire on Athenian freedom and law, that delicate Periclean balance whose other side was the uncontrollable dynamism of power, the ever-expanding empire? Or is there, on the other side of this opposition between peace and power, freedom and rule, a further reconciliation? I think that there is, and that it takes the form of erotic play. Let us return to the Theogony of the Birds.

This theogony lies at the play's core. Earlier Peisetairus had "explained" to the impressionable birds about the anciency and grandeur of their lineage, their power, and the great empire that they once held, and now should win back—all this buttressed by comic "proofs" based on wordplay, proverb, and quaint custom. Now, as if by a contagion of persuasiveness, the birds themselves trace their lineage and powers in a proud argument. They address themselves, as from an infinitely superior height and perspective, to "feeble mortals, like the generation of leaves, weak in action, figments of earth, weak shadowy tribes, wingless, creatures of a day, long-suffering mortals, of the substance of dreams. . . ." To these poor, weak creatures, the ageless and immortal birds will unfold, as no low sophist can, the mysteries of the universe, the one true cosmogony. Which indeed follows:

> First of all there was Chaos and Night, black Erebus and dank Tartarus. Earth, air, heaven did not exist. But in the beginning of time, in the endless bosom of Erebus black-winged Night gave birth to a wind-egg: from which, as the seasons passed, there was hatched Eros, bringer of desire, his back gleaming with golden wings; he moved like a whirlwind. And he—after he joined at night with winged Chaos down in vast Tartarus—produced our race as his chicks and brought it forth (then for the first time) to the light. But the race of immortal gods did not exist until Eros joined all things together, and from their various minglings heaven came forth, and ocean, and the imperishable race of all the blessed gods. So, in this way, we are far the eldest of all the blessed ones. (693– 703)

An account ensues, with more "proofs," of the abiding connection of the birds with love (don't lovers give ducky presents?), and of their prophetic skill, their power to confer blessings on humankind.

The Bird Theogony evidently parodies the style, and some of the content, of a mystical Orphic theogony with the great god Phanes perhaps springing, all-golden, from a Mystic Egg; with elements, too, of more scientific cosmogonies such as the pre-Socratics offered and perhaps some of the sophists, including Prodicus.[88] The parody is wild and funny and nonsensical, not least with golden-winged Eros being hatched from a great wind-egg[89] (a self-contradiction at the heart of things, yet no less incredible than the usual scientific explanations about the mixing and separating out of the four elements—or about antimatter and black holes); it is in keeping with the atmosphere of deception and delusion; but its special tendency is comic, Saturnalian. Frequently, in Old Comedy, Zeus is dethroned by some revolution, his power effectively transferred to Titans, or Plutuses, or Whirl (Dinos, in the *Clouds*). Since in the traditional Greek theogony according to Hesiod, Zeus and his Olympian world order were in fact latecomers who dethroned Kronos and defeated the Titans by force (as Kronos had earlier defeated and overthrown *his* father), a further revolution on Olympus was not only natural, but almost expected in the order of things. It is not as though

Zeus were the original, all-powerful creator; rather, the heavenly evolution of order from Chaos and Old Night, and the replacing of wild nature spirits like Whirlwind and Typhoon by the Olympians and the Olympian-begotten deities of grace and harmony and order, occurred in time and perhaps mirrored the human experience of evolving law, order, justice, and good government. Since Zeus stood for order in the family, the city, and the cosmos—an order that he symbolically maintained with his punishing thunderbolts—any revolution against Zeus could portend dizzying anarchy, a wild and dangerous cosmic freedom in which Titanic forces were once more released. There was always the danger of returning to Chaos and Old Night. In comedy, however, such revolutions are delightful. Since Zeus is the strict father who controls our behavior and denies our instinctual wishes, his overthrow portends a return to the Golden Age of Kronos, when pleasure ruled and utter happiness was the lot of men. That is the lost paradise for which we long. And what the birds promise is that by their true divinity they will make the earth once more into that blessed Garden where men can dwell happy and content. The only high god over them will be Eros, whose emissaries they are.

Of course this Saturnalian "revolution," being a customary part of comedy, would be received by its audience with a delighted sense of make-believe. How wonderful to participate, by festive license, in that temporary freedom from moral constraint and psychological inhibition! Comedy does return us briefly to the Golden Age of Kronos—though it insists paradoxically on continuing to hymn Apollo and the Muses and their Olympian order in lovely, reverent lyrics like those shortly to be sung by the same chorus of birds. (Zeus and Apollo were hymned by the hoopoe earlier; now birdsong rises for Pan and the Mountain Mother— woodland divinities, to be sure—and the song of swans for Apollo, the Graces, and the Muses.) Less positively, the Bird Theogony is marked not only as playful, but as linked with deception and delusion, by its midair atmosphere (more fully described in the *Clouds* earlier) in which fraud and confusion flourish, and especially by the connotations of *Chaos*, which is (1) the "yawning gap" of nothingness out of which things emerge and (2) closely related in Aristophanes' plays to the helpless "gaping" of people who are deluded by those smarter than themselves, or by their own foolish wishes. We are reminded, then, not only of the creative power of fantasy and rhetoric as these play upon people's minds and convert ideas into actions, but also of the delusory nature of this world picture too, of all theogonies and cosmogonies perhaps, and certainly of all artistic creations. Illusion teaches us the illusoriness of things. Or to put it differently: the highest existential philosophy is strictly for the birds.

At the same time, much of the Bird Theogony rings true to Greek belief and Greek experience. The portrait of man as feeble, evanescent, dreamlike, has many parallels in epic, tragedy, and lyric poetry—not least in Pindar's. *Erōs*, the passion of love, was a powerful god in the popular imagination, in art, and in cult. Too, the jokes in this play about the inattentiveness of the Olympian gods to human needs, the feeble excuses they make, and the questionable nature of their powers to foster agriculture and to inspire true prophecy, all ring of a popular skepticism, exacerbated by the pressure and confusion of war and given intellectual respectability by the teaching of the sophists. Was the dethronement of Zeus, the shift of power in the universe to the birds, only a playful fancy, a traditional Saturnalian pattern of transient revelry, a delightful piece of deception and playful illusion? Or (and the thought produces a dizzying sensation, in this play as in the *Clouds*, where Dinos takes the kingship)—was the revolution somehow for real?

What seems to be real is that mysterious, ongoing creative process by which our world was born from chaos, and by which we ourselves, whether we are statesmen or poets or confidence men, or some mixture of the three, continue to create actions out of words, campaigns out of daydreams, and kingdoms out of our imagination, much as rabbits emerge from a magician's hat by a stroke of the wand: only the magician is just pretending, whereas we seem somehow to perform the wonders and magic tricks of continuing creation. Perhaps every other freedom, including Athens' power of empire-building, springs from that first human freedom of self-definition and play, unhampered finally by restrictive laws. Men can take on "wings" of creative power, can take on something of divinity, even though from the birds' viewpoint, in which the poet shares, they also remain feeble, ephemeral creatures doomed to die. It is the same old paradox that Homer shows, and Pindar, and Sophocles. Like the birds, man occupies a middle position, midway between animal and god. Hence in the comic view he fortifies that midposition, in midair, adds wings to his comic padding of belly and buttocks and his phallus, and wars against the gods and the limits of nature with a success that we are denied by Homer and Pindar and Sophocles. In comedy the power of hope and the imagination, and of creative *erōs*, carries all before it. For the human imagination represented by Peisetairus is the cutting edge of that creative process that brought the ordered and ordering world of gods and men out of chaos and old night. It still continues, beyond Zeus' limited and limiting rule, into the spreading rule of Love.

Aristophanes knew, of course, quite as well as Pindar or Sophocles that *erōs* could draw people and nations into blind infatuation and destruction. And there is reason to think, as William Arrowsmith argues in his powerful essay, that the Athenians were, in fact, misled and destroyed by their blind erotic passion for world empire.[90] Such is Thucydides' view, and such the view we easily take with hindsight about the Peloponnesian War in general and the Sicilian venture in particular. Alcibiades, from whom Peisetairus is somewhat drawn, must have seemed the very personification of this guiding destructive *erōs*.[91] In part Aristophanes' play reveals the madness of imperial Athens; or better, it reveals the underlying Athenian and human wish for nothing less than everything. We recognize much of the delusion, the passion, even the lunacy of Athens beneath the conduct of the birds under Peisetairus' leadership and manipulation. And yet it is hard to believe, with Arrowsmith, that the play points a negative moral, urging the Athenians (and we might add, by Arrowsmith's reading, the Americans) to return to sane limits and fundamental values while there is still time. It is not just that Peisetairus' madness is triumphant in the play, conveying a sense of hope: but that the play *begins* precisely with a sense of discouragement and helplessness about Athens, and with an attempt to return to greener pastures (the "greening of Athens," so to speak), and it goes on from there. The movement of the play is erotic and hopeful in a way that does more, I think, than reflect delusion. I argued earlier that the rightness of wishing and hoping was an underlying premise of Aristophanes' comedies, that only within this larger experience of recovery and hope could comedy clarify our wishes in accordance with reality. What we need is not less imagination, not less play, not less creative passion than Alcibiades and his Athens represent, but somehow more. There is only one way to escape, and that way is forward.

What I am saying may sound unreasonable, as though I were committing Aristophanes himself to madness and delusion. Perhaps I am. The risk is always there. But we have to account somehow for the hopefulness and adventurousness of Aristophanes' comedy, which includes satire and parody but goes so far beyond them. My reading is also in keeping with the reading of other plays from which the loyalties emerge that were described earlier, especially the loyalty to Athenian and human freedom. It is true that this freedom is dangerous, that it is dynamic and uncontrollable, that it can reverse itself into tyranny abroad and perhaps at home. Plato perceived this later as the greatest risk inherent in democracy and, as a result, laid out (rather like Peisetairus) a totalitarian state in which such violent reversals would no longer be possible. His utopian Republic includes contradictions, much as Cloudcuckooland does. But Aristophanes remains loyal to Athenian, democratic freedom, as Plato and Peisetairus do not; and he does this not least because he perceives it as human freedom, and as rooted in that ongoing creative process at the heart of things of which the bird chorus sings. In the end, he is for that *erōs*, not against it; he celebrates life; and he follows Eros, as he follows Dionysus.

But while the positive, hopeful meaning of *erōs* still, as it dominates the *Birds*, remains in keeping with Aristophanes' central comic vision, it is equally true that the play belongs to a special moment in time: to 414 B.C. (though Aristophanes must have written much of it in 415); to the time when the great, mad Sicilian expedition had been sent out, was still in course, and might still have succeeded. Not that the hope behind the play is of world conquest: but this hope might have dimmed (together with Athenian hopes of world conquest) after the expedition failed in 413. The *Lysistrata* of 411 is beautiful and funny and touching, but it stays closer to home, it lacks the mad flight and scope of the *Birds*. That time was past. It is suggestive that Plato's *Symposium*, in which Aristophanes is given his great speech in praise of love's power of healing and recovery, had to be set back, for its dramatic date, to 416, the year before the Sicilian expedition: otherwise its unshadowed gaiety might have seemed implausible. The comic imagination, like the philosophical, transcends time; but it also knows (as the philosophical imagination did not always admit) that it is also *of* time, that it lives and changes in the course of time together with the city that fosters it. That Aristophanes' comedies accept the energies of time and change, including cultural change, change in tragedy, and even change in comedy itself (as I argue in the next chapter), speaks once more for Aristophanes' loyalty to that creative, golden-winged Eros emerging to build worlds out of the heart of darkness and empty, yawning space.

30   *Utopia Limited:* Ecclesiazusae

BY 392 or 391 B.C., when the *Ecclesiazusae* was produced, time had had its way with Athens and with Old Comedy.[92] After
the surrender and occupation of 404, the rule of the Thirty Tyrants, and
the restoration of democracy in 403, Athens showed resilience and (with
the amnesty) even good sense, but her dreams of glory, for the most part,
sank into the past. The polis portrayed in Aristophanes' last two plays
seems shrunk to bourgeois size. Its representatives are ordinary types,
men in the street. There are still vile politicians to satirize, like Agyrrhios,
who introduced the three-obol fee for attending the Assembly and who
had the further audacity to curtail the pay of comic poets; but these low
schemers lack the monstrousness of older villains. One almost misses
Cleon. The great change in comedy is that the chorus, its heart and soul,
is on the way out. It has not yet disappeared, to give way to irrelevant
musical interludes between acts; but because of the trouble and expense,
and a tendency toward realistic drama, its outfitting is now scanty, its
dramatic importance much curtailed.[93] Aristophanes himself was approaching sixty. Most critics believe that he, together with his comedy,
succumbed to what might be called "seriousness and weariousness," and
that the *Ecclesiazusae* and *Plutus* are no longer Old Comedy in form or
spirit, but rather Middle Comedy, looking toward the New.

I want to argue, with the dissenting minority, that Aristophanes is still
Aristophanes ("though much is taken, much remains") and that his Old
Comedy, though beginning to outlive itself, is still Old Comedy. The
Ecclesiazusae, about utopian schemes, is a test case. Have "seriousness
and weariousness" reduced comic fantasy to satire? Or (as I prefer to
think) has Aristophanes transformed potential satire into comedy? How
much vitality is there, and how much hope?

When the women first meet, in their borrowed men's clothes, to re-
hearse their strategy for the forthcoming Assembly, Praxagora's demonstration speech begins, like Lysistrata's, with the wretched state of public
affairs. Today we need footnotes to explain her references to decisions,

indecisions, and Assembly debates that went badly. Some of her criticisms sound familiar. The Athenians (she says) elect worthless leaders, resist sensible advice, are hard to satisfy, and seldom stick to resolutions. What seems comparatively new is her stress on private economic interests and their effect on politics. People always ask, "How will this measure affect *me?*" Individually and as pressure groups they support benefits for themselves and resist benefits for others. No wonder the commonwealth reels. The new three-obol Assembly fee typifies the general corruption. A great deal is "rotten" in the state of Athens.

No doubt Aristophanes is using the persona of "Praxagora" here to express his own real dismay at the sluggish, confused, irresponsible drift of Athenian politics. This is, as ever, the stuff of political satire. But he also makes us realize how readily such criticism turns into rhetoric, and tired rhetoric as well. Praxagora's opening gambit is the most trite of all: "If things were not so awful . . . I would not have spoken up."[94] The theatrical images, too, of rehearsing parts, going over lines, avoiding mistakes in delivery, and learning to make effective use of costumes, masks, and props, all serve to portray the Assembly debate as a special kind of performance. The conservative protest, possibly including Aristophanes' own, therefore begins to sound very artificial indeed, and very tired—a point underscored by the women's chorus later when they march off imitating the usual chorus of exhausted old men. They worry about getting their pay. It wasn't like this, they complain, in the good old days: nobody took money then for doing his civic duty; no, people used to come with a wineskin, a loaf of bread, two onions and three olives. Those were the days! But now, you'd think the assemblygoers were a gang of hired fruitpickers.

Back at rehearsal, though, we see how this tired criticism feeds a coup d'état. Praxagora moves with quick rhetorical sleight of hand from the proposition earlier advanced in the *Lysistrata*, that women are steady, conservative types (a proposition comically undermined by wine- and sex-jokes), to her revolutionary proposal to put the women in charge of everything. The turnabout may have been familiar from real life; what is new, I think, is the dramatization of how tiredness itself plays into the hands of revolutionaries. Things are such a mess (one can hear people saying it) that someone has to take charge, some strong and decisive Leader with new ideas.

People are thirsty, desperately thirsty, for new ideas. I use the metaphor advisedly: one of the women has already commented that men must drink heavily (something she appreciates) in the Assembly because they are always passing such drunken resolutions there. This is confirmed in Chremes' report of the Assembly meeting that ensues. He reports to Blepyrus, who has come out, during the interval, in his wife's nightie to take a shit. The scatological humor, splendidly prolonged, provides low

comic relief from political satire but also reinforces it with Shakespearean counterpoint: for Blepyrus, the old economic man, is so constipated
that he can't get on with the business of politics—can't even make it to
the Assembly. The Athenians, like Blepyrus, need relief. The agenda of
the Assembly consists simply of one item: how to save the polis. "I
move," says Euaion, "that the fullers provide free suits of clothes for
everyone who requires them with winter coming on. I further move that
any person who requires bed or bedding be lodged free of charge with
the tanners. Noncompliance to result in a three-rug fine." In one sense
these proposals are fantasy politics. They are as nakedly absurd as their
spokesman, who pretends to be dressed but is virtually nude. (The emperor has no clothes.) In another sense, these giveaway schemes involving other people's property can be seen as an extension of pork barrel
and welfare state politics as usual. Praxagora's communist revolution,
when it comes, will only take the process a step further—a giant step for
humankind, to be sure.

Is it relevant that the poet, like the politician, is under constant pressure to come up with new ideas? His efforts were suggested earlier, in the
"rehearsal" scene. Now the chorus make the connection explicit as they
introduce the formal agon:

> *Chor.* It is time to demonstrate what intellect can do. A clever inven-
> tion is what our city needs. Only see that you relate things never
> said or done before; people hate to look upon (*theōntai*) the old
> things time and again.
> *Prax.* I am quite confident that I shall give good advice. But what
> about the audience (*theatas*)? Will they be willing to put new
> things to the test, and not hold tight to what's old and familiar?
> That's really what worries me.
> *Chor.* As for our trying new things, don't be anxious on that score.
> That's what we like to do more than *anything*—and to disre-
> gard what's old. (576–87)

Aristophanes pauses here to joke with his audience, who like things new,
fast, and funny. In the present context, however, the joke seems painful.
On the one hand, it glances at the Assembly: always eager to hear something new, always ready to be taken in by clever new arguments, to back
off from some agreed-on policy. You can never say (the sarcasm is laid on
thick) that Athenians are afraid of novelty! And you can never say that
their firm loyalty to established ways will keep them from revolution.
Like the jurymen in the *Wasps*, the assemblymen here are criticized for
behaving like the audience at a dramatic entertainment. But, on the other
hand: are not the theater audience (what Plato would call the "theatroc-
racy") as fickle and unreliable as their counterparts in the Assembly?
Later, toward the end, the chorus will urge the judges not to forget this
play's merits merely because others came later, like courtesans who only

remember their last client. "What have you done for us lately?" The dreadful refrain of politics applies also to theater. The poet feels unrelenting pressure to come out with new ideas, new modes of entertainment. Earlier, in the *Knights*, he commented on the difficulty of satisfying this demanding and fickle public. How many older poets had failed, or just barely stood their ground! Now, more than thirty years later, Aristophanes feels the pressure. The imagined revolution, Praxagora's great (or not so great) idea, is motivated by a general weariness at Athens that is, not least, the poet's own.

Against this background of tired people, tired rhetoric, and the wish for novelty, Praxagora unfolds her communistic plan, sweeping objections aside or, better, using them to help her argument. (1) Land and possessions will be held in common (*koinōnein, koinos*). But what if people hold things back? No need: they'll have everything they want. But what if they want to give presents to girls? No need, for (2) women will be held in common too. But won't the beautiful ones be mobbed? No, because (3) the older, uglier women must be slept with first; likewise, the older, uglier, more ordinary men will get first crack at the women. But how will people know their own children? No problem, for (4) all men of a certain age will be regarded as fathers and hence treated with respect. (This point is arguable, so Praxagora hurries on.) Life will be easy. (5) The slaves will farm; *you* will dine. (6) There will be no more borrowing or lending of money and hence no more lawsuits. (7) Partitions will be broken down, the city will be one great dwelling place, and the old-time law courts and official colonnades will now be reassigned by lot as dining halls. In sum: "We'll provide everything in abundance for everybody."

Much of this is comic teasing, as the sequel will show. It is significant that Praxagora's presentation ends, in the *pnigos*, with a picture of comic frustration: youths returning from dinner will be enticed, by older women, with promises of luscious girls, but the older and uglier men will push ahead, insisting on their legal rights, so that the youths will just have to wait outside, masturbating, until the rest are through. This is almost self-parody. We are being teased; we may be disappointed. To appreciate the force of the teasing, though, we must realize how strong the nostalgia is to which it appeals; and here, once more, Plato is extremely helpful.

Scholars in the past have focused their energies on the *Prioritätsfrage*. How are these communistic schemes related to those of *Republic* 5–7, where the ideal state is reconstituted by means of "three waves" of reform: abolition of private property, abolition of the family, and the emergence of a philosopher-king? The first two only apply to the Guardian class, on whom Plato imposes an almost monastic discipline so that they will not be distracted from good "shepherding" by private needs, ambitions, or rivalries. More than that, he wants them to live, and feel, like one close family. Although his proposals take account of contemporary liberal thinking about women's capabilities and rights, giving them education and responsibility equal to men's, he uses sex as an instrument of state policy. All personal considerations are subordinated to the requirements of good breeding and efficient management and control. Nowhere is the divergence from democratic ways more striking than in this ordinarily most private sphere of sex, family, and home.

It seems unlikely to most scholars today that Aristophanes knew and parodied the *Republic* as we have it; unlikely too that Plato borrowed from Aristophanes. (Interestingly, when Plato introduces the subject of coeducational gymnastics, he treats laughter as an obstacle to be overcome by rational argument and habituation in the course of time.) Probably the two writers drew on a common source, or sources, for many were available.[95] Herodotus' history includes reports of distant nations whose lifestyles suggest utopian traits; for example,

> The Agathyrsi are the most luxurious of men. They enjoy abundance of gold, and they share their women for intercourse so they may all be brothers to one another, and so that, being all one family, they may not treat one another with jealousy or any kind of hostility. (4.104)

Although Herodotus always insists on the integrity of *nomos*, the need to respect one's own customs and those of other peoples, his explanation after the fact here betrays a certain envy of that tribal coherence that more civilized groups have lost. It is only a short step to the question "Why can't we civilized Athenians be more like the Agathyrsi?" Just so, many twentieth-century readers of Margaret Mead or Bronislaw Malinowski must have asked, "Why can't we be more relaxed about sex and childrearing, like the Samoans or the Trobriand Islanders?" It seems likely that long before Plato wrote anything, more than one sophist drew on comparative ethnology for a rigorous critique of Athenian individualism. Utopian ideas, as said earlier, were in the air. They must have grown in charm as Athens wearied of inner and outer competitiveness. But because, for us, their appeal is most strongly realized in Plato's *Republic*, it seems reasonable to begin there, and to work backwards.

For Plato shows, first, the power and beauty of utopian thinking. Although he argues that his "three waves" are not just wish-fulfillment fantasies (*euchais homoia*) but eminently practicable, because they are fully in accord with nature, he obviously enjoys the imaginative opportunity of working with a clean slate, unbothered by previously existing customs or institutions—or human tendencies. Still more, he enjoys the chance to put questions of value and desirability first, and to postpone questions of feasibility. He compares this procedure, with some self-irony, to day-dreaming:

Just do me this favor, for your part. Allow me to take a holiday (*heortasai*), the way idle people have the habit of treating their minds to a feast when they walk along by themselves. What do these people do? They don't wait to discover how the object of their ambition can be attained, but they let that question go, in order not to tire themselves out in asking whether this is feasible or not; instead, they simply assume that what they want is already *there*, and they make the rest of their plans accordingly, all the detailed arrangements for what they will do afterwards. Yes, it is a lazy business. (457e–458a)

Despite the irony, Plato knows and wants us to know that his "idle dreaming" is really a means of driving toward the center of reality, not away from it.

Second, Plato's utopian solutions express an overwhelming nostalgia for simplicity. They respond, that is, not to the ordinary desire that people have for freedom, choice, and responsibility, but to the equally human desire to escape from all these things when they become, or seem to become, psychologically overpowering and socially destructive. Plato wants to restore what E. R. Dodds called the "inherited conglomerate," the once seamless fabric of culture, tradition, and belief. More than that, he wants to return to something like tribal unity, to a time when people lived together with a common mind and heart, and a common sense of purpose—a little like Sparta, but without the corruption and rivalry for which Sparta was notorious. Hence Plato's utopia, for all its inventiveness, looks backward, not forward. It is a way of returning to the "hard Golden Age" of physical and moral discipline, social harmony, and piety toward the gods. The ruling elite will be spiritually akin to the "golden race" of old. The lower classes, not golden themselves (though making use of gold), will share in the contentment of that dispensation and in its secure order, which Plato calls justice.

Now, in *A Night at the Opera*, Groucho Marx, as Otis P. Driftwood, interrupts a musical impresario who is flattering a society lady: "Look here, Gottlieb, making love to Mrs. Claypool is *my* racket." Groucho is a fraud, he knows it, and (with rare honesty) he admits it; but when other, ordinary frauds enter in, things begin to seem crowded. In much the same spirit Aristophanes might have said to Plato or (more historically) to earlier utopian theorists, "Trading in fantasy politics is *my* racket." If anyone is going to chart the ideal future, untroubled by questions of feasibility, then it should be the expert in matters of "desire with hope," the comic poet. But Aristophanes, getting the bit between his teeth, goes further than Plato. He shows how the attraction of those utopian day-dreams is rooted in a human nature that wants more, not less; how, beneath the nostalgia for simplicity, there lurks a still deeper nostalgia for the "soft Golden Age," the utter happiness of the remembered world of very early childhood. Into that greater daydream, and out of it again, we must be teased.

Thus, to begin with communism of property: Praxagora first argues for it on moral and rational grounds, of social justice. She aims to remove great and harmful disparities of wealth (more evident in the fourth century than in the fifth) by abolishing private property. Yet the motives here set forth, of social justice, equality, and harmony, prove less important as Praxagora develops her plan than that other, deeper-rooted motive of returning to the protected world of childhood when all our needs (we feel) were satisfied easily and generously by an all-providing mother. Let me illustrate this appeal in a personal way by coming back to Oz. Here is a description of social and economic arrangements, taken from *The Emerald City of Oz:*

> There were no poor people in the Land of Oz, because there was no such thing as money, and all property of every sort belonged to the Ruler. The people were her children, and she cared for them. Each person was given freely by his neighbors whatever he required for his use, which is as much as anyone may reasonably desire. Some tilled the lands and raised great crops of grain, which was divided equally among the entire population, so that all had enough. There were many tailors and dressmakers and shoemakers and the like, who made things that any who desired them might wear. Likewise there were jewelers who made ornaments for the person, which pleased and beautified the people, and these ornaments also were free to those who asked for them. Each man and woman, no matter what he or she produced for the good of the community, was supplied by the neighbors with food and clothing and a house and furniture and ornaments and games. If by chance the supply ever ran short, more was taken from the great storehouses of the Ruler, which were afterward filled up again when there was more of any article than the people needed.
>
> Every one worked half the time and played half the time, and the people enjoyed the work as much as they did the play, because it is good to be occupied and to have something to do. . . .
>
> You will know, by what I have here told you, that the Land of Oz was a remarkable country. I do not suppose such an arrangement would be practical with us, but Dorothy assures me that it works finely with the Oz people.[96]

In all my compromises of growing up, all my accommodations to the economics and politics of what is called the "real world," I have never lost sight of that picture. It has remained a challenge for me, and often a reproach. In Oz, as in Plato's Republic, money is regarded as a source of division and struggle, and so is banished; but in Oz, the answer is not simplicity but magical abundance. Food, clothing, and a house are not enough. There must be games too, and ornaments—and jeweled ornaments at that (for Baum's descriptions all too often reflect the Gilded Age). Life is more than comfortable; it is luxurious. Realistic objections are introduced and answered briefly. People will *want* to work, to help and please one another. Yet in the end all this takes place in a magical, protected world, where Ozma cares for all the people as for her children. She recalls the good, nurturing mother who makes up from her abundance what might be lacking anywhere. Isn't this what we really want, underneath the daydreams of fantasy politics and the welfare state to which we, like the Athenians, keep returning?

My point, for now, is that Praxagora's scheme has deeper attractions than the more obvious ones of equality and justice. She offers (as Plato does not; and her world is lazier than Baum's) abundance and ease. The men won't even need to farm. Slaves will do that for them; they need only go in to dinner. Praxagora's word for it, *boskēsomai*, means that she will "feed them like cattle." The men will be pampered pets, rather like Odysseus' sailors whom Circe turned to swine. "They will all have everything." So we, as the audience, are teased into realizing that what, deep down, we have always wanted from life and from politics is nothing short of "everything." We are like Demos in the *Knights* (but only at first), when he lets himself be courted and pampered like a great big baby; or like Philocleon (but only briefly) when he lets himself be seduced by the comfort, ease, and luxury of his son's private welfare state; or like the refugees in the *Birds* (but only at first) when they are looking for the sort of country that they can wrap around themselves like a big, soft, warm security blanket. We are teased, as in all those other plays, with images of utter childish happiness. But as with Demos and Philocleon and Peisetairus, we are teased further, into moving on (if only to bigger and better fantasies), and to growing up. At the heart of this new teasing is the comic treatment of sex, and of sexual wishes.

Although Praxagora defends her proposal of sexual communism as a means of overcoming divisiveness in society, its appeal again reaches down to deeper-rooted desires. For what Praxagora seems to promise is a free and open sexual community presided over by a loving and generous mother. It all sounds Oedipal; no wonder an Oedipus joke appears later in the play. It is as though the normal (traditionally "male") adult wish for free and casual sex had been incorporated into that other childish longing for the "soft Golden Age." But, as so often, the promise of utopian bliss is extended and then snatched away, in a flurry of bureaucratization and comic frustration. Sex is not exactly denied, as in modern dystopias like Orwell's *1984*, but Praxagora's system gets quite out of control when it follows strict democratic logic to the point of insanity. Today we would say that it had been drafted by a committee.

The following episodes first illustrate what comes of abolishing private property. One man complies with the new law, marshaling his property in procession for the common storehouse; another man resists, with typical Athenian skepticism and disregard of law, but begins to *think* about compliance when the call comes to the general banquet. Is it the point that human nature will persist under a utopian regime—that problems are not waved aside as easily as Praxagora's sweeping logic would suggest? Or is the selfish man (who is not clearly punished) right in asserting that one should not go along with every new law like a dumb animal? It is not clear; Aristophanes is building slowly to an absurd climax. Sexual communism produces a wild and funny sexual disaster. A youth's assignation with a pretty girl, anticipated in a mawkish duet (a parody of the new, sentimental, almost Hellenistic love lyric), is prevented by an ugly old crone who claims first go at him. After the girl finally drives her away with pertinent insults—"You've got no sense. Can't you see he's not the age to sleep with you? You could more easily be his mother than his wife. If you succeed in putting this custom into practice, then you'll make the whole country full of *Oedipuses!*" (1038–42)—she yields before the onslaught of a second old hag, who resembles a goblin, and from whom the youth is rescued in turn—by a third hag, the oldest and ugliest of all, who looks like death warmed over. As the scene ends, he is carried into the house (still making sex and death jokes), to "row" for the two of them together. Evidently the new communism is in control.

These scenes may be hilarious (I have never seen them staged), but how do they affect our judgment of Praxagora's utopia? In younger days, now well behind me, I was tempted to read them as bitter satire. The inversion of normal sex relations seemed ugly and perverse—unlike so much later comedy, where the blocking character is expelled and the young lovers finally united. And worst of all, the nurturing mother imagined earlier seemed transformed here into the *mère terrible*, confronting her son in an Oedipal nightmare.[97] All this indicated dystopia. And yet I always had qualms about my negative reading of the episode, partly because it betrayed a male double standard (I had always enjoyed Aristophanes' dirty old men, even Philocleon, but evidently found his dirty old women too much to handle), but still more because I sensed, beyond satire, a promise of vitality. My wife, who has often complained of the mistreatment of the "Katisha" type by Gilbert and Sullivan, says that I might consider Mae West, who never stopped saying, "Come up and see me sometime." It is true that, as the youth's black humor affirms, sex and death are getting terribly mixed up. We end with something approaching necrophilia. And yet these hideous old women display an energy and vitality that the young pair, for all their sentimental eroticism, simply do not have. A triumph of the ugly-and-shameful (*to aischron*), their raw sexuality is closely akin to the Old Comedy itself, now *very* old comedy for Athens and for Aristophanes, yet a stronger response to the "seriousness and weariousness" of things than any newer, more polite and docile mode of entertainment could provide.

And the play ends with old-style comic teasing that blends celebration with hints, but only hints, of more frustration.[98] A drunken servant-girl comes out, fragrant with party atmosphere, to summon old Blepyrus to the feast together with all the spectators and (if they are favorable) all the judges, "for we shall provide everything." And Blepyrus, with two pretty girls in hand (is the new system working for him, after all?), responds to the call. "You must invite everybody," he says. "Old men, young men, boys. Tell them dinner's ready for all of them—if they'll just go home." It is the usual comic teasing, of the audience and of Blepyrus too, for after the chorus promise him the most mighty, massive, magnificent, and mouth-watering dish ever before or after compressed into a single compound word in comedy, they advise him to pick up some porridge for an after-dinner snack. Is he a comic scapegoat still? Or representative of a people bound to be disappointed in the end? We might think so; yet he goes off dancing to the (real?) victory dinner with the chorus, shouting Dionysian cries that sound as positive and as celebratory as ever.

Certainly, as we look back, the *Ecclesiazusae* seems heavy with satire. It makes us realize how much the fantasy politics of the welfare state are empowered by human and civic weariness and by deep-set, nostalgic wishes that grow strong in times of weariness. That is why people settle so readily for "Utopia limited," for communistic schemes and systems in place of true *communitas*. The scenes of political debate rehearsed and reported, Praxagora's inaugural address, the contribution episode, the crazy sex scenes, the final and familiar comic teasing about the party to which we may or may not all be invited—all this reminds us of how easily we fool ourselves with daydreams of comfort and are fooled by others too. And yet although this play does not end with the transformation of the body politic or the exaltation of the comic hero to godlike status, its final revelry, I think, conveys a spirit of vitality that goes beyond weariness, and hope that goes beyond disillusionment. We haven't got Utopia right, and the theorists haven't, and they probably never will. Only the Old Comedy, with its loyalties to the whole and comic truth, to human diversity and creativity, and to *communitas* (which is still strengthened by the sex play, the transvestism, and the topsy-turvy world), could tease us so effectively into seeing and accepting that truth. Yet we seem less tired and defeated at the play's end than at its beginning. Push weariness far enough—the weariness of Athens, of Aristophanes, of Old Comedy itself (which, as everybody knows, has outlived itself), and it will surprise you—will start to dance, or cavort, or chase some effete youth around the stage! Which is, to say the least, encouraging.

31   *Utopia Still Wanted:* Plutus

STILL more than Aristophanes' *Ecclesiazusae*, his *Plutus* has been banished by literary historians from the domain of Old Comedy. It has an insignificant chorus, and few songs; its setting is bourgeois; its concerns are with money, the effect of money on character, and social organization. All this has seemed a far cry from the wild, fantastic, political comedy of earlier years, and in some ways it is. Yet I would argue that if we look back at the *Plutus* from a play of the New Comedy, like Menander's *Dyskolos*, the differences remain more striking than the similarities, so that we may be tempted to think of the *Plutus* as Old Comedy, after all.

The *Dyskolos*, our only complete play of Menander to survive, is by no means his best. It lacks intrigue, and there is relatively little wit, subtlety, or fun in it. Yet its main concerns, which are ethical, are borne out by the other plays that survive in part, or through Terence's close adaptations; and as a fairy-tale comedy of sorts, it seems especially suitable for comparison with Aristophanes. Pan, who speaks the prologue, guides the course of events from behind the scenes so that the poor country girl, old Cnemon's daughter, who has honored him and the nymphs, will gain a prosperous marriage. Through confusion, mistake, and coincidence, everything turns out well; in fact this sentimental comedy of manners ends with a double wedding. But how does all this compare to Old Comedy?

I begin with the most obvious difference, the absence of a functional chorus. The play belongs entirely to the actors; only, between the acts, a troupe of "revelers" enters to sing and dance an interlude, and departs again. But whatever entertainment they offer remains extraneous. There is no animal masquerade, no comic teasing, no parabasis; in fact, there are no songs at all in Menander's plays, not even individual arias. The basic meter is the iambic trimeter of spoken dialogue, an instrument that Menander plays on with marvelous flexibility and control; scenes of heightened emotion are given in trochaic tetrameter, to flute accompaniment for "recitative." The songs will not reappear in comedy until Caecilius and Plautus reintroduce them at Rome, toward the end of the third century B.C.

Menander's settings are realistic, usually consisting of two houses on a city street. (The cave of Pan and the nymphs at Phyle, alongside two farmhouses, gives an exotic touch in the *Dyskolos*.) And people and places stay put. There is no voyaging to heaven or hell, no casual movement, even, from city to country and back again. The action too is realistic within its fairy-tale frame. There is no conversation, except in dreams, with gods or beasts or birds. Nature may be kindly or harsh, or a mixture of both (the rocks of Phyle are a dour setting, though honesty and virtue thrive there), but it has no tongue. What is real is love and friendship, human character, and money, not necessarily in that order. Human life can be improved, and generally, in Menander's comedies, it is; but it can hardly be said to be transformed.

New comedy is social, not political. It satirizes, not individual politicians or people about town (although these are occasionally referred to), but foolish or antisocial types: the miser, the misanthrope, the flatterer, the conceited man. It teaches that people should be considerate, tolerant, and generous. Often a man learns the hard way; he fails to appreciate his wife, or to trust his friend (male or female), and when he discovers the truth, he must repent of his pigheadedness in a storm of guilt and self-reproach; but still he is forgiven, and life goes on, much better than before. And these same private virtues, it is implied, improve society; they make the world go round. In the *Dyskolos* there is much stress on riches and poverty, and on the disparity of temper that can accompany them. Cnemon's stepson, Gorgias, the poor country boy who supports his mother, is by instinct suspicious of Sostratus, the idle young preppie whose business is (obviously) to corrupt innocent country girls. But after Sostratus explains that his intentions are honorable, and Gorgias apologizes for his harsh suspicions, the two become friends and allies; and when, finally, Sostratus is betrothed to the girl, and Gorgias is betrothed to Sostratus' sister, there is a reassuring suggestion that the disparity of rich and poor is being overcome—and with it, the greatest problem of fourth-century Athens. The resulting impression, I think, is deceptive in a way that Aristophanes' fairy-tale comedies are not. A little kindness, a little generosity—and the deep-lying problems of society fall away. It is like the satisfaction we feel at the end of Dickens's *Christmas Carol* when Old Scrooge is converted, gives generously to charity, tips a street-boy, and becomes the great and lasting benefactor of the Cratchits. Something like this may happen, now and then, and life may be the better for it; but it is not now, and never was, the economic answer.

Menander's chief interest is in the delineation and development of character.[99] We are invited to "place" each character in relation to some mean of conduct, or some deviation from the mean; for in this respect Menander's comedy is descended from Aristotle's *Ethics*, where the means and extremes of conduct are set out schematically, and from the *Characters* of Aristotle's student Theophrastus, in which various faulty types, like the miser, the braggart, the chatterbox, and the flatterer, are depicted with very amusing illustrations. Thus Cnemon, the title character of the *Dyskolos*, is the "bad-tempered man" who deviates by deficiency from the mean of agreeableness in society. He is also the self-willed misanthrope. His stepson Gorgias tends in the same direction, while Sostratus (and even more, Sostratus' friend in the first scene) tends to the opposite extreme of the *areskos*, or overly agreeable man, who resembles the flatterer.

The more inflexible and single-minded these extreme types are, the more they illustrate Henri Bergson's definition of the comic as the mechanical encrusted on human behavior. Their words, gestures, and actions are expressive of the disproportion and unbalance in their attitudes, and of the way their minds run along a single, undeviating track. They are all around us; they supply, with little need for invention, the stock types of New Comedy, or the comedy of humors, or of manners; and if Bergson is right, we learn from observing their foolish behavior how to become more balanced and sane ourselves and how to display the flexibility in our behavior that society requires if it is to move along without friction and disturbance. In this way the stock types are educational as well as comic, whether we see them on the stage or observe them (as Horace's father taught him to do) in ordinary life. But in Menander's plays generally, and in the *Dyskolos*, the more serious characters are not, or prove not to be, stock types. Their humanity and good sense consists, precisely, in the refusal to be stereotyped. Thus Sostratus and Gorgias are foils, at first, for each other's strengths and weaknesses; Sostratus is generous but too easygoing, and Gorgias is firm and independent but too prone to harsh judgments; but after they become friends, they influence each other's character for the good, so that Sostratus gets more backbone and Gorgias more friendliness. And Cnemon too moves toward greater individuality, if not greater balance, as the play develops. At first he is represented as a mere humor, a monster of disagreeableness who eats people alive if they disturb his misanthropic solitude. But we come to see him more as a person. His bark is worse than his bite. If he is misanthropic (a type often met in New Comedy), it is because he has been disappointed in people, has become cynical about human nature. His fall down the well and his rescue by Gorgias, his disaffiliated stepson (with an assist from Sostratus), teach him, first, that no man can be self-sufficient and, second, that human nature is not always self-seeking and vile. Not that he is converted altogether to sociability, like Scrooge (Menander is more realistic here than Dickens). He still wants to live alone. But he stops being the "blocking character"; he lets the others live and love; and he gives over his property, and his symbolic power with it, to the sensible Gorgias. The contrast with the unregenerate old scoundrel Philocleon, in Aristophanes' *Wasps*, could hardly be greater.

But the more serious scenes in the *Dyskolos* are balanced, in turn, by farcical scenes involving that low-life comic pair, the slave and the cook, Geta and Sicon. It is for them to complain, in time-honored fashion, about their aching backs; to bring in (with more complaints) a scrawny, wayward sheep for the sacrifice at Pan's cave; to disturb old Cnemon with their importunate requests for a large roasting pot; and even (for Sicon) to indulge in a little of the obscenity that, in general, is not found in New Comedy, and in particular, is never associated with the more serious and respectable characters. The farcical elements in the play balance, but also contrast with, the serious ones; there is something for everyone in the audience, for the more thoughtful and educated ones, and for the rest; but the different proprieties of speech and action are maintained, in accordance with the different levels of character and of intent.

Only once, I think, in the *Dyskolos* do the distinctions break down, in the manner of Old Comedy. This happens in act 5, in the revelry scene. Since the recognitions in New Comedy, both outer and inner, are usually completed by the end of act 4, the fifth act remains open; it can be used to ridicule a moral outsider (often the one person, not yet in the know, who prided himself on seeing and knowing everything); or it can be given over to celebration, with the slaves taking a strong lead. In the *Dyskolos* Cnemon's continuing self-isolation invites retribution from the slave and cook, mistreated earlier. They carry his bed outdoors while he sleeps, wake him up absurdly, and make fun of his helplessness. As the music plays, and a tipsy slave-girl describes the fun within, the old spoilsport must either join the party of his own accord or be compelled to join it. He decides to join in the dance. His conversion, perhaps, takes a further step. And something of the old comic revelry, beyond any power of moralizing (even about conversion), regains the comic stage.

It is, in all, a cheerful and respectable fairy tale. The good are rewarded, even those who (like Sostratus) make token efforts toward virtue. The bad, who are not really bad, but somewhat weak in Aristotelian ethics, can be improved by precept, by friendship, and by providential accidents. Rich and poor are brought together amicably; arrangements are made to share the wealth—especially after Sostratus' rich father has been given his lunch. The audience will be entertained, and duly edified, though we may doubt, as does the skeptical slave in Plautus' *Rudens* (a much wilder and funnier fairy-tale comedy, leading from Menander's *Dyskolos* to Shakespeare's *Tempest*), that the noble sentiments that they applaud will make much difference in their ordinary lives, outside the theater:

I've seen comic players before indulging in these noble sentiments,
and I've seen them applauded, when they showed the people such
splendid standards of behavior; still, when they went their ways,
each to his own home, not one man acted the way those actors told
him to. (1249–53)

Perhaps Gripus is too cynical. Perhaps, like Dickens's *Christmas Carol*
again, a Menandrian comedy like the *Dyskolos* will induce its spectators
to treat their wives or neighbors (though probably not their slaves) in
kindlier fashion during the next week. But the world, though ever so
slightly improved, will hardly be transformed.

And this is true, in the end, because the gods are absent from Menander's world, as they are absent, generally, from the fourth-century world
of philosophy and business. It is true that Pan appears to speak the
prologue, and that, as we infer, he stage-manages the play's happy coincidences; but he is not a dangerous and powerful god like Dionysus (or
like Venus, for that matter, in the *Rudens*). He is, rather, a tame and
sentimentalized divinity with features of Santa Claus. He differs little
from personifications of Ignorance or Chance who direct the benign
sequence of events in other comedies. If these vague, distant divinities
carry any weight, it is through the mediation of human character, which
the gods, as a slave says elsewhere, "have given the human race as garrison commander," since they are obviously unable to watch over human
affairs one by one. Respect character, use it rightly, and you will succeed.[100] There is a strong sense in Menander's plays that the gods help
those who (in a decent way, to be sure) help themselves. Religion is one
more area of life to be taken with moderation. That something divine
could irrupt wildly and dangerously into human life, turning it upside
down and answering to our deepest wish, for outrageous happiness—
and that this irruption, which transcends ordinary distinctions of propriety and morals, could be cause for the greatest revelry—is not an idea
that is represented on Menander's stage, or one that was present in the
mind of that respectable, bourgeois, fourth-century audience for whom
his plays were written.

On first view the *Plutus*, like the *Dyskolos*, is concerned
with money and character. Its hero's quest begins with a moral problem:
if honest men fail and the dishonest flourish, then should one teach one's
son to be honest or dishonest? Chremylus seeks an answer at Delphi; the
rest follows. Throughout the play, we are kept aware of the power of
money to control human and (it seems) divine affairs. Characters are
defined as honest or corrupt, generous or selfish; the moderate Chremylus, like Chremes in the *Ecclesiazusae*, anticipates Aristotle's mean. What

is more, he remains a serious, respectable person for most of the play, while the kitchen humor is left to his slave Cario, sometimes in counterpoint with his master's more serious comments.

All this comes close to New Comedy; and so, still more, does the waning of the chorus. It consists now of ordinary men, poor and suspicious, with no fancy costumes, nothing marvelous about them, and no special dramatic purpose; when Cario calls them in, they ask questions, raise objections, and express their pleasure at the prospect of Plutus' healing, but unlike the chorus of farmers in the *Peace*, they do nothing to help. Only, after Cario teases them, and then tells them that they will all be rich, they join him in performing a very funny, very dirty song and dance.[101] First he plays the Cyclops, and they play the bleating sheep and goats, and the followers of Odysseus who will blind the Cyclops; then he plays Circe and they play the oinking pigs, or (again) they get the upper hand, with Odysseus. It is as though the old Dionysian chorus of comedy or satyr play had returned for an instant with its mythic parody, its animal masquerade, its daemonic violence and sexuality, its wild comic reversals; but all this comes abruptly to an end. "But come now," says Cario, "leave off the fooling now and turn to another style, while I go to get some bread and meat, and to rest." And the chorus do leave off the fooling. They are uninvolved in the play's action from now on, except as an occasional cheering section. There is no parabasis. There are no teasing songs. There are musical interludes between episodes, marked by CHOROU in the manuscripts, as in those of Menander. It is as though their one wild revel were an anachronistic inset, a relic of popular custom like Shakespeare's rustic dances, but one whose vital comic meaning was now forgotten: all of which, taken together with the shift of content and ambiance, and the widening gap between the serious and the funny, makes us feel that Old Comedy was quite dead by 388 B.C., and that Aristophanes survived, perhaps by mistake, to usher in the New.

And yet as we come to know the *Plutus* better, its fairy-tale movement and healing god, its escalation of wishes, its rejection of Poverty's logical and moral arguments, and its final supplanting of Zeus himself by Plutus, all make us think that we might be reading (if not seeing) Old Comedy after all. Is it just possible that we are?

The fairy-tale movement is as clear and strong as ever. A problem is stated, and a solution sought; the oracle is consulted; Plutus is brought home, to be cured of his Zeus-sent blindness in the temple of Asclepius. As ever, human initiative joins with god-sent opportunity. The resistance to be overcome this time is embodied in the figure of Poverty, a wicked witch to be argued with and then dispatched. And despite the priestly frauds associated with it, and amusingly described, the healing power of Asclepius is portrayed as something very real.[102] The god intervenes with a saving power that is much more holy, much more deeply felt in the fourth century, than is the power of Pan or the other, allegorical divinities of Menander's plays. (The power and presence of the goddess Venus in Plautus' *Rudens* is comparable.) And what follows, after the description of the healing, comes closer to fairy tale than anything in Aristophanes, even in the *Peace*. Chremylus' house fills up, as described earlier, with unimaginable, comically exaggerated riches:

> Our shelves are stocked with cookie-rolls and sugar,
> the cellar's full of whisky and champagne;
> all the pots and pans in the cabinet
> are stuffed to the brim with thousand-dollar bills.
> You'd be amazed. We've got our own oil well
> in the back yard. Sweetly perfumed soap
> in all the bathrooms. Oranges in the attic.
> The dishes, cups, and saucers all have turned
> to sterling silver. And the paper plates
> to plătinum, with diamonds . . . .[103]   (806–14)

Afterwards a just man is rewarded, and a sycophant is punished, in fairy-tale manner;[104] and in a reversal of the *Ecclesiazusae* scenes, a nice (?) young gigolo escapes his financial enslavement to a rich, ugly old woman—except that, this time, she is included in the festive ending. And the play concludes with the universal triumph of the god Plutus, who has been installed in Athena's temple at Athens as a "new Zeus."

As many disconcerted critics have observed, the play moves from Plan A, to heal Plutus' blindness so that honest men will once again be rich, and dishonest men poor, to Plan B, whereby the coming of Plutus makes the whole world rich. How should this change of plan be understood?[105] One possibility, which I reject, is that Aristophanes has been careless. Another is that everyone, on becoming rich, will straightway become honest (I think of Shaw's Alfred Doolittle, drafted against his will into "middle class morality"); only this view is undercut by reminders, scattered throughout the play, that the rich are not, ordinarily, more moral than the poor, and that, indeed, when most people become rich, they become corrupted. Hence the third explanation, to which many would subscribe today: Aristophanes is being ironic, is casting doubt on the whole daydream of making people rich, happy, and virtuous at once.

But shifts of plan, and plot, have happened before: in the *Knights*, and in the *Clouds*; in the *Lysistrata*, where Plan B, the seizing of the acropolis, is superimposed on Plan A, the women's sex strike; and still more pertinently in the comic escalation of plan in the *Birds* and the *Ecclesiazusae*. In the latter play, as we just saw, the proposal to establish a calm, reasonable, and conservative caretaker government leads almost immediately to the creation of a revolutionary communist utopia in which private property and the family are abolished. And even more to the point, the fugitives' original wish in the *Birds*, to settle somewhere in peace and quiet, somehow produces out of itself a Super-Athenian Empire that will conquer the universe. Such a shift reflects the human tendency, which we all share, to rebound from rest into violent activity. Still more, I suggest, it reflects the healing power of comedy, which revives our capacity of wishing and hoping, so that we remember what we really want, and go after it.

In the *Ecclesiazusae* Aristophanes tested out the politics of "Utopia limited" against the older, deeper wish to have all our needs generously and effortlessly met, as in our infancy. The aims, morals, and compromises of a "hard Golden Age" like Plato's are simply not enough. So again, in the *Plutus*, it looks as though Aristophanes first thought of experimenting with a limited utopia, of the redistribution of wealth according to moral criteria; but the plan escalates.[106] Everybody is to become rich; everybody (so far as possible) is to become happy; and Plutus, enshrined ultimately in Athena's temple, is to bring prosperity and salvation to the whole state. What we thought we wanted was justice, the good to be rewarded and the bad punished. What we really wanted was for everybody to be outrageously happy. The vision is uncompromising and unfeasible; but Old Comedy, still true to its spirit, will settle for nothing less.

The rejection of Penia, or Poverty, goes closely with this shift of plan. A grim and frightening figure, like a tragic Fury, the beggarly Penia is there to be cast out in the spirit of old folk ritual. But her plea, which shows sophistic traits, is surprisingly strong. It begins with economic and social theory. In a situation where everyone was rich, who would work, and why? With no one working (for necessity is the mother of effort and invention), everyone would be worse off than before. Penia's argument is so cogent, and her cross-examining manner so overbearing, that in the end Chremylus can only reply, "You won't convince me, even if you convince me!" If feasibility studies and logical reasoning get in the way of utopian dreaming, then they must simply be thrown out, together with Poverty.

The other side of Penia's case is moral. She claims to make people virtuous as well as skillful; her followers are thin, brave, moderate, self-controlled and orderly. If a close connection exists, as she asserts, between scarcity, hard work, and morality, then Penia is pleading for the virtues of an older, more honest world in danger of disappearing. This was the world of Hesiod's *Works and Days*. It is the world of Prodicus' allegorical "Choice of Heracles," in which the hero rejects ease and pleasure for virtuous toil and the steep path to heaven (he would become the chief hero of Stoicism); and it is the world of Socrates, who embraced Lady Poverty in his life (like Saint Francis after him) and whose likeness Plato depicts in the figure of Eros in his *Symposium*, the needy but resourceful child of the beggarwoman Penia by the god Poros, or Plenty.[107] And finally, it is the world of the "hard Golden Age" described by philosophers and poets, from Plato to Virgil: the age ushered in by

Zeus, the strict father-god, to replace the "soft Golden Age" of Kronos, so that mortals might live, no longer in idleness, but in industry and virtue. But however right it sounds, Chremylus rejects the moral argument along with the economic one. "You won't convince me, even if you convince me!" Poverty's role is to be cast out. Comedy's role is to insist, without compromise, on the total recovery of the soft Golden Age, with all its riches and happiness, which may have been mislaid but were never really lost.

And this insistence on nothing less than everything is connected, I think, with the play's end, when everyone leaves the service of Zeus for that of Plutus: first Hermes, then a priest of Zeus, and finally Zeus himself! The implication may be satirical. Has money turned out to be more real, and more efficacious, in the present-day world than those elusive old Olympian gods? Or have riches led, as Penia warned that they would, to unrestrained *hybris*, the old sinful attempt to obtain mastery of things and defy the gods? Certainly these ideas are there, as ironic undercurrents. What takes center stage, though, is the replay of that old comic theme, the deposition of Zeus by a new Titanic power in the universe—in this instance, by Plutus.

The palace revolution in heaven may seem justified morally, because Zeus has not attended to his administrative business of rewarding the good and punishing the wicked. But that is just an excuse. Zeus's real crime is that he is the guardian of morality. It was he who established the Hesiodic system of scarcity, hard work, and virtue to which Penia appeals; and it is he whose dethronement now by Plutus signifies a return to the lost happiness of the soft Golden Age of Kronos. The same revolution was played out in the *Clouds*, in the *Birds*, and in many lost comedies by Aristophanes and other poets of which only tantalizing fragments remain.

At the same time, there is a suggestion toward the play's end that Zeus has been rejuvenated, not replaced:

> Priest ‚I think I'll join the rest, then. I'll say good-bye to Zeus the
> Savior, and I'll stay here myself.
> Chrem. Be assured. Everything will be fine, with the god's help, for
> Zeus the Savior is present here. He's come of his own accord.
> Priest In that case, everything is all right. (1186–90)

The sense here of divine providence recalls that of the *Peace*, where the gods who withdrew from Greek affairs because they were angry, and because they were being demythologized, could still be perceived, and celebrated, behind the present opportunity to grasp peace and happiness. In mythic terms, the *Plutus* gives us a new and rejuvenated Zeus.[108] It may be that a new Zeus was needed to bless the new, fourth-century world, where the old Olympian gods (like the old comic chorus) were somewhat out of date, and out of style; but there is a strong suggestion that Zeus was always there, always watching over Athens together with his daughter Athena, so that Plutus, in the end, is not his replacement, but rather a new guise in which he manifests his being. Hence the reassurance, felt throughout the play, that "everything is all right."

Our brief survey ends, as so often, with paradox. We have, with the *Ecclesiazusae* and *Plutus*, the impression that we have crossed a watershed in the history of comedy, and that we have come down into a valley of transition—what scholars, for convenience, have called Middle Comedy—on the other side of which rise the Menandrian hills. Yet even the *Plutus*, that seems so solidly grounded in the fourth century—that emphasizes social, economic, and ethical concerns, distinguishes serious elements from comic, and produces a halfhearted chorus only to let it fade away—even the *Plutus* exhibits a movement and a spirit that are of the Old Comedy, not the New. It rejects moral allegory, and moral purpose. It rejects philosophical compromise, rejects (as the *Ecclesiazusae* also did) "Utopia limited." In the Old Comic style, it escalates revolutionary change until Zeus himself is dethroned; yet it affirms the Olympian gods—the healing Asclepius, the present Savior Zeus—in a way that the philosophical New Comedy never can or will. The old revel song is still played out, into a new era. "Reports of my death," it might say, "have been grossly exaggerated."

Chapter Six

Old-and-New Comedy

Demeter, Persephone, and the young Triptolemos, to whom Demeter gives ears of golden corn, relief from Eleusis, ca. 440–430 B.C. Courtesy National Museum of Athens (no. 126).

32   *Aristotle and the Split in Comedy*

IT is hard to say just when Old Comedy died. The *Frogs*, which I discuss later, seems its swan song; in the *Ecclesiazusae* and *Plutus*, it has outlived itself; and before Aristophanes died, in the later 380s, he was writing something like Middle Comedy or even New. For our purposes, Aristotle's writings in the later fourth century, and especially his *Poetics*, supply the official coroner's report: Aristophanes is now relegated to the "older comedy." It is true that Aristotle admires him in principle, cites his wordplays, jokes, and scenes as examples of humorous effects, and may even, if Richard Janko's reconstruction of the lost *Second Poetics* is correct, have regarded him perceptively as a transitional figure between the old comedy of indecency and personal abuse and what Aristotle regarded as the new.[1] All the same, we must feel that Aristotle speaks for a new rational age, a changed literary sensitivity, a people "that knew not Aristophanes." His writings herald the failure of appreciation, and even of comprehension, that will be typical of later criticism. I want therefore to look more closely at that fourth-century incomprehension, and at the split it implies between refined and ordinary people in the comic audience, before returning to the fifth-century changes in comedy, in which Aristophanes played a strong part, and to his comedy's laughter in the face of its own threatened evanescence.

Let me begin by reviewing some of Plato's criticisms of tragedy and comedy, to which Aristotle's redefinitions and justifications in his *Poetics* are largely a response:

(1) In *Republic* 3 Plato argues against *mimēsis* as "representation," mainly on ethical grounds. For the young Guards, each of whom must learn to play his own role well, and to stick to it, any invitation to role-playing must be dangerous and misleading. Moreover, the strict self-control required of the Guards is endangered by emotional expression in the theater: by tragic heroes or heroines, for example, who wallow in

grief and self-pity, or even worse emotions; or by those low comic types whose indecency of word, gesture, and action offends against other people (characters onstage, but also living people who are satirized) and, even more, against themselves.[2] Sensible people must reject all such bad representations and bad examples. They will not enjoy such things except (a small loophole?) occasionally in play.

(2) In *Republic* 10 Plato expands his criticism of *mimēsis*, arguing that artistic representations are several degrees removed from Reality, as embodied in the eternal Forms, and also far removed from the consumer's practical knowledge of what things are for. He also bases the rejection of tragedy and comedy on more thoroughgoing psychological grounds than before.[3] The vicarious enjoyment, which we regard as harmless, of tragic emotions such as pity and grief surreptitiously lowers our threshold of emotional self-restraint, thus undermining the results of long effort and habit. And similarly, when we laugh (as we think, harmlessly) at the scurrilous clowns of the comic stage, we begin unconsciously to release that "clownish" part of ourselves that only wants an excuse to indulge its natural tendencies of indecency and hostility. It may be that Aristotle and other students of Plato had already begun to argue that such vicarious pleasures were harmless play, or even that they provided a safety valve for pent-up emotions (an early catharsis view). But Plato is unrelenting. These pleasures, he insists, are never harmless. They enter into the very soul. They weaken that self-government that education must bring and maintain, in the soul as in the state.

(3) In the *Philebus* Plato raises a different problem that later defenders of comedy must address. Most human pleasure, he argues, is mixed with pain. When we laugh at our friends' faults and pretensions, our laughter gives us pleasure; it is morally justified, we think; it may even be helpful to our friends; but all the same, it includes an element of painful *phthonos*, or envy. The point is strengthened by reference to comedy, for our laughter, which gives us so much pleasure, at the follies and misfortunes of characters on the comic stage, is clearly founded on envy, albeit a "playful envy," of the good fortune that these characters enjoy, or appear to enjoy.[4] What emerges when we laugh at the misfortunes of "Lamachus" or Strepsiades, or perhaps even at those of the typical misers, braggarts, or other "blocking characters" of later comedy, is pure *Schadenfreude*. There is a sting in our scornful laughter, but it is we ourselves who, more than we realize, feel the sting.

(4) In *Laws* 11, the proposed legislation to maintain public peace and order includes injunctions against the public expression of insult and invective so often arising out of disputes. And this definitely includes "making fun of" your opponent, which may seem harmless but always leads to trouble.[5] Nor will Plato tolerate insult and invective in sacred places, or on sacred occasions. This presumably rules out the *aischrologia* traditionally sanctioned by the rites of Demeter and Persephone, or

of Dionysus. (Aristotle, by contrast, in *Politics* 7, leaves a place for the teasing invective or *tōthasmos* of certain cults, though with the proviso that only youths of a certain age will be allowed to see and hear such things; the young must never, under any circumstances, be exposed to indecent and harmful impressions.)[6] And Plato closes another loophole when he says that playfulness in comic performance is no excuse:

No comic poet, *no* iambic or lyric poet is *ever* to be allowed, *either* in statement *or* in comparison, *either* when impelled by serious anger *or* when not so impelled, *ever* to insult or make fun of *any* citizen by name. (935e)

The rule is absolute. It rings out with negatives (*mē, mēte, mēte, mēte, mēte, mēdamōs*). Anyone who offends against it must be expelled from the country that very day. In short: there is absolutely no place for an Aristophanes in the well-ordered state.

And yet Plato leaves a loophole for comedy, whose redeeming educational purpose he described earlier, in *Laws* 7:

One must regard carefully and familiarize oneself with the area of things that pertain to ugly-and-shameful (*aischrōn*) persons and expressions of thought, and that are distorted in the various ways making for comic laughter (*epi ta tou gelōtos kōmōidēmata tetrammenōn*), whether in the language of speech or song, or dancing, or in the various comic representations (*mimēmata kekōmōidēmena*) of all these different things. (816d)

We learn things, Plato argues, from their opposites; so we can hardly learn to live serious and prudent lives if we are ignorant of ridiculous and foolish behavior. But how shall we gain this knowledge? Not, surely, through experience? Rather, we need comic representations to show us what foolish things we might inadvertently say or do. It follows that Plato's citizens will be allowed to watch comedies after all, provided, so to speak, that they take notes for their self-improvement.[7] Old Comedy, of course, with its indecency and invective remains beyond the pale. A later kind of comedy that makes fun of misguided and silly types, not individuals, and does so in a polite manner, is presumably available. But Plato is still wary; he adds further safeguards for the moral welfare of his citizens. The performers will be, not citizens, but foreign slaves hired for the purpose. No free person must ever be caught taking these comic performances seriously, let alone practicing them. Moreover, the performances must always be new and different, so that no single bad example, even in fooling, may impress itself on anyone's mind and character; for the danger is still there, and it is real.

Against this background of Platonic criticism, together with changes in comedy and in social and personal taste (about which I shall say more), we can understand how and why Aristotle redefines comedy as he does while attempting to justify its existence in philosophical terms. As critics have noted, he begins much earlier with a general justification of *mimēsis*.[8] *Mimēsis* is, in the first place, a form of relaxation and play that even serious and educated people need, and are entitled to, from time to time. Secondly, it is a learning activity natural for human beings. Children play instinctively at make-believe, and by imitating adult activities in play, they prepare themselves for adult work and adult living. Moreover, all humans take a certain intellectual pleasure in recognizing and identifying representations of this and that; the learning process that begins in child's play leads to serious and lifelong habits of study; and to the trained contemplative eye, even unpleasant and ugly things will have a certain theoretical beauty. (The scientist today, qua scientist, will enjoy studying the formation of cancerous cells under his microscope.)

In some such way we may be allowed to enjoy, and learn from, the representations of comedy once these have been redefined properly: "What is comic is a mistaking (*hamartēma*) and an ugliness (*aischos*) that does not give pain nor result in destruction, much as the comic mask is ugly and distorted but lacking in pain" (1449a34–37). What is implied, I think, in this very compact definition is, first of all, that comedy does not depict or satirize anything or anybody really bad, even if the villains are shown to fail. Rather, people are depicted who represent less serious character faults and who commit pardonable mistakes of a laughable sort because of those same faults—preoccupation with money, for example, or self-conceit.

Secondly, the laughter of comedy is harmless and not destructive. The point may be that in comedy, unlike tragedy, nobody is represented as undergoing real suffering or death; the blows of comedy are more humiliating (not to say noisy) than painful, and even humiliation is more tolerable in comedy than it is in tragedy, or in real life. But also, the new comedy, unlike the old, will never injure living people through insult or invective. Given these assumptions, we might not have to worry about the *Schadenfreude* of comedy and the inner pain, of envy or malice, that Plato found beneath its surface.

And third: what we laugh at, according to Aristotle, is a special subvariety of ugliness, a disproportion in human behavior that is precisely analogous to the distortion of the comic mask itself that the various characters wear. Once more, what is implied here is the educationally redeeming purpose of comedy, which even Plato admitted in *Laws* 7. When we observe, and laugh at, the various exaggerations and distortions of behavior in which the comic "characters" indulge, we recognize their degree of deviation—and the deviation of others around us, and, finally and most important, our own—from right proportion and from the moral and rational norm. "Would I ever do a thing like that?" we say to ourselves. But if our educated and civilized laughter includes a happy sense of superiority to human folly in its various manifestations, it is at the same time our own potential folly that we laugh at and, in laughing, decisively reject.

And there is a philosophical bonus, for Aristotle, in this comedy about foolish and ridiculous types of people. He says elsewhere that poetry is more philosophical than history because it describes the general truths of our human condition, whereas history tells about particulars, like "Alcibiades."[9] It was an extra count against Old Comedy that it made fun, quite literally, of Alcibiades. By contrast, the "new" comedy of Aristotle's time was more suitable as a learning device. And Aristotle himself, through his analysis of the ethical mean in different areas of life, and the attendant extremes of excess and defect—extremes that his student Theophrastus illustrated in his *Characters*, with comic genius—provided further material and inspiration for the comedy of manners, culminating in Menander.

I shall return shortly to Aristotle's *Nicomachean Ethics*, and especially to the standard of "liberal" humor established and defined there, which sheds further light on the definition of comedy and the comic in the *Poetics*. But first I want to emphasize how much Aristotle's insistence on what comedy *ought* to be, and was justified in being, kept him from having, let alone expressing in the *Poetics*, any adequate idea of what comedy had been or done. As Gerald Else has written,

> For comedy, the controlling factor is Aristotle's aversion to fifth-century Attic comedy, with its political orientation, its vituperativeness, and its foul language. Aristotle did not enjoy, he saw no reason to enjoy, political satire or unbridled attacks on individuals. His disapproval of this "iambic" kind of poetry . . . led him to a tendentious slanting of the definition of comedy (in chapter 5) and a gross distortion of its history (in chapter 4), including total suppression of the two most important persons in the story (according to our lights), Archilochos and Aristophanes.[10]

In Aristotle's defense we might say that the distortion came about, at least in part, through factors beyond his control. As we have it, the *Poetics* consists of lecture notes (and sometimes rather jumbled notes, at that); Aristotle may have deferred extensive discussion of comedy to the (now lost) second book of his *Poetics*; the historical sketch of the development of comedy is tangential to his main argument; and, besides, as Aristotle himself complains, comedy's official recognition and organization at Athens came too late for adequate records of its technical progress to have been maintained. We have no way, that is, of ascertaining who first introduced the masks, prologue, first and second actors, and so forth. And yet we may still complain that Aristotle's account is schematic and tendentious in the extreme. What concerns him is not what happened, but what *should* have happened as comedy moved toward the discovery and fulfillment of its own right nature. On the one hand, it

moved—it had to move—from the old-time exchange of rude, improvised verses to the invention and refinement of a genuine dramatic plot.
On the other hand, its tone and purpose shifted over the years from
irresponsible personal satire, or "iambizing," to the production of civilized entertainment marked by a harmless, good-natured, and even educational kind of humor.

Aristotle's account supplies two pivotal figures for this twofold development. First Homer, whose *Margites* is made an ancestor of comedy,
much as his *Iliad* is of tragedy: "It was he who brought to discovery the
form of comedy, taking not blame (*psogos*) but the comic (*to geloion*),
and making it into dramatic action" (1448b36–38). The *Margites*, a
mock epic regarded today as written long after Homer's time, had as its
hero a stupid fool who did everything wrong. Since presumably (it is
now lost) it combined harmless humor with a parodic plot based on
serious epic, Homer's name and authority seemed available for the double movement, at once artistic and social, that Aristotle wanted to see in
the development of comedy toward its *telos*.

The second pivotal figure is the comic poet Crates: "Of the writers
at Athens, it was Crates who first abandoned the iambic form (*idea*)
and began to make plots and dialogue of a general nature" (1449b7–9).
Here again a twofold progress is implied. Under the influence of Dorian
comedy, and especially of Epicharmus' witty Sicilian plays, Crates reshaped comic improvisations at Athens into a recognizable literary form
comparable to tragedy. At the same time, he moved from personal satire
that named individuals and gave people pain to a more pleasant and
more generally applicable kind of comedy that dealt (or so we might
assume) lightly and humorously with nonpainful "mistakings" in social
life.

Of Crates' actual life and work, we have little idea. A poet of the
generation before Aristophanes, he *may* have developed more sophisticated comic plots, under the influence of tragedy, and he is praised by
Aristophanes for his clever ideas, but it is hard to imagine that he could
have abandoned the indecency and invective of Old Comedy, as well as
its political interest, and still have survived. But since Aristotle ignores,
or means to ignore, Old Comedy, he simply identifies Crates' innovations
with the milder parodic or social comedy that he himself knew and liked
in the mid–fourth century. The result is a successful—and to us appalling—bypass operation around Aristophanes and his contemporaries of
genius, Eupolis, Cratinus, and the rest.

All this differs sadly from Aristotle's treatment of fifth-century
tragedy. Although he ignores Aeschylus, and although his appreciation
of Sophocles' and Euripides' plays differs widely from ours today, he
clearly recognized that with *Oedipus Tyrannus*, or *Iphigenia among the
Taurians*, Greek tragedy reached a height not to be surpassed. He clearly
enjoyed, and was moved by, his reading of Sophocles and Euripides, even

though he was not especially interested in the performance of their plays—let alone nostalgic for the fifth-century theater of Dionysus. He also notes many features of decline in later tragedy, such as the nonfunctional use of the chorus as mere entertainment (this is associated with Agathon), or the unbalanced innovations in musical performance.

By contrast Aristotle must have felt that the classical moment in comedy came in the fourth century, not in the fifth. And despite the redefinition of the aims and methods of comedy that he attributed to Crates, he must sometimes have regarded the old comedy of Eupolis, Cratinus, and Aristophanes, with all its scurrilous jokes and actions, as a kind of atavistic throwback to the pre-Crates period of careless, improvised, inartistic satire. Hence the puzzling omission of Aristophanes, whom he otherwise admired, in his historical sketch. It may be that he atoned for this omission, and this one-sidedness, in his *Second Poetics*, where he gave a fuller account of the aims and methods of comedy, and where he may even have introduced the idea, which some later Hellenistic scholars took up, that Aristophanes was a transitional figure in comedy, representing a happy mean between the excessive, too clownish laughter of the old comedy and the overseriousness of the new.[11] All the same, there must have been much in Aristophanes, as in the old comedy generally, that Aristotle instinctively disliked and rejected and that he could not justify against his master's strictures, or his own principles. The point will become clearer if we consider his discussion of liberal humor in the *Nicomachean Ethics*.

In Book 4 of the *Nicomachean Ethics* Aristotle justifies humorous and playful conversation, but with strong qualifications. Although play was never an end in itself for Aristotle as it was, in a high spiritual sense, for the older Plato, he regarded relaxation from serious occupations as a sometimes necessary thing, to be enjoyed in a humane and sociable manner. But even this seemingly trivial sphere of social interaction has its rules. It matters what sort of jokes you tell, or listen to, and in what way. The same standards of reasonableness and balance apply here as in other spheres, of ambition, agreeableness, getting and spending, and so forth.

Aristotle begins by describing the common excess of humor, or scurrility:

> Now those whose laughter is excessive seem to be scurrilous (*bōmolochoi*) and vulgar people (*phortikoi*). These strive to make people laugh any way they can, rather than to say decent things (*euschēmona*) or to avoid hurting the objects of their laughter. (1128a4–8)

The defect matters less; Aristotle mentions it to keep a humane balance in this area, as in others. "Those who neither say amusing things themselves nor like other people saying them seem to be boorish (*agroikoi*) and harsh." The mean is briefly described, but in rich, suggestive terms: "people who play in tune" (*hoi emmelōs paisdontes*), "people of ready wit" (*eutrapeloi*). The first metaphor is taken from singing tunefully or making harmonious music and is applied to persons who are orderly, harmonious, and fit, and to objects that are "in good taste, well-proportioned, suitable." For humor, the near opposite is the unsuitable joke, the joke in bad taste. The second metaphor implies a graceful flexibility of mind, like that of body. Since most people, Aristotle remarks, tend to fool around and joke beyond the limits of propriety, scurrilous folk are often called *eutrapeloi*; but still, coarse joking should never be equated with what is genuinely witty, clever, elegant, or smart.

In elaborating his definition of the mean, Aristotle suggests a strong split between the two classes of people who joke in different ways:

> Cleverness and tact (*epidexiotēs*) belong properly to the mean condition. And the clever and tactful man will say, and listen to, what is suitable to the reasonable (*epieikēs*) and the free-spirited (*eleutherios*) person; for certain things are proper for such a person to say, and to listen to, by way of sport, and the play of the free-spirited and educated man differs from that of the slavish-spirited and uneducated one. (1128a17–23)

Here then, as elsewhere in the *Nicomachean Ethics*, we find two groups: the civilized few and the philistine many. Refinement in humor both marks the civilized and is measured by their standard. Moreover, the man who offends against the proprieties of humorous discourse becomes degraded, like a free man falling into slavery, while the man who employs "liberal humor" preserves his dignity and maintains his spiritual and social position on the right side of the tracks.

Once again, then, indecency and invective must go. Aristotle illustrates the former by recalling the well-known change from the old comedy to the new: the older comic writers treated obscenity (*aischrologia*) as something funny, while the newer ones prefer suggestiveness (*hyponoia*); this "makes no small difference in the matter of decency." As for invective, Aristotle is still concerned, as he expands his account of right humor, with its power to hurt:

> So then: should the man who tells good jokes be distinguished by his not saying things unfit for the free-spirited person? Or by not giving pain to the hearer? Or (more positively) by his giving pleasure? Or is it the case that this sort of thing resists definition, since people differ in what they enjoy and in what they vehemently dislike?

But the same principle applies, we may say, to the jokes one listens to. For we may believe that a man would like, if he could, to do the things he enjoys hearing about; yet he clearly will not do just anything.

For the personal joke is a kind of insult, and certain kinds of insult are forbidden by legislators; so perhaps they should also ban (though they do not) all personal jokes. Accordingly, the man of elegant wit (*charieis*) and free spirit will act as a law to himself in this matter. (1128a25–32)

The succession of ideas, though somewhat elliptical, points to the need for a double censorship. On the one hand, attacking people gives more pain than pleasure and hence will be forbidden in the well-ordered state. On the other hand, making bad jokes damages the teller and the listener alike. Plato had stressed the psychological damage caused by indulging harmful emotions. What you enjoy listening to, you tend quickly to become. Aristotle merely observes that your character will be judged by the jokes you tell, or listen to, as much as by other forms of social behavior. You wouldn't think (he might say) of committing adultery? Then you'd better not be found enjoying adultery jokes. For your own good as well as that of the polis, you must practice a strong habitual restraint in these things, amounting virtually to self-censorship. And yet, as if to reemphasize the positive enjoyment and value of humor, Aristotle recalls the mean, condemns both extremes, scurrility and boorishness, and reiterates his initial proposition, "It seems that in life relaxation and play are necessary things."

Even without the specific contrast that Aristotle makes here to illustrate his conception of indecency, between the *aischrologia* of the old comedy and the *hyponoia* of the new, we might guess that many of his ideas about comedy, implied but never spelled out in what we have of the *Poetics*, were the same, but writ large, as those about joking in social gatherings. The invective and indecency of the old comedy, he would argue, gave offense to individuals, damaged the social fabric, and degraded the playgoers. The new comedy, by contrast, not only avoids aggressive and obscene humor but makes fun of foolish "characters" and extreme modes of behavior in a way that is both amusing and also positively educational. Perhaps it tends to overseriousness; but if so, this is because it appeals to, and reinforces, the moral standards held by the reasonable and educated man, who has learned, and who continues to learn, to live by the flexibility and good sense of the Aristotelian mean.

The ideal standard of liberal, refined humor going back to Aristotle has had an extraordinary influence on the mainstream of Western classical thought. I give two examples, from Cicero and Castiglione, that suggest why Aristophanes and the laughter of Old Comedy continue to be downplayed by upholders of this ideal, even to the present day.

In Book 2 of *De Oratore* Cicero discusses the orator's use of wit. Although he combines Peripatetic with Stoic ideas and adapts them to Roman needs and circumstances, he adopts the Aristotelian definition of the comic (*turpitudine et deformitate quadam continetur*) with its attendant qualifications and restrictions.[12] (Ugliness and distortion are indicated, but subtly, *non turpiter*.) Wit and humor, says Cicero's spokesman, are invaluable to the orator; they create goodwill in the audience; their cleverness is admired; they discommode one's opponent in several ways; they show the speaker to be *politus, eruditus, urbanus*; and, most of all, difficult and painful matters are dissolved in laughter:

> The special advantage of humor is that, where there was harshness of temper, bitterness, and anger it brings soothing, ease, and relaxation; and it dissolves, through fun and laughter, problems that engender hatred, that are not easily treated in debate. (2.58.236)

Yet wit, as Cicero himself knew through experience, is a dangerous weapon. In telling funny stories, one must avoid indecency; one must not give in to the temptation to become a mime or clown. That would be degrading, and would detract from the self-image that the good orator is careful to project, and on which his authority largely rests. In his verbal wit too he must not make fun of the wrong people—the wicked, or the wretched, or those who are generally loved—or else he will get the reputation of one who indulges scurrilous wit with no regard for person, place, or situation. Thus the orator Crassus was admired for his self-restraint in a defense case that he conducted with pervasive humor, but without verbal jabs at his highly regarded opponent, which would only have rebounded on the speaker:

> For he avoided offense to his opponent's worth and reputation (*dignitas*), and in so doing, he preserved his own. This is something that clever people and "wits" find most difficult, to take account of persons and times, and when remarks come to mind that can be delivered most facetiously, to keep these under control. (2.54.221)

The key word is control (*tenere*); the key concept is appropriateness— when, to whom, in what way, and how far. There are times when irritating opponents or stupid witnesses may be raked over the coals. But one's own *dignitas*, one's image and worth in the world's eyes, is always at stake and is more easily forfeited than many casual "wits" may realize.

Although Castiglione's definition and examples of the comic in Book 2 of his *Courtier* are drawn from Cicero, they are applied once again to the relaxed world of playful social intercourse that Aristotle was describing in Book 4 of his *Nicomachean Ethics*, and they richly, though unintentionally, illustrate Aristotle's view of laughter. Once again, propriety and tact are key requirements:

Many people can be found, though . . . who by talking too much sometimes overstep the bounds, or become foolish and inept, because they have no regard for persons, places, or times, for the demands of seriousness, or for the obligations of modest and decent behavior that they, of all people, ought most especially to maintain. (2.42)

The courtier will not employ verbal wit on just any excuse, or at any passing person or object, but will preserve limit and measure (*termine e misura*) in his biting satirical remarks. And again, in telling funny stories (which is generally a more agreeable business, as well as a safer one), he will be careful not to play the buffoon:

For indeed, it is not suitable that a gentleman should make faces, cry and laugh, or do different voices. We should attempt such imitations only in passing, inconspicuously, and on the sly, always maintaining the dignity of a gentleman, and never descending to dirty words or to gestures and actions that are less than honorable. (2.50)

A certain discreet mimicry is part of telling funny stories; but Castiglione's courtier, like Cicero's orator, must be careful to preserve his dignity: he must never allow himself to become a clown. Dirty words are out (this is a world where "ladies are always present"). Exaggerated grimaces, dishonorable gestures, are out. The undercurrent of humorous suggestion will be quite enough. An agreeable and truly civilized society, like that of Urbino, is characterized at once by the enjoyment of relaxation and humor and by the strong and constant restraints imposed on that humor in the name of *convenienza*, what "fits" the time and place, and what "is fitting" to the discourse and behavior of a gentleman.

Yet this admirable tone has its cost, in the effort (though this may become habit) of tact and self-restraint, and in the loss of those great belly laughs that aggressive and indecent joking so often affords. The broad humor of the stories narrated by Boccaccio, or by Chaucer, has greater healing power and includes a broader range of human nature and experience than the polite anecdotes and witticisms at which the ladies and gentlemen of Urbino permitted themselves to smile.

Polite comedy, the comedy of manners, carries a similar cost. It cannot, evidently, enjoy the cathartic effect that many have attributed to Old Comedy, of releasing strong tensions, pent-up feelings of anger, resentment, or indecency, in the body politic. Although I have suggested that Aristophanes employs this release as a preliminary catharsis, leading to larger comic recognitions for himself and his audience, still aggressiveness and indecency remain the building blocks of Old Comedy and are appropriately remembered as its distinguishing features. Again, in chapter 5, I described the loyalties of Old Comedy to the whole and comic truth, to the democratic diversity of human nature, and to the experience that modern anthropologists call *communitas*. By contrast the new comedy approved by Aristotle could never speak out with full comic *parrhēsia* or *libertas* about the follies and vices of a government or of powerful individuals; it could not speak for the underdog, or for the truth about things that the protester, the satirist, the prophet, the free press dare to voice—or the child who proclaims that the emperor has no clothes. Then too, a more civilized comedy whose chief appeal is to refined and educated people will scarcely give full recognition to the underside of human nature that we all share, let alone to our human diversity. Aristophanes wrote for an audience that was united by festive celebration and *communitas* transcending all differences of status or education. The Old Comedy of Dionysus is never in earnest, and hence can touch on the most serious and painful issues of private and public life. The comedy of manners perfected by Menander is basically earnest, sentimental, and moralizing—and never really goes to the roots of things. Its kitchen humor amuses the groundlings; its exaggerated "characters" reinforce the ethical norm. It assumes, and builds on, a split between humor and seriousness, between higher and lower elements in human nature, and between the more refined and intelligent members of the audience, for whom Menander ultimately writes, and the numerous but insignificant remainder.

It may be that if Aristotle developed his catharsis theory to its logical end, it came to follow this split in the audience.[13] As I suggested earlier, his purgation theory of tragedy and comedy was probably a first line of defense against Plato's attack on the theater for arousing and fostering harmful emotions. In Aristotle's opinion, the spectator's vicarious experience of the piteous and fearful events of tragedy, or of the laughable doings of comedy, would provide a harmless airing of otherwise dangerously pent-up emotions: of pity and fear, in the one instance; of malicious feelings stemming from anger, hostility, or resentment, or more likely, of the desire to say ridiculous things, and perform ridiculous (and indecent) actions, in the other. As a result the spectator would experience a pleasurable feeling of relief, and of restored emotional equilibrium. This emotional "purgation," which retains dim overtones of religious "purification" in the theater, would be somewhat analogous to the Corybantic treatment of hysteria through musical excitation and release, a form of homeopathic psychotherapy that Aristotle compared in turn to the physical use of purges to restore a physiological balance in the body.

Though brilliantly suggestive (and especially for followers of Freud), the double comparison has not seemed an altogether happy one. And Aristotle himself, under renewed attack from his teacher, may have retreated to a second line of defense, more evidently suggested by the *Poetics* as we have it, such that catharsis becomes something more like "clarification" of emotional situations, with emphasis on the ethical and rational lessons to be learned, and on the structuring techniques of tragedy—and on the somewhat different artistic techniques of comedy—by which the right emotional effect is produced and the right and appropriate kind of pleasure given.

Yet however much Aristotle refined his theory, the idea of emotional purgation is valuable, and it need not be lost. Perhaps the chief problem of later theorists consists in the difficulty of applying an extreme instance of psychotherapy, in the treatment of hysterics, to the ordinary experience of the tragic or comic theater. But Aristotle might have gone on to suggest that the nature and effect of catharsis would accord with the differing endowments, both moral and intellectual, of a divided audience. The ordinary, emotionally less balanced people watching *Oedipus* would experience a stronger release of pity and fear. The more educated, more balanced spectators would enjoy a quieter aesthetic and rational pleasure at the "clarification" afforded by the playwright's artistry and understanding. And so with comedy: most people would continue to laugh at the more farcical scenes, and at the words and actions of the more obviously ridiculous characters (though these would be more restrained in the new comedy than they were in the old); but the more refined, better educated people would smile with heightened understanding of—and superiority to—the ordinary mistakes and follies of human nature, including their own. If, by this change in comedy, the wilder and more "purgative" laughter was lost, that was part of the price exacted by the sometimes relentless progress of civilization.

Most later Greek and Roman theory of the comic and of the development of comedy follows closely after Aristotle and probably after his student Theophrastus, who wrote on both subjects.[14] Theophrastus emphasized the portrayal of character types in comedy, with their appropriate styles of speech (*ēthikē lexis*); his theory was influenced by the newer, fourth-century comedy of manners, and it helped in turn to bring that comedy to its perfection in Menander. Not surprisingly, in the critical discussions that followed, over the centuries, about the relative merits of Aristophanes and Menander or about their usefulness to the aspiring orator, Menander almost inevitably won both by the aesthetic criteria and by the ethical.[15] His various yet well-blended, understated style, his plots of general social significance, his use of character depiction and character contrast, his restrained, understated wit—all this was exactly what Aristotle wanted. If there had been no Menander for the Peripatetic theorists and their successors, he would have had to be invented.

This does not mean that Aristophanes and Old Comedy were never valued by the critics. Even Aristotle had high praise, scattered through-out his surviving works, for Aristophanes' creative play with words, his bold and striking metaphors, and his many uses of surprise; here we may trace the beginnings of an "incongruity theory" of the comic, which has rivaled the "scorn (or superiority) theory" to the present day.[16] And so, through later critical discussions, there was usually a minority voice praising the force, wit, and stylistic grace or charm (*charis, venustas*) of Aristophanes. Teachers of rhetoric praised his many flashes of wit and his usefulness as a model of the lofty style in oratory—although Menan-der was more apt for the middle or the plain style, or a pleasant blend of all three. Here is Quintilian's generous praise:

> The old comedy is almost unique in maintaining that pristine charm of the Attic tongue. It is most free-spoken, notable in the chastisement of vices, yet possesses great strength and effectiveness in its other aspects as well. For it is lofty, refined, and attractive. I can think of no other genre (after Homer, that is) more like to oratory or better suited to the production of orators. Among its many authors, Aristophanes, Eupolis, and Cratinus are outstand-ing. (10.1.65)

Quintilian praises the purity of Attic style to be found in the Old Comedy (it was much admired later by Atticists, both Greek and Ro-man), its eloquence in attacking vice, its forcefulness throughout, its loftiness of style (*grandis*), refinement of wit (*elegans*), and overall charm (*venusta*). Lovers of Old Comedy will be disappointed to find that Quin-tilian gives equally high praise to Menander, who he says supplies all the qualities needed in an orator; but at least there are good stylistic reasons for reading Aristophanes too.

Not all later critics took a monolithic view of Old Comedy. There was what might be called the "Three Bears" variant, according to which Cratinus was strong but too bitter (*pikros*) in his attacks, Eupolis good at plot construction but too mild, but Aristophanes was just right, combin-ing the vehemence of the one and the prevalent charm of the other. Such distinctions, though somewhat arbitrary, may have been variants of a more significant critical tradition going back to Aristotle himself, ac-cording to which Aristophanes would represent a mean between excess and deficiency in "the ridiculous," and Eupolis and the later Aristoph-anes would mark a transition from the older comedy to what was, for Aristotle, the new.[17] This minority tradition was more just to Aristoph-anes, and historically more accurate, than the more usual contrast with Menander that forced Eupolis, Cratinus, and Aristophanes together into the same unequivocal mold of "old comedy," distinguished mainly from new by its indecency and invective; and together with the appreciation (also going back to Aristotle) of stylistic grace notes in Aristophanes' work, it helped to justify his continuing existence in the orator's study and in the schoolroom.

Yet all this appreciation was outweighed by Aristophanes' failure to satisfy his critics' ethical expectations. Although the aggressiveness of comic invective (*loidoria*) might find some partial justification in the power with which it scourges vice, this advantage seemed nullified by the bitterness of Old Comedy, the pain it inflicts, and the sheer lack of discrimination with which it attacks people. (It is all very well, says the conservative Cicero, to go after vicious rabble-rousers like Cleon; but to attack Pericles—!)[18] This view was reinforced by the experience of Roman comedy and satire, and by Peripatetic theories of the history of comedy that traced it from primitive, almost childish play, through a stage of exaggerated license and defamation, to the point of forced submission to controlling laws that were socially and aesthetically advantageous.[19] People came, in time, to write "good" comedies—not like Aristophanes!

The best surviving example of the prejudice of the "gentleman and scholar" against Aristophanes and Old Comedy is furnished by Plutarch, in a formal comparison of Aristophanes and Menander, of which an epitome survives. " 'Coarseness,' he says, 'in words, vulgarity (*to phortikon*) and ribaldry are present in Aristophanes, but not at all in Menander; obviously, for the uneducated, ordinary person is captivated by what the former says, but the educated man will be displeased.' "[20] Earlier Plutarch has said that Aristophanes' puns are just plain silly. He contrasts such frivolities with Menander's evenness of style, which was nonetheless varied, flexible, and well adapted to the portrayal of different ages and character types. Actually, the literary appreciation of Menander is just, and we can see how critics reared on Menander might fail to enjoy or indeed to understand Aristophanes, much as the connoisseur of Beaujolais might listen incredulously to the praises of good Scotch whisky. (Something of the same prejudice, and the same incomprehension, is found in criticism of the Roman comic playwrights Caecilius and Plautus.)[21] Notice also that Plutarch divides the world into two groups. There are the educated people, whose standards are intelligent, sensitive, and well informed; and there are all the others (Plato and Aristotle would agree), whose judgment hardly counts.

Plutarch's aesthetic judgments in his comparison are more "scientific," his moral judgments more personal and more passionate. These end with a twofold condemnation of Aristophanes (in contrast with Menander's easy and pleasant wit):

> But the witticisms of Aristophanes are bitter and rough and possess a sharpness which wounds and bites. And I do not know wherein his vaunted cleverness resides, whether in his words or his charac-

ters. Certainly even whatever he imitates he makes worse; for with him roguishness is not urbane but malicious, rusticity not simple but silly, facetiousness not playful but ridiculous, and love not joyous but licentious. For the fellow seems to have written his poetry, not for any decent person, but the indecent and wanton lines for the licentious, the slanderous and bitter passages for the envious and malicious.

By this view Aristophanes is neither subtle nor witty. His characters are overdone, to the point of caricature. His jokes are pointless and absurd. What matters more is that they displease the moderate (*metrios*), sensible, educated person; their appeal is rather to licentious and malicious types. As Plutarch says, only the prospect of a play by Menander makes it "truly worthwhile for an educated man to go to the theater." Presumably such a person will enjoy mental relaxation while also allowing his educated habits and civilized perceptions to be reinforced. But Menander is also, Plutarch argues, the poet to recite at a civilized dinner party (where of course the rabble will not be present); and he is the poet for philosophers and scholars (*philologoi*) to read when their minds are weary with "concentrated and intense studies" and need refreshment.

And here is the problem in a nutshell. Aristophanes has passed into the guardianship of the *philologoi*, the more so because, as Plutarch complains elsewhere, "the old comedy isn't fitted for entertainment at symposia, since one needs a philologist to explain all the topical and personal references."[22] That is one obvious kind of incomprehension. As I said earlier, we owe an enormous debt to the editors and commentators whose "concentrated and intense studies" throughout the centuries have made it possible for us to read Aristophanes today and (for the most part) to understand the sense of what he is saying. Yet there remains another, even larger kind of incomprehension to which the scholar in his or her study—in the *phrontisterion*—is especially prone. For the scholar is too much cut off: from the living theater; from living comedy; from the broad laughter of ordinary people (of whom he or she is ultimately one); and worst of all, from the festive experience of life, and the celebratory, not cerebral, perspective from which Aristophanes and the Old Comedy are best enjoyed and understood. Even when Aristophanes is praised by the scholars and critics, as for his stylistic graces, he is somehow left out in the cold. *Laudatur et alget.* So it is all rather like Humpty Dumpty: once Old Comedy fell, and once the old festive experience, context, and perspective were lost, not all the king's editors, commentators, and critics, however great their merit, could put Aristophanes' laughter together again.

A somewhat extended comparison, with the fortunes of Rabelais, will suggest what power time and changing standards exercise over the enjoyment and understanding of comic writers. In his own time, in mid–sixteenth-century France, Rabelais's works were enjoyed by tens of thousands of general readers. Only a few bigots and "agelasts" rejected them as "prandial libertinism," or as materialistic or atheistic tracts. By the later seventeenth century, however, Rabelais's novel had become hopelessly obscure to the many, and a source of scandal, distaste, and sheer incomprehension to the more educated few.[23] La Bruyère writes, in 1690:

> There is simply no excuse for the filth that Marot and Rabelais threw around in their writings. Both had the genius, and the talent, to manage without it, even allowing for readers who would rather laugh at what they read than admire the author. Rabelais, above all, is *incomprehensible* [italics mine]; whatever else one might say of his book, it remains *inexplicable*, an enigma; it is a chimera, with the face of a beautiful woman and with feet or the tail of a serpent or some other still more misshapen creature—a monstrous jumble of refined spirit and intelligence together with dirt and depravity. When he is bad, he goes beyond the worst; his attraction is for the rabble. Where he is good, he reaches heights of excellence and refinement—a dish for the most delicate palate.[24]

If the "dirt" in Rabelais is inexcusable, the combination of beauty and ugliness in his novel passes all understanding. What one laughs at, for La Bruyère, is very different from what one "admires," just as the taste of refined and polite people is far removed from the casual likes or dislikes of the *canaille*. Rabelais is hopelessly Rabble-aisian.

So too, in the eighteenth century, Voltaire shows little or no appreciation of Rabelais, whom he compares unfavorably to Swift:

> In his extravagant and *unintelligible* book [italics mine], Rabelais has poured out vastness of mirth and even greater vastness of irrelevance; he has lavished erudition, filth, and sheer boredom on the book. For a good two-page story, you must suffer through volumes of stupidity. Only a few people of most peculiar taste pride themselves on their understanding and appreciation of the entire work; the rest of the nation laughs at Rabelais's jokes—and despises the book. People look to him as the chief of clowns and jesters; they are irritated to find that a man who had such great wit employed it so wretchedly: in short, we are speaking of a drunken philosopher who never wrote a word except when he was drunk.[25]

To Voltaire, the book is not just dirty; it is stupid and boring. Nobody wants to read it, nobody can make any sense of it, except for a few perverse Rabelais specialists. It was all a drunken bit of idiocy, really—an expense of spirit, or wit (which the Enlightenment could have put to better use) in a waste of nonsense.

In our own time, many people are reading Rabelais with new sympathy and appreciation. One reason is surely that in Western countries art and literature have become emancipated from the critical standards of neoclassicism and the Enlightenment. Another is that the wildest, most Dionysian comedy seems a modest response to the near chaos in which we live. But also, since we are in transition from one world to another—from books to computers, from industrial production to electronic transactions, from explorations of earth to ventures into space—we may come with renewed appreciation to the study of those writers and thinkers like Rabelais who, as someone once said, "had one foot in the Middle Ages and with the other saluted the rising sun of the Renaissance."

Rabelais is generally described at universities as a Renaissance humanist. Evidently he was excited by the new learning, by the rediscovery of the classics, by the new ideals of education. His interests and knowledge were vast. His works show an encyclopedic knowledge of law, medicine, architecture, military science, navigation, cooking, and fashions in games and dress. Above all, he was excited by the power and resources of language and the different and conflicting ways in which it can work, or play. In certain passages, such as Gargantua's letter to Pantagruel, or the description of Gargantua's reformed education, or of the antimonastic, ultracivilized Abbaye de Thélème, the liberal and optimistic ideals of the Renaissance emerge as beautifully as anywhere in the more serious writings of Erasmus or Montaigne or Castiglione (although we also sense the increasing pressures and disappointments in the face of which this early optimism seems to fade away). But all this, admirable though it is, remains only half of the story: for Rabelais's novel is equally rooted in the peasant culture and the festive customs and imagination of the Middle Ages. No one has caught the spirit of this other side of Rabelais better or more sympathetically than the Russian critic Mikhail Bakhtin. He shows how all the obscenity, the cursing and abuse, the thrashing and killing, the blasphemy and even the travesty of sacred things has a traditional, sanctioned place in festive liberties, in the free language of the marketplace, and above all, in the privileged, topsy-turvy world of carnival. More important, he reminds us time and again that all this "dirt" is not just negative, not just used satirically, but has its positive side always in the celebration of the body, of human life, and of the spirit of continuing regeneration of the world through time. "The negative derisive element was deeply immersed in the triumphant theme of bodily regeneration and renewal."[26] It is only when they are torn away from this two-sided festive context that Rabelais's images seem merely crude and dirty. So far,

Bakhtin seems absolutely right; I only miss, in his account of carnival, an acknowledgment of how all these festive practices were not just protected, but also strengthened and renewed in meaning by the official rites of the Catholic Church.

But what could the readers of a later, less colorful world make of all this? And what, more particularly, could the scholars do? They did what they could despite their disapproval: explained a great number of Rabelais's references to people, places, and things. But all too often they reduced large and ambiguous comic meanings to the kind of limited satire that is more easily understood. Explanations of the Picrocholine War in Book 1 are a case in point. On one level, we know (and here scholarship has been very helpful indeed) that the war takes place in Rabelais's own homeland of Chinon and can be read as an amusing allegory of local events in which Rabelais's father, the lawyer, was involved. On a second level, it suggests the wise and humane policies of Francis I and his advisers when faced with the expansionist ambitions and greed of Charles V. But on a third, still more universal level, Rabelais's comedy goes far beyond allegory, and beyond political commentary and satire. It celebrates the victory of all that is human and down to earth—of good eating and drinking, the love of life, and the enjoyment of peace—over those people, and those attitudes, that are hostile to peace and sanity and good living. The cakes whose refusal is a cause of war, the vineyards in danger of being ruined, belong to the feast, and the revelry, that life is (in the comic view) finally about.

Such larger comic meanings, which are reflected in the friendship of Pantagruel for Panurge, or again in the image of the Silenus box with its grotesque exterior and its inner treasure (an image that should not be mistaken for simple humanist allegory), are being rediscovered today and newly appreciated. In the words of Thomas Greene:

> A kind of fruitful perversity lies in fact at the basis of his art. The comic sense of Rabelais, unlike Molière's, unlike most comic writers', does not repose on a judicious common sense, observing from the solid center of experience the eccentricities of deviation. He does not command the assurance of the moderate sage, fortified by rational wisdom and an authorized ethic. He writes rather from the fringe of nonsense. He knew the secret folly at the heart of the universe, the wild uncertainty, the abyss of lunacy that underlies our rational constructions. He embraces that lunacy, both within and without us, and builds his comedy upon it. Beyond the immediate object of his laughter, in any given episode, lies that night of hilarious mystery which encloses his world. The greatest of his comic characters, Panurge, is precisely the incarnation of the universal perversity in things. Rabelais is so powerful and so disturbing a comic writer because he portrays human life as radically

irrational, vitally unhinged, sublimely grotesque. He knows that to be alive is to be paradoxical and finally incomprehensible. Thus his moral instinct, which is strong and healthy, recognizes the factitious element in the authorized morality based only on reason, and reaches for an unauthorized alternative.

But balancing the intuition of comic perversity there is an opposing intuition of moral and religious seriousness. The conflict of these intuitions never finds, fortunately, an explicit resolution, but it leads to a running dialogue of distinct narrative voices a little below the surface of the fiction. Mingled with the demonic voice, the voice of comic darkness and grotesquerie, is an angelic voice, gentle, grave, affirming a radiant and serene wisdom.[27]

I shall not press the parallel with Aristophanes, which is best left to the reader's imagination and further study. I wanted rather to suggest that the reasons why Aristophanes became incomprehensible to educated readers and critics ("the assurance of the moderate sage, fortified by rational wisdom and an authorized ethic") look very much like the reasons why Rabelais did, and that the resulting distortions in critical theory and practice have been very similar. I suggest, further, that it was only in our century, a time of unusual "comic sense," as of unusual vulnerability to chaos, that Aristophanes, together with Rabelais, could be rediscovered in his whole and joyful achievement, and generously admired.

A further, ironic connection exists between Rabelais's fate and that of Aristophanes. As Bakhtin shows, many episodes in Rabelais's novel are like comic performances, celebrating the victory of youth over age, of the new dispensation (in religion, politics, education, social life) over the old. Yet the forward movement, the Renaissance, that Rabelais celebrates would eventually sweep away the licensed festivities, and the festive meanings, of the Middle Ages on which his laughter was formed; it would usher in the ages of Reformation, scientific rationalism, neoclassicism, and the Enlightenment—to which Rabelais's novel would appear grotesque, disorderly, and incomprehensible. If the comic imagination accepts and celebrates the passing of time, that does not mean that time, in its ruthless flight, will return the compliment.

And so with Aristophanes: what we call his Old Comedy plays dangerously on the border of two worlds, the older world of folklore and rural festival and what might be called the Middle Ages of ancient Greece, and the newer world of the fifth-century Athenian Renaissance, with its encyclopedic learning, its wandering sophists (they might be called *umanistai*), and its new historical and artistic self-consciousness. Aristophanic comedy derives much of its brilliance and fun from the clash of cultures. It is really Old-and-New Comedy. But even as it celebrates time and change, it is subject to their ravages, just as the playwright's own body and mind are subject to aging and death. His comedies played their part in hastening the death of Periclean Athens and the birth of the fourth-century age of reason, in which already Old Comedy would no longer be performed, or enjoyed, or understood. I suspect that Aristophanes' later comedy was shadowed by an intense awareness of change and death, much as Rabelais's later books are shadowed, or Shakespeare's later plays, or Cervantes's novel. But although my last chapter must accordingly be shadowed by a sympathetic sense of time, loss, and death in the history of comedy, we must end by admiring the greathearted laughter of Old Comedy in the face of time, loss, and death, even including its own.

33 *Aristophanes' Old-and-New Comedy:* Clouds

DESPITE the minority view going back to Aristotle himself, according to which Aristophanes' comedy represented a mean between too great buffoonery and too great seriousness, Aristophanes seems increasingly to have been regarded as the champion of the old comedy as against the new, and hence as the prototype of the indecency and invective that became, in the literary handbooks, its distinguishing features. And yet if we look closely at Aristophanes' plays, we find that in his view "old comedy" was what his precursors had performed, and what his rivals, had they known better, should long since have outgrown. In the objective, long-range view we would place him in the sophisticated third generation of comic playwrights at Athens, the literary stratum that I have called Late Old Comedy III; so it would be accurate to speak of even his earliest extant plays, the *Acharnians* and *Knights*, as "Old-and-New Comedy." But it was the *Clouds* of 423, with its third prize, that seems to have made Aristophanes himself realize just how much his comedy fell between old and new, and how far Old Comedy had already traveled along the road of time.

One year earlier, in the parabasis of the *Knights*, Aristophanes had presented himself as a confident young writer, distanced by time and change from the *archaioi* (oldsters) who wrote before him. Here, in his first extant literary manifesto, he describes the war of time against the comic spirit. It is hard, he says, to keep pleasing the public. Although Magnes is still remembered for his colorful and funny plays, he was rejected towards the end after he lost his power of joking. Old Cratinus, once renowned for his comic energy and his catchy lyrics, has by now, as everyone knows, turned doddering and senile. And even Crates, whose dramatic economy and sophisticated conceptions (*asteiotatas epinoias*, "most urbane" inventions as against vulgar country stuff) were remarkable—well, Crates just hung in there, sometimes succeeding, sometimes not. Aristophanes relates this history partly to advertise himself (for he embodies all the aforementioned virtues), partly to justify his reluctance to direct his own plays before learning the theatrical ropes. But we may believe him when he says that the risk and challenge are great. In the first place, the comic poet must be inventive, must come up with new ideas, plots, choruses, lyrics, and dialogue, or else he will be accused of serving up the same old tired stuff, or of plagiarism, or else (if he has an occasional idea) of relying on someone else's brainpower. Such accusations were common, and they were expected. Aristophanes directs them against his rivals, who seem to have returned them in force. But in addition, however remarkable the poet's originality, he must maintain a consistently high level of joking, of fun, of sheer entertainment. In short, he must keep them laughing. As Aristophanes says, and discovered through experience, to succeed over the course of time is devilishly hard.

How well *did* Aristophanes succeed? In one sense, beyond all expectation: for eleven of his comedies have survived, to be read, translated, and sometimes performed after twenty-four hundred years, when those of his precursors and rivals have quite disappeared except for a few bushels of fragments. Unfortunately this undreamed-of success makes comparison impossible; we would give much for Cratinus' *Ploutoi*, or Eupolis' complete *Demes*, or something earlier by Magnes and Crates. In their absence we can only compare Aristophanes with Aristophanes; but it is very misleading to take his *Acharnians* as the oldest of Old Comedies, merely because it is our earliest extant play, and to go on from there.

Furthermore, we need to ask: how representative of Aristophanes' work, and how indicative of his artistic progress, are these eleven plays? A tentative grouping, with a few statistics, shows where we are on strong ground and where on weak.[28]

1. From the early period, 427–421, we have five plays out of ten, a five-year sequence that permits us to study Aristophanes most closely and follow his development as an artist. Within this period, the *Acharnians* (425) and *Knights* (424) seem most traditional; the *Clouds* (423) is an innovative comedy of ideas, on a more ambitious level (as Aristophanes himself argues); the *Wasps* (422) is also ambitious, but may have integrated new ideas even more successfully into the old farce and slapstick; the *Peace* (421) is a more relaxed, less ambitious play, reverting cheerfully and easily to an older style, more like the *Acharnians*.

2. From the middle period, 420–410, we have three plays out of some thirteen or fifteen: *Birds* (414), *Lysistrata* (411), and *Thesmophoriazusae* (411).

3. From the late period, 409–400, out of ten or twelve plays, we have only one, the *Frogs* (405).[29]

4. From the very late period, 399–?385, we have two plays out of six: the *Ecclesiazusae* (392 or 391), usually regarded as a transitional play between Old and Middle Comedy, and the *Plutus* (388), usually classified as Middle Comedy, on the way to New.

Certainly eleven Aristophanic comedies out of forty-one is a better proportion than seven Sophoclean tragedies out of ninety-two. Comparing Aristophanes to Aristophanes, Gelzer, Landfester, and Händel have been able to analyze formal components of his plays such as the epirrhematic agon, the prologue and exodos, and the parabasis, together with techniques of suspense and surprise, and to show Aristophanes' increasing mastery of these traditional forms and techniques as well as his increasing freedom of innovation from the early to the middle plays. What is harder to measure is the degree of advance marked by our two earliest plays. I believe, but cannot prove, that the travesties of the *Acharnians*, with their interplay of art and politics in image, metaphor, and stage action, were already highly sophisticated for Aristophanes' time, and that both the *Acharnians* and the *Knights* are more witty and thoughtful, and come closer to comedy of ideas, than has generally been recognized. But the absence of preceding and competing plays leaves us in the dark.

Similarly it is hard to say how far Aristophanes succeeded in his own time, and for what reasons—which may be different from succeeding in his own terms, or in ours. Are the best plays always the most widely appreciated? Byzantine editors and schoolmasters evidently preferred their trilogy of *Plutus*, *Clouds*, and *Frogs*, in that order; presumably, these plays seemed most accessible to literal interpretation, rhetorical study, and moral understanding. In our own time the *Lysistrata* is most often enjoyed and performed (though often with heavy-handed indecency), followed by the *Birds*, *Clouds*, and *Frogs*. I would say, if pressed, that the *Birds* is Aristophanes' greatest (extant) play, followed by the *Wasps*, *Clouds*, *Frogs*, and perhaps *Lysistrata*. But the votes of fifth-century judges, as best we know, give a different picture.

Aristophanes may have been most successful at the very beginning. After his *Banqueters* received second prize at the Lenaea, and his *Babylonians* first prize at the City Dionysia, both the *Acharnians* (thanks still to the director Callistratus) and the *Knights* received first prize at the Lenaea. Then the *Clouds*—surely a better play—received only third prize at the Dionysia. The *Wasps* and the *Peace*, more successful, still received only second prize (at the Lenaea and Dionysia, respectively). Overall, this is an impressive record for the early period; the more so because to be selected for performance was already an accomplishment. In the middle period the *Birds*—surely one of the greatest comedies of all time—received second prize at the Dionysia. In the third period, the *Frogs* received first prize at the Lenaea, thanks largely (it is said) to the patriotic sentiments expressed in its parabasis, and may have been awarded the further, very unusual honor of a second performance. All of which makes us ask: what do we mean by success? And what did Aristophanes mean? And what relation had this to the applause of his audience and the votes cast by the judges, mindful of that applause?

Aristophanes wrote for a mass Athenian audience, not for an intelligentsia, and certainly not for a dimly viewed posterity like our unimaginable selves. And he meant to keep that mass audience with him, however original and complex his new comedy of ideas might be. The audience of the *Acharnians*, sitting in the theater, needed to recognize and laugh at their own gullibility as assemblygoers and victims of rhetorical devices and disguises; the audience of the *Knights*, despite all ambiguities, were expected to show more intelligence than their stupid and gullible alter ego, the Demos or Sovereign People, who is preyed upon by demagogic flattery, deceit, and slander. What Aristophanes requires, and expects, is a shared imaginative understanding between himself and the audience, on which the shared victory for which his chorus prays can be constructed (581–94):

> Pallas, guardian of cities,
> who watch over our land, most sacred
> and most overcoming in war,
>   poets, and power:
> come to us now, and bring
> Victory, our co-worker in combat,
> friend to the chorus' song and dance,
> friend to our team, against all opponents.
> Come, then, reveal yourself to us:
> if ever you granted victory
>   to all these people here,
> then do, by all means, grant it now.

As knights, the chorus ask for victory against their enemy, the Paphlagonian (Cleon), in the internal struggle of Athens; as a comic chorus, they request victory for the play that they are performing; and both go closely with the external victory that Athena will grant to "these people here" (the Athenians in the theater) against their external enemies. The equation is impertinent, and probably traditional. In the *Acharnians* Aristophanes had already argued that Poet Power was a major national resource, comparable to control of the seas. A vote for Aristophanes—the "Lenaietan surge of applause" requested shortly before—will not only recognize true merit; it will also manifest that clear-sighted judgment that must carry Athens to victory over inner divisiveness and outer peril.

Aristophanes succeeded with the *Knights*, as with the *Acharnians*; the surge of applause came, and the first prize at the Lenaea. He was emboldened to write the more ambitious *Clouds* for the City Dionysia of

423. In it he made the "clouds" complain, in the parabasis, that the Athenians had chosen the "godforsaken tanner, the Paphlagonian" as general (for 423/22), despite the terrible weather portents, and as Aristophanes implies, despite everything he had shown them in the *Knights*. This is already a rueful admission that their shared victory, and perhaps the understanding behind it, remained incomplete; but Aristophanes still assumed, on the basis of earlier experience, that the audience would stay with him, getting his jokes and appreciating his new, very ambitious comedy of ideas. When they let him down, giving first and second prize to his (as he later says) undeserving rivals, it was a signal defeat—and a turning point, I think, in the self-awareness of Athenian comedy.

The question whether the *Clouds* succeeded or failed, and why, has been somewhat obscured by the question whether it succeeds or fails today; and this in turn has been clouded by two prejudicial considerations: the "Socrates problem" and the "revision problem."[30] Because, in the first place, Socrates has become a patron saint of philosophers and intellectuals, many classical scholars and teachers have, understandably, not much enjoyed the character called "Socrates," an archvillain and imposter, a practitioner of scientific humbug, and the enemy of religion, morality, and good old-fashioned education generally. They have also seen this caricature as leading to Socrates' trial and execution in 399 B.C. The formal charges against Socrates were that he corrupted the youth and did not believe in, or cultivate, the city's gods; in Plato's *Apology*, Socrates is less concerned with these overt charges, which (he argues) are easily refuted, than with the older and vaguer prejudices in people's minds, such as that Socrates pries into things in the heavens and under the earth, or makes the worse case into the stronger—slanders whose source cannot be identified except for "a certain comic poet." The reference is evidently to the *Clouds*. What Socrates here implies is that the slanders are ridiculous, once they are examined; but the nagging suspicion remains that Aristophanes, by poisoning men's minds against Socrates, contributed to his condemnation. Whatever the truth may have been—and Plato himself seems not to have blamed Aristophanes, but to have seen him as a generous and funny opponent of Socrates, a rival cathartist whose society Socrates might well have enjoyed[31]—it remains difficult, and often impossible, for intellectuals to appreciate the *Clouds* today when it makes fun of Socrates, much as it is difficult or impossible for twentieth-century Jews to appreciate Shakespeare's *Merchant of Venice* when it makes fun of Shylock. Yet it can be argued that Shakespeare was not anti-Semitic; that he holds little brief for the so-called Christians who bait Shylock, or for their crass, shallow, materialistic Venice; that Shylock, a major comic antagonist, rises nearly to the interest and sympathy of a tragic character (especially toward the end); and that the play as a whole is beautiful, truthful, and healing. If the Holocaust has made it generally unplayable and unenjoyable, then that is one more example of damage done by Hitler. Similarly with the *Clouds*: its brilliant fun-making of 423 has been shadowed forever by the trial and execution of 399, when the mood of Athens was dangerous—and when Aristophanes might well not have written his play. The irony remains, that the same play that an Athenian audience appears to have found too talky and intellectual, even too "Socratic" in subject matter and style, should so generally be regarded as anti-intellectual by the critics and teachers into whose judgment it has passed today.

Furthermore, appreciation of the *Clouds* is shadowed, in the scholarly world at least, by the question of revision. We know, on good evidence, that Aristophanes wrote a second version of the *Clouds*, presumably toward a performance that was not granted. What we have today is evidently this second *Clouds*. Just how much of the play was revised is subject to dispute; but the scholarly controversy, however uncertain its details, has seriously inhibited the enjoyment of the existing play and has provided an occasional means of denigration to critics who already disliked the *Clouds* instinctively—the "Socratic" prejudice again.

For my part, I admire the *Clouds* passionately. My first impulse, from which the present book began, was to defend the play against its detractors and to explain to the world how it was a great, funny, and very beautiful comedy. But since my plans, like those of Strepsiades, have gone somewhat astray, and since, for reasons of space, I have confined myself in this first volume to giving a general account of Aristophanes' comedy, and to establishing a perspective within which his plays generally, and the *Clouds* in particular, may be understood and enjoyed more fully, I wish merely to state, in summary outline, three propositions about the *Clouds* that I shall argue at length in the sequel:

(1) The *Clouds* is high comedy. It is more than satire, more than merely negative criticism of Socrates, or the sophists, or the new education. From what might have been mere satire, it grows into an imaginative confrontation of cultural change itself, the pain and confusion of transition from the old education to the new. Aristophanes enjoys and recognizes, without ultimately accepting them, the new techniques of argument and analysis. He is not anti-intellectual; he perceives the inadequacies of the old as well as the losses of wholeness and happiness incurred by the new; Dionysus is not, and cannot be, simply on the side of the old. The play inspires confidence about the power of the human mind, and the human spirit, to make its way through the confusion of generational conflict and cultural change. The pain of transition—which outside the theater contributed to the wish to make Socrates a scapegoat—is overcome hopefully by the triumphant laughter of comedy.

(2) The *Clouds* is a brilliant and successful comedy of ideas. It pours the new wine of later fifth-century conceptions, arguments, and concerns into the Old Comic wineskins without bursting them—much as Euripides, by whom Aristophanes was much influenced, integrated modern

ideas and issues into the mythic and symbolic framework of his trage-dies, subordinating thought to action, *dianoia* to *praxis*. The resilient Strepsiades, a different kind of hero but (like Monsieur Jourdain after him) a memorable one; his confrontations with Socrates, that magnifi-cent antagonist and imposter, which he wins through sheer stupidity and exuberance even more than loses; the beautiful songs (and dances) of the chorus of playful, teasing clouds, widely suggestive of the power of delu-sion and self-delusion in human life, and of the shifting mysteries of human and divine knowledge and existence; the development of a care-fully laid, quasi-Euripidean plot of escalation and reversal, through a series of confrontations including two brilliant, full-length agons—all this makes for superb comedy. We may believe Aristophanes when he swears (by Dionysus!) that this was his best play to date, and cost him the most work. It may (we do not know) have been a successful mutation in the development of Old Comedy. By a trick of fortune, at least, it is our first extant comedy of ideas.

(3) The play that we have is mostly identical with the play performed in 423 B.C. Obviously the first part of the parabasis has been rewritten as a criticism of the audience who, through the judges, gave the play third prize; I shall come to this shortly. Topical references date this revision to 419 or 418. Some slight changes, albeit big ones to the scholar's micro-scopic vision, have been made around the first agon, the contest between Right and Wrong: there is some change of speakers, and some removal of choral lyric and recitative (were the topical references outdated?) that was not replaced. Some more drastic change *may* have been made in the exodos, where Strepsiades burns down the *phrontisterion*, or "concen-tration camp," of Socrates; it is possible that Aristophanes substituted a more clear-cut, farcical, and violent ending for some less interesting, perhaps more ambiguous one. We cannot know; but the present ending is extremely well integrated into the play, both in diction and in its reversal plot, and it is hard, perhaps impossible, to imagine an alterna-tive ending for the *Clouds* that would be more satisfactory than what we have.

I offer these propositions as props, as supports. They show where I stand (and of course I am right on every count), but as said earlier, they require extensive confirmation. The proof of this particular pudding is ultimately in the eating—in the enjoyment of the play. Let me postpone the main argument, then, and return to the firmer ground of the revised parabasis, to consider Aristophanes' reaction to the *Clouds'* defeat.

Dropping their role, the clouds speak for their playwright in the first person:

> Spectators. I shall address you frankly,
> telling the truth. So help me Dionysus,
> so help me win, and be thought bright and clever,

it was because I looked to a bright audience
and because I thought this play was the most clever
of all my comedies, that I gave you the chance
to taste it first—the one I'd worked on hardest.
What happened then? My efforts were rejected;
low, ordinary types defeated me,
very unfairly.... (518–25)

From his usual vantage point, Aristophanes criticizes his last year's audience and judges. Their decision was wrong, and it was unjust. He gave them his most witty and intelligent comedy, on which he had worked hardest (a rare allusion to the effort of writing plays), and they chose "vulgar people" instead of him. Yet, rightly or wrongly, he had thought them an intelligent audience who could appreciate true wit; and even now, despite rejection, he promises not to abandon "the clever ones among you." He will remain loyal to their expectations and standards, and to his own.

He continues, as with the *narratio* of an argument for the prosecution (*not* the defense; it is they who are guilty of wrongdoing). He had, as he thought, received a sure pledge of his audience's intelligence when they enjoyed his *Banqueters* of 427, an earlier play about education. In it a "good boy," an old-fashioned son brought up on Homer and music, seems to have been contrasted with a "playboy," his prodigal, sophist-trained brother, who cared nothing for traditional culture or morals but was training to become a successful lawyer.[32] It is probably true that the success of his *Banqueters* encouraged Aristophanes to write his more ambitious *Clouds* along similar lines; but we may be skeptical when, after describing the earlier play as a "virgin effort," Aristophanes lists the several ways in which his *Clouds* is modest and decent, to wit:

1. It did not enter with a big, thick, red-tipped (dangling leather) phallus, to make the children laugh,
2. or crack jokes at baldheaded men,
3. or dance the *kordax*,
4. or have an old man hitting his neighbor with a stick while speaking, to hide poor jokes,
5. or come on brandishing torches (and making lunges with them at people),
6. or cry "Iou, Iou!" (exaggerated screams of counterfeit, comic pain).

But rather:

It came on stage trusting itself to stand
by its own wit. Yet I, although a poet
of such great standing, never put on (h)airs,
I never use the same old stuff to fool you

two or three times; but through my brains and skill,
I always bring you new and fresh ideas,
no two alike, every one of 'em brilliant.   (544–48)

And he gives further examples to prove his point. After hitting the
mighty Cleon in the belly (in the *Knights*, which is replete with food
images and belly laughs), he didn't kick him when down, didn't go on
repeating the same jokes; whereas "these people" keep on attacking
Hyperbolus over and over with the same old digs—the best of them
borrowed or stolen from Aristophanes. He concludes:

The man who laughs at that stuff needn't try
to like *my* plays. But if you people find
your spirits warmed by me and by my inventions,
then future ages will think—you've got good sense.

(560–62)

Should we take these critical statements at face value? Of course not. The
straightforward defense is a pose, inviting laughter. It is highly unlikely
that Aristophanes ever abjured all those vulgar effects, and certainly
not in the *Clouds*, where cries of "Iou, iou!" and beatings and torch-
brandishings are prominent. (In a performance at Catholic University in
Washington, the creditors were presented very appropriately as clowns,
with circus music and shenanigans.) Indeed, five lines after declaring that
he never laughs at baldheads, Aristophanes, who was bald, praises himself for not "putting on hairs." Of course he enjoys what we call vulgarity as much as anybody. If he gives it up, he does so in the manner of
Mark Twain: "It's easy to give up smoking. I've given it up a thousand
times." What he more seriously renounces as "vulgar" is not obscenity
or farce or slapstick but reliance on these things to cover the absence of
wit, or reliance on recent jokes that are then run into the ground. His
audience could always count on him not to sink to that level; but could
he, in turn, count on them?

We do not, of course, know the whole story. It may be that Aristophanes' prizewinning rivals in 423 wrote brilliant and very funny plays—in
which case the world has lost two comic masterpieces. But it seems more
likely that the *Clouds* got third prize because the audience found it too
talky, too intellectual, too full of ideas, with not enough knockabout
action and fun. They may, moreover, have failed to separate Aristophanes sufficiently from the sophistic arguments that he presents, exagger-
ates, and makes fun of. And unconsciously, they may have felt threatened by the serious issues that the *Clouds* so bravely confronts: cultural
and educational change, the demythologizing of religion, the evanescence of traditional authorities, and the emergence of a generation gap.
The comic catharsis may not have worked this time. Or more simply:
people may not have gotten the point.

What defeat, I think, brought home to Aristophanes despite his resilient humor was the insecurity of that shared understanding on which he relied, and which the success of earlier plays had seemed to support. A possibly unbridgeable gulf opens up between the clever people in the audience, the *sophoi* and *dexioi* who appreciate his wit, and the philistine others. And a gulf opens up between the belly laughs of what had become the "older comedy" and the less boisterous, more thoughtful and original laughter of Aristophanes' own old-and-new comedy, now increasingly self-conscious and possibly isolated.[33] To this threatening split in the audience, in comedy, and even in himself, Aristophanes responded in the fullest, most healing way possible. He wrote the *Wasps*.

The parabasis of the *Wasps* reflects further on the defeat of the *Clouds*. Ironically, in the preliminary verses of the little *kommation*, or beginning-of-intermission song, the audience are reminded to pay attention, not to miss good points as stupid spectators might: "That isn't your way!" What follows is another quasi-legal complaint against the audience who, despite all of Aristophanes' many benefactions (which he gladly enumerates) and his high moral character, had let him down:

> Yet though you found such a Liberating Hero
> to clear your land, this last year you betrayed him:
> the fresh ideas he sowed, you didn't take
> with a clear mind, and so you made them fruitless.
>
> (1043–45)

Yet the *Clouds* was an excellent play. By Dionysus, it was! If Aristophanes crashed, as in a chariot race, and broke his, er, *epinoia*, it was because he had outstripped his less ambitious rivals. The people who failed to "get it clearly" should be ashamed, not the poet, whom the intelligent (*sophoi*) commend. As for the rest, they had better appreciate original comedy in the future, and store up clever ideas, so that their clothing will be fragrant of cleverness, *dexiotēs*, all the year long.

What is remarkable here is Aristophanes' high good humor, his lack of bitterness. His response to the defeat of one old-and-new comedy, one superb comedy of ideas, is to write another. Indeed, as we saw, the bad judges are taken into the subject matter of the *Wasps*, together with the intelligent and clever young man who wants to reform them by means of a literary and social catharsis. But Aristophanes makes fun of the clever and intelligent people, including himself. They do not have the last word. The attempt to clean up the old, vulgar joking and farce fails as disastrously as does the social and political redemption of Philocleon. The play is a triumph of old farce and new ideas working in concert, of undivided old-and-new comedy—or what, to Aristophanes, was new comedy taken up into old.

Yet the threatened split remains, in comedy and in the audience; it is only reconciled momentarily in this warm and generous play. Already, in the prologue, a slave announces a new comic program with Aristophanic self-awareness:

> All right. Let's tell our audience the plot;
> but first, a few remarks: please don't expect
> anything very highbrow here, or look
> for low-down jokes stolen from Megara;
> we've not got slaves running up with baskets
> to throw some candy at the audience;
> not Heracles defrauded of his dinner;
> not Euripides camping it up again;
> not Cleon, though it seemed funny at first,
> chopped into mincemeat for the umptieth time.
> Only a little story with a point.
> It's not more clever than yourselves, but still
> it's brighter than your usual comedy. (54–66)

Aristophanes will steer a mean course between too highbrow (*mega*) comedy and too lowbrow (*Megarothen keklemmenon*; note the balancing pun). Presumably the *Clouds* was too "high" for its audience. Still, the emphasis goes the other way: it is on renouncing the old tricks, like throwing candy to the audience, or the tired old Heracles bit, or the once funny jokes about Euripides, or even Cleon, that are repeated over and over and over; all this is low and "stolen" laughter.[34] It is a kind of fraud—like what Cleon does! Aristophanes promises to give his audience more than trite, vulgar jokes. He also promises, rather trickily, that his "little story with a point" will not be (as the *Clouds* was?) more clever than themselves. And as if to prove it, he makes quite sure—or pretends to make quite sure—that the audience, this time, will not miss the point.

It is a short step from here to Aristophanes' claims in the parabasis of the *Peace*. He is the best (*aristos*, a pun) and most famous *kōmōidodidaskalos*. He reformed comedy by putting an end to his rivals' reliance on the old vulgar tricks: on (1) rag and louse jokes; (2) the starving Heracles bit (*ekeinous* implies that these stupid figures have receded into the dim comic past, although Aristophanes will use the starving Heracles six years later, in the *Birds*); and (3) the low-class slave bits, in which slaves run around, steal food, cheat their masters, get beaten, and trade insults on that seemingly inexhaustible subject. In short, Aristophanes has built up the art of comedy:

> He put away this low and foolish trash,
> and fortified the Art, and made it lofty
> with edifying wit, and great ideas,
> and joking not of your ordinary kind. (748–50)

Notice that "high" comedy (*megalēn, megalois*) wins this time. Its poet does not ridicule petty individuals, but attacked the great Cleon-mon-

ster; the lines are repeated from the *Wasps*, as if to assert a now established comic program. The poet is brave; he is persevering; he did not
abuse his success to seduce boys; in short, he

> gave little pain, and much good cheer,
> and everything in season. (764)

Is there a suggestion here, anticipating Plato and Aristotle, that comedy
should give pleasure and not pain? The *Peace* itself is clearly Old
Comedy; it contains a remarkable amount of obscenity, both sexual
and scatological; in its loose, playful structure it most closely resembles
the *Acharnians*; yet it shows a good humor, a mellowing of comic tone,
that looks forward to the good-natured laughter of Aristophanes' middle
plays: *Birds, Lysistrata, Thesmophoriazusae*. For all its nostalgic indecency, it evokes Aristophanes' power, now fully realized, to turn the
older comedy into something different and new.

To recapitulate, I believe that Aristophanes was right: that his *Clouds
was* an excellent play; that it successfully integrated the play of ideas into
the farce and fun of the (by then) old comedy; and that it tested, and still
tests, the perceptiveness of judges and critics. Secondly, I believe that
Aristophanes reacted to the defeat of his *Clouds* with disappointment
but also with comic magnanimity. He was not embittered; he could laugh
at his reforming self as well as at his incorrigible audience; and he managed to transform disappointment and frustration into a magnificent
sequel in which many of the same themes are replayed, with new results:
law and nature, the conflict of generations, the struggle of education
with stupidity. The formula is again complex, and it is (again, I think)
successful; so that in the *Peace* Aristophanes can look back as one who
has stood the test, has enlarged the realm of comedy, and may now relax
and celebrate, in fine good humor, the victory that has been gained.

If I am right, and Aristophanes responded bravely and generously to
the threat of time, change, isolation, and a growing split in things, then
his situation may be compared with Pindar's experience of change and
contradiction earlier in the century. For Pindar wrote celebratory odes
that belong, more than he may first have realized, to two different
worlds. On the one hand their way of conceiving and exploring the
world is still mythic and symbolic at heart, as opposed to what is abstract, conceptual, philosophical; on the other hand their treatment of
myth and history is intensely metaphorical, original in style, and individual in manner. In Pindar's odes private intuition meets with public
occasion; the generosity of poetic celebration responds to the generous
expression in history and sports of the god's gifts—and also of the sum-
moning patron's. But as Pindar explored old meanings and values (religious, moral, patriotic, familial) in striking new ways, he also came, as
John Finley has suggested, to realize the loneliness of his high-soaring
poetry, his arrows of song that "speak to those with understanding but

for the mass need interpreters."[35] Hieron's choice of Bacchylides over Pindar in 476 was a signal defeat. It seemed to show a failure of understanding on Hieron's part, a breach of agreement between patron and poet. Yet Pindar could not withdraw into willful privacy, for "social tradition and the setting of the epinikion as well as all personal attachment to the community and cult told him that his role was communal."[36] It is, again, a problem of the old-and-new: of a poet who puts the newest wine, of metaphorical thinking and expression, into the old celebratory wineskins of the victor's *kōmos*, but who is not always honored (or understood) in his own country, or in others.

Pythian 2, to Hieron, displays Pindar's magnanimous response to rejection and misunderstanding. He himself rejects bitterness; he will not batten on the satirist's hatred; he will not turn his back on *charis*, on the bright exchanges of gratitude and joy. From personal difficulties, as from the cloud of defeat inflicted by history (not least by the dynamic growth of Athens) on his beloved Thebes and its peaceful sister-state Aegina, Pindar turned with renewed conviction to the enduring realities behind myth, reaffirming joy after effort, achievement beyond vicissitude, and permanence the other side of historical and intellectual change. Though poet, family, or state grow old and weary, the "god-given brightness" does not fade but soars clear of things, giving meaning still to human effort and human life, and reason still to be grateful, and to celebrate.

Aristophanes belonged, more than Pindar, to the future. He was a child of imperial Athens, Pindar's "god-driven city." He was fascinated by the new rhetoric, the new tragedy, and the second-stage debates of the Sophistic Enlightenment at Athens; his plays present the clash of old and new ideas so vividly that he could be accused of "Euripidaristophanizing," perhaps of being himself a catalyst of intellectual change.[37] Yet his comedy remains rooted, like Pindar's epinician odes, in festive celebration and revelry. Its deep confidence is Dionysian and inherited; its rites of renewal antedate the material and intellectual riches of Periclean Athens; and it was, finally, the pride and confidence of those comic rites themselves that brought Aristophanes into the lists, not just to confront political and social change, as he had already in the *Acharnians* and *Knights*, but to confront even deeper, more disturbing problems of cultural and spiritual change, the evanescence of traditions and beliefs by which, among other things, the old comedy itself was supported. It is a remarkable tribute to Aristophanes' comic spirit, his loyalty to Dionysian hopefulness and "the dearest freshness deep down things," that he does *not* (as most people think) take a merely negative, satiric view of the sophistic movement and intellectual change in the *Clouds*, but rather plays out the old-and-new games of change with splendid impartiality and fun. The *Clouds* thus provided an adolescent rite of passage for Athens, and for the newly self-conscious Western mind, bringing it through a successful catharsis, as the hierophantic Socrates has often been thought to do but, in the view of his comic rival, could not.

I have suggested that the *Clouds'* defeat may, but only momentarily, have shaken Aristophanes' confidence in his comedy's cathartic power, as in the shared understanding on which this is based. If he felt defeated, and even isolated, he refused in good comic fashion to accept defeat, and he turned the threat of isolation, and of a split in comedy between high and low, into greathearted laughter. Yet Aristophanes must increasingly have felt, as the years went by, something like Pindar's sense of loss and dread: a sense that time and change were not on the side of Athens, or of social harmony, or of the civilized and good life as he had known it—or, with all these things, of the old comedy itself. As a private individual, a member of the Assembly, or even, one day, its president, Aristophanes must have felt enormous fear and sadness about what he saw around himself. Any thoughtful Athenian would. It is all the more remarkable that his comedy stays true to itself until the end: that it does not, like later comedy, fall into serious ethical moralizing, or combine humorous and serious elements in an uneasy mixture (not a compound), but fights off "seriousness and weariousness" every time, even its own, and even after the death of imperial Athens and the death, by every indication, of Old Comedy itself.

Comedy's power to jest in the face of death has often been admired. I think of Gilbert and Sullivan's *Yeomen of the Guard*, where the clown, Jack Point, literally jests in the shadow of the Tower of London. The anxiety of death, and of those things that lead to it—sickness and fighting and growing old—is universal; as Paul Tillich has shown, it is not a neurotic anxiety, but an existential one, to be faced by heroes, saints, and lovers—and comic poets? Another anxiety, greater and more threatening, is of social and cultural change: the death, this time, not of an individual, but of an entire society, or way of life. In Tillich's analysis, this would belong to the (also existential) anxiety of meaninglessness.[38] The old beliefs and traditions on which we draw for faith and courage appear to be subject, even as we ourselves are, to time, change, and death. Hence in their different ways poet and philosopher seek to grasp the things that are beyond time and change. For Socrates' student Plato, these are the eternal Forms, to be grasped in abstraction by the philosophic mind. For Pindar, it is the gods' underlying presence, beauty, and joy, which is revealed among men in special moments of flashing victory, and in the commemoration of these moments in the poet's brief and lovely song. And for Aristophanes? His great thesis (which this book has been about) is comedy's joyful vision, its gift of recovery and renewal, its powerful laughter in the face of every fear. The antithesis takes many forms, but it is ultimately the threat of a cultural and spiritual change in which every known and trusted value seems likely to disappear—including the values on which Old Comedy itself, like everything else at Athens, was founded. Aristophanes' first great synthesizing response—Old Comedy Meets Cultural Change, so to speak—was his *Clouds* of 423 and its rite of passage, which brings the Western mind, not safely but still joyfully, out of childhood into adolescence. Its complement is the *Frogs* of 405, which is comedy's Dionysian funeral rite for the older Athens, for Athenian tragedy, and very possibly for the older Athenian comedy as well.

34   *Festive Play Revisited:* Frogs

EURIPIDES' death in 407/6 B.C. gave the *Frogs* its first impulse. One comic idea, of staging an underworld agon between Aeschylus and Euripides, the old tragedy and the new, became joined with a second, that Dionysus himself would descend to Hades in order to retrieve a clever and creative poet.[39] His immediate desire is for Euripides; but comic heroes, like comic playwrights, often change purpose once their spirits have been revived. I believe that this renewal of spirit and perspective is the true center of the *Frogs*, from which all else follows: the confrontation of changing values in the agon, and the choosing of Aeschylus, not by the mind's critical discrimination, but by the deeper perceptiveness of a reawakened heart.

But whatever hope and confidence it achieves, the play takes its start from an overwhelming sense of death—the death of Euripides, and of tragedy, but also by implication the death that shadows all private and public life, all human achievement. As Dionysus explains to Heracles in the prologue, his quest began with a pang of longing (*pothos*) for the dead poet. "I was reading aboard ship, reading the *Andromeda* to myself, and suddenly a longing struck upon my heart, you can't imagine how strongly." Heracles grasps the erotic nature of *pothos*, but all too literally. Was it longing for a woman? For a boy, then? For a—man? Even the broad-minded Heracles is surprised when Dionysus' erotic passion turns out to be for the dead Euripides: that sounds like necrophilia. Still, as Dionysus' brother and an experienced Hades-traveler, he gives what advice he can about hotels, restaurants, difficulties along the way, and *Sehenswürdigkeiten* generally. But the misunderstood *pothos*, so difficult to explain, marks the beginning of the comic journey, first in sadness and loneliness but, after that, in "desire with hope."

The picture of Dionysus reading Euripides on shipboard is funnier and more poignant than people realize who can "read Euripides" today on airplanes (as I have often done). Probably the *Andromeda* of 412 B.C. seemed an escapist play; perhaps it was a tragedy of grace, like its companion piece, the "new *Helen*." Aristophanes parodied both plays admiringly in his *Thesmophoriazusae* of 411. But now, as it seemed, the beautiful *Andromeda* could not be revived in living performance (for Aristophanes could not have anticipated the popular fourth-century revivals of Euripidean plays). What is remarkable is that the *biblion*, the inanimate "book" or scroll with its ink-marks that can even be carried aboard ship and read there to oneself, still conveys so much of the play's erotic power. This is another tribute to Euripides. It also reflects his indulgence in erotic *pothos*, especially in his many escape odes. But even more, it raises questions of cultural change, and of life and death. What happens to a play when it becomes a text? And what kind or degree of immortality comes to good poets, or to bad ones, in the shape of a *biblion*? Can a playwright, by publishing, not perish?

Biblion jokes in Aristophanes are important, like computer jokes today. In the *Birds* the Athenians are depicted as pecking away at their books, and the bureaucrats and planners who invade Cloudcuckooland carry armloads of pamphlets, offprints, and legal documents. Although books may in practice have concerned only a philosophical, scientific, and artistic elite in the later fifth century B.C., they still were recognizable instruments of change, and to the comic imagination, as to the popular one, they took on a life of their own. There is a joke from a lost comedy about a young man who "has been corrupted by Prodicus or by some book."[40] The ink-marks pose a grave moral danger, like the professor! When, in the *Frogs*, Aristophanes includes among the sinners consigned to Hell "any person who copies out a speech of Morsimus," the immediate effect is satirical, and very funny; but the joke glances at the creeping ascendancy of written culture over oral. Again, the chorus assure the two competing poets that the audience may be relied on to appreciate all the fine points of their debate, for

> They are all set, in military order.
> Each person is equipped with his own text (*biblion*)
> and studies it, to get the clever jokes.[41]

Unfortunately this particular clever joke has sometimes been taken too literally—as though Aristophanes provided handouts! Scholars have been misled, or at best distracted, by their consuming passion to learn more about the circulation of written texts; and today, in the age of the photocopy machine run wild, the computer printout (ditto), and the video recorder, Aristophanes' fantastic picture, of thousands of Athenians diligently checking the spoken jokes against written copies in their laps, has lost its punch. And as usual, this wild and funny idea reflects troubling concerns. How much of a play can be captured in ink, enjoyed as literature? Is it possible that the playwright's subtleties can be caught better in the reading than in the performance? Should plays be studied? It is a great thing to be read on shipboard (or for that matter, at the

University of North Carolina) after you are dead; but might a living playwright, or the god of theater himself, be excused for wanting something more?

Euripides' death, which gave the *Frogs* its initial impulse, thus becomes linked with other kinds of death than that of tragedy, and other emotional concerns. On the one hand, it suggests the universal threat of each person's individual aging and death. Although comedy always jests, like Jack Point, in the shadow of that Tower, the *Frogs* carries an unusually heavy freight of dead bodies and jokes about death, from the corpse on its way to burial that refuses to carry some luggage for merely exorbitant pay ("I'd sooner—*come to life* again!"), to death itself and the "chariot on chariot, corpse on corpse" that Aeschylus hurls into the scales of critical judgment, weighing down the balance. Time, change, and death are everywhere. Even the immortal Dionysus complains, in the prologue, of stale jokes that make him feel a year older when he hears them. Aristophanes himself has grown a year older when the Lenaean festival returns in late January 405 B.C.

On the other hand, threats to the national life of Athens dwarf all such individual concerns. There was Alcibiades, brilliant and untrustworthy, yet whose naval and diplomatic strategy had revived the economic security and power of the Athenian empire; now, rejected again by the politicians, he had gone into self-imposed exile. And there was the aftermath of Arginusae, which must have seemed ominous even to a nonprophetic poet. As a modern historian tells it,

> Meanwhile [while Lysander revived Spartan strategy] the Athenians had squandered the fruits of victory. The crews of twelve sinking ships had not been rescued after the battle of Arginusae. The probable reason was that a storm made rescue impossible, but the thought of so many men floating unburied roused extremely bitter feelings. There had to be scapegoats and by an emotional vote in the Assembly it was decided to try all the generals together. In the heat of the moment they were condemned. The Athenians had sacrificed some of their commanders; more important they completely undermined the morale of the fighting forces at Samos. Lysander was able to take the initiative and sail to the Hellespont. The Athenians had to follow because the Hellespont was their vital life-line. At the battle of Aegospotami they were trapped into total defeat; only twelve ships out of 180 survived the battle.[42]

The *Frogs*, produced several months before Aegospotami, conveys a feeling of crisis unusual even for Aristophanes. It refers to the shortages of money, ships, and manpower, to internal dissension and bad politics, and, above all, to a sinking of morale. The "Alcibiades question" is introduced toward the play's end, amid much uncertainty. And Aristophanes seems especially to remember those corpses tossed in the sea near

Arginusae. Mention of the "battle of the meats," at which Xanthias was not present, may refer to them. Dionysus was present, supposedly, at the battle; he claims to have sunk twelve or thirteen ships—"and then I woke up," interjects the skeptical Xanthias. Perhaps the naval victory itself was like a good dream from which Athens had to wake up. In any event the corpses were unforgettable, and the politicians too, who could snatch defeat from the jaws of victory.

The financial shortages of Athens directly affected Old Comedy.[43] Money from the "private sector" was desperately needed for ships, even more than for comic choruses; Aristophanes used the same singers twice, first as an invisible chorus of frogs, and then as a visible chorus of initiates in tattered clothes—and he makes poetic capital out of all this. He also denounces that lowest of scum, the politicians who would cut the salary of comic poets in reprisal for their criticism. But the connection that Aristophanes perceives between plays and morale goes beyond personal pleading, however heartfelt. When, toward the play's end, he takes up political and military questions directly, it is "so that the polis, being saved, may present its choruses." This is not a joke, not an inversion of priorities. Song, dance, and festival are still an end in themselves. But they also provide Athens with a sense of purpose, of community, and even of identity.

Euripides' death, which triggered these concerns, must have shaken Aristophanes both personally and as a playwright, for he had accompanied modern tragedy through all its experiments and changes. The comic hero, Dicaeopolis or Trygaeus, imitated his tragic counterpart, as the clown imitates the acrobat; tragic speeches, gestures, and actions remained the foil against which Old Comedy played its preposterous games, reaffirming all that is low and silly, and yet somehow hopeful, in human life; and even when Euripides created a new and less dignified kind of hero, and a new, ironic, and very melodramatic kind of tragic plot, these still involved pretensions off which Aristophanes could score. The *Acharnians* kept pace with the *Telephus*. The *Thesmophoriazusae* parodied, even as it complimented, the "new *Helen*" and the *Andromeda*. Aristophanes may have looked to Euripides to set the pace, even more than he was aware. At the same time, Euripides' death may have made him realize, more than ever, how much that poet had been a catalyst of change, helping to dissolve many of the settled beliefs, traditions, and loyalties on which Athenian morale was nourished, and the Old Comedy with it. If Euripides' death posed the life-and-death questions with which every individual is concerned, and which he or she must answer in order to establish a real identity, yet the review of Euripides' work recalls older issues, of cultural change and "confusion worse than death," that had affected the identity of Athens, its past and present morale, and its very survival. The weight of these concerns, as they press down on the poet's mind and spirits, can be very heavy.

One obvious response to these pressures, and one that is implied in the Euripidean *pothos*, would be suicide. When we read Euripides' own escape odes, we often feel that he, or his characters, are more than "half in love with easeful death." The *Hippolytus* ode cited earlier, in which the chorus sing of their wish to fly like birds into the uttermost West, where life is beautiful like a fairy tale and free of trouble and pain, still awakens a stab of longing as we read it today; but in its context, it anticipates Phaedra's despairing suicide. Only the noose of death provides the release that she has so long sought. Similarly one attraction of Hades in the *Frogs* is the "resting places," *anapaulai*, about which Dionysus inquires, and which Charon announces as one of the station stops:

> Who's for the resting places
> from ills and troubles?
> Who's for the plain of Lethe? (185–86)

And suicide is recommended earlier, by Heracles, as a quick way to Hades. Dionysus rejects it because the details offend his sensibilities. Hanging, which Heracles first suggests, is too stuffy; hemlock makes your shins freeze; and if you throw yourself down from a tower—why, you might just bash out your brains! The incongruity jokes, which suit Dionysus' cowardly temperament, remind us that the comic hero is on the side of life. He resists the lure of suicide—and how could an immortal god commit suicide?—much as, in the *Knights*, the despondent slaves turned from thoughts of drinking bull's blood to the more hopeful plan of drinking wine.

Indeed, as Plato indicated in the *Symposium*, the impulse of erotic nostalgia can lead to the full comic movement that I have described as "desire with hope." Out of longing and even desolation, the comic hero decides what he really wants, and goes after it. Often the plan is changed, as in the *Birds*. Peisetairus and Euelpides (surely an auditory pun on *Euripides*) desire a quiet refuge, a place far from troubles and worries, and they go to the birds to find it; but once Peisetairus finds the escape realm and recovers his energy, he discovers what he really wants—to conquer the universe—and goes after it with the full imperial vigor of an Athenian. And so in the *Frogs*: the erotic longing for Euripides brings Dionysus down to Hades, where he discovers what he (and Athens) really wants and needs: which is not Euripides, but Aeschylus and the spirit for which he stands.

Dionysus' descent to the underworld offers diverse possibilities of parody and satire, which Old Comedy must often have exploited.[44] First, the comic hero undergoing the adventure can be contrasted with his serious predecessors. The fat, lazy, and very cowardly Dionysus of the *Frogs* is set against the steadfast Heracles, who for his last labor fetched Cerberus out of Hades; there may also be echoes of Orpheus seeking Eurydice, of Theseus trying to rescue Perithous, and perhaps of Dionysus bringing his mother Semele to Olympus. Such incongruous combinations as saffron robe and lionskin, buskin and club, must have been familiar from other burlesque sketches about Dionysus. Second, the hero's visit to Hades can become a vehicle for topical satire and comment, if prominent figures in the underworld are shown to behave like known, everyday Athenians. There is something of this in the *Frogs*, where Cleon and Hyperbolus are mentioned as patrons of the offended tradeswomen, but much less than we might expect. And third, Hades can provide a satiric foil, or corrective, to the present-day vices and follies of Athens. In Eupolis' *Demes* certain old-time statesmen were resurrected to judge and rebuke their unworthy successors; the nostalgia must have been strong, and the results hilarious. In the *Frogs*, by contrast, Aeschylus is escorted upwards only at the end, and his being chosen depends on a process of spiritual renewal that takes place in the rich underworld itself. Nostalgia matters, but only as a start.

Dionysus goes to Hades to retrieve his "clever poet," the fascinating Euripides; he ends up choosing, and bringing back, the enspiriting Aeschylus. But first the god must rediscover himself: who he is, what he values, and where his comic energies come from. My account owes much to Charles Segal, who has written very convincingly about the identity crisis that Dionysus experiences in this play, and about the clues taken from myth and rite that help him reassume his identity as god of theater, and especially of comedy.[45] It may be that for Aristophanes the identity crisis of the old comedy itself had to be resolved in mythic, poetic, and dramatic terms before that of tragedy—and of Athens—could be faced. Dionysus must learn to laugh and play again before he can judge, and he does this, as Segal has shown, by participating vicariously in his own rites and in those of Demeter and Persephone. I would only add that the rich underworld in which Dionysus finds himself is that of a fairy tale even more than myth or legend.[46] It is the place, not of suicidal negation of life, but where instead the "dearest freshness deep down things" may be reclaimed.

Many fairy tales describe the hero's descent to the rich though dangerous underworld. In the strongly archetypal story "The Three Feathers," the third and youngest prince, named Dummling, follows chance and intuition and goes down into the earth, where a powerful female toad bestows riches on him and one of her daughters, who turns into a beautiful woman. In a Hessian variant, Dummling finds a beautiful girl spinning linen, who turns into a frog when she joins him aboveground. When the frog arrives at the king's court, it cries out, "Kiss me and sink yourself down." Dummling takes the frog, kisses it, and jumps into the water with it; and it turns back, then and forever, into a beautiful woman. They reemerge and live happily ever after.

Freudian interpreters treating stories about toads or frogs (such as the better-known "Frog Prince") usually stress their sexual implications. The low, ugly creatures represent the sexual nature in oneself or others that frightens the growing child, making her or him shrink from the prospect of marriage. But this sexual emphasis, though sometimes very helpful (as in Bruno Bettelheim's analysis of "The Beauty and the Beast"),[47] misses deeper psychological and spiritual dimensions present in such fairy tales, as much so as in myths and legends. In the Jungian analysis, the cry "Versenk dich!" suggests the need for meditation, for sinking down into the unconscious. The toad or frog may stand for a particular aspect of the unconscious, the anima or animus, that has been ignored to the damage of the whole personality.[48] I would prefer myself to see the toads and frogs as representing our lower nature generally, including whatever gifts and energies have been lost to our dominant conscious thinking. But I would also like to go beyond psychological interpretation altogether and take the frog at least, since it moves easily between land and water, as a figure of transition, a mystical guide between the worlds of life and death—and for the comic poet, a figure of comedy itself as it shuttles or hops between the world of time and change and the other-world of timelessness, in which the religious or poetic imagination is still privileged to swim.

So in the *Frogs*: the creatures of the play's title accompany Dionysus as he crosses the Styx in Charon's boat. If we envision the actual staging, similarities with the fairy-tale aspects of the *Peace* become striking.[49] There, Trygaeus "flew" on the dung beetle from his own house, on the *logeion*, over some portion of the orchestra, and landed on Olympus, before the house of Zeus—another part of the *logeion*, or possibly the very spot from which he started. The mythic ride from earth to heaven is accompanied by the strongest reminders that this is make-believe. But the dung beetle, however wooden, is a powerful creature: it embodies that comic release, and those lower energies, that permit the comic hero Trygaeus to succeed where the tragic Bellerophon was shot down; and as we know from Egyptian myth, it is a supernaturally lucky creature that shares in the secret knowledge of life and death and is hence a figure of good luck, and of transitions.

In the *Frogs* Dionysus and his slave Xanthias make their way from Heracles' house, before the middle of the *skēnē* or perhaps to one side, down (literally by a few steps, I think, as well as symbolically) into the orchestra. On the way down, they meet the corpse being carried to burial. A little further on, they see Charon's boat, a large wooden car on wheels, probably propelled by attendants underneath and "steered" from above. Dionysus is taken on board; and while Xanthias runs around the "lake" (now the orchestra), his master "rows" around a half-circuit of the orchestra/lake and disembarks near the opposite side entrance, as at the "resting places" (*anapaulai*) on the way to Pluto's palace. There he is rejoined by Xanthias, and from there he enjoys the songs and dances of the Mystae, or initiates (who enter the orchestra from the first side entrance); then the two make their way, through comic difficulties onstage, to the palace—which may well be the same place they started from. So the journey to hell, as to heaven, takes people full circle. The dung beetle, however, is replaced by two similar and mutually complementary phenomena, the ship-car of "Charon" and the frogs who sing to Dionysus, accompanying his passage, but are never seen. Both ship and frogs have Dionysian associations, and both are closely connected with Old Comedy itself in its festive meanings and in its power to revive the human spirit, and even the divine.

Most obviously for an Athenian audience, the ship of Charon on which this Dionysus travels would recall the magic ship on which Dionysus regularly arrived at Athens or voyaged elsewhere. At the Lenaea, and probably by extension on other festive occasions, Dionysus was represented as arriving on a great ship-car, a wagon made to represent the magic ship, with sails and sailors; he was accompanied by a crowd of magical, subhuman creatures, and his car was followed by other floats or wagons from which these personages hurled indecencies and invective at the crowd. These licensed "jokes from the wagons" were a primitive survival. They show us the religious context of carnival from which the play forms of Old Comedy, its animal or daemon masquerade and its *aischrologia*, are derived (see the Appendix). The ship-car, once Dionysus mounted it, must have evoked a whole range of joyful and familiar responses in the audience, much as Santa Claus drawn by eight reindeer might today. If Segal is right, this Dionysus will gradually be reminded—and not least by references to the present Lenaea—of his divine identity; I would add that Old Comedy, with him, rediscovers its identity and laughing purposes.

But what (as Aristophanes might say) is the idea of the frogs? To begin with, they are an Old Comedy chorus, such as old Magnes was described as presenting, "dipping himself in frog-green," along with all the colorful choruses of birds, fishes, insects and the rest.[50] Aristophanes' principal and visible chorus will be that of the initiates (Mystae) in Hades. He may have avoided that title because Phrynichus had used it recently. He may have also chosen for financial reasons not to use a subsidiary chorus; the frogs will be sung by the same choristers who appear as Mystae later. Yet Aristophanes makes a comic and poetic virtue of necessity. The frogs' invisibility adds to their symbolic significance, as do the tattered clothes of the Mystae; all the more appropriately do they carry the play's title.[51]

Like many other Old Comedy choruses, the frogs are playful, teasing, and more than a little dangerous in their confrontation with the comic hero.[52] In this they especially resemble those irresponsible and childlike spirits, the teasing clouds who egg on Strepsiades in that play (and whose entrance song is sung partly offstage, before the clouds reveal themselves visibly and in female appearance to Strepsiades and to the audience). The frogs' chant should accompany Dionysus' rowing and set its pace, but it is hard to follow; the god has to row harder, and sing more vigorously himself, to keep up with them; and they perversely keep shifting rhythms on him, in what may suggest the manner of some modern poets. Yet the upshot is that they stimulate Dionysus to comically heroic efforts ending in a sort of victory, as he overmatches the frogs' chant and reduces them to silence. Garry Wills has suggested, I think convincingly, that to compete with the frogs' guttural singing and its accompanying *aulos* (flute or, better, shawm) Dionysus uses his own crescendo of belly rumbles and farts (and again, the parallel with Strepsiades' behavior in the *Clouds* is striking).[53] Perhaps Wills is right, and the frogs are "grossed out"; but still, as an Old Comedy chorus, they have given the god some of his own comic vitality back, and he needs just this in order to accomplish, and still more to redefine, his heroic purpose.

The first verses of the Frog Chorus, which evoke festive rites of the Anthesteria, are especially suited to the revival of Dionysus' sense of himself and his powers:

> Brekekekex koax koax,
> brekekekex koax koax,
> marsh-dwellers, offspring
>   of fresh waters,
> raise our cry of praise to the pipes,
> raise articulate song
>   (koax koax)—
> the shout of joy we've roused (*iachēsamen*) for Zeus's
> son Dionysus in the marshes,
> every time that hangover revel
> passes through our precinct on
> the holy Eve of the Pots.   (209–19)

The hangover revel (*kraipalokōmos*) on the second night of the Anthesteria should be placed in the larger context of that early spring festival, with its many life-and-death associations. The first day, the Pithoigia or Cask Opening, was when the new wine was broached, a time of great dangerousness that may have been countered by revelry. Perhaps the great wagons carrying casks of wine also carried Dionysian masquers who, as on other holidays, shouted apotropaic indecencies "from the wagons." The second day, the Choes or Feast of Jugs, was still more dangerous, a time when ghosts were abroad, when houses were protected by hasty charms, when each man drank in silent isolation at his own table and from his own jug—until, at the day's end, the citizens reeled off in a drunken mob to deposit their jugs, now wreathed with flowers, at the shrine of Dionysus in the Marshes (opened only once a year). By Greek custom, that second evening began the next day's festivities, of the Chytroi, the Feast of the Pots, a time to celebrate new life, flowers, and children. What the frogs evoke is a liminal time of transition between one ceremony and another, and between the death-shadowed second day of the Choes and the life-celebrating Chytroi. Our own Halloween and New Year's Eve preserve something of the carnival spirit—and the dangerousness—of just such times.

And these evocative verses establish the mutual relation between Dionysus and his Old Comedy chorus that Aristophanes means paradoxically to assert. On the one hand comedy's play and laughter were derived from Dionysian rite, and specifically from the *kōmos* or revel with which every Dionysian celebration ended, whether it was the goat sacrifice of the country (and later City) Dionysia or the great drunken hangover revel of the Anthesteria that the frogs say they witness each year from their privileged seats in the marshes. Tragic and comic competitions, increasingly formalized, were offshoots of these Dionysian revels, but comedy, the "*kōmos* song" with its choruses of frogs and other such daemonic creatures, most directly preserved—or had preserved up to now—its Dionysian nature. If comedy could play and laugh, it owed this freedom and energy to its patron god. On the other hand, at a time of national and theatrical decline and confusion, the god of theater himself might need to be recharged—and who could better do this than the god's own Old Comic animal-chorus? Even as he crosses the Stygian marsh to Hades, our Dionysus is revived and reinvigorated. He begins (but the process will take longer) to be god of the theater again, and especially of comedy. It is like the sacred moment, commemorated in Eleusinian myth and rite, when Iambe, through her cheerful indecencies, leads Demeter to laugh again, and then to take food and drink.

The frogs sing next of their own musical nature. Living down among the marsh reeds as they do, they are beloved by the Muses, by Pan with his reedy pipes, and by Apollo with his *phorminx*, a type of reed-bridged lyre. Wills argues that the frogs are not genuine songsters, but rather pretentious fakes, like certain modern dithyrambic poets; their defeat by Dionysus looks forward to Euripides' defeat by Aeschylus in the larger agon. Segal tentatively connects the frogs with the kind of buffoonery, unrooted in communal rites and beliefs, that Dionysus must learn to reject.[54] I want to raise a third possibility: that the frogs' song is meant to evoke the paradoxical beauty of what was now, to Aristophanes, the old comedy, whether of poets like Magnes or, as it was beginning to appear, of Aristophanes himself. The "swan-frogs," like comedy itself, combine the beautiful with the grotesque. And they sing comedy's swan song together with its old frog song—the lyric poignance and the *koax*—as it slips away toward the shore of death.

But there is more. The frogs who hop on land and swim in water, who raise up their heads to sing on bright, sunny days, but whose songs on rainy days come bubbling up from beneath the water, belong to both realms, of life and death, and move as liminal guides between the two. The "bubblesplashifications" of which they are so proud may suggest the ephemeral nature of all human creations, including the poetry of Old Comedy. All these things are like bubbles that swell to burst upon the air. And yet that song swelling up from the depths, and evoked presently by invisible singers, suggests that other power of imaginative creations, to live on and to move the spirit from beyond the waters of death—and with more force, and more true vitality, than the everyday chatter of the "living."

If I am right, then Aristophanes' frog chorus represents Old Comedy as it exists both in and out of time. Being subject to the "foot of time" (which Euripidean phrase seems to have caught Aristophanes' fancy as well as Dionysus'), the chorus of Old Comedy will someday come to an end, as Dionysus in this scene makes the frogs *stop*. As the money runs out in Athens, or the spirit, or the living sense of communal celebration, the chorus of Old Comedy will fall silent and disappear. And Old Comedy, like its earlier poets, and (eventually) like the present one, will slip over into the "invisible" realm of Hades. Everything does, and everything will: poets, plays, the polis, even the joy of those religious celebrations by which everything else is nourished. And yet like reeds growing from underwater, and like the frogs' song bubbling up from the depths on rainy days, what we love best in this mortal world is loved by the gods and nourished in their timeless world, where it finds deepest roots. The frog-swan song of Old Comedy comes now from the other side of time and death, to revive the god himself, and to *coax* him across the marshes, in his liminal passage.

Dionysus and Xanthias move on, through comically viewed scenes of Hell, passing the great sinners (these are evidently in the audience) and the she-goblin Empusa, the shape-shifter, whom Xanthias uses to terrify his "courageous" master. But then a change comes, of mood and tone. The two comic pilgrims hear, as was promised, a sound of flutes, catch sweeter airs, see torchlight gleaming in the dark underworld. The initiates are coming. And Dionysus and Xanthias, like the initiates themselves, fall quiet and (with the audience) listen.

The following scene could be called a "play of initiation" or an "initiation into play." It reflects the experience of the real initiates at Eleusis, not parodied here but transposed into the comic mode;[55] and it also reflects the closely related experience of Dionysian worship. If the god Dionysus was stimulated earlier to move on by one of his Old Comic choruses of frogs, he now emerges like an Eleusinian pilgrim out of darkness and a symbolic passage through death and underworld perils into a blaze of torchlight. And as the pilgrim is shown the central revelation, perhaps in the lifting up of a sheaf of wheat, of hoped-for joy and the rebirth of life out of death, so Dionysus and Xanthias rediscover in the deepest underworld the fullest and most joyful celebration of life, and of the gods' life-giving presence. This is the source of play generally, and of comedy's play in particular. If holidays, returning in their seasons, are a time for playing, joking, and teasing, as well as for being most deeply serious about life, it is because these are holy days, when the gods' timeless presence removes us, to laugh or cry or sing or dance, from the ordinary constrictions of time and space and the preoccupations of history. In the end people play because there is a time for playing. Dionysus is reinitiated vicariously into a joyful rediscovery of that god-given time. But equally, he and Xanthias represent a theater audience who see the mysteries through a theatrical representation and, indeed, through a comic veil. We are aware of Dionysus watching the chorus sing and dance, and commenting on it; he is a spectator, like ourselves; and this reminds us that if the gods give us laughter and play, yet play with its laughter may in turn give us back the gods or, in mythic and dramatic terms, restore them to themselves. Dionysus is revived by these echoes of the Eleusinian "Easter laughter," as he was by echoes of the Anthesteria hangover revel. Again he is drawn into the song; Dionysus the spectator becomes a participant in the play; and in this, and in his growing power to move on and back—on to Pluto's house, and back to the world of history and time—he is an example for us all to follow.

Iacchus, who is first invoked by the chorus, personifies the cry of joy, the great Alleluia given by the initiates of Demeter and Persephone. As he is portrayed here, closely conjoined with the goddesses, he also suggests Dionysus in one of his mystic embodiments (for Dionysus takes many shapes): the dance leader, tossing his myrtle-crowned head, stamping his foot in the "unbridled, play-loving rhythm" that is his due.[56] Terms for play and dance, *paisdein* and *choreuein*, are joined throughout this scene. Still more, as he leads the holy dance of the Mystae, the imagery of joy and rejuvenation associated with Iacchus comes very close to that usually belonging to Dionysus:

> Raise high our torches' flame!
> You have drawn near,
>   Iacchus, o Iacchus,
> nocturnal liturgy's
>   light-bringing star:
> meadows blaze with fire,
> old men vigorously leap,
> shaking off grief and pain

> and all the weight of cumulative years
>   for joy of the holy rite.
> Then lead us forth,
> with bright torches waving:
> over the flowering marshy plain
>   lead your dancers, lord!   (340–53)

Dionysus is often portrayed as the leader of torch-bearing dancers on the mountains. A Sophoclean chorus calls him "chorus leader of the fire-breathing stars, who watch over nightly voices," as though the entire universe took up the joyful dance.[57] So too the chorus of Euripides' *Bacchae* (the tragic opposite of the *Frogs*, almost contemporary with it) sing of Dionysus' gift of careless rapture, of newly invigorated feet that follow the god in dance, forgetful of age and time. The weight of returning years, so strong in the *Frogs*' prologue, is forgotten here in the celebration of the god's joy-bringing presence, in the sacred dance from which comedy and tragedy both grow, and which they do not (at least in the depths of things) forget.

Comedy's license to play and tease and joke, to make fun of individuals by name (*onomasti kōmōidein*), and to offer playful criticisms of public affairs and even of the polis, all originated in, and reflect, Dionysian celebration: much as the Eleusinian "joking at the bridge" relaxed the pilgrims' tension on their way but also preempted something of the joy and laughter that burst forth when their initiation was completed and they ran out to sing and play and dance in the fields, lighting up the night with their torches. It may be that in the earliest Old Comic performances, as in surviving Dionysian rites, a chorus entered (1) to hymn the god, or gods and (2) to chant teasing words at the bystanders, with a sung refrain. Although this grew into the full, very sophisticated and varied parabasis of Aristophanes' very late Old Comedy, something of the power and the fun of the old alternation of hymn and teasing invective can still be felt in it, and especially in the parabases of the *Knights* and *Clouds*.[58]

The "anapests," in which the chorus speak most closely (but still teasingly) for the poet, advancing his claims, are a later, playful, and increasingly sophisticated addition to the ABAB core of hymn and invective/teasing criticism; and it is very significant that in the *Frogs* Aristophanes detaches these anapests from their usual context and introduces them just after the hymn to Iacchus. It is as though he felt the need of a parabasis *before* the parabasis; or, differently, as though his claims, and those of Old Comedy, required their oldest and strongest comic setting if they were to be made at all.

In their first lyrics, the initiates invoked the god Iacchus; in the anapests, they exclude various wrongdoers and philistines who have not been initiated into the rites of poetic culture, and of comedy:

/ If any man is unversed in words like these,
      or of unsound mind,
I bid that man keep holy silence, and stay
      apart from our festive dances:
or if he never saw, or himself performed
      in, the generous cult of the Muses,
or never practiced the Bacchic initiation
      that bull-eating Cratinus gave,
or if he fails to put down the city's strife,
      or is ungentle to citizens,
and rouses the flame of hatred, fanning it
      from lust of private gain,
or traffics in his office to get bribes
      when Athens is under storm,
or betrays a fort or ships to the enemy,
      or sends forth contraband
wood or supplies (like damned Thorycion,
      the Aegina–Epidaurus route),
or organizes financial benefits
      for our enemy's navy,
or, from among the dithyrambic singers,
      shits on Hecate's statues,
or makes those most unkindly cuts of all
      in poets' salaries,
all because he, a politician, was mocked
      in *Dionysus' ancient rites*:
men like these I proclaim, and again proclaim, and a third time
      proclaim must stand apart
from our mystic dances. But *you*, awaken *your*
      singing and dancing;
rouse up an all-night celebration, to suit
      this joy-filled holiday.   (354–71)

As usual, the chorus leader makes preposterously self-advertising claims
on the poet's behalf. As he was a National Asset elsewhere, or a monster-
slaying Heracles, so here he has become a sort of bishop, the hierophant
presiding over comedy's mystic rite of initiation. As usual, the comic
poet's sense of self-importance becomes ridiculously inflated. And the
height of political crime and folly is marked by a certain scurvy politician, here unnamed, who in reprisal for comic lampooning introduced a
bill to cut the poets' pay. This is rather like building, in the catalogue of
sinners punished in Hell, from fraud, incest, father-beating, and perjury
to copying out a speech from Morsimus. We are put on guard; the Great
Comic View of Things is hardly disinterested. And yet however comically
exaggerated it is here, the metaphor of initiation reminds us that the

funmaking, the *onomasti kōmōidein* of Old Comedy *is* a privileged form of laughter, deriving its rights and upside-down authority from the worship of the gods. Anyone who would censor it directly or indirectly, or curtail its ancient rights, is an enemy of life and of the gods.

Comedy's ancient rite of making political comments as well as personal jokes belongs to its old-time festive authority, here reaffirmed. But the Athenian references in these anapests are also the beginning of a movement on back to Athens and its problems in space and time. The urgency of these problems is suggested by the references to money, ships, and defense fortifications, by the dangerous term *stasis*, denoting party factionalism and strife, and by the image of the city "under storm" (another reminiscence, perhaps, of Arginusae). If Aristophanes found the confidence to return to concrete political issues and face them squarely, it may be that this came from his own initiation into Old Comic joy and Dionysian (and Eleusinian) revival of spirit; certainly courage and perseverance are the qualities of which Dionysus, in the play, is most in need; and Athens, by implication, needs them too. Accordingly the lyrics following the anapests, which take the form of three bidding prayers, combine joyful affirmation of the gods' presence with an increasingly self-conscious feeling of need for their protection, and for their intervention, if good and happy things like comedy's own laughter are to survive in time.

Thus the first hymn affirms, behind the proclaimed right to "joke, play, and tease," the presence of the Savior Goddess (probably Persephone) who proclaims that she "*does* save the land, season unto season, even if Thorycion doesn't want it." The reference to that scoundrel Thorycion, here repeated, is an example of Old Comedy's privileged laughter. Fools and villains were always to be expelled from the happy, fruitful community. Yet the problems "in season," in time and place, are very serious, and even one politician can almost—but not quite—veto the gods' will that Athens be saved.

Again, in the second hymn, to Demeter, there is a note of seriousness, and of anxiety just barely overcome:

> Queen of holy sacraments,
> Demeter, stand beside us;
> save us, save your chorus;
> grant us still, through every day,
> to play and dance in safety.
>
> To say many things in fun,
> grant us, and much in earnest:
> and when we have joked and played
> worthily of your holiday,
> grant us to wear
>   bright ribands of triumph! (384–93)

Here the chorus prays for its own protection. The reference is partly to the physical safety of the pilgrims on their way to Eleusis from Athens, endangered for some years by marauding Spartans. One of Alcibiades' most popular feats had been to escort the Eleusinian procession safely on its way, in 407 B.C. But in Athens' threatened world of 405 Alcibiades was in exile, the road to Eleusis was closed again, and not just the chorus of Mystae but the singers and dancers of comedy itself may have felt the roots of their existence shaken. Perhaps that is why they pray, not just to play and joke, but to speak "many funny things, and many serious things too" (*geloia, spoudaia*). Would this be the voice of theater before its split into tragedy and comedy? Or, in a perilous world, and one in which tragedy itself seems to have lost its moral and spiritual authority (as will appear further in the great agon), must comedy combine seriousness with play? The point is only hinted at, but it matters greatly to the future identity of comedy.[59]

In the third song, to Iacchus, the chorus return to a lighter, more teasing mode—perhaps because they have reassured themselves about Demeter's saving protection. The appeal to Dionysus as "fellow traveler" in their songs and dances is appropriate not only because the god Dionysus was so closely connected with the Eleusinian rites under the guise of the mystic Iacchus, but also because Dionysus in the *Frogs* has been undergoing his own symbolic pilgrimage through death to rebirth, and he can be invited now to join his own dance, with the further stimulation of a certain erotic teasing:

> *Chor.* All together now,
>   summon the handsome god into our presence
>   with songs, our fellow pilgrim for the dancing.
>
>   Iacchus most revered, you who discovered
>   holiday's own sweet music, swell our progress
>   towards Our Lady,
>   and show us how, without effort,
>   you cover a long journey.
>   *Iacchus, lover of dancing, join in escorting me.*
>
>   It was you that, fostering our laughter
>   and for cheapness, ripped up this old shirt
>   and little sandal,
>   and it was you that showed us how
>   to play and dance with impunity.
>   *Iacchus, lover of dancing, join in escorting me.*
>
>   I looked aside just now; what did I see?
>   A sweet and charming girl younger than me
>   joining in the sport:

> when her shirt came open,
> a little breast came peeking out.
> *Iacchus, lover of dancing, join in escorting me.*

Xa. My ears are quite aglow
to hear that song; I'd like
to play and dance with her.
Di. And so would I.   (394–415)

The references to costume enjoy a nice ambiguity. They are, first, to the tattered clothes worn by the initiates, as a convenience in their journey, and also as an outward sign of *communitas*: the hundreds of pilgrims, rich and poor, male and female, are free and equal on this occasion, and they leave behind the badges of class and status that divide one person from another. (They are the kind of happy and confused crowd that I last encountered in Miami two years back, at the Orange Bowl parade.) But also, it suits Aristophanes' own comic chorus to wear old clothes at a time of financial stringency. It is done, as he says, for laughs and for economy. The two needs wonderfully coincide, and Aristophanes makes symbolic capital of them, as he did with the invisible frog chorus earlier. It is a fine comic touch when the absence of sufficient clothing—always a sign of some inadequacy in the state of things—supplies just the right touch, or rather sight, to entice Dionysus and Xanthias from the position of being mere spectators at the show. They are caught up, if not in the dance, at least in the teasing rhythm of the song.

And again, they are caught up in the simple, teasing verses that follow. I give only a few:

> Do you want us all together
> to laugh at Archedemus?
> At school his boyish nature
> was never—naturalized;
> but now he sways the people
> up there, where dead men flourish:
> in all their vicious actions
> his leadership is prized.   (416–21)

Here are more references to "real life" Athens, now seen from the vantage point of the initiates as a place of the living dead. The inversion by which the "corpses" are left above and the true vitality of Athenian life rests below is central to this play, and I shall say more about it; but what is more immediately striking is the old-fashioned playfulness of these verses. They are written in simple iambics, in a hand-clapping rhythm in which the audience could participate. They begin with an invitation to communal play and jesting; and again Dionysus and Xanthias find themselves joining in:

> *Di.* Do you think you could inform us
> of the place of Pluto's dwelling?
> We're foreigners who only
> just now have gotten here.
> *Ch.* You needn't go any distance,
> or think to repeat your question:
> you're at the very doorstep—
> that ought to be quite clear.　　　　(431–36)

As they join in the festive community, they get directions for continuing their journey—or rather, find that they have arrived just where they want to be. And as the chorus move into their last, very joyful dance and song—evoking their own torchlit dances, their revelry in the fields, and the true sunlight that only the blessed enjoy—Dionysus and his slave move on back toward Pluto's house, toward further comic (and human) misadventures, and, by implication, toward the Athenian world of time and change with which a comic poet, like a god renewed in spirit, must come to terms.

The scenes following the parodos are the wildest and funniest in the *Frogs*. Dionysus as Heracles is confronted by Pluto's servant Aeacus, who threatens him with horrible tortures for his (Heracles') earlier misdeeds. Here, after the sight of Heaven, are the threats of Hell. Dionysus, being a coward, is scared stiff; but being a comic hero, he persuades Xanthias to exchange costume and role with him. Then a servant appears, on behalf of her mistress Persephone, to invite Heracles to a banquet of rare meats, cakes, good sweet wine, and dancing girls; so Dionysus quickly takes his Heracles role back—just in time to encounter two ferocious landladies who invoke the entire political machinery of Hell against the offender Heracles. Again Dionysus changes roles; but when Aeacus enters with armed slaves, Xanthias-Heracles offers his slave to be tortured as evidence that he never came there before. This is too much for Dionysus, who reveals himself as "Dionysus, son of Zeus." Aeacus, understandably confused, uses a whipping contest to determine who is the god, for a god can't be hurt; and the confusion grows, for both are hurt. When I directed this scene once, I added to the confusion between levels of reality by telling the slaves to hit harder, so it would really hurt, if the *actors* playing Dionysus and Xanthias did not yell loud enough. Perhaps that was too modern. But the audience should not forget that an actor is playing Dionysus, who is playing his slave Xanthias, who is playing Heracles. It is no wonder that Aeacus is confused; the contest is inconclusive, and he must refer the question of Dionysus' identity to his master and mistress, Pluto and Persephone (a variation on the Eleusis theme earlier). They all go off, and the chorus deliver the parabasis.

When the play began, Dionysus was telling Xanthias not to make the usual clownish jokes about "Oh, my aching back," or about how the pressure was so great that he couldn't help it, he would just have to—the forbidden word pops up with double force—shit. Certainly, as Aristophanes said throughout his career, it is poor taste, and vulgar, to rely on buffoonery alone in the absence of comic ideas and comic wit; yet Old Comedy keeps returning, and rightly, to its base and basic self, and like Philocleon, it has always rejected efforts to clean up its act. Now the pressure is growing for comedy to be serious, perhaps even (as will appear) to adopt an educational role that tragedy has abdicated. All the louder are Dionysus' own stomach rumbles and explosive farts as, competing with the frog chorus, he crosses the Styx; and all the more splendidly vulgar is his behavior in these role-shifting scenes. I give one example (after Aeacus' horrible threats):

> *Xa.* What *have* you done?
> *Di.* My duty. Praise the Lord.
> *Xa.* You stupid fool. Won't you get up before
> some stranger sees you?
> *Di.* I can't. I'm feeling faint.
> Won't you apply a sponge around my heart?
> *Xa.* Here, take it, *you* apply it. What—? Ye gods,
> is *that* where your heart is?
> *Di.* It got frightened,
> it snuck right down into my small intestine.
> *Xa.* O thou of gods and men most vile—
> *Di.* Who, me?
> What's vile? Didn't I ask you for a sponge?
> No other person would have done it; no,
> he'd just have lain there, smelling himself.
> *That's* vile.
> But I got up. What's more, I wiped myself.
> *Xa.* Bravely done, by Poseidon!
> *Di.* Indeed it was, by Zeus!   (479–91)

There is the Old Comic hero in all his shamelessness, triumphant over ultimate humiliation. "But I got up. What's more, I wiped myself." It may be true that comedy will clean up its act, will become more serious, and will preserve sharper distinctions between levels of joking and seriousness in times to come: but not yet.

Or is this Old Comedy's last fling? Dionysus is stripped of Heraclean pretense, with very amusing results, but also as part of a symbolic initiation into his more god-like self; when he reappears, it will be in the god's solemn robe, and as visiting judge in the theater of the underworld.

Comedy too was stripped of pretensions for the whipping scene. Is its ancient rite of play finished when the clowns depart and the first half of the *Frogs* ends—a curtain-raiser, almost, to the second?

Certainly, against this background, Aristophanes surprises us with the seriousness of his parabasis, which he underlines himself in the first epirrheme:

> It is right that the sacred chorus should give good and useful advice and instruction to the polis. So: first of all, we think it right that all citizens should be made equal, and that every fear should be removed. (686–88)

The right of the "sacred chorus" to play and joke is here complemented by their other ancient right, to advise the community. Accordingly the first long recitative (B1) is a plea to forgive fellow citizens who made political mistakes, to release them from fear of suspicion and blackmail, and to enlist the help of all good citizens in a time of national peril (the storm at sea). In the second recitative (B2), the chorus advise the polis to return to the "gold standard" in choosing its leaders, as in minting its coins. They should choose good men, *chrēstoi*: not the low scoundrels who, in the old days, wouldn't have done as scapegoats, *pharmakoi*. The word is suggestive. It recalls the ritual origins of comedy, in which the invocation of the gods and their blessings was balanced by the expulsion of blighting influences, physical at first, then through mocking laughter. The ode and antode (A1 and A2) exemplify such playful invective. Cleophon is ridiculed as a barbarous-speaking noisemaker, Cleigenes as an ape-like little bath manager who adulterates the soap. Both are chosen because, as politicians and troublemakers, they exacerbate just those divisions in the community that the comic chorus is advising its public to correct.

In a sense communal solidarity is what Aristophanes has been advocating all along. It was symbolized in the *Lysistrata* by the gathering of wool from different sources so it could be spun and woven into a fine seamless coat. Here and elsewhere, the greatest defense of Athens against her external enemies is the preservation of inner unity and coherence, and the avoidance of *stasis*; and if, as we are told, Aristophanes' audience awarded the *Frogs* the unusual honor of a second performance, this may be because they were pleased, and moved, by the appeal to unity. Yet the political community here advocated should not be confused with the experience of *communitas* to which Old Comedy is basically loyal, and which is well represented in the depiction of the Eleusinian pilgrims, all equal in their human fun and seriousness, as in their tattered clothes. The experience of *communitas* comes in just such times, when differences of rank and status are waived; in turn it nurtures the ordinary, working, organized state in which such differences are necessary and (often) useful. Although the chorus plead for restored "equality" in the citizen body, their special wish is that all the good men, the *chrēstoi*, might work together for the common good; it is necessary that the *chrēstoi* take the lead in political affairs, and that the low scoundrels, men like Cleophon and Cleigenes, sink to the bottom where they deserve to be. In this way a natural hierarchy will be restored. As for the slaves, it was all right, even a good idea, to give citizenship to those who rowed at Arginusae: but enough is enough; that Saturnalia (it is implied) is over; it is time for right relations, and a proper hierarchy of roles, to be restored.

Is this, as many people think, the "true" Aristophanes showing his colors? Has he always been a conservative at heart? Or has he turned such because the life and spirit of Athens are now at stake? Either position is conceivable, but I am not convinced that either is true. Let me return to the closely related question of comedy and tragedy, and to the action of the *Frogs*.

In the scene following the parabasis a great change has taken place. It is a new beginning, a second prologue, given by two slaves. There is no more confusion about identities; Xanthias is fixed in his slave role and in the low humor appropriate to it; he and Aeacus are equally set off from their masters, of whom they make fun. Their business is to amuse the audience, to prepare the way for the great agon of Aeschylus and Euripides, which Dionysus is invited to judge as god of theater; and, that done, to get themselves out of the way.

One of the greatest differences between Old and New Comedy is that in the latter the comic business is left mostly to the slave and the cook. Scenes of sentimental love comedy, or of refined comedy of manners, are set off against scenes of low farce, or kitchen humor, as in Menander's *Dyskolos*. And even if, as often happens in Plautus, the slave takes charge of events and orders respectable citizens around, we are left in no doubt that this is a Saturnalian moment in things, and that the natural hierarchy of master and slave, magistrate and common man, seriousness and fun, will shortly (or outside the comic theater) be restored.[60] Or if, in Northrop Frye's formula, comedy takes us from the gray world into the green, the movement is still from one kind of law to another: from the unreasonable restrictions and biases of the old law to the greater freedom and flexibility of the new. We often feel, as we watch New Comedy and its successors, such as twentieth-century American musical comedy, that society has been improved by its comical shaking up; but we never feel that it has stopped being society.

Besides the disappearance of the functional Old Comedy chorus, the chief reason why the *Plutus* has seemed to belong to the later world of the new (or middle) comedy is that, for the most part, seriousness and joking are divided between the master Chremylus and the slave Carion. It is for the latter to crack jokes, to make irreverent and disrespectful remarks, to lead the chorus in an isolated vulgar dance and song, and to keep up a scurrilous running commentary on the serious action. But

Chremylus remains what he is, a serious, decent, and (perhaps) ordinary man, who is not carried away by sudden riches. He is a far cry from the crazy old heroes of Old Comedy, or its revolution-minded heroines. If he finds himself in a magical world where people get more money than they deserve, it is in spite of himself, and in spite of the bourgeois setting, and the bourgeois standards, into which comedy has begun to settle down. Seriousness and humor may have been combined in fourth-century comedy, but after Aristophanes—who perhaps remained a maverick to the end—they would no longer be confused.

If I have been looking into the future of comedy, it is because Aristophanes, in the *Frogs*, seems to be doing this too. At midpoint, his play suggests that the confusion of roles and styles, on which Old Comedy flourished, has been cleared up: that masters can once again be distinguished from slaves, and good men from bad; and that comedy has learned when to give serious advice, and when to joke. When Dionysus reappears, wearing his new, dignified robe as god of the theater, in company with Pluto, and when he takes his solemn seat to judge the agon between Aeschylus and Euripides, we might expect him (and Aristophanes with him) to make a good and true judgment about tragedy, and perhaps about Athens too. In the view of many critics he does just that. The choice of Aeschylus would correspond to the serious advice in the parabasis, to make use of good men, to restore order and community in the polis. And a basically funny play, perhaps the last wild fling of Old Comedy, would be followed by a basically serious one, hinting at the New. All this would be understandable under the circumstances. Whether Aristophanes gives us what is merely understandable is quite another question.

For all its hilarious moments (and there are many), the literary agon between Aeschylus and Euripides leans toward seriousness. The stylistic criticisms, with their more evenly matched parody, and culminating in the ridiculous weighing scene, are inset between the discussion of content, emphasizing moral and spiritual values or their absence, and the final questions put to the two poets. What should be done about Alcibiades? And how, in your opinion, can Athens be saved? Although this last discussion is inconclusive, like much that preceded it, the overall balance tilts from the start towards the moral wisdom and vitality found in Aeschylus' tragedies, and we are not surprised when Dionysus, as an intelligent judge of the theater, decides to bring Aeschylus, not Euripides, back to the upper world. Euripides' disappointment and outrage are comical. What can we say of Dionysus' choice, and Aristophanes' overall meaning?

To begin with the first stage of the agon, after the preliminary exchange of insults: Euripides' presentation makes it clear that he and Aeschylus live and think in different worlds. To him, and perhaps to many in the audience, Aeschylus is old-fashioned and often incomprehensible with his grandiloquent diction, archaic images, and complicated metaphors. This is a man who wants to impress his audience, not be understood by them. By contrast, Euripides claims that he himself thinned down the art of tragedy like a skilled physician, removing its swollen bombast; that he made his characters speak plainly and intelligently, instead of indulging in pretentious tragic silences; and that, by doing so, he sharpened the critical sensitivities of his audience. His star pupil (this tells against him, actually) is the versatile politician Theramenes, who shifts positions easily, wriggling out of difficulties. The shrewd mastery of language imparted by Euripides, as by the sophists and the teachers of oratory, is the key both to successful tragedy-writing and to the grasp of both private and public affairs that every Athenian naturally wants.

But Euripides' admission that poets should be admired for "making people better in the cities" plays into Aeschylus' hands. His tragedies, he maintains, made people better; Euripides' made them worse. Since Aeschylus' mind gravitates to concrete and symbolic instances, and not abstract definitions, he has some trouble conveying just how his plays produced, among other virtues, martial spirit, and just how and why this was a benefit; but when he asserts his place in a long line of poet-educators, the claim is impressive and convincing. Orpheus revealed holy rites and taught abstention from murder; Musaeus sang of healing and of oracles, Hesiod of farming and of the seasons; Homer taught what was good and useful (*chrēst' edidaxen*), like military order, discipline, and valor; and Aeschylus followed in Homer's footsteps. What does Euripides teach with his dramas of erotic passion, his "whores" like Phaedra and Stheneboia? He teaches honest women to kill themselves from shame. "But wasn't it true, what I wrote about Phaedra?" asks Euripides. It was, Aeschylus admits,

> But the poet should conceal what is bad, not bring it forth and produce it (*didaskein*) in public. For children have a teacher (*didaskalos*) to show them things, and young men and women growing up have the poets. So really we must say things that are good and useful. (1053–55)

The implied joke, that women are sex-crazed like Phaedra, opens a wedge between what is true and what is morally improving. Euripides presents himself as a realist: he portrays character the way it is, not as it should be; and his techniques, of diction or costume, are correspondingly realistic. Does Aeschylus' poetry match its claims, of artistic and human truth? Or is it simply outdated—like what we learned in school so long ago?

Aeschylus responds with further assertions, not analysis. His own high diction, his noble costumes, suited the larger-than-life figures that heroes and heroines ought to be; but Euripides has degraded his characters, dressing heroes in rags (a pathetic and contagious effect, now popular among taxpayers) and popularizing the practice of intellectual analysis, argument, and sheer chatter—something that, outside the theater, has emptied the wrestling schools and undermined military discipline. In short:

> What evils *didn't* this man start?
> Didn't he first bring bawds onstage,
> and women giving birth in shrines,
> and having sex with their own siblings,
> and saying, "To be is not to be"?
> No wonder Athens has to boast
> hundreds of minor bureaucrats
> and clownish apes who run for office,
> selling themselves with slick commercials:
> but no one *runs*, nobody's fit
> to bear the torch any longer.   (1078–88)

Dionysus pointedly concurs. He remembers laughing at a fat man who couldn't complete the Panathenaic torch race, but huffed, puffed, and panted, was beaten by bystanders, and finally blew out his torch and ran away. The image suggests the vanishing of an older way of life that was vital, holy, and glorious. The older tragedy, of Aeschylus, fostered such a life; modern tragedy, being nurtured on sophistry, made its physical health, its moral beauty, and the joy of its spiritual discipline disappear.

At this point the reader of Aristophanes at least may feel a sense of déjà vu, for the same conflict of old and new cultural values was represented in the first agon of the *Clouds*. There Socrates, not Euripides, was the catalyst of change, but the issues are much the same. In the contest of the two *logoi* that Pheidippides, the reluctant student, is left to watch, the Just Argument, or Right, speaks for the older educational system: for music and gymnastics, and for the morals and manners, and the right tone, that went with them. Although the speaker is old-fashioned, literal-minded, and ridiculous in many ways, yet his words turn poetic in the end, evoking the beauty of an older way of life, with young men running under the elm and plane trees in spring, that may now be lost forever. We feel something of Aristophanes' own nostalgia here. But the Unjust Argument, or Wrong, speaks second; he refutes the other easily with his sophistic logic-chopping, and with a cheerful, self-confident immoralism that is very funny; and when he wins, we are hardly surprised or shocked. Pheidippides goes on to study with Wrong, and to beat his father, and to argue, in a second agon, that father-beating is justified;

and Strepsiades, the father, comes to repent of his would-be wrongdoing and to burn down Socrates' place about his ears—but that is, or was, another story. Of significant resemblances, which suggests that it is a *continuing* story, I mention only two.

First, there is the joke about prayers. In the *Clouds* Socrates incorporates (among other things) the demythologizing tendencies of pre-Socratic science and the Sophistic Enlightenment. Thus he presents the clouds to Strepsiades as "your only true divinities"; he replaces Zeus and the Olympians with up-to-date explanations of meteorological phenomena and with scientific concepts, such as cosmic revolution, that the literal-minded Strepsiades imagines to be new gods who have taken over Olympus; and he swears by his new divinities: "By Chaos! By Respiration! By the Air!" In the *Frogs* the same joke is expanded, to begin a scene:

> *Di.* Now pray, the both of you, before you speak.
> *Aes.* Demeter, nurse of my intelligence,
>   may I be worthy of your mysteries.
> *Di.* Now *you* may offer incense.
> *Eur.* Thank you, no.
>   I pray to gods of quite another sort.
> *Di.* To private gods, just newly coined?
> *Eur.* That's it.
> *Di.* Well, make your prayers then, to your private gods.
> *Eur.* Ozone that nurtured me, Pivot of Tongue
>   and Power of Brain, and most perceptive Nostrils:
>   may I refute all arguments I meet.   (885–94)

Aeschylus was nurtured by Demeter and by the Mysteries whose joy the *Frogs* earlier celebrated. If his tragedies are inspired and inspiring, it is because they spring from a religious view of things. By contrast Euripides believes in abstract intelligence, which is bound up with the everyday ✓ material world ("higher thought" depends on how we breathe in and out) and which finds expression in speech, in the "turning pivot of the tongue." As in the *Clouds*, the sophistic air theory is contrasted with the cult worship of the Olympian gods, and the constant intellectual chatter of Euripides' characters and disciples is contrasted with the holy silence of the Mysteries, with the dignified silence of Aeschylus' tragic figures, which Euripides decried as silly, and even with Aeschylus' own angry silence in the face of the appalling Euripides.[61]

A late reference to Socrates more strikingly connects the *Frogs* with the earlier *Clouds*. When (to anticipate) Dionysus finally chooses Aeschylus over Euripides, the chorus praise his decision as right, sensible, and good for the community; they also interpret it as a rejection of Socrates and all his works:

It's nice, never to spend your time
with Socrates in stupid chatter,
spoiling the tragic art, as though
the music didn't matter;

for if you waste whole useless days
in quibbles of a pretentious kind,
scratching up bits of thought, it shows
you're simply—out of your mind.   (1491–99)

One implication here, which Nietzsche developed in his *Birth of Tragedy*, is that Euripides made the intellectual element in tragedy dominant, to the harm of its more basic "musical" nature, and did so under the influence of Socrates and the philosophers.[62] Today most people would argue that the charge against Euripides is unfair—just as it is unfair to make the poet directly responsible for what his characters say, regardless of the context—and that Euripides subordinates the element of *dianoia*, the rhetorical expression of ideas and arguments, to the more basic elements of *mythos* and *ēthos*, plot and character, as much as Aeschylus ever did. And yet Euripides remains a catalyst for change in his way, as Socrates in his. He exemplifies the power of new ideas in a popular medium. In his tragedies the older traditions of religion, democracy, and the family are subjected to conscious and often destructive scrutiny, just as in Socrates' teaching they are brought, without exception, before the bar of reason. It is no wonder that Aristophanes treats the two "learned doctors" in similar ways; nor that both times, in the *Clouds* and in the *Frogs*, he goes beyond satire to deal with deeper issues, of cultural and educational change, to which Socrates' teaching and Euripides' writing point.

Nevertheless the agon of the *Frogs* differs significantly in its procedure and outcome from the first agon of the *Clouds*. There the Unjust Argument spoke last, and he won, partly through sophistry and sheer brashness but partly too because what was new, vigorous, and Dionysian was on his side. His injunction to "skip, laugh, consider nothing shameful" could have been comedy's own. But in the *Frogs*, although the final decision is long delayed, Aeschylus has generally been given the last word, and the more telling argument; and while he is old-fashioned, he still possesses an energy of body and spirit that outmatches Euripides' rather effete intellectual stance, putting it to shame. Already Dionysus the character and judge leans to Aeschylus' side, and not least because the god Dionysus is this time on the side of the old, which is more vital and inspired than the new.

But Aristophanes himself has other reasons for siding with Aeschylus. The very existence of his own Old Comedy is bound up with the moral and spiritual strength of the older Athens, which Aeschylus helped to nourish (or so he claims, and there seems to be no reason to doubt him here). The city must be saved, "so it can present its choruses." But also, if the Old Comedy is to maintain its own irreverent and irresponsible ways, it requires as its foil the dignity and moral seriousness of the older ✓ tragedy. Therefore, if modern tragedy goes its unedifying way, then comedy in turn may need to change its nature, to alternate humor with seriousness, in order to take up the slack. It may even need to teach "good and useful things to the public"—as in the parabasis of the *Frogs*.

And yet the allegiance of Aristophanes' comedy is not so certain, for it has ironic affinities with the new intellectualism, and even with Euripides, as the teasing chorus suggest after the first section of the agon has been completed:

> Go at it, both of you. Speak out.
> Use old material and new.
> You may run the risk of expressing
>   subtle and bright ideas.
> If you're worried your audience might miss
> some clever sayings, out of ignorance,
> don't be afraid. It isn't like that any longer.
> They're disciplined likc soldiers now;
> every man has been issued his own book
> and quickly catches all the bright ideas.
> Their native aptitude is high,
> and now their mighty intellects
>   are sharpened to a point.
> Don't be afraid, then. Cover all your ground.
> You can be sure the audience is bright.   (1106–18)

To encourage the two contestants to do their best, the chorus praise the critical acumen of the audience, who may be relied on to get even the more subtle points of the subsequent debate. As said earlier, the picture of all those rows of intelligent and attentive spectators, each with his book in hand, following the more subtle details of literary analysis and parody, is wonderfully absurd. Only a scholar, with book in hand, could take it seriously—although the image hints at dreadful things to come. Yet the truth remains that Aristophanes required an intelligent audience who would "get the point," as they had notoriously failed to do when the *Clouds* was presented. The literary contest in the *Frogs* relies on wit and inventiveness, not on the old tricks of knockabout farce (which were renounced earlier, and then splendidly exemplified in the Dionysus–Xanthias scenes); it involves shrewd parody, and games involving critical notions; in short, it combines old things and new (*ta te palaia kai ta kaina*, 1107). As a writer of what we have called Old-and-New Comedy, Aristophanes profited from, and indeed required, the intellectual atmosphere of Athens that Euripides has just now claimed to foster. His plays, and especially the *Clouds* and the present *Frogs*, are comedies of ideas; and however deep-rooted they are (as I strongly believe) in religious celebration, they lay themselves open to the charge of "Euripidaristophanizing" that at least one competitor made against Aristophanes.[63]

It is hardly surprising, then, that Aeschylus' superiority cannot be established on grounds of style, for literary criticism tends toward relativism and, in the end, is just another one of those new forms of intellectual chatter that Euripides teaches and Aeschylus denounces.[64] Its method of close examination and "torture" (*basanisdein*) recalls the earlier whipping contest that failed to distinguish between slave and master, man and god. And similarly, despite all its fun, from the quibbling about prologues and versification to that wonderful parody of a typical aria of Euripides ("My lovely cock has flown away, has flown away . . ."), this section of the contest proves inconclusive. And so, really, does the nonsensical weighing scene, where words and phrases are thrown onto the critical scales. The joke here is on literary criticism itself, with all its pretentious jargon. It is, on one level, an insubstantial kind of chatter (albeit food for comedy; I would like to try something with "canons" and "cannons" today). On another level, as Cedric Whitman has shown, the scene has tragic implications.[65] Death is a heavier thing than persuasion, than all the play of words—perhaps including comedy's own. And death has weighed heavily in the *Frogs*, from the beginning. The death of the old tragedy, the old Athens, and even the old comedy, can no longer be ignored.

So Dionysus takes up the political problems that have been lurking in the wings. What should be done about Alcibiades? And how, practically speaking, can Athens be saved? Discussion of Alcibiades proves inconclusive. Euripides rejects him in pointed antitheses; Aeschylus indicates the tragic nature of the dilemma in symbolic language; and one is left wondering, as before, what should be done. And similarly with Athens: Aristophanes may indicate, by creating an impasse in the debate, that whatever answer Athens requires, it cannot be stated in terms that are both wise and clear, tragically comprehensive and politically decisive. Tragedy was never the handmaiden of practical politics, nor was meant to be. But it may be, if Wills's analysis of the passage in question is correct, that Euripides' cleverness is shown up finally as frivolous and irresponsible, while Aeschylus' silence, his refusal to give practical advice here and now, points to the prior necessity of Athens' spiritual regeneration—which the choice of Aeschylus and his old-fashioned religious, moral, and communal values will imply.[66] As Wills puts it,

> The mere willingness to listen to him, to its best self, its heroic past, will effect a salvation that no scheming could accomplish. This is what the "conversion" of Dionysus signifies. He did not get what he expected, but something better—not Euripides' devices, but the living Aeschylus. If Athens learns, like its festival god, to yearn

again after *that*, then it needs no further prompting on the externals of policy.[67]

It is in keeping with the difficult antithesis between silence and chatter, but also with comedy's own way of cutting through difficulties, that Dionysus, after all this lengthy and elaborate discussion, simply chooses the man whom his "soul desires":

Pl. It's judgment time.
Di. Then here's how I'll decide.
    I'll choose the person whom my soul desires.
Eur. Be mindful of the gods by whom you swore
    you'd bring me home, and choose your dearest kin.
Di. My tongue has sworn—and Aeschylus I'll choose.
Eur. What have you done, you utter villain?
Di. Me?
    Decided Aeschylus should win. Why not?
Eur. Shameful! And you can look me in the face?
Di. What's shameful, if the—audience don't think so?
Eur. Heartless man. Will you leave me here for dead?
Di. Who knows whether to be, be not to be,
    to breathe, perchance to dine, to sleep—a bedspread?

(1467–78)

So much for critical judgment. For Dionysus to give reasons, were they as plentiful as blackberries, would be to embroil himself once more in the sophisticated modern chatter that he has rejected; for he has simply experienced a change of heart. Originally it was his heart's desire that led him down to the underworld, to seek Euripides; but now that his sense of what he really wants has been clarified by the trip through Hades, his choice is reliable and sound, and Pluto, impatient for a decision, might have urged him, much as Virgil urges Dante as they near the summit of Purgatory and the Earthly Paradise, "lo tuo piacere omai prendi per duce," to take his pleasure for a guide.[68] The heart's reasons may be unspoken, like the ceremonies of Eleusis, and even unspeakable, but they are right in the end, and the reasonings of the critical intelligence, with all its Euripidean equivocations (now humorously turned against Euripides), are wrong.

Dionysus' experience of rediscovering his "soul" in Hades suggests that there is a certain truth in the Euripidean paradox, here parodied: "Who knows if life is death, and death is life?" (Compare the Euripidean heroines earlier who asserted, "Life is not life.") Certainly, the vitality that Dionysus rediscovers in the rich underworld makes ordinary Athenian life, and Athenian politics, seem ghastly by contrast, and Pluto urges Aeschylus, once he reaches the upper world, to tell Cleophon and the gang of tax experts to "go to hell" right away—in order, presumably, to end confusion between the living and the dead.[69] If Athens has been looking like a suburb of Hell—"I had not thought death had undone so many," Eliot says of the crowds streaming over London Bridge[70]—it seems reasonable to invert the proposition and find the true life of tragedy, and of Athens, down in Hades; still, life is life, wherever it may be found, and death is death.

The torchlight procession that escorts Aeschylus back to the upper world closes the play appropriately with an image of hope and not despair. In part this may reflect the fact that, by a special privilege, Aeschylus' plays had been "revived" at Athens.[71] Being performed is more vital, despite actors' changes and interpolations, than being read in a fixed text, whether on shipboard or elsewhere; hence the "revival" of Aeschylus suggests the living power of that great spirit beyond the grave. Beyond that, Aristophanes may have felt, with his own power of hopefulness, that Athens still showed vital signs, and that predictions of her death were exaggerated. Certainly he lived to see the city's remarkable recovery, once again, after the ships were beaten, the walls pulled down, and the Thirty Tyrants installed with the help of a Spartan garrison. But his point is not that the spirit of Athens is unquenchable, any more than that of tragedy—or even of comedy. It is rather that the light that goes out can be relit. In the course of time the festive torch, representing the spirit of an older Athens in all its beauty and vigor, can be blown out—just as a person's life can, in an instant, be breathed away. Only the gods have immortality. But for mortals, there is the hopeful glow of Eleusinian torchlight, lighting up meadows for singing and dancing the other side of death; and this bright glow, of life renewed, is reflected in the joyful procession that escorts Aeschylus back to the upper world. It is an inverted funeral rite, and it is a comic and Dionysian rite of passage for tragedy, for Athens, and for comedy itself—playing at initiation, and being initiated, once more, into a renewal of joyful play.

35   *Dionysian Rites of Passage*

T H E obvious tragic counterpart to the *Frogs* is Euripides' *Bacchae*, where Dionysus takes cruel revenge on the youthful tyrant
Pentheus, revealing himself as a god "most gentle . . . but also most
terrible." As a rite of passage, however, for Athens and for poetry, the
Frogs may also be paired with Sophocles' *Oedipus at Colonus*, written
shortly before Sophocles' death (to which Aristophanes briefly alludes)
in 406/5, and produced posthumously in 401 B.C.

The old, blind, wandering Oedipus of this play, supported literally and
figuratively by his two daughters, incarnates the sufferings and labors of
old age, which Sophocles also describes in one of the darkest odes in all
Greek tragedy. The winds howl, life's storms beat on his unprotected
head, as they do on Lear's. Yet he survives, through endurance, inborn
nobility, and a hidden grace of time; and he makes his way back into a
civilized community, of Athens, where Theseus welcomes and protects
him, and where, in the mysterious grove of the Eumenides at Colonus, he
is purified finally of his violent past. And then, by the gods' mysterious
gift (which balances their earlier violence against him, but comes, as he
complains, so very late), he makes his way into the transhuman condition of a Hero, with power extending beyond death to bless his friends
and curse his enemies. His mysterious "passing" at the play's end seems
a just fulfillment of his extraordinary heroism displayed in life. It also
suggests the mystery of death through which all people must pass, including Sophocles himself.

But the play is concerned with the fate of nations, not just individuals.
It presents an idealized Athens, young and vigorous like Theseus himself,
the Athens of panegyric that fights for the right and rescues helpless
suppliants. ("I lift my lamp beside the golden door.") But there are hints,
especially in the Polyneices episode, of a very different Athens filled with
envy, hatred, strife, and bloodshed, just like tragic Thebes; and indeed,
when the aged Oedipus promises recompense to Theseus for his kindness

and generosity, he reminds him, in extremely powerful language, that all things human are subject to the sway of time:

> Dearest son of Aegeus, it comes to no man,
> Only to the gods, not to grow old, never to die.
> All others are confounded by all-conquering time:
> It wastes the earth's power, wastes the body's:
> Honor dies, dishonor comes to bloom,
> And the same constant breath never, not even among
> Dear friends holds true, nor between the cities of man.
> For some today, for some in another time
> Joy comes to bitterness and round to love again.
> And as for Thebes, if now fair weather holds
> Between you and them, unnumbered time
> Shall bring unnumbered nights and days to birth,
> In which the concords of today
> Shall scatter from the spear over a little word.
> Then shall my sleeping, cold, and hidden corpse
> Drink their hot blood—if Zeus is still Zeus,
> If Phoebus is his son, if he is plain with me.[72]   (607–23)

Oedipus is speaking of the present good relations between Athens and Thebes, which could turn to bitter enmity someday (and did, long before the Peloponnesian War). But his words suggest that the bright, generous, and pious spirit of Theseus' Athens can also decline and fade, as all things human must.

If, in Sophocles' plays, one answer to time and change is the assertion of something unyielding in the hero's nature and will, whether this finds its outcome in Ajax' suicide, or Antigone's provocation of death, or in Philoctetes' or Oedipus' endurance and eventual triumph, what comparable answer can be made to the challenge that time and change pose for the beloved polis? One possible answer is that the gift of poetry keeps Athens alive. As Bernard Knox puts it,

> The Athens Sophocles knew in his youth is to die, but be immortal; he sings of it as he remembered it in its days of greatness and beauty, and this is how we remember it still. "Even if we lose," said Pericles, "the memory will live forever." The city of Sophocles' youth and manhood will put on immortality, like the old, blind man who has now become its citizen.[73]

Another possible answer is to affirm the gods' love for Athens, their abiding presence, and their imperishable gifts, as the chorus do in their lovely ode on Colonus (668–719). Dionysus and his divine nurses, the nymphs, walk there always; the Muses and Aphrodite cherish the place, Zeus and Athena watch over it, Poseidon and the Nereids grant it lasting blessings. The quiet grove, free of winds and storms such as beat upon old age; the narcissus blooming "day unto day, always"; the Cephisus, rich-flowing "for each day, always," from undiminished springs; the unconquerable olive, that neither old man nor young will overcome, but that flourishes forever: all these are images of something in the life of Athens that cannot grow old or die. Perhaps the chorus are wrong. Their affirmation is tinged with irony by Oedipus' warning, and by the audience's present experience of wartime desolation. In a play of Euripides such an ode would merely be nostalgic, a foil to present suffering, and present reality, which are one and the same. For Sophocles, however, the chorus may be right: there may be more to reality than is subject even to time.

Soon afterwards, the chorus wonder where the Athenian horsemen will catch up with the Theban kidnappers—perhaps near the precinct of Pythian Apollo, or else, perhaps,

> by the torchlit strand
> where the Two Queens nurture
> holy, majestic rites for mortals,
> for which the golden key
> of the Eumolpidae, their servants, is
> set upon men's lips.   (1049–53)

The saving revelation, evoked in images of bright torchlight along the sea, of Demeter's nursing care, and of the gold of divinity shining forth in human life, is kept in silence. And the place of Oedipus' burial or mysterious passing will also be kept in silence, a mystery to be handed down from father to son among the lords of Athens.

Sophocles does not make time, change, old age, and death seem easy. As a blind, helpless, wandering beggar, Oedipus continues to exemplify the stripping away of power and privilege, and the confrontation with the dark unknown, that every human being must undergo; and even after he straightens up (it is a remarkable moment in the theater) and leads Theseus and his daughters off, with god-inspired inner sight, Antigone and Ismene are left to mourn bitterly after his passing (which they do not see) and to suffer new involvement in the passions and struggles of Thebes. All the same, Oedipus' dying is depicted as the last of his transitions, for which all the others have prepared him. He has been purified by time and suffering, and by the rites performed on his behalf in the grove of the Eumenides. His heroism now reaches its fulfillment.

When the chorus pray to Aidoneus, lord of the "unseen" realm, and to Persephone that Oedipus' journey be made easy, their prayer could be for any dying person, even for Sophocles himself, who wrote these lines in extreme old age. But the rite of passage for Oedipus suggests a corresponding rite for Athens. Charles Segal, an outstanding scholar of transitions, puts it well:

The city too becomes involved in that passage between things human and things divine which centers upon Oedipus. For Sophocles, writing during Athens' near-exhaustion at the end of a long war, it may have seemed as if Athens was engaged in a perilous crossing between an old and a new existence, between material and spiritual greatness. Athens, like the aged Oedipus—and perhaps also the aged Sophocles—throws off the outer covering of its battered form to be reborn in the inner strength of its spiritual power. Its civilizing achievement is no longer in its might and dominion but in its spiritual radiance, its privileged openness to divinity.

Oedipus' grove, like Athens, is a place where new life arises in the midst of death. Close to death, like Oedipus, it holds a secret vitality that leads to rebirth. The singing nightingale in the sunless, windless grove, the beauty of the narcissus, the light of the crocus amid the dim foliage suggest a crossing of life and death not only for Oedipus and not only for Athens, but also for Sophocles' art: something in touch with the sources of vital energy that lie beyond human control, a promise of transfiguring brilliance in the midst of darkness.[74]

It may be that Sophocles envisaged Athens (and poetry with it) as needing to be purified through time and suffering, like Oedipus, and to pass through a kind of death. For the Periclean spirit does not remain, not even in living memory. The "immortality of song," once so strong a consolation for struggle and death, as in Homer and Pindar, itself becomes subject to time, change, and death. What remains is silence, and hope, and the Eleusinian promise (even though, as Knox indicates, the road to Eleusis could be barred by enemy squadrons) of light shining out of darkness the other side of death.[75]

I have suggested that in the *Frogs* the comic funeral rite of passage keeps pace with the tragic one. Euripides' death brings Dionysus to confront the world of death and corpses with Old Comic clowning, and to renew himself, and Aristophanes with him, at the deepest sources of the Old Comic spirit. As Dionysus competes with those croaking frogs from the marshes, and as he listens to the songs of the Mystae, his identity as god of comedy, and of theater, is renewed, and he finds the strength, not just to witness the agon of old and new tragedy, but to face the specter of cultural change at Athens, which could mean the death of the older polis. The joy of rediscovered play empowers Old Comedy to play out its last great game, as Dionysus chooses Aeschylus and brings him back in torchlit procession to the upper world. That is a proper comic outcome. It is festive, and it is impossible, and it is the heart's genuine desire. The inverted funeral procession is celebratory and affirmative as it ushers vitality back from the world of Hades. At the same time, it is a comic rite of passage for tragedy and for the older Athens, and for Aristophanes' own comedy too, which may join new seriousness with its fun after the old animal chorus has disappeared. Paradoxically, this very rousing "wake," which is Old Comedy at its liveliest, lights the way with its torches to Middle Comedy, and to New.

If the *Frogs* is a Dionysian funeral rite of passage for Old Comedy, the earlier *Clouds* was its rite of adolescence. As I explained earlier, the present book grew out of my simple wish to explain, once and for all, why the *Clouds* was and is an excellent play. What was needed, I felt, was less a clever new analysis of the *Clouds* than to establish a comic perspective by which the *Clouds*, together with other plays of Aristophanes, could best be appreciated. Hence these six essays, which are intended to stand by themselves, but which will also supply a prolegomena to the sequel, *Clouds of Glory*, or Old-and-New Comedy Meets Cultural Change—an encounter whose main ingredients have already been suggested.

But what, after all, would Aristophanes say about a professor of Greek in 1984 who sits at his desk, surrounded by books, trying to explain Aristophanes on a (now very old-fashioned) typewriter? Whatever he might say, books like my yellow Budé text and Stanford's red Macmillan commentary on the *Frogs* have produced an indescribable longing, or *pothos*, in my soul. Certainly I am glad to have the text, whether I read it here or on the airplane to New York; and I am glad that, because Aristophanes was not revived (as Euripides was) in the fourth century, the text is not cluttered up by actors' interpolations or by other theatrical changes.[76] Yet in itself it remains a lifeless thing, a kind of corpse. The more we love Aristophanes, the more we must feel the gulf between "the event and the text," and the more we must long to see Aristophanes performed in *some* fashion today—let alone to have been present, among an Athenian audience, in the fifth-century theater of Dionysus. Yet the paradox remains, that so much of the play's living delight still somehow breathes forth from the pages of these red and yellow volumes. Long ago, Antipater of Thessalonike caught this paradox in an epigram:

> Aristophanes' books, divine production,
> over which green Acharnian ivy waves,
> how much Dionysus your page holds!
> How your tales echo, filled with fearful graces!
> O comic writer, o far best in spirit,
> your hate, your laughter, matched the ways of Hellas.[77]

The epigram is full of contradictions, like its subject. How can a page "hold" Dionysus, god of escape and transformation? And how can the "graces" of comic tales be "fearful"? But Antipater catches it well. There *is* a poet, dangerous in passion, wildly funny in laughter, within or behind this book. And Dionysus binds these timeworn pages with the green ivy of immortality—the god's reward for the god-inspired service of creativity.

Often, in what has been called Aristophanes' afterlife or *Nachleben*, his book was read as no more than a book. To Galen it was "useful reading for students." To the princess Anna Comnena it was one more cultural adornment to be displayed. And however much, as teachers of Greek today, we try to revive the excitement and fun of an Aristophanic play, or as critics, to explain its "fearful graces," I still often realize, with a sinking feeling, that much of what we love and care about is lost forever.

In Fellini's film *The Clowns* a moviemaker and his crew are impelled by their nostalgic interest in old-time circus clowns to go around interviewing, filming, recording, trying to find out all they can. But everywhere their search is baffled by the transience of things. The great clowns yet surviving are very, very old, or forgetful, or sick, or near dying. People remember beautiful circus acts that can't be explained. Old photographs are hard to see; tapes are lost or broken. The more the camera crew search, the more their efforts seem doomed to futility, like human laughter itself lost in the mists of time.

Yet two curious things happen. One is that gradually the misadventures and frustrations of the camera crew begin themselves to be perceived as a comic act, a kind of clowning. And second, toward the end, when everything seems hopeless, the film erupts into a grand circus funeral for the clown Auguste, and amid the ridiculously exaggerated rites of wailing and mourning, the hearse explodes, the fire engines roar up, water is spouting everywhere, and everyone runs around madly, including Auguste, who has been roused from his coffin by all the noise and excitement: in short, from the funeral of the old clowning comes the clown's greatest triumph. The film almost ends with this celebration, this comic wake, amid the wine and the wild music, the cavorting animals, the fireworks and colored streamers. But the ending is quieter. Everything disappears, and Auguste is discovered alone. He misses his friend, Frou-Frou, the "Antoine"; he refuses to believe that Frou-Frou is dead; he plays a slow nostalgic trumpet call, and his friend reappears. The two play together in brief harmony in the silent circus, and then go out. It seems, once more, a comic rite of passage.

In some similar way the Greek professor who feels a *pothos* for Aristophanes is drawn imperceptibly, and through many misadventures and frustrations, into a world of clowning and of comic celebration. As he seeks, and rediscovers, what is vital and joyous in Old Comedy, he finds himself drawn by that vitality and that joy into the greater enjoyment of all comedy, wherever it is to be found: in Menander and Plautus, Shakespeare and Molière, the Marx Brothers and Tom Stoppard; and finds himself drawn, poor timid figure, from the shelter of his classical books into the ongoing dance of life itself that the god leads, crowned with green ivy. The first thing, it seems after all, is to dance and to celebrate. The right leg has to have its fling, and then the left. The rest will follow.

Appendix

From Ritual to Comedy

Comic chorus of "knights," Attic black-figure amphora, mid-sixth century B.C.
Courtesy Staatliche Museen zu Berlin, DDR (no. F 1697).

A   *From* Kōmos *to* Kōmōidia, *I*

THE term *kōmos*, from which *kōmōidia* comes, is best translated by the English word "revel."[1] Examples from private life are familiar from literature and vase painting. After a party, drunken people might "make their revel" homewards, staggering around the streets by torchlight, perhaps insulting helpless bystanders or beating them up or, like Alcibiades in Plato's *Symposium*, invading still another drinking party. Or else the *kōmos* might be a larger celebration, as of the athletic victories mirrored in Pindar's epinician odes. The victor was acclaimed and feasted in his home town; the climax of the celebration came when the victory ode was sung and danced in his honor by a well-trained *choros*. Pindar wrote "for a light-stepping *kōmos*."[2] He enjoyed, and his poetry reflects, the tension between the energy of the victory celebration and the restraint that gave it form and order, keeping it "light-stepping."

Literature and art are less helpful in describing the great public *kōmoi* attached to cult celebrations, and especially to the Dionysian festivals. We hear, for example, of what Aristophanes calls the "hangover revel" (*kraipalo-kōmos*), when the drunken populace who had been celebrating the Choes, or Feast of Tankards, brought their wreathed wine jugs back to the ancient sanctuary of Dionysus in the Marshes. We can imagine a straggling torchlit procession with much casual singing, shouting, and merriment. The older Dionysia of the country districts included the regular sequence procession–sacrifice–*kōmos*; it also included, from early times, informal performances of choruses (which came to compete with one another). Their sophisticated offspring, the Great or City Dionysia of Athens, at which tragedies and comedies were produced, began with the same rites on a grander scale: a procession, with many great wooden phalluses sent by tribute-paying cities, in which the god's image was escorted to his theater; then sacrifices; and in the evening a *kōmos* in the god's honor—again, we may assume, a torchlit "revel" with singing, shouting, and general merriment. We have no detailed description of this. As so often, a picture would be worth a thousand speculations! The point remains, that the *kōmos*, like the procession (*pompē*) earlier, was a regular part of the festival, giving honor to the god and entertainment to the populace.

Comedy, *kōmōidia*, takes its special name from the "revel song" generally. The Greek word (*kōmos* + *aeido*, "sing") keeps its derivation before our mind. (There is a secondary association, etymologically unsound but taken seriously by many ancient writers, between *kōmōidia* and *kōmē*, "village": for comedy began in the country districts and kept stronger roots there than in the city.) But the Old Comedy of Aristophanes' time was far removed from the simple "revel." Indeed a comedy might include a simple *kōmos*, a victory or marriage revel in the exodos, as the chorus conducted the hero offstage with a victory or marriage song. Similarly, the little phallic procession and song conducted by Dicaeopolis in the *Acharnians*, though it paradoxically lacks a chorus, still gives a depiction in miniature of the basic rites and play forms (a phallic procession and song, and a sacrifice, looking forward to a *kōmos*) from which comedy grew, and to which in its maturity it still looked back, for refreshment.[3]

It seems reasonable to trace comedy back to some such type or types of festive play. That is generally agreed, and that is where agreement usually ends. Aristotle, who was not much interested in ritual origins of drama and who took the usual scholar's view that where information is lacking, it is not worth speculating what may have happened, derives tragedy from the dithyramb and comedy from "those leading forth the phallic things" (presumably, the phallic song, but the indefinite plural suggests the larger ceremony, especially the procession that the song accompanied).[4] This is the "nuclear" theory, according to which comedy grew from a single rite. It is historically misleading, like the derivation of tragedy from the dithyramb; it cannot account for the varied elements found in Old Comedy; but it does give one good example of festive play, of the kind of combination of ritual and play forms from which comedy, like tragedy and satyr play, actually grew.

By "festive play" I mean the combination of two things that must have been inseparable from the first: the performance of a ritual activity and the expression of a play instinct. We see the latter most clearly in the behavior of children, who when left to themselves will sing or chant, move their bodies in rhythm, imitate the behavior of birds or animals or other children or their elders, dress up and "pretend" to be this or that, form little parades, and compete or fight with one another. We have rare and precious pictures of Greek children playing on the miniature *choes* given to them as presents at the feast of that name: we see them playing with balls or push-toys, or near a table of presents (much as children today find presents under the Christmas tree); but others display their inherited tendency to *mimēsis* by dressing up and forming a little parade, or *pompē*. Perhaps unconsciously, they parody the grown-up ritual. But their child's play reveals the inherent playfulness of even those ritual practices that grown-ups may have taken most seriously. For these regularly include such features as singing and dancing; animal or daemon masquerade, or the exchange of male and female clothing; processions to or from shrines and places of sacrifice; the use of sexual words, gestures, and actions usually kept hidden (from the carrying of phalluses to the exchange of obscene insults); and all manner of ritual *agōnes* or competitions, whether of running and other sports, or of mutual insult, or of song, dance, and music-making. All this is privileged play, intently and regularly performed, necessary to the well-being of the community. It remains, for all that, play: set apart in space and time from the ordinary work of the community, and calling upon (even as it develops) its most creative faculties. Play gives shape and meaning to work, and holiday to everyday, not vice versa.

Old Comedy grew out of elements of festive play. The phrase "festive play" is useful because it suggests a close union of play forms, holiday occasions, and ritual or religious intent; yet the meaning of this combination changes greatly with the times. Very broadly, I want to distinguish between three stages of festive play throughout the remainder of my discussion:

(1) In the first, or magical stage, the performance of specific rites, whether more or less serious, was (and in some societies still is) thought to have an immediate, direct, and necessary effect on the well-being of the community. The best known of these ritual types are those of "fertility magic" employed by agricultural and preagricultural societies (1) to induce fertility of crops, animals, and people, together with similar blessings, and (2) to expel or ward off blighting forces and disease. Sir James Frazer illustrated these fertility rites with a wealth of anthropological material gathered all over the world, in his *Golden Bough* (1925); and there is enough evidence for the existence of comparable practices in ancient Greece, like the carrying around of the Wreath of Plenty (*eiresiōnē*), and the casting out of a scapegoat, for us to supply the spirit and meaning of such ritual activities by use of analogies from Frazer and other sources. All these actions are magical, intended to affect nature directly. Still older and more basic are the procedures (from which Frazer also began, and for whose primitive stages Walter Burkert's *Homo Necans* [1979] gives a dark, coherent perspective) of human and animal sacrifice, with the rites preceding and following on the shedding of blood. A fourth, closely related category is that of catharsis, or purification, to remove stains from the household and the larger community.

(2) To some extent, the first stage included rites for dealing with spirits, especially the spirits of the dead, who unless rightly treated might return to trouble the living. It may also imply a greater or lesser belief in animism. But the second, or religious, stage was marked by the invocation of blessings from personal divinities through prayer and sacrifice. It

follows that ancient forms of festive play were now performed in honor of the gods, under their protection, and as a regular part of the feasts that now belonged to them. Cults of the gods provided a focus that drew a number of play forms together; for example, what I shall call a "carnival concentration" of festive play forms emerged in the rites of Demeter and (especially) Dionysus. Myths of the gods, often aetiological ones, gave the worshipers a new understanding of the traditionally prescribed words, gestures, and actions, giving to these a heightened meaning and power, but also increasing the participants' awareness of what they were about.

(3) There followed, inevitably, a later religious stage tending toward secularization. Much of the old magic became obsolete or fossilized; the play forms that were rooted in magical practices and confirmed in religious observances were increasingly valued as entertainment for their own sake. Holidays became customary excuses for having a good time. Artistic productions like tragedy and comedy became increasingly independent, self-aware, and separate from their origins in ritual action; so that, in time, they became quite secular, and quite serious. But this takes us well past the fifth century B.C., toward the present day.

What is remarkable about the festive play of Old Comedy is that though it belongs historically to my third stage, it still preserves so many features of ancestral meaning and power from the first and second stages—magical and religious features. Behind its persistent forms like the parabasis and the agon, we may easily imagine the origins of comedy, not in a single nuclear rite like the phallic procession and song, but in a variety of *groupings of festive play forms* that gradually coalesced. Among these would be:

1. The formation of a chorus of "revelers" who dressed up as animals or as daemonic creatures of some type, and sang and danced;
2. Such a chorus might move from place to place, perhaps carrying a green branch, or a phallus, or some other emblem of fertility. It might sing indecent or teasing songs, or insult passersby, or enter people's houses and ask for presents; hence the "trick or treat" combination that, even in ancient times, was largely taken over by holiday-making groups of children.[5]
3. Two choruses might conduct an agon, or mimed conflict, in words, gestures, or actions; each might be led by an *exarchōn* or "leader-out" of song and speech, who improvised antiphonal verses while the chorus joined in a refrain; or one chorus might split into competing semichoruses, each with its leader; or there might be an aggressive confrontation between a chorus and an individual (the first real actor separate from the chorus), who might be chased with stones or insults, very like a ritual scapegoat.
4. A chorus with its leader might imitate the celebration of a sacrifice

and feast, perhaps with much playfulness and parody. One or more characters—opponents, imposters, or just plain nuisances—might run in to demand or steal a share of the food; they were driven off with insults and blows.

5. The chorus might sing a victory or wedding song to celebrate the triumph of their leader, and march off joyfully.

From these early combinations of ritual and play elements it is easy to arrive at the basic, recurrent units of Old Comedy: the entrance song of the chorus (*parodos*), its festive songs and teasing verses directed at the audience or against individuals (*parabasis*, lesser ode/epirrheme combinations); the various kinds of informal *agon*; the episodes centering on a sacrificial feast; the festive finale of the *exodos* (or what since Cornford has usually been called the *kōmos* and *gamos*). The question remains: how do these elementary groupings come together to form a comic plot?

In his perceptive and influential book *The Origin of Attic Comedy* (1914; 2nd ed. 1934) Francis Cornford argued, first, that Aristophanes' comedies exhibited a "canonical plot-formula," normally consisting of prologue, parodos, agon, parabasis, sacrifice, feast, marriage *kōmos*; and second, that this plot formula "preserves the stereotyped action of a ritual or folk drama, older than literary comedy, and of a pattern well known to us from other sources."[6] He had in mind such rudimentary comic dramas as the English Saint George plays, or Punch and Judy shows, or the Thracian Mummers' Play, in which various characters fight, someone is knocked down and killed, a doctor revives him, and so forth—and the company takes up a collection from the audience gathered around. Cornford was surely right in thinking that early dramatic comedy must have been like this, with (1) a company of players making their entrance, (2) a performance involving various characters, and a fight (*agōn*), and its results, and (3) some appeal or address to the audience. Nonetheless it is hard to find a "canonical plot formula" of much extent in the mummers' plays surviving today; and more important, it is hard to find one underlying the plays of Aristophanes. These do all have a prologue and a parodos, but the agon may follow, not precede, the parabasis, or there may be more than one agon; the hero's success, rejuvenation, "resurrection," are common but not invariable; and many plays do not end with a clear *kōmos* and *gamos*. It takes a procrustean stretching and lopping to establish a regular Aristophanic plot. For a comparable experiment, try to find a "canonical plot formula" in the operas of Gilbert and Sullivan. The same character types appear, the same patter songs and ballads are heard, the same kind of fantastic situation, of conflict, of comic resolution, and move to a happy ending (usually with a *kōmos* and *gamos*), tends to repeat itself; and yet what makes a Gilbert and Sullivan opera is not a recognizable, canonical plot formula but rather a number of common elements, musical, literary, dramatic, and farcical, whose combinations bear a kind of "family re-semblance." The same thing could be said of Marx Brothers movies. Aristophanes' plays have much in common, and the more so by compari-son with later comedy of manners, or sentimental comedy; but their common features do not justify deriving them from a rudimentary folk drama with any unity and coherence of its own.

Cornford's theory of the development of comedy was further weak-ened by his attempt to derive the basic comic plot from a Dionysian death-and-resurrection pattern. Tragedy, he argued (following Gilbert Murray), imitated the suffering and death of the god in its hero stories and must once have played them out directly; comedy carries the pattern through to its ancient ending. The idea is tempting. What distinguishes comedy from (much) tragedy is the way it evades suffering and death, or leaps over them; like Falstaff, its hero was only counterfeiting. Yet the Old Comedy's triumph over death is not easily explained by Dionysian myth or religion. The ordinary worship of Dionysus provided ecstatic experience, a sense of communion with the god, and liberation from ordinary restraints; but the worshipers did not (like Demeter's mystics, or the followers of Near Eastern vegetation deities) trace their god's path through suffering and death to resurrection. That came later for Diony-sus, when his mysteries took on Orphic coloring. The normal myths of Dionysus current in the fifth century B.C. and represented in vase paint-ings are not about death and resurrection (although the baby Dionysus was "twice-born," from his dying mother and from Zeus): rather, they are about the liberation and renewal of energies in the vegetable, animal, and human world. Dionysus overcoming the pirates, Dionysus bringing Hephaestus back to Olympus, are the typical myths that stand behind Old Comedy, as they stand behind satyr play, so that these frequently show a Dionysian release of captives, a Dionysian triumph of vitality, a Dionysian renewal and transformation of ordinary life. But this is differ-ent from comedy's hypothetical growth from a rudimentary representa-tion of the death and resurrection of the god.

To form our ideas about the development of Greek comedy on the analogy of European folk and carnival plays is twice misleading. In the first place, though European holiday practices in the Middle Ages and the Renaissance kept a clear continuity with the old magical rites of a heathen time, yet these were taken under the wing of a Christianity that did indeed center around a pattern of death and resurrection. The old seasonal rites took on renewed power and meaning as part of the Chris-tian year: so that the lighting of fires at the winter solstice, and the Roman Saturnalian rites of December and of the New Year, became taken up in the revelry that spreads from Christmas to Epiphany, and beyond; and the wild celebrations of Carnival, when chaos briefly comes again, attached themselves to the Tuesday before the beginning of Lent, but also anticipated, in their merriment, the joy of Easter. We could say that for the Christian world the "Easter laughter" reaches backward, from its completed pattern of death and resurrection, to justify, even to sanction all the other occasions of old pagan laughter throughout the year. But this is not a power that Dionysus ever had.

In the second place, medieval and Renaissance Europe provide such a mass of evidence for the development of comedy from ritual and folk plays that a Hellenist must feel jealous. Furthermore, gifted and patient scholars, like Paolo Toschi and E. K. Chambers, have set this material in order for us. Their work demonstrates what Cornford's could not: a credible transition, stage by stage, from ritual practices to comic drama. No leap of imagination is required, or of faith. A recent book by Anthony Caputi (1978) very reasonably posits five steps, or strata, in the development of what he calls vulgar comedy: (1) the ritual revel, or holiday, (2) certain processional or ritual activities of rudimentary dramatic character, (3) more dramatic parts of ritual revels, or "dramatic exercises," (4) primitive, emergent plays, or "carnival plays," and (5) early, free-standing vulgar comedies.[7] The theoretical scheme is admirable, and it is well documented for England, France, and Italy. Not surprisingly, Caputi's attempt to apply it to ancient Greek comedy, filling his stages in with bits and pieces of secondhand evidence (like Aristotle's *phallophoroi*, for stage 2) and analogy (the Thracian Mummers' play dragged out still again, for stage 4), proves entirely unconvincing. So the question remains: how *do* we get from *kōmos* to Old Comedy?

Let me give a simplified three-stage sequence of my own that the surviving evidence supports, and that (especially for stage 2) owes much to the painstaking scholarship of Francisco Adrados. His *Festival, Comedy and Tragedy* (1975) is exceedingly complicated and difficult to read, but it is the only book I know that fills in the missing gaps with scholarly patience and care, and, in my opinion, gets the story right.

(1) My own first stage is that of *festive play*. From earliest times, the play tendencies innate in human beings (as they are in other animal species) found expression in a variety of ritual practices of more or less serious and magical intent: to promote the well-being of the community and the fruitfulness of nature; to drive out or avert bad and blighting influences; to find healing for the community and reconciliation with the world of animal nature (always disturbed by bloodshed) and with the spirit world. From the combination of ritual acts with the play instinct arose the *groupings of festive play forms*: the singing and dancing chorus, their animal or daemon masquerade, their phallic procession and song, their teasing of bystanders, their insult competitions, and so forth. From these groupings came the rudimentary forms of comic drama: the parodos, the agon, the parabasis, the exodos. But how these became combined in larger groups to form simple comic plays, we do not know. The Saint George and other such carnival plays at least help us imagine what comedy was like at this happy juvenile stage of development. This

is the real Old Comedy, or paleocomedy: the rude distant ancestor of the known form.

(2) My second stage is a long, intermediate one, in which two things happened. First, the festive play forms from which comedy arose took on new meaning and power from the worship of the Olympian gods. The hymns, prayers, and sacrifices were now made to them and in their honor, and such marked elements of comic drama as the phallic procession and song, the exchange of insults, and the combat or mock combat, were now performed in their honor and under their protection. The festivals of Demeter and especially Dionysus became a focus for rites pertaining to fertility and renewal; and although there was no single "carnival" among Greek festivals, Dionysus' worship attracted what I want to call a "carnival concentration" of such elements. (I explain this further in the next section.) Even without the fullness of a death-and-resurrection myth posited by Cornford (and to which the Eleusinian rites of Demeter and Persephone came closer), Dionysian myth and ritual were strong enough to draw together, with new authority, the elementary festive and play forms of comedy.

The other thing that happened during this second stage was a remarkable progress in artistry. We may follow Adrados in singling out four important aspects of this development.[8] (a) There was a general movement away from ritual action with direct practical intent, in the direction of entertainment. As groups of professional entertainers (who may, Adrados speculates, have grown out of religious associations, or *thiasoi*) became established, the rest of the community became less and less participants in the *kōmos*, more and more its "spectators." (b) The mimetic element, always inherent in festive play, became elaborated and increasingly important. The representation of the actions of gods and heroes developed, as ritual actions were given mythical and also historical explanations; the serious representations from which tragedy came were accompanied, from the first, by mythological burlesque, which would in time provide a unifying plot for satyr play and comedy. All these beginnings of mimetic drama were attracted to, and supported by, the festivals of Dionysus, as the god of ecstasy and transformation, of becoming for the time what one is not—hence the patron deity of actors. (c) Epic and narrative lyric poetry, which had themselves undergone a long development, greatly influenced the emerging forms of drama. The verbal element took on new importance; a prologue narrator joined the cast, and a messenger to describe offstage events. (d) The special genres—tragedy, satyr play, and comedy—became separated from their common matrix in ritual drama. Comedy, together with satyr play, inherited ancient elements of mythological burlesque, which it developed. Both comedy and satyr play were valued for keeping a balance with tragedy. But comedy also served as a repository for a number of old ritual elements that otherwise remained unused in drama, like the teasing of the audience, or the kicking out of imposters who interrupted the sacrifice and feast.

(3) All these things, taken together, formed a long intermediate stage in the development of Old Comedy from the rudimentary grouping of festive play forms (parodos, agon, and parabasis) to something like what we see in the plays of Aristophanes. Official state recognition of comedy came very late, in 486 B.C. For Aristotle, as for later scholars, that is where the official history of Old Comedy begins: for it achieved its artistic greatness under the threefold inspiration of state support (together with the generosity of ambitious citizens and the riches of the Athenian empire), of the literary and dramatic advances already made by Attic tragedy, and of the individual creative gifts of three generations of comic playwrights, stimulating each other in mutual competition. For Aristotle and his followers, this was the "old comedy," but at least it was taking the requisite steps away from casual "iambizing" toward a morally and artistically more responsible form of comedy. Yet this perspective of Aristotle's is misleading; it makes us forget how far Old Comedy had already come by 486. Indeed we would do better to refer to Late Old Comedy I, II, and III, much as we refer to the subdivisions of Late Minoan art. Aristophanes belongs to Late Old Comedy III—which says a lot about his achievement. We also do wrong to forget how tenaciously conservative this late Old Comedy remained. The new wine was poured into very old wineskins; there was always a tension between the unifying elements of "plot" and the largely independent shape and meaning retained by such old forms as the parodos, the agon, and the parabasis, through which, to the end of the fifth century B.C., the playful childhood of comedy, rooted in ritual observance and festivity, could still be seen, and felt.

The following brief studies of elements basic to Old Comedy, including phallic celebration, indecency-and-invective (*aischrologia*), satire, and masking, have two constant aims. One is to appreciate the distance traveled by Old Comedy from its ritual origins toward artistic independence and playful self-awareness. The other is to argue that Old Comedy distinctively retained, through all these changes, much of its ancient ritual power and meaning as festive play. I would like these investigations to be taken in the end as a tribute to Francis Cornford, who, though often wrong in the detailed application of his argument, seems to me to have been right in the things that really count. It is time to go back and take him seriously.

B   *Carnival Concentration: Halloween and Anthesteria*

I begin with carnival, as the most supportive environment for comedy; but I must begin negatively from where I am, in Chapel Hill. We rarely celebrate Mardi Gras here, since the community hardly observes Lent; even Catholics have (mostly) exchanged abstinence from meat for the desirable, but rather less tangible, intention of performing good works; and as the penitential force of Lent is weakened, together with the mounting experience of sadness and loss that reaches a climax on Good Friday, so too the great joy of Easter is attenuated. Only bright new clothes remain of it, and the hunting of Easter eggs. It follows that the excesses of Mardi Gras, which once anticipated that Easter joy, have no public place. Instead they have become a private idiosyncrasy, marked in our household by a large consumption of Pepperidge Farm cookies, with maybe an extra glass or two of wine.

For a sense of carnival, I depend on reports from places where that tradition is stronger: from Munich or Rio, or closer at hand, from New Orleans, with its wild street gatherings and jazz, its parades and floats, its masking and dressing-up and transvestism, all accompanied by a good deal of drinking and sexual license. It is a time to play. The sanctions are (at least nominally) Christian; they speak for a strong French Catholic tradition that brings New Orleans nearer to Munich or Rio than to Puritan Boston. On the one side, they are becoming secularized: unreflecting folk enjoy the fun and games for their own sake; more sophisticated people weigh the benefits of tourism against the costs of providing the festivities, and of keeping order, or perhaps think about the sense of urban pride and coherence that the city of New Orleans derives from this annual celebration. Economically, or psychologically, it "pays" to have the Mardi Gras. On the other side, the kings and queens of carnival, the maskers on their floats throwing gold and silver doubloons to the crowds, the pageants of Rex and Comus and Bacchus and the rest, revert in their play forms to old, pagan revelry, which has been sanctioned by the Christian calendar and presently resanctioned by economic and psychological use.

But how and when do we keep carnival in Chapel Hill? We have lost Mardi Gras; still more, we have lost the Feast of Fools and the rest of the Christian revelry that once stretched from Christmas to Epiphany and well beyond. There remain private celebrations, notably weddings, when we drink and dance and play; but I only know of two public occasions that keep the emotional force of carnival. One is New Year's Eve. This is still, at its core, what anthropologists call a liminal period, a dangerous in-between time of temporary disorder, when chaos comes again. On New Year's Eve it is right to wear funny hats, drink champagne with friends, blow on noisemakers, and sing "Auld Lang Syne." Excess is right as you ring out the Old Year, ring in the New. Even my puritan father, who never got drunk, would regale us every year with his wonderful *imitation* of a drunken man celebrating New Year's Eve. It was not a *kōmos*, but it was festive comedy.

Our second carnival time is Halloween. It has come (like many festivals) to belong mainly to the children, who dress up as ghosts and hoboes, witches and vampires, and go out to "trick or treat." There are (to most people's relief) fewer "tricks" than formerly, but most householders take care to be home on Halloween, to pretend to be scared by the wandering figures, and to fill their bags with popcorn, apples, chocolate bars, and a great variety of little candies. As a *quête*, the practice recalls the universal custom (well attested for ancient Greece) of groups of children, sometimes in greenery or animal disguise, "bringing fruitfulness" into the different households from the woods and fields, and asking for presents, and making more or less comical threats if these are not given. But what is unusual about Halloween is that its revelry is combined with something scary. The children frighten themselves and each other a little, even when they know they are only pretending. I have known shy, conservative college students to frighten themselves when they turned, for an evening, into hippies, gangsters, and prostitutes: their Jungian "shadow" was revealed. Last year I even frightened my wife, who is not timid, with a new red devil's mask and a black cape. And could it be that our hollowed-out pumpkins, grinning fiendishly with candlelight from their great eyes and teeth, are apotropaic magic—the nearest modern equivalent of the horrid Greek Gorgoneion?

Halloween comes from the Celtic Samhain, the feast of early winter.[9] Pagan revelry still seems right as the year turns cold and dreary, and dead leaves blow in the wind, and great fires are lit to compensate for the sun's weakening. Guy Fawkes Day in England comes close in spirit with its wandering urchins, its scapegoat figures, its bonfires. The old pagan revelry has gone through the usual stages, religious and secularizing. It has, first, been taken up into Christian celebration, for Halloween is All Hallows Eve, the eve of All Saints Day (1 November), which is directly followed by All Souls (2 November). It is the time when Christians pray, or used to pray, for the souls of the faithful departed; indeed the revelry of Halloween is the best psychological preparation for the high solemnities of All Saints. But today the Christian framework of this feast threatens to become obsolete. Not many hungover revelers move toward mass the next day. All Souls has become just one more peculiar observance of old-fashioned Catholics. For most people Halloween has become a traditional children's holiday, an occasion for entertainment—and one that, by the usual paradoxical reversal, is regulated more strictly every year; one almost waits for the Puritans to stamp it out. And yet the children's excitement, their exultation and alarm at their own disguising, still catches the old spirit of excitement and horror that prevailed at dangerous, liminal times, when spirits roamed abroad, when evil things were unconfined, when chaos came again. More than Mardi Gras, Halloween shows the other side of carnival, the wild and dangerous side. It lets us glimpse the fuller catharsis, not just of individuals releasing their darker selves, but of a community, a world slipping back (for a brief, limited time) into chaos and old night.

I have described these occasions partly to evoke a spirit and feeling of revelry that our society (and scholars not least) has largely forgotten today, and partly to suggest that in the absence of a designated carnival like Mardi Gras we may still speak of a "carnival concentration" of elements of festive play. Among these would be

1. eating and (especially) drinking in excess
2. loud noise, loud music
3. dressing-up and disguise; mask, costume, transvestism
4. sexual play; indecent words, gestures, actions
5. representation of demonic figures
6. processions or revels, by day and especially by night.

No one or two of these elements in isolation makes a carnival. We eat and drink excessively at Thanksgiving and Christmas, we parade and set off fireworks on the Fourth of July; but it takes a larger combination and concentration of these elements of festive play—rooted in pagan antiquity, nourished by Christian tradition, and still licensed by an increasingly secular society—to bring about that fullness of carnival experience that no private celebration could attain.[10] With this in mind, I want now to consider the Anthesteria, which displays the fullest "carnival concentration" of any known Athenian festival and suggests the kind of atmosphere on which Old Comedy thrives.[11]

By the fifth century B.C., the Anthesteria had become primarily a feast of Dionysus, with many Saturnalian features: drunkenness, masking, license, liberties taken by slaves and foreigners, a night-revel. Yet as

Burkert has shown, all this revelry must be seen against a somber background.[12] The opening of the new wine on the first day (the Pithoigia) was a dangerous act, like a blood sacrifice, that had to be hedged about with ceremonies of precaution. The second day, the Choes, was a "tainted day": all the shrines were closed, except for the shrine of Dionysus in the Marshes, which was opened for this one day; people chewed buckthorn and smeared their doors with pitch to ward off dangerous influences. Then there was the strange ritual of isolated drinking, which the Athenians explained by the myth of Orestes' reception at Athens. It was (as Halloween was once) an exciting but very dangerous time to be gotten through. The revelry of the Choes flirted with chaos. It must have been a great relief to come past it into the fun and games, the swinging and flower celebrations of the Chytroi, the third and last day of the festival.[13]

One aspect of the Anthesteria strongly suggestive of carnival is the drinking, which must have gone on fairly steadily, or unsteadily, beginning with the tasting of the new wine, continuing through the ceremonious drinking of the Choes ceremony, of about 2.5 liters per person— for some, taking the form of a drinking bout with prizes, such as Aristophanes describes toward the end of his *Acharnians*—and reaching its height in the great "hangover revel" to the shrine of Dionysus in the Marshes. This excessive drinking, encouraged and even prescribed by ritual, must have been taken as a cheerful gift of Dionysus, especially as the more dangerous and uncanny aspects of the feast fell into the background; but perhaps it was heightened by them too. People celebrate life more intensely when death and specters are in the background. Probably, though we do not know the order of events, the *kōmos* took on a sexual meaning also by association with the mystic "sacred marriage" between Dionysus and the Queen in the Boukoleion. Perhaps the Dionysian revel also became a wedding procession for the god (represented by a mask) and his bride, as they were escorted from the shrine in the marshes back to the Boukoleion. In comedy, as Cornford argued, the *kōmos* and *gamos*, revel and marriage, often go together; and such wedding revels as those of Trygaeus in the *Peace* or Peisetairus in the *Birds* may reflect, and draw on, the wedding revel of Dionysus and his bride.

Another, still more striking carnival aspect is the "joking from the wagons" at the Anthesteria. It was the custom—later borrowed by the Lenaea—for Dionysus' revelers to move through the town in carts, insulting passersby in a coarse, unrestrained fashion. This is an example of *aischrologia*, the magical combination of obscenity and insult that promotes fertility and wards off bad influences—as well, of course, as making everyone feel better. It seems likely that these revelers wore disguises. There were grotesque masks, which could frighten children. The disguises gave free rein to invective and obscenity, but they may also have represented daemonic creatures like satyrs—spirits of fertility, but also fearful powers that lurk in the background of ordinary life. The masked revel must have included its "devil dancing." It may be that these strange figures burst into people's houses and demanded hospitality. This would be a familiar aspect of carnival; it ended formally when a general cry rang out, "Depart ye Keres: the Anthesteria is over!"[14] A number of revelers may simply have daubed their faces with wine lees, as a simple disguise and as a tribute to the new wine and to Dionysus. Perhaps they rode on the same wagons that had brought in the great jars (*pithoi*) of new wine. The drinking, the masquerading, the wagon procession and revel, the hurling of insults and obscenities at the passersby, all taking place under Dionysus' patronage but against a background of darker and older rites, involving danger and catharsis: all this makes up a strong "carnival concentration." We still have to flesh out the scholarly notices today, with the help of Mardi Gras, or of Halloween.

As the "revel song," comedy drew strength and meaning from many Dionysian and pre-Dionysian rites. But if we may follow a joke of Aristophanes, the players of Old Comedy sprang in part from these same *trygodaimones*, the "wine lees daemons" impersonated by the revelers on the wagons with their wild, coarse, drunken joking.[15] When Aristophanes, in other places, refers to his comedy as *trygōidia*, he means this as a parody of *tragōidia*, its tragic sister-form (and originally the sacred goat song); but the comic word also draws on old and familiar rites of Dionysus and hence affirms comedy's license to proclaim the whole and human truth.

Significantly, the last day of the Anthesteria was, or at least became, a children's festival. It celebrated a rite of passage for three-year-olds, as they emerged from the perils of infancy in the direction of adulthood and citizenship; they were crowned with spring flowers; they also each received a little *chous* and a little table of presents. As said earlier, these miniature *choes* provide the best pictures we have of the games and fun of small Athenian children. Is there a universal tendency for religious festivals to turn into mere occasions for family cheerfulness, present-giving, and entertainment? How strange it would be if only decorated Easter eggs remained to tell the story of our own spring festivities. And yet the images of children's play on the little painted *choes* still catch the essential thing about carnival, which is festive play. It is the very heart of holiday-making, and of Old Comedy.

C   Dionysus and the Phallus

THERE was no Dionysian "carnival" among the Athenian festivals, although the Anthesteria comes closest to one, with its drinking and its drunken night-revel, its masking, and its licensed mix of obscenity and invective "from the wagons," a feature that the Lenaea appears to have copied. Whatever the specific origins of Attic comedy—and I shall argue that it has many diverse sources in play and ritual—it came to flourish in a carnival-like atmosphere created by the fusion of various fertility and purification rites under the patronage of Dionysus as the god of vegetation, wine, ecstasy, and catharsis. In this section, I consider the meaning of the phallic songs and processions associated with Dionysus; in the next, the meanings of *aischrologia*, "obscenity-with-invective," which his rites share with those of Demeter.

Although representations of the male and female genitalia were displayed on various ritual occasions or used in what must once have been rites of sympathetic magic to promote fertility, and perhaps sometimes in rites of aversion, the phallic procession became especially associated with Dionysus.[16] On the Great Dionysia, large phalli sent by all the tributary states were carried in procession, almost as though Athens had summoned to her own use the masculine forces of the empire. But the phallic procession and phallic song go back to simpler, more primitive ceremonies of the local "rural Dionysia." One of these is reproduced playfully in Aristophanes' *Acharnians*.[17] When Dicaeopolis recovers peace, though for himself and his family only, the first thing he does is to celebrate his private "country Dionysia" with his family and slaves: he sets up a little procession, emphasizing that the phallus must be held "erect" behind the basket-bearer (his daughter), and he sings a little comic song in honor of "Phales, companion of Bacchios, fellow reveler (*synkōme*)." It is an innocuous song, only slightly indecent, a celebration of the recovered joys of the peaceful countryside; but its joking about drinking and sex evokes two qualities of the country Dionysia: the formal celebration of sexuality in the form of the personified phallus, in a so-called phallic song (*to phallikon*) to go with the phallic procession; and the drunken revel that would normally follow—whose hangover, says Dicaeopolis, will be cured by a good bowl of hot peace soup the next morning. Of course his private celebration is, in this play, a very funny parody of what should have been a public Dionysian celebration in the country. In a way it emphasizes how much things are out of joint. But Aristophanes also draws on the energies and meanings of festival, here of the country Dionysia, later on of the Anthesteria (and especially the Choes), to undergird the celebratory meanings of his play.

We shall ask later what Aristotle knew, and what he meant, when he derived comedy from "those leading off the phallic things." For now, I want to call two earlier witnesses. Here first is Herodotus, describing a phallic procession of "Dionysus" in Egypt:

> Everyone, on the eve of the festival of Dionysus, sacrifices a hog before the door of his house. . . . In other ways the Egyptian method of celebrating the festival of Dionysus is much the same as the Greek, except that the Egyptians have no choric dance. Instead of the phallus they have puppets, about eighteen inches high; the genitals of these figures are made almost as big as the rest of their bodies, and they are pulled up and down by strings as the women carry them round the villages. Flutes lead the procession, and the women as they follow sing a hymn to Dionysus. There is some sort of religious explanation for the size of the genitals and the fact that they are the only part of the puppet's body which is made to move.[18]

Herodotus' main concern here is that of an ethnographer and student of comparative religion. In his view Dionysus, like most of the Greek gods, came from Egypt (where the priests consulted by Herodotus identified him with their Osiris); it appears that the seer Melanthus introduced Dionysus' name, sacrifice, and phallic procession into Greece. This last seems quite normal to Herodotus, like the ithyphallic herms whose origin he accounts for soon afterwards. For him, as for his Greek audience, there is nothing surprising or shameful about exaltation of the phallus. It may be, though, that those Egyptian puppets with their huge phalluses wagging up and down would have struck him as funny, as something that would amuse his readers; at the same time, the description brings out something very primitive underlying the familiar practice taken for granted by fifth-century Greeks. The old sexual magic was still there. It was still potent, though it had been taken under the protection of Dionysus some time before. Only the historian realizes that it was not such a long time, after all.

An earlier witness, Heraclitus, finds the phallic procession more offensive: "If it were not Dionysus for whom they march in procession and chant the hymn to the phallus (*aidoia*), their action would be most shameless (*anaidestata*). But Hades (*Aidēs*) and Dionysus are the same, him for whom they rave and celebrate Lenaea."[19] Writing in the late sixth century B.C., Heraclitus is a pre-Socratic philosopher and a religious puritan. Here he objects to the basic indecency of the phallic procession and song, illustrating this by a typical play on words: the "revered and shameful" parts (*aidoia*) are exhibited as an object of worship and publicly celebrated in a way that would have to seem "most irreverent and shameless" (*anaidestata*)—if it were not sanctioned by tradition and, underlying this, by a deeper philosophical meaning that Heraclitus himself perceives and expresses with yet another wordplay. But the objection is still strongly felt. Why this obscene mummery? Why parade on festive occasions what any sane person knows enough to conceal? It is improper, and it is unworthy of the god. Like other pre-Socratic theologians, and especially Xenophanes, Heraclitus wants to purify the worship of the gods and the way men think about them. He dislikes the old sex and violence. His criticism of what we might call messy fertility rites goes along with his criticism, preserved in another quotation, of purification through blood sacrifice, which he compares to washing oneself clean by wallowing in mud.[20] His humor, playing on literal and figurative meanings of *catharsis*, does not conceal his scorn.

We have come, after Frazer and Jane Harrison (1908), to see the phallic procession and song as an obvious species of fertility magic, designed to promote the fertility of land and people and perhaps secondarily (for the phallus has apotropaic uses, most notably against the evil eye) to ward off dangerous or blighting influences.[21] These magical procedures had for some time been incorporated in Dionysian cult, to Heraclitus' disgust. Their obscenities of language and gesture and their inversion of normal behavior were now sanctioned by the god's patronage and given new meaning. Here Heraclitus' remarks are to the point: for, even more than by obscenity, Dionysian religion was characterized by ecstatic madness. The verb *lēnaïsdō*, from the same root as the Lenaea festival, basically denotes, not drinking (although this element was added, and became a popular and very noticeable component of Dionysian festivals), but the imitation, in wild, ecstatic dancing, of the Maenads who accompany Dionysus. Again, Heraclitus objects to all this irrational behavior as a darkening of men's souls and of their concept and worship of divinity, but he has the right idea when he subordinates the phallic rites to those of the people (originally, the cult associations of women) who "do mad things." For the essence of Dionysian worship was ecstatic dancing and the tearing and consumption of raw flesh that gives a feeling of joy and power beyond the human. The release of inhibition given through sexual gesture and expression belongs to the much greater release of ecstatic dancing in communion with the god. It may be that the original purpose of these cathartic rites was to ward off madness, envisaged in the form of possession by dangerous spirits; the act of *mimēsis*, enacting just such spirit-possession under the ordered conditions of religious ritual, was itself the chief means by which madness was warded off, lucidity regained.[22] But in such cathartic rites as these, life and death came close together. Dionysian ecstasy must have seemed to Heraclitus a crazy "drowning" of the soul, akin to drunkenness—another Dionysian feature. He may finally be right about the paradox. The celebration of life, of sexuality, in the phallic procession and hymn, is bound up in Dionysian ritual with the experience of ecstasy that belongs to death. Life sinks into death and rises from it again. That is the oldest, deepest meaning of religious rites. Heraclitus dislikes their messiness, but he sees deeper into their meaning, and their origin, than the holiday crowd who were simply enjoying a traditional time for having fun, joking about sex, and getting drunk. His criticism suggests to us the real inner unity of meaning and effect that a Dionysian festival like the Anthesteria or the Lenaea still retained, beneath its jovial surface, in the sixth and fifth centuries B.C.

How Dionysus took over the old magical rites, making them his own, is now speculation.[23] As a foreign vegetation god, he took over the realm of viticulture, which seems to have been "open" for him in the Greek world, and established himself well before Homer's time as the god of wine and giver of its joys, parallel to Demeter and her gift of grain; the two became closely joined in worship. But Dionysus was also the god of ecstatic dancing, of the "cathartic" madness that wards off daemon-possession and insanity. It seems likely that this aspect gave his worship the tremendous drive and quick expansion that it experienced throughout the Greek world, and that enabled it to take over many features of fertility rite, like the celebrations of Phales, that once existed independently. That is how what I have called a "carnival concentration" came about in Dionysian festivals like the Anthesteria and Lenaea. This is the environment in which comedy, together with tragedy, can flourish. It is ironic that Heraclitus, who disliked and feared this appalling mixture of blood and sex, drunkenness and madness, should have seen the point of the Dionysian rites as few scholars, or theologians, have after him.

D   Aischrologia

THE phallic procession and song had both a positive and a negative side in fertility ritual; still more did the mix of invective and obscenity conveyed in the Greek term *aischrologia*, "ugly-and-shameful talk." Normally the word denotes the use of indecent expressions, words referring to sex and excretion that were ordinarily suppressed in conversation. (Curiously, one symptom of extreme sickness or senility could be—and, I am told, still is—a flood of uncontrollable obscenities.) But under certain ritually sanctioned conditions, what was normally forbidden becomes right and proper. People shouted out obscene words, performed obscene gestures, handled obscene objects. All this must have given a powerful experience of psychological release and healing. So too must the other side of *aischrologia* have done, the expression of insult and invective, perhaps against bystanders, as in the Dionysian mockery "from the wagons," or perhaps against some rival group or team.[24] The combination of obscenity and invective is especially potent. It became a chief element of Old Comedy; we think inevitably of Freud's account of those aggressive and obscene "Tendenzen" that civilization so greatly inhibits, to our psychic cost and pain, and whose release through joking brings a discharge of pent-up feeling in strong, sudden laughter. All this is true. The more polite and civilized we are, the more true it is. Still, if we overemphasize the psychological release thus afforded to individuals and even to a society, we may be distracted from older, more central meanings of *aischrologia*. We need to recover a sense of it as magic, as powerful "medicine" that promotes fertility, wards off bad influences, reconciles the sexes, even resolves deep-set conflicts and tensions in the universe. We need also to understand how the old fertility magic could take on new meaning in religious myth and ritual. Let me illustrate these different possibilities and levels of experienced meaning with three examples: (1) the "fruitful contest of the sexes" described by Victor Turner as part of the Wubwang'u ceremony of the Ndembu people; (2) the Egyptian ceremony of festal sailing to Boubastis described by

Herodotus; and (3) the joking from the bridge, or *gephyrismos*, on the pilgrimage to Eleusis. After that, I shall ask how far, and on what level or levels, *aischrologia* promotes a "carnival" experience in the rites of Demeter and of Dionysus.

(1) To begin with the Ndembu: Turner describes how the men and women "cheerfully revile one another" on the occasions of the gathering of medicine for the Twin Ceremony and the splashing of a patient with this same medicine:

> The songs, at both phases, are in serial order. First, members of each sex belittle the sexual organs and prowess of members of the opposite sex, and extol their own. The women jeeringly assert to their husbands that they have secret lovers, and the men retort that all they get from the women are venereal diseases, a consequence of adultery. Afterward both sexes praise in lyrical terms the pleasures of intercourse as such. The whole atmosphere is buoyant and aggressively jovial, as men and women strive to shout one another down.[25]

This last is shown in a splendid photograph. Whatever the men and women are doing, or think they are doing, in these scurrilous and indecent songs, they are clearly having a very good time. I quote further from the same passage in Turner, since his comments apply to most rites of this "shameless" nature:

> First, before singing the ribald songs, Ndembu chant a special formula, *"kaikaya wo, kakwawu weleli"* ("here another thing is done"), which has the effect of legitimizing the mention of matters that otherwise would be what they call "a secret thing of shame or modesty" .... The same formula is repeated in legal cases concerning such matters as adultery and breaches of exogamy, where sisters and daughters or in-laws (*aku*) of the plaintiffs and defendants are present. Ndembu have a customary phrase explaining *Wubwang'u* songs. "This singing is without shame because shamelessness is [a characteristic] of the curative treatment of *Wubwang'u*" .... In brief, *Wubwang'u* is an occasion of licensed disrespect and prescribed immodesty. But no sexual promiscuity is displayed in actual behavior; indecency is expressed by word and gesture only.

Several things are important here. First, the Ndembu are conscious of the reversal by which ordinary taboos and inhibitions are waived. Second, they know that this reversal belongs to a healing process. Third, they use a proper formula to mark the entry into that other time and place, that other world, where indecency and impropriety are right. But, fourth, even this expression has built-in limitations. The rite of shamelessness does not degenerate into a general sexual orgy; the sexual mimesis in word and gesture is "medicine" powerful enough to answer the need. Most Greek rites with which we shall be concerned will show a comparable liberation *up to a point* and within a larger, fixed ritual order. The same will hold true of Old Comedy, insofar as it grows out of ancient rites.

The Ndembu rites are perceived as healing—we would say, as cathartic. Obviously, they evoke and resolve tensions between the sexes—a consummation always devoutly to be wished. Difference, conflict, antagonism between male and female are acted out, and they turn into their opposite: into a celebration of the harmonious union of the sexes. Yet this play of sexual conflict and resolution enacts something larger in society, in the universe.[26] The birth of twins threatens a disturbance in things, an interference by dangerous spirits that must be dealt with. The shameless sexual joking, which in its own way is evoked by the birth of twins, works by a kind of sympathetic magic to play out the larger conflict in things, to resolve the larger tension. Hence it is cathartic in a sense far transcending the psychological healing of individuals or even of a society: like so many ritual acts the world over, it helps bring the world order once again out of chaos. Oddly enough, the holiday waiving of ordinary restraints, of ordinary shame, is ultimately a means of reinforcing the basic order of things on which shame, like other restraints and limits, must finally depend.

(2) When Herodotus describes the sailing to Bubastis for the festival, he does not account for its meaning as a modern anthropologist like Victor Turner would. He does, however, set it against a background of fastidious religious observance and concern with cleanliness and purity that makes its carnivalesque indecencies all the more striking:

> The procedure at Bubastis is this: they come in barges, men and women together, a great number in each boat; on the way, some of the women keep up a continual clatter with castanets and some of the men play flutes, while the rest, both men and women, sing and clap their hands. Whenever they pass a town on the river-bank, they bring the barge close inshore, some of the women continuing to act as I have said, while others shout abuse at the women of the place, or start dancing, or stand up and hitch up their skirts. When they reach Bubastis they celebrate the festival with elaborate sacrifices, and more wine is consumed than all the rest of the year.[27]

It is the usual "carnival concentration" of elements: the noisy procession, with loud singing and dancing; the massive eating, implied by elaborate sacrifices, and drinking; and especially the indecencies, which are not only permitted by the holiday but an essential part of its effect—presumably as a fertility rite, but perhaps also (we are not well informed) as a rite of reversal. The *aischrologia* reported here would have been shocking as well as titillating to Herodotus' Greek audience, for the Egyptian women indulged in it publicly, in company with men, rather than in private women's rites like the Thesmophoria, from which men were strictly excluded. Shocking too would have been the women's public exposure of their genitalia, or *anasyrma*, which DeSelincourt politely translates as "hitch up their skirts." It is an aggressive, an apotropaic gesture; to Herodotus, it must have suggested something basic in carnival observances that his more civilized Greek contemporaries had largely outgrown, or tamed. Herodotus has a double aim, here as elsewhere: to instruct and to entertain. As a "historian," he reports on Egyptian religious customs and argues for their antiquity; he believes the Greek gods and rites are generally derived from the Egyptian. Characteristically, he treats the latter with humor and irony but also with respect. It is always amusing to hear how differently the Egyptians do things; sometimes their customs are the reverse of the Greek; but underneath comic difference, Herodotus perceives an underlying sameness. Sir James Frazer would do no less. *Our* indecencies are more restrained, and their potential shock value is overlaid with familiarity; *their* indecencies are really obscene— and to the modern reader of Herodotus, they are a reminder of what potency *aischrologia* had in the old fertility rites. The ordinary Egyptian simply enjoyed this merrymaking, like the Greek festivalgoer; it gave him or her a chance to have fun. The scholar-priests whom Herodotus consulted could always produce a mythic, doctrinal explanation to make religious sense of gross indecencies in the rites; Herodotus was satisfied, though we would not have been, with the ex post facto explanations. The truth is that obscenity helps crops and children to grow, keeps off blighting forces, placates bad spirits, renews the order of things out of disorder and chaos. It helps the world go round.

(3) The experience is different when, making indecent jokes or gestures, people imagine themselves to be participants in a god's story. Although certain details of the Hymn to Demeter reflect and explain aspects of the Eleusinian Mystery preparations and rites, the initiates consciously participated in the myth of the Mother Goddess who loses her Corn Daughter to the rich underworld, wanders the earth in grief for her, so that nothing grows, and eventually recovers her, so that the natural process of life and growth can continue. So the pilgrims to Eleusis moved from fasting to food and drink, from effort to relaxation, from sadness to laughter, from seeking to finding, from darkness to light. How should we account for indecencies this time, in such a solemn ritual? The "joking from the bridge," or *gephyrismos*, was famous, although few details are known. Apparently, as the procession of pilgrims crossed the Cephisus River, a man with veiled head (or a woman, or very likely a man in woman's clothes) made jokes against individuals. This was ritual *aischrologia*. It marked a significant moment of transition. It also provided an emotional respite, a time of relaxation in what must have been, for many, a wearisome and hungry journey.[28] But within its imaginative

setting, the coarse joking and laughter reflected, and was sanctioned by, the moment in the myth when Iambe's joking makes the mourning goddess to laugh. (In another version, it is the primitive Baubo who makes Demeter laugh by the sudden comic gesture of the *anasyrma*; obscene joking is the verbal equivalent, and sometimes accompaniment, of the basic obscene gesture of self-exposure.) If Demeter's laughter anticipates the final joy of her reunion with her daughter, the merry laughter of the pilgrims anticipated the fuller joy that would come when their initiation was complete, when they would run out into the meadows to dance and sing and play like happy children.

Here, where we see festive laughter a little *from the inside*, as the anthropologist tries to do with his Ndembu celebrants, and as we cannot do, despite Herodotus' details, with the sailing to Boubastis, we see that the meanings of laughter in old fertility rites were confirmed but also changed as they were taken up into the more developed Olympian worship. This was no ex post facto rationalization of ritual through myth. The myth did help to sanction the old elements of ritual, such as the indecent joking at the bridge; and these kept their old functions of releasing tension, promoting community. But festive joking was raised to a higher power. It celebrated life's basic goodness and hopefulness. It had much in common with the popular forms of playing and joking that later became attached to the high moments of the Christian calendar: to the Christmas season, to Carnival (before Lent), to the time after Easter, to Corpus Christi. There are times in the religious year, of any faith, when such playing and joking are absolutely right, and when, while still giving the age-old pleasure, they draw their fullest meaning no longer from magic but from religion.

I could multiply examples of *aischrologia* from Greek rites, but the range of meanings and value that we have indicated in these three examples would hardly be extended.[29] Let me limit myself to two further observations.

The first is that the most striking instances we know of *aischrologia* in the Athenian rites belonged to women's ceremonies involving strong fertility magic, mostly located within the sowing season of early October. The old Stenia gave, with its license, a synonym (*steniasdein*) for "satirizing." At the Thesmophoria, when the women celebrated a private three-day holiday (or longer, outside of Athens; and note that their organizing of female assemblies, under female officials, provided an unusual experience of counterculture, on which Aristophanes would draw heavily), the verbal indecencies went together with the seeing and handling of "unspeakable things."[30] These were, presumably, models of male and female organs. I prefer, as an excluded male, not to pry further into the secrets of the Thesmophoria: they were evidently fertility magic, taken under the protection of Demeter. As Froma Zeitlin has pointed out, the women's licentious joking went with the reverse extreme, the fasting of a day of mourning (the Nesteia) and the strict abstinence from sexual intercourse that this festival, like many others, required.[31] The power of sexuality denied, or rather postponed, enhanced the festive celebration of maternity; the permitted indecencies of word and gesture celebrated and strengthened the sexual union and the "good birth" resulting from it; yet both together may, as Zeitlin suggests, have been "modeled on the scenario of the goddesses" and thus "integrated into the ensemble of the festival."[32] Once again, we have a sense of the old "strong medicine" at work, but with enhanced meaning, social and religious, for the participants.

My second and last observation, drawn from the Eleusinian Haloa, is that even the women's Demetrian rites, when they took on a carnival intensity, tended to be associated with Dionysus, if not drawn into his sphere. There were many links between Demeter and Dionysus: the companionship of corn and wine, the identifying of Dionysus with the "Iacchos" shout of the pilgrims to Eleusis, the joining of the Dionysus-child with Demeter and Persephone in rite and explanatory myth. Now the Haloa shows a "carnival concentration" of elements. There was massive eating and drinking; prostitutes were welcome; as a scholiast to Lucian tells it, speaking of the Eleusinian Haloa (but its main features must have been common to other Haloa, in city or country):

> A women's rite is included here at Eleusis, with many forms of playing (*paidiai*) and joking (*skōmmata*). Entering in by themselves the women can say what they want without fear. Indeed, they say the most ugly-and-shameful things (*ta aischista*) to one another on this occasion, and the priestesses go up to the women and in their ear, privately—like a ritual secret—counsel them to try adulterous affairs. But all the women loudly proclaim, to each other, shameful and irreverent things (*aischra kai asemna*), while they hold up indecent sexual images, both male and female.[33]

Notice that we may distinguish here between two kinds of *aischrologia*. The indecent "play and joking" takes the form of mutual insult and invective, while the second example is of pure obscenity, evoking the power of sex for its own "prostropaic" or apotropaic sake. But more: the scholiast goes on to report a tradition connecting the rite with Dionysus.

He makes it a joint rite in honor of Demeter, Kore, and Dionysus, and connects it, rather dubiously, with the cutting of the vines and the preparation of the new wine. (To some degree this shows a confusion with the country Dionysia, a winter rite close in time to the Haloa.) What is especially interesting is the aetiological myth that he relates:

1. The obscene male images symbolize the act of sowing (generation), since Dionysus' gift of wine sharpens desire for sexual intercourse.
2. Dionysus gave the gift of wine to Icarios; he was killed by shepherds

ignorant of the effect of wine; because of this, and because they attacked Dionysus himself, they were driven mad, and they became fixed "in the shameful posture" [of ithyphallic aggression]; on consulting an oracle, they were told that they could be relieved of madness if they made clay images of the genitals and dedicated these. So they did. Their trouble was removed; the present holiday is a memorial of their experience and trouble.

Now, as an explanation of the Haloa rites, all this sounds spurious. We may doubt that the fertility rites of the threshing floors, obscenity and all, had any original connection with Dionysus—least of all the private women's rites. In time, however, it seemed natural to make such a connection. Corn and wine ceremonies went side by side; phallic ceremonies connected the two, giving a similar experience of licensed joking and release; and most of all, as god of release, Dionysus became associated with the *cathartic experience* produced by what I have called the "carnival concentration." Obscenity belonged to Demeter in its function of promoting fertility, and also to Dionysus; but in its other function, of warding off the madness that excessive repression of instinctual feelings can bring, it came to belong especially to Dionysus, as the god who causes or averts madness. His friendly invasion here of Demeter's realm was late but appropriate. The god who best combined the old vegetation magic with the more recently arrived (but still very primitive) power of catharsis had become—with no lessening of Demeter's authority and majesty—the chief god of carnival, and the chief patron of festive comedy.

E

Comedy's Emergence from Festive Play: Aristotle and Horace

ARISTOTLE mentions the ritual origin of comedy but then drops the subject quickly.

> Now tragedy came from a beginning that consisted of improvisation—and so did comedy; tragedy came from the people leading off the dithyramb, and comedy from those who led off the phallic things (*ta phallika*) that are still practiced even today in many of the cities—and it [tragedy] developed little by little, what could be seen of it, as people carried it forward; after many changes it came to a halt, once it achieved its true nature (*physin*). (1449a9–15)

The reference is tantalizingly brief. We want to know so much more about the phallic songs and ceremonies that survived into Aristotle's time, and about their ancestors, and just how comedy grew from these and other roots in ritual and festive play.[34] But Aristotle hurries on. For now, he is mainly interested in tragedy; the remarks on comedy are parenthetical, mainly for the sake of the parallel. If he witnessed a phallic survival, it can only have led him to reflect, with much satisfaction, on how far comedy had come since its rude beginnings. His whole emphasis is on the gap between improvisation and art (a gap that, in the case of the dithyramb and tragedy, modern scholars have filled in with bits and pieces of evidence, and with reasonable speculations). What mattered to Aristotle was that, in time, the exchange of improvised verses became converted into a more musical and theatrical art by gifted people who, each following his own bent, organized the different genres. Songs were prepared in advance, written down and learned. An actor was added to the basic chorus; in time, masks were developed, and prologues, and a second and third actor were added, so that tragedy could reach its full growth (*physin*) as a literary and dramatic form. Something like this must have happened to comedy, although the details were not available to Aristotle. What mattered, he thought, in any case was the scheme of organic development, not the dim and casual beginnings.

But the development of comedy that Aristotle had in mind was two-fold. It was artistic, but it was also moral and social. Plato had criticized comedy for (among other things) its admixture of the painful; people felt the sting of envy and so rejoiced in the misfortunes of others and in inflicting discomfort on them. In response, Aristotle worked out a justification of comedy that included, alongside other elements like the famous *catharsis*, a redefinition of the genre to conform with a redefinition of "the comic," *to geloion*. It still fell under the broad category of the ugly-and-shameful, *to aischron*, but with limitations:

> What is comic is a mistaking and something ugly that does not give pain nor result in destruction, much as the comic mask is ugly and distorted but lacking in pain. (1449a34–37)

I discuss this conception in section 34; what matters for now is that it is quite opposed to the kind of festive abuse and invective that we have been considering—and that surely contributed much to the development of Attic comedy in mood as well as form. Aristotle does recognize an early stage of satire, which he refers to as "blame" (*psogos*) and "iambizing" (*iambisdein*). The former term is contrasted with the poetry of praise, hymns and encomia, in which, Aristotle says, began the *mimēsis* of "serious" people that was later to issue in tragedy. Satire, by contrast, is negative; it centers on "blame" (though still according to the norms of a given society); and as a casual, almost conversational form, it primarily uses the iambic meter, which is very close to ordinary spoken prose. When Aristotle speaks of early poets who "iambized one another," he is referring to a protogenre that he judges inferior from both an artistic and a moral viewpoint. It was undeveloped, and it was uncivilized. But in the *Margites*, an epic about a stupid nonhero that was (for Aristotle) the ancestor of comedy as the *Iliad* and *Odyssey* were the ancestors of tragedy, Homer showed the way to expressing, in appropriate dramatic form, the genuinely "comic":

> It was he who brought to discovery the form of comedy, taking not blame but the comic, and making it into dramatic action. (1448b36–38)

The right development took time, but once Homer had given the clue, it was bound to follow. The Dorians get credit next. They claimed comedy for their own invention, and we tend today to give them credit for developing certain stock figures and situations of farce that came into Attic comedy; but Aristotle sees the Dorians, and especially the Sicilian writers, Epicharmus and Phormis, as having developed comic plots of a general nature, which the poet Crates then introduced at Athens:

> Of the writers at Athens, it was Crates who first abandoned the iambic form and began to make plots and dialogue of a general nature (1449b7–9)

Again, the abandonment of the "iambic form" implies a double progress: from the casualness of comic speech still recalling its primitive, improvised beginnings, to a recognizable literary form that is worthy to be a companion to literary tragedy; and from personal satire that names individuals and gives pain, to a more generally applicable and pleasant kind of plot that deals, lightly and humorously, with nonpainful "mistakings" in society. Once we have reached Crates' comic plots, we are nine-tenths of the way to the fulfillment of the *physis* of comedy: nearly, we might say (though Aristotle did not read his plays), to Menander.

But what of Aristophanes? Aristotle leaves him out of this account (to be sure, a sketchy one, perhaps to be supplemented and modified in a projected, fuller treatment of comedy in a *Second Poetics*): as though he were an embarrassment, and as though Old Comedy as we know it were an anachronism, a throwback to some more primitive time of satirizing and licentious play.[35] Yet there are hints elsewhere that Aristotle admired Aristophanes as a writer; and while his Peripatetic successors maintained a strong contrast between "old comedy" and "new comedy"—the former distinguished by its obscenity and personal invective, which clearly went out of style, or became impermissible, around the end of the fifth century—they also credited Aristophanes with a number of literary and dramatic virtues that set him among the great models of rhetorical style.

The two approaches, never quite reconciled, resurface curiously in Horace's accounts of the satiric aims and methods of Lucilius, and of his own. He begins *Satires* 1.4 with a statement that Lucilius' satire "depends wholly" in spirit on the satirical freedom, *libertas*, of Old Comedy:

> Eupolis, Cratinus, and Aristophanes and the other Old Comedy poets set down with great freedom and frankness (*multa cum libertate notabant*) anyone who deserved to be called villain or thief, or who was notorious for being an adulterer, or a hit man, or whatever. Which is where Lucilius comes from.

Here the essence of Old Comedy seems to consist of its hunting license. Aristophanes and his contemporaries had complete "freedom" to attack evildoers by name, though implicitly in the service of society; the verb *notare* connects their work with that of the Roman censor, who struck immoral people from the Senate list. Horace goes on to criticize Lucilius as a careless writer and to give a quite different definition of his own literary and social aims in writing satire: he wishes to be, not a public policeman or informer, but an educator, or better a self-educator who observes and jots down the actions of mistaken and foolish people to his own advantage. Horace is ironic in his defense, ironic too in his question whether satire is to be considered poetry; but although his satire remains more aggressive, and sometimes more personal, than he openly admits, he has succeeded in giving a broader social, literary, and educational meaning to the ideal of *libertas* than Lucilius or his admirers may have wished. It may, in fact, approach the Aristotelian ideal of "liberal" humor as opposed to raw satire. Horace had been a college student in Athens, and his ethical and literary standards owe much to his study with the Peripatetics. But so does his view of Old Comedy expressed in a later satire, which brings out a strong sense of its virtues as a model for good literary satire:

> It isn't enough to make your audience laugh, with great, wide grins (though there is skill in this too); brevity is required . . . and a form of speech that is now vehement, now casual and joking; now playing the part of a high orator and poet, now of a clever wit, who spares his strength and draws it out to a point. The comic (*ridiculum*) cuts through great affairs better and more effectively than the sharply aggressive (*acri*). By this, the writers of Old Comedy held the stage; in this, they deserve to be imitated. (1.10.7–17)

(Writers whom, Horace goes on, these self-styled new critics have never actually read.) His point here is that the defenders of Lucilius who traced his *libertas* back to Aristophanes and the rest had only a kind of handbook learning; they identified Old Comedy with fierce, outspoken satire, but they ignored those other dramatic and rhetorical qualities that gave it true wit, charm, and excellence. It was (as good satire ought also to be) closer to the rapier than the bludgeon. If this Aristophanes was a great deal better than the popular image of "Aristophanes," Horace may have learned from the Peripatetics to do him justice.[36]

Still, in a scholarly tradition going back to Varro, the mainstream of Roman verse satire, with Lucilius as its founder, was long believed to be characterized by the quality of personal abuse, *onomasti kōmōidein*, derived from the Old Comedy: "Among the Romans, satire is defined as a poem that uses invective now and criticizes men's faults in the style and manner of old comedy: such as Lucilius, Horace, and Persius wrote."[37] The prevailing Roman view was that Athenian Old Comedy in its license of abuse went to shameful excesses and had in the end to be repressed by law. Cicero, in his *Republic*, voiced the shock of a Roman gentleman, and a conservative politician.[38] It is one thing, he says, for a writer of Old Comedy (he evidently has Aristophanes in mind) to attack such low, subversive demagogues as Cleon, Cleophon, or Hyperbolus; but to attack Pericles? To slander a famous general and statesman of such *auctoritas*, and on the public stage? That is as bad "as if our very own

Plautus or Naevius had attacked the Scipios, or Caecilius had attacked Cato"—which is just the kind of outrageous, antisocial behavior that the Twelve Tables guarded against when they established the death penalty for purveyors of public slander against individuals.

Richard LaFleur has shown how much Horace was aware of the implications of that law for satire, as well as the temper of the times and the new principate; he might joke about the "law of satire," playing on its different literary and social meanings, and cling to his satirist's right of self-defense against attacks, but essentially, he moved away from the old, personal satire toward a broader commentary on society and on human nature.[39] In doing so he changed the norm of *libertas*, making it more inward and personal, and he modified the traditional *lex generis* while making his satire conform more nearly to the spirit and letter of the public law. Not only did his satire move away from the abusive spirit of "Eupolis, Cratinus, and Aristophanes" and closer to that of New Comedy, of Menander and Terence, but under his direction Roman satire may have seemed to undergo the self-correction that elsewhere, perhaps following a Peripatetic source, he attributes to Greek comedy:

> After that came Old Comedy, not without much praise: but liberty fell away into license and into random violence that needed to be curbed by law. Law, then, was imposed; and the chorus, on losing its right to inflict damages (*sublato iure nocendi*), shamefully fell into silence. (*Ars Poetica* 281–84)

The picture is unfair. Two major differences between New Comedy and Old were the disappearance of the chorus (except for song-and-dance interludes) and the abandonment of *aischrologia*, personal abuse with obscenity; Horace suggests that once the latter was removed—free speech having gone too far—the chorus simply had nothing left to say. It is unfair, and it is unhistorical. But it probably reflects a generally accepted version of the history of Greek comedy: freedom grown to dangerous excess, then curtailed by law.

I suggest that the same version served as a model for the imaginative picture of popular lampooning that Horace gives in *Epistles* 2.1, to Augustus. I examine this in detail because it roots the development of this *Fescennina licentia* in popular festivals, exactly as we would expect Aristotle and his successors to have done for Greek comedy:

> The men of old, strong farmers and easily contented, used to relax their bodies after harvest time by making holiday, and to rest their minds, too, that endured harsh toil by looking hopefully to its end. Together with their loyal wives and their dear children, companions of their work, they now offered their dues: a pig for Mother Earth, milk for Silvanus, flowers and wine for our Genius who remembers that life is short. And Fescennine license, found for

these holidays, poured forth its rustic taunts in alternating verses, and free expression (*libertas*), presented every year as the seasons turned, enjoyed its childlike, amiable play—until that funmaking changed into savage and open madness, parading through honorable households with impunity and threats. Those harassed by the bloody tooth felt pain; others, untouched themselves, took thought for the general welfare; and

> at last a legal penalty was found
> by which writers of libel all were bound,
> and they, unwilling to be liable,
> wrote poems more reliable and sound.   (139–55)

Here again we see three stages, of play, excess, and regulation. The first is festive play. Horace's picture joins realistic traits with more idealizing ones: his nice, simple, family-loving peasants might have stepped right out of Virgil's *Georgics*,[40] and their sacrifice is simple and pious; the holiday, returning in the year's cycle, permits them to relax in body and spirit after all the long work of plowing, sowing, caring for the crops, and finally harvesting them. The *Fescennina licentia*, the exchange of rude and indecent verses, probably improvised on the spot, fits easily and naturally into this context. It is like what children do. Horace's phrase *lusit amabiliter* evokes the charming play (*paisdein*) of a little child, much as, earlier in the epistle, he compared the Greek amateur spirit after the Persian Wars to the playing (*luderet*) of a small girl under her nurse's care.

There is, the epistle suggests, a time for careless play and a time for growing up. In its second stage (we might almost say, its violent adolescence), what seemed a tolerable, even charming play form turned into something worse, a widespread attack on individuals that raged through noble houses; the wording implies Horace's outrage at this breach of privacy and at the idea, also voiced by Cicero, that great men should have been attacked. Hence the satirist has to be restrained by law like some mad dog or ravening wolf. Society protects itself by laws against defamation, against *mala carmina*. The Roman satirist was thus restrained; Lucilius, we might guess, was something of a privileged exception, but even he had to be careful and to justify his satire against criticisms of its lawlessness. Horace follows him, more fully abandons the old childlike *libertas* of personal invective, more fully accedes to the letter and spirit of the law. But he seems to have been encouraged by the reflection that Greek comedy, in its time, had done the same.

The idea of the *malum carmen* is significant for Horace's purposes, and for ours.[41] In the Twelve Tables, it seems to have connected the two ideas, disparate for us but closely interrelated for the Romans, of witchcraft and defamation. Pliny (*Historia Naturalis* 28.17) indicates that people were punished for practicing sorcery, whether against crops or persons (*qui fruges excantasset . . . qui malum carmen incantasset*); Cicero (*De Republica* 4.12) has Scipio link witchcraft with defamation under a single penalty (*si quis occentavisset sive carmen condidisset, quod infamiam faceret flagitiumve alteri*). It looks as if the law against defamation had been subsumed under the more general law against bad magic. The two were more closely connected than they are today. To get hold of someone's name and revile it has always constituted an attack on that person, but the early satirist seemed to do worse: to use his verses as an evil charm, like sticking pins through a wax image, that could shame or wound or even kill. The archetypal satirist is very dangerous. His distant offspring, the modern satirical poet, is still suspect, still seems to have a power, at least latent, of bad magic.

All this Horace renounces, through a cheerful pun on *mala carmina / bona carmina* that he had used previously, in *Satires* 2.1. There he claimed that his poetry was "good and charming," not at all like those "bad charms" that the law forbids. He was appealing, of course, to the aesthetic judgment of good critics and, not least, of Augustus; but there was also a strong suggestion that his poetry is "good magic." The metaphor is taken from Plato, writing about Socrates' use of philosophy. In *Epistles* 2.1, however, it almost goes beyond metaphor. Horace has just finished justifying the poet as the best educator of youth, who teaches them morality and effective religious prayer, shaping their tender speech and turning their ear away from indecent talk (*ab obscenis . . . sermonibus*). All this illustrates the *bonum carmen*, the exact opposite of the irresponsible and dangerous *malum carmen* of the unbridled satirist.

What a reversal is here. For us the Fescennine verses, whether sung at a harvest festival or (as they are preserved for us) at a general's triumph or at a wedding, are a form of good magic: their playful obscenity encourages the crops to grow, or the marriage to be fruitful, or else (as in the case of the triumphing general) it is apotropaic magic, warding off the evil eye that threatens human happiness and success. Horace is right: this was the raison d'être of the old invective and obscenity that became the distinguishing mark of Old Comedy, and later of Lucilian satire. It is sad that history and criticism should result in their rejection as "bad magic." Horace wished to distance Roman culture as far as possible from its rustic origins, from that *agresti Latio* that the manners and civilized values of *Graecia capta* happily captured in their turn. He especially wanted Latin literature to shake off the *vestigia ruris*, the crudities left over from those rustic beginnings. His etymology for "comedy" was probably the "country village song," from *kōmē*: he would like it to be more grown-up, civilized, and "urbane"; in fact, he would like to get away from stage spectacles and the uneducated popular audience altogether. Better to write plays for educated readers! It is an eloquent and moving plea, for good art and for good patronage, but it has left *kōmōidia*, the old "*kōmos* song," far behind.

F   *From Magic to Art:*
Satirical Abuse

A T *Acharnians* 1150–73, Aristophanes' chorus sings a
little insult song against some trivial person named Antimachus:

> As for Antimachus,
>   the son of Psakas (Drip),
>   the bureaucrat, the music man, the heel,
> May Zeus above send him an awful fate!
> (What does he do? Underwrites the show
> last year, then cheats me of my final meal)—
> if only I could see him
>   lusting for roasted squid one day,
>   piping hot, epiphanizing
>   out of the sea,
>   ready to land upon his plate:
> just as he's about to eat it, a
> dog will snatch it up, and run away!
>
> That's one disaster, and
> for night I've got another planned:
>   overheated after polo,
>   as he's jogging off to bed,
>   I'll have that drunken thug Orestes
>   come and punch him in the head!
> And when he tries to grab a stone
>   and hit that mugger with one shot,
> I'll have him lay his stupid hand
>   upon some fresh-made doodly-squat
> and, brandishing that squishy thing on high,
> hurl it, and hit—Cratinus in the eye!

To many academic readers, this song has seemed gratuitous, an arbitrary way of filling the time between the departures of Dicaeopolis and Lamachus, to feasting and war respectively, and their triumphant/ignominious returns. Its beginning bears traces of the ancient *malum carmen* just now discussed. An individual is singled out by name and cursed to utter destruction. And why? He has failed in hospitality, failed to give "me" (the chorus) a dinner after last year's play. But the curse is a work of art.[42] Aristophanes describes, with relish and succinctness, a punishment that will fit the crime: Antimachus' own longed-for dinner will be snatched away at the last moment by a greedy dog. As if that were not enough, he will be beaten up by a crazy thug; and, in a great comic moment—the ancestor of all pie-throwing scenes—he will throw a piece of dung instead of a rock, miss Orestes, and hit—Cratinus (the comic poet, Aristophanes' rival). The little indirect hit is beautiful, something to be cherished. It is a great moment of comic art.

Although the personal lampooning of Antimachus and Cratinus, the mix of invective and (mild) scatology, and the dramatically uncalled-for insult song are typical features of Old Comedy, they provide a good starting point for us to look back and see how far Old Comedy had come from its primitive beginnings in magic and improvisation. We cannot trace its full development from ritual to play and from magic to art, any more than Aristotle could do, or cared to do; but we can use this one distinctive element of insult and invective as a measure of the distance covered.

Contrast with Aristophanes' song a legendary bit of satire described by Robert Elliott in his book *The Power of Satire*. According to Irish tradition, the poet Cairpre Mac Edaine had been treated inhospitably by King Bres Mac Eladain, who offered him only a bare hut to sleep in and three dry cakes to eat. Cairpre responded with a magical curse:

> Without food speedily on a platter,
> Without a cow's milk whereon a calf thrives,
> Without a man's habitation after the staying of darkness,
> Be that the luck of Bres Mac Eladain.[43]

Here too, the punishment fits the crime; but the poem is a magical curse, genuinely intended to harm the king and not very different from making a wax image of him and sticking pins into it. This is a *malum carmen*, black magic worked against the king. It may be that, as Elliott suspects, the verses formed part of a fertility ceremony. Inadequate kings or chiefs have to be killed, at least symbolically; and blighting forces are averted or cast out of a community in the person of a scapegoat who is mocked and beaten and sometimes put to death. This procedure, whether apotropaic or purifying, is the negative counterpart of blessing the new crops and praying for their increase and for general prosperity. But magic and scurrilous verses were not limited to approved occasions and social purposes in ancient Ireland. A free-lance satirist like Aithirne the Importunate could go about from place to place as a general nuisance and blackmailer; if he was refused good food and drink and shelter—and other people's wives to sleep with—he would shame people, even to death, with his scurrilous verses.[44] There the "magical" and "defamatory" aspects of satire, forbidden in Roman law, still belonged together; a man might be cursed in verses like those above, and be ridiculed for faults, real or imagined, in a way that drove him out of the community and hence to suicide. Magic and ritual had not grown into genuine art, or genuine play.

I would argue that they do so in three ways: (1) through growing adherence to social norms of behavior and judgment; (2) through institutionalization of limits, including those of ritual; and (3) through the emergence of artistic ability and self-conscious design.

(1) Homer's epics provide an influential model for the strict control of insult and invective in the service of the values of an aristocratic society. Werner Jaeger has demonstrated the importance in Homer's world of *aretē*, "excellence," but also of *aidōs* and *nemesis*, "awe" or "shame" before others, together with "respect" for what they may think of one's behavior and, conversely, "indignation" at others when they behave in a base or unworthy manner.[45] These are norms of any shame culture; it is like the way we are brought up as children, being told that this is "nice," that is "not nice." It follows that good conduct will be praised in public and bad conduct blamed. Indeed a degree of insult can benefit the community, as when Hector charges his brother Paris with being an idler and a coward: he is trying to rouse him to action against the enemy, and (for a time) he succeeds. Insults may also be used with almost ritual propriety in preparations for personal combat. But they easily get out of hand, as in the quarrel between Agamemnon and Achilles; and on no account can ordinary folk, in Homer's world, be allowed to insult their betters and get away with it. After the disguised Odysseus is taunted by Euryalus among the Phaeacians, he retorts angrily, and receives handsome amends. When, back at Ithaca, he is taunted by the goatherd Melanthius and by the shameless serving-woman Melantho—do the "black" names suggest some ritual function of abuse, or of the scapegoat?—he waits his time, then retaliates. But the best example of the limitations on personal satire comes in *Iliad* 2, in the Thersites episode.

Thersites, we are told, used often to rail against Achilles and Odysseus. On the present occasion, he rails against Agamemnon, charging the king with greed, lust, and laziness in words that seem almost a parody of those that Achilles used earlier. Homer brings out the disorderly nature of Thersites' abuse. He rails *ou kata kosmon*: that is, with no sense of right order in language or tone or social fitness. What he says has some truth to it, but coming from Thersites, it is disruptive to Homeric society; so Odysseus rebukes, threatens, beats, and silences him, to the great satisfaction of the army.

Thersites might, we feel, have been a "licensed fool" in the army, a privileged satirist who could spur on the attack against the enemy, as in Arab armies described by Elliott. Or he could have been a powerful poet-satirist like Aithirne and his kind, whom nobody would dare offend. But he has no such privilege. Homer's moral and social world has no place for the uncontrolled mocker. On the contrary: Thersites is treated as a kind of scapegoat.[46] Homer describes him as being *aischistos*, the most ugly-and-shameful among the Greeks, a lame, squinty-eyed, near-bald, pointy-headed hunchback. He likes to make fun of the Greek chieftains but is himself a more suitable object of mockery. Perhaps, in Odysseus' beating him, and still more in Odysseus' threat to strip off the clothes "that cover your genitals" and send him wailing to the ships, we catch an echo of ancient scapegoat rituals in which some ugly man or criminal (or both) was stripped and beaten on the genitals or chased with stones, and sometimes even killed. Perhaps such a scapegoat enjoyed a temporary license to say and do as he liked, before his time was up. Thersites is not cast out in any such primitive or magical way. Rather, he is a "scapegoat" in the metaphorical sense we would use today, someone whose humiliation helps to restore the sense of unity and harmony that makes for community. At the end of *Iliad* 1, Zeus and Hera and the other gods laugh at the lame Hephaestus bustling about, and they forget their quarreling and unhappiness. Now, in *Iliad* 2, order is symbolically restored to the army after the disastrous quarrel of the chiefs: partly through a military "ordering," and partly through the repudiation of disorder in the person of the discomfited Thersites, the would-be satirist. Homer's account cannot have been typical, but it helped to set a norm for the control of satirical, personal abuse in the interest of public values and public order.

(2) So long as people live together in a community like the Greek polis, there will be mockery, and the fear of being mocked, and the danger that mockery will get out of hand, causing serious disturbance or bloodshed. To permit it within bounds poses a difficult problem for any society, large or small. Gregory Nagy, arguing that "in societies where blame poetry was an inherited institution, there must have been clearly defined traditional limits for degrees of insult," cites as evidence for such control the custom of common meals at Sparta described by Plutarch:

> They became accustomed to make fun of each other playfully but without scurrility (*paisdein . . . kai skōptein aneu bōmolochias*), and also to endure being made fun of without taking it hard. For it seemed an especially Spartan thing, to put up with mockery. But if

it became too strong, a person could beg off, and the other would make an end of his teasing.[47]

The arrangement seems somewhat idealized. As members of fraternities and comparable small societies know, a certain amount of teasing can help educate individuals to perceive themselves as members of a close group—although it easily turns to something really painful, a form of hazing. In Plutarch's view the discipline of accepting social teasing from one's peer group was character-forming, like the other, more physical forms of "Lycurgan" discipline imposed on Spartan cadets; but there were clear limits. Teasing was not to descend into "scurrility." The word *bōmolochia* came eventually to denote what we call "vulgarity," a low level of humor, often including the obscene. Its original meaning, however, was "ambushing around the altar"; *bōmolochoi* were like those imposters and nuisances in Aristophanic comedy who interrupt a sacrificial feast and try to make off with some of the food.[48] The term would include a free-lance satirist and blackmailer (like Aithirne the Importunate) who demanded food and services from his potential victims. Spartan discipline had no room for such disreputable practices. Indeed, Plutarch claims, if the teasing became too painful for the receiver, he had only to say so, and it stopped there. We may be skeptical; but the description suggests the importance of drawing a line somewhere for teasing, as for other potentially disruptive forms of behavior.

At first glance the kinds of ritual mockery connected with Dionysian and other festivals ignore such limits. Their *aischrologia* combined invective with obscenity, and it was personal. Yet the whole point was that it was out of ordinary time. Whether the revelers wore masks of satyrs or sileni or other daemonic creatures or simply stained their faces with soot or vermilion, making them unrecognizable, they behaved with the special license of the god's crew, and their personal abuse belonged to the other-time and other-space of religious festival. It was a time when one could have his cake and eat it too: could enjoy, at least vicariously, the expression of aggressive and obscene sentiments, without being really hurt by the insults that came one's own way—for festive mockery *did not count* in the ordinary world. And this immunity from pain was carried into the theater, into organized "comedy." It is hard for us to believe that Aristophanes' victims—Cleonymus, for instance, but also Cleon, or Socrates—did not feel pain at the insults thrown at them. Perhaps they did. Cleon for one fought back, tried to silence the comic poet. But what mattered was that the holiday license made the insults *different*, so that the victims could not really lose face. It was only later, when laughter lost much of its festive meaning, that serious and educated people like Aristotle or Horace or Plutarch came to believe that scurrilous attacks lay at the very root of Old Comedy. Horace says that the old chorus "shut up shamefully" once it lost its power to offend. The reverse was true: once the old chorus disappeared, the licensed mockery went with it; it needed the festive spirit for its support.

(3) Long before Aristophanes wrote his comedies, satirical abuse in Greece had come to be subordinated largely to social norms, as "poetry of blame," and to be controlled by institutional or at least ritual bounds. At the same time, it had increasingly become a form of art. To follow Aristotle and see early satire as artless "iambizing" is to lose perspective. The iambic or choliambic poetry of Archilochus and Hipponax, the great early satirists, was already a sophisticated form; the great Hellenistic arbiters of taste like Callimachus paid it the tribute of imitation. How far had Archilochus and Hipponax come on the journey from magic to art, and from ritual to play?

We have mostly fragments, but enough to make a judgment. When Hipponax builds up a horrendous picture of things that should happen to a man who did him wrong—he will be shipwrecked, cast up naked and belching seaweed on a foreign shore, to fall a slave to vicious savages—it is not a magical curse designed to produce any such literal result, but an imaginative picture expressive of Hipponax' feelings: "These things I should like to see."[49] It is not magic, but art. Hipponax would have recited the poem to an audience who appreciated its wit, its force, its wonderfully controlled buildup of images; the creation of a publicly shared art form became an end in itself, supplanting and perhaps sublimating the desire of an aggrieved man for vengeance over his betrayer. The audience would laugh at the imagined victim; perhaps they would also laugh at the exaggerated vehemence of the bad-wish poem. Just the other day I read with pleasure a very similar poem in which "the other woman" (who was presumably trifling with the poet's husband) was invited to experience a number of discomforts and humiliations.[50] Revenge can be sublimated into art.

Again, when Hipponax suggests in a poem that a certain man be "pelted and whipped with fig branches like a scapegoat (*pharmakos*),"[51] he does not intend that the man should literally be made into a ritual victim, a scapegoat, to promote society's welfare. Rather, the picture is *artistic* cursing; it does justice to his feelings; and it is meant, not to bring about magical results, but to be enjoyed by an audience, perhaps of friends, or perhaps a larger festal gathering where insult poetry is traditional, expected, and—like the "poetry of praise"—appreciated as an art.

So too with Archilochus, who has erroneously been converted into the figure of the archetypal satirist who hounded personal enemies to death through his shaming invectives. We begin to see (although the evidence, again, remains fragmentary) that Archilochus' famous *iambus* was a public performance; it was connected with, or at least derived from a ritual occasion, in honor of Demeter or Dionysus; and it was produced for the *entertainment* of a group. Martin West has even cast doubt on the historical existence of Archilochus' target "Lycambes" and his daughters. Could they have been traditional figures of fun? We cannot know; but our fragments suggest that Archilochus often assumed the persona of a satirist.[52] Once he uses "Charon the carpenter" as a mouthpiece for his satiric comments on life. The new Cologne Epode has the form of a dramatic monologue; it may include a low-life portrayal of "Neobule" and her sister, but it equally includes a comical, low-life picture of the poet himself and what happened to him in his efforts at lovemaking. The one thing it is *not* is a serious story, with serious intent—however much scholarly ink has been spilt in recent years over the exact nature of the sexual climax with which the poem ends.

Whether Archilochus addresses himself nominally to an individual or to the general public, he is still putting on a show, and his *iambus* is something like a vaudeville act or music-hall "turn." As West describes it:

> He ridicules or denounces particular persons or universal types, in an amusing or entertaining way, or he tells tales of titillating sexual adventures or other low doings. He may represent himself as something of a clown, he may assume a different character altogether, at least at the beginning of the performance. Archilochus can become Charon the carpenter, or a father speaking to his daughter; Hipponax can become a back-street burglar or a grumpy old peasant; Semonides can perhaps become a prostitute or a cook. Simple actions appropriate to the character can be portrayed, and there are some indications of a phallus being worn.[53]

When we read the fragments of Archilochus or Hipponax, we are struck by the freedom with which "low doings" are described in them. No wonder Henderson has been able to mine them for examples of obscene expressions later used in Old Comedy.[54] What we miss, necessarily, is the sophistication and artfulness of the *iambus* as an early species of comic representation, or *mimēsis*. Here, in rudimentary form, are many of the elements of Aristophanic comedy. Aristotle blessed the time when comedy abandoned its "iambic form," but with Archilochus, we have come a long way from the Irish poet's magical curse on the inhospitable king, and a long way toward Aristophanes' little insult song against the inhospitable Antimachus.

And yet even in this last there is a touch of magic, and a touch of ritual. The song about Antimachus is more than a cheerful musical interlude between comic episodes. It has a special rightness, or rite-ness, where it stands. In a comedy that celebrates peace, that affirms the goodness of peace in the face of war, and does so in terms of good food, drink, sex, festivity, and country pleasures, the teasing little ode retains an apotropaic function: someone has to lose his "dinner," someone has to fail—as Lamachus, the antagonist, fails on a grander scale—if the good is to win out. The ode is very far from a magical imprecation against an enemy. It is playful, teasing, and funny—a comic gem. Yet, as an insult song, it plays an ancient and valued part in the comedy, and it helps maintain that deep balance between positive and negative—between the celebration of good things and the casting out or aversion of bad things—that is rooted in fertility ritual, adapted to the festivities of Dionysus, and at the very core of Aristophanic comedy. Play derives at length from ritual, and art from magic, and in Aristophanes' comedy both have come a long way; but the nurturing bonds have not yet been severed.

G   *From Ritual to Play: Parabasis and Agon*

A M O N G more than two hundred items in a recent exposition called Celebration, at the Renwick Gallery in Washington, representing rites of passage and other festive occasions the world over, I noted a nineteenth-century mask and costume of tree-bark cloth embellished with leather, paint, beads, and other elements of decoration. The trousers and jacket are brightly painted with symbolic figures, from suns to triangles, in red and black; the mask is basically wolflike, with tiger's eyes and strange snout, fangs, and long red tongue. To an unaccustomed visitor, it is two-thirds alarming and one-third ridiculous. I give the catalogue description:

> Costumes such as this one were worn during the Feast of Corpus Christi in the central provinces of Panama by masked and costumed men performing the Danza Cucua or Bark-Cloth Tree Dance. These dancers were *cholos*, men of Indian descent who lived in the rural, mountainous regions but came to town during this festival to cavort in the streets and beg for alcoholic drinks (*aguardiente*) from the spectators.
>
> Townspeople liked to believe that these masked "devils" were part of the performers' Indian heritage, but the tradition of the dance stems, in fact, from Christian origins. The sun and the crowns on the mask's trailer may well relate to Christian symbolism.[55]

For lack of evidence and experience, I shall not attempt to convey the effect of these masked dancers on their audience—let alone their own sense of rite and play from the inside! May we, however, infer a fairly typical sequence of events and meanings in the history of animal masquerade?

(1) It began, I suggest, with a kind of "devil dancing" that preceded

the influence of the Christian religion, whether in Central America or (perhaps) in old Europe. In the sacred dance, masked and costumed worshipers moved out of ordinary time and space into a special, sacred world, of the *illud tempus*, where they became identified with the daemonic creatures whose nature and movements they reenacted in song and dance.

Such dances the world over have many meanings and functions. The daemons may be powerful spirits like tribal ancestors who need to be evoked, dealt with, and once again safely dismissed back to their spirit world on regularly recurring occasions; or they may represent powerful and dangerous forces in the world—sometimes evil forces, justly called "devils," but more often ambiguous ones involving some potency in physical or human nature. Although this "dancing out" of daemons is serious and intense, it also has, as the mask shows, a comic side, and may from very early times have evoked from grown-ups as well as children a kind of half-frightened laughter. From being ugly and grotesque, such masks have the greater power. It is easy today to imagine masked dances as cathartic in the psychological sense for both the dancers and the bystanders, as dark and dangerous aspects of the human psyche were brought to light and given expression. The relief thus afforded must have been worth dozens of hours of psychotherapy. But this personal catharsis cannot, for primitive people, be separated from the sense of social renewal following on such an experience of the irruption of anarchic forces, or from the still larger sense of a world order that threatens to break apart from such a daemonic invasion, when temporary chaos comes again, but is then reborn into order and renewed vitality, stronger than ever for the interruption, the chaotic interval.

(2) In time, this ancient dancing was taken under the protection of the great Christian feast of Corpus Christi. This is the last of the three great feasts, of Easter, Pentecost, and Corpus Christi, that celebrate, in spring and early summer, Christ's resurrection and its results, the coming of the Holy Spirit upon the Christian community and the gift of the Eucharist, which is the living center of that community. Processions on Corpus Christi in honor of the Eucharist were traditional, joyful events; they included (from that exuberant sense of joy) much carnivalesque material; it was also a good time to put on mystery plays, which were the seed of later medieval drama. (These plays were basically serious, but they included comic figures like Noah's wife, and comic scenes like Mary Magdalene's wrangling with a perfume-seller, that were capable of further, independent development.) We could say that the great Christian feast provided license for carnival fooling, for different types of play. Its holiday freedom came, paradoxically, to include those very pagan devil-dancers of old. Whatever their ancient meanings were, they must have become forgotten, degenerating largely into a form of sport. People knew that because it was Corpus Christi, and tradition, it was somehow all

right for these masked figures to "cavort" in the streets and ask for drinks, and be given them.

(3) There are parallels the world over for this kind of play. Our children, as said, keep up the practice on Halloween in a simple "trick or treat" form, which still shows a little of the old dangerousness. (I am tempted to get a group of faculty together next year in devil masks and visit the Administration Building. It might help renew the life of the University!) What is basic to the universally enjoyed play form is disguise and "cavorting." People hide their faces, and their ordinary selves, beneath masks and perhaps also costumes; this gives them a chance, not just to express foolish and indecent things, but to become, for the time, something different from their usual selves. Of course, the experience of otherness lacks much of its ancient force, as we move away from ritual, from the sacred dance. Drinking has to replenish the motive force of modern carnival behavior. The *cholos* in the tree-bark costumes were largely playing, and they knew it, and so did the bystanders who would draw back from them—and buy them drinks. We do not know—an anthropologist would have to ask—how much this festive disruption of order, this licensed fooling, ran counter to the ordinary life of the village.[56] Perhaps it just exaggerated a familiar rowdiness. But we might guess that, for dancers and onlookers, the custom kept a little of its ancient power and force. Strange energies were let loose for the time, and were played out, and life—the life of the individual, or the society, or perhaps the cosmos—was better for it.

What I have just been describing is a *kōmos* or "revel" of the sort from which comedy universally springs. It brings us back imaginatively to the "carnival concentration" of elements of festive play at the Dionysian celebrations. The formal Dionysian *kōmos* was a nighttime revel, usually lit by torches and accompanied by much drinking, singing, and shouting, as at the Choes. But *kōmos* elements must have entered into the daytime festivities too: the great procession of wagons at the Anthesteria, led by the figure of Dionysus on his ship-car; or the Lenaea procession, which also had "joking from the wagons," or the great phallic procession of the City Dionysia. In all of these, as in the comedies performed at the Lenaea and the City Dionysia, many strange, frightening, and ridiculous daemonic figures must have appeared, whose origin and meaning went back long before the coming of Dionysus into the Greek-speaking world—much as the animal masquerade of those bark-cloth dancers conveyed "strong medicine" from a time well before the regularization of the feast of Corpus Christi, to which it had become attached, and from which it took on new license and new meaning.

Did the Greeks have animal dancers? Certainly they did; but the origins of the comic choruses of birds and beasts, fishes and insects, are lost in obscurity. Vase paintings show a tradition going well back before state recognition of Old Comedy in 486 B.C.; there are bird-choristers, horses with their riders, and dolphin- and ostrich-riders; but though these pictures suggest the entertainment value of bird and animal choruses, they give no indication of the original meaning or force of such dances in a ritual context.[57] They are simply play. To imagine what the earlier "revel" of such a chorus might have been like, we must go to literary sources and to ritual survivals formally unconnected with drama. One of these, discussed by Pickard-Cambridge, is a *kōmos* of so-called *boukoliastai* at Syracuse, which formed part of the worship of Artemis Lyaia:

1. They wore simple disguises, including wreaths and stags' horns, and they held throwing-staffs;
2. they carried, or had attached to their clothing, great loaves of bread with animal-figures on them, wallets full of various seeds, and wine in a goat-skin, which they poured out for many who met them;
3. they sang songs, in a contest of some kind;
4. the winner of the contest received the bread and stayed in the city;
5. the losers went around the villages, singing funny songs, invoking blessings for the local people of health and success, and collecting sustenance for themselves.[58]

Clearly, the *kōmos* as reported here had taken on a complex form, involving both fertility rites and common forms of play. Food and wine were celebrated and shared; there was a competition or *agōn* of songs (as, on other occasions, there might be a sports contest); and the losers had to go around the villages in a *kōmos* of their own (which may originally have been an independent one), invoking blessings on the people they visited but also singing comic, probably insulting, songs and practicing an adult version of "trick or treat." All this was play, felt to benefit the community, sanctified by tradition and put under the protection of Artemis. As often, there was an aetiological myth to explain the rite: it was a regular thank-offering to Artemis for reconciling competing factions at Syracuse. But we may imagine that the revel was older than that, and had cathartic meaning. Artemis Lyaia is the goddess who "gives release." Her ecstatic worship was taken over in many places by Dionysus, also called Lyaios. Her stag's-horn dancers must once have been ecstatic worshipers, who forgot their human selves as they danced out the life of animal nature for the goddess; from there the chorus declined into bringers of fertility, then into customary players. The end of the tradition, as reported, is perfectly harmless. The beginnings have disappeared.

I mention the animal dancers first, partly because they help us imagine the origins of the animal choruses of Old Comedy, but also because they give a perspective that is helpful when we come to those other ancient figures of revel who "bear the phallus." Aristotle, as said earlier, derives comedy from "those who led off the phallic things" (*ta phallika*). We are to imagine a rudimentary *kōmos* of people wearing some phallic emblem and singing a phallic song; their "lead-off man" eventually separated himself from the chorus and became the first actor, in comedy's formal development. Aristotle mentions also that such phallic rites were practiced in his own time in the Greek cities. For him they were living evidence of the sort of occasion and practice out of which comedy (despite lack of historical records about its early development) must have sprung. We hear elsewhere of such survivals: of *phallophoroi*, who carried a large phallus; of *ithyphalli*, who wore one attached to their persons. Both groups were masked to some extent; both sang, danced, and played. In later times they must have been figures of fun, like modern clown troupes who attach themselves to parades. Their old-time potency, and menace too, must have been forgotten. Yet again, an account of the *phallophoroi* by Semus of Delos bears Aristotle out, giving us some idea of the kind of rudimentary *kōmos* from which "comedy" grew. As reported, these *phallophoroi*

1. wore thick cloaks, and instead of masks, great thick wreaths of flowers and ivy over their foreheads;
2. they entered the theater, in procession, singing a "new song" to Dionysus;
3. and they ran up to various individuals and made fun of them;
4. while the phallus-bearer continued on his way, covered with soot.[59]

Here, as usual, is the phallic procession, with a kind of masking; here, too, the combination of invoking the god and festive insult of the bystanders that is so common in fertility rites. Like phallic worship generally, it has come under Dionysus' protection. What we see, as this *kōmos* enters into the theater and plays there, is a rudimentary form of the parabasis of Old Comedy: not itself an ancestor, but, as Aristotle saw, a (somewhat) primitive survival of the kind of ancestral *kōmos* out of which comedy grew.[60]

Early Corinthian vases, but also Attic ones, show another *kōmos* group: the much-discussed "fatbelly" dancers with padded bellies and buttocks.[61] This seems to have been another protocomic chorus. The normal costume of a fifth-century Athenian comic actor derived from these beginnings: a basic leotard stuffed before and behind, and equipped with a visible though not very extensive sewn-on phallus, over which a chiton and himation or other special garments could be worn. In historic times, this was a traditional clown's costume to make people laugh; it suggested a celebration of food and sex quite suitable to the Dionysian festival. We may imagine that the fatbellies were originally fertility spirits, impersonated by revelers. But like the animal masquerade and the phallic song, they were drawn into the carnival rites of Dionysus, who as a god of vegetation and ecstatic worship drew sexual and fertility rites and even older cathartic rites to himself. What was once powerful and dangerous magic had become, under the patronage of established religion, a traditional and fairly harmless form of play—still felt, nonetheless, to improve the spirit and well-being of the community.

Old Comedy is conservative, keeping old forms alongside new ones, and in some of these forms we catch glimpses of the shape that still older comedy took. Most obvious of these is the parabasis, where the play's action rests while the chorus "come forward" to speak to the audience, partly on behalf of the playwright, whose personal and artistic claims and comments they voice, and partly in their play roles as knights, clouds, wasps, birds, or whatever. For readers today, the most interesting part is the "parabasis proper" or "anapests," the address on behalf of the playwright in some long meter (often, but not always, anapestic), introduced by a brief lyric section and closed by a rapid-fire *pnigos*, or "choker." It seems likely, however, that the ABAB sequence represents the older parabasis form.[62] It consists of a tight, responsive "syzygy" of ode and epirrheme, antode and antepirrheme, the odes being sung, the epirrhemes, in longer, patter-song meters, being recited to flute music by the chorus. The combination is artistically very satisfying, and must have seemed so to the Greeks. Its appeal is suggested by Aristophanes' frequent use, in the later part of his comedies, of an additional, "secondary parabasis" in this ABAB form, as though he enjoyed using the older, simpler play form in addition to the more sophisticated and artistically elaborated seven-part parabasis, which tends to be integrated thematically and imagistically into the play in which it appears.

In the *Knights*, the *Clouds*, and (a little differently) the *Birds*, this ABAB portion of the main parabasis keeps a simple balance between lyrical evocation of the gods in the ode and antode and a more casual, teasing commentary on politics or play-invitation to the audience in the epirrheme and antepirrheme. The hymns to the Olympian gods seem especially traditional in the *Clouds*, where Socrates has just demythologized the gods and substituted new forces of nature in their stead, and in the *Birds*, where Peisetairus is building a bird empire to disrupt the Olympian order. The basic pattern must be very old. It corresponds to the two sides of fertility ritual: the invocation of positive blessings, and the expulsion or aversion of blighting influences; the latter takes the form either of personal satire or of an increasingly general, but still very playful, satirical or critical commentary on modern life. The balance, which is very successful still today, reminds us of Semus' description of the simple *kōmos* of the *phallophoroi*, who sang a hymn to Dionysus and then ran forward and recited mocking verses, presumably improvised ones, at the bystanders. In the *Frogs*, where Aristophanes' comedy seems to be seeking and claiming its own roots in festive play, the chorus of Eleusinian initiates sing hymns to the gods, especially Demeter and Dionysus-Iacchus, and follow these with brief little teasing verses against individuals. This is not the regular syzygy of ode and epirrheme, but more than any other example, it shows the ritual function and the essential rightness of personal teasing in the context of festival play.

Although in the "parabasis proper" the chorus speak on behalf of the poet and sometimes even in the first person singular, they tend in the ABAB sequence to speak in their roles as Acharnians, knights, clouds, and so forth, albeit with the light self-awareness of comic choristers who are playing a role. Thus they may give a cloud's-eye view of Athenian politics, or they may explain the symbolism of their wasp-like costume so that the audience will not be confused. All this is playful, but it is also highly sophisticated play, integrated into the structure of high comedy. What seems older and simpler is the teasing appeal of a comic chorus to the judges for their vote. Thus the bird chorus, in its playful second parabasis, promise riches and fruitfulness to the judges if they are given first prize, but otherwise—they had better look to their heads! Similarly, in an antepirrheme (the rest of the syzygy was abandoned in revision), the cloud chorus promise fair weather—not too much rain, not too little—to the judges if they win first prize; but otherwise, they will smite the growing vines with terrible hailstorms, and if someone holds a wedding feast, there will be a monstrous deluge! These passages have a "trick or treat" quality that must have been very familiar to the audience. Their playfulness suggests the rudimentary begging-*kōmos*, or *quête*, like that of the Syracusan *boukoliastai*, or of children's groups bringing in blessings from woods and fields the world over. Their stress on crops and marriage recalls again the two-sidedness of fertility ritual: to invoke blessings, and to cast out or avert blighting influences through satire or teasing. In these sections of the parabasis, and in other teasing songs that stand by themselves, Aristophanes' chorus perform a function out of which the rest of comedy may have grown.

Next to the parabasis, the agon holds most tenaciously to its formal structure. Most typically, in the plays we have, one actor speaks against another in epirrhematic form; epirrheme and antepirrheme are introduced by short lyric verses and a very few longer lines of encouragement from the chorus.[63] It may be that this usual sequence has taken the place of an older ABAB syzygy in which one chorus sang and its leader spoke for it, and then the other chorus and its leader, in equally matched competition. The closest that Aristophanes comes to this is in *Lysistrata*, where the two choruses of men and women sing and speak against each other; and here the stylized battle of the sexes seems to reclaim its ancient ritual function of promoting the land's welfare. Another possible arrangement is suggested in the *Acharnians*, where the chorus divide into two parties, the one favoring Dicaeopolis, the other opposing him and taking Lamachus as their champion. Although the two parties do not sing against each other, it is easy to imagine a formalized agon between semichoruses, each with its own leader. Perhaps the antagonists of the formal "epirrhematic agon," like the two Arguments of the *Clouds*, or Philocleon and Bdelycleon in the *Wasps*, emerged from the two leaders of competitive choruses or semichoruses. The sense of a ritual combat between teams must have been stronger in the older comic structures, but it is still highly marked in the more developed agons—the more so because, as Cornford has argued, the two antagonists so often are champions of the Old and the New, whether this is the old and the new education, or the old and new gods, or, by implication, a struggle between the Old King and the New King, the Old Year and the New.

There are traces also of another early agon that may have served the development of Old Comedy. As the leader of a chorus separates from it and becomes an actor, he may speak in opposition to the chorus and, at least symbolically, fight against it. When we watch the chorus of fierce old Acharnians march onstage in pursuit of Dicaeopolis, whom they attempt to stone, and who has to argue his defense against their strong opposition, we feel for a moment that this is an ancient scapegoat ritual. There are parallel instances in the *Knights*, the *Wasps*, and the *Birds*, and (rather differently) in the *Thesmophoriazusae*. The chorus often express, and demonstrate, their anger against some individual; a mimed physical combat may precede a verbal combat, defense, or demonstration. The hero may thus be treated as an antagonist or imposter or scapegoat (to use Cornford's terms); if he is right, and lucky, he will succeed in casting his opponent in these roles instead of himself.

Scholars have speculated on the growth of comedy from a rudimentary *kōmos* form, perhaps combining the basic units parodos–agon–parabasis and ending with an exodos.[64] The chorus, that is, march into the theater; they play out some kind of formal contest; and they address the spectators with song and teasing recitative. Perhaps they conclude with a victory song such as Aristophanes sometimes gives us in his festive exodos. But all this is speculation. What matters is that as comedy grew to its full stature under the influence of tragedy, old play forms like the parabasis and the agon were expanded and integrated into a very complex and full artistic structure. A prologue was added, and perhaps a new kind of parodos, and a sequence of plot episodes from a variety of literary and dramatic sources. The plots of Old Comedy seem, from old times, to have taken the shape of mythological burlesque—not so differently from satyr plays—and so they inherited an increasingly strong unity of theme and action from the tragic representations of myth that they parodied. At the same time, such ancient components of comedy as the parabasis, the agon, and the teasing songs kept something of their independence: they were always wanted, and felt to be right; and often older forms, like the secondary parabasis, continued alongside the new, more sophisticated ones. Accordingly, there is always a tension in Aristophanes' comedies, between integrating elements of artistic imagination and dramatic action that draw the play together and persistent kinds of song, scene, and action that go back to ancient ritual and play, and are still felt to be somehow right, complete, and satisfying in themselves.

I give one last example of comedy's fidelity to its nourishing roots. The last part of an Aristophanic comedy is often decried as "episodic," as though, his business done, the playwright had to fill in the time until the festive ending with various casual scenes and character types—probably "Doric" ones. Recently critics have become more aware of artistic ties between these later scenes and the earlier parts of the play. I have argued, in my account of the *Peace*, for the central importance of recovery and celebration of good things in that play, as elsewhere. The artistic arrangement of such scenes, the balance they keep (for instance, between teasing song and farcical action), is itself impressive. But sometimes, too, the later portion of a play may be centered on that very ancient cluster, the "imposters at the sacrifice." That is, the hero celebrates a sacrificial feast, marked by prayers for various blessings, and for continued success for himself (and, it is implied, for Athens). His feast is interrupted by a series of nuisances, who want mainly to get some of the food being cooked. Of course the list of imposters can always be renewed by adding new types, and individuals; this is good contemporary satire and great fun; in the *Birds*, it reaches an all-time high. Yet here once more, we feel an ancient balance characteristic of fertility ritual, between the positive evocation of blessings and the negative insulting and beating off of bad influences in the form of imposters, or scapegoats. There may even be traces of something still older: of the type of ritual that Walter Burkert has described, in which initiates try to reach, or steal, part of the sacrificial meat and to run away with it, at great risk.[65] We admire the sophistication of Aristophanic comedy, the more so as we regard it against the background of its hypothetical origins in the simple, rudimentary *kōmos*; but at the same time, we continue to feel, and to be impressed by, the power and meaning of ancient ritual actions working through the play forms of comedy. It still, through change, exercises the old catharsis. It still pleases the gods, reconciles us with the spirit world, makes things to grow.

H *From* Kōmos *to* Kōmōidia, *II*

THE preceding studies in the development of comedy could have been fleshed out with corroborative detail until they became a book in themselves. That was never my intention. I wanted to give some measure of the distance between the rudimentary Greek *kōmos*, of which we have some glimpses, and the Old Comedy of Aristophanes, which I have described as "Late Old Comedy III." This distance came about partly through the sequence found in many societies, of magic–religion–secularization, and partly through the great artistic achievements of seventh, sixth, and fifth-century Greece in narrative epic, lyric, and (especially) tragedy, the support of a rich and powerful polis, and the genius of generations of Old Comedy writers building on these traditions and stimulated by each other's work. All this taken together accounts for much of the sophistication, the intellectual grace, the self-conscious and reflexively playful artistry of Aristophanes' comedy.

Still more urgently, I wanted to show the continuing vitality of the old *kōmos* tradition through change. This is something for which critics and scholars have gradually lost their feeling since the first two decades of our century, when the Cambridge Anthropologists flourished and Jane Harrison first wrote about Greek rituals, Gilbert Murray about epic and tragedy, and Francis Cornford about comedy, beneath the magical shade of the Golden Bough. Their studies could be misleading or downright wrong. They relied too much on analogies from one society to another; they confused historical periods; they stretched the evidence too far. Yet they had a remarkable feeling for the atmosphere of cult practice and belief out of which Greek poetry and drama arose, and in which they continued to thrive. By contrast, there is something bloodless about the work of later, neo-Aristotelian scholars who have turned away from concern with ritual origins. Their readings are too literary, too much centered on surviving texts. Has the time come to renew our feeling for ancient drama in its festival setting? Would the treatment of tragedy and comedy be less desiccated if we once again felt the lifeblood of ritual flowing through these forms, giving them energy and vitality?

What has been hard, given the fragmentary state of Greek antiquities and especially of the early stages of comedy, has been to understand the continuing power of old ritual forms through historical and religious changes. In so trying, I have been heartened by E. K. Chambers's *The Medieval Stage* (1903), which traces the origin and development of English festival customs and their influence on drama with a fullness of circumstantial detail and evidence, and always in historical perspective. Supplemented by later works like C. L. Barber's *Shakespeare's Festive Comedy* (1959), Chambers suggests how we might (though without pressing particular analogies too far) build bridges between the early Greek *kōmos* and civilized *kōmōidia*.

Consider the Feast of Fools in medieval Europe, which Chambers describes at length.[66] Its "carnival concentration"—the eating and drinking, the shouting and bell-ringing, the dressing-up, riding about, and exchanging of insults—took its special shape from the burlesquing of normal religious ceremonies. Minor clerics stood outside the church with wine bottles and glasses in hand; the altar was censed with old shoes set afire, or with pudding and sausage; an ass was led through the church as the congregation brayed a mighty "Hee-haw" in place of the usual responses. The closely related celebration of the Boy Bishop is defined still more obviously by status inversion. A choirboy (or on other days, a subdeacon or other low-ranking cleric) received the staff of authority, the *baculus*. He delivered a mock sermon, gave orders for the day to his new "inferiors," took up a collection for food and drink. For a brief time, the order and discipline of the church, hence of society, were turned upside down.

Such play forms are instinctive; they will break out in most social groups at one time or another. But the story told by Chambers of their historical and religious shaping, and their eventual secularization, is a fascinating one. He traces them back to the pagan celebrations of early winter, first held around November, in northern Europe, and then, as the autumn feast became a harvest festival, drawn to a different point in midwinter near to the solstice. This midwinter revelry was strengthened in turn from later Roman and Christian sources, and given new meanings. As a New Year rite, the Roman Kalends made 1 January a Saturnalian time; in their turn, the Christian holidays between Christmas and Epiphany gave a special focus for revelry. Christmas itself was a time for feasting and play, until the Reformation. Its religious joy gave occasion for the old Saturnalian customs, the *libertas Decembri* and winter feasting. A religious feast, of the Circumcision, occurred on 1 January. Epiphany, as much as Christmas, was a time of present-giving and revelry. But amid the Twelve Days from Christmas to Epiphany, December 28 stood out: the day of the Holy Innocents, commemorating the children slain by Herod. By a natural association, this became the time of reversals par excellence, the third and climactic day of the Feast of Fools, the post-Christmas revelry.

It is not enough to see these Christian holidays as a thin cover and excuse for old pagan celebrations. Certainly many old customs held their ground, barely changed in appearance. A few still do: the lights of our Christmas trees, which ought to be candles, still revive the sun's power at its lowest ebb. Yet the old revelry takes on heightened meaning from Christianity, not just protection. That slaves should talk back to masters, or sit down and be waited on by them, was old Saturnalian practice, a rite of status inversion suited to the New Year, then falling into mere holiday custom. It was revived and given new meaning by the Christian teaching of human brotherhood, and by the Christian paradoxes of reversal, that the last shall be first, and the first last. The theme of the Feast of Fools was the *Deposuit* (taken from the *Magnificat*): *Deposuit potentes de sede et exaltavit humiles,* "He has put down the mighty from their seat and has raised up the lowly." Perhaps the most striking symbol of this reversal was the lowly ass. He was present when Christ was born; he carried him with his mother on the Flight into Egypt (which is closely associated with Herod and the Holy Innocents); he carried him into Jerusalem on Palm Sunday. So he has a right to be honored, to bray in church once a year. The jester's cap itself had its origin in the festive custom of wearing ass's ears.

The ancient *kōmos* survived in many forms. Some were closely regulated, and relatively harmless; thus the boy-bishop of Mainz took a regular part in church services, but also "paid a visit with his company to the palace of the Elector, sang a hymn, and claimed a banquet or a donation."[67] This is the usual *quête,* a bringing round of blessings with just a faint touch of "trick or treat." By contrast there is the group of students who went about to various houses by torchlight for their amusement (*causa solacii et iocosa*) in Paris of 1367, fell out with the watch, and were beaten and imprisoned.[68] In this case one feels that the feast of Saint Nicholas, patron of students, was only a thin excuse for the old, pre-Christian play instinct, and that these revelers could have been noisy, drunken Athenian *kōmastai* from a fifth-century vase, or from a comedy.

The holiday revels were always suspect to the higher clergy, partly for their obvious pagan elements and partly because their customary indecencies, insults, and other abuses always threatened to get out of hand and become full-scale riot—as they sometimes did. The Reformers eventually succeeded in putting them down. Such festivities were expelled from the churches; even Christmas celebrations were outlawed, for a time. But the new bourgeois society that produced Protestants, and Puritans, also produced townspeople who liked their customary fun. Some of these created informal companies, like the French *sociétés joyeuses*, who elected Lords of Misrule and carried on the revels.

May we pause here to compare this story of the Feast of Fools with that of the Dionysian carnivals considered earlier? Surely, *mutatis mutandis*, the basic stages of development are alike. In both instances, a variety of festive play forms from older, "pagan" days, which took their shape from seasonal celebrations and agricultural fertility rituals, became attracted in turn to a form of religious worship that provided them with a new focus in time, with continuing license, and, besides justification, with a new sense of heightened meaning. I have lingered over this comparison with Chambers's evidence because it matters greatly. The nonsense play of the Feast of Fools was not only tolerated by medieval Christianity; it expressed an important aspect of its joyousness, enhanced by the teachings of the Founder. In a similar way, I have argued, the "carnival concentration" of old festive play forms found more than a focus and an excuse in Dionysian worship. They took on heightened meaning and power from Dionysus' myth and cult—from the religious experience, not exactly of a shared resurrection, but of liberation, transformation, and deep-set renewal in companionship with the god. In both instances, too, secularization of the play forms set in as religious belief and worship declined, or became more ethical, rational, and anthropocentric—however one regards the change. Dionysus became a tame god, the Dionysia an excuse for merrymaking; and even comedy became more an expected entertainment than an honored rite of celebration and catharsis. I think it likely that the *phallophoroi* and *ithyphalli* mentioned by Aristotle as showing the origin of comedy were late groups just like those *sociétés joyeuses*, guilds of townspeople who carried on the outward forms of carnival in a more bourgeois, economic, and secularizing age.

From the background described so fully by Chambers, I turn to C. L. Barber's book *Shakespeare's Festive Comedy*. In it Barber traces the Saturnalian experience of Shakespeare's comedies, offering release and clarification, back to popular forms of entertainment rooted in festival. The May-game and Midsummer rites, the bringing in of blessings from field and woods, the casting out of scapegoats, the masking and disguise, the mimed contests (as of Winter and Summer, or Carnival and Lent), and the festive abandonment or inversion of rank and status—all enter into Shakespeare's bright comedies, occasioning their fun and shaping their festive meanings. Perhaps Barber's surest example is the role of Falstaff in both parts of *Henry IV*.[69] A complex figure, Falstaff is descended partly from the medieval character Vice, and partly from the Plautine *senex* and *miles gloriosus*; but still more, he functions as a Lord of Misrule, presiding over the inversions of law and morality at Cheapside (which are played out in counterpoint to the nobles' rebellion against

King Henry). In the end, of course, Falstaff is cast out, like an embodiment of Carnival when it reaches its end, or like one of Frazer's temporary kings who enjoys great power and comfort for a limited time and then is put to death. It is like Shakespeare to make us feel the pathos of Falstaff's fall from favor, which foreshadows his death. He took on too much personality for a ritual mock king and scapegoat. Perhaps, in his creator's eyes, he also took on something of the essence of festive comedy itself, which (together with the rites on which it was nourished) was drawing to an end. Hence these tears—though festive comedy, like Falstaff, tends to "counterfeit" its death.

From the studies of Chambers and Barber (or from those of Toschi on the origins of Italian plays, or of Bakhtin on Rabelais' debt to the French carnivalesque tradition), we may return with renewed confidence to the insights of Francis Cornford about the ritual origins of Aristophanic comedy. We ought not, certainly, to strain the comparison between the Christian European experience and that of ancient Greece. The annual observance in Christian churches of the major events, of Christ's birth, suffering, death, and resurrection, has of itself a natural dramatic cast, which was easily taken up in liturgical dramas like the *Quem Quaeritis* plays; expansion followed, and consolidation of smaller units into greater ones, and, eventually, the development of an independent vernacular drama. Again, the Christian liturgical year was ordered so well and so powerfully as to absorb, with little effort, a great variety of earlier seasonal and agricultural rites, and to attract groupings of festive play elements such as attach themselves to periods of carnival. All this, as said, supports the old revels, provides the atmosphere in which comedy flourishes, and even associates a measure of mockery, indecency, and inversion with the joy that is at the heart of traditional Christian worship. We cannot, evidently, find anything like this in ancient Greece. The myths of Dionysus may be about liberation, but they are not organized dramatically around an experience of death and resurrection; they never generated liturgical dramas (although a case can be made for the existence of such plays earlier in the Near East); they never provided a basis for organizing the Greek festive calendar, including its carnivals, around unifying occasions that gave meaning and relation to the rest. Even so, without straining the analogies, we may find encouragement in the story of English, of Italian, of French festive comedy, to affirm the existence of such a pattern of development as I have described for Old Comedy, and to reaffirm Cornford's argument that Old Comedy not only sprang from ritual but inherited from ritual its central and organizing meanings. And its power.

In chapter 1 I discuss the three insights of Cornford that I regard as most valuable to the reading of Aristophanes. He brought out, first, the balance of positive and negative elements in the parabasis and elsewhere, going back to the complementarity of hymn and invective, or teasing, in fertility ritual; hence the subordination of satire to comedy. Second, he insisted on a central conflict between the Old and the New, originating in ritual combats and seasonal or agricultural magic, and developed by Aristophanes in a remarkable dialectic—which Cornford hardly began to explore, and which should warn us against the fallacy that Aristophanes, as a conservative, must inevitably side with the old against the new. And third, Cornford showed that many characters in Aristophanes' plays take on larger roles and meanings against a ritual background. What Aristophanes makes of Cleon or of Socrates may seem more comprehensible in comic terms if we think again of what Shakespeare does with Malvolio, or Shylock, or Falstaff, and against what background.

If I were revising Cornford's book today, I would give more weight to other features of Old Comedy, like the fat and phallic hero (a very Dionysian figure, especially when he gets something to drink), or like the violent confrontation between the chorus and an individual whom they pursue, try to stone to death, and so forth. This agon is ancient; and through its traditional playing out of anger, hostility, and violence, it contributes much to the cathartic effect of Old Comedy. I would also put more emphasis on the celebratory sacrifice and feast, which imposters interrupt, and somewhat less on the *kōmos* and *gamos* (which are not always apparent) at the play's end. Certainly, when the chorus celebrates the hero's victory, escorting him offstage with a song of triumph, or a marriage song, or both, this festive exodos seems to preserve the *kōmos* at the heart of the *kōmōidia*. At other times, however, it is the parodos, not the exodos, that best conveys the ancient spirit of revelry and celebration.

Let me close with one last statement by Barber on Shakespeare that applies well to Aristophanes:

> A great many detailed connections between the holidays and the comedies will claim our attention later, but what is most important is the correspondence between the whole festive occasion and the whole comedy. The underlying movement of attitude and awareness is not adequately expressed by any one thing in the day or the play, but is the day, is the play. Here one cannot say how far analogies between social rituals and dramatic forms show an influence, and how far they reflect the fact that the holiday occasion and the comedy are parallel manifestations of the same pattern of culture, of a way that men can cope with their life.[70]

Surely Barber is right. I have been arguing that comedy comes from *kōmos* in spirit, not just in name; that it inherits its forms, its meanings, and its power from ritual celebrations of life that pass through Dionysian worship into popular forms of entertainment. In one sense the old *kōmos* lives on in comedy the way our distant ancestors, those sometimes disreputable folk, live on in our (superficially) civilized selves. In another sense Aristophanes' *kōmōidia* reenacts the old *kōmos*, still *is* the old *kōmos*, since, despite and through its new religious and historical meanings, and despite and through its new sophisticated art and self-awareness, the spirit of celebration that empowers its laughter and shapes its dance steps remains the same.

Abbreviations

AJP	*American Journal of Philology*
BICS	*Bulletin of the Institute of Classical Studies,* University of London
CO	*Classical Outlook*
CP	*Classical Philology*
CQ	*Classical Quarterly*
CR	*Classical Review*
CW	*Classical World*
G&R	*Greece and Rome*
GRBS	*Greek, Roman and Byzantine Studies*
HSCP	*Harvard Studies in Classical Philology*
JHS	*Journal of Hellenic Studies*
PCPS	*Proceedings of the Cambridge Philological Society*
RhM	*Rheinisches Museum*
SP	*Studies in Philology*
TAPA	*Transactions of the American Philological* Association
WS	*Wiener Studien*
YCS	*Yale Classical Studies*

Notes

Throughout the notes I have referred to basic modern texts, commentaries, and translations simply by author's or editor's name, without date. These are treated separately at the beginning of the Bibliography.

CHAPTER 1

1. Compare the way satyrs leap and fool around on vase paintings during some task: Brommer (1959) 14–15, fig. 6, esp. 52, fig. 49 (Pandora rising from the earth while satyrs dance around with big hammers). The scene is evidently taken from a satyr play.

2. On the historical background see Kagan (1974) 305–49. Sicking (1967) demolishes the old *Festspiel* view and underscores the doubts and shadows. On timing and intention, see Dover (1972) 137:

> *Peace* . . . was performed only ten days before the formal conclusion of the peace-treaty of 421, and although Aristophanes may have conceived its central idea before the battle of Amphipolis (in the summer of 422), at which both Kleon and the Spartan Brasidas were killed, he had time to work it out in detail after general feeling had turned in the direction of peace. Thus Trygaeus is not the mouthpiece of a far-sighted minority lamenting the continuation of an apparently unending war, but a man who performs on a level of comic fantasy a task to which the Athenian people had already addressed itself on the mundane level of negotiation. The progress of events made the play more of a celebration than a protest.

The most careful account of the structure of *Peace* is given by Landfester (1977) 153–92. On its festive imagery see Moulton (1981) 82–107; also the appreciative treatment (with American Indian comparisons) by Horton (1977/78).

3. Dover (1972) 133 defines Theoria as "attendance at festivals and games" and Opora as "the season at which fruit is gathered." There have been many evocative renderings, including Erntesegen and Festfreude (Seel 1960), and Fruttidora and Festa (Russo 1962).

4. On the accumulation of festive images generally, and the reversal from unpleasant sensations to pleasant ones, see Whitman (1964) 109–14, Henderson (1965) 63, Reckford (1979), and Moulton (1981) 82–107. On the countryside as an idealized *Wunschbereich*, see Heberlein (1980) 84–95.

5. The construction and odd placing of Hermes' speech (see Gelzer [1960] 151–53, 253: it is only half of an epirrhematic agon, and it comes neither after the parodos nor in a *diallagē*) highlights the absence of conflict; cf. Peisetairus' speech in *Birds* 462–626, where he carries all before him. And no real debate on peace and war was needed (thus Gelzer, 169–72). On the fictional content of Hermes' speech see Ste. Croix (1972) 236–37. Landfester (1977) 171 points out

that Hermes' later comments about Peace complete the present statements: not just Pericles but *all* Athenians are made responsible for the war's dragging on. Athenians and Spartans, demagogues, the Athenian demos itself, all finally share the guilt.

6. The lead editorial of *The New Yorker* for 30 December 1972 compared the experience of the Vietnam war to living in a tunnel: "But instead of seeking the light we have been growing used to the tunnel life. The tunnel life has got to our brains and our spirits. Not only have we lost our sense of the way out; we are losing our memory of what life used to be like." But the same issue included a wonderfully heartening essay about Oleg Popov, the star clown of the Moscow Circus.

7. Aristophanes draws on the Aesopic fable of the eagle and the dung beetle (Hausrath no. 3); see Trygaeus' remarks to his child at 127–134, and the story that Philocleon begins at *Wasps* 1446–49; the fable motif from *Wasps* is reversed completely in *Peace* (Reckford [1977] 310–11). There is a later reference at *Lys.* 692–95. The dung beetle is a helpful creature in folktale: see Thompson (1977) 153 on type 559. Fraenkel (1962) 53–57 discusses the traditional report of enormous Etna beetles mentioned by a scholion; they were an emblem of Etna, probably (like the Egyptian scarab?) bringing good luck. On the dung beetle's grotesqueness, which "completes ... the figure of Trygaeus," see Whitman (1964) 106–9; cf. also Kenner (1970) 26–27 on the daemonic power felt beneath certain *Seelentiere*. For the parody of Euripides' lost play *Bellerophon* see Rau (1967) 89–97.

8. On the comic significance of excrement, including its throwing (which underlies the euphemism "mudslinging"), see Bakhtin (1968) 147–52, chap. 2 passim (esp. 175–76 and 221–26). "Excrement was conceived as an essential element in the life of the body and of the earth in the struggle against death" (224). *O belle matière fécale!*

9. On catharsis see chapter 2, n. 3.

10. See Barber (1959) 4–10; also 124, on *A Midsummer Night's Dream*; and 139: "The exorcism represented as magically accomplished at the conclusion of the drama is accomplished, in another sense, by the whole dramatic action, as it keeps moving through release to clarification."

11. See n. 3 above. Norwood (1931) 231 n. 1 describes *theōria* as "a jolly expedition to some sacred celebration—exactly what 'pilgrimage' meant to Chaucer. But that word has now associations of solitariness and toil which make it useless here."

12. Of special interest among the miniature *choes* listed and described by Van Hoorn (1951) are those depicting (1) children with presents; (2) children dressing up, playing at religious processions, even imitating actors (e.g. no. 854, with a boy dressed as a comic actor holding a torch: from Athens, 430–410); and (3) children as part of the mythical/Dionysian world, such as a boy in a chariot drawn by three fawns (early fourth century), and a boy greeting a little panther that reminds me of Tigger (no. 35, ca. 420). The *choes*, big or small, give an introduction to the *kōmos*, especially for the Anthesteria; see Immerwahr (1946) and for depictions of masquerades, including comic or pre-comic ones, Breitholtz (1960) 193–96.

13. I owe this description to Robert Sutton.

14. For some surviving manifestations of "Easter Laughter" in the later Mid-

dle Ages, including eggs and ballgames even in churches, see Chambers (1903) 128 and n. 4. Herter (1947) 5 applies the term to the privileged merrymaking of Greek festival.

15. See the remarks of the Corinthian spokesman in Thuc. 1.70.8–9. The Athenians, he says, are always acquiring new possessions, never resting; "their only idea of a holiday is to accomplish the business at hand."

16. For criticism of the numerous and costly festivals see Ps.-Xenophon, *Ath. Pol.* (Kalinka) 2.9 and 3.2, and the comments of Gomme (1962b) 46–47; cf. also Plut. *Per.* 11.4, where Pericles provides "continual spectacles, public feasts, and ceremonial processions" to gain political acclaim. My colleague Philip Stadter points out (in his forthcoming commentary) that "The festivals could be set by the religious calendar, but the amount spent and the number of days of celebration could be determined by the assembly, magistrates, or individual holders of liturgies." For further details see Mikalson (1975) and, for a good overview of the Athenian festive cycle, Parke (1977); Deubner (1932) is still valuable for his detailed citations and pictures.

17. For a hypothetical description of how tragedy and comedy arose from play forms and from ritual see Adrados (1975); my own views about comedy are developed in the Appendix here.

18. On keeping order in the theater (*eukosmia*) see Pickard-Cambridge (1968) 69–70, 273.

19. On the structure and experience of Greek festivals generally, see Burkert (1977) 163–78 and Parke (1977) 13–25 (the nearest term to "feast" is not *heortē*, "holiday," but *thysia*, which denotes both sacrifice and the resultant consumption of meat). As Parke notes (15), ancient sources tend to explain the origin or *aition* of a festival; they do not give—what we badly want, and what was once obvious—a description of the full event. Pieper (1973) 25 reminds us how far popular experience of the feast differs from scholarly tabulation:

On the one hand, real festivity cannot be restricted to any one particular sphere of life, neither to the religious nor to any other; it seizes and permeates all dimensions of existence—so that from a mere description of the proceedings we cannot easily tell whether a festival is "really" a social, economic, athletic, or church event, a fair, a dance, or a feast. Until I was eight years old I thought that Whitsun simply meant country fair, because our village would celebrate both the same day.

20. Among those scholars who have described and interpreted Dionysian myth and cult, I have found Farnell (1909), Otto (1965), and Jeanmaire (1970) the most helpful—the latter especially for Dionysus' assimilation to Olympian and civic religion, his appropriating of cult ceremonies belonging to other gods, notably Artemis, and the cathartic nature of his worship. Since Euripides' *Bacchae* offers the fullest depiction of Dionysian worship in both its tame and its wild aspects, Dodds's introduction and commentary (1960) remain extremely valuable; also numerous books and articles, especially Winnington-Ingram (1969) and now (with an extensive bibliography including several modern approaches to Dionysus) Segal (1982).

21. On the Return of Hephaestus as a protocomic myth and its representations in art and literature, see Pickard-Cambridge (1962) 171–73, 194, 265; also Brommer (1959) 29–32, fig. 20 (taken from a satyr play by Achaeus). Wall paintings from Dionysus' precinct, either from the hall or from the later temple,

are described by Pausanias 1.20.3 as including the (comic) Return of Hephaestus together with the (tragic) Punishment of Pentheus and Lycurgus, and the god's finding of Ariadne; cf. Pickard-Cambridge (1946) 28–29.

22. This beautiful fifth-century red-figured vase was in the Castle Ashby collection (no. 38) when I contemplated it for two rapt hours by permission of the Marquis of Northampton in April 1970. He has since died, and the collection has been dispersed. A stamnos in the British Museum (E452) by the Eupolis Painter (ca. 450–440) shows two women, also joyful and relaxed, perhaps worshiping Dionysus' image at the Lenaea. For fuller references see Beazley (1963) 2:207.

23. For the conduct of the Great or City Dionysia, see Deubner (1966) 138–42, Pickard-Cambridge (1968) 57–101 and nn., and Parke (1977) 125–35.

24. Finley (1955) 134–36 contrasts fr. 63, the quieter spring poem for Athens, with fr. 61 (wild storm and ecstatic dance).

25. Pickard-Cambridge (1968) 60.

26. For the remains and the reconstruction of the earlier theater precinct, see Pickard-Cambridge (1946), esp. 1–29; Travlos (1971) 537–52 gives a good modern summary with bibliography. Although the fine Lycurgan *peribolos* wall, encompassing shrine and theater, came later, the earlier precinct was also set apart from its surroundings, and the audience felt a part of it: see the remarks of Jeanmaire (1970) 45 and Walcot (1976) 4–5. We must remember that, as Pickard-Cambridge points out (13), the Greeks used the term *theatron* more narrowly than we do, of the place where the spectators sat (auditorium), not including the orchestra and *skēnē*. I use "theater" more freely, to include all three.

27. For the full account see Pickard-Cambridge (1968) 57; for phallic rites, see my Appendix, section C and nn.

28. See Dover (1972) 138: "If the chorus, divided between two or more ropes, has its backs to us when the hauling scene begins, we can think of it more as the spearhead of a great host which includes us, the audience, and the world beyond us."

29. For Aristophanes' use of the *mēchanē* see Dearden (1976) 75–79; for the Euripidean procedures parodied, Hourmouziades (1965) 150–53.

30. Sifakis (1961) 7–14 is basically right about Aristophanes' play with his audience and the absence of such "illusion" as realistic drama demands, but he fails to account for the comic exploitation of variations in psychological involvement, imaginative participation, acceptance of stage conventions, and similar matters. Cf. the discussions of Dover (1972) 55–56, 59–65; Bain (1977) 95–96, 208–22; Gelzer (1979) 280–81; and McLeish (1980) 79–92. Aristophanes especially enjoys referring to stage procedures and playing up "the inconsistency between what was actually seen and what was supposed to be conveyed by a scenic convention" (Hourmouziades [1965] 64).

31. Lysimache, whose name means "Looser of Battle," was a priestess of Athena Polias and the probable inspiration for Lysistrata (see section 27 and n. 40).

32. For possible scenarios of eating or non-eating, see Reckford (1979) 195–98 and nn. The suggestion of Landfester (1977) 184 that the choregic dinner is anticipated and brought onstage, seems worthy of Aristophanes but theatrically

dubious; cf. also Händel (1963) 160, n. 4. I suspect a grand array of delectable stage "foods" that cannot (the point is symbolic) be consumed in fact—just yet.

33. I have borrowed the concept from Fontaine Belford's "realife," with much gratitude.

34. Barber (1959) 3.

35. Barber (1959) 16.

36. The criticisms of Cornford are best summarized in Pickard-Cambridge (1927) 329–49.

37. The parabases of *Knights* and *Clouds* offer the clearest surviving examples of what may have been the original ABAB pattern: (A) prayers for victory, salvation, etc.; (B) the chorus expressing their (dramatically assumed) mood or nature. Cf. Händel (1963) 105–6.

38. On the children's parts in *Peace*, probably played by child actors specializing in song, see Russo (1962) 226–27.

39. See section 10 for further reflections on *Peace* and fairy tale. Zarabouka's adaptations include the *Birds, Lysistrata,* and *Frogs* (1977) and *Plutus* (1978), as well as *Peace* (1977).

40. On the second parabasis, see the discussions of Seel (1960) 134–40 and Heberlein (1980) 96–106. Interestingly, *Comarchides* recalls the leaders of the competing *kōmoi* at the rural Dionysia, where comedy began (cf. Deubner [1932] 136–37).

41. This being comedy, Dicaeopolis "moves" quickly and easily from city to country and back again: cf. Russo (1962) 81–82, recalling the magic drink that says, at 198, "Go where you will."

42. Pieper (1952) 24. For a fuller account of the meanings of festival, and of its power to keep alive the memory of its own religious origins, see Pieper (1963), esp. 39–41, 63–64.

43. "Sacred laughter" in Greek cult, myth, and art has not been studied sufficiently. On comedy's laughter and the gods see Seel (1960) 15, 124–29; also Dover (1968) 127–28; on the gods' own laughter, Friedlander (1934); on the easy popular association of pious belief and broad joking, Kleinknecht (1937) 62, 69 (*religio* and *lascivia* "oft ineinanderspielen"). In my opinion Ehrenberg (1951) 263, esp. 116–22, overemphasizes irony and unbelief, both popular and in comedy.

44. On the Iambe episode in the Homeric Hymn to Demeter, its "proper epic decorum," and parallels from other mythologies (e.g. Amaterasu the Japanese sun goddess made to laugh and rejoin the gods), see Richardson's commentary (1974) 213–17. West (1974) 23–24 sees Iambe's jests as "the mythical prototype of some ritual raillery of a comic, insulting and probably indecent sort, which must have borne the name *iamboi*." Iambe is associated in the hymn with qualities of warmth and healing (*iainō* means "to warm, melt, relax"); I see her also as a personification of Demeter's own heartwarming creativity and nurture: cf. line 65 (how Demeter once cheered the Sun); also 435 and the suggestive names of Persephone's companions in 418–21.

45. Richardson (1974) 213–17, esp. 216–17; see also Friedlander (1934) 16.

46. Frye (1957) 163–86, to be supplemented now by Frye (1965), esp. 103–5, on participation and detachment, and 115–17 on desire and levels of reality; both passages are particularly relevant to this chapter.

CHAPTER 2

1. References are to Freud's 1905 essay on wit and the unconscious (Freud 1963). Mauron (1964) provides a basically Freudian but more balanced treatment of laughter, wit, and comedy, with less emphasis on the "tendencies" satisfied and more on "inoffensive wit" with its play and silliness: "Dans le rire de l'enfant, c'est l'énergie mobilisée par l'angoisse qui est épargnée, dans celui de l'adulte, c'est généralement l'énergie mobilisée par les exigences d'un compartement 'normal' " (20–21).

2. For Aristophanes' associating of dreams with comedy see section 20 with bibliography there cited, especially Paduano (1974).

3. My *daimonion* forced me to excise a second appendix, on tragic and comic catharsis, from this already long volume; I make brief remarks here and in section 32 but defer more serious consideration (together with bibliography) to volume 2. Aristotle would excuse the procedure. For tragic catharsis: traditional views and issues are reviewed by Golden (1973), who maintains the "clarification theory" (1976); I continue to find a modified "purgation theory" both suitable to (at least the early) Aristotle and highly suggestive of the religious– psychological powers of Old Comedy. Much helpful material exists in commentaries on the *Poetics*; I have relied heavily on Else (1967), despite disagreements, especially about catharsis, and Lucas (1968); Lain Entralgo (1970) is extremely helpful. On comic (and again, tragic) catharsis: some speculations of Cooper (1922) may now be replaced by Janko (1984), a scholarly reconstruction of *Poetics* 2; unfortunately, there is little evidence about the actual emotions affected. I intend to study this problem further.

4. See Aristotle *Rhet.* 2.6 on shame and its causes.

5. In his basically Freudian treatment of obscenity in Aristophanes, Henderson (1975) emphasizes the satisfaction of hostile and sexually aggressive impulses through jokes but finds "no indication of the kind of guilty, inhibited, and repressive feelings so characteristic of later societies" in regard to sexuality (5); I disagree, and hence see a stronger release through comic laughter. A splendid complaint about inhibition (of eyes, ears, tongue, hands, feet, and mind) survives from a tract of Antiphon the Sophist (87 B 44, fr. A, col. 2 [Diels–Kranz]), who appears, not coincidentally, to have practiced dream-interpreting and psychotherapy (87 A 6, 7).

6. Cf. the remarks of Levin (1969) 4 on Kenneth Grahame's "Olympian" adults and "Saturnian" children in his book *The Golden Age*; also Frye (1957) 171:

> The total *mythos* of comedy, only a small part of which is ordinarily presented, has regularly what in music is called a ternary form: the hero's society rebels against the society of the *senex* and triumphs, but the hero's society is a Saturnalia, a reversal of social standards which recalls a golden age in the past before the main action of the play begins . . . this ternary action is, ritually, like a contest of summer and winter in which winter occupies the middle action; psychologically, it is like the removal of a neurosis or blocking point and the restoration of an unbroken current of energy and memory.

7. Boston Museum 10.185, from Cumae. For fuller references see Beazley (1963) 2:550.7. On sexual humor in Greek art see Vermeule (1969), an excellent

introduction to the topic that does not take itself too seriously.

8. The fullest, most suggestive treatment of the comic hero is that of Whitman (1964), who refers frequently to the grotesque juxtapositions of beast–man–god; see also the good remarks of Reinhardt (1938) 265–66 on the contradictory nature and fairy-tale energy of the comic hero: "So ist er kühn und feige, überlegen und unterlegen, leidend und obsiegend, dumm und schlau, wahnsinnig und erfinderisch, Narr und Genie zugleich, dem Eindruck jeder kleinsten komischen Gefahr ebenso masslos preisgegeben wie von der Idee, der sich in ihm inkorporiert, besessen bis zu jenem Grade, der Berge versetzt" (266).

9. On comedy's self-assertion on behalf of average citizens against the gods, against political, military, or intellectual superiors, and against social constraints generally, see Dover (1972) 31–41; on the vicarious demolition of authority figures and intimidating people see Sutton (1980a) 35–43, 72–77 and (with a bow to Adler on inferiority and superiority feelings) 83–92.

10. For Dicaeopolis playing Telephus, see sections 16–18 and nn.

11. This discussion appeared earlier as the opening section of Reckford (1974). Among several good readings I found Bacon (1959) and Dover (1966) most helpful, although Dover argues that the myth's chief affinities are with folklore generally, not comedy. The dramatic date of the *Symposium* is 416, the actual date of composition around 384; cf. Dover (1965): the famous topical reference to the *dioikismos* of Mantineia in 385/84 may be a playful anachronism by Plato, outdoing Aristophanes at his own game. Might this tribute have just followed Aristophanes' death?

12. My perception of *erōs* here and elsewhere owes much to Rollo May (1969), not only for his discussion of sex and passion (in chaps. 2 and 3, esp. 73, 77–81), but for his account of wish, will, and intentionality (esp. in chaps. 8 and 10), which has become fundamental to my understanding of comic catharsis.

13. See Weil (1957). Although Weil disparages the positive value of carnal union in Aristophanes, she well catches the sin–grace rhythm.

14. For Empedocles see O'Brien (1969), esp. chap. 9, "The Zoological Stages," 196–236; 227–29 discuss the *Symposium* myth.

15. The contrast between the Socratic/Platonic catharsis and the Aristophanic is developed in greater detail in Reckford (1974) 58–64.

16. See Dover (1966). For the style, content, and background of Greek fable I am indebted to the work of a former student, Joseph Ewbank (1980). All references are to Hausrath's Teubner edition of *Corpus Fabularum Aesopicarum*.

17. Typical examples of archaic Greek thinking about *elpis* are collected by Nisetich (1977): Sophocles, Theognis, Semonides, Solon, Aeschylus, and especially Pindar (243–49; I would add Simonides 8 [West] to the list). Nisetich argues that *elpis* is dangerous because it is both emotional and intellectual (251); in sum: "In archaic poetry *elpis* is either ambivalent or bad. As we follow it from Hesiod to Pindar and beyond, the ambivalence becomes less prominent and *elpis* tends to appear more frequently as a delusive power" (252).

18. See Dodds (1957) 41 and n. 72, citing Theognis 637–38 and Soph. *Ant.* 791–92.

19. Cf. also Hesiod *Works and Days* 455–57 on idle daydreaming; 495–501 picks up the theme. For a later version, see Theocritus 21, the dream of the golden fish versus the need to work.

20. See the discussion and bibliography in West's commentary, p. 169 (he finds

some inconsistency in Hesiod's symbolism). There is a helpful comparison with Theognis 1135ff.

21. On the name and characteristics of Märchen, see Bolte and Polivka (1930) 1–39. The quotation and definition are from p. 4.

22. Thompson (1946) 7–8. (He gives full definitions of, and distinctions between, folk tale, fairy tale, and legend; my colleague Terry Zug has clarified these further for me.)

23. For an excellent account of style in fairy tale, see Lüthi (1970) 47–57; see also his chap. 5, on symbolism in fairy tale: feelings and relations are externalized.

24. Tolkien (1965) 55–70.

25. Bettelheim (1976); but see Lüthi's warning (1970) 138 against too limited psychological or sociological interpretations of fairy tale. Bettelheim's special concern with the child's need to extricate himself (or herself?) from Oedipal predicaments might well be supplemented today by discussion of pre-Oedipal problems.

26. The best introduction is von Franz (1978); I have learned much also from her other books, *The Feminine in Fairytales* (1976), *Individuation in Fairytales* (1977), and *Shadow and Evil in Fairytales* (1980).

27. Lüthi (1970) 70.

28. Bettelheim (1976) 73.

29. On beginnings see Bolte and Polivka (1930) 13–16 (from which I take my examples); on endings, 24–35. Von Franz (1978) 28 speaks of a "rite de sortie"; see also Bettelheim (1976) 61–64, on beginnings and endings.

30. From *Die Piccolomini* (1799), act 3, scene 4; cited by Bolte and Polivka (1930) 84.

31. Lüthi (1970) 77.

32. Brief surveys of the available material are found in Aly (1928) and Bolte and Polivka (1930) 41–56, 108–22; there is some scattered material in Carpenter (1946) and in writings on Herodotus and Pindar, but see the caution given by Nilsson (1941) 16–22: the humanizing and rationalizing changes acting upon the *Märchenmotive* and excluding the more fantastic ones make it very difficult to examine, let alone isolate, that element in Greek mythology.

33. Aly (1928) 267–68.

34. The principal early sources for the Bellerophon story are Homer *Il.* 6.155–211, and Pindar *Ol.* 13.60–92 (Snell); cf. also Pindar *Isth.* 7.44–47. I have not seen the fullest modern discussion, R. Peppermueller, *Die Bellerophontesage. Ihre Herkunft und Geschichte* (diss. Tübingen, 1961).

35. Euripides' *Stheneboia* and *Bellerophon* are reconstructed tentatively by Webster (1967) 80–84, 109–11.

36. Zielinski (1885); see esp. 12–17 on the *Birds*, 20–34 on Schlaraffenland. See, however, the cautions of Schmid (1946) 437, n. 6 about using the term *Märchenkomödie*: he finds it appropriate, in Zielinski's sense, only insofar as Aristophanes uses motifs from several types of Märchen; but generally, in the sense that the heroes' plans could not be carried out in reality; so also 437–38, the fairy-tale solution to troubles is *only meant ironically* (italics mine).

37. Thompson (1946) 278 n. 12 criticizes von Hahn's assumption of a direct relationship between modern folktales and ancient Greek myths; see now the excellent review of the relevant scholarship by Richard Dorson in his foreword to

Dorson and Megas (1970). He concludes:

Still, the themes and motifs of narrative folklore forms flow freely back and forth between epic, legend, fairy tale, and ballad, and all are permeated with folk belief. In the light of these studies, Greek mythology can be understood as a literary and artistic revision of oral folk traditions that floated freely in Homer's day and are floating still today. The continuity is not from classical myth to present folktale within Greece, but from a European body of folklore that existed then and exists now, always in flux and yet remarkably pertinacious, which nourished the myths. (xli–xlii)

38. On Schlaraffenland in Old Comedy see section 28 and nn.; see also Sutton (1980a) 55–67, "Visions of Cockaigne."

39. Zielinski (1885) 41–42; cf. Lüthi (1970) 77, quoted earlier.

40. Zielinski (1885) 1.

41. On Christ and Saint Peter in Märchen, see Thompson (1946) 135 (a combination of wonder tale, pious legend, and humorous story).

42. Cf. type 460A of the folktale, "the journey to God to receive reward"; see also Moulton (1981) 101–6, on *Peace* as a quest-romance (following Northrop Frye's definition).

43. See chapter 1, n. 39.

44. For Dionysus and the fairy-tale world see Bonner (1910); Kenner (1970) 42–43, discussing the Phineus Cup in Würzburg (ca. 520) with the lion, panther, and two deer drawing Dionysus' chariot, and the wine-giving spring; Simon (1969) 288; Jeanmaire (1970) 224; Sutton (1980a) 55, 63–66 and nn.; see also the comparable scenes on children's *choes* (chapter 1, n. 12, above). But see Otto's warning (1933) 95: "Everything has been transformed. But it has not been transformed into a charming fairy story or into an ingenuous child's paradise. The primeval world has stepped into the foreground."

One special locus of Dionysian fantasy in myth and cult is the magic ship-car (*Wunderschiff*) that brings wine, vegetation, and all good things: see Nilsson (1906) 270–71; Burkert (1972) 223–24; Simon (1983) 93–94. See also Slater (1976) and Davies (1978) on the "symposium at sea," when the wine cup becomes a ship taking one on a wondrous voyage.

45. See the excellent discussion of nonsense, logic, and fearful emotion in Sewell (1952), passim; also my further remarks in section 24.

46. "Full Moon" is from the original *Mary Poppins* (1934); I quote with permission from pp. 103–4, 108, 115 of the Harcourt Brace & World edition, *Mary Poppins and Mary Poppins Comes Back* (New York, 1962). P. L. Travers has also written *Mary Poppins Opens the Door* (1943), *Mary Poppins in the Park* (1952), and—faithful to her vision over long years—a coda, *Mary Poppins in Cherry Tree Lane* (1982); Mary Shepard has continued to provide her splendid illustrations.

47. Many of Travers's reflections on myth appear in issues of *Parabola*, to which she is a contributing editor. She gives a remarkable interview in Cott (1981) 193–238.

48. For fairy-tale motifs in satyr plays, see Guggisberg (1947) 68–74 and Sutton (1980b) 151–53 (e.g., Hermes' magic flute and "cap of Hades" in *Inachus*).

49. On satyr play generally, see Guggisberg (1947); Seidensticker (1979), with a good comparison of satyr play and comedy, 247–49; and Sutton (1980b).

50. Many details, barely glanced at here, may be found in R. G. Ussher's fine

commentary on the *Cyclops* (1978). For the probable dating, close to Euripides' *Hecuba* of 425/24, see Sutton (1980b) 108–20 (with good general discussion, 95–133). Konstan (1981a) well brings out (1) the uncivilized nature of the satyrs, with their "undifferentiated eroticism" (97), as of the isolated Cyclops, and (2) the importance of their alliance with Odysseus, the representative of civilized transactions.

51. See Seidensticker (1979) 223 on the "Ausgelassenheit und kindliche Begeisterungsfähigkeit" of the satyrs.

52. On Dionysus and wine (with its powerful ambivalence) see Otto (1965) 143–51.

53. See Sutton (1974) 177:

Secondly, there is an escape from the preeminently adult vision of life as tragedy, characterized by a rich sense of life's moral ambiguities, back to a singularly childlike view of life characterized by this polarization into simple good and simple evil. I say "childlike" because the satyr play often appropriates the viewpoints of Märchen and fairy tales as well as their formal elements. Therefore in a very real sense the satyr play allows us to view the world through the eyes of a child, temporarily relieving us of the burden of adulthood.

Cf. also his remarks on satyr play and comedy (173).

54. This identification, though traditional, has no clear basis in the text of *Knights*: see Dover (1959) 198–99.

55. The Latin words *voluptas* and *voluntas*, often confused textually (as in Lucretius), show a similar, very significant connection of meaning.

56. Lucian *The Dream* (or *The Cock*) 5.

57. On the *Knights* generally, see Pohlenz (1952); Newiger (1957) 11–49 (still the best introduction to Aristophanes' use of personification and metaphor in the *Knights*); Whitman (1964) 80–103; Vaio (1969), esp. part 2, "Food and Eating in the *Knights*" (a thorough treatment of the language, metaphors, and dramatization of food in the play); and Landfester (1967) esp. 83–104 (reviewing different approaches and possibilities of interpretation) and (1977) 56–58 (unusual in his rejection of the pessimistic-ironic interpretation).

58. For the Athenian political background, and a corrective to the anti-Cleon view fostered by Aristophanes and Thucydides, see Connor (1971).

59. The comic use of riddles and oracles, recognition and reversal, may be compared with their epic or tragic uses. For the possibility of specific parody of Sophocles' *OT* see Knox (1979a) 120–22 (arguing for a date of 425 B.C. for the *OT*); see also Landfester (1967) 75–78.

60. *Reminiscences of Tolstoy, Chekhov and Andreev, by Maxim Gorky*, trans. K. Mansfield, S. S. Koteliansky, and L. Woolf (London: The Hogarth Press, 1948) 98–100.

61. See Bakhtin (1968) chap. 2 on the language of the marketplace, esp. 162–63 (on tripe, stomach, and intestines) and 193 (on "the carnival role of butchers and cooks, of the carving knife, and of the minced meat for dressings and sausages"). See also n. 63 below, on the archetypal Magic Cook.

62. On the name Agoracritus see Pohlenz (1952) 125–26. He sees a shift from one who "grew big in the *agora*" (marketplace) to one who was "approved in public assembly"; I prefer a closer association, one who "makes his market in the public assembly." Notice that in 1256–58, just before revealing himself as

Agoracritus, the sausage-seller asks to be Demos' new "Phanos, secretary of lawsuits"—a jab at an informer, but is there a hint of Aristo*phanes* behind the scenes?

63. On the Magic Cook see Cornford (1934) 87–89 (where he is compared to the Doctor), 164–65, 188–89. Aeschylus' satyr play *Dionysou Trophai* may have involved Medea and Silenus in a magic operation similar to the rejuvenation of Demos. Although Dohm (1964) 34–36 argues that our sausage-seller is not a cook, his account of early cooks and their implements (esp. 31–34) and their ancientry (1–10) is suggestive for the *Knights*; see also his account of cooking roles in *Peace* and other plays (48–56).

CHAPTER 3

1. Literally: "for while many people attempted her, she bestowed her favors on few" (517, a sexual metaphor).

2. For the statistics of theatrical competition see Russo (1962) 25–55.

3. The "gleaming forehead" may also recall the ivy crown awarded to the victorious poet.

4. Halliwell (1980) gives an excellent account of the relations between poet and *didaskalos*; he also brings out the importance of encouragement and patronage for the apprentice poet (see the earlier remarks of Croiset [1909] 47–48).

5. *Clouds* 530–32, from the revised parabasis.

6. On the role and functions of the *didaskalos*, which gradually became specialized and separate, and on the official records, see Ghiron-Bistagne (1976) 125–36.

7. For the invaluable help and patronage of Lucius Ambivius Turpio, see the prologues to Terence's *Heautontimoroumenos* and *Hecyra* (latest version), esp. 9–27: Turpio had a financial stake in Terence's success, but he was a generous ally too; there was a point when, under severe criticism and attack, Terence might have stopped writing plays altogether, from sheer discouragement.

8. Although lack of evidence has prevented most scholars from speculations about the working playwright, see Arnott (1962), esp. 109–10; Taplin (1977a) 12–15; Blume (1978) 30–45; McLeish (1980) 25–37; Stanford (1983) 64–75.

9. See Pickard-Cambridge (1968) 84, citing Plato *Laws* 7.817d (*epideixantes tois archousi*), and the discussions of Blume (1978) 31 (who doubts, n. 64, that manuscripts were submitted for approval), and McLeish (1980) 30. Gelzer (1971) 1517–18 argues that the poet must have presented choral songs at least, since the chorus requires a lengthy preparation.

10. For the statistics see Russo (above, n. 2) and Geissler (1925); on the special problems of the 422 Lenaea see Russo, 191–93. Philonides is listed officially as *didaskalos* for both plays, but Aristophanes may have given him the *Proagon* (which dealt with cultural issues) to produce under his own name as well as direct. (Does *Wasps* 1018–20 hint at this tricky procedure, as well as alleging that Aristophanes gave secret help to earlier poets in their productions?)

11. Cf. Cratinus, fr. 237 (Edmonds): Cratinus says at the end of his *Chirons* that he "barely finished this play in two years of hard work"—but he challenges the other poets to match it in a lifetime!

12. See Pohlenz (1952) 103, 127–28 (the capture of Sphacteria did not affect

the main plot of the *Knights*); but I wonder: might Aristophanes have used Eupolis' help (as the latter claimed afterward) against their common enemy, under pressure of time?

13. The scholion on *Acharnians* 6 is discussed by Connor (1968) 53–59 (on Theopompus, fr. 94 [Jacoby]). He opts for a historical event: Cleon tried influence-peddling in connection with a minor readjustment of the tribute, but was found out, forced to surrender the bribe. One difficulty, I think, is the vagueness of the "islanders" who allegedly bribed Cleon; another is the context of *Ach.* 6, set among otherwise dramatic and musical references; also, "vomited up" suggests a vulgar comic scene. (Is it possible that Theopompus, fr. 93—the knights hated Cleon because he accused them of military desertion—could have been derived from another comic play? Here, in the scholion on *Knights* 226, is the same vagueness; see Connor, 50–53.) For an event in *Babylonians*, see Van Leeuwen (1908) on *Ach.* 6. Let me try a further suggestion: if Dionysus was the comic protagonist of *Babylonians* (a suggestion of Norwood [1930] that has been ignored), and if Dionysus got into trouble with bribe-seeking demagogues, notably Cleon, then he may have made them "vomit up their ill-gotten gains" like wine; compare Odysseus and the Cyclops.

14. See Murray's remarks (1933) 86 on how modern topical jokes might be misconstrued by later scholiasts who failed to get the point.

15. Further examples of late inserted references to recent events are the capture of Sphacteria, in the *Knights*; mention of the Salaminia (recalling Alcibiades suddenly) in the *Birds* 145–47; and very recent political and social references in *Thesm.* (see Dover [1972] 170–72).

16. For the situation behind the *Peace* see Kagan (1974) 305–49, and chapter 1, n. 2, above.

17. For changes in the *Frogs* see Gelzer (1960) 26–31 and n. 1 (reviewing earlier discussions), Russo (1962) 311–36 (lines 71–85, 786–95 are written after Sophocles' death, and 1257–60 have been substituted for 1252–56—aside from the question of a larger shift of ideas), and Dover (1972) 180–83.

18. On these *Eccl.* verses see Russo (1962) 339.

19. See Calder (1958) on the single performance and its implications.

20. On theatrical activity in the demes, at the rural Dionysia (where it all started), including performances and (in the fourth century and later) revivals of Old Comedy, see Ghiron-Bistagne (1976) 86–97.

21. See the enviable assemblage of box-office statistics and deductions about Shakespeare's audience in Harbage (1941).

22. The Pronomos Vase is an Attic krater, ca. 400 B.C., in the National Museum in Naples (no. 3240); the quotation is taken from Ghiron-Bistagne (1976) 86, who cites H. Froning, *Dithyrambos und Vasenmalerei* (Würzburg, 1971), 4–14.

23. Written scripts for actors' use are assumed by Page (1934) 112–15, "Excursus on the Progress of a Text from Poet to Publisher" (see also 98–100, "Excursus on the Prompter"), and by Gelzer (1971) 1552 (perhaps people had just their own parts, and errors were made when these were assembled into a copy of the whole play); so also Chancellor (1979) 137–38. For oral instruction by the *didaskalos*, including stage directions, see Taplin (1977b) 15 and Stanford (1983) 68: "Actors and choruses probably learned their words orally, not from written

scripts, though presumably—but it is not absolutely certain—the poet-dramatist-director had a written version. The supreme value of the written text was that it preserved plays after the performances."

24. Stanford (1983) 68–75.

25. Stanford (1983) 75.

26. Aristotle advises dramatists to think themselves into their characters (*Poet.* 1455a31–32) and to adopt the poses and movements of the characters and actions they are describing (*Poet.* 1455a29–30); see Stanford (1983) 7–8 (citing Eur. *Suppl.* 180–83) and 88.

27. Previously, rehearsals were held in public buildings or, more likely, in private houses, used or rented (Antiphon 6.11): Blume (1978) 38.

28. Russo (1962) 135 suggests that *Knights* 973–96, a mocking little song at Cleon, might actually have been sung around Athens, much as, e.g., Cratinus' songs had been sung at dinner parties (*Knights* 529–30).

29. Page (1934) 112–13 argued that after alterations in the original manuscript text were made at rehearsals, by the poet or another (an interesting suggestion, that the poet may have used a scribe's help at this point), "a fair copy was made for the prompter . . . and after the performance sent to the publisher." But there is no evidence for this simple arrangement, let alone for a prompter. Russo (1962) 377 argues from the revised *Clouds* and *Frogs* that the published comedies must have been based on "esemplari" that had *not* been arranged in advance by the author for publication in book form. Cf. Taplin (1977a) 15 on the reading and circulation of tragedies: at least one copy was preserved, probably in the dramatist's family, or less probably, in an official collection (n. 3). McLeish (1980) 34 sums up the process reasonably: "The final script (possibly only existing in the actors' memories, not fully written down) would now be fixed, to remain largely unchanged until after the performance, when it might be revised and published, taken on tour by the actors, shelved and later revived, or—like *Clouds*—rewritten for revival but not produced."

30. On Aristophanes and books see sections 34 and 35.

31. From *Little Gidding*.

32. Horace *Epistles* 2.2.128–40.

33. Tom Stoppard, "The Event and the Text": the subject, not formal title, for a talk/reading on 7 March 1983 at the Library of Congress.

34. The tape of Stoppard's remarks on *Rosenkrantz and Guildenstern* was lent to me by John L. Sweeney. I am grateful to my colleague J. Kimball King for Stoppard bibliography, especially interviews; Tynan (1977) and Hunter (1982), who gives outlines of the plays, provide a good general introduction to Stoppard's work.

35. Patrick Hurley, in private conversation and speaking to my Classics 114 class, September 1979.

36. Quoted by Mel Gussow, *New York Times*, 31 October 1975, 21.

37. On Stoppard and Ayer see Tynan (1977) 97–103.

38. Aelian *Var. Hist.* 2.12: Socrates stood up, to let people see the resemblance—and the difference?—between the fictional "Socrates" and himself.

39. The phrase is Tynan's (1977), but he puts too much stress on Stoppard's detachment, as Hunter (1982) points out in his last section, on "caring" (197–214).

40. I had the good fortune to see *Earnest* and *Travesties* performed in close succession, on 16 and 30 March 1984, by the Playmakers Repertory Company in Chapel Hill.

41. Interview with Charles Marowitz, *New York Times*, 19 October 1975, 2:1.

42. On the development of *Rosenkrantz and Guildenstern* see Tynan (1977) 69–74.

43. "Ambushes for the Audience: Towards a High Comedy of Ideas," *Theatre Quarterly* 4 (May–July 1974) 3–17 (quoted, 16).

44. Quoted by Tynan (1977) 92. (The idea of the "human pyramid" comes out of *Rosenkrantz and Guildenstern*: Tynan, 91.)

45. For the bow and arrow, and a similar absurd buildup in Stoppard's *After Magritte*, see Tynan (1977) 44–45.

46. Quoted by Mel Gussow, "Stoppard Refutes Himself, Endlessly," *New York Times*, 26 April 1972, 54. For further comments on the original writing of the play, see Marowitz (above, n. 41) 2:5.

47. Tom Stoppard, *Artist Descending a Staircase* (a radio play first produced on BBC Radio 3 on 14 November 1972), in *Albert's Bridge and Other Plays* (New York: Grove Press, 1977), 85–86.

48. Richard Ellmann, summarizing the story in the (London) *Times Literary Supplement*, 12 July 1974, 744. Stoppard found the fuller account in Ellmann (1959) 435–72; a few details are now added in Ellmann's new and revised edition (1982) 426–59.

49. I add a hitherto unnoticed curiosity. In the original Zurich production of *Earnest*, John Worthing was played by one Tristan Rawson. Mix him up serendipitously with Tristan Tzara, and the rest will follow!

50. This and subsequent quotations are taken from *Travesties: A Play by Tom Stoppard* (New York: Grove Press, 1975).

51. We should now add *playwrights*, whom Stoppard unmasks and yet (at their best) defends in *The Real Thing* (1982).

52. See Gussow's interview (above, n. 46), 54: "I write plays because writing dialogue is the only respectable way of contradicting yourself. I'm the kind of person who embarks on an endless leapfrog down the great moral issues. I put a position, rebut it, refute the rebuttal, and rebut the refutation. Forever. Endlessly." See also Stoppard, "Playwrights and Professors," in the (London) *Times Literary Supplement*, 13 October 1972, 1919–20, esp. 1920: "A play is not the end product of an idea; the idea is the end product of the play." Many similar statements, quoted in Hunter (1982), can be illustrated from the various plays.

53. The 1984 Chapel Hill performance: see above, n. 40.

54. On *Acharnians* generally: I am indebted to Douglass Parker for letting me read and use his unpublished book, "The Unity of the Acharnians" (1962); Whitman (1964) 59–80 and Edmunds (1980) are helpful. On the political background and the play's meaning, see also Forrest (1963) and the refutation by Ste. Croix (1972) 369–70.

55. On feathers and food, and related images see Whitman (1964) 67–75; on the staging of the great *synkrisis* scene (1095–1142) see Harriott (1979). (I suggest that music would enhance the actions. And notice the large visible props, including spear and sausage.)

56. For the reconstruction of Euripides' *Telephus* of 438 B.C. see Handley and

Rea (1957); for its parody in *Acharnians*, see also Rau (1967) 19–42; for the further parody in *Thesmophoriazusae*, see Miller (1948), Rau (1967) 42–50, and Rau (1971) 344–47.

57. Text and interpretation are difficult. For the feather falling and giving a last speech see Dale (1961) and Fraenkel (1962) 35–42; for Lamachus speaking, Dover (1963) 23–25; Sommerstein (1978) 390–95 argues persuasively that the feather does not speak, but Lamachus bids farewell to it as to a dear love.

58. On Aristophanes' use of wordplays and puns see Whitman (1964) 98–99, 260 (the "demiurgic" power of puns), 272 (puns, parodies, double images).

59. But Dunbar (1970) 269–70 argues that Lamachus may have been a *stratēgos* by 425 B.C., *Acharnians* 1073–74 notwithstanding. Lamachus later appears rehabilitated after his death, in *Thesm.* 839–41.

60. See Whitman (1964) 76 on *Katagela*: "It stands at the end of the passage as a kind of distillate of all that has been said, less in the context than the embodied essence of the context. That is wit, no doubt, but it is also wit with lyrical imagistic force."

61. On *spondai* see Edmunds (1980) 5 (an inversion of whole and part); see also Kleinknecht (1937) 49, on *Lys.* 203–4, where something divine is felt in the cup of wine, and Moulton (1981) 91 on *harpasai* (the manuscript reading) in *Peace* 300: "his words conflate the notions of rescuing Peace, and also of drinking her, as one would a toast." Rabelais would proclaim wine's divinity, from the cry "De vin!"

62. For *choiros* see Henderson (1975) 131–32.

63. For the "Megarian device" see *Ach.* 738; for low "laughter stolen from Megara," *Wasps* 57; the scholion on the latter cites Eupolis' *Prospaltioi*: "The joke is licentious and extremely Megarian." But this standard gibe should not be used as evidence for the supposed origin of Old Comedy in Doric farce at Megara: see Breitholtz (1960) 55–71.

64. The dating and force of the Megarian decree are much debated, especially in relation to other decrees and the normal effects of war; the usual view, of an Athenian embargo on Megarian goods, with devastating results, is challenged by Ste. Croix (1972) 225–89, esp. 231–44, 383–86 (on *Ach.* 515–23). In a forthcoming article in *GRBS*, "Plutarch, Charinus, and the Megarian Decree," my colleague Philip Stadter argues that Plutarch identified the Charinus decree with the Megarian decree, establishing a state of hostility with Megara, although different features of the decree may be brought out in different reports (and the Megarians, in their account, seem eventually to have replaced the provocation of Anthemocritus' murder, a very serious matter, with the Aristophanic theft of Aspasia's whores). "The Megarian decree which can be reconstructed from the two accounts voted a general exclusion from Attica and the Athenian empire on pain of death, with particular reference to the Athenian agora and the harbors of the empire. In addition, it contained clauses declaring enmity with Megara, requiring the generals to swear to invade Megara twice a year and ordering the public burial of Anthemocritus."

65. On figs and fig trees see Henderson (1975) 117–18; on sycophants and related words and images, Taillardat (1962) 423–25. See also the *Phanai* joke in *Birds* 1694–1705 and the *sykophantria* in *Plutus* 970–71: Süss (1964) 311 remarks on the obscene meaning, and Henderson, 135, suggests that she might be an erotic tease.

66. In *Lys.* 700–703 a nice girl who is invited to a party but can't come turns out to be a Copaic Eel.

67. On *akhos, Akhilleus,* and the *Akhaioi* see Nagy (1979) chap. 5, esp. 91–93 (contrasting *Khari-laos* and *khar-* derivatives!): Achilles endures grief, and he causes grief among the people. Cf. now Parker (above, n. 54), and *Ach.* 176–77, 200; also 563, 832–33.

68. For the *Telephus* parody see above, n. 56. Handley and Rea (1957) 24 point out that whereas the real Telephus (apparently) arrived in disguise, Dicaeopolis gets disguised in front of the audience; also (33, following Erbse) that the "disguise" in *Acharnians,* only assumed after the discovery (393–479), "adds merely tragic tone to the speech and not the concealment which was its original object."

69. Euripides, fr. 706 (Nauck).

70. There is a comic suggestion that Cleon's charge against Aristophanes, of insulting the polis in the presence of foreigners, has come out of the *Telephus*; cf. fr. 712 (Nauck), "he says bad things of our entire polis." For Aristophanes' further comments on his dealings with Cleon, see *Wasps* 1284–91 (Cleon gave him a good beating, and everybody just stood by and laughed at his discomfiture; so he "played the ape" a little—for the time being).

71. I am assuming that Aristophanes uses two doors, two houses (see Russo [1962] 104–5); one of these will do for Dicaeopolis, the other (in turn) for the two "misery specialists," Euripides and Lamachus—who might also be played by the same actor.

72. Dale (1956) 124 explains the joke. Euripides is "persuaded to 'eccycle' and so be outside and conversable while remaining indoors undisturbed." (She compares the similar joke of *Clouds* 181–99.)

73. Hourmouziades (1965) 101–2 makes the interesting suggestion that *Ach.* 418 and 427 refer to tragic *masks,* presumably hanging from a pole or arrayed on a board.

74. On costume in Aristophanes and its varied uses, I rely on Stone (1981), esp. 127–43 on the basic garment and padding, worn beneath further embellishments or disguises. On the power of the comic (as against the tragic) hero to manipulate his world through the use of costume and props, or to expose the ignorance and pretension of his enemies, see Foley (1980) 115–16.

75. Dover (1963) 8–13 doubts that Aristophanes "intends us wholly to imagine the Persians as disguised Athenians"; so also Chiasson (1984). I believe, however, that the two eunuchs are unmasked as Cleisthenes and Strato. The beard, though Persian, is inappropriate to the eunuchs and hence a giveaway; cf. Chiasson on the "sham eunuch." Dicaeopolis will pull off the beard, revealing the Cleisthenes mask underneath; perhaps he will do the same with Strato. But we are also aware (this is part of the joke) that beneath this pretense at mask and costume are real Athenians—comic actors, who, together with the actor playing the Great Eye, may have nodded "by mistake" in Greek fashion.

76. The suggestion that Aristophanes himself played Dicaeopolis was advanced by Bailey (1936) after having been put forward tentatively by Merry and Starkie; it is generally doubted today (see Ste. Croix [1972] 363); the statement in the *vita* that Aristophanes played the Paphlagonian/Cleon in the *Knights* tends if anything to discredit both identifications. See, however, the suggestion of Landfester (1977) 43–44 that the comic hero, not called "Dicaeopolis" before

line 406, would be thought by the audience to be Aristophanes himself. Earlier poets, including Chionides, Crates, Pherecrates, and Cratinus, are said to have acted in their own comedies (as Aeschylus and Sophocles acted in their own tragedies).

77. See Kennedy (1963) chap. 2, 26–51, "Techniques of Persuasion in Greek Literature before 400 B.C."

78. See McLuhan (1965) 15–16 on the hypnotic power of media, especially when the public is unused to them; also 285–86, on the (onetime) power of film, and 18: "The serious artist is the only person able to encounter technology with impunity, just because he is an expert aware of the changes in sense perception."

79. For the philosophical and psychological implications of Gorgias' Encomium of Helen, see Segal (1962). My translations are from Gorgias 82 B 11 (Diels–Kranz).

80. For Aristophanes' knowledge and use of rhetoric, see Murphy (1983): but he sees him as opposed to the new art, not enjoying it—or else as using it for propaganda in his drama of ideas; 99–104 has a detailed rhetorical analysis of Dicaeopolis' speech, which Murphy sees as combining features of dicanic and deliberative oratory. See also the interesting comments of Walcot (1976) 42 on the common elements in oratory and acting, and their mutual influence.

81. According to Ghiron-Bistagne (1976) 125, *trygōidia* is a neologism created by Aristophanes to designate comedy, whose prize is (or, better, was) a skin of wine. Is there a reference to the "masquerade" that consisted of smearing one's face with wine lees?

82. But Lamachus may have been a general already: see above, n. 59.

83. The fullest account of the parabasis, its structure and functions, is given by Sifakis (1971); see esp. 36–37 on the freedom of the chorus to shift their point of view, as when they speak for the poet in the third person, or identify themselves with him in the first person (as in *Ach.*), or when they shift from a narrower to a broader group, or vice versa.

84. As Edmunds (1980) 15 says: "Whether *apodyntes*, 'stripping,' is literal, of removing the himation, or whether it is metaphorical, the chorus is doffing its persona in order to speak for the comic poet, just as Dicaeopolis has already done." But if the stripping is only partial (cf. Ketterer [1980], who argues for literal stripping, but only of the *tribōn*, not the mask), so, I think, is the poet's self-revelation in this parabasis, and elsewhere.

85. I do not agree with Dover (1972) 14 n. 5, that references to producer and poet in this parabasis might be to Callistratus, the actual *didaskalos* (as Rennie argues in his commentary, 11–21, 143–44, 185–89); but Aristophanes, who (not Callistratus) was attacked by Cleon, may be pretending to "reveal" himself gradually from beneath the "disguise" of the *didaskalos* technically in charge of the production. This further level of play and dramatic awareness should be added to the whole Telephus business.

86. On the uncertain question of Aristophanes' connection with Aegina, see Schmid (1946) 176 and Gelzer (1971) 1397. Aristophanes presumably had property in Aegina; was it acquired after 431? His father might have come from Aegina to Athens, but this cannot be proved.

87. Aristophanes may refer specifically to the portrayal in the 426 *Babylonians* of the Athenians' gullible subservience to clever speakers; cf. fr. 68 (Kock) and the comments of Norwood (1930) 6–7.

88. The clause *deixas hōs dēmokratountai* has two possible meanings: (1) Aristophanes showed how the allies were ruled—and treated badly—by the demos-leaders of Athens (the ironic implication, cf. Rogers, xxii); or (2) the political comedy exhibits democratic freedom in action—what the allies should appreciate in Athenian democracy. I tend to read Aristophanes' statement as overt appreciation of democracy (2), with a tinge of irony (1).

89. We need to remember also that the two "girls" were probably played by two boy actors (as Rogers suggests), which must have provided a further element of silliness and make-believe.

90. Kerr (1967) 29.

91. From the Author's Preface to Trudeau (1975).

92. Segal (1961) (and see section 34, below).

93. An odd thought: if Aristophanes actually played Dicaeopolis (though this has seemed unlikely; see n. 76, above), would he have been eligible to win the prize for best first actor, which was awarded at the Lenaea after 442? Could he have won—and claimed, towards the play's end—prizes both as actor and as successful poet? That would have been hubristic—and worthy of Dionysus!

94. Ghiron-Bistagne (1976) 106; the picture from the red-figured vase at Tarentum, ca. 440–430 B.C., is used by Ghiron-Bistagne as her frontispiece. She also cites (107) Lucian *Necyom.* 16, on the actor taking off his beautiful costume. See also Trendall and Webster (1971) on plate IV.7a, a grave relief of a famous poet, perhaps Aristophanes: "The sadness of the poet contrasts with the gaiety of the slave-mask on his lap."

95. I assume that the comic actor normally wore an unobtrusive, coiled-up phallus: the long, red-tipped, dangling or erect type was saved for unusual comic effects; see Stone (1981) 72–126.

96. See the good comments of Lenz (1980) 20 on the double distortion both of the bad *Ausgangslage* and of the fantastic solution. This distortion provides a recognition of what was distorted and also of itself. "So wird satirische Kritik . . . zugleich geleistet und gemildert."

97. See Tolkien (1965) 58: "*Mooreeffoc* is a fantastic word, but it could be seen written up in every town in this land. It is Coffee-room, viewed from the inside through a glass door, as it was seen by Dickens on a dark London day; and it was used by Chesterton to denote the queerness of things that have become trite, when they are suddenly seen from a new angle."

98. Sparkes (1975) discusses the difficulties of visualizing (1) Aristophanes' props, which "can be thought of as naturalistically made or fantastically exaggerated" (122), and (2) objects from ordinary life that characters mention; his article contains warnings against easy and common types of misunderstanding, together with useful examples of common objects supported by archaeological evidence; see also Sparkes (1962), on the Greek kitchen.

99. For reservations and the need to exercise care in using Aristophanes as a source for historical events or social customs see Dover (1968) 128–30, Ste. Croix (1972) 232–36, and Chapman (1978).

100. The "critical idea" and the "comic theme," terms partially derived from Mazon (1904), are carefully defined and distinguished from one another by Koch (1968); note his statement (69) that the comic theme is not a direct presentation of the idea, as a *Tendenzschrift* would be, but rather its transformation into comic fantasy, creating its own structured world. But Aristophanic comedy re-

mains basically serious by this view, as in the similar views of Massa Positano (1967), Ste. Croix (1972) 355–71, and Kindermann (1979). For a fine, thoroughgoing criticism of the dominance of the critical idea or satirical purpose, or its splitting off from comic entertainment, see Lenz (1980).

101. Murray (1933) 10 saw obscenity as just a ritual remnant. He pointed out, rightly, that obscenity needs the background of traditional ritual: "Without that background the play becomes consciously obscene instead of simply taking the indecency in its stride." But he failed to realize how much that "background" was still alive for Aristophanes. Similarly, Wilamowitz (1927), despite many valuable explanations of obscene passages in his *Lysistrata* commentary, tended to write off obscene jests as crowd-pleasers (57–58) and found them annoying. The important contribution of Süss (1954), esp. 143–44 on Aristophanes' often *casual* use of obscenity, should be remembered gratefully.

102. Jaeger (1935).

103. Gelzer (1979) 276; see also 270, on how Aristophanes' comic criticisms represent not "eine Fortsetzung der Politik mit andern Mitteln, sondern eine Beurteilung der Politik von einem Punkte ausserhalb ihrer selbst aus."

104. Chesterton, from a poem beginning "Old Noah he had an ostrich farm" and ending "But I don't care where the water goes if it doesn't get into the wine," in *The Collected Poems of G. K. Chesterton* (New York: Dodd, Mead, 1980).

105. The line is of course arbitrary, since many significant critical contributions were made before 1945: e.g., by Reinhardt (1938).

106. I take this term from Ruthven (1979) chap. 1, "Books as Heterocosms."

107. On the artistry and the artistic unity of Aristophanes' plays see now Moulton (1981), who concludes (144), "Aristophanes' verbal art, in metaphor and pun, co-ordinates and unifies his plays far more than the actions in his plots, in an Aristotelian sense." Aristophanes' rich play with metaphors may now be studied with the help of Taillardat's fine compilation (1962).

108. Whitman (1964); add now Whitman (1982) 132–59 ("Aristophanes and the City: or 1/Everybody").

109. Whitman (1964) 7 (after pointing out that Jaeger's view of Aristophanes' educational mission went beyond any simple notion of moral or political didacticism). See also 259: "Although the art of Aristophanes is generally recognized as a compound of the fantastic and the realistic, interpreters have on the whole based their views on the realistic and satiric element, and dismissed, or better subsumed, the fantastic aspect as simply the mode appropriate to comedy, the vehicle by which the satirical message is conveyed."

110. See Kraus (1963) 457, for a view that has become fairly general: "Die wehmütige Ironie, die die illusionären Triumphe des komischen Helden über die Schäden der Zeit durchdringt . . . ."

111. Cf. Ruthven (1979) 13 on the autarchic ideal: "diplomatic relations between art and reality are broken off, and the whole world exists only to end up in a book." But this should be balanced against the continuing need to maintain the integrity of literature, to "prevent it from being treated as a defective system of philosophy, an ineffectual mode of moral exhortation, or a substitute for religion" (12).

112. One, two, or three doors? The range of scholarly opinion is remarkable. I tend to agree with Newiger (1965) (two doors sometimes required, three probably available) and Dover (1972) 21–24 (two or three doors; he argues for flexibil-

ity); but Dale (1957), Webster (1970), and Dearden (1976) 19–30 argue for only one door. Arnott (1962) 104–5 gives a *non liquet*. According to Hourmouziades (1965) 49, a second building seems required by several Euripidean tragedies, and perhaps also a subsidiary opening.

113. Taplin (1977a) 12–28 reminds us that the received text is only a libretto of the performance; he argues (1) that the stage action can be recovered to some extent from the text, and (2) that the scenic presentation is essential, "an inextricable element of his communication and hence of his meaning" (p. 2). Recent writers on Greek tragedy show a heartening concern with visual elements: see, for example, Rosenmeyer (1982), esp. 45–74, on Aeschylus, Seale (1982) on Sophocles, Bain (1977, 1981), and Mastronarde (1979). The essays and reviews of Bernard Knox over the years (collected in Knox [1979]) have helped us maintain a sense of tragic *theater*; so too the new series of Oxford translations edited by William Arrowsmith.

114. Cf. Bain (1981) 44–46, on the use of extras: the text of comedy, a less realistic genre than tragedy, contains less of the action. Taplin (1977a) 31, n. 1, admits some exceptions in comedy (props, movements, etc.) to his general theory that there was no significant stage action that was not reflected in the words; see also Taplin (1977b) 129.

115. Taplin (1977a) 4.

116. On the quick and easy movements of comedy, see Süss (1954) 123 (Aristophanes' "dramatische Sorglosigkeit und Unbekümmertheit" continues through his latest plays) and Gelzer (1979) 284.

117. On the quick, easy movements of Dicaeopolis in *Ach.* see Russo (1962) 81–82. Seel (1960) 31 speaks of the "beglückende Naivetät dieser Dramaturgie."

118. On the "dramatic illusion" see chapter 1, n. 30.

119. Arnott (1962) 62–63 argues that Aristophanes parodies Euripides' self-conscious efforts at realism: cf. 49–50 (the regular stage altar "right here"), 72–75, 114–22. For Euripides' tendency to greater realism in depicting settings, see Hourmouziades (1965) 125–27; but he argues (93–108) that Euripides does not strain to make the *ekkyklēma* realistic; in the *Heracles*, Euripides "does not attempt to disguise the fact that his resort to this expedient is dictated by purely technical needs" (100).

120. Arnott (1962) 65.

121. My colleague Kimball King tells me that *The Real Thing* is largely a response by Stoppard to critics who have accused him (1) of not being concerned with politics and (2) of not being concerned with ordinary, messy human emotions. This play deals wittily and feelingly with both issues.

122. I have used and quote from *The Tempest* in the Arden series, ed. Frank Kermode, 6th ed. (London: Methuen, 1964).

123. For an excellent account of music and catharsis in *The Tempest* see Brower (1962) 95–122.

CHAPTER 4

1. Most general treatments of the *Wasps* have focused on Aristophanes' satirical treatment of Cleon and the jury courts, the artistry of the dog trial scene, and the nature and significance of the wasp chorus; exceptions are Whitman

(1964) 143–66, emphasizing generational conflict and *nomos* versus *physis*; Vaio (1971), who brings out the structural unity of the play, especially the close relation of the early and late scenes; and Paduano (1974), who argues for a shift of sympathy to Philocleon, despite the ideological views, largely represented by Bdelycleon, that Aristophanes wanted to maintain. (Paduano is also very good on Philocleon's psychology.) My own view of the play was set out earlier (Reckford 1977); it comes closest to that of Douglass Parker in his 1962 translation. See also now Lenz (1980). In a forthcoming article in *TAPA*, David Konstan will delineate the underlying political issues of the *Wasps* more sharply than I have done, and the class conflict which, he argues, Aristophanes evades through his comic strategies.

2. The speakers whom I call Xanthias and Sosias are actually anonymous, and the distribution of lines between them is not always certain.

3. The phrase is MacDowell's. On joke and dream in the prologue see Paduano (1974) 49–70; on the technique of Aristophanes' slave prologues, Händel (1963) 185–89.

4. Erich Segal (1973) argues that the ancient derivation of *kōmōidia* from *kōma*, "deep sleep," as well as from *kōmos*, "revel," and *kōmē*, "village," may have some intuitive rightness: comedy is the "song of deep sleep." See also Breitholtz (1960) 49 and Sifakis (1971) 82.

5. The riddle game was an ancient and popular form of entertainment for the Greeks. It had many forms: see Athenaeus, *Deipnosophistae* 10.448b–459b. Some riddles, like our word games or quiz programs, required quick recall of information ("Quote a line from Homer beginning and ending with the letter *alpha*"); others resembled modern riddles in requiring a solution that depended on the perception of analogies, or the use of wordplay, to solve puzzling verbal or pseudo-logical problems. It is an easy step from such *griphoi* and *ainigmata* to comic allegory.

6. For dreams, jokes, and wit I have used Freud (1938, 1963). For the larger context of psychological theory I have used his *General Introduction to Psychoanalysis* (Freud 1953); 246–48, on dream jokes in relation to puns and riddles, are especially relevant, although he does not find dream jokes funny (247). A good Freudian analysis of the jokes in the prologue is given by Paduano (1974) 49–70. Those interested in a Freudian psychoanalysis of Aristophanes himself may consult Dracoulides (1967) for the poet's aggressive rage, his need for sexual compensation, his sexual inhibitions, his egocentrism, narcissism, and anal eroticism, and his dislike of *joie de vivre*. I make no comment.

7. I believe that Aristophanes is making a playful but significant connection between *hypokrinomenon*, "interpreting dreams" (53), and the actor, *hypokritēs*, who "interprets" a play's action or "answers" to another or others: cf. *Wasps* 1279; also *Ach*. 401, where Euripides' servant answers what seems a riddle (how can Euripides be "in and not in"?) as a good actor would. On the terminology of interpreting, "answering," and acting, see Pickard-Cambridge (1968) 126–29, Ghiron-Bistagne (1976) 115, and Buttrey (1977).

8. On dreams in antiquity and Greek attitudes toward them, see Dodds (1957) 102–34; the theory and practice of dream interpretation is discussed and exemplified in *Artemidori Daldiani Onirocriticon Libri V*, ed. R. A. Pack (Leipzig, 1963); for a good translation with notes see White (1975). For reputable psychiatrists and their antecedents (as against street-interpreters and charlatans) see

Lain Entralgo (1970), chaps. 1–2, esp. 101–7. Both are descended from the *oneiropolos*, a subspecies of prophet specializing in dreams.

9. For the missing obsession (there is a lacuna at *Wasps* 76–77), Sider (1975) has suggested *philarchos*, "desirous of office"; this produces a wordplay in the next line.

10. I am allowing, of course, for the distortions of dreams in what is called secondary elaboration, the reconstruction by the awakening consciousness.

11. For Freud see above, n. 6. My view of dreams in this passage owes much to Sewell (1952); for example:

Dream, the halfway house of disorder in the mind, runs its material together, making curious unions and analogies; but . . . it leaves the total mind still in possession of its sense of personality and detachment. It does not impair the integrity of the individual. The dreamer can still wake up and say with Bunyan, "I awoke and, behold, it was a dream." The dream tends toward oneness but the mind is separate from the process and can, on waking, set the dream into words, thereby establishing a measure of control over it and communicating it to other minds. (53)

12. For the Puer Aeternus see von Franz (1970).

13. Cf. *Peace* 43–48 (a would-be clever young man guesses the symbolic relevance of the dung beetle), and the digs at literary criticism, with all its machinery, in the agon of the *Frogs*.

14. Bergson (1925) 59–60.

15. For tragic parody see Rau (1967) 150–52 (on Philocleon's monodic lament), 152–55 (tragic silence preceding an outburst of grief); also Harvey (1971), especially on the influence of Euripides' Phaedra on the representation of Philocleon.

16. The best general account of the wasps is still that of Weber (1908) 127–66: the wasp traits are appropriate to irritable veterans and jurymen, but traits of bees (honeymaking, beehives) are freely added. See also Newiger (1957) 74–80. On the wasp costume, with a "sting" projecting from the hip, see Wilamowitz (1971) 302, and *Wasps* 225; although the sting strongly suggests the phallus, the two need not be equivalent in fact, *pace* Newiger (p. 80) and Ruck (1975) 32–40 and nn. (I doubt that the sting could be drawn forward through the legs and extended like an erect phallus, as Wilamowitz, 303, believed.) On the *kentron*, a point or goad, often identified with the phallus in Aristophanes' plays, see Henderson (1975) 122 (but only applied tentatively to the *Wasps*). Mazon (1904) 67–68 suggested that the visible sting would recall the form of the penalty stylus, or *enkentris*. Although MacDowell, 192–93 (on *Wasps* 427), denies the existence of, or comic reference to, a "stylus" used by jurors to draw the penalty line, I still suspect that Aristophanes equates the stylus, the sword, the sting, and the erect phallus as symbols of male potency.

17. The structure of *Wasps* is unusually agonistic: see Vaio (1971) 347–48. Gelzer (1960) 19–20 treats *Wasps* 334–402 as a first agon, despite some irregularity (the *antipnigos* is lacking), and he sees *Wasps* 403–525 as an early epirrhematic agon. I prefer to take 526–727 as the main agon, to which the previous conflicts and (tentative) compacts lead.

18. On the sword see Wilamowitz (1971) 304, and Sommerstein (1977a) 264–65: "Here the presence of the sword on stage can be traced for more than 200 lines. At 523 Philokleon vows to fall on the sword if defeated in the agon; at 654

he threatens to kill his son, a threat which is much more credible if he is armed; at 714 he has difficulty in holding the sword; and at 756–57, as Barrett has seen, . . . he unsuccessfully attempts to stab himself, and probably lets the sword fall." If Sommerstein is right (p. 265), there is a contrast not only with tragedy but with Paches' suicide in court, as related by Plutarch (*Arist.* 26.3, *Nic.* 6.1).

19. In general, my terminology and analysis of the "epirrhematic agon" follow Gelzer (1960); occasionally he notes the addition of *E*, a *sphragis* or closing judgment.

20. For definitions of play and game see Huizinga (1955) 1–75 and the full and splendid analysis of Caillois (1979); for play and law (litigation as an *agōn*, bound by fixed rules, sacred in form) see Huizinga, 76–88. My notions of play and game, to be developed in this chapter, owe much to Sewell (1952), Miller (1973), and the dissertation of my former student Fontaine Belford (1974).

21. From Gorgias' Encomium of Helen, 82 B 11, section 13 (Diels–Kranz).

22. Thuc. 2.40.2–3 (Pericles), 3.38.3–7 (Cleon).

23. One unusual technical meaning of the term *proagōn* is the "official preview" at which poet and actors would present themselves before the public and announce what plays they were to perform (Pickard-Cambridge [1968] 67–68). I use the term here in another sense, which Pickard-Cambridge (1962) 204–7 adopts from Zielinski: "The business of this scene is to single out and present the disputants in the coming agon to the audience, to calm them (and often the chorus, which at first sides with one of them) down to the debating point, and generally to arrange the terms of the debate, to which, often after a violent beginning, the scene leads" (204–5). See also Händel (1963) 70–71 (the form should not be isolated) and, for *Wasps* 403–525 as a proagon, Landfester (1977) 128.

24. See Bonner (1922): not much wit survives in Athenian forensic oratory, but there are indications that it emerged in informal exchanges and in speeches composed by the litigants themselves.

25. Aristotle *Rhet.* 2.2.

26. Significantly, the term *anapeithein* is the first used to denote bribery, at *Wasps* 101: a cock has allegedly been bribed to awaken Philocleon late. Thus the second meaning, "to persuade someone to change his mind" (MacDowell on *Wasps* 101), is shadowed at 116 and elsewhere by the notion of bribery. At 784 the two ideas most closely coincide: Philocleon gives in largely because of his son's substantial promises.

27. See Boegehold (1967) on Lycus as the neighboring hero to what may have been Philocleon's favorite law court. As a figure of wrath and power, the wolf hero may have been Philocleon's patron, even though he was not a religious functionary of the administration of justice.

28. On the actual trial of Laches (probably in 425) and its relation to the play see Wilamowitz (1971) 284–99, esp. 284–85, 297. Aristophanes is our only source for this trial, which probably occurred soon after Laches' return from Sicily in 426/25 (Thuc. 3.115). Landfester (1976) 31–32 argues that Laches was probably not acquitted.

29. Russo (1962) 194 makes the interesting suggestion that the proud young Bdelycleon might have worn "la maschiera fisionomica di Aristofane." Why not, indeed?

30. For magic cooking and political therapy see section 12.

31. Dover (1967) 22–23 argues that there may have been nothing unusual about Cleon's face to develop, as in a modern political cartoon, though other forms of symbolism could be used; perhaps Aristophanes used an exceptionally hideous mask, pretending it fell short of the real Cleon. For an actual cartoon of the time, a vase painting that apparently depicts Cleon as a masturbating Sphinx against which the hero Oedipus (Brasidas?) bravely advances, see Brown (1974).

32. The term "watchdog of the people" recurs in fourth-century speeches: see Dover (1972) 96–97. Aristophanes is also mindful of Hesiod's advice, at *Works and Days* 604, that the farmer should keep a jagged-toothed dog (*kyna karkharodonta*) and feed it well, to ward off thieves.

33. Add that Cleon came from the deme *Kydathenaiōn*. So, for that matter, did Aristophanes.

34. Becker (1973) 105–24 and passim describes the *causa sui* passion or project as "an energetic fantasy that covers over the rumbling of a man's fundamental creatureliness" (107); thus the psychoanalytic movement as a whole was Freud's "personal vehicle for heroism, for the transcendence of his vulnerability and human limitations" (109).

35. On games and play see above, n. 20. Miller (1970) 42–49 points out that while psychologists like Berne and Chapman use the metaphor "games people play" to analyze unfortunate ways of human behavior, implying that a healthful life would be beyond games, psychiatry may itself be a "metagame"—and still more, the author's playful examination of all this!

36. Herman Hesse, *Magister Ludi* (*The Glass Bead Game*), trans. from the German (*Das Glasperlenspiel*, 1943) by Richard and Clara Winston (New York: A Bantam Book, 1970).

37. On Horace *Epistles* 2.2 see Reckford (1969) 119–22.

38. See von Franz (1970) 16 on a man cured by a Freudian analysis: "This man was in a way more cured than my analysand, but on the other hand, it seems to me that such a terrific disillusionment makes one ask whether afterwards it is worthwhile going on living? Is it worthwhile just to make money for the rest of one's life and get small bourgeois pleasures?" Differently, Becker (1973) 202 poses a new question for the science of mental health: what is the "best," most life-enhancing illusion under which to live? It would be "a lived, compelling illusion that does not lie about life, death and reality" (204).

39. For the serious moral verses parodied in *Alice*, and for much other background information, see Gardner (1963).

40. Sewell (1952), passim.

41. For the "failure" of the 423 performance of the *Clouds* and for Aristophanes' response see below, section 33.

42. For the comic reversal of the *Wasps* generally, see Vaio (1971). See also Mauron (1964) 29 (against Bergson) on the genuine and needed vitality that can be expressed by "reversibility" in comedy; this is far from the mechanical and deterministic.

43. On Philocleon's reversion to low, aggressive humor see Paduano (1974) 190–96.

44. My student Joseph Ewbank kindly referred me to the following fables in *Corpus Fabularum Aesopicarum*: on the impossibility of changing your own nature, or that of others, Hausrath nos. 50, 237, 93, 109; on the idea "Stick to

your own trade," nos. 198, 99. I suggest also that Philocleon turns out to be the proverbial "asshole that defies cleaning" (*Wasps* 603–4), *pace* Edmunds (1978).

45. Borthwick (1968) 44–46 suggests that Philocleon's Pyrrhic dance movements, a defensive crouch followed by an offensive leap, may be symbolic of his rise and fall; see also MacCary (1979): Philocleon's erotic and Dionysian rejuvenation is supported by ithyphallic and related elements of meter, rhythm, and dance.

46. Cf. the prominence of the Dionysian escape theme in satyr plays: Seidensticker (1979) 243, Sutton (1980b) 147.

47. The story is in Artemidorus 4.24; it is cited by Freud in his *Interpretation of Dreams* and again in his *Introductory Lectures.* Alexander had lost precious time in besieging Tyre; he was anxious and disturbed; one night he dreamt of a satyr dancing on his shield, and Aristander, the dream-interpreter, divided *satyros* into *sa-Tyros,* "Tyre is yours." With this encouragement Alexander quickly took the city.

48. In *Wasps* 1283, there is a splendid pun on *glōttopoiein* (referring to cunnilingus) and *gelōtopoiein,* "to make laughter." Was Ariphrades a would-be comedian?

CHAPTER 5

1. The line is arbitrary, and the 1938 essays of Reinhardt (1960) and Gomme (1962a) would not be contained by it; both made a breakthrough toward a new conception of Aristophanes' artistic aims and impartiality. The "conservative" view was itself a step forward from that of Aristophanes as an oligarchic partisan or hanger-on.

2. Thuc. 2.43.

3. Thuc. 6.89–92.

4. The only attested law of censorship is the "psephism of Morychides," 440/39–437/36: see Norwood (1931) 26–29 and Schmid (1946) 40–41. Although Syracosios may have proposed a similar decree in 415, there is no evidence that it was ever in force. Lefkowitz (1981) 106 is skeptical about the existence of any censorship law, since "there appears to be no reference to legal censorship outside commentaries on old comedy."

5. From *Comedians,* by Trevor Griffiths (New York: Grove Press, 1976), 20.

6. *Comedians,* 33.

7. *Night and Day: A Play by Tom Stoppard* (New York: Grove Press, 1979), 99–100.

8. See Pickard-Cambridge (1962) 183–84.

9. Ps.-Xenophon, *Ath. Pol.* 2.18 (Kalinka). On the "old oligarch" (a pamphlet best dated during the Peloponnesian War, ca. 424 B.C.) and comedy see Gomme (1962b) 43–45; Moore (1975) 55 argues that a reference to a specific law banning attacks on "the people" in comedy "is not necessary linguistically, and poses serious problems historically." Nor is there any necessary connection between this alleged law and the Morychides Decree of 440/39.

10. Steffen (1956) suggests (1) that a specific law against satirizing the state and the people in the presence of foreigners may have been passed after the

Babylonians of 426, at Cleon's instigation (but this sounds like guesswork on the part of scholiasts); (2) that Cleon hauled Aristophanes before the Boule, but he got off scot-free or with a small fine—the case need not have gone further; and (3) that Cleon tried to make use of existing laws, specifically the *graphē adikias eis ton dēmon* (action for wrongdoing against the People) and perhaps the *graphē hybreos dia logōn* (action for verbal assault). Of these actions, I think the former more likely, not least because of Aristophanes' insistence on his "right-doing," *to dikaion*.

11. See *Wasps* 1284–91, a funny but somewhat sardonic sketch that anticipates Jack Point's refrain in *Yeomen of the Guard*: "They don't mind it so long as you're funny."

12. See Dover (1972) 96, "a judicious blending of reproof and reassurance," and 98–99; also Dover (1974), passim.

13. *Clouds* 557–59.

14. Chesterton (1959) 46–47, from chap. 4, "The Ethics of Elfland."

15. I owe "hand" and "handle," and probably a host of unconscious borrowings, to Douglass Parker's magnificent translation of *Lysistrata*.

16. See the sensitive comment of Seel (1960) 85–86 on *Lys.* 590: "Hier also ist die Grenze dessen, was an Ernstem in die Komödie soeben noch eingehen konnte, äusserlich gewahrt, aber eben doch tatsächlich überschritten." Cf. also *Lys.* 37–38 (Athens is in danger of perishing; Lysistrata won't say it, but her interlocutor must get the idea, *hyponoēson*); 387–98 (cries of wailing when the Sicilian Expedition was proposed); and 512, "Our hearts would be grieving within, but we would question you, laughing cheerfully." Is this similar to Aristophanes' behavior as a concerned citizen/comic playwright?

17. See Stewart (1965) 203–7 on the importance of forgetting false dignity, and on the ridiculousness of sex as one example of Aristophanes' "constructive anarchy" (203).

18. *The Rape of the Lock*, 117–18.

19. On this drinking scene, see the good remarks of Moulton (1981) 74–76; the passage "perhaps hints at the broader usefulness of comedy in general" (74).

20. Whitman (1982) 135.

21. Thuc. 2.37.2, 2.41.1.

22. *Republic* 557b–d.

23. See Seel (1960) 167–69 on the human power of self-experiment and playing with possibilities; comedy provides "die reinigende und entkrampfende Freisetzung dieses Spieltriebes."

24. The concept of *communitas* is explained by Turner (1969), esp. chaps. 3–5; for a further account see Turner (1974) 231–71.

25. The Ndembu rite: Turner (1969) 97–106.

26. Turner (1969) 178–81 (quoted, 178).

27. Turner (1969) 179.

28. Turner (1969) 177.

29. For this political and social ambivalence of Saturnalian festivals, see Kenner (1970) 93–94: they may be used as a safety valve for revolutionary tendencies or may give the spark to actual revolution. (She cites Lucian's *Saturnalian Letters* 21 and the Menippean tradition that portrayed great figures humbled in the afterlife, and humble ones exalted.) For Cox (1969), the implications of celebration and fantasy for social change helped bridge the great gap of the

1960s between hippie dreamers and radical activists. Kunzle (1978) 39–94 shows how the power of imagination has worked historically in different political directions: "The [World Upside Down] Broadsheet could, without basic changes in its form or content, be made to appeal at once to the political conservative, the dissident, and the lover of fantasy and nonsense" (88); and "Revolution appears disarmed by playfulness, the playful bears the seed of revolution" (89). For "Women on Top," see (in the same volume) Davis (1978) 147–90, with useful notes and bibliography.

30. Turner (1969) 201.

31. The number 13,000, used here and elsewhere, is an approximation, taken from *Plutus* 1083.

32. Cf. the German concept of the *Festgemeinde*, which Old Comedy variously reinforces: Reinhardt (1960) 270.

33. Sommerstein (1977b) gives a detailed and convincing account of the immediate historical background and probable dating of *Lys.* and *Thesm.* See also Dover (1972) 168–72 on *Thesm.* and the reminder of Gelzer (1979) 286 that, when Aristophanes wrote *Lys.*, inner tensions at Athens may have been even more serious than external pressures.

34. On the prayers in *Thesm.* 295–311 see Kleinknecht (1937) 33–37: they parody religious ceremonies for a popular assembly; the religious and political forms are set in a comic, inappropriate context; but humor and seriousness—even religious seriousness—are nicely blended.

35. It would be helpful if we had the whole of Eupolis' *Demes*, which may have taken a more political and partisan approach after the events of 413; see Rivier (1966) on this play, probably produced ca. 412.

36. On the structure of *Lysistrata* and the connections or parallels between *oikos* and *polis*, the domestic and political spheres, see the several good accounts by Vaio (1973), Newiger (1980), Henderson (1980), Moulton (1981) 48–80, esp. 48–58, and Foley (1982) 6–13. On the wide-ranging wool imagery, which includes sex, see Whitman (1964) 207–8 and Moulton, 53–58.

37. Foley (1982) 6–13, esp. 11.

38. If Srebrny (1961) is correct in thinking that the play should end with 1273–94 (which would then follow, not precede, the two monodies), this would bring out, more than ever, the harmonious joining of the sexes in a festive exodos emphasizing reconciliation—and Lysistrata's achievement. I follow Srebrny; so does Henderson (1980) 217.

39. In her unpublished 1979 lecture "Aristophanes' *Lysistrata*: The Tragic Heroine Re-created," Lois Hinckley argues that Aristophanes shows women moving (1) from a position of weakness to one of strength, (2) from one-sidedness to duality, and (3) from separation to complementarity.

40. Lysistrata was probably modeled on Lysimache, a priestess of Athena Polias: see Henderson (1980) 187, following D. M. Lewis, who pointed out in 1955 that Lysimache was still in office in 411 B.C.; Henderson adds that at 554 Lysistrata virtually calls herself Lysimache, and (p. 188) he indicates Lysistrata's thematic affinities with Athena. Cf. the earlier reference to Lysimache in *Peace* 992.

41. See Zeitlin (1982) 194–200 and, for a related but somewhat different approach, Moulton (1981) 110–45.

42. Cf. Knox (1979b).

43. See Zeitlin (1982), esp. 186–89.

44. According to Parker (1956–57) a well-constructed secondary world may be judged by (1) the solidity and variety of the developed structure, (2) its relation to reality, and (3) its viability. Tolkien's *Lord of the Rings* (for example) admirably passes the test.

45. I refer mainly to the first fourteen Oz books, written by L. Frank Baum between 1900 and 1919. These and later books, together with miscellaneous Oziana, are reviewed by Greene and Martin (1977); see also Hearn's introduction to *The Annotated Wizard of Oz* (1973). Hearn's collection of critical essays on Oz and the Oz books (1983) contains articles by (among others) Marius Bewley, S. J. Sackett on utopian features of Oz, Hearn himself, and Brian Attebery; the last is especially good on Oz and America. See now my review of Hearn (1983) in *The Baum Bugle* 28, no. 1 (Spring, 1984).

46. Baum (1960) 24.

47. For a view similar to mine but perhaps more objective see Sackett (above, n. 45) 220. Besides being influenced toward goodness in a conventional sense, he says,

we can also say that they would have been influenced to believe in the freedom of the individual, in the voluntary acceptance of responsibility, in progressive prison reform, in the proposition that money is relatively unimportant in life, in the possibility of making a better world, in the pleasures of work, in the significance of contentment, in nonconformity, in the superiority of man to machine, in the need for permitting both sexes to share equally in the good life, in the folly of war, in reverence for life, in a truly substantial education, and in the need for the intellect and the emotions to be brought into harmony.

48. The International Wizard of Oz Club, Inc., incorporated as an educational association under the laws of the state of Illinois. Its publication, *The Baum Bugle*, is included in the annual *MLA International Bibliography*.

49. Wagenknecht (1929), esp. 29–30.

50. Sale (1978) 223–43.

51. Cited by Wagenknecht (1929) 30 from *Tik-Tok of Oz* (Chicago: Reilly & Lee, 1914) 161–62.

52. I refer, despite its several merits, to Charles Reich, *The Greening of America* (New York: Random House, 1970).

53. My account is taken from Hesiod's *Works and Days* 109–201; imitations in Greek and Latin literature (together with relevant scholarship) seem almost endless. For general background and differences of detail between versions of the myth, see Gatz (1976) 1–86; for life under Kronos-Saturn, 114–28. The psychological interpretation by Peter Smith (1980) of the sequence of ages in Hesiod is suggestive for Old Comedy as it draws upon childhood memories and fantasies of that "golden age": see esp. 156–57 and n. 28.

54. See Dante, *Purgatorio*, 22.64–72, 28.139–48.

55. Pindar *Ol.* 2.68–75, trans. Finley (1955) 63–64.

56. Havelock (1957) chaps. 1–3. The progressive view of civilization is best grasped today not from fragments of the pre-Socratic philosophers and the Sophists, but from the second half of Lucretius' *De Rerum Natura*, Book 5.

57. Demokritos 68 B 275–78 (Diels–Kranz).

58. There were imaginary "Republics" before Plato; Aristotle *Pol.* 2.7–8 cites the writings of Phaleas of Chalcedon (with equalization of property among citizens, but no sharing of wives or children) and, especially, Hippodamus of Miletus. See Hadas (1935) on early utopian stories that may have been sources for Herodotus' account of the Scythians and other distant people like the Agathyrsi (4.104), and that probably anticipated the travel stories of the fourth century and the Hellenistic Age.

59. See the eloquent discussion by Dodds (1957) chaps. 6–8.

60. Solmsen (1975) chap. 3; see esp. 71–74, on the *Hippolytus* passages.

61. On the choral ode, *Hippolytus* 732–75, see Reckford (1974b) 325–27 and nn.

62. From the 1939 MGM movie *The Wizard of Oz*, with music and lyrics by Harold Arlen and E. Y. Harburg.

63. See Havelock (1957) 87–103, "History as a Compromise." Plato's nostalgia for the security of the Golden Age seems strongest in *Polit.* 271c–272d: in the reign of Kronos, the god and the *daimones* cared for men as shepherds care for their sheep.

64. Telecleides, fr. 1 (Kock; Edmonds). My translation of this and the following comic fragments is very free, to catch their spirit today.

65. See the warning of Heberlein (1980) 19–22 that plays like Cratinus' *Ploutoi* should not be imagined as thoroughly independent *Märchenkomödien*, since they may keep the extra-dramatic situation as their main point of reference.

66. Pherecrates, fr. 130 (Kock; Edmonds). Cf. also his *Metalles* (with a rich underground kingdom discovered by the Miners?), fr. 108 (Kock; Edmonds).

67. Crates, fr. 14–15 (Kock; Edmonds).

68. Cratinus, fr. 160–68 (Edmonds), supplemented and improved now by Austin, pp. 39–44.

69. Carrière (1979) 104. He argues that comedy is losing its function of mediating effectively "entre la cité réelle et l'idée d'un bonheur instinctif et immédiat."

70. Bibliography on the *Birds* is extensive. I have especially used Whitman (1964) 167–99 (a brilliant essay entitled "The Anatomy of Nothingness"), Newiger (1970) 80–103 (no one simple allegorical meaning), Arrowsmith (1973), and Hofmann (1976).

71. On the danger that quiet-loving gentlemen will withdraw from Athenian politics, see Connor (1971) 175–80 and, on Aristophanes and the fantasy of escape, 180–83. We might compare Cicero's concern about the seductions of Epicureanism in late republican Rome.

72. On the name see Gelzer (1971) 1461 and references. Although the manuscripts also give Peisthetairos and Pisthetairos, the best reading appears to be Peisetairos. (I would add that the play on the tyrant Peisistratos is important.)

73. The word *basileia*, as here accented, means "princess," not "royal power." Although Newiger (1970) 92–97 sees her as a real goddess, corresponding closely to Athena, I like the idea of Zielinski (1885) 51–52 that she is the princess of fairy tale whom the hero marries. Hofmann (1976) 147–58 argues interestingly that Basileia is split into two people: the old Hera, left to Zeus, and the new Hera, taken by Peisetairos. (The resulting suggestion of incest seems appropriate to Old Comedy.)

74. Whitman (1964) 178; Shakespeare's owl, on the other hand, urges his hearers toward hunting and/or erotic activity with his persuasive "To it! To woo!": see M. C. Bradbrook in *Shakespeare Quarterly* 33 (1982) 94–95.

75. See above, n. 61. Blaiklock (1954) 104–5 writes feelingly about birds and the escapist mood ("Oh for the wings of a dove . . .").

76. In the October 1971 Playmakers production of the *Birds* at the University of North Carolina, in the outdoor Forest Theater (directed by Patricia Barnett, and using the English adaptation by Walter Kerr), "Over the Rainbow" was played at the beginning, to set the mood. This was absolutely right.

77. On wings and sexuality see Arrowsmith (1973) 135–37, 164–67.

78. On *polypragmosynē* and its opposite, *apragmosynē*, in the Peloponnesian War period see Ehrenberg (1947) 46–56.

79. Thuc. 1.70; Pericles seems to respond to this criticism of Athens (which is also unwilling praise) in his Funeral Oration, Thuc. 2.38–39.

80. This powerful antithesis, with its wide-ranging implications for American history, is taken from Leo Marx (1967).

81. "Building a Rainbow," poster by Studio One (Norristown, Pa.), 1972.

82. The phrase "the greenlaw world" is based on "the green world" of Northrop Frye (see below, n. 87); there is also an inside joke, since we live in what is called the Greenlaw House in Chapel Hill. (It was built by Edwin Greenlaw, a distinguished professor of English, after whom Greenlaw Hall, the English Department building, has officially been named.)

83. On *nomos* and *physis* in the *Birds* see Whitman (1964) 175–78, 185–86, and Arrowsmith (1973) 157–64.

84. Unfortunately we cannot compare Pherecrates' *Savages* (*Agrioi*) of 420 B.C. In that play (see Plato *Prot.* 327c) the Athenian misanthropes apparently find themselves among real savages, outside the pale of civilization, so that Athens, for all its folly and vice (*ponēria*), looks good by comparison. Was Pherecrates satirizing escapist fancies and the myth of the noble savage?

85. "Birds' milk" was a proverbial *adynaton*, or "impossibility."

86. This should be seen as a sequel to, and further comment on, the father-beating scene in the *Clouds*.

87. Frye (1957) 163–86 sees Shakespeare's romantic comedies especially as displaying a movement from the normal world to the green world and back again (182–84): "The green world has analogies, not only to the fertile world of ritual, but to the dream world that we create out of our own desires" (183). See also Huizinga (1955) 100: "We might, in a purely formal sense, call all society a game, if we bear in mind that this game is the living principle of all civilization"; and 211: "real civilization cannot exist in the absence of a certain play-element."

88. On the parabasis generally, and its background of theogonies and cosmogonies, see Hofmann (1976) 177–96; he rightly emphasizes Aristophanes' own creativity and fun. For the possible travesty of an Orphic theogony (less well known than Hesiod's classic *Theogony*) see Guthrie (1966) 69–147, esp. on the World Egg and Aristophanes' use of it (95–96), and on Phanes, who is given other names, including Dionysus and Eros. (I wonder: did Aristo*phanes* take a special interest in that potent god?)

89. For the possible symbolism of the wind-egg see Whitman (1964) 184.

90. Arrowsmith (1973); see also his introduction to his translation of the *Birds*.

91. Arrowsmith (1973) 134–35 (Alcibiades' device was a figure of Eros armed with the thunderbolt: Plut. *Alc.* 16.1), 140–45.

92. On the *Ecclesiazusae* generally, see Wilamowitz (1927) 203–20, Heberlein (1980) 51–61, 125–30, and Foley (1982) 14–21 (on the creation of an essentially domestic utopia). I am much indebted to Ussher's introduction and commentary; also to Parker's introduction to his spirited translation, and to his notes.

93. For the diminished role of the chorus in *Eccl.* and (still more) in *Plutus*, moving toward the interludes of New Comedy, see Dover (1972) 193–95.

94. On Praxagora's sophistic rhetoric, using "eroded" ideas ("einen Abnutzungseffekt," 55), and her using the farmer ethos as a masquerade, see Heberlein (1980) 53–60.

95. See Ussher, xv–xx, on Aristophanes and Plato, and (n. 4) on a possible predecessor, the Socratic Antisthenes who also wrote a *Republic.* For earlier utopian accounts and theories see above, n. 58.

96. L. Frank Baum, *The Emerald City of Oz* (Chicago: Reilly & Lee, 1910), 30–31.

97. The phrase *mère terrible* is taken from Mauron (1964) 120–23; Dracoulides (1967), esp. 151–53, attributes this to Aristophanes' "regressive period," with renewed submission to the phallic mother. With better comic sense, Murphy (1972) 179 compares a fragment of a vase by Asteas: "Ajax, attacked by Cassandra and an elderly priestess, clings in terror to a statue of Athena."

98. The usual view of the ending of *Eccl.* is ironic and negative: Blepyrus is frustrated, the promises of the new regime come to nothing; see Wilamowitz (1927) 219–20 and Süss (1954) 289–97. Much depends on the dancing girls. Ussher (on 1112–83, 1125–27, 1128–40) thinks that Blepyrus enters with the girls and dallies with them; I prefer to think that Praxagora has provided them for her aging husband, in the spirit of the new legislation. This may add to the comic teasing; but if Blepyrus goes off dancing with the girls, as he is bidden, the ending would seem fairly positive.

99. For a fuller account of character contrast and character development in the *Dyskolos* see Reckford (1961).

100. Menander *Epitrepontes* 1084–99 (Oxford Classical Texts ed.); Onesimus' homily should not, however, be taken as identical with Menander's own thinking on the subject.

101. See Silk (1980) 150 on Aristophanes' retreat to a "low lyric base" in *Plut.* 290–321, something that could not be carried into later comedy.

102. Roos (1960) 55–97 argues that Aristophanes treats Asclepius with great respect and stays close to the actualities of temple healing; only the slave Cario is scurrilous.

103. For a fuller translation and comment see above, section 9. Heberlein (1980) 178–80 suggests that a Midas motif, indicated earlier at 287, is present in 812–17; he may be right, but I would not exaggerate the skepticism here.

104. As Konstan (1981) 381 says, "The sycophant's problem is not that he will fare worse under the golden age, but that he is by nature unfit to enjoy it."

105. The problem of the two issues of *Plutus*, fair distribution of wealth and universal prosperity, and of the relation between the two, was raised by Süss (1954) 298–313 and has provoked many thoughtful answers, usually stressing Aristophanes' ironic or realistic intention: see Newiger (1957) 155–78, Flashar (1967), Maurach (1968), Willetts (1970), and Konstan (1981); the fullest ac-

count is Heberlein (1980) 61–66, 130–82.

106. Contrast Plautus' *Rudens*, where, as Konstan (1983) argues, private property is respected and universal justice is affirmed: "It is the utopia of the ancient city-state" (93).

107. Like Aristophanes' speech in the *Symposium* (see section 8, above), Diotima's parable of Eros and his parents Poros and Penia at 203a–204a appears to be a tribute to Aristophanes, who may recently have died; it clearly recalls the *Plutus*, even as it transforms the Penia scene into a praise of the Socratic life.

108. See Cornford (1934) 25–27 on the New Zeus in *Plutus*, and 20–31 on new gods and new kings generally. Our understanding of this and related issues is much impaired, however, because we lack earlier plays for comparison, like Cratinus' *Ploutoi* or, for that matter, Aristophanes' first *Plutus*.

CHAPTER 6

1. The idea is not new: Cooper (1922) 24 asks why Aristotle should not have found "the turning-point between the earlier (not the archaic) and the later comedy where it is even now most apparent, in the time, and even in the works, of Aristophanes himself?" Else (1967) 311 finds Cooper's argument "plausible" enough but thinks there is insufficient evidence to decide. But now Janko (1984) has raised the questions anew: (1) did Aristotle assign Aristophanes to "middle" comedy, as he appears to have done in several sources deriving from Hellenistic scholarship? and (2) was Aristophanes thought "to constitute the happy mean between 'old' and 'new'"? Janko argues (86–87, 201–8, esp. 242–50) that the tripartite division of comedy, which originally omitted Menander, goes back to a theory of Aristotle's according to which Aristophanes could have represented the mean; see 247, on the "subtle position . . . that Cratinus is pure 'old' comedy, but Aristophanes and Eupolis partook of it only for some time," a view that may have become crudely simplified in later theory. This would accord, not only with my own view of Aristophanes' Old-and-New Comedy, but with what I believe to have been *his* view of his own achievement: see section 33. Then, after Menander was discovered (Janko, 248–50), the older tripartite division would have been changed to the one used at present, with "middle" comedy (between Aristophanes and Menander) falling into that limbo, and Aristophanes being pushed back into the "old." And the lines of critical judgment would have hardened against Aristophanes.

2. See esp. *Republic* 3.395e–396a, part of a larger section on *mimēsis*: the Guards should not imitate unfitting things that would influence their minds and characters for the worse.

3. See esp. *Republic* 10.606c (in the context of a renewed, more objective attack on *mimēsis*) and my remarks in section 6.

4. *Philebus* 48a–50e. Hackforth (1972) 92–93 has a good discussion of what *phthonos* and the "playful *phthonos*" of comedy mean in this section.

5. *Laws* 11.934d–936a, on verbal injury. No ridicule of citizens will be allowed, even without passion, as happens in comedy (935c–936a), although if the supervisors of youth approve, there may be some playful satirical songs (presumably for social purposes). Only honored men over fifty may compose *enkōmia* and *psogoi* with utter freedom.

6. Aristotle *Politics* 7.1336b3–23. Young people will not be allowed to be spectators of iambic performances or of comedies until they reach the right age to attend drinking parties and are sufficiently educated so as not to be harmed by such things (20–23).

7. Plato, *Laws* 7.816d–e, in the larger context of education.

8. Else (1972) argued for a continuing dialogue between Plato and Aristotle on the subject of *mimēsis*; he suggests (56–57) that Aristotle may have written a proto-*Poetics* around 360, when he was teaching rhetoric at the Academy, and that Plato revised his criticism of *mimēsis*, in *Rep.* 10, to respond to Aristotle's challenge. Else's forthcoming posthumous book on Plato's and Aristotle's poetics will include a very lucid account of *mimēsis*.

9. See *Poetics* 1451b5–11. Aristotle significantly illustrates the point by the example of the comic poets of his day, who use random names for character types rather than "make fun of individuals as the *iambopoioi* do."

10. For the argument see Else (1967) 139–63, 183–203, 309–14; he makes the interesting point (139–40) that *iambizon allēlous* suggests an exchange of banter or abuse between individuals or groups and hence would belong to the pre-poetic stage, of improvisation. The summarizing quotation is taken from Else's forthcoming book, by courtesy of Peter Burian.

11. For the existence once of the *Second Poetics*, and for a patient and (I think) convincing reconstruction of its shape and contents from the *Tractatus Coislinianus* and other late sources going back to Peripatetic tradition, see Janko (1984).

12. Cicero's discussion of wit, humor, and "the laughable" (*ridiculum*) in *De Oratore* 2.54–71 is derived from Peripatetic and Stoic sources; see Kennedy (1972) 223–24 and nn. The definition quoted above is taken from 2.58.236.

13. On Aristotle and catharsis, see chapter 2, n. 3, above, and add Lord (1982) 105–79, who sets the question against the background of Aristotle's general views of music and education in *Politics* 7–8. (Lord is concerned to show that any catharsis of pity and fear provided by tragedy cannot be precisely analogous to the catharsis of pathological enthusiasm by homoeopathic means; and he doubts, 175–76, that Aristotle ever held a doctrine of comic catharsis.) For the double audience see Aristotle *Pol.* 1342a18–22 and Lord, 147 (with n. 68): "the more fundamental distinction is plainly that between the musical education or culture of the citizen class of the best regime and the musical entertainment of its noncitizen class, between a music that serves the leisured pastime (*diagogē*) of mature citizens and a music that serves the relaxation (*anapausis*) of the vulgar." Using later material to reconstruct the argument of the *Second Poetics*, Janko (1984) 136–51 finds additional support for a modified purgation theory of tragic catharsis: (1) potentially excessive emotions are given vicarious expression in tragedy, and thereby relieved (*hyphairei*); and (2) they are brought into a more balanced condition, of *symmetria*. Evidently (143–44), comedy had a cathartic effect on the emotions too, but this is hard (at present) to specify; Janko refers to the narrower (shame, overconfidence) and the broader (indecency) interpretations of Lucas and other scholars. I conclude that Aristotle used the idea of a catharsis of laughter broadly but may not have pinned it down to treatment of specific emotions; he was more concerned to show in what artistic ways laughter could be shaped in order that the proper pleasure of comedy (and probably, as with tragedy, the reestablishment of emotional equilibrium) could be achieved.

14. On Theophrastus and the Peripatetic tradition see Plebe (1952) 9–11, 31–48. Theoretical discussions of the (imagined) origin of comedy emphasized festive country play connected with the vintage and attributed some initially redeeming social value to personal satire, but looked for, or invented, historic laws restricting the excessive liberty of *onomasti kōmōidein*. Insofar as he repudiates the Old Comedy with its invective, Horace seems to follow the Peripatetic tradition more closely than Cicero does (Plebe, 77).

15. The critical discussions contrasting Aristophanes with Menander are well summarized by Quadlbauer (1960), who emphasizes (40) that these judgments should be studied, not in isolation, but as part of a continuing discussion whose terms keep changing.

16. Although, as Quadlbauer (1960) shows, later praise of Aristophanes (much of it surviving in prosaic hypotheses of his plays and scholia vetera) was mostly aesthetic, citing his elevated and forceful diction, his wit, and his elegance and grace (*charis*), occasional judgments in his favor are ethical: for instance, that he made comedy more useful and dignified. The suggestion of Cooper (1922), esp. 90–91, that appreciation of Aristophanes in the later sources (more than that of Old Comedy generally) may go back to Aristotle, gains much support from the detailed reconstructions of Janko (1984).

17. See above, n. 1.

18. Cicero, *De Re Publica* 4.11; and, on the abandonment of lampooning living individuals by name in Roman satire, see LaFleur (1981).

19. For an imaginative but probably traditional poetic reconstruction of the development of comedy along Peripatetic lines see Horace, *Ars Poetica* 281–84 and *Epist.* 2.1.139–55 (given, with comments in the Appendix, section E).

20. The text and translation of the "Summary of a Comparison Between Aristophanes and Menander" (= 853a–854d) are taken from Plutarch, *Moralia*, vol. 10, trans. Harold North Fowler, Loeb Classical Library (Cambridge: Harvard University Press, 1960). See the discussions of Plebe (1952) 104–9 and Quadlbauer (1960) 64–68.

21. Cf. the comparisons between Caecilius and Menander in Gellius *Noct. Att.* 2.23. The modern reader, and especially the lover of Plautus, will give greater appreciation to Caecilius' playful, almost operatic expansions of language and feeling; similarly, we may be justified in seeing Plautus as altogether a match for Menander if we compare *Bacchides* 494–572 closely with Menander's *Dis Exapatōn* 11–63, 89–112 (in *Menandri Reliquiae Selectae*, ed. F. H. Sandbach [Oxford, 1972]), from which they are adapted. It was, however, Gellius who gave Aristophanes the wonderful title *homo festivissimus* (Quadlbauer [1960] 69).

22. *Symposiaka* 712a, in Plutarch's *Moralia*, vol. 9, trans. Edwin L. Minar, Jr., Loeb Classical Library (Cambridge: Harvard University Press, 1961). In addition to minding the obscenity and other things, Diogenianus (not Plutarch) says, "What is more, just as a special waiter stands by each guest, at the banquets of the great, so everyone would need his own scholar (*grammatikon*) to explain the allusion: who is Laespodias in Eupolis, and Cinesias in Plato, and Lampon in Cratinus, and so on with all the persons satirized in the plays. Our dinner party would turn into a schoolroom (*grammatodidaskaleion*), or else the jokes would be without meaning or point."

23. On the fortunes of Rabelais after the sixteenth century see Bakhtin (1968) 101–44.

24. La Bruyère, in *Les caractères*, ed. Robert Garapon (Paris: Classiques Garnier, 1962), 82. I thank Professor Alfred Engstrom for this and the following reference.

25. From no. 22 of Voltaire's *Lettres philosophiques*, in George R. Havens, ed., *Selections from Voltaire*, rev. ed. (New York and London: Appleton-Century, 1930), 73. Voltaire's prejudice against Aristophanes becomes more explicable if we read the article on atheism in his *Dictionnaire philosophique*, where he accuses Aristophanes of preparing the hemlock for Socrates (by writing the *Clouds*).

26. Bakhtin (1968) 75; cf. 321, on how sexual life, eating, drinking, and defecation "have been transferred to the private and psychological level where their connotation becomes narrow and specific, torn away from the direct relation to the life of society and to the cosmic whole."

27. Greene (1970) 10–11.

28. More conservative than Geissler (1969), Russo (1962) 49–51 cites twelve comedies between 427 and 421 but only twenty-five between 420 and 388. The point remains, that the earlier creative period was more intense.

29. Gelzer (1979) 286–87 would put the *Frogs* with comedies of the second period. I see it more as a transitional piece between Aristophanes' later middle period and his late period.

30. For a good introduction to the "Socrates problem" I recommend Dover (1968) xxxii–lvii and Nussbaum (1980); for the "revision problem," Dover, lxxx–xcviii, and Newiger (1957) 143–52.

31. For Socrates and Aristophanes as rival cathartists, see Reckford (1974a), esp. 58–64.

32. For Aristophanes' *Banqueters* see the excellent edition of the fragments with notes by Cassio (1977).

33. See Carrière (1979) 138: "Le jugement esthétique d'Aristophane sur ses rivaux annonce le jugement morale qu'Aristote portera sur l'ensemble de la Comédie Ancienne. La Comédie Ancienne ne meurt pas parce qu'elle s'effondre dans l'obscenité, elle meurt parce qu'elle tend a s'éloigner de la 'vulgarité.'"

34. Breitholtz (1960) 64 believes that the comic treatment of Cleon and Euripides here referred to exemplifies higher comedy, as against low, Megarian fooling (nuts and Heracles); but the point is rather that these personal jokes usually remain on, or (outside Aristophanes' plays) sink back to, a low, commonplace level.

35. Finley (1955) 34, 92–103; and cf. the remarks of Nagy (1979) 239–41 on how the poetry of praise (*ainos*) has a built-in ideology of exclusiveness but also a base for communication in a celebrating group, the *kōmos*.

36. Finley (1955) 103.

37. In Cratinus, fr. 307 (Kock), a shrewd spectator refers to somebody (apparently Aristophanes) as *hypoleptologos, gnōmodiōktēs, euripidaristophanizōn*. The first two words, "equipped with oversubtle arguments" and "hunter-down of cleverly stated ideas," suggest specific ways in which Aristophanes has been transformed into an intellectual and very modern poet like Euripides. The judgment is, naturally, unfavorable.

38. Tillich (1952) 32–63 and passim.

39. On the writing and performance of the *Frogs* see Russo (1962) 311–36; on the coherence of its plan and structure, despite changes, see Süss (1954) 138–41 and Fraenkel (1962) 163–88. Despite the arguments of Hooker (1980), I believe that the Aeschylus–Euripides contest in Hades and the *katabasis* theme were closely integrated with each other from the beginning. Newiger (1970) 278–80 remarks that the *Frogs*, in contrast with the *Birds*, is an old-fashioned comedy, giving the impression "eines bewussten Zusammenfassens all dessen auf, was die Alte Komödie in Form und Inhalt ausmacht." It would probably help if we had (1) Aristophanes' *Gerytades* (probably before 408: see Geissler [1969] 61), in which a delegation was sent to the poets in Hades, and a goddess, perhaps Ancient Poetry, was brought back from there; (2) Phrynichus' *Mystae* (possibly in 407: see Geissler, 63); and (3) Phrynichus' *Muses*, which won second prize after the *Frogs* and in which, Schmid (1946) 210 suggests, the Muses were judges and Sophocles probably won the crown.

40. Aristophanes, fr. 490 (Edmonds). In the Greek, the corrupting "book" comes first, then the more usual personal agents, "Prodicus or one of the chatterers."

41. See Woodbury (1976) on the humor and incongruity in both passages, Dionysus reading aboard ship and the audience (allegedly) provided with texts of Aristophanes; I would add that Aristophanes is exploiting the fun and confusion of a new technology (like "computer literacy" today) starting to take over: cf. the book jokes in *Birds* 974–89, 1024–25, 1036; in Plato, fr. 173 (Edmonds), a man is reading the instructions of a cookbook to himself (this is obviously very funny) in the wilderness. Aristophanes associates Euripides' tragedy-writing with much reading of books: cf. lines 943 and, very significantly, 1409: Euripides "can throw in—all his books!"

42. Meiggs (1975) 374.

43. On the financial pressures see Ghiron-Bistagne (1976) 83–84: an emergency measure of 405 seems to have provided for two *chorēgoi* each for tragedies and comedies, and this looks forward to the replacement of the *chorēgia* around 315 or 310 by an administrative *agōnothesia*. But Gelzer (1971) 1484 argues that the *synchorēgia* of 405 was only for the Dionysia, not the Lenaea, despite the scholiasts' guesses.

44. In the absence of other plays (n. 39, above), we may contrast the *Demes* of Eupolis, where four statesmen return from the past to give Athens good practical advice and lead the city to political, military, and judicial reformation and rejuvenation. For text and bibliography see Austin (1973) 84–94; Rivier (1966) gives a good account of the play. It would be nice to compare Cratinus' *Chirons*, where Solon apparently returned to give good advice (Rivier, 138).

45. Segal (1961). Although we differ in emphasis, I am thoroughly indebted to this essay, and also to the sensitive and moving treatment of *Frogs* by Whitman (1964) 228–58.

46. Radermacher, 37–47, catches something of the fairy-tale atmosphere of *Frogs* and compares it with *Birds* and *Peace*, although he will use the term *Märchenkömodie* only with strong reservations (46–47); cf. sections 9 and 10, above.

47. Bettelheim (1976), esp. 277–310, "The Animal-Groom Cycle of Fairy Tales."

48. Von Franz (1978) 33–82, on "The Three Feathers" and related stories.

49. I have generally followed the suggestions of Russo (1962) 325–32 about the staging of the *Frogs*, especially for Part 1. We are ignorant of how Charon's boat was managed; Cary (1937) 53 suggests that "Aristophanes was a little alarmed by the clumsiness of the stage boat, as he was by that of the stage beetle in the *Peace*, and so he turned it into a joke. Charon stands in his traditional position at the stern of the boat, paddle in hand, and directs the operations, while his boat is hauled up on to the stage." I agree about the clumsiness and the joke, but I see no reason why the boat, probably a *currus navalis* (Radermacher), need be hauled up on the stage.

50. Cf. *Knights* 523. At that play's end (1406), Agoracritus appears in a frog-green robe or *batrachis*, to dine in the Prytaneion. Was the color a sign of hope or merely of luxury?

51. There is no evidence that the frogs are seen: Charon only says, 205–6, that their songs will be heard; a scholiast to 209 calls them an unseen, subsidiary chorus. If this is true, Aristophanes would have avoided the expense and trouble of visible frog-dancers in green costumes (an expense that Ussher [1979] 7 believes to have been offset by the rags of the Mystae). For further discussion see Dover (1972) 177–78 and MacDowell (1972) 3–5, both leaning toward visibility; I am not convinced that the song of an invisible frog chorus would be hard to hear, any more than that of the (at first) invisible cloud chorus, which MacDowell mentions, at *Clouds* 275–90, 298–313. Add that the chorus of Mystae may be invisible at first as they begin to sing, invoking Iacchus, before their torch-bearing entrance: see Händel (1963) 37 and n. 19. Although Carrière (1977) 26–31 also prefers visible frogs, his remarks on the use of subsidiary choruses to mark an important movement in comedy, as in tragedy, are helpful.

52. Spatz (1978) 122 seems right in treating the frog chorus as one of the old comedy choruses hostile to the hero, over which he must triumph: "The duet, in effect, is a telescoped comic paradus [*sic*] in which Dionysus, like Dicaeopolis or Pisthetaerus, triumphs over the opposition."

53. Wills (1969a) argues for a competition not in volume, rhythm, or violence, but in beauty (farting versus croaks); MacDowell (1972) 4–5 adds the criterion of persistence, by which Dionysus wins.

54. Wills (1969a); Segal (1961) 210–15, 228–30.

55. Händel (1963) 42 suggests that the chorus may have been extended beyond twenty-four to convey a sense of Eleusinian inclusiveness, with old and young people, men and women; then some are sent off at 440–47. (If he is correct, the procedure would resemble that of the *Peace*.) Händel also insists (38–39) that these festive rites in the (comic) underworld should not be thought identical with the Eleusinian rites above ground: they have their own forms, ceremonies, and intentions. Perhaps Seel (1960) 132 puts it best: "Beides ist gemeint, der Hörer steht immer zugleich innerhalb und ausserhalb der Spiel-Illusion, so auch das Lied: es ist ebenso sehr kultisch wie aristophanisch, ebenso Tradition wie Selbstaussage des Dichters." For Eleusis and the Mysteries, see Mylonas (1961) and Burkert (1972) 275–323.

56. The Iacchus cry is often connected with the birth of a child (Iacchus? Plutus?); see Burkert (1972) 307–14. This may be connected with Dionysus' reexperiencing of *paisdein* in Hades. For Iacchus as Dionysus in Eleusinian representations see Simon (1983) 32–33; for connections between Eleusis and the

Lenaea (which may be reflected in the *Frogs*) see Pickard-Cambridge (1968) 35–36 and Segal (1961) 218–19.

57. Sophocles *Antigone* 1146–48 (leading up to the cry *Iacchon*, 1154).

58. See Fraenkel (1962) 201–4 on the ancient element of religious cult lyric in the parabasis of Old Comedy, and on the (popular) iambic teasing song.

59. In one view, which is consonant with Old Comedy, play acts as a central metaphor in which the ideas of seriousness and nonseriousness both inhere: see Miller (1973) 103–8. In the other, play and seriousness are treated as antithetical. The distinction is crucial.

60. See the excellent and very funny account by Erich Segal (1968), which focuses on the more cheerful plays such as *Menaechmi* and *Mostellaria*. More troubling issues, together with some questioning of traditional Roman values or of accepted contradictions in Roman social practices, are raised by Konstan (1983) in his analytical studies of Plautus and Terence.

61. See Whitman (1964) 243 on the theme of silence versus speech.

62. Socrates' influence on Euripides was suggested earlier by the comic poet Telecleides, fr. 39, 40 (Edmonds; Kock); see also Callias, fr. 12 (Edmonds; Kock).

63. On "Euripidaristophanizing" see above, n. 37; also Gelzer (1971) 1546–47: Aristophanes shared the traditional conservatism of comedy but was so fascinated with new ideas that he seemed caught up in the *Zeitgeist*.

64. Segal (1970) 158–62 suggests that Aristophanes may be making fun of Protagoras' minute criticism, which could find many "mistakes" and contradictions in a piece of poetry. To "test" poetry closely (*basanisdein*, *Frogs* 802, 826, 1123) was equivalent to the kind of human "torture" for which Xanthias offered his supposed slave at 616–25. And the results may have seemed to Aristophanes equally inconclusive and (except for comic purposes) unsatisfactory. (I hope that no serious literary critic who may read this note will take it personally.)

65. Whitman (1964) 243.

66. MacDowell (1959) gives lines 1443–44 and 1446–47 to Euripides, thus producing a balance of serious advice between Aeschylus and Euripides. I am, however, convinced that Wills (1969b) is correct in maintaining that 1442–50 and 1463–65 should be omitted as spurious and highly inappropriate to the speakers, the context, and the play as a whole. I also accept Wills' reinterpretation of 1462 (which he defends, 49–51): "*You* should not speak here—so long as you send your blessing up from here (by speaking above)."

67. Wills (1969b) 57.

68. Dante, *Purgatorio*, 27.131. By traversing the terraces of Purgatory, Dante's will has been purified and disciplined until it is fully "libero, dritto e sano" (140) in what it desires and chooses. Hence, in canto 28, Dante recovers the experience of play in the Earthly Paradise. Desire with hope, *disio con speme*, is the great theme of the *Purgatorio*; I have borrowed it, *mutatis mutandis*, for Aristophanes' comic catharsis, in chapter 2 and elsewhere.

69. See Whitman 256–58, on the ambiguities of life and death.

70. T. S. Eliot, *The Waste Land*, 63, in *Collected Poems 1909–1935* (New York: Harcourt Brace, 1936); cf. Dante, *Inferno* 3.55–57 (cited in Eliot's note).

71. See Cantarella (1970) 227–48: single tragedies of Aeschylus were revived, by a special decree, as early as 425; this procedure should not be confused with the revivals of "old tragedy" generally (but mostly plays of Sophocles and Euripi-

des) after 386. Ghiron-Bistagne (1976) 127 cites *Ach.* 9–12, *Vita Aeschyli* 12, and, very suggestively, Philostratus' life of Apollonius 6.2: "Hence the Athenians called him the father of tragedy *and invited him, though dead, to the Dionysia* [italics mine]. For the plays of Aeschylus, by decree, were performed and made victorious anew."

72. The translation is by the late Robert A. Brooks, who directed and played Oedipus in the 1957 Harvard production (in Greek) of *Oedipus at Colonus.* Cf. Ajax' very serious but also ironic or deceptive remarks in *Ajax* 646–83 about time's power and the necessity of yielding to it. The two Sophoclean speeches, early and late, are strangely complementary.

73. Knox (1964) 155–56.

74. Segal (1981) 374–75.

75. See again Knox (1964) 155: "The power of Athens is dying; that inviolate peace of the grove at Colonus and of the Attic landscape had been breached and ruined ... the way to Eleusis, the processional road, was barred by Spartan patrols; the olive trees of the Attic farms had been chopped down."

76. No revivals of Aristophanes' plays are known from the fourth century B.C. or later (until the Renaissance); the official performances of "old comedies" at the Dionysia in 339 and 311 were revivals of middle comedy to be followed by revivals of Menander and his contemporaries: see Pickard-Cambridge (1968) 83 and Ghiron-Bistagne (1976) 42–52. But Old Comedy could be revived in the demes: cf. the records of the Dionysia at Aixone (Ghiron-Bistagne, 95–96). In retrospect, the comment of Schmid (1946) 450 seems unintentionally ironic: "Dies war ein Vorteil im Sinn der Reinhaltung der Texte von jenen Schauspielerinterpolationen, unter denen der Euripidestext zu leiden hatte."

77. *Anth. Pal.* 9.86, quoted by Schmid (1946) 456.

APPENDIX

1. The best account of *kōmos* and related terms is by Ghiron-Bistagne (1976) 207–38, who makes good distinctions between the *kōmos*, as one of the "carnivalesque processions" found at different festivals, and the *pompē* or sacrificial procession proper (though the latter might be parodied); see especially her remarks on how festive masqueraders identify themselves with mythological figures who may act out a predramatic sequence like the Return of Hephaestus (216–21). Speculations follow about the development and differentiation of genres; these may be supplemented from Adrados (1975) and, for comedy, from Herter (1947), Pickard-Cambridge (1962) 132–229, Breitholtz (1960), Händel (1963) 289–310, Gelzer (1966) 55–78, and Landfester (1979) 361–67.

2. Pindar *Ol.* 14.16–17 and passim.

3. For the stimulus given to theatrical and literary developments by Dionysian celebration see Jeanmaire (1970) 220–331 (esp. 302–3, on comedy) and Giangrande (1963); Herter (1947) well summarizes the movement from ritual and magic to play.

4. For phallic rites, see section C of this Appendix; for Aristotle's statement, see section E of the Appendix, and nn.

5. The best surviving example of trick-or-treat is the Rhodian swallow song in Athenaeus *Deipn.* 8.360b–d; the fertility wreath, *eiresionē*, was carried around

by children who received gifts: see Parke (1977) 76; Harrison (1908) 190 gives comparable examples. On the *agermos* generally, see Burkert (1977) 166–67. The account given in a scholion to Theocritus of Artemis' masqueraders, the *boukoliastai* at Syracuse who wore horns on their heads and brought wine, fruits and blessings, is especially suggestive for the comic revel; see Nilsson (1941) 202–3 and Pickard-Cambridge (1962) 155–57 and nn.

6. For the strengths and weaknesses of Cornford's theory see section 4.

7. See my review of Caputi (1978) in *Classical and Modern Literature* 1 (1981) 147–52.

8. Adrados (1975) 306–15 and passim.

9. For Halloween and the Celtic Samhain see Turner (1969) 181–83: a seasonal expulsion of evils and renewal of fertility associated with cosmic and chthonic powers, taken up into Christian festival and rite. We should remember that Halloween may once have coincided with the Celtic New Year, a potent combination: see Frazer (1925) 633–34 on fire rites long celebrated on the Isle of Man, and, on the beginning of winter and New Year's customs generally, Chambers (1902) 228–73.

10. For such a "carnival concentration" see Chambers (1902) 249–73 on New Year's customs: winter processions, sometimes riotous; remnants of animal masquerade; transvestism; election of a mock or temporary king; involvement of children, who receive presents; commemoration of ancestors.

11. No Greek holidays survived quite like the Roman Saturnalia, at which, as Scullard (1981) 205–7 describes it, shops, lawcourts, and schools were shut for up to seven days (by Cicero's time) around the winter solstice, informal clothes and soft caps were worn, public gambling was allowed, masters waited on servants, a mock king was chosen as Master of the Revels, presents were given, and extra wine was served out for the household. The Attic Kronia was less significant and faded into a mere holiday for slaves: see Parke (1977) 29–30; but Nilsson (1906) 35–40 cites reports of other saturnalian holidays in Greece, such as the Thessalian Peluria.

12. On the Anthesteria see Nilsson (1906) 267–71: a feast of souls older than the cult of Dionysus, and spread throughout Ionia; see also Harrison (1908) 32–76, especially on the darker side of the feast, Deubner (1932) 93–123, Burkert (1972) 326–69, and Simon (1983) 92–101. Parke (1977) 119–20 puts it well: to the ordinary Athenian "the occasion must have felt like Hallowe'en—an occasion mainly for jolly parties with perhaps at times a somewhat eerie atmosphere to it and certain old traditional games all of which simply added spice to the occasion." Of special interest are the great figures, carnival giants or monsters, carried aloft in Dionysian revel processions: see Breitholtz (1960) 156–57 (figs. 14–15), 229 nn. 118–19 and Van Hoorn (1951) 20–22.

13. See Immerwahr (1946) for vases illustrating the *kōmos*, and esp. 251–54 on the transitional evening between Choes and Chytroi.

14. For *kēres*, death-spirits or "goblins," see Harrison (1908) 163–212, and now Parke (1977) 116–17; for *Karioi*, "Carians" (ancient inhabitants of the land?), see Burkert (1972) 250–55. Van Hoorn (1951) 20–21 is uncertain, but one of his *choes* (102, ca. 420, from Athens) shows a *kēr* seizing the *chous* of a little boy with a wreath of flowers who defends his property with a stone. What matters in any case is the masquerade: of mummers on wagons, and of people who, whether masquerading as specters or Carians, came into houses and de-

manded entertainment. See Burkert 253–54, catching the spirit well: "Das Ineinander von Lustigkeit und Ernst ist beim Maskentreiben besonders augenfällig: ausgelassenes Gelächter auf einem Hintergrund von Erschrecken und Grausen." Cf. Adrados (1975) 372–74 on carnival masks of demons, devils, or souls of the dead that "present a character half terrifying, half clownish."

15. *Clouds* 296; cf. Burkert (1972) 253–54 and nn. 18, 19: could the Dionysian mummers with their grotesque forms and frightening masks have been called *trygodaimones*? If so, the comic players inherit their festive masquerade and their comic liberty.

16. On phallic rites taken over by Dionysus see Nilsson (1906) 261–66, comparing cults of Demeter, Hermes, Artemis, and Priapus; see also Otto (1965) 164–65.

17. *Acharnians* 241–83; see above, section 5.

18. Herodotus 2.48 (De Selincourt trans.).

19. Heraclitus fr. 116 (= 22 B 15 in Diels–Kranz), discussed by Kahn (1979) 264–66; Dionysus (sexual vitality) and Hades (death) are made equivalent in a typical riddling statement, and Dionysus, as the god of drink and madness, is associated (again through wordplay) with death.

20. See Kahn (1979) 266–67 on fr. 117 (= 22 B 5 in Diels–Kranz). Heraclitus objects to purification through blood sacrifice, to praying to images, and possibly to every kind of traditional cult action.

21. By the usual view, the phallus is a negative charm against evil spirits (cf. also magical abuse) as well as a positive agent of fertilization: thus Cornford (1934) 49; but Nilsson (1941) 108–9 argues that though it has a positive healing force, it is not apotropaic, not a *fascinum*. For a different view, connecting the phallus with rites of compensation and with transference of aggression, see Burkert (1972) 82–84.

22. The healing quality of the phallic procession is indicated by a story cited by Pickard-Cambridge (1963) 57 and n. 6 from a scholion on *Ach.* 243: "In Athens, as in some other places in Greece, the god was not well received, and the men of Athens were smitten with a disease from which (it was said) they only freed themselves (on the advice of an oracle) by manufacturing *phalloi* in honour of the god." Cf. the aetiological account of indecency at the Haloa in section D of this Appendix.

23. See the excellent account by Jeanmaire (1970) chap. 1 (5–56) and passim of vegetation rites taken over by Dionysus, especially from Artemis.

24. Adrados (1975) 294–95 emphasizes that *aischrologia* often took an agonal form, as a contest between two bands or choruses (cf. 296–97 on choral *agōnes* of entertainment, including wedding songs). See Harrison (1908) 136 on fighting, abuse, and quarreling at women's festivals, as well as joking. On cultic obscenity generally as a background to Aristophanes, see Henderson (1975) 13–18.

25. Turner (1969) 78–79, with photograph.

26. Cf. the strategy of *Lysistrata*, discussed in section 27.

27. Herodotus 2.60 (De Selincourt trans.); and cf. Frazer (1925) 67 on ribald songs and immodest dances by women in a cleansing ceremony (to bring rain) of the Baronga in southeast Africa.

28. On ritual jesting and Eleusis see Richardson (1974) 214–16 (and my section 5).

29. Many instances of indecency in cultic language and act are cited by Nilsson (1906). I have not seen H. Fluck, *Skurrilen Riten in griech. Kulten* (diss. Freiburg, 1931), often cited by scholars.

30. On indecent talk and gestures at the Stenia and Thesmophoria see Deubner (1966) 53 and n. 3, 57–58; at the Haloa, 61–67; the long scholion to Lucian is quoted at 61, n. 5. Dracoulides (1967) 151–52 describes a licentious women's gathering still extant in the village of Monoklissia, in eastern Thrace, on 8 January: women officials take charge for twenty-four hours; there are songs, dances, phallic processions (with peas and sausages), much eating and drinking, and many sexual jokes and gestures.

31. Zeitlin (1982) 138–53 and nn.

32. Zeitlin (1982) 149.

33. Deubner (1966) 61 n. 5. The aetiological explanation of overt sexual rites at the Haloa, while not historical, suggests the psychological release and healing that such occasional expressions of obscenity may provide—an important aspect, I would argue, of comic catharsis.

34. On Aristotle and the beginnings of comedy see the good discussions of Breitholtz (1960) 34–54 (esp. 50–54 on *ta phallika*), Pickard-Cambridge (1962) 33–45, and Jeanmaire (1970) 43. Despite the doubts of Else (1967) 163, who proposed *phaula*, the reading *phallika* is generally accepted today and connected with the discussion of the *kōmos*: see Giangrande (1963), esp. 4 n. 1.

35. For Aristotle's treatment of Old Comedy in general and Aristophanes in particular see section 32 and nn.

36. *Satires* 1.4 may reflect a tradition of the preferred mean in comedy: if the old comedy of Eupolis, Cratinus, and Aristophanes was too free-spoken and aggressive in personal attacks, the new comedy lacks force of spirit (*quod acer spiritus ac vis / nec verbis nec rebus inest*, 46–47); against this background see *Satires* 1.10.7–19, where Old Comedy is seen in retrospect as alternating forceful, spirited poetic language with subtle and humorous understatement.

37. This definition of satire comes from Diomedes, a fourth-century grammarian (485 [Keil]).

38. Cicero *Rep.* 4.11–12.

39. LaFleur (1981): an excellent treatment of the subject and, in its reminders that Horace *did* lampoon living persons by name, a useful corrective to the overgentle view of Reckford (1969) 32–40.

40. Cf. Virgil's imaginative reconstruction of early comedy in *Georgics* 2.380–92: first Greek—the goat sacrifice, primitive plays in competition through the country villages (*pagos et compita circum* = *kōmas*), drinking, jumping on wineskins—all this an accurate description of the Country Dionysia; and then Roman—improvised verses (*incomptis*; cf. *compita* and *kōmas*), play and laughter, "horrendous" masks, invocations of Bacchus in songs and other rites, all promoting fertility and increase.

41. On the *malum carmen* see LaFleur (1981) 1816–19 and nn.

42. On the stylistic virtues of the Antimachus ode and its integration into the play see now Moulton (1981) 18–24.

43. Elliott (1960) 62: this was the legendary first satire of Ireland. On the development of ridiculing verse away from magical satire see Elliott, 3–99, esp. 87–99; as he says (18), "Social sanctions have replaced the deadly powers once commanded by the poet, but the shadow of these powers is still discernible."

44. Elliott (1960) 27–32.

45. Jaeger (1954) 7.

46. *Iliad* 2.211–77. Nagy (1979) 259–64 treats Thersites as a bold representative of "blame poetry" against whom laughter and abuse are turned, and also (279–80) as a *pharmakos*. It seems that in the *Aithiopis* he was killed by Achilles. One is hardly surprised.

47. Plutarch *Lyc.* 12.6, cited by Nagy (1979) 245 as evidence that "In societies where blame poetry was an inherited institution, there must have been clearly defined traditional limits for degrees of insult" (244). On blame poetry generally, see Nagy, 222–64.

48. On the term *bōmolochos* see Nagy (1979) 245 n. 3.

49. Hipponax 115 (West).

50. Elisavietta Ritchie, "Elegy for the Other Woman," in Ritchie (1982).

51. Hipponax 5–10 (West).

52. On the *iambus* see West (1974) 22–39. Aristotle evidently ignored the "mimetic" element in the *iambus*, its indirection, and its use of personae; see Nagy (1979) 259 on the degree to which the *iambus* got away from blame poetry.

53. West (1974) 33.

54. Henderson (1975) 18–23.

55. Smithsonian Institution (1982) 72 (color illustration, 22). See also Turner (1982), the excellent companion volume of essays on festivity and ritual.

56. The problem of social disruption is raised, and partially answered, by Abrahams and Bauman (1978) 193–208.

57. On animal dances and masquerades, and their incorporation into Attic comedy, see Pickard-Cambridge (1962) 151–62 and, with a helpful review of different theories, Giangrande (1963) 21–24 and n. 1. I agree with the view of Herter (1947) 9 n. 26, 18, that these dancers are derived from ritual presentation of theriomorphic daemons that gradually became playful: "Je mehr sich im Laufe der Zeit der magische Character dieser Tänze verlor, desto freier konnte sich der Spieltrieb entfalten und besonders leicht das burleske Element entwickeln, das in den derben Gestalten der niederen Geister von Feld und Flur und in der Kraftäusserung ihres Lachens angelegt war" (7).

58. Pickard-Cambridge (1962) 155.

59. Pickard-Cambridge (1962) 137; but see the warning of Breitholtz (1960) 114–15 that Athenaeus' sources may have been late and that he may have confused various amateur groups with one another, losing sight of their chronological or formal differences.

60. See Herter (1947) 16–19 on surviving phallic rites, and 37 on Aristotle's view: comedy did not develop out of phallic songs but rather replaced the traditional presentations of the *phallos* singers, which continued along their separate path.

61. On "fat men" at Athens, Corinth, and elsewhere see Pickard-Cambridge (1962) 139–40, 169–73: Attic comic actors and chorus probably came from Attic padded dancers, not Corinthians, though there may have been cross-influence in the sixth century.

62. I disagree here with Sifakis (1971) 64, who argues that only the anapests were originally called "parabasis," then the whole was named after the part. Why should not the central ABAB syzygy have been the original parabasis? The best

account is that of Händel (1963) 84–111, who thinks that the main parabasis must first have offered a contrast between (1) odes praying for victory, salvation, and the like, and (2) epirrhemes in which the chorus made their special nature or mood felt; later on mocking songs were added to the play, and a second parabasis to contain them.

63. For definition and development of the epirrhematic agon I have relied heavily throughout this book on Gelzer (1960), who drew on and refined the work of earlier scholars, including Bergk and Zielinski.

64. Which form was older, parabasis or agon? And how did they come together? The question is much debated, and there is no agreed-on answer. Perhaps, as Pickard-Cambridge (1962) 161–62 suggests, the "epirrhematic structure" (ABAB) is the oldest element in the old sequence of parodos–*agon*–epirrhematic structure; Gelzer (1960) 209 finds no indication that one form grew out of another, or that there was any connection between the epirrhematic syzygy of the parabasis and the epirrhematic agon (see also 203–12 on the parabasis). In the end, Gelzer speculates (227–29; see also 229–37) that comedy came together from three main groupings: (1) the parodos, epirrhematic agon, and exodos, involving actors and chorus, and once involving the *diallagē* (reconciliation); (2) the parabasis, of the chorus; and (3) the iambic scenes of Part 2 and perhaps the prologue.

65. Burkert (1972).

66. Chambers (1903) 274–335; see also 336–71 on the Boy Bishop.

67. Chambers (1903) 351.

68. Chambers (1903) 363.

69. Barber (1959) 192–221.

70. Barber (1959) 6.

Bibliography

EDITIONS CHIEFLY USED

BASIC TEXTS

Aristophane. Edited by Victor Coulon. French translation by Hilaire Van Daele. 5 vols. Paris: "Les Belles Lettres," 1923–30.
Scholia in Aristophanem. Edited by W. J. W. Koster and D. Holwerda. Groningen: Bouma's Boekhuis, 1960–.
Comicorum Atticorum Fragmenta. Edited by Theodorus Kock. Vol. 1. Leipzig: Teubner, 1880.
The Fragments of Attic Comedy. Edited by John M. Edmonds. Vol. 1. Leiden: Brill, 1957.
Comicorum Graecorum Fragmenta in Papyris Reperta. Edited by Colinus Austin. Berlin and New York: De Gruyter, 1973.

EDITIONS WITH NOTES OR COMMENTARY

Dover, Kenneth J. *Aristophanes: Clouds.* Oxford: Clarendon Press, 1968.
Holzinger, Karl. *Kritisch-exegetischer Kommentar zu Aristophanes' Plutos* (1940). New York: Arno Press, 1979.
MacDowell, Douglas M. *Aristophanes' Wasps.* Oxford: Clarendon Press, 1971.
Merry, W. W. *Aristophanes: The Birds.* 4th ed. Oxford: Clarendon Press, 1904.
Neil, Robert A. *The Knights of Aristophanes.* Cambridge: Cambridge University Press, 1909.
Platnauer, Maurice. *Aristophanes: Peace.* Oxford: Clarendon Press, 1964.
Radermacher, Ludwig. *Aristophanes' Frösche.* Revised by Walther Kraus (1921). Graz, Vienna, and Cologne: H. Böhlaus, 1967.
Rennie, W. *The Acharnians of Aristophanes.* London: E. Arnold, 1909.
Rogers, Benjamin B. *The Comedies of Aristophanes.* 11 vols. London: G. Bell & Sons, 1902–16.
Sommerstein, Alan H. *The Comedies of Aristophanes: Acharnians, Knights, Clouds.* Warminster: Aris & Phillips, 1980–82.
Stanford, W. B. *Aristophanes: The Frogs.* 2nd ed. Basingstoke and London: Macmillan, 1963.
Starkie, W. J. M. *The Acharnians of Aristophanes* (1909). *The Clouds* (1911). *The Wasps* (1897). Reprinted Amsterdam: Hakkert, 1966–68.
Ussher, R. G. *Aristophanes: Ecclesiazusae.* Oxford: Clarendon Press, 1973.
Van Leeuwen, J. *Aristophanes.* 11 vols. Leiden: Sijthoff, 1893–1906.
Wilamowitz-Moellendorff, Ulrich von. *Aristophanes: Lysistrate.* Berlin: Weidmann, 1927.

TRANSLATIONS

The dramatic and literary insights of translators are too often ignored by scholars. I am indebted to the translations and notes of William Arrowsmith (*Clouds, Birds*), Richmond Lattimore (*Frogs*), and Douglass Parker (*Acharnians, Wasps, Lysistrata, Congresswomen*) in the University of Michigan series, edited by W. Arrowsmith (1961–, recently republished by Mentor). Rogers's translations, cited above (see Editions with Notes or Commentary), still retain a fine Aristophanic flavor, with help from Gilbert and Sullivan. For the general reader I can also recommend the translations of Aristophanes' plays by David Barrett and Alan H. Sommerstein (Penguin Books, 1974, 1978), and of *Clouds, Women in Power,* and *Knights* by Kenneth McLeish (Cambridge, 1980).

OTHER ANCIENT SOURCES

Corpus Fabularum Aesopicarum. Edited by August Hausrath and Herbert Hunger. Vol. 1, 2nd ed., 1970; vol. 2, 1959. Leipzig: Teubner.

Fragmente der griechischen Historiker. Edited by F. Jacoby. Berlin: Weidmann, 1923–50.

Die Fragmente der Vorsokratiker. Edited by H. Diels and W. Kranz. 6th ed. Berlin: Weidmann, 1951–52.

Grammatici Latini. Edited by H. Keil. Leipzig: Teubner, 1855–1923.

Iambi et Elegi Graeci. Edited by M. L. West. Oxford: Clarendon Press, 1971–72.

Tragicorum Graecorum Fragmenta. Edited by A. Nauck. 2nd ed. Leipzig: Teubner, 1889.

GENERAL BIBLIOGRAPHY

Abrahams, Roger D., and Bauman, Richard. 1978. "Ranges of Festival Behavior." In *The Reversible World*, edited by Barbara A. Babcock, 193–208. Ithaca and London: Cornell University Press.

Adrados, Francisco R. 1975. *Festival, Comedy and Tragedy* (1972). Translated by Christopher Holme. Leiden: E. J. Brill.

Aly, Friedrich. 1928. "Märchen." In *Paulys Realencyclopädie der Klassischen Altertumswissenschaft*, edited by Georg Wissowa, 14.1:254–81. Stuttgart: Alfred Druckenmuller Verlag.

Arnott, Peter. 1962. *Greek Scenic Conventions in the Fifth Century B.C.* Oxford: Clarendon Press.

Arrowsmith, William. 1973. "Aristophanes' Birds: The Fantasy Politics of Eros." *Arion*, n.s. 1, no. 1:119–67.

Bacon, Helen. 1959. "Socrates Crowned." *Virginia Quarterly Review* 35:415–30.

Bailey, Cyril. 1936. "Who Played 'Dicaeopolis'?" In *Greek Poetry and Life: Essays Presented to G. Murray*, edited by C. Bailey, et al., 231–40. Oxford: Clarendon Press.

Bain, David. 1977. *Actors and Audience: A Study of Asides and Related Conventions in Greek Drama*. Oxford: Oxford University Press.

———. 1981. *Masters, Servants and Others in Greek Tragedy*. Manchester: Manchester University Press.

Bakhtin, Mikhail. 1968. *Rabelais and His World*. Translated by Hélène Iswolsky. Cambridge, Mass., and London: MIT Press.

Barber, C. L. 1959. *Shakespeare's Festive Comedy*. Princeton: Princeton University Press.

Baum, L. Frank. 1960. *The Wonderful Wizard of Oz* (1900). New York: Dover Edition.

Beazley, J. D. 1963. *Attic Red-Figure Vase-Painters*. 2nd ed. Oxford: Oxford University Press.

Becker, Ernest. 1975. *The Denial of Death*. New York: A Free Press Paperback.

Belford, Fontaine M. 1974. "Comedy's Play." Ph.D. dissertation, University of North Carolina, Chapel Hill.

Bergson, Henri. 1925. *Le rire*. Paris: Librairie Felix Alcan.

Bettelheim, Bruno. 1976. *The Uses of Enchantment: The Meaning and Importance of Fairy Tales*. New York: Knopf.

Blaiklock, E. M. 1954. "Walking Away from the News." *G&R*, ser. 2, no. 1:98–111.

Blume, Horst-Dieter. 1978. *Einführung in das antike Theaterwesen*. Darmstadt: Wissenschaftliche Buchgesellschaft.

Boegehold, Alan L. 1967. "Philokleon's Court." *Hesperia* 36:111–20.

Bolte, Johannes and Polivka, Georg. 1930. *Anmerkungen zu den Kinder u. Hausmärchen der Brüder Grimm*. Rev. ed. Vol. 4. Leipzig: Dieterich.

Bonner, Campbell. 1910. "Dionysian Magic and the Greek Land of Cockaigne." *TAPA* 41:175–85.

Bonner, Robert J. 1922. "Wit and Humor in Athenian Courts." *CP* 17:97–103.

Borthwick, E. K. 1968. "The Dances of Philocleon and the Sons of Carcinus in Aristophanes' *Wasps*." *CQ* 18:44–51.

Breitholtz, Lennart. 1960. *Die Dorische Farce im Griechischen Mutterland vor dem 5 Jahrhundert. Hypothese oder Realität?* Acta Universitatis Gothoburgensis, 66. Uppsala: Almquist & Wiksells.

Brommer, Frank. 1959. *Satyrspiele. Bilder Griechischer Vasen*. Berlin: De Gruyter.

Brower, Reuben A. 1962. *The Fields of Light* (1951). New York: A Galaxy Book.

Brown, Edwin L. 1974. "Cleon Caricatured on a Corinthian Cup." *JHS* 94:166–70.

Burkert, Walter. 1972. *Homo Necans. Interpretationen Altergriechischer Opferriten und Mythen*. Vol. 32 of *Religionsgeschichtliche Versuche und Vorarbeiten*, edited by Walter Burkert and Carsten Colpe. Berlin and New York: De Gruyter.

———. 1977. *Griechische Religion der Archaischen und Klassischen Epoch*. Vol. 15 of *Die Religionen der Menschheit*. Stuttgart and Berlin: Verlag W. Kohlhammer.

Buttrey, T. V. 1977. "*Hypo* in Aristophanes and *hypokritēs*." *GRBS* 18:5–23.

Caillois, Roger. 1979. *Man, Play, and Games* (*Les Jeux et les Hommes*, 1958). Translated by Meyer Barash. New York: Schocken Books.

Calder, William M., III. 1958. "The Single Performance Fallacy." *Educational Theatre Journal* 10:237–39.

Cantarella, Raffaele. 1970. "Aristoph. *Plut.* 422–25 e le Riprese Eschilee" (1965). In *Scritti Minori sul Teatro Greco*, 227–48. Brescia: Editrice Paideia.

Caputi, Anthony. 1978. *Buffo: The Genius of Vulgar Comedy*. Detroit: Wayne State University Press.

Carpenter, Rhys. 1946. *Folk Tale, Fiction and Saga in the Homeric Epics*. Berkeley, Los Angeles, and London: University of California Press.

Carrière, Jean Claude. 1977. *Le choeur secondaire dans le drame grec*. Paris: Klincksieck.

———. 1979. *Le carnaval et la politique*. Annales litteraires de l'Université de Besançon, 212. Paris: "Les Belles Lettres."

Cary, A. L. M. 1937. "The Appearance of Charon in the *Frogs*." CR 51:52–53.

Chambers, E. K. 1903. *The Medieval Stage*. Vol. 1. Oxford: Oxford University Press.

Chancellor, Gary. 1979. "Implicit Stage Directions in Ancient Greek Drama: Critical Assumptions and the Reading Public." *Arethusa* 12:133–52.

Chapman, G. A. H. 1978. "Aristophanes and History." *Acta Classica* 21:59–70.

Chesterton, Gilbert K. 1959. *Orthodoxy* (1908). Garden City, N.Y.: Image Books.

Chiasson, Charles C. 1984. "Pseudartabas and His Eunuchs: *Acharnians* 91–122." *CP* 79:131–36.

Connor, W. Robert. 1968. *Theopompus and Fifth-Century Athens*. Cambridge: Harvard University Press.

———. 1971. *The New Politicians of Fifth-Century Athens*. Princeton: Princeton University Press.

Cooper, Lane. 1922. *An Aristotelian Theory of Comedy*. New York: Harcourt, Brace.

Cornford, Francis M. 1934. *The Origin of Attic Comedy*. 2nd ed. (1st ed., 1914). Cambridge: Cambridge University Press.

Cott, Jonathan. 1981. *Pipers at the Gates of Dawn: The Wisdom of Children's Literature*. New York: Random House.

Cox, Harvey. 1969. *The Feast of Fools*. Cambridge, Mass.: Harvard University Press.

Dale, A. M. 1969a. "Seen and Unseen on the Greek Stage: A Study in Scenic Conventions" (1956). In *Collected Papers of A. M. Dale*, edited by T. B. L. Webster and E. G. Turner, 119–29. Cambridge: Cambridge University Press.

———. 1969b. "A Heroic End" (1961). In *Collected Papers*, 170–72.

Davies, Mark I. 1978. "Sailing, Rowing and Sporting in One's Cups on the Wine-Dark Sea." In *Athens Comes of Age: Papers of a Symposium*, 72–75. Princeton: n.p.

Davis, Natalie Zemon. 1978. "Women on Top: Symbolic Sexual Inversion and Political Disorder in Early Modern Europe." In *The Reversible World*, edited by Barbara A. Babcock, 147–90. Ithaca and London: Cornell University Press.

Dearden, C. W. 1976. *The Stage of Aristophanes*. London: The Athlone Press.

Deubner, Ludwig. 1966. *Attische Feste* (1932). 2nd ed., rev. by Bruno Doer. Darmstadt: Wissenschaftliche Buchgesellschaft.

Dodds, E. R. 1957. *The Greeks and the Irrational* (1951). Boston: Beacon Paperback Edition.

——, ed. 1960. *Euripides' Bacchae*. 2nd ed. Oxford: The Clarendon Press.

Dohm, H. 1964. *Mageiros*. Zetemata, 32. Munich: C. H. Beck.

Dover, Kenneth J. 1959. "Aristophanes, *Knights* 11–20." *CR* 9:196–99.

——. 1963. "Notes on Aristophanes' *Acharnians*." *Maia* 15:6–25.

——. 1965. "The Date of Plato's *Symposium*." *Phronesis* 10:2–9.

——. 1966. "Aristophanes' Speech in Plato's *Symposium*." *JHS* 86:41–50.

——. 1967. "Portrait-Masks in Aristophanes." In *Kōmōidotragēmata: Studia Aristophanea viri Aristophanei W. J. Koster in Honorem*, 16–28. Amsterdam: Hakkert.

——. 1968. "Greek Comedy." In *Fifty Years (and Twelve) of Classical Scholarship*, edited by Maurice Platnauer, 123–58. 2nd ed. Oxford: Blackwell.

——. 1972. *Aristophanic Comedy*. London: B. T. Batsford.

——. 1974. *Greek Popular Morality in the Time of Plato and Aristotle*. Berkeley and Los Angeles: University of California Press.

Dracoulides, N. N. 1967. *Psychanalyse d'Aristophane*. Paris: Editions Universitaires.

Dunbar, Nan V. 1970. "Three Notes on Aristophanes." *CR*, n.s. 20:269–73.

Eastman, Max. 1921. *The Sense of Humor*. New York: Charles Scribner's Sons.

Edmunds, Lowell. 1978. "Aristophanes, *Vesp.* 603–4." *AJP* 99:321–24.

——. 1980. "Aristophanes' *Acharnians*." *YCS* 26:1–41.

Ehrenberg, Victor. 1947. "Polypragmosyne: A Study in Greek Politics." *JHS* 67:46–67.

——. 1951. *The People of Aristophanes*. 2nd ed. Oxford: Blackwell.

Elliott, Robert C. 1960. *The Power of Satire: Magic, Ritual, Art*. Princeton: Princeton University Press.

Ellmann, Richard. 1959. *James Joyce*. New York: Oxford University Press.

Else, Gerald F. 1967. *Aristotle's Poetics: The Argument*. Cambridge: Harvard University Press.

——. 1972. *The Structure and Date of Book 10 of Plato's Republic*. Heidelberg: C. Winter.

Ewbank, Joseph B. 1980. "Fable and Proverb in Aristophanes." Ph.D. dissertation, University of North Carolina, Chapel Hill.

Farnell, Lewis R. 1971. *The Cults of the Greek States*. Vol. 5 (1909). Chicago: Aegean Press.

Finley, John H., Jr. 1955. *Pindar and Aeschylus*. Martin Classical Lectures, 14. Cambridge: Harvard University Press.

Flashar, Hellmut. 1975. "Zur Eigenart des Aristophanischen Spätwerks" (1967). In *Aristophanes und die Alte Komödie*, edited by H.-J. Newiger, 405–34. Wege der Forschung, 265. Darmstadt: Wissenschaftliche Buchgesellschaft.

Foley, Helene P. 1980. "The Masque of Dionysus." *TAPA* 110:107–33.

——. 1982. "The 'Female Intruder' Reconsidered: Women in Aristophanes' *Lysistrata* and *Ecclesiazusae*." *CP* 77:1–21.

Forrest, W. G. 1963. "Aristophanes' *Acharnians*." *Phoenix* 17:1–12.

Fortenbaugh, W. W. 1975. *Aristotle on Emotion*. New York: Barnes & Noble.

Fraenkel, Eduard. 1962. *Beobachtungen zu Aristophanes*. Rome: Edizioni di Storia e Letteratura.

Franz, Marie-Louise von. 1970. *The Problem of the Puer Aeternus*. Zurich: Spring Publications.

―――. 1978. *Interpretation of Fairytales*. 4th ed. Irving, Tex.: Spring Publications.

Frazer, Sir James G. 1925. *The Golden Bough*. Abridged ed. New York: Macmillan.

Freud, Sigmund. 1938. *The Interpretation of Dreams* (1900). 3rd English ed. In *The Basic Writings of Sigmund Freud*. New York: The Modern Library.

―――. 1953. *A General Introduction to Psychoanalysis*. Translated from the rev. ed., by Joan Rivière (1920). Garden City, N.Y.: Doubleday Permabooks.

―――. 1963. *Jokes and Their Relation to the Unconscious* (*Der Witz und seine Beziehung zum Unbewussten*, 1905). Translated by James Strachey. New York: The Norton Library.

Friedlander, Paul. 1969. "Lachende Götter" (1934). Reprinted in *Paul Friedlander. Studien zur Antiken Literatur und Kunst*, 3–18. Berlin: De Gruyter.

Frye, Northrop. 1957. *Anatomy of Criticism*. Princeton: Princeton University Press.

―――. 1965. *A Natural Perspective: The Development of Shakespearean Comedy and Romance*. New York and London: Columbia University Press.

Gardner, Martin, ed. 1963. *The Annotated Alice: Alice's Adventures in Wonderland and Through the Looking Glass*, by Lewis Carroll. Cleveland and New York: Forum Books.

Garton, Charles. 1972. *Personal Aspects of the Roman Theatre*. Toronto: Hakkert.

Gatz, Bodo. 1967. *Weltalter, Goldene Zeit und Sinnverwandte Vorstellungen*. Hildesheim: Georg Olms.

Geissler, Paul. 1969. *Chronologie der Altattischen Komödie* (1925). 2nd ed. Berlin: Weidmann.

Gelzer, Thomas. 1960. *Der Epirrhematische Agon bei Aristophanes*. Zetemata, 23. Munich: C. H. Beck.

―――. 1966. "Dionysisches und Phantastisches in der Komödie des Aristophanes." In *Probleme der Kunstwissenschaft II: Wandlungen des Paradiesischen und Utopischen*. Berlin: De Gruyter.

―――. 1971. *Aristophanes der Komiker*. Suppl. 12 in *Paulys Realencyclopädie der Klassischen Altertumswissenschaft*, edited by Georg Wissowa. Stuttgart: Alfred Druckenmuller.

―――. 1979. "Aristophanes." In *Das Griechische Drama*, edited by Gustav Adolf Seeck, 258–306. Darmstadt: Wissenschaftliche Buchgesellschaft.

Ghiron-Bistagne, Paulette. 1976. *Recherches sur les acteurs dans la Grèce antique*. Paris: "Les Belles Lettres."

Giangrande, Giuseppe. 1963. "The Origin of the Attic Comedy." *Eranos* 61:1–24.

Golden, Leon. 1962. "Catharsis." *TAPA* 93:51–60.

―――. 1973. "The Purgation Theory of Catharsis." *Journal of Aesthetics and Art Criticism* 31:473–79.

―――. 1976. "The Clarification Theory of *Katharsis*." *Hermes* 104:437–52.

Gomme, Arnold W. 1962a. "Aristophanes and Politics" (1938). In *More Essays in Greek History and Literature*, edited by David A. Campbell, 70–91. Oxford: Blackwell.

_____. 1962b. "The Old Oligarch" (1940). In *More Essays in Greek History and Literature*, 38–69.

Greene, Thomas M. 1970. *Rabelais: A Study in Comic Courage*. Englewood Cliffs, N.J.: Prentice-Hall.

Guggisberg, Peter. 1947. *Das Satyrspiel*. Zurich: Leemann.

Guthrie, W. K. C. 1966. *Orpheus and Greek Religion* (1935). Rev. ed. New York: The Norton Library.

Hackforth, R. 1972. *Plato's Philebus*. Translated with an Introduction and Commentary. Cambridge: Cambridge University Press.

Hadas, Moses. 1935. "Utopian Sources in Herodotus." *CP* 30:113–21.

Halliwell, Stephen. 1980. "Aristophanes' Apprenticeship." *CQ* 74:33–45.

Händel, Paul. 1963. *Formen und Darstellungsweisen in der Aristophanischen Komödie*. Heidelberg: Carl Winter.

Handley, E. W., and Rea, John. 1957. *The Telephus of Euripides*. University of London, Institute of Classical Studies, Bulletin Suppl. 5.

Harbage, Alfred. 1961. *Shakespeare's Audience* (1941). New York and London: Columbia Paperback Edition.

Harriott, Rosemary. 1979. "*Acharnians* 1095–1142: Words and Actions." *BICS* 26:95–98.

Harrison, Jane Ellen. 1908. *Prolegomena to the Study of Greek Religion*. 2nd ed. Cambridge: Cambridge University Press.

Harvey, F. D. 1971. "Sick Humour: Aristophanic Parody of a Euripidean Motif." *Mnemosyne* 24:362–65.

Havelock, Eric A. 1957. *The Liberal Temper in Greek Politics*. New Haven: Yale University Press.

Hearn, Michael Patrick, ed. 1983. *The Wizard of Oz*, by L. Frank Baum. The Critical Heritage Series. New York: Schocken Books.

Heberlein, Friedrich. 1980. *Pluthygieia. Zur Gegenwelt bei Aristophanes*. Frankfurt: Haag und Herchen.

Henderson, Jeffrey. 1975. *The Maculate Muse: Obscene Language in Attic Comedy*. New Haven and London: Yale University Press.

_____. 1980. "*Lysistrate*: The Play and Its Themes." *YCS* 26:153–218.

Herter, Hans. 1947. *Vom Dionysischen Tanz zum Komischen Spiel*. Iserlohn: Silva-Verlag.

Hofmann, Heinz. 1976. *Mythos und Komödie. Untersuchungen zu den Vögeln des Aristophanes*. Hildesheim and New York: Georg Olms.

Hooker, J. T. 1980. "The Composition of the Frogs." *Hermes* 108:169–82.

Horton, Andrew C. 1977/78. "Festive Comedy and Sacred Clowns: Pueblo Indian Drama and Aristophanes' *Peace*." *CO* 55:88–92.

Hourmouziades, Nicolaos C. 1965. *Production and Imagination in Euripides*. Vol. 5 of *Greek Society for Humanistic Studies*, ser. 2. Athens: Greek Society for Humanistic Studies.

Huizinga, Johan. 1955. *Homo Ludens: A Study of the Play-Element in Culture* (1938; 1st Eng. ed., 1950). Boston: A Beacon Paperback.

Hunter, Jim. 1982. *Tom Stoppard's Plays*. New York: Grove Press.

Immerwahr, Henry R. 1946. "Choes and Chytroi." *TAPA* 77:245–60.

Jaeger, Werner. 1954. *Paideia*. Vol. 1. Translated from the 2nd German ed. (1935) by Gilbert Highet. Oxford: Blackwell.

Janko, Richard. 1984. *Aristotle on Comedy: Towards a Reconstruction of Poet-*

ics II. Berkeley and Los Angeles: University of California Press.

Jeanmaire, H. 1970. *Dionysos: histoire du culte de Bacchus*. Paris: Payot.

Jung, Carl G. 1959. "The Phenomenology of the Spirit in Fairytales" (1948). In *The Archetypes and the Collective Unconscious*, translated by R. F. C. Hull, 207–54. Bollingen Series 20. New York: Pantheon Books.

Kagan, Donald. 1974. *The Archidamian War*. Ithaca and London: Cornell University Press.

Kahn, Charles H. 1979. *The Art and Thought of Heraclitus*. Cambridge: Cambridge University Press.

Kennedy, George A. 1963. *The Art of Persuasion in Greece*. Princeton: Princeton University Press.

———. 1972. *The Art of Rhetoric in the Roman World*. Princeton: Princeton University Press.

Kenner, Hedwig. 1970. *Das Phänomen der Verkehrten Welt in der Griechisch-Römischen Antike*. Bonn: Rudolf Habelt.

Kerr, Walter. 1967. *Tragedy and Comedy*. New York: Simon & Schuster.

Ketterer, Robert C. 1980. "Stripping in the Parabasis of *Acharnians*." *GRBS* 21:217–21.

Kindermann, Heinz. 1979. *Das Theaterpublikum der Antike*. Salzburg: Otto Muller Verlag.

Kleinknecht, Hermann. 1967. *Die Gebetsparodie in der Antike* (1937). Hildesheim: Georg Olms.

———. 1975. "Die Epiphanie des Demos in Aristophanes' 'Rittern' " (1939). In *Aristophanes und die Alte Komödie*, edited by H.-J. Newiger, 144–54. Darmstadt: Wissenschaftliche Buchgesellschaft.

Knox, Bernard M. W. 1964. *The Heroic Temper: Studies in Sophoclean Tragedy*. Berkeley and Los Angeles: University of California Press.

———. 1979a. "The Date of the Oedipus Tyrannus of Sophocles" (1956). In *Word and Action: Essays on the Ancient Theater*, 112–24. Baltimore and London: The Johns Hopkins University Press.

———. 1979b. "Euripidean Comedy" (1970). In *Word and Action*, 250–74.

Koch, Klaus-Dietrich. 1968. *Kritische Idee und Komisches Thema*. 2nd ed. Bremen: Verlag Friedrich Rover.

Konstan, David. 1981a. "An Anthropology of Euripides' *Cyclops*." *Ramus* 10:87–103.

———. 1981b. "The Ideology of Aristophanes' *Wealth*." *AJP* 102:371–94.

———. 1983. *Roman Comedy*. Ithaca and London: Cornell University Press.

———. forthcoming. "The Politics of Aristophanes' *Wasps*." *TAPA*.

Kraus, Walther. 1975. "Aristophanes—Spiegel einer Zeitwende" (1963). In *Aristophanes und die Alte Komödie*, edited by H.-J. Newiger, 435–58. Darmstadt: Wissenschaftliche Buchgesellschaft.

Kunzle, David. 1978. "World Upside Down: The Iconography of a European Broadsheet Type." In *The Reversible World*, edited by Barbara A. Babcock, 39–94. Ithaca and New York: Cornell University Press.

LaFleur, R. A. 1981. "Horace and *Onomasti Komoedein*: The Law of Satire." In *Aufstieg und Niedergang der Römischen Welt. Geschichte und Kultur Roms im Spiegel der neueren Forschung*, edited by Hildegard Temporini, 2.31.3:1790–1829. Berlin and New York: De Gruyter.

Lain Entralgo, Pedro. 1970. *The Therapy of the Word in Classical Antiquity*.

Edited and translated by L. J. Rather and John M. Sharp. New Haven and London: Yale University Press.

Landfester, Manfred. 1967. *Die Ritter des Aristophanes.* Amsterdam: B. R. Grüner.

———. 1976. "Beobachtungen zu den *Wespen* des Aristophanes." *Mnemosyne* 29:27–32.

———. 1977. *Handlungsverlauf und Komik in den Frühen Komödien des Aristophanes.* Berlin and New York: De Gruyter.

———. 1979. "Geschichte der Griechischen Komödie." In *Das Griechische Drama,* edited by Gustaf Adolf Seeck, 354–400. Darmstadt: Wissenschaftliche Buchgesellschaft.

Lefkowitz, Mary R. 1981. *The Lives of the Greek Poets.* London: Duckworth.

Lenz, Lutz. 1980. "Komik und Kritik in Aristophanes' *Wespen.*" *Hermes* 108:15–44.

Lever, Katherine. 1956. *The Art of Greek Comedy.* London: Methuen.

Levin, Harry. 1969. *The Myth of the Golden Age in the Renaissance.* Bloomington and London: Indiana University Press.

Lord, Carnes. 1982. *Education and Culture in the Political Thought of Aristotle.* Ithaca and London: Cornell University Press.

Lucas, D. W., ed. 1968. *Aristotle, Poetics.* Oxford: The Clarendon Press.

Lüthi, Max. 1970. *Once Upon a Time: On the Nature of Fairy Tales* (1968). 3rd ed., translated by Lee Chadeayne and Paul Gottwald with additions by the author. New York: Frederick Ungar.

Lynch, William F., S.J. 1965. *Images of Hope.* Baltimore: Helicon Press.

MacCary, W. Thomas. 1979. "Philokleon *Ithyphallos*: Dance, Costume and Character in the *Wasps.*" *TAPA* 109:137–47.

MacDowell, Douglas M. 1959. "Aristophanes, *Frogs* 1407–67." *CQ*, n.s. 9:261–68.

———. 1972. "The Frogs' Chorus." *CR* 86:3–5.

McLeish, Kenneth. 1980. *The Theatre of Aristophanes.* New York: Taplinger Publishing Co.

McLuhan, Marshall. 1965. *Understanding Media: The Extensions of Man.* New York and London: McGraw-Hill Paperback.

Marx, Leo. 1967. *The Machine in the Garden: Technology and the Pastoral Ideal in America.* A Galaxy Book. New York: Oxford University Press.

Massa Positano, Lidia. 1967. "Aristophane e il comico." In *Kōmōidotragēmata, W. J. W. Koster in honorem,* 82–107. Amsterdam: Hakkert.

Maurach, Gregor. 1968. "Interpretationen zur Attischen Komödie." *Acta Classica* 11:1–24.

Mauron, Charles. 1964. *Psychocritique du genre comique.* Paris: Librairie José Corti.

May, Rollo. 1969. *Love and Will.* New York: W. W. Norton.

Mazon, Paul. 1904. *Essai sur la composition des comédies d'Aristophane.* Paris: Hachette.

Megas, Georgios A., ed. 1970. *Folktales of Greece.* Translated by Helen Colaclides. Foreword by Richard M. Dorson. Chicago: University of Chicago Press.

Meiggs, Russell. 1975. *The Athenian Empire.* Oxford: The Clarendon Press.

Mikalson, Jon D. 1975. *The Sacred and Civil Calendar of the Athenian Year.*

Princeton: Princeton University Press.

Miller, David L. 1973. *Gods and Games* (1970). New York: Harper Colophon Books.

Miller, Harold W. 1948. "Euripides' *Telephus* and the *Thesmophoriazusae* of Aristophanes." *CP* 43:174–83.

Moore, J. M. 1975. *Aristotle and Xenophon on Democracy and Oligarchy*. Berkeley and Los Angeles: University of California Press.

Moulton, Carroll. 1981. *Aristophanic Poetry*. Hypomnemata, 68. Göttingen: Vandenhoeck & Ruprecht.

Murphy, Charles T. 1938. "Aristophanes and the Art of Rhetoric." *HSCP* 49:69–113.

———. 1972. "Popular Comedy in Aristophanes." *AJP* 93:169–89.

Murray, Gilbert. 1964. *Aristophanes: A Study* (1933). New York: Russell & Russell.

Mylonas, George E. 1961. *Eleusis and the Eleusinian Mysteries*. Princeton: Princeton University Press.

Nagy, Gregory. 1979. *The Best of the Achaeans*. Baltimore and London: The Johns Hopkins University Press.

Newiger, Hans-Joachim. 1957. *Metapher und Allegorie. Studien zu Aristophanes*. Zetemata, 16. Munich: C. H. Beck.

———. 1975a. "Retraktationen zu Aristophanes' 'Frieden.' " In *Aristophanes und die Alte Komödie*, edited by H.-J. Newiger, 225–55. Darmstadt: Wissenschaftliche Buchgesellschaft.

———. 1975b. "Die 'Vogel' und ihre Stellung im Gesamtwerk des Aristophanes" (1970). In *Aristophanes und die Alte Komödie*, 266–82.

———. 1980. "War and Peace in the Comedy of Aristophanes" (1975). Translated by Catherine Radford. *YCS* 26:219–37.

Nilsson, Martin P. 1941. *Geschichte der Griechischen Religion*. Vol. 1. Munich: Beck.

———. 1957. *Griechische Feste von religiöser Bedeutung mit Ausschluss der Attischen* (1906). Stuttgart: B. G. Teubner.

———. 1961. *Greek Folk Religion*. Reprinted from *Greek Popular Religion* (1940). New York: Harper Torchbooks.

Nisetich, Frank J. 1977. "The Leaves of Triumph and Mortality: Transformation of a Traditional Image in Pindar's *Olympian* 12." *TAPA* 107:235–64.

Norwood, Gilbert. 1930. "The *Babylonians* of Aristophanes." *CP* 25:1–10.

———. 1963. *Greek Comedy* (1931). New York: Hill & Wang.

Nussbaum, Martha. 1980. "Aristophanes and Socrates on Learning Practical Wisdom." *YCS* 26:43–97.

O'Brien, D. 1969. *Empedocles' Cosmic Cycle*. Cambridge: Cambridge University Press.

Otto, Walter F. 1965. *Dionysus: Myth and Cult*. Translated with an Introduction by Robert B. Palmer. Bloomington and London: Indiana University Press.

Paduano, G. 1974. *Il giudice giudicato*. Bologna: Il Mulino.

Page, Denys L. 1934. *Actors' Interpolations in Greek Tragedy*. Oxford: The Clarendon Press.

———. 1973. *Folktales in Homer's Odyssey*. Cambridge: Harvard University Press.

Parke, H. W. 1977. *Festivals of the Athenians*. Ithaca: Cornell University Press.

Parker, Douglass. 1956–57. "Hwaet We Holbytla." *Hudson Review* 9:598–609.
———. 1962. "The Unity of the Acharnians." Unpublished monograph.
Pickard-Cambridge, Sir Arthur W. 1927. *Dithyramb, Tragedy and Comedy*. Oxford: The Clarendon Press.
———. 1946. *The Theatre of Dionysus in Athens*. Oxford: The Clarendon Press.
———. 1962. *Dithyramb, Tragedy and Comedy*. 2nd ed., rev. by T. B. L. Webster. Oxford: The Clarendon Press.
———. 1968. *The Dramatic Festivals of Athens*. 2nd ed., rev. by John Gould and D. M. Lewis. Oxford: The Clarendon Press.
Pieper, Josef. 1952. *Leisure: The Basis of Culture*. Translated by Alexander Dru with an introduction by T. S. Eliot. New York: Pantheon Books.
———. 1973. *In Tune with the World (Zustimmung zur Welt, 1963)*. Translated by R. and C. Winston. 2nd ed. Chicago: Franciscan Herald Press.
Plebe, Armando. 1952. *La teoria del comico da Aristotele a Plutarco*. Università di Turino, Publicazioni della Facoltà di Lettere e Filosofia, 4.1.
Pohlenz, Max. 1952. *Aristophanes' Ritter*. Nachrichten der Akademie der Wissenschaften in Göttingen I., Philologisch-historische Klasse, 5. Göttingen: Vandenhoeck & Ruprecht.
Quadlbauer, Franz. 1960. "Die Dichter der Griechischen Komödie im Literarischen Urteil der Antike." *WS* 73:40–82.
Rau, Peter. 1967. *Paratragodia*. Zetemata, 45. Munich: C. H. Beck.
———. 1975. "Das Tragödienspiel in den *Thesmophoriazusen*." In *Aristophanes und die Alte Komödie*, ed. H.-J. Newiger, 339–56. Darmstadt: Wissenschaftliche Buchgesellschaft.
Reckford, Kenneth J. 1961. "The *Dyskolos* of Menander." *SP* 58:1–24.
———. 1967. "Aristophanes' Ever-Flowing Clouds." *Emory University Quarterly* 22:222–35.
———. 1969. *Horace*. New York: Twayne.
———. 1974a. "Desire with Hope: Aristophanes and the Comic Catharsis." *Ramus* 3:41–69.
———. 1974b. "Phaedra and Pasiphae: The Pull Backward." *TAPA* 104:307–28.
———. 1976. "Father-Beating in Aristophanes' *Clouds*." In *The Conflict of Generations in Ancient Greece and Rome*, edited by Stephen Bertman, 89–118. Amsterdam: B. R. Grüner.
———. 1977. "Catharsis and Dream-Interpretation in Aristophanes' *Wasps*." *TAPA* 107:285–312.
———. 1979. " 'Let Them Eat Cakes'—Three Food Notes to Aristophanes' *Peace*." In *Arktouros: Hellenic Studies Presented to Bernard M. W. Knox*, edited by Glen W. Bowersock, et al., 191–98. Berlin and New York: De Gruyter.
Reinhardt, Karl. 1960. "Aristophanes und Athen" (1938). In *Tradition und Geist*, edited by Carl Becker, 257–73. Göttingen: Vandenhoeck & Ruprecht.
Richardson, N. J., ed. 1974. *The Homeric Hymn to Demeter*. Oxford: The Clarendon Press.
Ritchie, Elisavietta. 1982. *Raking the Snow*. Washington: Washington Writers' Publishing House.
Rivier, André. 1966. "L'Esprit des *Dèmes* d'Eupolis." In *Mélanges offerts à M.*

Georges Bonnard, 129–49. Université de Lausanne, Publications de la Faculté des lettres, 18. Geneva: Librairie Droz.

Roos, E. 1960. "De Incubationis Ritu per Ludibrium apud Aristophanem Detorto." In Opuscula Atheniensia 3:55–97. Lund: Gleerup.

Rosenmeyer, Thomas G. 1982. The Art of Aeschylus. Berkeley, Los Angeles, and London: University of California Press.

Ruck, Carl A. P. 1975. "Euripides' Mother: Vegetables and the Phallos in Aristophanes." Arion 2:13–57.

Russo, Carlo. 1962. Aristofane Autore di Teatro. Florence: Sansoni.

Ruthven, K. K. 1979. Critical Assumptions. Cambridge: Cambridge University Press.

Ste. Croix, G. E. M. de. 1972. The Origins of the Peloponnesian War. London: Duckworth.

Sale, Roger. 1978. Fairy Tales and After. Cambridge, Mass., and London: Harvard University Press.

Schmid, Wilhelm. 1946. "Die Altattische Komödie." In Griechische Literaturgeschichte, edited by W. Schmid and O. Stählin, 7.1.4:1–470, in Handbuch der Altertumswissenschaft, edited by W. Otto. Munich: Biederstein Verlag.

Scullard, H. H. 1981. Festivals and Ceremonies of the Roman Republic. Ithaca: Cornell University Press.

Seale, David. 1982. Vision and Stagecraft in Sophocles. Chicago: University of Chicago Press.

Seel, Otto. 1960. Aristophanes oder Versuch uber Komödie. Stuttgart: Ernst Klett.

Segal, Charles P. 1961. "The Character and Cults of Dionysus and the Unity of the Frogs." HSCP 65:207–42.

———. 1962. "Gorgias and the Psychology of the Logos." HSCP 66:99–155.

———. 1969. "Aristophanes' Cloud-Chorus." Arethusa 2:143–61.

———. 1970. "Protagoras' Orthoepeia in Aristophanes' 'Battle of the Prologues.'" RhM 113:158–62.

———. 1981. Tragedy and Civilization: An Interpretation of Sophocles. Cambridge, Mass., and London: Harvard University Press.

———. 1982. Dionysiac Poetics and Euripides' Bacchae. Princeton: Princeton University Press.

Segal, Erich. 1968. Roman Laughter: The Comedy of Plautus. Cambridge, Mass.: Harvard University Press.

———. 1973. "The Etymologies of Comedy." GRBS 14:75–81.

Seidensticker, Bernd. 1979. "Das Satyrspiel." In Das Griechische Drama, edited by G. A. Seeck, 204–57. Darmstadt: Wissenschaftliche Buchgesellschaft.

Sewell, Elizabeth. 1952. The Field of Nonsense. London: Chatto & Windus.

Sicking, C. M. J. 1967. "Aristophanes Laetus?" In Kōmōidotragēmata, W. J. W. Koster in honorem, 115–24. Amsterdam: Hakkert.

Sider, David. 1975. "Aristophanes, Wasps 74ff.: The Missing Vice." CP 70:125–26.

Sifakis, G. M. 1971. Parabasis and Animal Choruses. London: The Athlone Press.

Silk, Michael. 1980. "Aristophanes as a Lyric Poet." YCS 26:99–151.

Simon, Erika. 1969. Die Götter der Griechen. Munich: Hirmer.

———. 1972. Das Antike Theater. Heidelberg: F. H. Kerle.

_____. 1983. *Festivals of Attica*. Madison: University of Wisconsin Press.

Slater, W. J. 1976. "Symposium at Sea." *HSCP* 80:161–70.

Smith, Peter. 1980. "History and the Individual in Hesiod's Myth of Five Races." *CW* 74:145–63.

Smith, Sidney. 1977. "The Golden Fantasy: A Regressive Reaction to Separation Anxiety." *International Journal of Psycho-Analysis* 58:311–24.

Smithsonian Institution. 1982. *Celebration: A World of Art and Ritual*. Catalogue of an Exhibition by the Office of Folklife Programs and the Renwick Gallery of the National Museum of American Art. Washington: Smithsonian Institution Press.

Solmsen, Friedrich. 1975. *Intellectual Experiments of the Greek Enlightenment*. Princeton and London: Princeton University Press.

Sommerstein, A. H. 1977a. "Notes on Aristophanes' *Wasps*." *CQ*, n.s. 27:261–77.

_____. 1977b. "Aristophanes and the Events of 411." *JHS* 97:112–26.

_____. 1978. "Notes on Aristophanes' *Acharnians*." *CQ*, n.s. 28:383–95.

Sparkes, B. A. 1962. "The Greek Kitchen." *JHS* 82:121–37 and plates iv–viii.

_____. 1975. "Illustrating Aristophanes." *JHS* 95:123–35 and plates xii–xvii.

Spatz, Lois. 1978. *Aristophanes*. Twayne's World Authors Series, 482. Boston: G. K. Hall.

Srebrny, Stefan. 1975. "Der Schluss der *Lysistrata*." In *Aristophanes und die Alte Komödie*, edited by H.-J. Newiger, 317–23. Darmstadt: Wissenschaftliche Buchgesellschaft.

Stanford, W. B. 1983. *Greek Tragedy and the Emotions*. London and Boston: Routledge & Kegan Paul.

Steffen, Victor. 1956. "Qua Lege Fretus Cleon Aristophanem in Iudicium Deduxerit?" *Eos* 48, fasc. 2 (*Symbolae Raphaeli Taubenschlag Dedicatae*, 2):67–73.

Steiger, Hugo. 1934. "Die Groteske und die Burleske bei Aristophanes." *Philologus* 89:161–84, 275–85, 416–32.

Stewart, Douglas J. 1965. "Aristophanes and the Pleasures of Anarchy." *The Antioch Review* 25:189–208.

Stone, Laura M. 1981. *Costume in Aristophanic Comedy*. New York: Arno Press.

Stow, H. Lloyd. 1936. "The Violation of the Dramatic Illusion in the Comedies of Aristophanes." Ph.D. dissertation, University of Chicago.

Süss, Wilhelm. 1954. "Scheinbare und Wirkliche Incongruenzen in den Dramen des Aristophanes." *RhM* 97:115–59, 229–54, 289–316.

_____. 1975. "Zur Komposition der Altattischen Komödie" (1908). In *Aristophanes und die Alte Komödie*, edited by H.-J. Newiger, 1–29. Darmstadt: Wissenschaftliche Buchgesellschaft.

Sutton, Dana F. 1974. "Satyr Plays and the Odyssey." *Arethusa* 7:161–85.

_____. 1980a. *Self and Society in Aristophanes*. Washington: University Press of America.

_____. 1980b. *The Greek Satyr Play*. Beiträge zur Klassischen Philologie, 90. Meisenheim am Glan: A. Hain.

Taillardat, Jean. 1962. *Les images d'Aristophane*. Paris: "Les Belles Lettres."

Taplin, Oliver. 1977a. *The Stagecraft of Aeschylus*. Oxford: The Clarendon Press.

———. 1977b. "Did Greek Dramatists Write Stage Directions?" *PCPS*, n.s. 23:121–32.

Thompson, Stith. 1977. *The Folktale* (1946). Berkeley, Los Angeles, and London: University of California Press.

Tillich, Paul. 1952. *The Courage to Be*. New Haven and London: Yale University Press.

Tolkien, J. R. R. 1965. "On Fairy-Stories" (1947). In *Tree and Leaf*, 3–84. Boston: Houghton Mifflin.

Travers, P. L. 1962. *Mary Poppins and Mary Poppins Comes Back* (1934, 1935). New York: Harcourt, Brace and World.

Travlos, John. 1971. *Pictorial Dictionary of Ancient Athens*. New York: Praeger.

Trendall, A. D. and Webster, T. B. L. 1971. "Old and Middle Comedy; Phlyakes." In *Illustrations of Greek Drama*, 4:116–44. London: Phaidon.

Trudeau, G. B. 1975. *The Doonesbury Chronicles*. With an introduction by Garry Wills. New York: Holt, Rinehart & Winston.

Turner, Victor. 1969. *The Ritual Process: Structure and Anti-Structure*. Ithaca: Cornell University Press.

———. 1974. *Dramas, Fields, and Metaphors: Symbolic Action in Human Society*. Ithaca and London: Cornell University Press.

———, ed. 1982. *Celebration: Studies in Festivity and Ritual*. Washington: Smithsonian Institution Press.

Tynan, Kenneth. 1979. "Withdrawing with Style from the Chaos—Tom Stoppard" (1977). In *Show People*, 44–123. New York: Simon & Schuster.

Ussher, Robert G., ed. 1978. *Euripides' Cyclops*. Rome: Edizioni dell'Ateneo & Bizzarri.

———. 1979. *Aristophanes*. Greece and Rome: New Surveys in the Classics, 13. Oxford: The Clarendon Press.

Vaio, John. 1969. "Studies in Aristophanes, Knights." Ph.D. dissertation, Columbia University (1966). Ann Arbor, Mich.: University Microfilms.

———. 1971. "Aristophanes' *Wasps*: The Relevance of the Final Scenes." *GRBS* 12:335–51.

———. 1973. "The Manipulation of Theme and Action in Aristophanes' *Lysistrata*." *GRBS* 14:369–80.

Van Hoorn, G. 1951. *Choes and Anthesteria*. Leiden: E. J. Brill.

Van Leeuwen, J. 1908. *Prolegomena ad Aristophanem*. Leiden: Sijthoff.

Vermeule, Emily. 1969. "Some Erotica in Boston." *Antike Kunst* 12:9–15, with plates.

Wagenknecht, Edward. 1929. *Utopia Americana*. Seattle: Folcroft Press.

Walcot, Peter. 1976. *Greek Drama in its Theatrical and Social Context*. Cardiff: University of Wales Press.

Weber, H. 1908. *Aristophanische Studien*. Leipzig: Theodor Weicher.

Webster, T. B. L. 1967. *The Tragedies of Euripides*. London: Methuen.

———. 1970. *Greek Theatre Production*. 2nd ed. London: Methuen.

Weil, Simone. 1957. "The Symposium of Plato" (1951). In *Intimations of Christianity among the Ancient Greeks*, edited and translated by E. C. Geissbuhler, 106–31. London: Routledge & Kegan Paul.

West, Martin L. 1974. *Studies in Greek Elegy and Iambus*. Berlin and New York: De Gruyter.

White, R., trans. 1975. *The Interpretation of Dreams*, by Artemidorus. Park Ridge, N.J.: Noyes Press.

Whitman, Cedric H. 1964. *Aristophanes and the Comic Hero*. Cambridge: Harvard University Press.

————. 1982. *The Heroic Paradox*. Edited with an introduction by Charles Segal. Ithaca and London: Cornell University Press.

Wilamowitz-Moellendorff, Ulrich von, ed. 1958. *Aristophanes Lysistrate* (1927). Berlin: Weidmann.

————. 1971. "Über die *Wespen* des Aristophanes" (1911). Reprinted in *Kleine Schriften*, edited by Akademie zu Berlin und Göttingen, 1:284–99. Berlin: Akademie Verlag.

————. 1975. "Zu Aristophanes' 'Fröschen' " (1929). In *Aristophanes und die Alte Komödie*, edited by H.-J. Newiger, 357–63. Darmstadt: Wissenschaftliche Buchgesellschaft.

Willetts, R. F. 1970. *"Blind Wealth and Aristophanes," An Inaugural Lecture*. Birmingham: The University of Birmingham.

Wills, Garry. 1969a. "Why are the Frogs in the *Frogs*?" *Hermes* 97:306–17.

————. 1969b. "Aeschylus' Victory in the *Frogs*." *AJP* 90:48–57.

Winnington-Ingram, R. P. 1969. *Euripides and Dionysus*. Amsterdam: Hakkert.

Woodbury, Leonard. 1976. "Aristophanes' *Frogs* and Athenian Literacy: *Ran.* 52–53, 1114." *TAPA* 106:349–57.

Zarabouka, Sophia. 1977. *Aristophanē EIRĒNĒ. Diaskeuē gia Paidia*. Athens: Kedros.

Zeitlin, Froma I. 1982a. "Travesties of Gender and Genre in Aristophanes' *Thesmophoriazousae*." In *Reflections of Women in Antiquity*, edited by H. Foley. London, Paris and New York: Gordon & Breack Science Publishers.

————. 1982b. "Cultic Models of the Female: Rites of Dionysus and Demeter." *Arethusa* 15:129–57.

Zielinski, Th. 1885. *Die Märchenkomödie in Athen*. St. Petersburg: Kranz.

Index